Henry Wilder Foote

Annals of King's Chapel from the Puritan age of New England to the present day

Volume I

Henry Wilder Foote

Annals of King's Chapel from the Puritan age of New England to the present day
Volume I

ISBN/EAN: 9783741123566

Manufactured in Europe, USA, Canada, Australia, Japa

Cover: Foto ©ninafisch / pixelio.de

Manufactured and distributed by brebook publishing software (www.brebook.com)

Henry Wilder Foote

Annals of King's Chapel from the Puritan age of New England to the present day

ANNALS

OF

KING'S CHAPEL

FROM THE PURITAN AGE OF NEW ENGLAND
TO THE PRESENT DAY

BY

HENRY WILDER FOOTE

IN TWO VOLUMES

VOL. I.

BOSTON
LITTLE, BROWN, AND COMPANY
1882

PREFACE.

THIS work owes its origin to a series of afternoon discourses on the History of King's Chapel, given by the author in the course of his parish duty some years ago, at a time when the ill-considered iconoclastic attempts to destroy the scanty remnants of former history surviving in Boston were directed against this historical building, and when it seemed important to revive the knowledge of its place in our local annals. The request of the parish that the discourses should be published made necessary the further studies which have resulted in this work. It has been prepared in vacation seasons, and amidst the engrossing calls of professional cares from which it has taken time that could ill be spared; and a considerable further delay has resulted from causes beyond the author's control, but greatly to his regret.

Dr. Greenwood's valuable History of King's Chapel, published in 1833, has been for almost fifty years the sole authority on the substance of the eventful chapter in the ecclesiastical history of New England which it treats, although, as the present writer has found, some of those who have treated these subjects have not always been punctilious in acknowledging their debt to Dr. Greenwood's pages. In presenting the subject to a new generation, however, it has seemed necessary to follow a different method from that adopted by my predecessor, who confined the narrative almost exclusively to the path marked out by the records of the church. A multitude of historical publications during the half century that has intervened have thrown new light on the whole course of the history, and more and more illustrate its importance as a factor in shaping events in New England before the Revolution, and in preparing the way for that consummation. The writer cannot hope to have explored the whole mass of materials, though he has sought to do this so far as they were within his reach, and to base his work on original sources. The story has been told, as much as possible, in quotations from contemporary authorities.

A portion of Chapters II. and III. has been already published in the "Memorial History of Boston," Vol. I., Chapter X., and some other fragments of the material used have been printed elsewhere.

The unique position of King's Chapel in our political and religious history seems to justify and even to demand the treatment of our subject, not merely as a chapter of the local and parochial Annals of Boston, but in its broader aspects as the centre around which were grouped the manifold relations of Great Britain to the Province of Massachusetts Bay. For nearly forty years it was practically the sole representative of the churchly and loyal traditions of the Mother Country among the children of the Puritans; and during the succeeding half century, until the Revolution, it retained its pre-eminence in this regard. Its history since that era, — from the time when for thirty years it stood alone for religious convictions, and "the first Episcopal Church in New England became the first Unitarian Church in America,"[1] through the period when its ministers, from Dr. Freeman to Dr. Peabody, adorned the faith which they preached, — deserves as careful record. For almost two centuries the parish has worshipped on the same spot, among the graves of the founders of New England, and for more than a century and a quarter in the beautiful church which perpetuates in Boston the ecclesiastical work of the school of Sir Christopher Wren, — whose solid walls and worshipful interior are no unfit emblem of the generations whose religious home it has been.

[1] In appropriating these words of Dr. Greenwood, the writer is not unmindful of the facts mentioned in Chapter I. concerning the early attempts to plant the Church of England in Maine and New Hampshire. These disappeared, however, from the memory of men, so that Humphreys in 1730 and King's Chapel somewhat later, under Dr. Caner, stated the claim without being disputed, it even being asserted at that time to be "the oldest Church in British America."

PREFACE.

A narrative so closely interwoven with the most intense controversies which have rent New England, theologically and politically, for two centuries, cannot pursue a peaceful course, and it would be too much to hope that the writer will satisfy critics on subjects which still excite strong differences of feeling. He has endeavored, however, to treat his theme in an historical temper, and, while himself a descendant of the Puritans and loyal to their noble memory, not to deal unjustly by those of a different church which, during most of the period covered by the present volume, was struggling for a foothold as a dissenting form of faith in Massachusetts.

The chief sources of information are, of course, the records of the church. These have been preserved almost entire, the first entries being in a parchment-bound folio, 1686-1719, containing all that we possess of records and accounts for that period, somewhat heterogeneously mingled. Seven thin folios, besides various ledgers and account books, comprise the following period till 1776. Since the Revolution, the records have been kept with even greater care; but, as containing less of general interest, these will be more sparingly drawn upon in the narrative. The King's Chapel Registers of Births, Marriages, and Deaths are also of much value. Their fortunate recovery in 1805 from Dr. Caner's heirs, after having been lost for thirty years, gives emphasis to the importance (which may here be urged) of putting them in print beyond the chance of destruction.

The quotations from papers and records are uniformly given in the *spelling* of the original; but the *punctuation* has been adapted to the sense in every case.

As the early records have never been printed except in fragmentary selections, it seemed desirable to bring them within the reach of antiquaries, and to insure their preservation, — especially as they are important to the early history, not only of the particular parish of King's Chapel, but of the whole body of churches now constituting the Protestant Episcopal Church in the United States of America, which also derive their descent from the Church of England. The rule has therefore been adopted, at the risk of encumbering these pages as a continuous narrative, of printing substantially *the whole* of these records down to the Revolution, omitting only such formal matters as (*e.g.*) the lists of persons present at each meeting of the Vestry, etc.; and although many trivial matters are thus preserved, it has seemed best to run the risk of erring on that side rather than to leave it uncertain whether some matters of importance might not be inadvertently omitted. In this the writer trusts at least, in the words of Dr. Greenwood, to be "almost sure of the favor of antiquaries, to whom facts are never unimportant or dull."

The kindness of many friends has laid the author under much obligation. He would especially acknowledge his indebtedness to the Rev. George E. Ellis, D.D., to Messrs. Charles Deane, Henry H. Edes, and Charles C. Smith, for their unfailing sympathy and assistance; to Professor William R. Ware and Messrs. J. Rogers Rich and Robert S. Peabody for artistic suggestions; and to Messrs. John Ward Dean, William H. Whitmore, and Justin Winsor for valuable aid. The family papers which Mrs. F. E. Weston has enabled him to incorporate in the closing chapters of Vol. I., similar aid for Vol. II. from Mrs. M. A. Elton and from the Right Rev. W. S. Perry, D.D., Bishop of the Diocese of Iowa, from the families of Dr. Greenwood and Dr. Peabody, and from the Rev. James Freeman Clarke, D.D., and the permission to quote from the records of Christ and Trinity Churches, require specially grateful acknowledgment. The printed materials which have been consulted are in part referred to in the notes; but more particular expression should be made of indebtedness to the invaluable genealogical labors of Savage and Wyman, to the Bibliography appended to Dr. Dexter's "Congregationalism, as seen in its Literature," and to the Historical Collections of the American Colonial Church, Vol. III., containing the materials relating to the Church of England in Massachusetts previous to the Revolution, collected in England by the late Rev. Francis L. Hawks, D.D., from the MS. treasures of the Lambeth Library and of the Society for Propagating the Gospel in Foreign Parts, and published in 1874 under the accomplished editorship of Dr. Perry. These papers (quoted in the notes as "Church Docs. Mass."), of which only a small

PREFACE.   xi

portion had before been printed, supply much information upon the period covered by the present volume, and have been freely used to illustrate our narrative. The author regrets that he has not had the advantage of consulting the promised History of the Episcopal Church in America, soon to appear under the same editorial care.

To Messrs. Samuel Adams Drake, and William H. Whitmore, to Messrs. Roberts Brothers, publishers of Mr. Drake's "Old Landmarks of Boston," and to Messrs. J. R. Osgood and Co., publishers of the "Memorial History of Boston," for the permission to enrich these pages with many of the illustrations used, thanks should be recorded; and also to Messrs. Thomas G. Appleton and R. H. Gardiner for the engraved portraits of Mr. Samuel Appleton and Dr. Gardiner, to Messrs. William B. Swett and George R. Minot for permission to copy the likenesses of Mr. and Mrs. Charles Apthorp, and of the Rev. James Freeman, which will all appear in the second volume, and to Miss Sarah H. Clarke for a sketch of the "Governor's Pew," which, elaborated by Mr. Donald Black, has made it possible to reproduce that interesting feature of the church in Provincial times.

By heliotypes and woodcuts, it has been endeavored to present the most characteristic features of King's Chapel. These are in great part prepared for this work; most of the autographs also being fac-similes from the records of the church. The list of illustrations of a subject so rich in historical associations might have been greatly extended from portraits of members of the parish by Copley and Stuart, and by earlier and later artists; but such personal illustrations have been of necessity limited to the likenesses of some of the persons commemorated by monuments on the church walls.

To the members of the parish whose generous aid has made this publication possible, and particularly to Mr. J. Randolph Coolidge, and to the former and present Wardens, — Messrs. George C. Richardson, Arthur T. Lyman, and Thomas B. Hall, — the writer would express his sincere thanks for their interest and encouragement. He desires to associate with them the name of their colleague, the late Mr. Edward Pickering, and the memory of other friends who continued the best traditions of character in the church which they loved, and which they strengthened by their presence.

The abundance of material has constrained the author to enlarge the original scope of the work so as to include two volumes, of which the first is now published; while the second is in the press, and will be completed as soon as other duties will permit.

KING'S CHAPEL,
  Forefathers' Day, 1881.

NOTE TO CHAPTERS IX. AND X.

While these pages are in the press, I am indebted to the Rev. Edward J. Young for the fact that the records of the First Parish in Cohasset, which was formerly a part of Hingham, contain the following record of deaths: —

"1728. March 1. The Rev. Samuel Miles, Pastor of King's Chappel in Boston, aged 65.

"1729. Oct. 6. The Rev. Henry Hairis, minister of King's Chappel, Boston, 42."

It was customary at that time to record in Parish Books, in the Congregational Churches, events of general importance as well as the special incidents which happened in the Society and the Town. These entries show that the death of a minister of King's Chapel was thought to be of sufficient consequence to find a place in the Parish Records of this little precinct of Hingham, where also both ministers were probably known on account of Mr. Myles's family connections in Swanzey, and the attempt to plant the Church of England in Scituate.

CONTENTS.

CHAPTER I.
INTRODUCTORY. — THE PURITAN COMMONWEALTH.
1620–1664.

Relation of the founders of Massachusetts to the English Church. — The Church of England in Virginia and Maine. — Religious system of the Puritans. — Abortive attempts to modify it 1

CHAPTER II.
EPISCOPACY PLANTED IN BOSTON.
1667–1686.

Controversies within the Puritan Church. — Edward Randolph. — Arrival of Rev. Robert Ratcliffe. — Founders of King's Chapel . . 31

CHAPTER III.
CHURCH AND STATE UNDER SIR EDMUND ANDROS.
1686–1689.

The opposing elements face to face. — The South Church an unwilling host. — The first Revolution. — Downfall of the policy of King James II. 58

CHAPTER IV.
THE CHURCH TAKES ROOT.
1689–1701.

Rev. Samuel Myles. — His early ministry. — He brings from England the bounty of King William and Queen Mary. — Affairs of the Church. — Lord Bellomont, Governor and Vestryman 95

CHAPTER V.

GOVERNOR DUDLEY AND THE CHURCH.

1702-1709.

Accession of Queen Anne. — Arrival of Governor Dudley and Rev. George Keith. — Rev. Christopher Bridge, the King's Lecturer. — Unquiet relations between the ministers. — Noted parishioners . . 147

CHAPTER VI.

THE CHURCH ENLARGED. — A BISHOP SOUGHT.

1709-1714.

Arrival of Rev. Henry Harris. — Sir Leoline Jenkins's Fellowship. — Enlargement of King's Chapel. — Mr. Brattle's organ. — Sir F. Nicholson's ecclesiastical commission. — The Society for Propagating the Gospel in Foreign Parts. — Petition for an American Bishop. — Queen Anne's Death 192

CHAPTER VII.

FIGHTINGS WITHOUT AND FEUDS WITHIN.

1714-1722.

Accession of King George I. — Mr. Harris's Voyage home. — Noted Parishioners. — The Church of England planted in Newbury, Braintree, and Marblehead. — Governor Shute. — Friction between Episcopacy and Puritanism. — A strife in print begins 236

CHAPTER VIII.

THE CONTROVERSY WAXES. — CHRIST CHURCH.

1724-1734.

Mr. John Checkley and his pamphlet war. — The Rector of Yale College declares for the Church of England. — Christ Church built. — Its first minister 285

CHAPTER IX.

THE THREE CLERGYMEN.

1724-1728.

Dissension between Dr. Timothy Cutler and Rev. Henry Harris. — The Massachusetts Synod thwarted. — Struggle for seats in the Board of Overseers of Harvard College. — Accession of King George II. — Close of Mr. Myles's ministry 326

CHAPTER X.

THE BISHOP'S COMMISSARY.

1728-1737.

Governor Burnet and the Church. — Rev. Roger Price succeeds Mr. Myles. — His commission as Commissary of the Bishop of London. — Death of Mr. Harris. — Noted Parishioners. — Governor Belcher and the Church. — Rev. Thomas Harward, the new King's Lecturer. His differences with Mr. Price. — His death. — Question about his successor 375

CHAPTER XI.

THE CHURCH UNDER LAW.

1692-1740.

Provincial Laws providing for public worship. — Quakers and Baptists. — King's Chapel and Christ Church, in the long struggle to free churchmen from taxation for support of Congregational parishes. — The Petaquamscut Purchase. — The pamphlet strife renewed. — Within the Church. — Mr. Checkley receives orders 438

CHAPTER XII.

TRINITY CHURCH. — A CLOSING EPOCH.

1737-1747.

Rev. Addington Davenport succeeds Mr. Harward. — Trinity Church built. — Its first minister. — Obsequies of Queen Caroline. — Relation of the Church to Whitefield and the Great Revival. — Mr. Price and the Hopkinton mission. — Church Records. — Rev. Stephen Rowe, King's Lecturer and Schoolmaster. — Governor Shirley. — Commissary Price's relations to Rev. William Hooper. — Close of his ministry at King's Chapel. — His family. — His parishioners 480

ILLUSTRATIONS.

	PAGE
The Provincial Governor's Pew	*Frontispiece*
Sounding Board	1
Part of Initial Letter, carved work in the present Church	1
Vassall Monument (*Heliotype*)	12
First page of earliest Record book (*Fac-simile*)	31
Record of first meeting, June 15, 1686 (*Heliotype*)	45
The first King's Chapel	58
Arms of Nicholson	61
Governor Andros	62
Arms of Captain Hamilton	70
Great Seal of New England under Andros	76
Note from the Records on the Rebellion against Andros (*Fac-simile*)	82
Arms of Andros	84
Railed pews, 1694	95
Foxcroft Arms	106
King William and Queen Mary (*Heliotype*)	121
Chancel of the present Church (*Heliotype*)	122
Inscription on base of Communion flagon	122
Communion flagon, 1694	123
Arms of Mountfort	123
Stamp on cover of books given by King William III.	124
Communion plate given by King William and Queen Mary	124
Arms of Bellomont	141
Governor Bellomont	142
Seal of the Society for Propagating the Gospel in Foreign Parts	147
Arms of Dudley	149
Joseph Dudley	150

xviii   ILLUSTRATIONS.

	PAGE
Titlepage of Sermon by Rev. George Keith (*Fac-simile*)	153
Checkley Arms	179
John Nelson	180
Old Communion Table, 1686	192
Pulpit, 1717	236
Arms of Shute	267
Three Pence, Massachusetts Currency	268
Map of 1722, showing King's Chapel	284
Royal Arms, from cover of prayer book given by King George III. to King's Chapel	297
Christ Church	326
Part of titlepage of a Funeral Sermon by Dr. Caner	374
The Province House	375
Governor Burnet	376
Arms of Burnet	379
Price Coat of Arms	388
Arms of Belcher	397
Initial Letter of Mr. Harward's sermon	438
Old Trinity Church	480
Davenport Arms	482
Country homes of Revs. Roger Price and James Freeman (*Heliotype*)	517
Shirley Monument (*Heliotype*)[1]	548
Ornament from cover of old Bible	551

[1] The Shirley Monument is given, with the Vassall Monument, at p. 12.

AUTOGRAPHS.

	PAGE		PAGE
S. Mavericke	14	Charles Hobby	175
William Blaxton	15	Ed. Lyde	178
Richard Gibson	17	Jo. Nelson	181
Fran: Champernowne	18	Tho. Newton	182
Robert Ratcliffe	42	Savill Simpson	183
Benjamin Bullivant	46	Wm. Tailer	184
Ed. Randolph	55	East Apthorp	234
F. Nicholson	60	John Jekyll	244
E. Andros	62	Cyprian Southack	246
Samll Sewall	63	Fras. Brinley	248
Fra. Foxcroft	104	George Cradock	249
Sam: Ravenscroft	104	Samll Shute	267
Edward Gouge	114	Jno. Checkley	290
Nicholas Tippett	114	W. Burnet	377
Giles Dyer	122	Rog. Price	391
Benjamin Mountfort	123	Edm. London	391
John Indecott	128	Henry Harris	393
Bellomont	143	J. Belcher	397
J. Dudley	150	Addington Davenport	481
Samuel Myles	164	Thos. Greene	496
Chris. Bridge	164		

ANNALS OF KING'S CHAPEL

FROM THE PURITAN TIMES TO THE LAST ROYALIST RECTOR.

A STUDY OF THE PLANTING OF THE ENGLISH CHURCH IN NEW ENGLAND.

"*And kings shall be thy nursing fathers, and their queens thy nursing mothers.*" — Is. xlix. 23.

ANNALS OF KING'S CHAPEL.

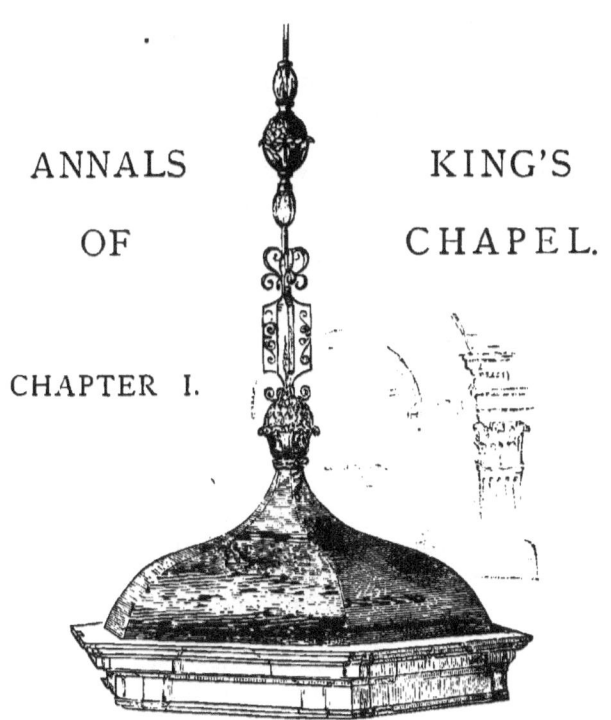

CHAPTER I.

INTRODUCTORY.—THE PURITAN COMMONWEALTH.

KING'S CHAPEL, in Boston, represents historically and locally what, at the time, was regarded as the unwelcome and intrusive appearance of the Church of England amid a community of expatriated Englishmen whom circumstances had alienated from it. Our review of the history of that edifice, its origin and uses, must therefore start from a reference to those circumstances.

The religious controversies which divided Protestantism in the seventeenth century played a great part in the settlement of the New World. Even where commerce was the leading motive for emigration, the religious temper of the time did not abandon the struggling colonists to the rude exposures of an unchurched wilderness. French Protestants colonized Florida in 1567; the Church of Holland emigrated to New Amsterdam in 1614, with the Dutch; the Reformed Church to New Sweden in 1638; the Church of

England to Virginia, with Raleigh's colonists, in 1587, and again at the permanent settlement of that colony in 1607, continuing there the Established Church until the Revolution. To this day, the multitude of religious "denominations" in America is largely a monument of fading, if not obsolete, controversies which drove their founders across the Atlantic two centuries and a half ago. But it will be conceded that, while the foundations of the American nation were thus largely laid in faith and prayer, it was pre-eminently so with New England. To the Pilgrims of Plymouth belongs the eternal glory of having planted their colony purely for religion; to the Puritans of Massachusetts Bay, the high honor that they built their political edifice on the corner-stone of faith. Nor can it be doubted that the religious fervor and constancy which gave its supreme quality to their work caused it to succeed where less exalted spirits failed.

The rulers of the Church of England did, indeed, intend to exercise sway over the new colonies. Chaplains were often sent with colonists, to represent the State religion and to keep up at least its outward forms.[1] The first religious service held on New England soil was in the abortive colony sent out to settle "within the river of Sachadehoc, by the Honorable Sir John Popham, Kt., Lord Chief-Justice of England," under George Popham and Rawlay Gilbert. The old chronicler relates that, on Aug. 9, 1607, being

> "Sonday, the chief of both the shipps, with the greatest part of all the company, landed on the island where the crosse stood [which Captain George Weymouth had erected], the which they called St. George's Island, and heard a sermon delivered unto them by Mr. Seymour, his preacher, and soe returned abourd againe."[2] Ten days later, "they all went ashoare where they had made choise of their plantation, and where they had a sermon delivered unto them by their preacher."

After which the government was organized, "Richard Seymer, preacher," being sworn an assistant. But, with the failure of the colony, these echoes of the liturgy of the Church of England soon died away, and gave place to the sighing of the vast forest and the wash of the sea on the solitary coast.

---

[1] An Indian was baptized at Roanoke Island, Aug. 13, 1587. The first English Communion in the New World was celebrated in Virginia by Robert Hunt, June 21, 1607.

[2] "The Historie of Travaile into Virginia Britannia, etc. . . . Collected by William Strachey, Gent. London: Hakluyt Society, 1849," p. 169. Strachey's original authority is first printed by Rev. B. F. De Costa in Mass. Hist. Soc. Proc., May, 1880, pp. 82–117. The places named are Monhegan island and the peninsula of Sabino.

It was reserved for a more austere type of religion to Christianize the wilderness. The Pilgrims of Plymouth, in 1620, brought with them the simplest form of church government and worship. The Brownists had separated from the Church of England on conviction; nor were they so gently entreated as to win them back to its fold.[1] John Robinson, though in early life "soured with the most rigid principles of the separation,"[2] had softened during the tarry at Leyden. His followers had gone so far as to say: —

"To ye confession of fayth published in ye name of ye Church of England & to every artikell thereof wee . . . assent wholly. . . . Wee judg itt lawfull for his Majesty to apoynt bishops. . . . The authoryty of ye present bishops in ye Land wee do acknolidg so far forth as ye same is indeed derived from his Majesty untto them."[3]

But, in spite of these concessions, James I. would say only that he would "connive at their separatism," and not molest them so long as they gave no public offence. But to allow and tolerate them "under the great seal," he should not consent; and when they emigrated from Holland they were not bound even by these articles, which had been the uttermost that their conscience could concede.

Thus Independency, which was to grow into New England Congregationalism, was planted with sturdy vigor by the Pilgrims at Plymouth. Three years later they were visited by Rev. William Morell, who had come over with Robert Gorges in 1623, when that son of Sir Ferdinando Gorges sought to set up his authority over the territory on the Bay of Massachusetts, called "Massachusiack." Morell had a commission from the ecclesiastical courts of England to exercise a kind of supervision over

---

[1] Dexter's "Congregationalism of the Last Three Hundred Years" gives a full survey of the opinions of Browne: "The one original, urgent, controlling thought, which grew to be a burden upon his soul which he could no longer carry, was that of the laxness, the corruption, the practical ungodliness of those parish assemblies of all sorts of persons, which were the only churches that the Church of England knew. . . . It was mainly because the Bishops justified this state of things, that he declared they could not be Christ's ministers." His followers could neither worship God according to their consciences in England, nor easily leave it. "The humble Petition of her highnes faithful Subiects falsly called Brownestes . . . to passe peaceably into the province of Canada . . . and there remayning to bee accounted her Ma^{tes} faithfull and loving Subiects, to whom wee owe all dutie and obedience in the Lord," probably, soon after the passage of the cruel law of 1592 against the Puritans, received only contempt. — *N. E. Hist. and Geneal. Reg.*, xiii. 259.

[2] Mather's Magnalia.

[3] Articles from the Church of Leyden, 1617, sent to the Great Council of England, "to bee considered of in respeckt of their judgments occationed about theer going to Virginia Anno 1618." — *N. E. Hist. and Geneal. Reg.*, xxv. 276.

the churches which were or might be established in New England, that the spread of Puritanism might be restrained. But he did not even mention his commission till just before leaving Plymouth for England.[1]

The Plymouth colony represented the principle of absolute separation from the National Church.[2] Not so the great Puritan party, which was destined to found a nation in the New World, and to live there with transplanted vigor after the downfall of its hopes with the Commonwealth. Although there were in it many degrees of alienation from the ruling spirit in the Church, its great vision was still of the National Church, purified of its corruptions and reformed to the simplicity of the gospel. The attitude of the Puritan party toward the National Church is expressed thus: —

"We have not separated ourselves, simply and absolutely, from the communion of any particular church whatsoever, even the Roman itself, so far forth as it is Catholic, but only from their errors, wherein they had first separated themselves from their predecessors." [3]

It was in this spirit that the leaders in the great Puritan emigration went forth. Higginson, in presence of his children and other passengers whom he had called to the stern of the ship to take their last sight of England at Land's End, said: —

"We will not say, as the Separatists are wont to say, on their leaving England, Farewell Babylon! Farewell Rome! But we will say, Farewell dear England! Farewell the Church of God in England, and all the Christian friends there! We do not go to New England as Separatists from the Church of England, though we cannot but separate from the corruptions in it; but we go to practise the positive part of church reformation, and propagate the Gospel in America." [4]

He concluded with a fervent prayer for the king, and for the Church and State in England.

But the most impressive statement of the spirit and wish of the Puritan leaders is found in " the humble request of his Majes-

---

[1] He wrote a Latin poem while at Plymouth, which, translated, ends —
"To see here built I trust
An English Kingdom from this Indian dust."

[2] The grounds for this position are stated in Governor Bradford's "Dialogue between Old Men and Young Men," concerning "the Church and the Government thereof." — *Mass. Hist. Soc. Proc.*, 1869-70, pp. 396-464.

[3] Bramhall's Vindication, quoted in Anderson, Col. Ch., i. 20.

[4] The authenticity of this, which is first reported by Cotton Mather in his "Magnalia," is doubted by Dr. Palfrey; but it accords with the "Humble Request" so closely as to seem every way probable. The distinction is drawn between the divine and the human element in the Establishment.

ties loyall Subjects, the Governor and the Company late gone for New England; to the rest of their Brethren in and of the Church of England," put forth by Winthrop and his associates on their departure in 1630:[1] —

"*Reverend Fathers & Brethren*, — The generall rumour of this solemne enterprise, wherein ourselves with others, through the providence of the Almightie, are engaged, as it may spare us the labour of imparting our occasion unto you, so it gives us the more incouragement to strengthen ourselves by the procurement of the prayers and blessings of the Lord's faithful servants: For which end wee are bold to have recourse unto you, as those whom God hath placed nearest his throne of mercy; which as it affords you the more opportunitie, so it imposeth the greater bond upon you to intercede for his people in all their straights; we beseech you therefore by the mercies of the Lord Jesus to consider us as your Brethren, standing in very great need of your helpe, and earnestly imploring it. And howsoever your charitie may have met with some occasion of discouragement through the misreport of our intentions, or through the disaffection, or indiscretion, of some of us, or rather amongst us; for wee are not of those that dreame of perfection in this world; yet we desire you would be pleased to take notice of the principals and body of our company, as those who esteeme it our honour to call the *Church of England*, from whence we rise, our deare Mother, and cannot part from our native Countrie, where she specially resideth, without much sadness of heart, and many tears in our eyes, ever acknowledging that such hope and part as we have obtained in the common salvation, we have received in her bosome, and suckt it from her breasts; wee leave it not therefore, as loathing that milk wherewith we were nourished there, but blessing God for the parentage and education, as members of the same body, shall alwayes rejoice in her good, and unfainedly grieve for any sorrow that shall ever betide her, and while we have breath, syncerely desire and indeavour the continuance and abundance of her welfare, with the inlargement of her bounds in the kingdome of Christ Jesus."

Such words from such men are to be understood in their serious, simple sense; and the fact that they soon took the Separatist ground is explicable without any cloud on their good faith.[2]

---

[1] Hutchinson's History of Massachusetts, i. 487, 488.

[2] White's "Planter's Plea" answers the objection, "that religion indeed and the colour thereof is the cloake of this work, but under it is secretly harboured faction and separation from the Church, ... renouncing our Church as a limbe of Antichrist. ... The men are far enough from projecting and erecting of this Colony for a Nursery of Schismaticks." Cotton Mather says: "They were able to distinguish between the *Church of England*, as it *contained* the whole *Body of the Faithful* scattered throughout the kingdoms, tho' of different Persuasions about some *Rites* and *Modes* in Religion. ... And the *Church of England*, as it was *confined* unto a certain Constitution by *Canons* which" etc. ... "By the Light of this *Distinction* we may easily perceive what *Church of*

The letter itself reads as a solemn farewell from men going out from one spiritual home to build another. "The Church of England at that day was a local, National Church, . . . without any pretension to any Catholic or universal character."[1] The large liberty of self-government which their charter gave must have included to their minds the right to organize religion for themselves. Indeed, this right was their controlling motive. The voyage across the Atlantic was enough to convince them how impracticable it was to carry the ceremonials of the National Church into the wilderness. It showed them, too, as week after week passed upon the deep, that the gulf between them and England insured their freedom to do what they should deem best for religion, — not only to cast off the things which had affronted their conscience as Puritans, but to start clean and free.[2] Not without some effort of a few to resist the course of things

---

England it was that our *New-England* exiles called *Their Mother*. Though their *Mother* had been so harsh to them as to turn them out of Doors, yet they highly honoured Her, believing that it was not so much her *Mother*, but some of their angry *Brethren*, abusing the Name of their Mother, who so harshly treated them; and all the harm they wished her was to see her put off those *Ill Trimmings* which at her first coming out of the Popish *Babylon* she had not so fully laid aside." — *Magnalia*, i. v. 20.

[1] In his "Reasons to be considered," etc., Governor Winthrop says: "What can be a better work, and more honorable and worthy a Christian, than to help raise and support a particular church while it is in its infancy?" It is evident from his letter Oct. 27, 1629 (Life and Letters, i. 354), that before embarking there was earnest consultation, with godly ministers, how far the obligations to the English Church would be dissolved by going to New England. See Hon. R. C. Winthrop's paper in Mass. Hist. Soc. Proc. January, 1881.

Rev. J. Higginson's attestation to Mather's "Magnalia" says: "By this *Essay* it may be seen that a *farther Practical Reformation* than that which began at the first coming out of the Darkness of *Popery* was aimed at and endeavoured by a great Number of Voluntary Exiles that came into a *Wilderness* for that very end, that hence they might be free from humane *Additions* and *Inventions* in the Worship of God, and might practise the *positive part* of Divine *Institutions*, according to the Word of God."

[2] The exigencies of party warfare compel a class of writers to this day to misjudge the Puritans. Chalmers (Political Annals, p. 152) says: "Before December, 1630, two hundred had perished [in Boston]. Humanity will drop a tear over the graves of the dead, though she cannot altogether approve of the savage fury with which they deserted their native land when it required the aid of their exertions." Anderson (Col. Ch., i. 127) admits that "if they had been treated with forbearance or generosity, or even with bare justice, they would have rejoiced to remain within the fold" of the Church. Yet he calls New England Puritanism "a despotism as intolerant as any which the world ever saw." And again (ii. 183) he says: "Nevertheless, to meet with any one document in the early annals of New England, not marred and blotted by the decrees of spiritual tyranny, is a fact which demands thankful acknowledgment." . . . Of the noble Governor of Plymouth he says (ii. 193): "Few passages are to be found in which this hatred of Puritans against the Episcopal Order is expressed in more awful terms than in Bradford's History. The bitterness of his rancor, upon hearing of the downfall of the Bishops, is only equalled by the falseness of his prophecy that they should never be restored."

did the changed ecclesiastical constitution become fixed for New England. Already, in 1623, the London adventurers had sent over "a preacher, though none of the most eminent and rare," to Plymouth. John Lyford there made dissension, set up a separate Church, to which "he would minister the sacrament by his Episcopal calling;"[1] and, being expelled for gross immorality, became, in 1627, minister of the unsuccessful colony at Cape Ann. Probably Roger Conant and the "old planters" at Naumkeag were of that mind. When Higginson and his colleagues arrived at Salem, in 1629, they found the majority decidedly in favor of the simple church polity already devised at Plymouth; and the plain yet impressive rite by which the pastor and teacher of the Salem Church were set apart for their sacred office marks the adoption by the Massachusetts colony of the Congregational order.[2] Yet it at once became evident that there was a strong enough party opposed to such a radical policy to occasion serious trouble. The brothers Browne,[3] observing that the ministers did not at all use the Book of Common Prayer, and administered baptism and the Lord's Supper without the ceremonies, and proposed to use church discipline on scandalous persons, "gathered a company together, in a place distinct from the public assembly, and there, at sundry times, the Book of Common Prayer was read."[4] Before Governor Endicott, they

"Accused the ministers as departing from the orders of the Church of England, that they were separatists and would be anabaptists; but for themselves, they would hold to the orders of the Church of England. The ministers answered for themselves, they were neither separatists nor anabaptists; they did not separate from the Church of England, nor from the ordinances of God there, but only from the corruptions and disorders there; and that they came away from the common prayer and ceremo-

[1] Bradford's History, etc., — 4 Mass. Hist. Soc. Coll., iii. 171-196.

[2] See the account in "New England Congregationalism in its Origin and Purity: Illustrated by the Foundation and Early Records of the First Church in Salem, etc. By Daniel Appleton White. Salem: 1861." The original Covenant, pp. 12, 13, is of singular beauty. On the influence of Plymouth upon Massachusetts in 1629 and 1630, see Mr. Deane in Mass. Hist. Soc. Proc., October, 1870, pp. 398, 400.

[3] One a lawyer, the other a merchant, and both among the first patentees. See "Archæologia Americana," iii. lxxiv-lxxvi,

the account of John and Samuel Browne from Roxwell, in Essex, members of Parliament, etc., 1640-43; also pp. 52-54, account of the proceedings concerning them, in the Company's Records, A. D. 1629.

[4] The geographical difficulties of some English writers are illustrated by a passage in Anderson, Col. Ch., i. 362, where he disputes "what Bancroft has said respecting the Puritan Settlers of New England." The fact is, that Mr. Bancroft is speaking of the Pilgrims of Plymouth; so that the case of the Brownes of Salem, which Anderson cites against him, is not pertinent.

nies, and had suffered much for their non-conformity in their native land, and therefore being in a place where they might have their liberty, they neither could nor would use them, because they judged the imposition of these things to be sinful corruptions of the word of God."[1]

This answer met general approval, as well as that of the Governor and Council; and as the speeches and practices of the brothers tended "to mutiny and faction, the Governour told them that New England was no place for such as they, and sent them both back for England."

Nor were they alone. Of the four ministers who had been sent over by the Massachusetts Company, while Higginson and Skelton thus led the way to the later congregationalism, and Ralph Smith was so rigid a separatist that he was forbidden to exercise his ministry in the colony, Francis Bright was too much a churchman to remain where the Puritan tendencies so developed, and soon returned to England, as did perhaps a hundred others who were not prepared to give up the forms of the English Church. When the great emigration with Winthrop arrived in 1630, they found the new ecclesiastical type crystallized into a form for which they were already prepared.

"It had been their way in the old country, so far as it was permitted, to supplement the usual and obligatory ministries and observances of the National Church by a kind of congregation within the congregation, — a company of men and women covenanting each with the other and all with the Invisible Head to live by the divine grace and in all mutual love and fidelity. Sunday afternoons and on week days[2] these congregations listened to lectures and joined in free prayers under the spiritual leadership of ministers, some of whom still served in the English Church, while

---

[1] Morton's N. E. Memorial, p. 147. Much is made of such transactions by critics of the Puritans, on the ground that they were in violation of the alleged principles on which the colony was founded. But those principles are correctly stated in a sermon entitled: "*Ne Sutor ultra Crepidam*: Or, Brief Animadversions upon the New-England Anabaptists, etc. By Samuel Willard, Teacher of a Church in Boston. [Vice-President of Harvard College.] Boston, 1681." He thus meets the Charge: "Our practices are contrary to the Design of our first Planters, who left all for Liberty of Conscience, and we are the children of those that felt the lash of Imposition, and yet will show to others the like severity. "*Answer:* I perceive they are mistaken in the design of our first Planters, whose business was not Toleration, but were professed Enemies of it, and could leave the World professing they *died no Libertines*. Their business was to settle and (as much as in them lay) secure Religion to Posterity, according to that way which they believed was of God. If (therefore) this People parted with so much, and were at such charges for their liberties, why then do the Anabaptists trouble them, who had neither scot nor lot in that charge? Let them go and do the like, and we shall not so molest their Churches as they have shamelessly done by ours."

[2] Rev. John Cotton's weekly service in St. Botolph's was continued in the "Thursday Lecture" of the First Church.

others had overtaxed the patience of their bishops and had been silenced for non-conformity with the ceremonies, which seemed to these earnest Protestants inseparably associated with the corruptions of Rome. Gradually these congregations became the realities of the living present, the old ritual was positively an offence to their fervid spirits, the Church was again the two or three met together in the name of Jesus."[1]

So in the new world " it was inevitable that the new communion should replace the old, and an extreme simplicity supplant an extreme formalism."

But if there had been any doubt in the case, the ministers exiled to Massachusetts by their Puritan convictions would have fixed the new ecclesiastical type. At least ninety University men — three fourths of them from Cambridge, and the main part ejected clergymen — impressed a character on Massachusetts which it has never lost. There was no town so small, just snatched from the encompassing wilderness, that it did not have an educated leader.[2] In this sense the English Church trained the founders of New England; but what shall be said of those whose hardness drove out these men, " choice grain sifted from a whole nation"? No just estimate is possible of the causes which fixed the character of the New England Church order, without emphasizing the effect of the spiritual tyranny of the heads of the Church of England during the years of the great emigration. Even John Cotton had written a letter to Bishop Williams, Jan. 31, 1624, — " a very gentle and touching plea to be forborne with" : —

"My forbearance of the ceremonies was not wilful refusal of conformity, but from some doubt in my judgment (which I confess is very shallow), and from some scruple in conscience, which is weak. . . . I have thus far gained (what by conference, what by study, what by seeking unto God) *as of late to see the weakness of some of these grounds against kneeling, which before I esteemed too strong for me to dissolve.*"[3]

But he was harried out of the kingdom at last.

Thomas Shepard, afterward the godly minister of our Cambridge, had an interview with Laud while Bishop of London.

---

[1] Rev. R. Ellis, D. D., Sermon on the "Two hundred and fiftieth Anniversary of the First Church." Dr. Ellis adds: " It is touching to note how careful they were, for a time at least, not to discredit or in any way disparage the Church which they seemed to have outgrown; and yet none the less it dropped away from them, as the husk from the ripe fruit, and as time went on became to their fervid spirits a hindrance and a stumbling-block."

[2] See a paper by Prof. F. B. Dexter on "The Influence of the English Universities in the Development of New England," in Mass. Hist. Soc. Proc. for February, 1880.

[3] See N. E. Hist. and Geneal. Reg., xxviii. 137.

The angry Bishop said: "I'll have no such fellows prate in my diocese. Get you gone, and make your complaints to whom you will." "So away I went, — and blessed be God that I may go to Him!"[1] "My arm shall reach him there," said the wrathful Laud, when he heard of the escape to New England of Rev. John Davenport. The persecution of such holy servants of God forced the conviction on the Puritan mind that the whole system was wrong which gave such power to a hierarchy. Unless virtue were a lie, and conscience inspired by Satan, they felt that the authority so used and the spirit nursed by prelacy were unchristian. The very virtues of the primate — his sincere religion and his narrow zeal — made him the chosen instrument for accomplishing this result. It has been keenly said: —

"New England has perhaps never quite appreciated its great obligations to Archbishop Laud. It was his overmastering hate of non-conformity, it was the vigilance and vigor and consecrated cruelty with which he scoured his own diocese and afterward all England, and hunted down and hunted out the ministers who were committing the unpardonable sin of dissent, that conferred upon the principal colonies of New England their ablest and noblest men. Indeed, without Laud, those colonies would perhaps never have had an existence. His dreadful name is linked to our early story by sickening memories of terror and brutal insult and grief, of darkened firesides, of foul prisons opened to receive saints instead of felons, of delicate women and little children set adrift in the world without shelter or protector, of good men — scholars, apostles — fleeing for their lives, under masks, under false names, skulking in the guise of criminals, from the land they were born in."[2]

The establishment of the New England colony had been at first regarded by the Court as a happy purging of "virulent humors from the politic body;"[3] but the colony was now estab-

---

[1] See Shepard's own account of this scene in Increase Mather's "Discourse concerning ... Tithes, etc., pp. 25-27, or, [the Maintenance Due to Those that Preach the Gospel.]"

[2] Tyler, History of American Literature, i. 204. There was a grim humor in the proposal of the House of Commons, when the turn of the Puritans had come, to send Arch-Bishop Laud to New England, in April, 1643. Increase Mather's introduction to "Johannes in Eremo" says: "That eminent Person, Dr. *Tillotson*, the late Arch-Bishop of *Canterbury*, did, not above four years ago, sometimes express to me his Resentments of the Injury which had been done to the first Planters of *New-England*, and his great dislike of Arch-Bishop *Laud's* Spirit towards them.... Had the *Sees* in *England*, fourscore years ago, been filled with such Arch-Bishops and Bishops as those whom King *William* (whom God grant long to Live and to Reign!) has preferred to Episcopal Dignity, there had never been a *New-England*." — *Mather's Magnalia*, iii. 10.

[3] Carew, Masque at Whitehall, Feb. 18, 1633; quoted by Palfrey, i. 393. The feeling crops out in the private letters of the time: —

"18th Sept. 1635. Sir Henry Vane

lished on secure foundations. The watchful primate soon sought to bar the way to this house of refuge. Already, 28th February, 1633, came an "order for discharge of ships bound for New England," — "(2) That they cause the Prayers contayned in the Booke of Common Prayers established in the Church of England, to be sayde dayly at the usuall howers for morning and Evening Prayers, and that they cause all persons aboard theise said Shippes to be present at the same."[1] In February, 1634, the Star Chamber prohibited the escape thither of "persons ill-affected to the religion established in the Church of England, . . . of ministers who are inconformable to the ceremonies and discipline of the Church," and "all that had already gone forth . . . forthwith to be remanded back."[2] "It was deemed unsafe to Church and State to suffer such a constant receptacle of discontented, dangerous, schismatical persons to grow up so fast."[3]

The ship "Griffin," in September, 1634, brought a commission from the king to change the government of New England and transfer it to the Archbishop of Canterbury, Bishop of London, and others, with power to settle "the clergy government or the cure of souls, tithes, to appoint magistrates, levy fines, inflict penalties, and send home the refractory to England."[4] All but

also hath as good as lost his eldest son, who is gone into New England for conscience' sake; he likes not the discipline of the Church of England; none of our ministers would give him the Sacrament standing: no persuasions of our bishops nor authority of his parents could prevail with him; let him go; but he has more sons, but those also bred up at Leyden." — *Mass. Hist. Soc. Proc.*, 1871-73, p. 246 (from Cal. State Papers).
[1] N. E. Hist. and Geneal. Reg., viii. 137.
[2] N. E. Hist. and Geneal. Reg., viii. 135.
[3] Heylin, quoted by Anderson, i. 401.
[4] Charles's Commission for regulating plantations, "to the right reverend father in God, our right trusty and well-beloved counsellour, William [Laud], by the providence of God Archbishop of Canterbury, primate and metropolitan of all England," said: "Wee, being graciously pleased to provide for the ease and tranquillity of the said subjects, and reposeing assured confidence in your fidelity, wisdom, justice and providence, . . . to you, or to any five or more of you, do commit and give power of protection and government, as well over the said English colonies already planted as over all such other colonies which by any of our people of England hereafter shall be deduced into any other like parts whatsoever. . . . And for relief and support of the clergy, and the rule and cure of the soules of our people living in those parts, and for consigning of convenient maintenance unto them by tythes, oblations, and other profits accrewing, according to your good discretion, with the advice of two or three of our bishops, whom you shall think fitt to call unto your consultations, touching the distribution of such maintenance unto the clergy, and all other matters ecclesiasticall, and to inflict punishment on all offenders or violaters of constitutions and ordinances, either by imprisonments or other restraints, or by loss of life or members, according as the quality of the offence shall require; . . . and also to ordain judges, magistrates, and officers for and concerning courts ecclesiasticall." — *Hutchinson's History*, i. 503.

one of the ministers met on the following January 19th, and to the question, "What ought we to do if a general governor should be sent out of England?" all agreed that "we ought not to accept him, but defend our lawful possessions if we were able; otherwise to avoid or protract." In December, 1634, all persons were prohibited from emigrating unless they had taken the oaths of supremacy and allegiance, and could prove their "conformity to the orders of discipline of the Church of England." The royal ordinances of 1637 and 1638 required an examination, both moral and religious, of those designing to come to New England, before they could leave the kingdom, to insure the detention of those who were not on the side of Church and King.

The plot against Massachusetts thickened when, on the surrender of the Charter of the "Council for New England," a decree of *quo warranto* was issued against the Massachusetts Company. John Mason was appointed Vice-Admiral of the whole territory, and success seemed near for his schemes and those of Gorges for transforming the colony into a stanch buttress of the Stuart Church and State. But Mason died in 1635; the political horizon in England darkened more and more, and, though the surrender of the Massachusetts Charter was fruitlessly demanded once and again, the peril passed.

It does not fall in our province to relate how the convulsions which shook down throne and bishops in the mother country reacted on the history of this colony.[1] But it is interesting to note that the only public memorial here preserved of the connection of the Massachusetts men with the resistance to the Star Chamber, in which John Hampden was the most conspicuous leader, is in the beautiful monument still existing in King's Chapel to Samuel Vassall, a brother of the early colonist, "one of the original proprietors of the lands of this country, a steady and undaunted asserter of the Liberties of England in 1628. He was the first who boldly refused to submit to the tax of Tonnage and Poundage, an unconstitutional claim of the Crown arbitrarily imposed: for which (to the ruin of his family) his goods were seized and his person imprisoned by the Star Chamber Court. He was chosen to represent the City of London in two successive Parliaments which met April 13 and Nov. 3, 1640. The Parliament in July, 1641, voted him £10,445 12s. 2d. for his damages, and resolved that he should be further con-

---

[1] Palfrey's "History of New England" traces this connection with great interest and power.

sidered for his personal sufferings; but the rage of the times and the neglect of proper applications since have left to his family only the honor of that Vote and Resolution. He was one of the largest subscribers to raise money against the Rebels in Ireland."[1]

Thus our Puritan forefathers had no love for the institutions of the English Church, and gladly would have kept the salt sea between them and that ecclesiastical organization which was so associated in their minds with all that was intolerant and oppressive. They had fled from that church on a long journey and at the price of bitter sacrifices. It had driven them out from the England which was their home, and which they loved. It is not strange that when they once enjoyed the freedom which they had obtained with so great a price; when they had established a commonwealth disposed according to their own ideas of the Divine Law, based on their interpretation of the Bible, and ordered from beginning to end, as they believed, so as to establish a Church knit together by vital piety, and a State all compacted of holy souls, — they should have dreaded the intrusion of their old enemy; that they should have flouted at the old days hallowed by the Church, and hated the form of Common Prayer, and taught their children to be fiercely intolerant in the new home to that which had been so intolerant to them in the old home. Tolerance is a plant of slow growth; and they whose memory still smarted with the scars of wrongs which had driven them or their fathers from their native country could scarcely be expected to welcome the Book of Prayer and the surpliced priest. Yet it was inevitable, in the nature of things, that even in the early days of the colonial history some few steadfast members of the Church of England should find their way hither. The intense glow of the Puritans' faith has cast into shadow the quiet religion of a sober, moderate English type which in scattered spots along the coast tended its lowly and flickering light; but we can distinguish enough to know that there were those who preferred the old way to the new.

The little group of "Old Planters" had no religious sympathy with the new-comers.[2] These men seem to have been the remnants of the fruitless attempt under Gorges to colonize the

---

[1] The monument proudly refers for all these facts to "the Journal of the House of Commons," and states further that "He was the Son of the gallant John Vassall, who in 1588, at his own expense, fitted out and commanded two Ships of War, with which he joined the Royal Navy to oppose the Spanish Armada."

[2] See Mr. C. F. Adams, Jr.'s, chapter in "Memorial History of Boston," i. 63.

coast of Maine. Some of them were men of loose character and little religion; but others were of a better type.[1]

Thomas Morton of Mt. Wollaston was a stanch advocate of Episcopacy; so were Thomas Walford at Charlestown, and Samuel Maverick at Noddle's Island, where he had built a fort. Maverick impressed the Puritans as "a man of a very loving and curteous behaviour, very ready to entertaine strangers, yet an enemy to the Reformation in hand, being strong for the Lordly Prelaticall power over this Island."[2] He was destined to play an important part in subverting the Puritan supremacy in later years, when aggrieved by the treatment which he had received.[3]

Samuel Mavericke

William Blackstone, the original settler on the peninsula of Tri-Mountain, who "claimed the whole peninsula upon which Boston is built, because he was the first that slept upon it," was an ordained clergyman, "who had left England, being dissatisfied there and not a thorough conformist; but he was more dissatisfied with the non-conformity of the new-comers." He told them that he "came from England because he did not like the Lords Bishops; but he could not join with them because he would not be under the Lords Brethren."[4] He removed in 1635 from Bos-

---

[1] Rev. G. E. Ellis, D. D., has pointed out that the Prayer-book seems to have been but little valued or used. Even the inventory of William Blackstone's library does not mention it. See, on this point, Mr. Winthrop's paper in Mass. Hist. Soc. Proc., January, 1881. If rarely possessed by dissenters from Puritanism, it may have been due to the rarity of portable copies. Only two of the thirty-six editions printed during the reign of Charles I. were of this kind.

[2] Johnson's Wonder-working Providence, etc., 2 Mass. Hist. Soc. Coll., ii. 86.

[3] He was born about 1602, was found here by the Massachusetts Company in 1630, and admitted freeman in 1632, but on account of his opinions never held office. He had a grant of land in Maine from the President and Council of New England, in 1631. He "was ordered to reside in Boston, and forbidden to entertain any *strangers* for a longer time than one night, without leave of the civil authority, under penalty of £100, March 4, 1635, and convicted of aiding Thos. Owen in breaking prison, September, 1641." After the Restoration he went to England, and in 1664 was appointed one of the Commissioners "for reducing the Dutch at the Manhados; visiting the Colonies in New England, hearing and determining all matters of complaint, and settling the peace and security of the country." He resided, after the recall of the Commission, in New York, and died there before May, 1676. Josselyn gives a painful account of his brutal conduct to a female slave. (See Mass. Hist. Soc. Coll., vii. 307 n.; J. Wingate Thornton's Review of Peter Oliver's Puritan Commonwealth). His eldest son was named Nathaniel. Samuel Maverick, another son, married Rebecca, daughter of Rev. John Wheelwright, 1660, and died at Boston, 10 March, 1663¾. The two Samuels have been strangely confounded. See the Will of Samuel Maverick, Jr., March 28, 1663¾, and Power of Administration on the same, 14 March, 1663. — *N. E. Hist. and Geneal. Reg.*, viii. 378; xvi. 333; xii. 155.

[4] Mather's Magnalia, iii., i. xi. Blackstone, or Blaxton, graduated at Emanuel College, Cambridge, — A. B. 1617; A. M. 1621.

ton to a place six miles north of Providence, where he lived a secluded life, "neere Master Williams, but far from his opinions." Johnson's "Wonder-working Providence" says of him: —

William Blaxton B.A. 1617-18 [handwritten annotation]

He "betooke him . . . to till the Land, retaining no simbole of his former profession but a Canonicall Coate." Tradition further relates that "he had a great library, was a great student; there is a hill now called *Study Hill*, on which he loved to walk for contemplation. He rode his Bull for want of a horse to Boston and elsewhere. He sometimes came to Providence and preached there; the first time to one man, two women, and a number of children, whom he invited and collected around him by throwing apples to them. But he did not preach often."[1]

While Puritan Independency was thus consolidating itself, the Church of England was established both on the south and north of New England. Virginia had been colonized by adherents of that church order. The poet Crashaw, preacher at the Temple, in a sermon before the Virginia colonists (Feb. 21, 1609-10), said: "Suffer no Brownists nor factious Separatists: let them go and convert some other heathen; and let us see if they can constitute such churches really, the ideas whereof they have fancied in their brains. And when they have given us such an example, we may then have some cause to follow them; till then we will have our patterns from their betters."[2] The earlier colonists of Virginia had hospitably treated Puritan emigrants; but in 1632 the Assembly laid the English penalties upon all who dissented from the Episcopal Church as there established, and in 1662 the same Assembly "imposed a fine of 2,000 lbs. of tobacco on 'schismatical persons' that would not have their children baptized; and on persons who attended other religious meetings than those of the Established Church a penalty of 200 lbs. of tobacco for the first offence, of 500 lbs. of tobacco for the second offence, and of banishment for the third offence. Marriage was not tolerated under any other form than the Prayer-Book. No one, unless a member of the Established Church, might instruct the young, even in a private family. Any ship-

---

[1] See 2 Mass. Hist. Soc. Coll., x. 170-173; N. E. Hist. and Geneal. Reg., xiv. 31; Bliss's History of Rehoboth; Fifth Report of Record Commissioners, Boston, 1880, pp. 1-5. The autograph is kindly furnished by Mr. C. W. Tuttle.

[2] See Waddington's Congregational History, p. 170, where also are given, pp. 171, 172, the Rules of the Virginia colony to compel attendance on Divine service. The contrasts between the Massachusetts and the Virginia types of religion are well set forth in Prof. F. B. Dexter's paper already cited.

master who should convey non-conformist passengers to Virginia was to be punished. . . . As late as 1741 penal laws were enacted in Virginia against Presbyterians and all other dissenters."[1] But the contrast in religious spirit was very striking between this free and jovial colony and that planted by the Puritans. It was found that of the preachers who came to Virginia "very few of good conversation would adventure thither; . . . yet many came, such as wore black coats, and could babble in a pulpit, roar in a tavern, exact from their parishioners, and rather by their dissoluteness destroy than feed their flocks."[2]

More promising was the endeavor to settle the Church of England on the northern border of Massachusetts. In 1628 Captain Christopher Levett was appointed by royal commission Governor of New England, and was authorized to raise contributions and benevolences in England, "to build a city there and call it York," upon the present site of Portland.[3] But he died before any such result was reached.

The early settlers in Maine had no sympathy with Puritanism. "Mr. Henry Jocelyn, Gent.," who was in Scarborough as early as 1636, a son of Sir Thomas Josselyn, Kt., and brother of the traveller Josselyn, was a prominent opposer of the Bay government.[4]

Rev. Robert Jordan early settled in Maine as "an itinerant preacher to the people," and, marrying the only child of Mr. John Winter of Richmond's Island, became a large landed proprietor. He was known as "an Orthodox devine for the Church of England, and of great pt^y and Estate," and was "the soul of the opposition to Massachusetts, for which, and for baptizing children, he was more than once arrested."[5]

In 1637 Rev. Richard Gibson preached at Saco, where William Gorges had, in 1636, established an organized government and drawn up "a book of rates for the minister." Before May,

---

[1] See Tyler, History of American Literature, i. 91, and Campbell's History of Virginia. Whatever may be said against the Puritan treatment of the Quakers, it is fully paralleled by similar proceedings in the Virginia colony, as is reluctantly admitted by Anderson, ii. 27.

[2] John Hammond's "Leah and Rachel," 1656, quoted in Tyler, i. 62. The degraded condition of the Church in the Southern colony is painfully disclosed in "Papers relating to the History of the Church in Virginia." Edited by Drs. Hawks and Perry.

[3] Calendar of State Papers, Colonial, 1574-1660; i. 45, 47, 87. The name of "city" was at that time only applied to an episcopal seat.

[4] N. E. Hist. and Geneal. Reg., ii. 204; xxi. 202. The name of "John Michell, a Minister," appears on the Privy Council Register, June 27, 1638, as having money due him from Sir F. Gorges upon his adventures in Laconia. Jenness, Transcripts, etc., p. 29.

[5] See Rev. W. S. Bartlet's Frontier Missionary, p. 72; N. E. Hist. and Geneal. Reg., xiii. 221.

1642, Mr. Gibson removed to Strawberry Bank, now Portsmouth. The Piscataqua settlement was distinctively Church of England. The worship was regularly held here and glebe land set apart, and the first church built for that form of worship, as early as 1638. In an inventory of goods, in 1633, mention is made of "one communion cup, a psalter, communion cloth, and two service books, and again of one great bible, 12 service books, of a flaggon, and of cloths for communion table."

Mr. Gibson was "a good scholar, a popular speaker, and highly esteemed as a gospel minister;" but he was expelled by the Bay Colony in 1642 for denying its jurisdiction, and organized Episcopacy became extinct in New Hampshire for ninety years.[1]

Richard Gibson.

The fishermen of the Isles of Shoals held out stubbornly against the Puritan rulers of the Bay, encouraged by Gibson, but were compelled to receive a sound Puritan divine.[2] There were laymen, also, who shared the feeling of Richard Vines of Saco, who wrote to Winthrop: —

"I like Mr. Jenner, his life and conversation, and alsoe his preaching, if he would lett the Church of England alone; that doth much trouble me, to hear our mother Church questioned for her impurity vpon every occasion. . . . For my part I profes my selfe to be an opposite to Church covenant and seperacion, holding it sufficient that I am all ready a member of the Church of England, and so consequently of the Church of Christ, and soe capeable of the benefitts of his sacraments."[3]

The man of gentlest blood among these scattered Churchmen was Francis Champernowne, descended from a "clarous and

---

[1] Mr. Gibson had been in amicable relations for a time with the Massachusetts authorities. A letter from him to Governor Winthrop, Jan. 14, 1638–39, is preserved, complaining of the charges against Mary Lewis, of Saco, whom he has married, that "when she came from England some 2 yeares agoe, shee so behaued her selfe in the shipp, that the block was reaved at the mayne yard to have duckt her." — 5 *Mass. Hist. Soc. Coll.*, i. 267. The chapel was used for Congregational worship by Mr. Parker in 1642, and Queen's Chapel, named for Queen Caroline, was not established till 1732. One relic of that time is to this day preserved in Portsmouth, however, in the title "Wardens," still used in Congregational church affairs. See "Adams's Annals of Portsmouth" for 1640; N. H. Prov. Papers, i. 43, 111, etc.; Four Sermons by A. P. Peabody, 1859, pp. 44–46; and Rev. Jas. De Normandie's Historical Sketches of Portsmouth, N. H., in "Boston Transcript," Nov. 12, Dec. 26, 1873, and Jan. 7, 1874.

[2] Hubbard delights to chronicle the drunkenness and profanity of the Shoals and Piscataqua people. On the other hand, they fully returned the dislike.

[3] Jan. 25, 1640. See 4 Mass. Hist. Soc. Coll., vii. 340.

knightly family" of Devonshire, nephew by marriage to Sir F. Gorges, from whom, Dec. 12, 1636, his father received a grant of two tracts of land in the "Province of New Sommersett in N. E.,"

Fran: Champernowne

— now the Gerrish and Cutts Islands, and a tract on the mainland in Kittery and on the edge of York. The gift was transferred to the son, who came to the Piscataqua settlement in 1636, at the age of twenty-two, and passed many years on a large estate which he bought in the town of Greenland in 1640. As a councillor in the Gorges government, he was opposed to the rule of Massachusetts, and later was a member of the Council of Cranfield and his successors. He had retired to Cutts Island, where he lived till his death in 1687, an uncompromising royalist and churchman, and a recognized leader by birth and character.[1]

There is material for romance in these lives of Englishmen who kept alive their old-fashioned loyalty to Church and King, among uncongenial neighbors; but they could do nothing against the masterful purpose with which the Puritan authorities ruled them during the troubled years of Parliament and Commonwealth.[2]

The ecclesiastical system of the Puritans took its distinctive character by a natural reaction from all that had heretofore been forced on them against their conscience. No word of set forms was allowed in their prayers, but only the "conceived" prayer, which had hardly been tolerated in their old churches. Even the Lord's Prayer had been so superstitiously used that it was omitted now.

"They would share no white surplice with Romish priests, but would minister in the scholar's black gown of Geneva. Like the early disciples, they would gather about the sacramental table rather than kneel about

---

[1] See in N. E. Hist. and Geneal. Reg., xxviii., an account of him by C. W. Tuttle, to whom we are indebted for the autograph. Mr. Tuttle's forthcoming Life of him will contain much unpublished material. There is a striking sonnet on his grave by John Albee, which concludes: —

"Here rest the bones of Francis Champernowne;
The crest of ancient Norman kings he bore.
His fathers builded many a tower and town,
And ruled in England after Hastings' gore;
Now o'er his grave the lonesome forests frown,
And sailless seas beat the untrodden shore."

[2] The fragmentary notices of them which survive are gathered up in C. R. Batchelder's History of the Eastern Diocese, 1876.

the altar, lest haply men should say 'they worship the bread and the wine.' They will have no funeral prayers, but will bear their dead to the last resting-place and lay them away in touching silence, lest they should be thought to pray for the departed spirit, and say masses in the ancient manner. They will not only lay aside the marriage ring as heathenish, but by a strange revulsion they will have marriage a civil service, to be performed not by the minister, but by a magistrate. They cannot quite refuse to sing; but there shall be no instrument save the human voice, and such rough psalmody as was supplied to the Puritans of Amsterdam by Henry Ainsworth, — their tunes, some ten in number, oftenest York, Hackney, Windsor, St. Mary, and St. Martyn's."[1]

They would not use the title "Saint" even in speaking the names of places; yet it was keenly noted that they applied it to the members of their own communion, using the New Testament language, with which their critics were perhaps less familiar. The fondness for Scriptural or other significant names soon gave a special flavor to the new generation.[2] Separate from the Church of England they did not deem themselves, but only "from the corruptions in it." Its form of prayer had no divine authority in their sight; its order of bishops as superior to presbyters was held by the whole Puritan party to be in no wise established by Christ. They were free in a New World to lay their foundations by the line and plummet of Holy Writ, as best they could read it, without feeling that they went out of communion with all Christian men.[3]

In 1637 some of the Puritan ministers in England wrote over to their brethren here, inquiring about reports which had come concerning new opinions of theirs, among them "that a stinted form of prayer and set liturgy is unlawful." The question was felt to be "very hard to make any handsome work upon;" but an answer was prepared, and the course of events in England soon brought the inquirers to the same opinion with those whom they had criticised.

The preface to the "Platform of Church-Discipline Gathered out of the Word of God, And Agreed upon By the Elders and Messengers of the Churches Assembled in the Synod At Cambridge, in N. E., in 1649," says: —

[1] Rev. R. Ellis, D.D., Sermon in Commemoration of the Two Hundred and Fiftieth Anniversary of the Founding of the First Church in Boston.
[2] Hutchinson says that the first three baptized in the Boston church were Joy, Recompence, and Pity. Maj.-Gen. Atherton named children Rest, Thankful, Hope, Watching, Patience, Consider, etc.
[3] On the advice of Rev. John White, the Congregational model of church government was adopted by the Dorchester colony before leaving England. See Palfrey, i. 318; Two Hundred and Fiftieth

"For though it be not one Native Country that can breed us all of one minde ... yet ... we, who are by nature English-men, do desire to hold forth the same Doctrine of Religion (especially in Fundamentals) which we see and know to be held by the Churches of England, according to the truth of the Gospel. ... Yea, moreover, as this our profession of the same Faith with them will exempt us (even in their judgements) from suspition of Heresie, so (we trust) it may exempt us in the like sort from suspition of Schism. ... It is true, indeed, the National Covenant doth justly engage both Parties faithfully to endeavour the utter extirpation of the Antichristian Hierarchy, and much more of all Blasphemies, Heresies, and Errours. Certainly, if Congregational Discipline be Independent from the Inventions of men, is it not much more Independent from the delusions of Satan?"

The Lord's Day began at sunset on Saturday. Through its hours no one was permitted to leave or enter the town, the gates on the "Neck" being shut and the north ferry watched, while throughout the country travelling was strictly prevented. Nor was it allowed, "even in the hottest days of summer, to take the air on the Common," or on the wharves adjacent to the houses; while fine and imprisonment awaited those who, meeting in the street and conversing there, did not disperse at the first notice.[1] In 1677 the Court ordered that any person making a noise during the day, or misbehaving in the meeting-house, should be "put in a cage, to be set up in the market-place," and be kept there till examined and punished.[2]

Their religious services began at nine in the morning by "wringing of a bell,"[3] and were not essentially different in their arrangement from the Congregational order to-day, except that they were longer. The pastor began "with solemn prayer, continuing about a quarter of an houre." The teacher then read and expounded a chapter, after which one of the ruling elders, setting the pitch with his pitch-pipe, "dictated" a psalm, which was sung after him, line by line. A sermon or *extempore* exhortation by the pastor followed, in either case given without

---

Anniversary of the First Church in Dorchester, 1880.

[1] Bennett's History of N. E.; Mass. Hist. Soc. Proc., January, 1861, 115, 116.

[2] A mariner thus records his visit at a later day: "... In Boston they are very Strict Observers of the Sabath day and in Service times no Persons are allow'd the Streets but Doctors; if you are found upon the Streets and the Constables meet you they Compell you to go either to Church or Meeton as you Chuse, also in Swearing if you are Catcht you must Pay a Crown Old Tenor for Every Oath being Convicted thereof without farther dispute." — *N. E. Hist. and Geneal. Reg.*, xxiv. 63; *Captain Goelet's Journal*.

[3] In Boston by 1641, and in Salem as early as 1638, but in most places by beating a drum, blowing a shell or horn, or hoisting a flag. Dexter's "Congregationalism," etc., p. 452.

notes,[1] and the teacher concluded with prayer and benediction. Once a month the Lord's Supper followed, to which church-members alone remained, although others might look on if they wished. The ministers and ruling elders sitting at the table, the pastor and teacher divided the service between them, following the same order which is still observed in the Congregational churches. At 2 P.M. the congregation again met.[2] The pastor opened with prayer, and a psalm was sung; after which the teacher expounded a chapter and preached, praying before and after sermon. Then ensued baptism of children of church-members, after which one of the deacons saying, "Brethren, now there is time left for contribution; wherefore, as God hath prospered you, so freely offer," the congregation filed before his seat, dropping into a wooden box their contributions for the ministers and for the poor, "the Magistrates and chiefe Gentlemen first, and then the Elders, and all the congregation of men, all single persons, widows, and women in absence of their husbands."[3] Various church business followed, as the admission of members, etc., concluding at a late hour with a psalm and prayer and benediction.[4] No Scripture was read unless accompanied with a full exposition, without which it was stigmatized as "dumb reading."[5]

To the rare visitors who came hither for business or curiosity, and who were not in sympathy with the bare ritual of the Church of Calvin, the day, its forms of worship, and the religion of the people which it precisely expressed were repellent. It is to such unfriendly critics that we are indebted for our detailed accounts.[6]

[1] In 1681 Nathaniel Mather wrote to Cotton Mather: "I had forgot to say to yourselfe, by any means get to preach without any use of or help by your notes. When I was in N. E., no man that I remember used them except one, and hee because of a special infirmity, the vertigo, as I take it, or some spice of it." — 4 *Mass. Hist. Soc. Coll.*, viii. 34.

[2] In places where the people were widely scattered the intermission was shortened, so that they could conveniently remain to the second service.

[3] In Boston the ministers were paid by voluntary contributions. In some places the boxes were carried about at the end of long poles. Bennett's "History of New England;" Mass. Hist. Soc. Proc., 1861, 115.

[4] Lechford's Plaine Dealing, 3 Mass. Hist. Soc. Coll., iii. 76-78.

[5] The Labadist missionaries, in 1679, say that, attending a day of fasting in a church, "in the first place a minister made a prayer in the pulpit of full two hours in length; after which an old minister delivered a sermon an hour long, and after that a prayer was made and some verses sung out of the psalm. In the afternoon three or four hours were consumed with nothing but prayers, three ministers relieving each other alternately: when one was tired, another went up into the pulpit." — *Long Island Hist. Soc. Coll.*, i. 380.

[6] Lechford and Josselyn were Episcopalians. Lechford says in his preface: "Now that the government at New Eng-

But the holy day had a more sympathetic side to the people whose choice treasure it was. There was strictness in their worship and homes and lives; yet it was not the severity of bigots, but the austerity of God-fearing men who had forsaken all they held dear for what they deemed His service. The Puritan Sabbath began with the quiet shadows which preceded its dawn; it filled with its peace the streets of the little town, and added a holy beauty to the glory of the year or its pensive decay. The grave men and women who filled the "meeting-house" were fed with strong meat, and rejoiced therein; but it is doubtful how far the weaker brethren and babes were ministered to with "the sincere milk of the Word." "In the homes there is, till sundown, a hushed and sober tranquillity, though we may be sure that young hearts, and older ones too, had their joyousness."[1]

By this, more than all else, were knit the fibres of the Puritan community, religious, self-sacrificing, wise, far-seeing, generous in its poverty, with the strong virtues which grow on rocky soil, which did uncomplainingly the rugged tasks of planting the wilderness, and readily flowered in the heroic qualities that have made and saved a nation.

When the need arose, the churches adopted declarations of faith; but they were left to a merciful largeness in the beginning, as in the first covenant of the Salem and Boston churches.[2] In 1648 the synod which framed the Cambridge platform of Church discipline endorsed the Westminster confession; and the synod of 1680 prepared the Boston confession. These two

---

[1] land seemeth to make so many Church-members so many Bishops will be plaine by this ensuing Discourse." But John Cotton, in his "Way of Congregational Churches Cleared," says: "Let no man think he [Thomas Lechford] was kept out of our Churches, for maintaining the authority of Bishops. For we have in our Churches some well-respected Brethren, who doe indifferently allow either Episcopall, or Presbyteriall, or Congregationall Government, so be it that they governe according to the rules of the Gospel. Neither do we disturb such, nor they us, in our communion with them."

[1] Rev. G. E. Ellis, D.D., in an address in Boston before the Young Men's Christian Union, March 17, 1877, says: "All is so still that you might hear a bumblebee through the town, save as a thoughtless or a thoughtful rooster pays his tribute to St. Peter. The household ovens were heated on Saturday, so that the beans and brown bread and Indian pudding are taking care of themselves. All the inhabitants are gathered in their meeting-houses." McKenzie's "History of the First Church in Cambridge," p. 85, well says: "They were not morose, sour, tyrannical. There were some such, it may be; there are now. Men of bigoted temper, long-visaged, sullen, are to be seen any day in our streets. They are not Puritanic, they are badly human; not a reproach to the fathers, but a sorrow to us."

[2] Felt's misstatement that it is "proved that our first [Salem] church, at their outset, had articles of faith," — a point insisted on by the late S. M. Worcester, D.D., in his discourse at Plymouth and elsewhere, — is refuted in Judge D. A. White's "New England Congregationalism."

documents became the foundation of the Congregational church polity.

Thus was planted New England Congregationalism, the only system, it is safe to say, by which such a community as that of Massachusetts could have been organized.[1] In twenty years forty-two churches in as many towns had been planted by it, each a centre of that independent, self-developed life out of which America has grown. Its divinely ordained function in the order of Providence is shown by the fact that its essential principles are the foundation of every Protestant community in the land to-day.[2] From its fundamental thought, that all Christian men are "kings and priests unto God," sprang popular government in Church and State.

But although the Massachusetts Colony was founded on a definite religious idea, it could not entirely keep out those persons who were not in full sympathy with it. They came for trade and profit, as the colony grew prosperous; and, being here, found themselves excluded from places of honor, disqualified to vote, and under an ecclesiastical censorship which must have been in the highest degree irritating to those out of sympathy with it. Many of the children even of the early settlers could not meet the tests for admission to the church when they grew up; and as baptism could not be had for the children of those who were not church-members, a generation arose who were largely excluded alike from religious and civil privileges.

This state of things waxed worse and worse, as years went by. But even in the earliest days there were those who had little sympathy with the rigid spirit of the Puritans, — some who desired the Established Church of England because they had been born and bred in it and cared for it, and some, doubtless, who

---

[1] This is strongly stated by Hon. R. C. Winthrop in his oration at Plymouth in 1870.

[2] Even the American Episcopal Church, in its mode of electing and supporting ministers and in its representative system, has engrafted these principles on the alien methods of the Church of England. "Democracy," said John Cotton, "I do not conceyve that ever God did ordeyne as a fitt government eyther for church or commonwealth. If the people be governors, who shall be governed?" But John Wise expressed the idea of the system when he wrote, "That the People, or Fraternity, under the Gospel, are the first Subject of Power; ... that a Democracy in Church or State is a very honourable and regular Government according to the Dictates of Right Reason. And therefore, That these Churches of New-England in their ancient Constitution of Church Order, it being a Democracy, are manifestly Justified and Defended by the Law and Light of Nature. It has the best ballance belonging to it of any Church-Government in the World. Other Governments have generally too high a Top, and are very lop-sided too." This tract ("Vindication of the New England Churches") was issued again in Boston on the eve of the Revolution, in 1772. See Dexter's "Congregationalism," etc., p. 498.

desired it, not because they loved it more, but because they hated it less than the rigid system under which they were living. Whenever a favorable opportunity should occur, it was certain that an effort would be made for wider freedom by demanding equal privileges for the old Church in the new country.

But when this opportunity might come would depend on the condition of ecclesiastical affairs across the water. The close connection of the two countries in religious matters must be carefully borne in mind, in order to understand the full significance of the two abortive attempts which preceded the successful introduction here of Episcopacy.

The first occasion came when, after the downfall of Episcopacy, the struggle between Presbyterianism and Independency was at its height in England. John Milton's sonnet line —

"New Presbyter is but old Priest writ large" —

expresses the mind of our forefathers. But it seemed likely in 1642 that the Independents in England would be overborne by Presbytery; and if so, then must their sympathizers in New England go under too. This was the moment chosen by William Vassall to push for the doing away of church distinctions here. Vassall was a man of fortune, who had come over with Governor Winthrop in 1630, and had been one of his assistants, but had almost immediately returned to England, — possibly from dissatisfaction with the tendencies to Separatism which he witnessed, and when he came back did not come any nearer to Boston than Scituate. The charitable judgment on him is, that he was "a gentleman of high and honorable feelings, who looked with contempt on many of the narrow notions of the day." But Winthrop's own judgment of him is, that he was "a man never at rest but when in the fire of contention," "of a busy and factious spirit, and always opposite to the civil governments of this country and the way of the churches."[1] At his instigation a Remonstrance and Humble Petition was addressed, by Samuel Maverick, Robert Child, and five others, to the General Court, representing —

"That they could not discern in this colony 'a settled form of government acc. to the laws of England;' that 'many thousands in these

[1] See Drake's Boston; Sumner's East Boston; Winthrop's New England. Cf. Colonel Aspinwall on "William Vassall no Factionist," in Mass. Hist. Soc. Proc., March, 1863. S. Deane's History of Scituate, pp. 366-369, contains a notice of Vassall and his estate in Scituate. The fate of the petition is related in "New England's Jonas cast up at London," — 2 Mass. Hist. Soc. Coll., iv. 107-120.

plantations of the English nation' were 'debarred from all civil employments,' and not permitted 'so much as to have any vote in choosing magistrates, captains, or other civil and military officers;' and 'that numerous members of the Church of England, . . . not dissenting from the latest and best reformation of England, Scotland,' etc., were 'detained from the seals of the covenant of free grace, because, as it was supposed, they will not take these churches' covenants.'"

They asked to be relieved from these grievances, and signified that otherwise they should "be necessitated to appeal to the honorable Houses of Parliament" for relief.

"They hoped," they said, "should their requests be granted, to see the now contemned ordinances of God highly prized; the gospel much darkened break forth as the sun at noon-day; Christian charity and brotherly love, almost frozen, wax warm; jealousy of arbitrary government (the bane of all commonwealths) quite banished," — and many other ensuing blessings and benefits.

Copies of this paper were sent flying abroad through Massachusetts and the other colonies. The difficulty which it was foreseen this would make with the Presbyterian party in England was met by the calling, by the General Court, of a Synod at Cambridge to consolidate the churches, and the Remonstrance was answered in a carefully drawn "Declaration," which indulged in contemptuous description of the seven unfortunate signers, of whom another [1] said: —

"The persons were of a linsey-woolsey disposition: some for prelacy, some for Presbytery, and some for *Plebsbytery*, but all joined together in the thing they would, which was to stir up the people to dislike of the present government."

"And these are the champions," said the General Court, "who must represent the body of non-freemen. If this be their head, sure they have an unsavoury head, not to be sweetened with much salt."

After a solid reply in argument to the petition, they reminded the petitioners of the issue of Roger Williams's recent experiment in Rhode Island, where variance had come, and church and civil state had been overthrown, instead of being established.

"Such peace, unity, prosperity, etc.," they say, "is that which we may expect, if we will cast off the rules of God's word, the civill prudence of all nations, and our owne observation of the fruit of other men's follies, and hearken to the counsell of these new statesmen. From which the Lord deliver us, and all the seed of Israell to the comeing of Xt Jesus. Amen."

[1] Johnson's Wonder-working Providence, etc.

The petitioners insisted on appealing to England; and finally, denying the jurisdiction of this government, were heavily fined, and their papers seized. When Child at last reached England, he found the political conditions so changed that Presbyterian sympathy could no longer help him; and so the movement came to nought. The Commonwealth followed, and Massachusetts had leisure to consolidate into what was an independent people in all but name.[1]

Such was this people, as firmly rooted in habits and convictions as ever men were, when the determined movement of the English government to break down Puritan exclusion here, if not to crush Puritanism altogether, began. The people of Massachusetts could not know how base and false was the ruler who had come to the throne, as it seemed, by such wonderful Providence, and after a discipline of adversity which must have seemed to the God-fearing Puritans to be a divine chrism for his office. Charles II. promised also, while believing the liturgy to be "the best extant," that it should be revised by men of different persuasions; that the scruples against the cross in baptism and the surplice should be respected; and that subscription should not be required for university or ecclesiastical positions. It appeared that though royalty and episcopacy came back to England, the Puritan principles had established their equal right to exist in the bosom of the Church. This hope should mollify our judgment of the adulatory terms in which the General Court addressed the king in July, 1660.[2]

A second address claimed to be an "Eucharistical approach

---

[1] The difference between the Independent and the Presbyterian ideas is well stated by Dr. Dexter, "Congregationalism of the Last Three Hundred Years," etc., pp. 459-462. Its points were: the "terms of membership of the Church," whether a regenerate membership or a comprehensive State Church; "the silent power of assent accorded to the brotherhood;" and the power of synods, which, in the New England system, were "for advice and the moral power of persuasion only, while Presbyterianism held that they exercise the Gospel authority of Christ over the many congregations of the one Church." Thomas Hooker thus defines Independent: "The word in its fair and inoffensive sense imports thus much: 'Every particular congregation, rightly constituted and completed, hath sufficiency in itself to exercise all the ordinances of the Church.'" The Independents feared despotism; the Presbyterians anarchy, — each from the other.

[2] One touching sentence shines in this address: ". . . That we might therefore enjoy divine worship without humane mixtures, without offence to God, man, our owne consciences, with leave but not without teares departed from our country, kindred, and fathers' houses into this Pathmos; in relation whereunto we do not say our garments are become old by reason of the very long journey, but that ourselves, who came away in our strength, are, by reason of long absence, many of us become grey-headed, and some of us stooping for age."— *Hutchinson Papers*, ii. 46 (*Prince Reprint*).

unto the best of kings." It says: "There wee besought your favour by presenting to a compassionate eye that bottleful of teares shed by us in this Jeshimon. Here we also acknowledge the efficacie of Regal influence to qualify these salt waters."[1]

It soon became evident that all these hopes were baseless, and that if New England escaped it would be only distance that would save her. The last dream of a united Church of England faded, and organized dissent first came into being, on the failure of the Savoy Conference. The Act of Uniformity, May 17, 1662, enforced the strictest conformity, and made St. Bartholomew's day memorable by the ejection of more than two thousand pious clergymen. By this act, "for the first time since the Reformation, all orders except those by Episcopal hands were disallowed."[2] In 1664 was passed a law

"Which subjected any person above sixteen years of age, who should attend any religious worship other than that allowed by the Church of England, where five or more persons besides the household were present, to an imprisonment of three months for the first offence, and of six for the second. If he should offend a third time, he was liable to transportation for seven years to some of the American Plantations, except New England and Virginia; and, if he should make his escape thence, he was to be adjudged a felon, and suffer death without benefit of clergy."[3]

During the reign of Charles II. nearly eight thousand nonconformists died in English prisons. In 1660 Leverett wrote from England: "Episcopacy, common prayer, bowing at the name of Jesus, sign of the cross in baptism, the altar and organs, are in use and like to be more. The Lord keep and preserve his churches, that there may not be fainting in the day of trial!" Every blow at Puritanism in the old home struck an answering knell in the new. In the Diary of John Hull we read: —

"Nov. 30 (1660). A small ship arrived from England, Mr. Trumball master, and brought intelligence of the bishops' countenancing the old

---

[1] Hutchinson doubts if this paper was sent, but Anderson (Col. Ch., ii. 214) gives it, dated Aug. 7, 1661, signed by Endicott in the name of the General Court of Massachusetts, from the original MS. in the State Paper Office, "as a sample of the train of thought and language prevalent in that day." It is substantially as in Hutchinson, omitting the clause which he states was objected to by the General Court. It contains the following paragraph: —

"Royal Sir, — Your just title to the Crown enthronizeth you in our consciences; your graciousness in our affections: that inspireth unto Duty, this naturalizeth unto Loyalty; thence we call you Lord, hence a Saviour. Mephibosheth, how prejudicially soever misrepresented, yet rejoiceth that the King is come in peace to his owne house."

[2] Dexter, "Congregationalism of the Last Three Hundred Years," etc., p. 667.

[3] Anderson's Col. Ch., ii. 258.

liturgy, and inventions of men, in the worship of God, and the face of things looking sadly toward the letting in of Popery; as if, when they had been now twenty years conflicting, and a great part of them in bloody war, for reformation, they should all upon a sudden be sent back again, as sometime Israel in the wilderness, ready to enter into Canaan, yet for unbelief and disobedience sent back to the Red Sea, and to wandering forty years, to consume that generation that would not learn and do the work of their generation."[1]

The king's letter of June 28, 1662, brought by Bradstreet and Norton, said: —

"And since the principal end of that Charter was and is the freedom of liberty of conscience, we do hereby charge and require you, that freedom and liberty be duly admitted and allowed; so that such as desire to use the Book of Common Prayer, and perform their devotions after that manner as Established here, be not denied the Exercise thereof or undergo any prejudice or disadvantage thereby, they useing their Liberty peaceably without disturbance to others; and that all persons of good and honest lives and conversations be admitted to the Sacrament of the Lord's Supper, according to the said Book of Common Prayer, and their Children to Baptism."

It expressly excluded Quakers from toleration, but enjoined "only consideration to be had of the wisdom, virtue, and integrity of the persons to be chosen, and not of any faction with reference to opinions and outward profession; that all freeholders of competent estate, not vicious in conversation and orthodox in religion, though of different persuasions concerning church government, should have their votes." About this time the report came from England to Massachusetts that "a Bishop, with a suffragan," had been appointed for the colonies.[2]

---

[1] Archæologia Americana, iii. 196. The revival of Episcopacy in the mother country reanimated the old feeling against its form of prayer. June 6, 1663, Mr. Higginson wrote to the Legislature "that the Common Prayer-book may be cited against the impenitent, as the heathen poets were by an Apostle." Governor Winthrop's story about the mouse which nibbled the leaves of a Prayer-book, but spared those of a Greek Testament and a Psalter bound in the same volume, is paralleled by Cotton Mather's tale of the possessed girl whom he had in his house, who called the Prayer-book "her *Bible*, and put a more than ordinary Respect upon it. She could read the *Scriptures* in that Book; but if any shewed her the very same Scriptures in the *Bible* it self, she would rather die than read them," etc.

[2] Hutchinson's History, i. 225, *n*. The letters of the Dutch W. I. Co. acquaint Governor Stuyvesant in 1664 with the rumor then afloat that the King of England was about to send commissioners to install bishops in New England "the same as in Old England." "We believe that the English who mostly left England [to escape the government of bishops] will not give us henceforth so much trouble." *New York Col. Docs.*, ii. 235, 409. Mag. of Amer. Hist., Oct. 1879, p. 627.

The Court adopted a temporizing policy, ordering a Thanksgiving " for the safe and speedy return of the public messengers sent to England, together with the continuance of the mercies of peace, liberties, and the Gospel." At the same time a day of fasting and humiliation was appointed, to be kept a month later, " on account of the afflictive and low estate of the cause and people of God universally, with the prevailing power of Antichrist over the reformed churches beyond the seas, together with some public rebukes of God among ourselves."

In July, 1664, appeared four commissioners,[1] with powers to hear and determine all matters of complaint, and settle the peace and security of the country. Among them was the same Maverick who had been fined and imprisoned here more than twenty years before, who now had the satisfaction of commending to the General Court that they "would further consider of His Majesty's letter." An order was passed enfranchising " from henceforth all Englishmen being twenty-four years of age, householders, and settled inhabitants, and presenting a certificate under the hands of the ministers or minister of the place where they dwelt, that they were orthodox in religion and not vicious in their lives, and also a certificate from selectmen . . . that they were ratable to yearly value of 10s." But as few besides church members paid this yearly value, it still left the power in the churches. The commissioners reduced New York, and visited the other colonies before the decisive conflict;[2] then, returning, acquainted the Court "that such as desire to use the Book of Common Prayer be permitted so to do without incurring any penalty, reproach, or disadvantage, — it being very scandalous that any persons should be debarred the exercise of their religion according to the laws and customs of England, by those who were indulged with the liberty of being of what profession or religion they pleased."

But not even royal authority, by such instruments, could change the rooted habit of this people. The Court replied that " the use of the Common Prayer-book would disturb their peace and present enjoyments; " they would not have been " voluntary ex-

---

[1] The commissioners were Colonel Richard Nichols, of the Duke of York's household, Sir Robert Carre, George Cartwright, and Samuel Maverick.
[2] Jenness (Transcripts, etc., p. 48) gives a petition to the commissioners from "part of the inhabitants of Portsmouth and Strawberry Bank": "The contrary party have kept us under hard servitude, and denyed us in our publique meeting the Common prayer, Sacram^{ts}, and decent buriall of the dead contrary to the Laws of England and his Maties lre sent by Simon Broadstreet and John Norton in the yeare 1662." It is signed by Francis Champernowne and others.

iles from their dear native country . . . could they have seen the Word of God warranting them to perform their devotions in that way, and to have the same set up here. And as to ecclesiastical privileges they had commended to the ministry and people here the word of the Lord for their rule." The commissioners shrewdly replied: "Though you commend to the ministers and people the word of the Lord for their rule, yet you did it with the proviso that they have the approbation of the Court; and we have great reason both to think and say that the king and his council and the Church of England understand and follow the rules in God's Word as much as this corporation." But the Court yielded nothing, refusing in the name of the king to recognize the authority of those who claimed to represent him. They were recalled to England, and though the Colony was ordered to send agents to answer the charges against it before the king, the danger was again postponed. But there were now disintegrating forces working within the body politic in the same direction.

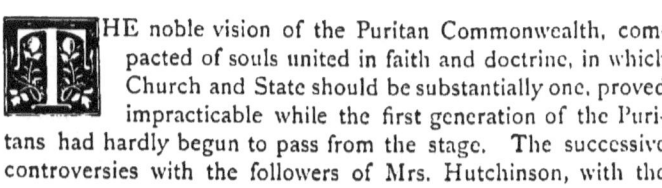

FIRST PAGE OF THE EARLIEST RECORD BOOK.

CHAPTER II.

EPISCOPACY PLANTED IN BOSTON.

THE noble vision of the Puritan Commonwealth, compacted of souls united in faith and doctrine, in which Church and State should be substantially one, proved impracticable while the first generation of the Puritans had hardly begun to pass from the stage. The successive controversies with the followers of Mrs. Hutchinson, with the

Baptists, and with the Quakers, demonstrated more and more clearly the impossibility of such accord of the whole population on religious questions as was vitally necessary for the permanence of the Theocracy. The fixedness with which the policy of repression was pursued until the English Government interfered, although ineffectual to do more than postpone the religious disintegration which nothing could ultimately prevent, had one further effect of immense importance. It secured time to impress on the community a marked character which two centuries since elapsing, with all their modifications of faith and of the population, have not been able to efface. During half a century the Puritan spirit had exercised a predominant sway, while the new community was hardening into its fixed character. The Boston of 350,000 inhabitants to-day, with its mingling of many races and all religions and no religion, is marked profoundly by its inheritances from the temper, spirit, and belief of the Boston which, at the close of the seventeenth century, was a little town of less than 7,000 souls.

The period of forcible repression of dissent from the Established Church of New England, in which the Quaker and the Baptist conquered by enduring, was succeeded by a period in which the protesting bodies gained a firm and recognized footing in Boston.

For twenty years the two "Old Meeting-houses" in which Cotton and Wilson ministered accommodated the whole population.[1] But, on account of the growth of the town in numbers, a second church was formed in 1650, with the consent of the First Church.[2] The fame of its two most eminent ministers gives it special distinction: it has been called "the Church of the Mathers," four of its early pastors having belonged to that family, who held the pulpit for seventy-three out of the first ninety-one years of the church history.

But the era of peace within the Puritan ecclesiastical community was now rudely broken by the formation of the third church in Boston. The growing sentiment that "all baptized persons, not scandalous in life and formerly excommunicated,

---

[1] See the histories of the First Church of Christ in Boston by Rev. William Emerson, 1812, and Arthur B. Ellis, 1881, and the memorial volume containing the addresses on its quarter-millennial celebration, and the historical sermons of Rev. Rufus Ellis, D. D.

[2] The "North Church" was burned in 1676, but was soon rebuilt. This later edifice, though in a condition to last many years longer, was destroyed for fuel by the King's troops during the siege of Boston in 1775. The congregation then united with the New Brick Church in Hanover Street, retaining the name and records of the Second Church.

ought to be considered members of the church in all respects, except the right of partaking of the Lord's Supper," though strenuously opposed by lovers of the old way, had finally induced the Court of Massachusetts to call a General Council in 1657, which met at Boston, delegates from Connecticut also taking part. This Council determined that those who had been baptized in infancy were therefore to be regarded as members of the church, and entitled to its privileges, with the exception of the Lord's Supper, including baptism for their children. Such an innovation on the earlier practice roused yet more bitter opposition. A second Synod was found to be necessary in 1662, at which this decision was substantially reaffirmed. Vigorous protest was, however, made by some of the most eminent pastors, who published writings in opposition; and among them Rev. John Davenport of New Haven, "the greatest of the anti-synodists." The churches of Massachusetts were divided among themselves, whether to receive or reject the conclusions of the Synod. In the First Church of Boston a majority favored them, but the influence of their pastor, the venerated Wilson, preserved the peace. His death, Aug. 7, 1667, at the age of seventy-nine, left a vacancy which was filled by the choice of Mr. Davenport, then seventy years old. The prominent position of this eminent man as an advocate of the stricter side in the controversy then agitating New England occasioned the most earnest opposition to his settlement. The church was divided, the former minority becoming the majority. Mr. Davenport accepted their call and came to Boston, where he died little more than a year after beginning his ministry. But the dissatisfied minority did not rest here. Twenty-eight in number, with one member of the Charlestown Church,[1] they met at Charlestown, probably to avoid, by holding their meeting in another county, the law which required that the magistrates should be consulted before forming another church. Their application to the First Church to be dismissed for this purpose was refused, whereupon they called a council of other churches, by whose advice they organized themselves in due form as the "Third Church in Boston." The publication of protests and counter-protests enlisted the whole colony on one side or the other, as it was seen that "the favorers of the old church were against the Synod, and those of the new church were for it."[2]

Nor was the opposition confined to words. It is probable that the "imprisoning of parties," to which a letter of Randolph

[1] Rev. Thos. Thatcher, their first minister.   [2] Wisner, "Old South Church," 1830.

refers, indicates that the members of the new church were punished in this way for proceeding without the consent of the authorities. Governor Bellingham, being strenuous for the First Church, of which he was a member, summoned his Council to prohibit the erection of the new meeting-house. The Council, however, was unwilling to take this extreme ground, and the consent of the selectmen of Boston being obtained to the erection of "another Meeting-House in this town," the Third (or South) Church was built on what is now the corner of Washington and Milk streets. The land for the purpose was given by Madam Norton, who, though the widow of a former minister of the First Church, was in warm sympathy with the seceders from it.

The dissension agitated the "House of Deputies," who, in 1670, adopted a report from "a committee to inquire into the prevailing evils which had been the cause of the displeasure of God against the land," explicitly condemning the transaction by which the new church was constituted, "as irregular, illegal, and disorderly." But the next election reversed this action, and the new General Court, being chosen with reference to this very question, adopted a contrary vote by a decisive majority.

The troubled waters, however, subsided but slowly. The old church refused to have any ecclesiastical relations with its rebellious daughter. Three times it denied dismission to the wives of the brethren who had withdrawn to form the new church, who naturally wished to follow their husbands; nor was it until the forebodings of an invasion of the ecclesiastical unity of New England by the dreaded Episcopacy of the mother country grew into certainty, that the breach was healed. In May, 1682, Edward Randolph wrote to the Bishop of London: —

"We have in Boston one Mr. Willard, a minister, brother to Major Dudley; he is a moderate man, and baptizeth those who are refused by the other churches, for which he is hated. There was a great difference between the old church and the members of the new church about baptisme and their members joyning in full communion with either church; this was soe high that there was imprisoning of parties and great disturbances, but now, heereing of my proposals for ministers to be sent over, . . . they are now joyned together, about a fortnight ago, and pray to God to confound the devices of all who disturbe their peace and liberties." [1]

Meantime, the period of active persecution of obnoxious modes of faith had closed; the two heresies which had been

[1] Hutchinson's Collection of Papers, ii. 271.

most strenuously resisted, the Baptist and the Quaker, had rooted themselves in the soil, in spite of all opposition. The former built a place of worship in 1680, which, though closed for a time by order of the General Court, was soon peaceably occupied. The Quakers had a regular place of meeting as early as 1677, and in 1697 they erected on a lot in Brattle Street the first meeting-house built of brick in Boston.

But bitter to the strict followers of "the old way" as were these indications of the relaxing Puritanism, the rooting of the Church of England here was most bitter of all.

The people of the sturdy Puritan stock are not blameworthy for desiring to keep the country of their own way of belief, if they could. For nearly half a century they had had the opportunity to grow far toward an independent nation on that ecclesiastical basis, and the presence of the Church of England would be a perpetual sign that this state of things was ended. Nor is it strange that they feared many evils from the admission of the Book of Common Prayer which never came to pass. But they resolutely shut their eyes to the fact that there were those among them who had an equal right with themselves to such religious institutions as they might choose. The Church of England had the misfortune to be, in the estimation of the mass of New-Englanders, a part of the tyranny of the Stuarts. If it had been more free from such associations, perhaps they would have feared and hated it less, nor would some of its earliest promoters have been so zealous in its behalf.

The controversy in the reign of Charles II. could end only in one way. Englishmen must surely have the rights of Englishmen in an English colony; and among these none was dearer to some than the right to worship God according to the hallowed and familiar form established in England itself. Yet although there were not a few in Boston who desired it, " most of the inhabitants," says Hutchinson, " who were upon the stage in 1686 had never seen a Church of England Assembly." Edward Randolph discovered, in his first visit here in 1676, that there were laws forbidding the observance of " Christmas day or any like festivity,"[1] "the solemnization of marriage by any person but

---

[1] The law of 1651 enacted: "For preventing disorders arising in several places within this jurisdiction, by reason of some still observing such festivals as were superstitiously kept in other countries, to the great dishonour of God and offence of others: It is therefore ordered by this Court and the authority thereof, that whosoever shall be found observing any such day as christmas or the like, either by forbearing labour, feasting, or any other way upon any such account as aforesaid, every such person so offending shall pay for every such offence five shillings as a

a Magistrate," and confining the suffrage to church-members, as well as on other points which contravened the Royal prerogative. The result, partly of Randolph's persistency in his frequent crossings of the ocean, and partly of the King's own growing certainty of the intractable stubbornness of the people with whom he had to deal, was a steady pressure on our ancestors to alter their laws in these regards. In November, 1678, the General Court appointed a Fast Day, to beseech the Lord "that he will not take away his holy gospel, and it be his good will yet to continue our liberties, civil and ecclesiastical, to us and our children after us." The times were dark indeed for them, — Charles Stuart on the throne, and they too weak to resist him with open war.

"The thoughtful observer," says Dr. Greenwood, "will mark the strange processes by which the human mind is often forced to the most simple and excellent conclusions. He will see arbitrary power from another country contending against arbitrary power here, and the results of these conflicting and angry authorities to be toleration, liberty, and peace."

In 1679 a number of persons residing in Boston petitioned the King "that a Church might be allowed them for the exercise of religion according to the Church of England." Not until 1681 was the law which forbade the keeping of Christmas repealed. That sturdy Puritan, Samuel Sewall, wrote in his diary for Sunday, Dec. 25, 1681 : —

"Mr. Randolph and his new wife sit in Mr. Joyliffe's Pue [in the South Church] ; and Mrs. Randolph is observed to make a curtesy at Mr. Willard's naming *Jesus*, even in Prayer-time."[1]

fine to the county." — *The Charters and General Laws of the Colony and Province of Massachusetts Bay*, etc. Boston: 1814. Chap. L., sec. 2.

Bradford, of Plymouth, relates that, in 1621, "One ye day called Chrismas-day, ye Govr caled them out to worke (as was used), but ye most of this new-company excused themselves and said it wente against their consciences to work on yt day. So ye Govr tould them that if they made it mater of conscience, he would spare them till they were better informed. So he led away ye rest and left them ; but when they came home at noone from their worke, he found them in ye streete at play, openly, — some pitching yᵉ barr, and some at stoole-ball, and shuch like sports. So he went to them and tooke away their implements, and tould them that was against his conscience that they should play and others worke. Since which time nothing hath been attempted that way, at least openly." Governor Winthrop, indeed, begins his Journal on "Easter Monday, March 29" [1630] while his fleet was still "riding at the Cowes." But the church days did not cross the sea with him.

[1] This was in the same church where Judge Sewall afterward did public penance for his part in the Witchcraft trials. It is to be feared that some unfriendly eyes were open watching their neighbors' sins, when they should have been shut for meditation on their own!

The good man (for that he was, after the stern old pattern) wrote four years later: —

1685. "X^r 25, Friday. Carts come to Town, and Shops open as is usual: some somehow observe ye day; but are vex'd I believe that ye Body of ye People profane it, and blessed be God no authority yet to compell them to keep it."

"X^r 28. Cous. Fessenden here Saith he came for Skins last Friday, and was less Christmas-keeping than last year, fewer Shops shut up."

In those four years events had marched fast in Boston, and on the other side of the water.

Edward Randolph, "his shuttle of mischief being," in 1682, on this "side of the ocean, still working in its loom of hate and revenge,"[1] — doubtless, also, of loyalty to King and Church, after the high-handed fashion of loyalty with which such a man would serve a Stuart king, — wrote two letters to the Bishop of London, urging measures to establish the Church of England here:[2] —

"In my attendance on your lordship, I often exprest that some able ministers might be appoynted to performe the officies of the church with us. The maine obstacle was how they should be maintayned. I did formerly and doe now propose, that a part of that money sent over hither, and pretended to bee expended among the Indians, may be ordered to goe towards that charge. Since wee are here immediately under your lordship's care, I with more freedome press for able and sober ministers, and wee will contribute largely to their maintenance; but one thing will mainly helpe, when no marriages hereafter shall be allowed lawfull but such as are made by the ministers of the Church of England."

And, July 14, 1682,[3] besides urging the bringing a *quo warranto* against the Massachusetts charter, to "disenable many . . . of the faction . . . from acting further in a public station," he says: —

"Wee have advice . . . that your lordship hath remembered us and sent over a minister with Mr. Cranfield; . . . the very report hath given great satisfaction to many hundreds whose children are not baptized, and to as many who never, since they came out of England, received the sacraments. . . . If we are misinformed concerning your lordship's sending over a minister, be pleased to commiscerate our condition, and send us over a sober, discreet gentleman. Your lordship hath now good security,

---

[1] Rev. Dr. G. E. Ellis.
[2] Hutchinson's Papers, ii. 271, May 29, 1682.
[3] Hutchinson's Papers, ii. 280. Randolph to Bishop of London.

as long as their agents are in England, for his civil treatment by the contrary party; he will be received by all honest men with hearty respects and kindness, and if his majesty's laws (as none but fanatics question) be of force with us, we could raise a sufficient maintenance for divers ministers out of the estates of those whose treasons have forfeited them to his majesty."

No wonder that good Mr. Sewall and his Puritan fellow-worshippers with him looked darkly on the man who was busy among them with such thoughts as these. For though they could not read his thoughts or the letters which their descendants can read, they knew him as one who hated their ways and looked on them as more than half rebels, and met their resolute wills with a will every whit as resolute for high prerogative in Church and Crown as they had against it. Still the "sober and discreet" minister did not come. Randolph wrote again, and described the religious condition of the country at this time: —

"New Eng^{ld} is devided into 7 small colonyes or Gouernm^{ts}, at present managed by men of weake and inconsiderable parts; most of them having different Lawes and methods of executing them. They are devided into Presbyterians, Independants, Anabptists, Quakers, seauenth day men, who are some of them in all gouernm^{ts}: Such of the Church of England tho' the chief men and of good parts not appearing soe till a regulation in governm^t from hence directed. Our chiefe colony is that of Boston, made so by a continuall concourse of people from all parts; they driue a great trade in ye world, and in deed give Lawes to all the rest; here all is managed by their Clergye, without whom the magistrates venture not to act, as in the late example of this gov^r. upon receipt of his ma^{ties} letter, et^c. Here noe children are baptised but the children of church members: some giue a larger latitude and admit the gran-children of C members, others the children of such who own the church and promise to liue under their watch.

"But none in any of the colonyes are admitted to the Eucharist but as are in full communion. All are obliged, by one way or other, to maintaine the ministry: some by weekly contributions at their meeting-houses; Anabaptists and Quakers pay not under that notion, but are rated in towne rates, which also is really for that intent."[1]

Randolph went and came again. Meantime, in the neighboring domain of New Hampshire a governor less able than Randolph and Andros, but as overbearing and resolute to crush out

---

[1] Tanner, MS. xxxii. 5, in "Papers relating to the History of the Church in Massachusetts," 1676–1785, edited by W. S. Perry, D. D., 1873.

opposition in State and Church, was illustrating before the observant watch of the Massachusetts Colony what they might expect when their turn should come. In the intervals of Randolph's absence from New England, Governor Cranfield supplied fresh fuel for the flame.

"Touching Ecclesiasticall matters," he wrote, "the attempting to settle y² way of ye Church of England I perceive wilbe very grievous to ye people. However Mr Mason asserted y^t their Inclinacons were m^{ch} y^t way. I have observed them to be very dilig^t and devout in attending on y^t mode of worship wch they have been brought up in, and hath been so long settled among them and seem to be very tenacious of it, and are very thankfull for His Maj^{sties} Gracious Indulgence in those matters." [1]

And again: —

" . . . tis my humble opinion, that it will be absolutely necessary to admit no person into any place of Trust, but such as take ye Sacrament and are conformable to the Rites of the Church of England, for others will be so influenced by their Ministers as will obstruct the good Settlement of this place, and I utterly dispair (as I writt in my former to yor Lordps) of any true duty and obedience paid to his Maj^{ty} untill their Colledge be suppress and their Ministers silenced; for they are not only Enimies to his Maj^{ty} and Government, but Christ himself, for of all the Inhabitants of this Province, being about ffour Thousand in number, not above Three Hundred Christned by reason of their Parents not being Members of their Church. I have been this 16 Months perswading the Ministers to admitt all to the Sacrament and Baptisme, that were not vitious in their lives, but could not prevaile upon them, therefore with advice of the Councell made this inclosed Order. Notwithstanding they were left in the intire possession of their Churches and only required to administer both Sacraments, according to the Liturgie of ye Church of England, to such as desired them, which they refuse to doe, and will understand Liberty of Conscience given in his Maj^{ts} Commission, not only to exempt them from giving the Sacrament according to the Book of Comon Prayer but make all the Inhabitants contribute to their Maintenance, although they refuse to give them the Sacrament and Christen their Children, if it be not absolutely enjoyned here, and in other colonies, that both Sacraments be administered to all persons that are duly qualified, according to the form of the Comon Prayer, there will be perpetual dissentions, and a totall decay of the Christian Religion." [2]

In New Hampshire Cranfield tried to put these principles into practice with no more success than was to be looked for when

---

[1] Jenness's Transcripts, etc. p. 126; Edward Cranfield to Committee for Foreign Plantations, Dec. 1, 1682.

[2] Jenness's Transcripts, pp. 147, 148. Cranfield to Committee for Foreign Plantations, Jan. 16, 1683.

the Governor chose to strike against the Puritan rock. In December, 1683, he ordered the ministers to admit all persons not scandalous to the sacrament and to baptism, and to use for these sacred offices the English liturgy when desired, under penalty; and he commanded Rev. Joshua Moodey, of Portsmouth, to read this order from his pulpit. A few days later he sent Moodey notice that he with some of his coadjutors — who, if tradition is to be believed, could scarcely claim to be "not scandalous persons " — " would receive from him the sacrament according to the liturgy of the Church of England the next Sunday." Moodey declined to violate his conscience, and went to prison for it with a stout heart. Nothing is so stimulating to religious convictions as the sight of a worthy martyr; and the latent Puritanism was doubtless quickened in many lukewarm spirits in Boston, when the news spread like wildfire as to what had been done, just beyond their jurisdiction, by the overbearing Governor who had been seen in their own streets.

In October, 1683, Randolph brought the threatened *quo warranto* against the charter, which, in October, 1684, was abrogated at last. The liberties of the Puritan State had fallen, with those of the ancient boroughs of England and of the city of London, before the corrupt decision of courts which were the tools of the Stuart tyranny. And Massachusetts was now a Royal Province, to be ruled by a Governor sent from over seas, — a representative of the King, who must needs have, therefore, a sort of vice-regal court, and must worship after the forms of the Established Church. Still a little further delay; for Charles II. was summoned to the bar of the King of kings, — in that sudden hour of which John Evelyn has left so impressive an account. Charles died in February, 1685. Just before his death he had shown what his temper toward New England was, by appointing the brutal Colonel Piercy Kirk to be governor with unlimited authority. He was to have a council of his own appointment, and all lands granted here were to pay a royal quit-rent. One of the three Boston churches was to be seized for the service of the Church of England, — a point on which Randolph's persistency with the Royal Council and the prelates had succeeded. But James II. soon found that he should need Kirk for a tool of oppression in England. In the year's delay which yet intervened, the following record from the Journals of the Privy Council show what preparations were making there: —

"Nov' 1685: Ordered, that . . . his Ma:s stationer do forthwith provide and deliver to the Right Rev. Father in God, Henry, Lord Bp. of

London, . . . six large Bibles in folio, six Common-Prayer Books in folio, six books of the Canons of the Church of England, six of the homilies of the Church, six copies of the xxxix Articles, and six Tables of Marriage, to be sent to New-Eng., and there disposed for the use of his Ma's plantation, as the said Bp. of London shall direct." [1]

Meanwhile, in Boston, things went on as of old: —

"1685. Thorsday, June 4th, Mr. Mather preaches from Isa. xiv. 32. Doct., — The Church of God shall stand and abide forever. Probable that N. E. Church shall doe so.[2]

"[Nov. 12, 1685.] The Ministers of this Town Come to the Court and complain against a Dancing Master who seeks to set up here, and hath mixt Dances, and his time of Meeting is Lecture-Day; and 'tis reported he should say that by one Play he could teach more Divinity than Mr. Willard or the Old Testament. Mr. Moodey said 'twas not a time for N. E. to dance. Mr. Mather struck at the Root, speaking against mixt Dances." [3]

On May 15, 1686, there entered Boston Harbor a vessel "freighted heavily with wo" to "the Bostoneers," as Randolph called them. For this "Rose" frigate brought a commission to Joseph Dudley as president of Massachusetts, Maine, Nova

---

[1] Journals of the Privy Council, quoted in Palfrey, iii. 484.

[2] Sewall's Diary. The quotations from this authority are made from the original MSS. A Public Fast proclamation had been issued on May 27, which said: "In respect of afflictive Sicknesses in many Places, and some Threatenings of Scarcity as to our necessary food, and upon other Accounts also, we are under solemn Frowns of the Divine Providence; being likewise sensible that the People of God in other parts of the World are in a low Estate."

[3] The next year was published "AN ARROW against *Profane and Promiscuous* DANCING: *Drawn out of the Quiver of the* SCRIPTURES. *By the Ministers of Christ at* Boston in New-England. Judg. vi. 31, ' *Will you plead for Baal?* Let him plead for himself.' ' *Chorea est Circulus cujus Centrum est Diabolus.*' Gulielm-Parisiensis." "It is granted that *Pyrrical* or *Polemical Saltation* . . . may be of use. Nor is the question, whether a sober and grave *Dancing* of Men with Men, or of Women with Women, be not allowable, . . . in due season, and with moderation. . . . But our question is concerning *Gynecandri-cal Dancing*, or that which is commonly called *Mixt* or *Promiscuous Dancing.*" Besides the argument from Scripture, they objected for these reasons: "Petulant Dancings" were invented by the Devil, and after him the Heathen; even the graver Heathen condemned it; it cannot be sanctified by Prayer; this is a time when God calls us to mourn; and God's wrath against dancing has been shewn. Answering to its defenders, they met "Plea 3, — *Children are much pleased with this Exercise*," — with the "*Ans.*, That we believe; but if it suit with their corrupt natures, that 's a sign it is evil. No doubt but that if a Stage-play were set up, many Children would be as much pleased with it as now they are with the Dance."

The Churches were appealed to for Discipline, that "we shall not be much or long infested with a *Choreutical Dæmon.*" Corol. 2 was: "*Such Church-Members in N. E. as have sent their Children to be* Practitioners or Spectators of mixt Dancing between Young Men *and Maidens have cause to be deeply humbled.* . . . If our Fathers should rise out of the Graves, they would not own such Children."

Scotia, and the lands between: she also brought the Rev. Robert Ratcliffe, the first minister of the English Church who had ever come so commissioned to officiate on this soil.

Boston Decembr 31. 1686

Robert Ratcliffe

As the new-comers saw it, the town was well fitted to be the capital of British America. The rude castle, a league below, saluted the king's ships as they passed. Three picturesque hills gave a unique character to the peninsula, of which two — one crowned by a windmill, the other by a fort — were parted by a deep curving bay, shut in from the outer harbor by a sea-wall on which cannon frowned; while the third, the lofty green summit to the northwest, was capped by a beacon-pole. On landing, they went up a short, broad street, paved with rough pebble, to the wooden market-building and town hall, whose upper story contained a library and other public rooms, while below was the Exchange, partly open to the weather. From this centre two great streets stretched away, — the one to the north, the other to the south. "This latter windeth about like a huge serpent, its Head being by the Towne Hall, and close by the cathedral of all their meeting-houses, while its Tail loseth itself somewhere on the Neck, near a league distant, where standeth the gallows."[1] A few houses still bore the type of the English mansion, in memory of which they had been erected by the gentry among the first settlers; but mostly they were plain and bare. "Their houses are generally wooden," wrote the Commissioners in 1664, "their streets crooked, with little decency and no uniformity; and there neither dayes, months, seasons of the yeare, churches, nor inns are known by their English names." Yet its busy shore and homes nestling among gardens blended thrift and wealth with comfort.

---

[1] Although the ingenious letters purporting to be by Rev. Robert Ratcliffe, and published in the "St. Chrysostom's Magazine" for December, 1874, and January, 1875, could not be regarded as genuine, for the reasons given in an editorial note to Sewall's Diary, i. 141, they are an interesting study of this period. It may be properly stated here that they are now known by the present writer to have been the literary *jeu d'esprit* of the late Peter Oliver, Esq., and were published with no intent to deceive the public. The sudden demise of the magazine in which they appeared prevented a proposed statement in its pages of their authorship, which has been delayed until a fit opportunity. We have been permitted to consult other letters in the series never published.

EPISCOPACY PLANTED IN BOSTON. 43

The Puritan diarist, who has left an invaluable chronicle of this period, supplies the record of the ensuing ecclesiastical steps, not without ample indication of the course of his own sympathies: —

"May 16 [1686]. Mr. Randolph at Meeting, sate in Mr. Luscombe's Pue.

"1686. Tuesday, May 18. A great Wedding from Milton, and are married by Mr. Randolph's Chaplain at Mr. Shrimpton's, according to y.ᵉ Service-Book, a little after Noon, when Prayer was had at ye Town House: Was another married at ye same time; The former was Vosse's son. Borrowd a ring. Tis sᵈ they having asked Mr. Cook and Addington, and yy declining it, went after to ye President, and he sent yᵐ to yᵉ Parson."[1]

No sooner had Dudley assumed his office than Mr. Ratcliffe waited on the Council, and Mr. Mason and Randolph proposed that he should have one of the three Congregational meeting-houses for the service.[2] This, however, was denied; but he was allowed the use of the library room in the east end of the town house, which stood where the Old State House now stands.

Mr. Ratcliffe was a graduate of Oxford, where he took his B.A. at Exeter, Oct. 16, 1677, his M.A. June 15, 1680, and his B.D. July 16, 1691. He is thus described by Dunton:[3] —

"Mr. Ratcliff was the Parson that came over with the Charter, who was a very Excellent Preacher, whose Matter was good, and the Dress in which he put it Extraordinary, he being as well an Orator as a Preacher. The next Sunday after he landed he preach'd in the Town-house, and read Common-Prayer in his Surplice, which was so great a Novelty to the Bostonians that he had a very large Audience; and myself happening to go thither for one, it was told about Town, as a piece of Wonder, That

---

[1] Hutchinson says: "I suppose there had been no instance of a marriage lawfully celebrated by a layman in England when they left it. I believe there was no instance of marriage by a clergyman after they arrived, during their charter, but it was always done by a magistrate, or by persons specially appointed for that purpose." In September, 1685, a French minister had been reprimanded for presuming to perform the marriage service. May 29, 1686, after the wedding above described, Dudley issued a proclamation authorizing this clerical function. For a specimen of the marriage license then used see in 3 Mass. Hist. Coll., vii. 170.

[2] "If the demand," says Dr. Palfrey, "had been for the use of the building for a mass, or for a carriage-house for Juggernaut, it could scarcely have been to the generality of the people more offensive." This is a strong statement. The Established Church of England can hardly have been to them quite on the level of idolatry or paganism; but that it was profoundly distasteful as a form of religion, besides that its intrusion was a gross invasion of the rights of property, is not to be denied.

[3] Letters, p. 187. Cf. a similar account in his "Life and Errors." The commissioners in 1665 had a chaplain, but "he had been directed not to use his surplice."

Dr. Annesley's Son-in-Law was turn'd Apostate: So little Charity have some Men in New-England for all that have a larger Charity than themselves. Dr. Bullivant, and Mr. Gouge, and Mr. Tryon were constant hearers at this New Church; but for my own part, I went but once or twice at the first, tho' Mr. Ratcliff (as I have said before) was an Extraordinary good Preacher."[1]

"Wednesday, May 26. Mr. Ratcliffe, ye Minister, waits on ye Council; Mr. Mason and Randolph propose y^t he may have one of ye 3 Houses to preach in. That is deny'd, and he is granted ye East end of ye Town House, where ye Deputies used to meet; untill those who desire his Ministry shall provide a fitter place.

"Sabbath, May 30th, 1686. My son reads to me in course ye 26th of Isaiah, — In that day shall ye Song, etc. And we sing ye 141 Psalm both exceedingly suited to ye day wherein therein to be Worship according to ye Chh of Engld as 'tis call'd, in ye Town House by Countenance of Authority. Tis defer'd till ye 6th of June at what time ye Pulpit is provided; it seems many crowded thether, and ye Ministers preached forenoon and Afternoon. Charles Lidget there. The pulpit is movable, carried up and down stairs, as occasion serves."

There for the first time the liturgy was publicly read, — and on June 15, 1686, "the Church of England as by law established" was organized in Boston, — as appears from the first record in the parchment-bound folio constituting the earliest record-book of King's Chapel.

Besides Mr. Ratcliffe and Mr. Randolph, were present Captain Lydgett, Messrs. Luscomb, White, Maccartie, Ravenscroft, Dr. Clarke, Messrs. Turfery and Bankes, and Dr. Bullivant. It was voted to defray the expenses of the church by a weekly collection at evening service. Dr. Benjamin Bullivant and Mr. Richard Bankes were elected the first church-wardens. It was also voted humbly to address the King and the Archbishop of Canterbury and the Bishop of London, "to implore their favor to the church, and that all other true sons of the Church of England might join in the same." Also: "Agreed, that Mr. Smith

---

[1] The Council Records show that "at a Council held in Boston July 1, 1686, Mr. Robert Ratcliff's paper desireing an honourable maintainance and good encouragement (sutable for a Minister of the Church of England) was read and thereupon *ordered:* That M^r. Liscomb and others do consider and make Report (of what his Auditors have agreed) to the Councill. 12th July. — Mr. Atturney Generall's paper relating to an annuall provision for M^r. Ratcliffe, and shewing what were raised amongst his Auditors (which amounted to about 50 lbs. per anm) was received. July 26, 1686. — In answer to M^r. Ratcliff's desire for maintainance pursuant to the letters of the Right Honble the Com^{tee} for Trade bearing date the 30th of October, 1685. It is *ordered:* That the Contribution money Collected in the Church where he performs divine service, be solely applied to the maintainance of M^r. Ratcliffe."

Boston in N: England June 15th 1686

Att a meeting wherein were present ye Gent: following
vizt: mr: Ratcliffe our minister
Edward Randolph Esqr: one of his Majesties Councell
Captaine Lydgett
mr: Luscomb
mr: White
mr: Mauerick
mr: Ravenscroft
Doctor Clerke
mr: Tenfry
mr: Banks
Doctor Bullivant

Agreed. That every Sabath day after evening Sermon, shall be made a publique Collection by the Churchwardens for the time being for the service of the Church, to be continued until some publique and settled provision be made for the same

Agreed. That Doctor Benjamin Bullivant, & mr: Richard Banks, are elected Churchwardens, & to Continue until Easter next.

Agreed. That Edward Randolph Esqr, Capt: Lydgett, mr: Luscomb and Dr Bullivant with our minister, should waite on ye Presidt & Councell to treate about our Church affaires.

Agreed. That an humble address be made to his Majestie, and to be signed by the Gentlemen as above named, to implore his Majesties favour to our Church, and it is Consented that all other true sons of ye Church of England, may joyne with us in the same.

Agreed. That in the same method, a Letter be sent to ye Right Revd father in God, the Lord Arch-Bishop of Canterbury, and another to the Reverend father in God, the Lord Bishop of London to implore those Prelates favour towards our Church.

Agreed. That mr: Smith the Joyner do make 12 formes, for the service of the Church, for each of which he shall be payd 4/s

Agreed. with the said mr Smith the Joyner, that this church will give and allow unto him 20/s Quarterlie, every Quarter, for in Consideration of his cleaning, placing and removing the Pulpitt, formes, table &c, and doing all other things which shall be Convenient, and Necessary in our time of Publique Assembling.

the Joyner do make 12 formes for the servise of the Church, for each of which he shall be paid 4*s.* 8*d.*; and that the said Mr. Smith be paid 20*s.* quarterly for placing and removing the Pulpit, formes, table, etc., and dooing all other things which shall be convenient and necessary in our place of publique Assembling."[1] Dr. Greenwood says: —

"These accommodations were intended to furnish the library room in the town house in a decent manner for the performance of divine service. This was truly an humble beginning for those who made such high pretensions as did these zealous royalists and churchmen. As they assembled in the east end of the town house, and looked round on their twelve forms and their movable pulpit, they must have felt the contrast between such a tabernacle and the solemn old cathedrals at home; and have felt, too, that they were among a people who, though of the same blood with themselves, were strangers to their mode of faith and worship, despising what they esteemed most sacred, and setting at nought the power which they deemed unquestionable. It is hardly to be supposed that these feelings were calculated to conciliate them toward the Congregationalists, or that the condition in which they found themselves was favorable at the time to their growth in Christian humility or charity; for truths taught by experience are learned slowly. That they even had the town house for their worship is, however, a proof that the colonists were to a very considerable degree overawed and restrained by the attitude which the mother country assumed towards them."[2]

Boston in New England, July 4th, 1686. — Att a meeteing wherein were present ye Gent following, vizt.: Mr Ratcliffe our minister; Edward Randolph, Esqr.; Mr Turfry; Mr Proctour; Mr White; Mr Steph: Wissendunke; Mr Thomas Brindley; Mr Ravenscroft; Capt. Lydgett; Mr Luscomb; Dr Clarke; Mr Maccartie; Mr Mallett; Mr Banks, Dr Bullivant, } churchwardens.

Agreed, To pay m^r Ratcliffe our minister 50^l p annu Salary besides what ye Counsell Shall thinke fitt to Settle on him; and if m^r Buckley, chaplain to his Majesties Frigatt the Rose, shall please to assist m^r Ratcliffe, he shall receive for his paynes 20,' a weeke.

Agreed, That m^r Smith the Joyn^r doe make a readding table and Desk, and that he be payd his bill for Joyners worke done for the Church.

Agreed, That a Cushion be bought for ye Pulpitt.

Agreed, That a sober and fitt pson be Sought after for a Clarke.

Agreed, That there be a Sacrament the 2^d Sabath in August next.

Agreed, That the Counsell be addressed unto, to give us Libertie and authority by a briefe, to passe through the Whole territory of his

---
[1] The heliotype is a fac-simile of the record of this meeting.
[2] Greenwood, p. 24.

46   ANNALS OF KING'S CHAPEL.

Majestic in New-England, and therein to Collect and Receive all Such voluntary Donations as all psons whatsoever shall be disposed to give us for and towards ye Building of a Church in Boston, to be erected for the Service of God, and for the use of the Church of England as p Law Established.[1]

Agreed, That the prayers of ye Church be said every Wednesday and Friday in the yeare, for the present, in the Library chamber in ye town house in Boston, and in the Summer Season to beginne at 7 of the Clock in the morneing, and in the Winter Season at 9 of the Clock in the Forenoone.

Of these founders of King's Chapel Dr. Benjamin Bullivant, the first warden, should have special mention. He came to Boston about 1685, a physician from London; was made attorney-general, as being of a noble family, according to Dunton, who knew him in London.[2] Nov. 9, 1686, the Council appointed

Ben Bullivant   Churchwarden

him the first clerk of the Superior Court, or "Clerk of the Assize;" and he took the oath of office, which is regularly entered upon the records of the court. He had been created attorney-general before July 26, 1686.[3] He is described as "a witty apothecary, a medical lawyer, and an honest politician." Dunton says, with some historical inaccuracy: —

"I must consider him both as a gentleman and a physician. As a gentleman, he came of a noble family, but his good qualities exceeded his birth. He is a great master of the English tongue, and the Northampton people find him a universal scholar. His knowledge of the laws fitted him for the office of attorney-general, which was conferred upon him on the revolution in Boston. It is true he sought it not, but New England knew his worth, and even forced him to accept of it. While he held this place of attorney-general, he was so far from pushing things to that ex-

---

[1] The Council Records contain no reference to such an application, and no such brief appears to have been issued until 1688. Perhaps the rumor of Governor Andros's impending arrival, which Randolph knew by July 28, changed the plans of the churchmen.

[2] He is supposed to have brought a wife from England. His daughter Hannah was baptized Jan. 3, 1686, at the Old South Church, but neither he nor his wife are in the printed list of members.

[3] The attorneys under the old charter were usually, like Bullivant, men of other employments, and not of legal training. "A law was passed, in fact, in 1663, excluding 'usual and common Attorneys' from a seat in the General Court." — *Washburn's Judicial History of Massachusetts,* pp. 51, 88, 93.

EPISCOPACY PLANTED IN BOSTON.

tremity, as some hot spirits would have had him, that he was for accommodating things and making peace. His eloquence is admirable; he never speaks but 'tis a sentence, and no man ever clothed his thoughts in better words.

"I shall next consider him as a physician. His skill in pharmacy was such as had no equal in Boston, nor perhaps Northampton. He is so conversant with the great variety of nature that not a drug or simple escapes his knowledge, so that he never practices new experiments upon his patients except it be in desperate cases, where death must be expelled by death. This also is praiseworthy in him, that to the poor he always prescribes cheap but wholesome medicines, — not curing them of a consumption in their bodies and sending it into their purses, nor yet directing them to the East Indies to look for drugs when they may have far better out of their gardens."[1]

His name appears signed to various public documents.[2] With two fellow-parishioners he was associated with the immediate outbreak of the Revolution,[3] and suffered with Andros. His petition to King William sets forth that he was, " on 18th April last, violently seized and kept close prisoner over eight weeks without mittimus, and then discharged, after giving £3,000 bail;" that he had been "hindered repairing to London by

---

[1] John Dunton's Journal, 2 Mass. Hist. Coll., ii., 105, 106.

[2] "M.ʳ Greene, — I am commanded by M.ʳ Secretary Randolph to give you notice that you doe not proceed to print any Almanack whatever, without haveing his approbation for the same." Nov. 29, 1686.
With Chas. Lidgett, Antho. Haywood, and Fra. Foxcroft, he signs the proclamation for 30th Jan. 1688/9.
When a proclamation was issued by Governor Andros ordering a general thanksgiving on the birth of "a prince, which being a great blessing bestowed on their Majesties and all his Majesty's dominions," Dr. Bullivant sends "to Mr. Cotton Mather, minister in Boston: "Suffolk, ss., N. England: In his Majesty's name you are hereby required to cause the above-written proclamation to be publickly read in the congregation on the next Lord's day after you shall receive it, and that you do then and there publickly stir up your hearers to the solemn work of the day, as is required by the same, and hereof you are not to fail." — Sept. 1, 1688. See 4 Mass. Hist. Coll., viii. 663, 3 do. i. 84, Mass. Hist. Proc.,

1871-73, 11; Hutchinson's History, i. 372, n.

[3] In "The Revolution in New England Justified," etc., Boston, 1691, the Deposition of John Winslow (who brought the news of William's landing at Torbay) says: "As were going, I told the Sheriff I would choose my Justice. He Told me I must go before Doctor *Bullivant*, one pickt on purpose (as I Judged) *for the business*. Well, I told him, I did not care who I went before, for I knew my cause good. So soon as I came in, two more of the Justices dropt in, — *Charles Lidget* and *Francis Foxcroft*, — such as the former, *fit for the purpose;* so they asked me for my Papers; I told them I would not let them have them by reason they kept all the news from the people. So when they saw they could not get what I bought with my money, they sent me to prison for bringing *Traiterous and Treasonable Libels* and Papers of News, notwithstanding I offered them security to the value of two thousand pounds." (See Andros Tracts, i. 78.)
"One Pothecary *Bullivant*, a memorable Justice (and *something else!*)," says Cotton Mather.

multitudes of unjust actions on purpose to impede his address to his Majesty;" and he prays "to be commanded to the king's royal presence to answer in the King's Bench these unjust suits, without which he is in danger to have his estate torn in pieces."[1] He returned again to Boston, and, having been made an attorney by Dudley, acted as Thomas Maule's legal adviser in his trial at Salem, Nov. 11, 1696, but later went back to England.[2]

[1] I am indebted to W. Noel Sainsbury, Esq., for the above petition, probably written in February, 1690. See Bullivant's Journal, in Mass. Hist. Proc., 1878, p. 101.

[2] He spoke for the Quaker Maule "modestly and with respect," says Judge Sewall; who also records, "Oct. 19, 1698. Mr. Bullivant was with me to take leave." There is a letter from him from Northampton, England, Feb. 18, 1710-11, in which he says: "I have now and then A Letter from Boston from such surviveing friends as I have there, and more particularly from Colloncll Dudley theyr present gouvernour." — *Dunton's Letters*, p. 94.

Of the other founders of King's Chapel *Thaddeus Maccarty*, warden in 1695, belonged to the artillery company, 1681. He died in Boston June 18, 1705, aged 65, and his widow Eliza died June, 1723, aged 82. They had children, — Charles, Francis, 1667, Thaddeus, 1670, Margaret, 1676, and Samuel, baptized at Roxbury, 1678.

Samuel Ravenscroft, warden in 1689, belonged to the artillery company, 1679; married Dionysia, daughter of Major Thomas Savage. In 1689 he was one of the wardens of the church, and that prevented the baptism of his two youngest children (born November, 1686, and June, 1688) at the Old South Church, to which he had belonged, and where his three eldest are recorded. Perhaps his churchmanship led to his imprisonment at the revolution in April, 1689. He united as warden in the loyal address to King William, but he probably removed in a short time.

Dr. John Clark, physician, son of Dr. John who had come to Boston from Newbury, and had married Martha, sister of Sir Richard Saltonstall. The son was freeman, 1673, and representative in 1689. He died Dec. 17, 1690. His daughter married Rev. Cotton Mather as a second wife; his son Dr. John was prominent in public affairs.

George Turfry (or Turfree), of Saco, 1685, was a man of distinction, a captain and representative that year; who was in the Assembly in which Thomas Danforth, one of the Massachusetts Assistants, was President. He removed to Boston before 1695. His will was probated Nov. 17, 1714. His son Edward died Jan. 8, 1703⁄4, under which date Sewall praises his character.

Charles Lidgett was son of Peter, partner of John Hull, who calls him "an accomplished merchant." The father died April 25, 1676. His widow married John Saffin. Charles was born March 29, 1650; artillery company, 1678; called colonel, 1689. April 26, 1687, he was an Assistant-Justice of the Superior Court, with Dudley as Chief-Justice. His sister Elizabeth married Lieut.-Governor John Usher. He died in London, July 13, 1698. He married (1) Bethia Shrimpton; (2) Mary, daughter of William Hester, of London.

Captain William White was one of the commissioners to receive contributions for the church in 1688. With Luscomb, Maccarty, Bullivant, and Lidgett, he is in the list of richer tax-payers in 1686. See Mr. Whitmore's chapter in "Memorial History of Boston," vol. ii.

Of the four additional persons present at the second meeting, *Thomas Brinley*, son of the first Francis Brinley, of Newport, R. I., was born in that town. He removed to Boston in 1681, was a member of the Ancient and Honorable Artillery Company, and "a founder of King's Chapel." In 1684 he went to England and married Catharine Page, dying there in 1693.

Cranfield, writing from Boston to Sir Ll. Jenkins, May 14, '84, mentions "*Mr. Stephen Wesendouke*, a Wine Cooper." (Jenness's Transcripts, p. 158.) He may have been brother of Warner Wesendunk. In 1693 he terms himself "merchant of London," but was resident in

EPISCOPACY PLANTED IN BOSTON.

The earliest financial records are as follows: —

Anno Domini 1686, Benjamin Bullivant and Richard Banks, Dr.

June 20	To Cash Rec^d this day at ye Collection	£3. 11. 00.[1]
August 8	To Cash rec^d at ye Sacrament	1. 3. 00.

1686. P Contra are Creditors:

July 6	By money p^d John Usher Esqr for this booke	00. 09. 00.
„ 13	By money p^d Mr Buckley for his Last weekes paines[2]	01. 00. 00.
August 8	pd for one Gallon of tent 8/ and bread 6^d	00. 08. 6.
„	pd Mr Maccartie for the outside of ye pulpit Cusheon and Silke	01. 07. 00.
„	pd Mrs Buckley for makeing fringe and Tassells and Silke	00. 10. 00.
„	pd Mr Shippen makeing ye Cusheon, for ye feathers, pillow and Case	00. 16. 00.
„	pd Mr Buckley more for Silke	00. 01. 00.
Sept. 20	pd Mr Smith in full for a table and 12 formes	03. 08. 00.
„	pd for wood delivered the old Eluthera man and woman[3]	00. 10. 00.
Novemb^r 1	By Money p^d Capt St Loos chaplin[4]	03. 00. 00.
„	By money given a poore man in Necessitie	00. 02. 00.

Boston Decemb^r 31, 1686. — Rec^d of Benjamin Bullivant and Thaddeus Maccartie the Sum of twenty pounds and fourteen shillings in full of the Collection money resting in their hands this day, I say received p me

ROBERT RATCLIFFE.

Memorandū y^t m^r Ratcliffe gave of the above Sum, and at the same time, unto m^r Josiah Clerke, minister for his afternoone Lecture, Tenn pounds. As attests

BENJAMIN BULLIVANT.

An early administration of the church offices outside the town house is recorded in Sewall's *Diary:* —

Boston as late as 1707. See Sewall's Diary, i. 133, *n*.

Mr. Mallett was, perhaps, Thomas Mallard; Boston Artillery Company, 1685; conjectured by Savage to have removed to New Hampshire.

[1] The account is regularly kept from this time, and varies from this sum to £1 18s. 9d. On the 22d of October the balance of the collections made up to that time, remaining from necessary expenses, is ordered to be paid to Mr. Ratcliffe. The whole amount of collections was £48 8s. 4d.; expenses, £19 14s. 6d.; paid Mr. Ratcliffe, £28 13s. 10d. Mr. Ratcliffe's receipts for this sum in two several payments are given.

[2] Several other payments to him for sermons are recorded.

[3] In July, 1686, many Huguenot families had "arrived from Eleutherea, one of the Bahamas Isds, having been spoiled by the Spaniards and Driven of Naked and destitute." — *Mass. Archives*, cxxvi. 200.

[4] Captain St. Lo commanded the "Dartmouth."

"Aug. 5 [1686]. M' Harris, boddice-maker, is the first buried with Common Prayer: he was formerly Randolph's landlord."

The first observance of the Lord's Supper was held on the second Sunday of August. This, too, was noted by the observant Puritan eye: —

"Sabbath-day, Aug' 8. 'Tis s^d ye Sacramt of ye Lord's Super is administered at ye Town H."

There were other signs of the change which had come upon New England. Mr. Sewall, who was captain of the train-band, wrote: —

"Friday, Augt 20. I was and am in great exercise about ye Cross to be put into ye Colours, and afraid if I should have a hand in 't whether it may not hinder my Entrance into ye Holy Land." [1]

"Sept' 15 [1686]. Mr. David Geffries marries Mrs. Betty Usher before Mr. Ratcliffe.

"Friday, Nov! 5 [1686]. One Mr. Clark preaches at the Town-House. Speaks much against the Presbyterians in England and here.[2]

"Satterday, Nov! 6. One Robison Esq!, that came from Antego, is buried; first was had to the Town-House and set before the Pulpit, where Mr. Buckley preaches. The President and many others there. Common-Prayer used.

"Friday, Nov! 12. Jn° Griffin is this week buried with the Common-Prayer: Which is the third funeral of this sort, as far as I can learn."

The Episcopalians set about the undertaking of a church for themselves, without delay, and did not scruple even to ask gifts from the unfriendly.

"Augt 21, Mane. Mr. Randolph and Bullivant were here. Mr. Randolph mention'd a Contribution toward building them a Chh, and seem'd to goe away displeas'd bec. I spake not up to it." [3]

But Randolph had other designs for them, involving the seizure of one of the Congregational meeting-houses, and the support of the Church of England at the cost of those who hated it.

His brief partnership with Dudley speedily gave place to hos-

---

[1] The cross, which Endicott cut from the ensign in 1634, as given to the king by the Pope, and so "a superstitious thing and a relic of Antichrist," had been discontinued by laying aside all the ensigns in March, 1635.

[2] Rev. Josiah Clarke, chaplain of the fort in New York, seems to have come as an assistant to Mr. Ratcliffe, but did not remain long. Sewall notes: "April 7, 1687.— Weare sails, in whom Mr. Clark, the Church of England Minister, goes."

[3] Sewall, *Diary*.

tility, as the possession of coveted power gave the pliant son of stern old Thomas Dudley the opportunity to displease all parties in serving himself. Randolph wrote to the Lords of Trade and Plantations, July 28, 1686: —

"The proceeding of the governor and councill . . . are managed to the incouragement of the independant faction and utter discountenancing both the minister and these gentlemen and others who dare openly profess themselves to be of the Church of England, not making any allowance for our minister, more than we rayse by contribution amongst ourselves."

Randolph had supposed it to be part of the implied contract with Dudley, that the Church of England was to be installed in power on his accession. But the following letter gives a vivid picture of his disappointment, as well as of the difficulties with which the new church had to contend: —

"BOSTON, NEW ENGLAND, Augt 2nd, 1686.

". . . As to Mr. Dudley, our President, he is a N. Conformist minister, and for several years preached in New Engl^d till he became a magistrate, and so continued for many years ; but, finding his interest to faile among that party, sett up for a King's man, and, when in London, he made his application to my Lord of London, and was well liked of by some about his late Matie ; whereupon he was appointed for this turn to be president, who, at my arrival, with all outward expressions of duty and loyalty, received his Maties Commission, sweetened with liberty of conscience ; and now we believed we had gained the point, supposing the President our own for ye C. of Eng. At the opening his Mati^{es} commission, I desired Mr Ratcliffe, our minister, to attend the ceremony and say grace, but was refused. I am not to forget that in the late Rebellion of Monmouth not one minister opened his lipps to pray for the King, hoping the time of their deliverance from monarchy and popery was at hand. Some time after ye settlement of ye gov^{nt}, I moved for a place for the C. of England men to assemble in ; after many delays, at last were gott a small room in ye town house, but our Company increasing beyond the expectation of the gov^{nt}, we now use ye Exchange, and haue ye Commonprayer and two sermons euery Sunday, and at 7 a-clock in ye morning on Wednesdays and Frydays the whole service of ye Church ; and some Sundays 7 or 8 persons are in one day baptis'd, and more would daily be of our communion had we but the countenance and company of the President and Council, but instead thereof wee are neglected and can obtain no maintainance from them to support our minister. Butt had we a gen^a gov^r we should soon haue a large congregation and also one of the churches in Boston, as your Grace was pleased to propose when these matters were debated at ye Councill Table.¹ I humbly remind your Grace of the money granted formerly for evangelizing the Indians in our neighborhood. It's a great pitty that there should be a considerable stock in this country (but how imployed I know not) and wee want 7 or 800£, to build us a church. Their ministry exclaim against ye common prayer, calling it man's invention, and that there is more hopes the whoremongers and adulterers will go to heaven than those of ye C. of Eng. By these wicked doctrines they poison the people, and their ministry carry it as high as ever. . . . Your Grace can hardly imagine the small artifices they haue used to prevent our meetings on Sundays, and at all other tymes to serve God. They haue libelled my wife and our Minister, and this is done (as credibly believed) by ye minister of the frigott; yett it's countenanced by the faction, who haue endeauored to make a breach in my family, betwixt me and my wife, and haue accomplished another design in setting up and supporting Capt. Georg, Commander of the 'Rose' frigott, against me. . . .

" . . . It is necessary that ye gou^r licence all their ministers, and that none be called to be a pastor of a congregation without his approbation. By this method alone the whole Country will easily be regulated, and then they will build us a church and be willing to allow our ministers an honorable maintenance.

"Wee haue a sober, prudent gent. to be our minister, and well approved; but, in case of sickness or other casualtyes, if he haue not one soul from Eng^d to helpe him, our church is lost. 'Tis therefore necessary that another sober man come ouer to assist, for some tymes 'tis requisite that one of them visit the other colonyes to baptise and administer the Sacrament; and in regard we cannot make 40^{lb} a yeare start by contributions for support of him and his assistant, it would be very gratefull to our church affaires if his Matie would please to grant us his Royall letters, that the 3 meeting-houses in Boston, which seuerally collect 7 or £8 on a Sunday, do pay to our Church Warden 20s. a weeke for each meetinghouse, which will be some encouragement to our ministers, and then they can but raile against ye Service of ye Church. They haue great Stocks, and were they directed to contribute to build us a Church, or part from one of their meeting-houses, Such as wee should approue; they would purchase that exemption at a great rate, and then they could but call vs papists and our Minister Baal^s Priests." ²

In a letter to Archbishop Sancroft, July 7, 1686, he had given the same arguments with some added touches: —

"'To humour the people our minister preaches twice a day, and baptises all that come to him, — some infants, some adult persons. We are

---

¹ See Hutchinson's Collection of Papers, pp. 549, 550, of the original edition; ii. 291, 292, of the Prince Society's reprint.

² Tanner MSS., xxx. 97, quoted in Perry's "Papers relating to the History of the Church in Massachusetts," p. 653.

now come to have praiers every Wednesday and Friday mornings on their exchange, and resolve not to be baffled by the great affronts, — some calling our minister Baal's priest, and some of their menisters from the pulpit calling our praiers leeks, garlick, and trash. We have often moved for an honourable maintenance for oure menister; but they tell us those that hire him must mainetaine him, as they maintaine their owne menisters, by contribution. Of a president and eighteen members of the councell, there is onely myselfe, since Mr. Mason's departure for England, that is of the Church of England, and 'twas never intended that that charge should be supported by myselfe and some few others of oure communion. . . . Having all redie brought upon myself so many enemise, and to all my crimes added this one as the greatest in bringing the letherdge and cerimonise of the Church of England to be observed amongst us."[1]

In another letter Randolph again urged the necessity of building a church at Boston:[2] —

"Wee have at present 400 persons who are daily frequenters of our church; and as many more would come over to us, but some being tradesmen, others of mechanick professions, are threatened by the congregationall men to be arrested by their creditors, or to be turned out of their work, if they offer to come to our church."

He pressed the question of the employment of the funds of the Society for evangelizing the Indians, and told how the commissioners "would not suffer Aaron, an Indian teacher, to have a bible with the common-prayer in it, but took it away from him." He continues: —

"We want good schoolemasters, none being here allowed of but of ill principle; and, till there be provision made to rectifye the youth of this country, there is noe hopes that this people will prove loyall. The money now converted to private or worse uses will set up good and publick schooles and provide maintenance for our minister, who now lives upon a small contribution, and are yet forced to meet in the town-house. I cannot omit to acquaint Your Grace how tender-conscienced members of our old church — for soe they are distinguished from the other 2 churches in Boston — are. Not long since I desired them to let their clerk toll their bell at 9 o'clock Wednesdays and Fridays, for us to meet to go to prayers. Their men told me, in excuse for not doing it, that they had considered and found it intrenched on their liberty of conscience granted them by his Majestyes present commission, and could in noe wise assent

---

[1] It almost seems as if Randolph, in his misspelling, had purposely anticipated the phrase with which a form of prayer has sometimes been stigmatized by those who love it not, as a "lethargy."

[2] Oct. 27, 1686. Hutchinson's Coll. of Papers, pp. 552, 553. The number of attendants must be greatly exaggerated. Randolph's statements are seldom to be accepted without question.

to it. The necessity of a church and publick schooles and encouragement of ministers presses me to give Your Grace this trouble, which I humbly intreat Your Grace to remember to effect, least the small beginnings of the Church of England, settled here with great difficulty, fall to the ground and be lost for want of tymely relief and countenance."

Randolph's letters, says Dr. Greenwood, "not only let us far into the spirit of the times and the men of the times, but show the perfect calmness and conscientiousness of his own tyranny in a way which, however exasperating that tyranny was to our fathers, is to us, at this distance of time, only amusing. Nothing could be more graphic than their strong and natural touches. We see the Bostonians angry and abusive, the ministers railing in their pulpits against the English Liturgy, in terms which few ministers would use now of the prayers of the most degraded heathen; and on the other hand we have the usual steady and undoubting arrogance of Randolph, who talks of making the three Congregational churches support the Church of England, in ways as oppressive as those which compelled the fathers of that generation to fly from their native land."[1]

It is evident enough, from the letters of the most resolute enemy that New England had, that the church was pushed here by Randolph in no small degree as a political engine, rather than for religious and devout ends. The clear-sighted and conscientious Puritans who were opposed to him saw this very plainly. The wonder is not that they opposed the church so championed, but rather that it took root at all under such malign auspices. It was at bottom nothing less than a deadly strife which of two opposing principles should govern Massachusetts. The unanimous mind of those who came here to execute the court policy was expressed by Governor Cranfield, of New Hampshire, who, in a letter dated at Boston, June 19, 1683, wrote to "Sr Lyonell Jenkinns," —

". . . There can be no greater evill attend his Maj^{tie} affairs here, then those pernicious and Rebellious principles which flows from their Collige at Cambridge which they call their Uniuersity, from whence all the Townes both in this and the other Colonys are supplyed with ffactions and Seditious Preachers who stirr up the people to a dislike of his Maj^{tie} and his Goum^t. and the Religion of the Church of England, terming the Liturgy of our Church a precident of Superstition and picked out of the Popish Dunghill; so that I am humbly of opinion this Country can never bee well

[1] History, pp. 28, 30.

EPISCOPACY PLANTED IN BOSTON.

settled or the people become good Subjects, till their Preachers bee reformed and that Colledge suppressed and the severall Churches supplyed with Learned and Orthodox Ministers from England as all other his Maj^ties Dominions in America are.

"The Country growes very populous, and if Longer left ungoverned or in that manner as now they are I feare it may bee of dangerous consequence to his Maj^ts concerns in this Part of the World. . . . If the Boston Charter were made void and the Cheif of the ffaction called to answer in their owne persons for their misdemenors and their Teachers restrained from Seditious preaching, it would give great encouragement to the Loyall Party, to shew themselues, who haue hetherto beene kept under and greatly oppressed and from all places of proffitt and trust. . . ."[1]

A school of historical students has sprung up in this country who teach that the Massachusetts policy was a self-seeking and hypocritical one. The fact simply was that the Massachusetts policy was imperious, as it was necessary to be when in collision with imperiousness, and its assertors were in a way sagacious, as those must be who have to outwit unprincipled craft; their course was narrow, as a sword must be if it is to have a cutting edge. The Puritan idea tended to make men freemen; the courtly idea of the court of Charles II. tended to make them slaves. In that interest the courtier party here bent all their efforts to break the Puritan idea to atoms. On the other hand, the Puritan idea was based on the supposition that this would be a colony of Puritans, — that they could keep out everybody else. And so, when the land filled up with churchmen and loyalists, the injustice followed that there was a multitude of disfranchised persons; thus it came to pass that the courtier party, in fighting against liberty, were obliged to fight for liberty here. To our forefathers these men seemed wholly evil; but as dispassionate historical students we should judge them more fairly.

The soul of the court and crown party was Edward Randolph, rewarded by his present success for his unwearied journeys between England and America, in which he consumed, in voyages across the Atlantic, at least a year out of the ten between 1676 and 1686. At his first visit the magistrates seem to have miscalculated his power, and thought to put him off, as they had done so many evil-wish-

[1] Jenness's Transcripts, etc., p. 150.

ers before; but he was the messenger who took away the charter, and now had his hour of triumph, enriching himself and humiliating his enemies. He was called "The Evil Genius of New England" and "her Angel of Death." His portrait has been fixed in immortal colors in our literature, "as he appeared when a people's curse had wrought its influence upon his nature."[1] Yet a just judgment of him declares "that his excessive zeal for the interests of the Crown and for the Church of England, his undaunted courage and uncompromising spirit, were the chief causes of his great unpopularity. . . . His career in New England may be characterized as meteoric in many respects."[2]

"In the whole of his arbitrary course it can easily be conceived that he was actuated by a sense of duty toward his sovereign, who was also the sovereign of these colonies, and who, Randolph might well imagine, was not treated here with the deference and obedience which were his due. He considered that the Bostonians were stiff-necked, refractory, and rebellious, and that he ought to curb and turn their spirit. They, on the other hand, looked upon him as the myrmidon of a tyrant and a hateful spy, and said that 'he went up and down seeking to devour

---

[1] Hawthorne's Legends of the Province House. Cotton Mather's characteristic summary of his end is not supported by evidence: —

"Of *Randolph* I said a good while ago, that *I should have a farther Occasion to mention him.* I have now done it. And that I may never mention him any more, I will here take my *Eternal Farewell* of him, with Relating That he proved a *Blasted Wretch*, followed with a sensible *Curse* of GOD wherever he came, — Despised, Abhorred, Unprosperous. Anon he died in *Virginia*, and in such Miserable Circumstances that (as it is said) he had only Two or Three *Negro's* to carry him unto his Grave." — *Parentator, quoted in Andros Tracts,* iii. 129.

[2] Mr. C. W. Tuttle in Mass. Hist. Proc., 1873-75, p. 241. Mr. Tuttle states that Randolph was son of Edmund Randolph, Doctor of Physic, and of Jane Master, of Canterbury, both parents being of gentle lineage. He married Jane Gibbon, whose brother married a granddaughter of Captain John Mason. He brought his four daughters to New England before 1684, to make a permanent home. "3d, 10th (being friday) Mr. Randall's wife was buried in Boston alamode England." He says, "The troubles of 1681 broke my wife's heart." In 1685 Mr. Randolph had been lately married to a gentlewoman related to the family of the Hydes. (N. E. Hist. and Geneal. Reg., vii. 58. Tutor Noadiah Russell's Diary. Mass. Hist. Proc., 1880, p. 257. 4 Mass. Hist. Coll., v. 142.) After the revolution of 1689 he was imprisoned with the other leaders, and finally sent to England. He seems later to have been "Surveyor-General of the Customs on the Continent of America" in 1697-98. (N. Y. Col. Docs., iv.) He visited Boston in May, 1698 (R. I. Rec. iii. 339). See Andros Tracts, iii. 211, 212, 237.

The feeling against Randolph is expressed in a letter from S. Bradstreet, May 18, 1680, to the Privy Council, 3 Mass. Hist. Coll., viii. 391. Hutchinson relates that the day after his arrival in Boston in October, 1683, a terrible fire occurring in the richest part of the town, it was believed by some to have been set by his procurement.

EPISCOPACY PLANTED IN BOSTON.

them.' He despised their prim and exclusive congregationalism, and they abominated his stately and formal episcopacy. He was arbitrary after his fashion, and they were so after theirs. If he had not been excited by their inveterate opposition to what he deemed alone true and venerable, he probably would not have troubled them as much as he did. If they had not been too weak at that time to resist the royal power, they would not have borne his arrogant interference for a day." [1]

The congregation of the Church of England in Boston was now organized and established, and would soon have had a church of its own but for a new political event. On Dec. 20, 1686, Sir Edmund Andros superseded Dudley, and became the first Royal Governor of the Province.

[1] Greenwood's History, p. 20.

THE FIRST KING'S CHAPEL.[1]

CHAPTER III.

CHURCH AND STATE UNDER SIR EDMUND ANDROS.

O those who are seeking in history for the costume and drapery of courts and courtly personages, the story of New England is bleak and bare as her own granite hills. A narrow fringe of English settlers of the middle class on the edge of a forest wilderness, whose monotonous shadows seem to darken and weary their spirits, parted by the vast wash of Atlantic seas from the conspicuous stage on which nations were enacting the tremendous drama of the seventeenth century, wresting their daily bread from a grudg-

---

[1] The illustration is taken from the "Memorial History of Boston," where it is enlarged from the little vignette showing this original wooden edifice, with Beacon Hill beyond, given by Dr. Greenwood in his "History of King's Chapel," as taken from an old print of Boston of 1720. It is really taken from what is known as Price's View of Boston, of a date probably a few years later than 1720. The later issue of 1743 is now the only one known.

CHURCH AND STATE UNDER ANDROS.

ing soil, remote from culture, dependent only on themselves to keep alive the traditions of civilization which they have brought with them,—such was New England in its first age. There were 21,000 English here before 1643. After that emigration ceased, and for forty years the people grew together, and the peculiarities which were gristle when they left England toughened into bone.

Life was grim and hard, but it was cheered by an heroic spirit. In the same regions where now we find the greatest beauties of Nature they saw

> "A waste and howling wilderness,
> Where none inhabited
> But hellish fiends, and brutish men
> That Devils worshipped."[1]

Now and then there was a rare gleam of showy splendor, but this only set off the bareness of common times.[2] But at last Boston was to see a pale shadow of the State-and-Church pomps to which it had been a stranger. They were the first of the long procession of more or less needy English office-holders who came to America as to a gold mine, usually returning disappointed. Younger sons, with better blood than brains, broken-down court-hangers-on, wearing here as new the second-hand clothes of royalty; soldiers whose poor success on European fields gave small promise of glory in a more difficult country; men unlike in many things, jealous of one another, but all agreeing in disliking and despising the Puritans,—such were the men, for the most part, who tried to govern here during the ninety years of Provincial History. Of them all, the earliest were far the ablest. They can only dimly be called out of the mists of nearly two centuries. West and Palmer are representatives of the mere money-hunter,—the class whom Cotton Mather called, in a zoölogical metaphor, "Roaring Lions and Ranging Bears."

There is another group of gay rufflers with profligate habits of drink and debt and oaths. They made chilly efforts to be

---

[1] Wigglesworth's "God's Controversy with New England," in Mass. Hist. Proc., 1871-73, p. 83. Upham's "Witchcraft," i. 7, 8, vividly describes the effect of the primitive wilderness on the imagination of the early settlers.

[2] At the funeral of Elder Thomas Leverett, Governor, dying in office, buried March 25, 1678-79, "Mr. Wm. Tailer and four others carried a Banner Roll each at one corner of the Herse. Mr. Charles Lidgett, the Back [piece of his armor] before the Herse, ten others carrying other pieces of his armor." Mr. Lynde was one of four "to carry Banners mixt with the Banner Roles above."—*New England Historical and Genealogical Register*, iv. 128.

convivial amid the austerities of New England, and to make Boston like Whitehall.[1]

The little group of rulers, who hardly took the trouble to wear a silken glove over the mailed gauntlet, stand in the centre of this company. Here may be named the second in command to Andros, Colonel Francis Nicholson, a curious illustration of how mingled is the web in many characters. Nicholson is a marked illustration of how much religiosity can consist with how little true religion. A zealous high-churchman, a generous giver to the Church and harsh to other persuasions, he could neither control his temper nor his tongue nor his moral conduct. In New York and Virginia, in command of great expeditions against Canada, he was the same man.[2] He was supposed to owe his promotion largely to his churchmanship, as he had not received a military training.

Ffr: Nicholson

Mr. Commissary Blair accused him in Virginia of passionate temper, great profanity, and licentiousness, giving instances: "I really came at last to consider him as a man of the blackest soul and conscience that I had ever known in my life."[3] Those who saw his other side called him "a true son, or rather nursing father, of the Church of England in America." One wrote of him: —

"When I do think with myself of Governor Nicholson, I do call him the Right hand of God, the father of the Church, and more, a father of the poor. An eminent Bishop of that same character being sent over here with him will make Hell tremble, and settle the Church of England in these parts forever."[4]

---

[1] Sewall describes one of their efforts in that direction: "Friday, Sept. 3. Mr. Shrimpton, Capt. Lidget, and others come in a Coach from Roxbury about 9 a'clock or past, singing as they come, being inflam'd with Drink. At Justice Morgan's they stop and drink Healths, curse, swear, talk profanely and baudily, to ye great disturbance of ye Town and grief of good people. Such high-handed wickedness has hardly been heard of before in Boston."

[2] See his character in Anderson's Col. Ch. ii. 403.

[3] Hist. Coll. Amer. Colon. Church, Virginia, pp. 78–80.

[4] Mr. Nicholas Moreau to Bishop of Litchfield. Ibid. p. 31. Nicholson was subject to excessive fits of passion so far as to lose the use of his reason. After he had been in one of these fits while he had the command of the army, an Indian said to one of the officers, "The General is drunk." "No," answered the officer, "he never drinks any strong liquor." The Indian replied, "I do not mean that he is drunk with rum. He was born drunk." (N. Y. Hist. Soc. Proc., 1868, —

His name will appear again in our narrative, and his escutcheon was with reason hung in gratitude on a pillar in the little church.[1]

The capable instrument of a despotic cause, himself imperious, quick-tempered, alien in every feeling from the Puritan ways, Andros had been a page in his boyhood in the Royal Household, and had shared the exile of the Stuarts. They knew him well, and found him faithful and an able soldier in Dutch and American service. His earlier career in New York, and later in Virginia after New England had done with him, does not fall within our story. But it is worth noting, that, whereas here he made his bitterest enemies by his zeal for the Church, in Virginia he found the churchmen his greatest enemies.[2] His portrait represents a

ARMS OF SIR FRANCIS NICHOLSON, 1693.

Colden Letters). The Council of Virginia petitioned the Queen, May 20, 1703, "for relief of our selves and other your Majesty's good and Loyall Subjects of this country from the many great grievances and pressures we lie under by reason of the unusuall, insolent, and arbitrary methods of Government as well as wicked and scandalous examples of life which have been now for divers years past put in practice by his Excellency Francis Nicholson," etc. Yet not long before, the Society for Propagating the Gospel, etc., had voted: "That the thanks of this Society be given to Colonel Francis Nicholson, Governor of Virginia, for the great service he has done towards the propagation of the Christian Religion and the establishment of the Church of England in the Plantations, and particularly for his having contributed so largely towards the foundation of many churches along the continent of North America." Anderson, iii. 44.

[1] How much he was in Boston at this early period does not appear; but in the reference to his Arms in the list of ornaments of the Church, in 1733, the mention of him as "Lieut.-Governor" indicates that he was thus honored from the beginning. He was Lieut.-Governor of New York while Andros was Governor of New England. On the accession of William and Mary he became Lieut.-Governor of Virginia, 1690–1692, and in 1694 Governor of Maryland. In 1698 he succeeded Andros as Governor of Virginia, but was recalled in 1705 at the urgency of the clergy, led by Commissary Blair, who is justly venerated for his self-sacrifice and zeal in organizing the Church in Virginia. In 1710 he was appointed General, and commanded the successful expedition against Port Royal; and in 1711 led the land forces against Canada, without result. In 1713 he was Governor of Nova Scotia, and in 1720, receiving knighthood, he was appointed Governor of South Carolina, "when he conducted himself with a judicious and spirited attention to the public welfare; and this threw a lustre over the close of his long and active career in America. Returning to England, June, 1725, he died at London, March, 1728." See Campbell's "History of Virginia," pp. 368, 369; Washburn's "Judicial History of Massachusetts," p. 128.

[2] See Historical Collections of the American Colonial Church of Virginia, pp. 10, 32. Dr. Blair charges him with not caring to supply the country with

soldier of the best cavalier type, in shining armor and lace cravat, with a huge, flowing, curled wig and a courtly, stately

ministers, or to follow Governor Nicholson's "good example."

[1697]. "*Sir* E. ANDROS *no real friends to the* CLERGY, *as appears by what followeth:* . . . It is a common maxim among his friends that we have nothing to do with the Bishop of London nor no church power." He gives a painful account of Andros's dissensions with Nicholson, Governor of Maryland, who had come about the College affairs: "At first, Sir Edmund tried to make him weary by dryness and frowns, and asking uncivil questions, demanding the reason how he came to leave his Government, or what he had to do in Virginia to amuse the people?" Finally, he set on a Colonel Park to challenge him to a duel.

bearing, closely modelled on the likeness of Charles II. or James II.[1]

The proceedings of the new Governor in the State were paralleled by his course in ecclesiastical affairs. On the very day of his landing he endeavored to *Samuel Sewall* make an arrangement with the ministers for the partial use of one of the meeting-houses for Church-of-England worship.[2] The pithy, condensed entries in Sewall's Diary give us an invaluable picture of the course of the negotiation and of subsequent events.

". . . it seems speaks to ye Ministers in ye Library abt accomodation as to a Meeting-house, yt might so contrive ye time as one House might serve two Assemblies.

[1] The engraving whose use is kindly permitted by the publishers of the "Memorial History of Boston" is copied from the portrait given in the Andros Tracts. The inveteracy of ancient grudges is illustrated by the recent refusal of the Comptroller of Connecticut to hang the portrait of Andros with those of the other governors in the State House. Without disparaging the good looks of the others, it is safe to say that one of the handsomest is thus banished. He was descended from a Northamptonshire family, whence his great-great-grandfather removed to Guernsey in the 16th century. He was born in London, Dec. 6, 1637. During the exile of the Stuarts, he served in the army of Prince Henry of Nassau and remained loyal. In 1660 he was made Gentleman in Ordinary to the Queen of Bohemia, — "the Queen of Hearts," — the only daughter of King James I., whose romantic history is well known. In the same year he came to America as major of a regiment of foot. Here he distinguished himself against the Dutch. In 1672 he was major of Prince Rupert's Dragoons and commander in Barbadoes. In 1674 he inherited his father's estates, succeeding him as Bailly of Guernsey, and was sent by the Duke of York to govern his new province. Returning to England to refute charges of dishonesty in the administration of New York in 1681, he was knighted. In June, 1686, he was commissioned Governor of New England, and in April, 1688, his commission was enlarged to cover "all the English possessions on the main land, except Pennsylvania, Delaware, Maryland, and Virginia." After the revolution here in April, 1689, he was kept prisoner at the Castle, being foiled in two attempts at escape, until February, 1690, when he was sent to England, and was there released by an order in Council, because "no person could be found ready to sign or own the charge against him." He was Governor of Virginia from 1692 to 1698, when "for quarrelling with Dr. Blair he lost his government." See the full and lucid account of his life and family by Mr. Whitmore, in the Introduction to the Andros Tracts. The "Boston News-Letter," May 3, 1714, says: "By Letters from London of the 24th of February, we are inform'd that Sir *Edmond Andrews*, sometime Governour of New-York, New-England, and Virginia, Dyed that Week in a good Old Age."

[2] The commission from James II. to Sir Edmund Andros said: "And for the greater ease and satisfaction of our loving subjects in matters of religion, we do hereby wil and require and command that liberty of conscience be allowed to all persons, and that such especially as shal be conformable to the rites of the Church of England be particularly countenanced and incouraged." — 3 *Mass. Hist. Coll.*, vii. 147.

"Monday, Decembʳ 20, 1686. Govʳ Andros comes up in yᵉ Piñace. Govʳ was in a Scarlet Coat, Laced. Several others were in Scarlet.

"Tuesday, Decʳ 21. There is a Meeting at Mr. Allen's of ye Ministers, and four of each Congregation to consider what answer to give ye Govʳ; and 'twas agreed yt could not with a good Conscience consent yt our Meeting-House should be made use of for ye Comon-prayr worship.

"Decʳ 22. . . . In ye Evening Mr. Mather and Willard thorowly discoursed his Excellency about ye Meeting-Houses in great plainess, shewing they could not consent: This was at his Lodging at Madam Taylor's; He seems to say will not impose.

"Friday Xʳ 24. About 60 Red-coats are brought to Town. . . .

"Satterday, Xʳ 25. Govʳ goes to ye Town-House to Service Forenoon and afternoon, a Redcoat going on's right hand and Capt. George on ye left. Was not at Lecture on Thorsday. Shops open to-day generally and persons about yʳ occasions. Some but few Carts at Town with wood thoᵘ ye day exceeding fair and pleasant. Read in ye morn ye 46 and 47 of Isa."

So ended what must have been an exciting week in the little Puritan community. But they were thankful that things were no worse. Mr. Sewall doubtless expressed the general mind when meeting Governor Andros at Capt. Winthrop's: —

"Friday Jan. 7ᵗʰ 168⁶⁄₇. I thankfully acknowledged ye protection and peace we enjoyed under his Excellencie's Government."

The Puritans knew very well the temper of the men whom they were fighting. The controversy was one which no soft words would heal. That little group of men "in the library of the town house" brought the antagonist forces face to face.

Confronting the new power which was bent on subverting the cherished system of the colony was a little company, resolute, uncompromising, devoted to the Puritan idea, — the five ministers of Boston. They were the steel point of the spear which Massachusetts held steadily before her breast, ever on the guard, though not as yet thrusting against her enemy. The clergy had possessed a supreme influence from the beginning of the colony. The ablest men had found in that profession their largest opportunity. Many a man whose ambition led him later into public life set his foot first on that firm stepping-stone to power. George Downing, who passed from his Cambridge study of theology, by way of a chaplaincy in Cromwell's army, to success as one of the wiliest politicians in England, whose baseness in betraying his former friends to a traitor's death when he joined

Charles II. was only paralleled by his refusal to allow his mother the pittance needed in her old age; Joseph Dudley, nursed in the bosom of Massachusetts, and turning to give her the deadlier sting with talents and powers which made him one of the ablest men of his time; William Stoughton, the rich, sour old bachelor, who never repented of his dark part as judge in the Salem witchcraft tragedy, and whose character is crabbedly portrayed on the walls of the Cambridge dining-hall, — these, and such as these, began as New England ministers.

The sceptre of dominion was to pass forever from the Massachusetts clergy with the generation now on the stage. But the five ministers of the Boston churches are worthy to wield it. They face Andros, when he demands one of their churches, with a will as resolute as his own. Four of them were now nearly fifty years of age; the fifth made up for the brevity of his twenty-four years by a precocity which was the wonder of the town. Two were joint-ministers of the First Church, two of the Second, and one of the Third, or South, Church.

Rev. James Allen, an ejected minister and Oxford Fellow, came to New England soon after the accession of Charles II. At the period of our narrative he had been eighteen years a minister of the First Church, having been installed as its teacher Dec. 9, 1668, at the same time that Davenport was inducted as its pastor. He was destined to continue in his sacred office until his death, Sept. 22, 1710. John Dunton says of him: —

"He is very humble and very rich, and can be generous enough when the humor is upon him."[1]

"He was equally moderate and lenient in his concessions to others, on the score of individual freedom, as he was strenuous for the enjoyment of his own rights. He was willing to render to Cæsar all proper tribute; but he was unwilling that Cæsar, in the capacity of civil magistrate, should interfere in holy things. [He] enjoyed a long, virtuous, and happy life of seventy-eight years, forty-six of which he had been a member, and forty-two a vigilant ruler and instructor of the Church. His wealth gave him the power, which he used as a good Bishop, to be hospitable."[2]

His colleague, Joshua Moodey, was a man of the stuff of which martyrs are made, and had himself shown a willingness to die, if need be, in this very cause. During his imprisonment by Cranfield at Portsmouth, he wrote from prison a letter worthy to be enrolled with the Acts of the Martyrs: —

[1] Life and Errors, 2 Mass. Hist. Coll., ii. 101.
[2] Emerson's First Church, p. 156.

"The good Lord prepare poor New England for the bitter cup which is begun with us, and intended (by man at least) to go round. But God is faithful; upon whose grace and strength I beg grace to hang and hope." This letter he signed "Christ's prisoner and your humble servant."[1]

After three months' incarceration he had come to Boston, and had been invited to remain as Mr. Allen's assistant. It is not less to his honor that in 1692 his opposition to the witchcraft delusion was to cause his removal again from Boston, returning to Portsmouth, where he died July 4, 1697.

Of the renowned ministers of the Second Church — the Mathers, father and son — the son has given a fantastic tinge to the name, which clouds over his real claim to honorable memory. Cotton Mather had grave faults, — his conceit of learning, his credulity, his monstrous part in the witchcraft tragedy. But lovers of books ought to judge leniently of the man who wrote more than three hundred! And the part which he played in his later years in the introduction here of inoculation for small-pox, when the fury of the mob imperilled his very life, entitles him to grateful remembrance. When he stood before Andros, only twenty-four years old, his faults were not yet so evident, and his promise seemed to have no limit.

The father, Increase Mather, was President of Harvard College, and one of the most eminent who have ever filled that office; a powerful preacher to the age of eighty-five; agent of Massachusetts at the court of King James II. and at that of William and Mary, where his distinguished reception testifies to the impression which he made on nobles and princes. He lived to be the last possessor of the almost absolute power of the old Puritan clergy. When he faced Andros he was the very incarnation of the Puritan temper. He addressed a town-meeting in Boston when there was question of giving up the charter, in 1683-84, and openly counselled that they should return Naboth's answer when Ahab asked for his vineyard, — that they would not give up the inheritance of their fathers. Randolph, who knew men thoroughly, paid Increase Mather the compliment of hating him and fearing him as he did no other man here. "The Bellowes of Sedition and Treason," he called him; and when, after the downfall of the Andros tyranny, Randolph was safely lodged in prison, and had leisure to contemplate the bringing to nought of his fifteen years of busy scheming, he wrote from the "Goal

[1] Mass. Hist. Coll., v. 120.

in Boston, May 16, '89," to the Governor of Barbadoes: "...
They have not yet sent to England, expecting Mather, their
Mahomett."[1] The Mathers were also quite capable of a hatred
which they perhaps thought to be only righteous indignation.
Increase Mather, with all his dignity, showed this in his famous
letter to Governor Dudley, nearly twenty years later, in which
he raked together all Dudley's political and personal sins in a
pile of red-hot coals, by no means of the kind which the
apostle commands to heap on an enemy's head.[2]

It is not difficult to imagine what was the temper of such men
when they saw that nothing but their firmness and skill could
save from destruction all that they held dearest.

Last of the five ministers was he of the South Church, — Rev.
Samuel Willard, son of Major Simon Willard, one of the principal citizens of Concord, and prominent in civil and military life.
He had been a Fellow of Harvard College and subsequently the
second minister of Groton, where his ministry was ended by the
destruction of the town by the Indians in March, 1676, when
he removed to Boston. From Sept. 6, 1701, to Aug. 14, 1707,
he filled the office of Vice-President of Harvard College, while
retaining his pastorship. He died Sept. 12, 1707.[3]

"Well furnished with learning," says Dunton, he "has a natural fluency of speech and can say what he pleases." During
the witchcraft delusion he bore himself prudently and firmly.
Pastor of three of the special judges of that tribunal, "he has as
yet," says a contemporary, "met with little but unkindness, abuse,
and reproach from many men." Calef says that once "one of
the accusers cried out publicly of Mr. Willard, as afflicting of
her." He published many works, of which the chief was in
1726, — his "Complete Body of Divinity," the first folio volume
published in this country.

These were the men who, with a constituency of laymen behind
them, had to foil Andros and Randolph if they could.[4]

Of those who were with these ministers, — the shaft to their
spear-head, — we can now call up only few and shadowy
glimpses. We know, indeed, the names of a few of the gentlemen who were on the side of the native cause; but with the

---

[1] Hutchinson's Collection of Papers, ii. 315.
[2] See the correspondence, 1 Mass. Hist. Col., iii. 127, 131.
[3] See the notice of his life and writings in Dr. S. A. Green's Historical Address at Groton, 1876.

[4] The lofty bearing which these Puritan ministers could assume is shown in their answer to the Quaker, George Keith, just after this time, when he challenged them to a public disputation as teachers of a "Doctrine false and pernicious." See "Memorial Hist. of Boston," i. 208.

exception of Judge Sewall there is hardly one whom we can vividly picture to ourselves. The great men of the former generation had passed away. With the death of that grand old Commonwealth soldier, Governor Leverett, nine years before, the last of the men of the heroic group had gone. Danforth and Cooke were the strongest of the leaders. The most venerable figure whom we now see is Simon Bradstreet, full of years and of dignity. When Andros was overthrown in 1689 he was placed at the head of the government, though weighed down with the snows of ninety years. We prize the few words in which the Labadist missionaries describe him, — "an old man, quiet and grave, dressed in black silk, but not sumptuously." Venerable, but not forcible, his memory was long cherished, largely because he had the happy fortune to linger the last survivor of a band of remarkable men. He seemed to concentrate in himself the dignity and wisdom of the first century of Massachusetts life.

But the strength of the opposition which the ministers headed was really the same that made the strength of the Revolution, and again of our own War for the Nation. It was the tough persistence of the common people. The yeomen of New England knew perfectly what they wanted; and they wanted no bishops nor tithes, nor forced loans of their churches. They might bend a little for a moment, but they would only spring back the stiffer; and they would never break!

The strange chance by which the Old South Church was brought — in this earlier time of revolution as well as ninety years afterward — into a representative attitude as the special antagonist of the alien influences is strikingly exemplified in the person who stands in history as the typical Puritan of his time. It is not because Samuel Sewall was the most prominent man in Boston; for that he was not, at the time where we are, though he was a man of wealth and influence and of the real Puritan character. But it is, above all, because he *kept a diary!* His ink had a wholesome human tincture in it which has prevented it from fading through two centuries. Judge Sewall is the Pepys of New England: his diary is as quaint and racy, and as full of delicious bits of self-revealing, though unstained. But how unlike to that other Samuel in all the nobler aspects which are mirrored in those brown old pages, — his prayerful temper, his loyalty to God and to the God-fearing Puritanism which he loved so well!

The Governor, perhaps expecting advice from England, waited

three months with a patience hardly in accord with his impetuous character, and showed himself a good churchman in the shorn observances in the town hall. Sewall records: —

"[1686–87]. Tuesday, January 25. This day is kept for s^t Paul, and ye Bell was rung in ye Morning to call persons to service; The Govr (I am told) was there.

"Monday, January 31. There is a Meeting at ye Town house forenoon and afternoon. Bell rung for it; respecting ye beheading Charles ye first. Govr there."

But when the solemn days of the Church at the close of Lent drew nigh, there seemed a special unfitness in their celebration by the representative of the King and by the authorized ritual of England in a place devoid of all sacred associations, with a few "benches and formes," while around the Governor were commodious houses of worship tenanted by a style of religion which at home had not even the legal right to exist.

No reason is given why the South Church was selected to be the very unwilling host of the new Episcopal Society; but it may be conjectured that it was either because it was the nearest to where Sir Edmund lived, — in what was then called "the best part of the town," and near where the Province House afterward stood, — or because the South Church only had *one* minister, while each of the others had *two;* that is, twice as many persons with troublesome tongues. Then, too, Randolph had doubtless told the Governor how the South Church rose out of a bitter quarrel, and he may have thought that the two other churches would look on its vexations with more composure of spirit. To be sure, in 1682, when ominous clouds were gathering over the prospects of New England Puritanism, the First Church had proposed to the South Church "to forgive and forget all past offences," and to live "in peace for time to come." But it may well have been supposed that the old gulf had not wholly closed. Sewall again notes in his diary: [1] —

"Tuesday, March 22, 168⁹⁄₇. — This day his Excellency views the three Meeting houses. Wednesday, March 23. — The Govr sends Mr. Randolph for ye keys of our Meetingh. y^t may say Prayers there. Mr. Eliot, Frary, Oliver, Savage, Davis, and my self wait on his Excellency; shew that ye Land and House is ours, and that we can't consent to part with it

---

[1] Mar. 3, 1686–87, the new militia officers were commissioned. Of these, Major Lidgett and Captains Luscomb, Haywood, White, and Ravenscroft were churchmen. Sewall notes that if Nelson and Foxcroft had not refused, they would have taken the place of the only two who were not.

to such use ; exhibit an extract of Mrs. Norton's Deed and how 'twas built by particular persons as Hull, Oliver, 100£ a piece, etc.

"Friday, March 25, 1687. The Govr has service in ye South Meetinghouse ; Goodm. Needham [the Sexton], tho' had resolv'd to ye Contrary, was prevail'd upon to Ring ye Bell and open ye door at ye Governour's Comand, one Smith and Hill, Joiner and Shoemaker, being very busy about it. Mr. Jno. Usher was there, whether at ye very Begining, or no, I can't tell."

During the remainder of Andros's administration, — that is, for a little over two years, — the Episcopalians had joint occupancy of the South Church with its proper owners.

This enforced tenancy of the South Meeting-house caused some of the most picturesque passages in our religious history. We quote Sewall : —

"Monday, May 16, 1687. This day Capt. Hamilton [of the Kingfisher] buried wth Capt. Nicholson's Redcoats and ye 8 Companies : ['Tis said the North Bell was toll'd as he was dying]. Was a funeral sermon preach'd by ye Fisher's Chaplain ; Pulpit cover'd with black cloath upon wch scutcheons ; Mr. Dudley, Stoughton and many others at ye Comon Prayer, and Sermon ; House very full, and yet ye Souldiers went not in."

This gallant officer's escutcheon[1] kept his memory fresh on the walls of the little church in the New World, while his brother's fame is enshrined in Westminster Abbey.

CAPT. HAMILTON'S ARMS.

As a matter of policy, it was obviously unwise for Andros to irritate the town by forcing his form of worship into a meeting-house against the will of its owners. He had to build his own church at last. But we should greatly err if we should measure his act by the standard of toleration in our own day. It was something, indeed, for which the Puritan congregation had reason to be grateful, that they were allowed to worship at all in their own meeting-house by the representative of a government which at home had set so many marks of scorn on dissenters. Nevertheless, on the special days of the Church they were subjected to grave inconveniences. On Easter Sunday, 1687, the Governor and his suite met there again at eleven, sending word to the proprietors that they might come at half-past one ; "but it was not until after two that the Church service was over ; "

---

[1] I am indebted to Colonel J. W. Chester for the coat-of-arms. For a notice of Captain Hamilton's distinguished family and career, see p. 94.

owing, says Sewall, to "the Sacrament and Mr. Clarke's long Sermon; so 'twas a sad sight to see how full the Street was with people gazing and moving to and fro, because they had not entrance into the house."

The Puritan diarist, to whose invaluable pages we are indebted for the history of this obstinate contest, follows it further, step by step, with his pithy narrative, till the end of October, 1688: —

"Monday, Ap. 4. . . . In the Even Mr. Willard, Eliot, Frary, and Self have great debate about our meeting for the Lord's Supper.

"Tuesday, May 10. Mr. Bullivant having been acquainted that May 15th was our Sacrament-day, he writt to Willard that he had acquainted those principally concern'd, and 'twas judg'd very improper and inconvenient for ye Govr and his to be at any other House, it being Whit-Sunday and they must have ye Comunion, and y^t 'twas expected should leave off by 12, and not return again till yy rung ye Bell yt might have time to dispose of ye Elements. So remembring how long yy were at Easter, we were afraid twould breed much confusion in ye Afternoon, and so on Wednesday concluded not to have our Sacrament, for saw 'twas in vain to urge their promise. And on ye 8th of May were out past One a pretty deal. May 15, Goes out just ½ hour after one; so have our Afternoon exercise in due Season. But see yy have ye advantage to lengthen or shorten ye Exercises so as may make for yr purpose.

"Wednesday, June 1. A privat Fast of the South-Church was kept at our house. Mr. Willard pray'd and preach'd in the morn; Mr. Cotton Mather pray'd first in the afternoon; Mr. Moodey preach'd and pray'd; Mr. Willard dismiss'd with a Blessing. Mr. Willard's Text, Deut. xxxii. 36, — For the Lord shall judge his People, etc. Mr. Moodey's Text, Ps. xlvi. 10, — Be still, etc. Occasion of the Fast was the putting by the Sacrament the last Turn, and the difficult circumstance our Church in above others, regarding the Church of England's meeting in it."

"Sabbath, June 12 [1687]. Lord's Super at ye South Chh. But Chh of E. men go not to any other House; yet little hindrance to us save as to ringing the first Bell, and straitning ye Deacons in removal of ye Table."

After a few months, the pressure of imposition on one side and of resistance on the other grew more urgent.

"Octr 16th [1687]. Had ye Sacrament today at ye North-Chh; Mr. Ratcliff also had ye Sacramt, and Sent to Mr. Willard yesterday to leave off sooner. To wch Mr. Willard not consenting, Govr sent for him in ye night.

"Sabbath, May 20. Mr. Willard preach'd in ye Morn from Heb. xii. 4. 'Have not yet resisted unto bloud etc.' In ye Afternoon rain'd exceeding hard, so yt I doubt many staid to hear yᵉ service who had not been wont.

"Sabbath, June 3. Sir Wᵐ¹ not abroad in yᵉ forenoon; in yᵉ Afternoon hears Mr. Mather; so ye Whitsuntiders have not his company."

The watchful Puritan spirit, which notes with disgust Shrove Tuesday sports coming in, Feb. 15, 168⁶/₇, marks every innovation of the Church "which the fathers came over to avoid":

"Wednesday, Julij, 6 [1687]. Waited on his Excellency to Cambridge. Eleven Bachelors and seven Masters proceeded. Mr. Mather, President, pray'd forenoon and after-noon. Mr. Ratcliff sat in ye Pulpit by ye Governour's direction. Mr. Mather crav'd a Blessing and return'd Thanks in ye Hall.²

"Monday, Augᵗ 1, 1687. Mr. Lidget buried a Daughter yesterday in ye Even, with ye Service-Book.

"Tuesday, June 5ᵗʰ, 1688. Mr. Nathl. Newgate marries Mr. Lynd's Daughter before Mr. Ratcliff, wᵗʰ Chh of Engld Ceremonies. Mr. Payson and Mr. Farwell his Bridemen; a great wedding.

"Apr. 13, 1688. It seems Mr. Watter and Elisha Odlin were fined last Wednesday 13.4ᵈ apiece for refusing to lay yʳ hand on yᵉ Bible in swearing.

"May 10. Mr. Dudley and his Son call here. I speak to him abt ye mode of Swearing, if no remedy might be had; of wᶜʰ had no encouragemᵗ, but said Lifting up ye Hand was ye handsomest way.

"Thorsday, June 7ᵗʰ [1688]. Mr. Dudley and Stoughton call here. In comes Mr. West and hath one Mr. Newton a newcomer sworn an Attorney. Mr. Dudley asked for a Bible; I ask'd if it might not be done without. He laughd, and, seeing a Bible by accident, rose up and took it."³

---

¹ Sir William Phips had arrived.

² The College seems to have been at a low ebb of scholarly spirit and aids. The Labadist missionaries who visited Boston in 1682, on entering the college building say they "found there eight or ten young fellows sitting around, smoking tobacco, with the smoke of which the room was so full that you could hardly see; and the whole house smelt so strong of it that when I was going up stairs I said, This is certainly a tavern. . . . They could hardly speak a word of Latin, so that my comrade could not converse with them. They took us to the library, where there was nothing particular." Such as it was, however, the college was the stronghold of Congregationalism, and was to be captured if possible. See Long Island Hist. Soc., i. 384.

³ "A brief Discourse Concerning that Ceremony of Laying the Hand on the Bible in Swearing," by Samuel Willard, was published at London, 1689. It lays down, "That all Religious Worship not Commanded by God is forbidden; that all Symbolical Ceremonies enjoyned Men in Religious Worship are made Parts of Worship, and consequently, if not Commanded, forbidden. Imposing such, is infringing liberty of conscience. It is a sin not to avoid things indifferent. No Practice of holy and good Men is sufficient to warrant my Practising after them, or ought to satisfy my Conscience. He that invokes such a thing as his Helper in his Prayer, doth certainly make it of the Object which he prays unto, — i. e. it is Idolatry."

CHURCH AND STATE UNDER ANDROS.

The press had always been under censorship; and heretofore it would have been difficult to obtain leave to publish any book in favor of Episcopacy. But now the tables were turned.[1]

"Friday, Apr. 6 [1688]. The Exposition of ye Chh of Engld Catechise, by ye Bishop of Bath and Wells, comes out printed ⅌ Richd Pierce, with ye 39 Articles."

On the other hand, such writings as those of Increase Mather against the innovations were published abroad. In his "Testimony Against several Prophane and Superstitious Customs Now Practised by some in New-England, The Evil whereof is evinsed from the Holy Scriptures, and from the Writings both of Ancient and Modern Divines," Mather says: —

"The last Year Promiscuous Dancing was openly practised and too much countenanced in this Degenerated Town. There was, in the day of it, a Testimony published against that Evil, by the Ministers of Christ in this place; amongst whom I am the least." He testifies against "Health-drinking, Dicing, Cards, and such like Games, Christ-mass-keeping, New year's Gifts, Candlemas, Shrove-Tuesday, *The Vanity of making* Cakes *on such a Day*, Cock-scaling, the Superstition of Dedicating Days to Saints. *New-England* was and ever ought to be *a Land of Uprightness*. But shall men do such things in a Land of Uprightness, where the Word of God and the Ministers of God have taught them better?"[2]

The Governor did not intend, however, to confiscate the meeting-house into which he had intruded.

By the side of this soldierly, mail-clad figure, among these shabby genteel courtiers who make up his little court, had appeared like a ray of pure sunshine in the scene a refined lady of gentle birth and breeding, — perhaps the first of her degree since the lovely Lady Arbella Johnson "took New England on her way to Heaven." Robert Mason wrote to Sir Edmund Andros from Great Island, Aug. 13, 1687: "I shall be extream glad to heare of my good lady's safe arrival, which so soon as I shall understand, I will make a speedy journey to Boston to kiss her hands."

Sewall records: "Oct. 17, 1687. 'Weare' Arrives, in whom

---

[1] The instructions to Sir E. Andros, April 16, 1688, enjoin that "forasmuch as great inconveniences may arise by the liberty of printing within our said Territory, under your Government, you are to provide by all necessary orders that no person keep any printing-press for printing, nor that any book, pamphlet, or other matter whatsoever be printed without your especiall leave and license first obtained." — *Docs. relating to Colonial Hist. of N. Y.*, iii. 548.

[2] Published in London, 1687.

comes the Governour's Lady." It is related as noteworthy that "when Lady Andros arrived at Boston in 1687, she and her husband, the Govr, rode in a coach," — the first, perhaps, which had been seen on this peninsula.

But soon the same shadow which fell on Lady Arbella fell upon this, the only woman in the picture. Four months only passed, and the bright scene darkened.

A young poet[1] of the time, not seeing the revolution which smouldered beneath the surface of society, wrote to console the Governor: —

> "And You Great S^r, among the joyes of Life,
> Loose the sweet Solace of a vertuous Wife.
>
> . . . .
>
> . . . Here no Martiall Ensigns fly,
> But wear the badge of Loyalty;
> Here no dismall tragick sight,
> That may the Fairer Sex affright,
> Unles the Trophies of your Right.
> No (may we humbly guess), she hither came
> To soften your heroic flame,
> The dazzling lustre of your virile Mien
> Her Aspects rendering placid and serene."

On Jan. 21, 1687–88, one of the little court wrote of "the great griefe and sorrow wee are in for my Lady Andros, who since Tuesday last was sevenight hath been extreamly ill, and soe continues almost at the Court of Death, and is a greate affliction to his Excellency who is most passionately concerned. If it should please God to call her to himselfe, wee should all have a greate losse of a right good and vertuous Lady."[2] The Puritan ice melted somewhat in sympathy: —

"Sabbath 22^d [Jan. 168⅞]. My Lady Andros was prayed for in Publick, who has been dangerously ill ever since the last Sabbath . . . About the beginning of our afternoon Exercises, the Lady Andros expires."

"Apr. 6, 1688. . . . The Lady Andros died Jan^e 22; buried Feb. 10, generally lamented . . ."[3]

---

[1] I am indebted to Dr. F. E. Oliver for these lines from an unpublished MS. of Benjamin Lynde, H. C., 1686, who succeeded Sewall as Chief-Justice of the Province. See "The Diaries of Benjamin Lynde and Benjamin Lynde, Jr.," etc. Boston: Privately printed. 1880.

[2] Trumbull's Conn. Records, iii. 437, quoted in Andros Tracts, i. xxxix.

[3] Sewall's Diary and Letter-book. Colonel Andros had married Marie Craven, sister of Sir William Craven, February, 1671. He married, 1691, Elizabeth Crispe, widow of Christopher Clapham. She died August, 1703, and he married, April 21, 1707, Elizabeth Fitzherbert, who surviving him died February, 1716-17.

CHURCH AND STATE UNDER ANDROS.

The rigid Puritan diarist gives us an unconscious glimpse into his feelings of indignant sorrow for New England, in his account of this impressive scene: —

"Feb. 10, 168$\frac{7}{8}$. Between 4 and 5 I went to y^e Funeral of y^e Lady Andros, having been invited p̄ ye Clark of ye South-Company. Between 7 and 8 (Lychns illuminating ye cloudy air) The Corps was carried into the Herse drawn by six Horses. The Souldiers making a Guard from y^e Governour's House down ye Prison Lane to ye South-M. House, there taken out and carried in at ye western dore, and set in ye Alley before ye pulpit wth six Mourning women by it.[1] House made light with candles and Torches; was a great noise and clamor to keep people out of ye House, y^t might not rush in too soon. I went home, where about nine a clock I heard ye Bell toll again for ye Funeral. It seems Mr. Ratcliffe's Text was, — Cry, all flesh is Grass. The Ministers turned in to Mr. Willards. The Meeting House full, among whom Mr. Dudley, Stoughton, Gedney, Bradstreet etc. 'Twas warm thawing weather, and the wayes extream dirty. No volley at placing the Body in the Tomb. On Satterday, Feb. 11, the mourning cloth of the Pulpit is taken off and given to Mr. Willard."

Tradition reports that she was buried in what is now the King's Chapel burying-ground, in the tomb which afterward belonged to Dr. Church of Revolutionary note. She may well have desired to be laid near the spot destined for the house of prayer of her own people.

Everything was novel and strange in this solemn night-service in the great meeting-house with its unwonted illumination. "But when we approached with our solemn march and Flashing Tapers, the great Bell tolling a mournful Dirge, all became hushed, and way was respectfully made for the afflicted mourner as he followed the coffin alone into the Church, notwithstanding the dislike and fear the People have for him."[2] By most of them the grand funeral office must have been heard for the first time.

---

[1] In New Jersey, in the last century, "the official mourning women were six in number, each wearing a white turban or high, white-veiled hat." — *Mag. of Am. Hist.*, November, 1879.

[2] The extract is from one of the letters under the pseudonyme of Rev. R. Ratcliffe. The poet already quoted wrote, in his elegy on Lady Andros's death: —

"Welcome, Great Guest! surrounding echoes said,
And he was thought but little more than dead
That had not roused, and, at her passage spread
Displayes of joy; when just before
Loud peals were sent from every shore,
But now, enrang'd, All haile! bright spirits say,
Who on their hov'ring wings convey
Through heavenly vaults the blessed soul away,
And leave us mortals here below to gaze
On its exalted virtues which did shine,
Beaming an impress of Divine. . . .
Her lasting Pyramid shall be the extended land,
Which thence ennobled we will call
Her place of Buriall.
Altho' her birth the other England gave,
New England fame enough will have
In that 'twas here she had her grave."

Perhaps a dying request of his gentle lady that her lord would end this unseemly strife with the stubborn Puritans, hastened his action; and he must surely have desired to see the church erected near the spot which her burial had made for him indeed "God's acre." Within six weeks the authority to raise contributions was accorded by a brief, March 24, 1688, and the list of subscribers shows no less than ninety-six names.[1]

OBVERSE.   REVERSE.

GREAT SEAL OF NEW ENGLAND UNDER ANDROS.

They first tried to purchase a site from Sewall, but in vain: —

"March 28, 1688. Capt. Davis spake to me for Land to set a Chh on; I told him could not, Would not, put Mr. Cotton's Land to such an use, and besides 'twas entail'd. After, Mr. Randolph saw me, and had me to his House to see ye Landscapes of Oxford Colledges and Halls. Left me with Mr. Ratcliff, who spake to me for Land at Cotton-Hill for a Church wch were going to build. I told him I could not, first because I would not set up that wch ye People of N. E. came over to avoid; 2^{ly} ye Land

---

[1] "*By his Excellency.* Pursuant to a resolve in Council, I do hereby appoint and authorize you, Capt. Anthony Howard, Capt. William White, and Mr. Thaddeus Mackerty, to ask and receive the free and voluntary contribution of any the inhabitants in the town of Boston, towards the building and erecting of a house or place for the service of the Church of England; and in the doing thereof to desire the assistance of such persons, of either congregation or neighborhood, as may be proper to accompany you therein; and of what you shall so receive to keep a distinct account, to be disposed of by you to that use accordingly; for which this shall be your warrant." 3 Mass. Hist. Coll., i. 84. The original document probably perished in the fire which consumed many valuable papers in the office of the late Hon. James Savage, in 1825.

was entail'd. In after discourse I mention'd chiefly the Cross in Baptism, and Holy Dayes.

"Satterday, Apr. 14 [1688]. Mr. West comes to Mr. Willard from ye Govr to speak to him to begin at 8 in ye morn, and says this shall be ye last time ; they will build a house. [So] We begin ab^t ½ hour past 8. Yet ye people come pretty roundly together. 'Twas Easter-day, and ye Lord's Super with us too."

Notwithstanding the Governor's promise, it proved as flexible as "the royal word" of the Stuarts whom he served; and in June the long further delay led to hot remonstrances and an angry dispute between the high-tempered soldier and the Puritan owners of the South Church, who were stubborn for their rights : —

"Thursday, May 24th [1688]. Bell is rung for a Meeting of ye Chh of Engld Men, being in y^t language Ascension day.

" 1688, Sabbath, June 10. Sacr^t wth us finis^h, so y^t got home just about a quarter past 12 p̄ ye Dial. Govr angry yt had done so late, and causd ye Bell to be rung ab^t a 4^r past One ; 'twas rather more before ye Bell had done. So 'twas about a quarter past Three before our Afternoon Bell Rung, ab^t 1½ hour later than usual.

"Satterday, June 23. Capt Frary and I goe to his Excellency at ye Secretarie's Office, and there desired y^t He would not alter his time of Meeting, and y^t Mr. Willard consented to no such thing, neither did he count y^t 'twas in his power so to doe. Mr. West sd he went not to ask Mr. Willard Leave. His Excellency askd who ye House belonged to : we told Him ye Title to ye House was on Record. His Exc. turnd to Mr. Graham and sd, ' Mr. Attorney, we will have y^t look^d into.' Govr s^d if Mr. Willard not ye Parson, so great an Assembly must be consider'd ; we sd He was Master of ye Assembly, but had no power to dispose of ye House, neither had others, for ye Deed expressed ye Use 'twas to be put to. Govr complaind of our long staying Sabbath-day señight ; sd 'twas ye Lord's Super, and had promis'd to go to some other House on such dayes. Mr. Randolph sd he knew of no such promise, and ye Govr seemd angry, and said He would not so break his word for all ye Massachusets Colony, and therefore to avoid mistakes must give in writing what we had to say ; we answerd Mr. Randolph brought not any Writing to those he spake to. Govr sd we went off from ye old Chh against ye Governm^t, and ye Land ye House Stood on was bought clandestinely, and y^t one should say he would defend ye work with his Company of Soldiers. Mention'd folk's backwardness to give, and ye unreasonableness ; because if any stinking filthy thing were in ye House we would give something to have it carried out, but would not give to build y^m an house. Said came from England to avoid such and such things, therefore could not give to set y^m

Hott Dispute with Gov: r about Meeting House South.

up here; and ye Bishops would have thought strange to have been askd to contribute towards setting up ye New-England Churches. Govr said God willing they would begin at Eight in ye Morning, and have done by Nine; we said 'twould hardly be so in ye Winter. Mr. Graham sd if they had ye Service by Candle-light what was that to any? And y^t ye service apointed by ye Chh for morning could not be sd after Noon.

"Sabbath, June 24. We read and sing in course ye 57th Psal. Altastchith. They have done before Nine in ye morn, and about ¼ after One in ye afternoon; so we have very convenient time. July 1. — Govr takes his olde time again after our coming out, and Sir Wm Phips's Chaplain preaches. We were a little hurried and disapointed in ye morning, ye Bell ringing about ¼ before Nine."

In this dispute the Governor's private sorrow may have wrought hardly upon his patience. But the most striking illustration of the bitter conflicts of feeling which arose between the old religious party and the new is afforded by the account of the funeral of Edward Lilley, who had "left the ordering of this to his executors." There was an indecent conflict at the burial between Mr. Ratcliffe and Deacon Frairy in behalf of the family, for which the Deacon suffered severe legal penalties. The account of this scene is graphically given from the Puritan side: —

"I hinted to Capt. Sewall the story about Deacon Ffraery covented and bound over with sureties for forbidding Ratliff to read Comon-prayer at the grave of old Lilly. The relations desired Capt. Frary to speake, and had requested the parson to forbear before hand, when at the House. But he went on, and being hindered complained to Justice Lidget, Ffoxcraft, and Bullivant, who so treated Mr. Ffraery. Now when the deceased did not desire it, and left the buriall to the Execut^{rs} and they forbade it, meethinks it should not bee imposed; and what a case are wee all in! King, the Attorney, saith it will cost him 100 mark, and that hee is bound to do his duty (I mean Ratliff is), and the King's Proclamation will not relieve him. Captain Frary is bound to the good Behaviour, and wilbe so for a 12 month. (A fearful reproach and snare.) What does the proclamation for liberty of Conscience doe, if such impositions are allowed! This is a very tremendous thing to us. And the shutting up shops on Christmas Day, and driving the Master out of the school on Christmas Holy daies are very grievous. These *Raptim* in my lect^e on Thursday."[1]

---

[1] Mather Papers, p. 370-71, in a letter from Rev. Joshua Moodey, 8th of 11th mo., 1688 (Jan. 8, 1688-89). This scene is depicted in an animated passage in the "Vindication," etc., by Increase Mather, London, 1689, reprinted in Andros Tracts, ii. 65: "Such was his *Zeal*, that he came with *Gown* and *Book* to settle a Laudable custom in that Barbarous Country." This case was deemed of sufficient im-

CHURCH AND STATE UNDER ANDROS. 79

The last record by Sewall concerning the joint occupancy of the South Church reads: —

"Oct' 28 [1688]. N. It seems ye Gov' took Mr. Ratcliff with him [to Dunstable] ; so met not at all distinct in our House y" day. Several of y'" w'" us in ye afternoon. Col. Lidget, Mr. Shetlock, Farwell, in our Pue ; went to Contribution."

It is pleasant to know that, High Churchmen though these men were, they were Christian enough to join in the worship of the Puritans, and to contribute for its support, — an example of charity which it is to be hoped some of those with whom they communed would have been willing to imitate in turn.

A glimpse of the kindly relation which Mr. Ratcliffe strove to maintain with his Puritan neighbors, given just before Sewall's departure for a visit to the mother country, closes for a time his record of events in Boston : —

"Wednesday, Oct' 24, 1688. In y° afternoon coming out of Town, I met Mr. Ratcliff, who ask'd me if I were going for England ; he ask'd when. I said in Capt. Clark. He pray'd God Almighty to bless me, and said must wait upon me."

It is a chapter of outrageous wrongs which Andros wrote here, and there is cause for lasting regret that the origin of so good a thing as religious freedom under the stern old Puritan régime should have been sullied by his despotic acts. But it is satisfactory to remember that ninety years later King's Chapel willingly expiated this injustice by opening its doors wide to the Old South Congregation, when dispossessed of their own church by the later revolution. It should be said, too, that the character both of Andros and Randolph doubtless had a better side than they showed to these troublesome (as they must have seemed to them) and rebellious colonists. They were pupils in a bad school, — the household of the Stuarts.[1] These advocates were

portance to be reported to the Privy Council in England. As there is no record of any other interference of this kind by the minister of the Church of England, it is reasonable to suppose that he had a reason for his course. It may be that Lilley had joined the new Episcopal society, though his friends had not. That he had preferences in this direction seems to be indicated by the fact that his name is found among the subscribers for building the new church. Sewall describes the ordination of Theophilus Frary as deacon of the South Church, Nov. 8, 1685.

[1] Randolph was probably in the family of the Duke of York before he became James II., while Andros had begun life as a page to Charles I. They were loyal to Church and King after the old High Tory fashion. Randolph is described by Dr. Ellis as "a persistent and pestering, if not unscrupulous, man." Of Andros, Mr. Whitmore, in his "Andros Tracts," says there is "no evidence that he was

not such as wise men would have chosen; but the cause which they were advocating, though blindly, was of the best, and doubtless not a few of those who first met in this way had a spirit worthy of the cause. "In the most contentious and stormy periods," says Dr. Greenwood, "I doubt not that a holy calm was shed upon the heart of many a worshipper as he offered up his prayers in the way which to him was best and most affecting, — and perhaps the way in which, long years ago, he had offered them up in some ivy-clad village church of green England, with many dear friends about him, now absent or dead."

The enforced tenancy of the South Meeting-house did not wait to be brought to a close until the downfall of Governor Andros, in April, 1689. The fact that the first wooden church was already nearly finished at that time is sufficient proof that the interference with property which gave such offence was a temporary though high-handed obedience to supposed necessity, and not a step towards confiscation. The foundations of the new building had been laid before the middle of October, 1688. Sewall wrote: —

"Tuesday, Octr 16. This day the Ground-sills of ye Chh are Laid, ye stone-foundation being finished. Octr 17. — This day a great part of ye Church is raised [Mr. Cotton Mather not there]."[1]

Sir Edmund had delayed too long. The building which at an earlier day must have been accepted as a proper recognition of the State and the religion which the Governor represented, was now considered to be his reluctant concession to public opinion. One of the complaints most urged against him before James III. and William III. was, "That the Service of the Church of England has bin forced into their Meeteing Houses."[2] Gov-

---

cruel, rapacious, or dishonest," nor immoral; and "a hasty temper is the most palpable fault to be attributed to him." But the domineering will of both Andros and Randolph came out in its harshest colors when brought in such collision with the will of the Puritans, which was as unyielding as the granite of New England itself.

[1] Sewall's notice of Mather's absence would indicate that the other ministers of the town, and the diarist himself, and probably other leading persons were present, according to the friendly custom of the period, to help in the "house-raising." This seems to show that the occupation of the burial-ground was not regarded as an invasion.

[2] Hutchinson, i. 356, remarks that "this was an equivocal expression." He had "made use of a meeting-house against the wills of the proprietors, but after their service was over, and compelled no Congregationalist to join him." Sir Edmund's own Report of his Administration, to the Lords of the Committee for Trade and Plantations, says: "The Church of England being unprovided of a place for theyr publique worship, he did, by advice of the Councill, borrow

ernor Danforth writing to Governor Markham of Pennsylvania, in 1698, describes in too glowing colors " the equanimity and civility which we shewed to our Brethren the Gentlemen of the Church of England in Boston, who with their Minister, after that he arrived, had the free use of our Great Court House, as also the spacious new Meeting-house in Boston for divine service, our hours of worship being so fixed as not to interfere with theirs."

Thus, after fruitless attempts to buy a piece of Cotton hill, the Governor and Council seem finally to have used their authority, as the supreme governing body, to appropriate a part of the corner from the old burying-ground, which probably was then but thinly tenanted. Ill-natured question is sometimes made of the rightful tenure of this spot by the church, but the question seems to be fairly answered by two facts: first, only the smaller moiety of the land on which the present King's Chapel stands was obtained at that time, the other portion having been bought from the town when the present church was built, at an exorbitant price, sufficient to cover the fair value of all the land; second, if the town had power to sell to the church in 1749, the Governor and Council, being the only lawful authorities at the time, had the right to convey a piece of the public land in 1688. If it had not been so considered, the act would surely have been at least impugned, if not annulled, after the overthrow of Sir Edmund Andros. But no attempt to do so appears, even in Sewall's Diary.

Doubtless the Council proceeded with due regard to legal forms; it may be giving " a grant of the land under the seal of New England and in the King's name to Mr. Ratcliffe and his successors, making the office of Rector of King's Chapel a sole corporation, as is the case with Vicars in England."[1]

Here the modest little church was built at a cost of £284 16s.,

the new meeting-house in Boston, at such times as the same was unused, untill they could provide otherwise; and accordingly on Sundays went in between eleven and twelve in the morning, and in the afternoone about fower; but, understanding it gave offence, hastened the building of a Church, wch was effected at the charge of those of the Church of England, where the Chaplaine of the Souldiers prformed divine service and preaching." — *N. Y. Docs.*, iii. 722, 726.

[1] This was the supposition of the late Peter Oliver, Esq. But there is an unfortunate gap in the records of the Council for 1687-89; and if the deed was given it was probably carried to England by Mr. Ratcliffe. The charges against Andros and others, given in Andros Tracts, i. 149-173, from Mass. Archives, Inter-Charter Papers, xxv. 255, bring together everything which could be collected by the Committee of Seven, but make no mention of the taking of land for the church, which they would surely do if that had been regarded as a usurpation. The selectmen of Boston, by their deed of additional land to the wardens

or $1,381.24. To defray this expense, ninety-six persons throughout the colony had contributed £256 9s., the balance being given by Andros on his departure from the country, and by other English officers later. The church remained, however, without pews, although it had a "pulpit cushion with fringe, tassel, and silk," until 1694, when the pews were paid for by a subscription of £53.

With poetical justice, Andros and Randolph did not enter the building which they had done so much to obtain. They were punished for their misdeeds of oppression by not enjoying their *good* deed, or seeing the emblem of that form of religion established which they really cared for. The church-book, on the next page to that which states the cost of the house, contains a "Note." There can be little doubt where the sympathies of the writer lay. If he was the senior warden it is not strange, as Dr. Bullivant had been one of those imprisoned.

The records of the church do not state how the land was procured, or of whom; when the building was formally dedicated, or by whom, if at all. It is evident, however, from certain entries in them, that worship was first held in it on Sunday, June 30, 1689, and that day may therefore be considered the dedication-day of King's Chapel. It stood on a corner of the old burial-ground, covering the space now occupied by the tower and front part of the present building.[1] This burial field, in

---

and vestry in 1748, recognized their ownership of the original lot, as was pointed out by the late N. I. Bowditch. See "Fifth Report of Record Commissioners," 1880, p. 9. I am indebted to Mr. P. H. Sears for evidence from the Massachusetts Archives that a grant of public lands in Yarmouth even to a private owner by the Andros government was respected as valid by the later authorities.

[1] Erected in 1754.

which sleeps some of the most precious dust which ever was sown in a "God's Acre" here or anywhere, is said by doubtful tradition to have been bequeathed to the town for this use by Isaac Johnson, the husband of Lady Arbella. Tremont Street was then a lane, travelled by cows going to pasture on the Common, among graves, or scattered houses, or open fields. The Common itself at that time seems to have extended nearly to School Street. Opposite to the site of the church were two or three homesteads, and about half way between Beacon Street and the entrance to Pemberton Square was the estate of Mr. Sewall. There the land rose in a ridge called Cotton hill, "distant from other building and very bleake." The school-house stood where the chancel and pulpit of the present church are, and on the opposite corner was Captain Penn Townsend's house. Sewall writes, July 24, 1688: "Tis finally said that the Church shall be set between the School House and Capt. Townsend's corner, many of the Council urging it, so that it might not stand just full up with Mr. Moodey's gate, where it would have wholly cut off the way between my fence and John Coney's, and have stood upon the cartway that now is into the ground."[1]

The civil administration of Governor Andros in New England is a subject aside from the province of this narrative, yet our theme is so closely intertwined with it that it is difficult to keep them completely parted. In the steady Stuart policy, if the political method by which James II. was being made absolute master of New England was the *warp* in the dark web, the churchly method was the *woof* in it; and the secular and religious threads cross and recross and mutually support each other.

The government of Andros lasted two years and four months. Carrying out implicitly the orders of the royal master who had chosen him for his trusted instrument,[2] he sought to make unmistakably clear the doctrine of the absolute dependence upon the Crown of every person in New England. The English law of the time held that in the forfeiture of the charter all rights under it lapsed to the Crown, as the original owner of the territory. Neither college, town, nor landowner had any rights which were not dependent on the king's sole pleasure.

---

[1] 4 Mass. Hist. Coll., viii. 517. The supreme authority of the Governor in such matters is recognized by a petition in the Mass. Archives, addressed to Sir E. Andros by the French congregation, Oct. 25, 1687, for the use of the Latin Schoolhouse on Lord's Days. They so used it until 1715.

[2] His character is well summed up by Mr. Whitmore. Andros Tracts, iii. ix, x, and J. R. Brodhead's "The Government of Sir E. Andros," etc., p. 20.

Accordingly, while in England the last Stuart king was hastening toward his destruction in a course which is unrolled before us in the splendors of Macaulay's stately page, Andros was making it clear to every New Englander that the sixty years of vigorous growth in independent life were annulled, and that the colony which had been treated by Cromwell almost as an independent State was only a Proprietary domain. The people had heretofore taxed themselves by act of their legislative assembly: now the Governor and his Council laid rates and duties. They had heretofore made their own laws: the Governor and Council relieved them of that responsibility. They had deemed themselves owners of the land they lived on: they now found that it would be necessary to pay for new grants to the Crown as proprietor of the farms they or their fathers before them had cleared. And the hungry office-holders who came with Andros — Randolph at their head — extorted heavy fees from them for services which they would have preferred to dispense with, even if offered *gratis*. The Governor said: "An Indian deed is no more than the scratch of a bear's paw." "You must not suppose," said Dudley, "that the rights of Englishmen follow you to the end of the earth." Such were the endurances which were laid on the neck of this unyoked and unyokable people.

ARMS OF ANDROS.[1]

In judging Andros, we must not forget that he was simply the faithful servant of his master. All personal charges against him fell unproved, when in England, after his overthrow, he was confronted with the agents of the colony. And William III., a good judge of men and servants, though he did not send him back to New England, gave him the government of Virginia.

However despotic the policy of James in the internal affairs of these colonies, his foreign policy as the ruler of the English nation must be approved. Catholic though he was, and bigot, and son of a French mother, James was an Englishman. He saw that the way to meet France on this continent was not by the barricade of loosely-joined colonies, but by the solid masonry of a single government. He saw how Canada fared under a single governor-general. It was a good example, not only for strength, but for " his own arbitrary rule." Hence his consoli-

---

[1] These arms, which were hung up in the church, are taken from the seal of Andros. See Heraldic Journal, i. 141.

CHURCH AND STATE UNDER ANDROS.   85

dation first of Massachusetts, Connecticut, Rhode Island, and New Hampshire under Andros; and hence, in April, 1687, his addition to this Dominion of New York and the Jerseys. Viewed as a great measure of national policy, this was wise; but for the separate interest of Massachusetts, and for carrying out the Massachusetts idea, it would be fatal, — merging all that was distinctive therein in the larger and incongruous mass. If James had ruled a little longer, he would have had all the colonies in America under a single Viceroy.

This idea was an imperial thought. It had in it infinitely more of the instinct of a great national government than any policy of England on this continent for the ninety years which followed. But it fell to pieces, through the partial triumph of the Massachusetts policy, on the downfall of Andros. The separate colonies resumed their autonomy provisionally: the government of William granted their separate charters again in a modified form. The "Dominion" had burst like a bubble, leaving the potent elements of Puritanism to work unhindered, till the time should be ripe for a new nation to grow together out of these scattered fragments.

The people of Massachusetts were essentially the same in 1689 that they were in 1775. Whether, if James II. had not been dethroned, they could have held out in their feebleness and without the other colonies against Great Britain, or whether they would have had the fate of the Scotch covenanters, cannot be told. But the wrath of the common people burned so fiercely that they were ready for rebellion or revolution. The signal was given by the news on April 4, 1689, of the landing of William of Orange at Torbay. A fortnight elapsed of sultry, oppressive silence; then with one loud crash and blinding glare the whole sky was filled with lightnings. By 8 A. M., on April 18, the town was full of rumors, and by 9 the drums were beating and the streets full of armed men. Captain George and Dr. Bullivant were soon seized, while Andros and Randolph with others took refuge in the fort on Fort Hill. About noon, above twenty native companies being assembled at the town house, "a declaration of the Gentlemen, Merchants, and Inhabitants of Boston," etc., drawn up by Cotton Mather, was read from the balcony. But the issue was by no means decided, as the town lay between the frigate and the fort, each ready for battle. At this critical moment, when no one seemed willing to head so perilous a venture, Mr. John Nelson, a fellow-churchman with Andros, but a lover of liberty, took command of the impatient militia and led them against the fort just in time to intercept the Governor's escape, and by a bold advance capturing the sconce, turned its guns against the fort and compelled a surrender. The Governor was lodged in Mr. Usher's house; but next day the country-folk from far and near swarmed raging into the town, demanding his imprisonment in the fort. Only the prompt action of the gentry in taking the head of the uprising preserved the form of a government and prevented bloodshed, which must later have brought a terrible retribution. Meantime, most of Mr. Ratcliffe's leading parishioners[1] were lodged in the old stone gaol on Prison Lane, which is described by an unfortunate tenant as "the nearest resemblance to a hell upon earth." Its outer walls were of stone three feet thick, its unglazed windows barred with iron, "the cells partitioned off with plank, the doors covered with iron spikes, the passage-ways like the dark valley of the shadow of death."[2] Here Randolph and others remained from April till January, when they were sent to England by royal command and "in no gentle mood."

A daring deed had been brought to pass. No wonder that Danforth wrote to Mather, "I am deeply sensible that we have a wolfe by the ears." The penalties of treason were hanging over their heads. It was well for the Colony in that hour that Increase Mather was safe in England, to parry at the Court of William every thrust of their enemies, and to win for them another Charter which, if less good than the former one, would yet be broad enough to enable Massachusetts under its protection to gather her strength for the Revolution of 1776.

The storm of that time had well nigh driven the little ark of the church from its anchorage. Even now, after the lapse of nearly two centuries, it is impossible to read the "Andros Tracts" without feeling the ground-swell of those waves of passion which tossed so fiercely in the little town of Boston. In July, 1689, Rev. Robert Ratcliffe returned to England.[3] "Mr. Ratcliffe follows his business close," Sewall wrote thence to his wife, Aug. 3, 1689; and as late as May 28, 1692, Charles Lidgett wrote from London to F. Foxcroft: "Mr. Ratcliffe last week in town gives you his Service, has a Mind once again upon lit-

---

[1] Besides Andros and Randolph, Lidgett, Trefrey, Bullivant, Foxcroft, White, and Ravenscroft.

[2] See Drake's Hist. of Boston, p. 635.

[3] Mr. Ratcliffe must have gone to England before Andros, as is evident from the following entry on the records: "July 27, 1689. By disbursements for the accommodation of Mr. Ratcliffe for his voyage home, as appears by several bills on file, £11 4s. 8d." He seems for some time to have cherished the hope of returning to Boston, even after taking a living in England.

tle incouragm¹ to leave a Sure Benefice here for another Strowl into America."¹ But we are unable to trace his later history. It is unlikely, in the angry state of public feeling, that there was any public dedication, or perhaps any consecration at all, of the wooden church.² The very building seems to have been in danger, for in those days there was such a power as the "Boston Mob." A pamphlet published in London in 1690, " New England's Faction Discovered, by C. D.," states that —

"Though at the time of the Revolution most of the Principal Officers in the Government were of the Independent and Presbyterian Party, yet their malice and fury was not shewn to any of them, but only used and exercised against those of the Church of *England*, whom (as well the Governour as other officers of the Government and principal Members of that Church) they seized and most barbarously imprisoned. The church itself had great difficulty to withstand their fury, receiving the marks of their indignation and scorn by having the Windows broke to pieces and the Doors and Walls daubed and defiled with dung and other filth in the rudest and basest manner imaginable, and the Minister for his safety was forced to leave the country and his congregation and go for England." ³

A vigorous pamphlet in reply, however, entitled " A Vindication of New England," denies that there was anything more in this than " the breaking of a few Quarrels of Glass by mischievous boys." But a petition is preserved, signed by Mr. Ratcliffe's successor and the church wardens, and addressed to King William III., which would indicate something more serious: " Our church, by their rage and fury, having been greatly hurt and damnified, and dayly threatned to be pulled down and destroyed; our minister hindred and obstructed in the discharge of his duty and office." ⁴

The church however survived, to be fostered by the care and honored with the gifts of the successive monarchs of England,

¹ N. E. Hist. and Geneal. Reg., xxxiv., 80.

² Dr. Greenwood thinks that the following dates from the old record-book may give some light. Under the date of March 20, 1687, there is the last regular entry of the weekly contribution till after Andros's deposition. On the 30th of June, 1689, these entries are again resumed. It will be remembered that on the 23d of March, 1687, Andros took possession of the South Church, and on the 18th of April, 1689, was deposed. July 1, 1689, there is an entry of 20s. paid to Mr. Miles, and 5s. to the "Clerke," and July 5, of £1 15s. 0d. to "Mr. Wm. Smith for Benching the church." He adds: "Putting these dates together, I think it almost certain that worship was first performed in the wooden church on the last Sabbath and day in June, 1689."

³ Andros Tracts, ii. 212.

⁴ See " The Humble Address," etc., in the next chapter. The Puritan satisfaction at this reverse of the church's fortune was vented in the "Vindication": " 'Tis notorious they went a *begging* to all the Congregations in the Town for Money to Erect their Edifice, which they call a Church (tho', by the way, it was never *Consecrated*). Several Non-Conformists gave towards it (as the Indian

from William and Mary to George the Third. Under the long ministry of Rev. Samuel Myles it won the respect, if not the love, of its neighbors. The plain building was the only place in New England where the forms of the Court church could be witnessed. The prayers and anthems which sounded forth in the cathedrals of the mother country were here no longer dumb. The equipages and uniforms which made gay the little court of Boston brightened its portals. Within, the escutcheons of Royal governors hung against the pillars; at Christmas it was wreathed with green; the music of the first organ heard in New England here broke the stillness of the Sabbath air.

The religious struggle of twenty-five years was over. If it be asked which party won in it, the answer must be, — both. The despotism of Andros was overthrown; the charter never was restored in its first fulness, but its work had been wrought; a people had been trained to great traditions of freedom, and these survived eighty-six years more and then burst into blossom and fruit. On the other hand the religious despotism of Puritanism was broken forever. Baptists, Episcopalians, Quakers, might henceforth worship as they would; to-day, everything, anything, or nothing may be believed where for nearly sixty years the Calvinism of New England was all in all.

It may be inferred that Mr. Ratcliffe carried with him such records as had been kept during his three years' ministry, from the absence of any record between July 4, 1686, and the following: —

worshiped one whom he feared else would hurt him). Such contributors (we suppose) Expected no great reward of their bounty in the *other* World, and now they see they are like to have none in *this*. Thus *at their own Charge* they built an *House;* but can the Tounsmen of *Boston* tell at whose charge the *Land* was purchased?

"The truth of the matter is this: There could never be found amongst them to make a sufficient Congregation to *that way*, untill the change of the Government powered in some strangers who were to raise (to themselves) Estates amongst them. Before *that*, those of *that way* who had any visible sense of Religion usually joyned in worship with the Churches of *New-England* as finding nothing in those Administrations to offend their Consciences, tho' perhaps not enough to please their *Appetite*. Besides if any one appear to be a man fearing God, they receive him to the *Lord's Table*, notwithstanding his being *Episcopal*. Or if at any time there were any number of *that way*, they could never find *Clergie-men* to undertake the care of their souls. . . . Persons, indeed, that will Drink, Sweare, Fornicate, practise and preach up (the honest games of) Cards, Dice, etc., have never found New England a good Fishing Ground. And others that have had more *Grace* have also (for the most part) had more *Witt* than to Cross the Ocean for a Dwelling in so *cold a country*. And this is all the Interruption that ever the Church of England found in those parts of the World." — *Andros Tracts*, ii. 36, 45.

BOSTON, July, 1689.   Laus Deo.

A memorandum of sure, honest, and well-disposed persons that Contributed their assistance for and towards erecting a Church for God's worship in Boston, according to the Constitution of the Church of England as by law Established.[1] The sums following were first collected:

	£	s.	d.		£	s.	d.
Doct Benjamin Bullivant	20	00	00	Edward Crook	1	00	00
Lt Col. Nicholas Paige[1]	20	00	00	Stephen Minott[37]	1	00	00
Lt Col. Charles Lidget	15	00	00	Joseph Short	1	05	00
Majr Anthony Haywood[2]	10	00	00	Mercy Hunt	0	05	00
Thaddeus Mackarty	7	10	00	Wm Hunt[38]	2	00	00
Francis Foxcroft[3]	10	00	00	Thomas Fareweather[39]	0	10	00
Samuel Ravenscroft	5	00	00	John White[40]	0	10	00
Edward Hill	6	00	00	George Raison[41]	1	00	00
Capt Wm White[4]	7	00	00	Nathaniel Nudigate[42]	2	00	00
Andrew Dolbury[5]	10	00	00	Lancelot Lake[43]	5	00	00
John Nelson[6]	5	00	00	Joshuah Broadbent[44]	2	00	00
Thomas Brinley[7]	5	00	00	Samuel Lynd[45]	1	00	00
Wm Brinley[8]	2	00	00	Duncan Cambell[46]	1	00	00
John George[9]	3	00	00	Sargent Walker	0	12	00
Capt P. Bowdon[10]	5	00	00	James Adkins	1	00	00
Richard Harris[11]	2	00	00	Edward Randolph, Esqr	5	00	00
Robert Johnson	2	00	00	John Conney, Junr[47]	1	01	00
Wm Hobby[12]	2	00	00	Benjamin Mountfort[48]	2	02	00
George Monck[13]	1	02	00	Robert Gutteridge[49]	0	10	00
Anthony Checkley[14]	3	00	00	Richard Rogers	1	00	00
James Sherlock[15]	5	00	00	John Colton	0	10	00
Edward Lilley[16]	3	00	00	Richard Crispe[50]	1	00	00
Benjamin Davis[17]	3	00	00	John Foy[51]	1	10	00
Giles Dyer[18]	5	00	00	Savil Simpson[52]	1	00	00
Francis Burroughs[19]	5	00	00	Edward Smith	1	16	00
George Pordage[20]	5	00	00	John Dole	1	10	00
Lt Veazey[21]	1	00	00	John Baker	1	04	00
Thomas Luscombe[22]	5	00	00	Ralph Dordant[53]	1	00	00
Nathaniel Baker[23]	0	18	00	Capt John George[54]	1	02	00
Thomas Stanbury[24]	1	10	00	Warner Wesendunck[55]	2	00	00
Harry Clark[25]	1	00	00	George Hollard[56]	0	12	00
Mr Belchamber	3	00	00	Edward Thomas[57]	1	04	00
James Hooper	5	00	00	Wm Gilbert[58]	0	10	00
Gilbart Bant[26]	1	00	00	Isaac Jones[59]	0	12	00
Thomas Harris	1	00	00	Daniel Allen[60]	1	00	00
Thomas Gold, the founder[27]	0	12	00	Thomas Mallet[61]	0	06	00
Thomas Walker	0	10	00	Abram Blish[62]	0	06	00
Thomas Clark[28]	1	00	00	David Harris[63]	0	06	00
Benjamin Alford[29]	2	00	00	Jarvas Ballard[64]	0	12	00
John Ware[30]	2	00	00	James Meeres[65]	0	06	00
Wm Ardell[31]	1	00	00	Nath. Shepcoat[66]	0	06	00
Andrew Marriner[32]	1	00	00	Thomas Winsour[67]	0	06	00
John Parmeter[33]	1	01	00	Richard Talley[68]	0	06	00
Xpher Goff	1	04	00	Abram Smith	0	06	00
Thomas Cooper[34]	1	10	00	John Wooddy	0	06	00
James Lloyd[35]	1	00	00	Joseph Hilliard	0	06	00
Roger Kilcup[36]	0	10	00	Wm Huff[69]	0	06	00
	£199	06	00	turned over	£50	03	00

[1] Notwithstanding the sarcastic insinuations of their opponents to the contrary, it is probable that the greater part of these subscribers really favored the Church of England. The absence of prominent New England names is no-

The continuation of the names of the Contributors to the Church.

	£	s.	d.
Brought from t'other side	249.	09.	00
Stephen Wesendunck [10]	5.	00.	00
Thomas Dudley	2.	00.	00
	£256.	09.	00

Cost of the house to Carpenters	£260.	00.	00
" " " "	9.	00.	00
Maj! Haywood's bill	15.	16.	00
	£284.	16.	00

Note there was some other charge in painting the window frames by Tho. Child wch demanded nothing for.

Maj! Haywood undertooke wth Carpenters and the accompt was balanced wth him when Capt. Ravenscroft and Foxcroft Was Churchwardens.^{a}

	£	s.	d.
Sir Edmund Androse, K! left for the Church service	30.	00.	00
Capt. Francis Nicholson left	25.	00.	00

The Governor and Lieut.-Governor were faithful to the church in the change of fortunes which befell them and it.

---

ticeable. Dr. Bullivant and other founders of the church have been already noticed. See pp. 45-48, *ante.* Richard Bankes, first Junior Warden (see pp. 44, 45), may have been the person of that name who took the oath of fidelity at Scituate in 1643. His removal to York, Me., prior to November, 1645, indicates his sympathy with the Episcopal preferences of that settlement. He had various land-grants there and held offices between 1649 and 1679. He married Elizabeth Alcock, of York, and had four sons. If he was the Warden, he must have been living in Boston in 1686, but probably returned to York, as he is supposed to have perished with two sons in the Indian massacre there in 1692.

^{a} Here follows the note of which a fac-simile is given on p. 82.

[1] Came to Boston, in 1665, from Plymouth, in Devon, England. Served in Philip's war, 1675. Captain and Colonel of Artillery Company, 1693. He married a niece of Governor Dudley. He died in 1717.

[2] Boston, 1671; one of those authorized to receive contributions for building the church. A contribution to ransom him from captivity is mentioned in the records. See p. 118.

[3] Warden, 1689. See p. 105.

[4] See p. 48. Dunton's Letters, p. 81, calls him "a Worthy Merchant, who crosses both the Torrid and the frozen Zone, midst Rocks and Swallowing Gulfs for gainful Trade; piercing the center for the shining Oar, and th' Oceans Bosom to rake Pearly Sands; a Merchant who by Trading has clasp'd Islands to the Continent, and tack'd one Countrey to another; Nor was his skill in Merchandizing all; His Knowledge both of Men and Things was Universal; And to have heard him talk of any subject, you wou'd have thought he had engross'd all knowledge, and that the seven Liberal Sciences took up their Residence within his Brest."

[5] Boston, 1677. Mariner. His wife Elizabeth joined the Second Church July, 1691, and had daughter Elizabeth baptized July 12, 1691.

[6] Warden, 1705-7. A relative of Sir Thomas Temple, Artillery Company, 1680, Captain and one of the leaders in capturing Andros, 1689. On account of his churchmanship, he was not trusted as his merits deserved. The story of his romantic and gallant career will be related later. See p. 179.

[7] Son of Francis Brinley, of Newport,

1652, and belonging to a Loyalist family. Artillery Company, 1681. He married in England Mary Apthorp. He died of small-pox, 1693.

⁸ Younger brother of Thomas, died 1693, unmarried.

⁹ Of Boston. One of the first members of Brattle-Square Church, February, 1700. His widow Lydia, daughter of Rev. Samuel Lee, became third wife of Rev. Cotton Mather, July 5, 1715.

¹⁰ Probably Pierre Baudouin, the Huguenot refugee and founder of the Bowdoin family.

¹¹ Merchant. Died April 12, 1697. Had wife, Elizabeth, and several children.

¹² Warden in 1693 and in 1699-1701. A Boston merchant. He was father, by his wife Ann, of Sir Charles Hobby, to be noticed later, and of several other children.

¹³ Vintner at the sign of the Blue Anchor. Dunton's Journal honors his genial disposition: "A person so remarkable, that had I not been acquainted with him, it would be a hard matter to make any New England man believe that I had been in Boston. There was no house in Boston more noted than George Monk's, or where a man might meet with better entertainment; he was so much the life and spirit of the guests that came to his house, that it was almost impossible not to be cheerful in his company."

¹⁴ Merchant. Son of William, of Preston Capes, Northamptonshire. Baptized July 31, 1636. Captain Artillery Company. Married (1) Hannah, daughter of Rev. John Wheelwright; (2) Lydia, widow of Benjamin Gibbs, and daughter of Joshua Scottow. He was chosen, 1689, Attorney-General, but superseded before the Witchcraft infatuation. He died Oct. 18, 1708.

¹⁵ Of Portsmouth. Appointed Counsellor, 1684; made by Andros Sheriff of Suffolk, 1687; imprisoned April, 1689; sent to England February, 1689-90.

¹⁶ Was in Boston, 1670. A cooper. He may have been brother of Samuel (Boston, 1686), at whose funeral a famous dispute occurred. See p. 78.

¹⁷ Was in Boston, 1670. Son of William (apothecary, who was a man of wealth, enterprise, and discretion, commander of a troop, commissioner in 1653, etc., and one of the founders of the Third Church). Merchant. A major, Artillery Company, 1673; freeman, 1690; one of the founders of Brattle-Square Church. He died Nov. 26, 1704.

¹⁸ Warden, 1690, 1696-98. Artillery Company, 1680; Colonel and Sheriff of the colony. Dudley's first Council, May 25, 1686, appointed him "Receiver of the Duties upon wines and other Liquors imported," and Aug. 26, "Deputy Receiver of his Majesty's Customs." He was "allowed 12d. in the £ for all publick moneys he hath or may receive." He died Aug. 12, 1713. His will names his wife Hannah and children, Giles and Elizabeth Raisin, a widow, whose son George also subscribed. Sewall records his death "after long Languishing, about 6 M. Church-Bell rings just before the School Bell, so both ring together. Augt 14. Am invited to be a Bearer to the Sheriff. I enquired of Mr. Secretary whether there was a Sermon; he told me yes, Mr. Harris was to preach, and seem'd to make no doubt of [my] going to hear him: I now begun to be distress'd." Judge Sewall accepted a pair of gloves for his sake, but refused to be a bearer, and though he followed in the procession, would not go into the church.

¹⁹ Was in Boston, 1685; Artillery Company, 1686; a merchant from London. He married, for second wife, widow Elizabeth Heath, Dec. 29, 1709. Dunton says he was "the first person that welcomed me to Boston, formerly a hearer of my reverend father-in-law, Dr. Annesly. He heaped more civilities upon me than I can reckon up; offered to lend me monies," etc.

²⁰ Also spelt Portage. Merchant. He married Elizabeth, daughter of Simon Lynde. Savage thinks he removed from Boston, probably from the province. His daughter Hannah, born Feb. 13, 1687, married, Sept. 16, 1714, James Bowdoin, and was mother of James, Harvard College, 1745, President of the Convention of 1780, and second Governor of Massachusetts.

²¹ Probably of Braintry, and a brother of Rev. William Vesey, whose apostasy from Puritanism is recorded by Sewall. It may have been he who was fined in 1696 "for plowing on the day of Thanksgiving," and whose cow was distrained for taxes for the support of the Congregational minister, to which he objected

as being a member of the Church of England. See Sewall, June 2, 1713.

[22] Brother of Major Humphrey Lyscom, or Liscom, merchant, who died 1688. One of the brothers was among the founders of the church in 1686.

[23] He was of Yarmouth, eldest son of Francis, of Boston, who came in the "Planter," 1635.

[24] Son of Thomas and Martha, of Boston, born Oct. 15, 1642, baptized in First Church, Nov. 30, 1645.

[25] Warden, 1691. If this was Henry Clark, of Newbury, he was son of Nathaniel. He married, Nov. 7, 1695, Elizabeth, daughter of Stephen Greenleaf.

[26] Sea-captain, of Boston. His wife was named Mercy. Their daughter Mary was born April 28, 1689, etc. He was carried prisoner to England in the "Mehitabel," February, 1689-90.

[27] Thomas Gould, of Boston, married, Sept. 10, 1656, Frances Robinson. Their daughter Ann, born about 1685, married, Feb. 27, 1703, Nathaniel Green.

[28] Probably the person mentioned in N. E. Hist. and Geneal. Reg., xv. 15; not recorded by Savage, who gives four others of the name. He was born at Salisbury, Co. Wilts, Dec. 22, 1645. He married Rebecca, widow of Capt. Thomas Smith, and had daughters Anne, born Sept. 1, 1694, married John Jeffries, and Jane, married Rev. Benjamin Colman.

[29] A Boston merchant, probably son of William (merchant in Salem, 1635, who came from London, 1634, a member of the Skinners' Co. He favored the party of Wheelwright; was disarmed by General Court, removed to New Haven, but returned after 1654, to Boston). Artillery Company, 1671. He married Mary, daughter of James Richards, Esq., of Hartford. He had been a prisoner in Barbary, and after return was a man of importance in Boston. He died 1710. His son John founded the Alford Professorship of Natural Theology, etc., at Harvard College.

[30] Of Dedham. He married Dec. 10, 1668, and removed to Wrentham. A freeman, 1677, and representative for Wrentham, 1689.

[31] Boston, 1687; merchant. Removed to Portsmouth, and was Sheriff of New Hampshire under Andros, and later. He was ordered to bring his accounts to the Council at Portsmouth, Jan. 19, 1696-97, and in April, '97, it was ordered that " in case ye said Ardell refuse to pay " the balance, " that the Secretary give warrant to the present sheriff to take it by distress." May 21, '97, he was ordered to be apprehended for refusal to pay; but on May 27 appeared to answer his contempt, saying that Mr. Usher gave him the contrary order; and was dismissed on acknowledging contempt, paying his balance and charges, and promising reformation. Dec. 14, 1697, he was summoned before the Council for breaking open the King's stores at New Castle, under order from Lieut.-Gov. Usher, and was put under bonds to appear at next Quarter Sessions. He was appointed high sheriff Jan. 15, 1698-99; but July 31, 1699, was discharged from his office, " the Council having advised his Excellency to remove Wm Ardell from being High Sheriff of this Province, as being a person who lives remote; also a great Swearer, given unto drinke and abusive in his drinke, and of no visible Estate in this Province, and therefore very unfitt for the place of High Sheriff." See Prov. Papers of N. H., ii., 203, etc.

[32] An inscription in the Granary burying-ground reads: " Priscilla, daughter of Andrew and Ruth Marriner, aged 2 years and 3 mos., died July 9, 1690."

[33] Of Boston. Housewright. By wife Judith had Judith, born Feb. 14, 1667, etc.

[34] Of Boston. One of the founders of Brattle-Street Church. Merchant. (Perhaps son of Josiah, Boston, Cordwainer.) Married Mehitabel, daughter of James Minot, and niece of Lieut.-Governor Stoughton. His son, Rev. William Cooper of Brattle-Square Church, Harvard College, 1712, was father of Rev. Samuel Cooper, D. D., Harvard College, 1743, also of Brattle Square, and of William, the celebrated town-clerk of Boston for fifty years.

[35] A Boston merchant, probably from Bristol, who came about 1670 to Newport, but in 1673 was fixed at Boston. He died 1693. He married (1) Griselda, daughter of Nathaniel Sylvester, of Shelter Island; (2) Rebecca, daughter of Gov. John Leverett. He was grandfather of Dr. James Lloyd, whose son James was United States Senator.

[36] Of Boston, perhaps son of William (Boston, 1649, called a seine-maker).

Freeman, 1690. He died Oct. 1, 1702, aged 52.

³⁷ Of Boston, grandson of George (of Dorchester, born Aug. 4, 1594, at Saffron Walden, Co. Essex; an early settler; freeman, April 1, 1634; representative 1635–36; ruling elder 30 years). He was born Aug. 10, 1662; married Dec. 1, 1686, Mary, daughter of Christopher Clark, and had twelve children. He was one of the founders of Brattle-Square Church. He died 1732. Savage says: "The reputation of his great-grandson, George R., Harvard College, 1778, is fixed in one generation by most amiable character, and for the succeeding by his works on our history." A genealogy of the Minot family is given in N. E. Hist. and Geneal. Reg., i. 171, 256.

³⁸ Of Boston. By his wife Sarah had Thomas, born March 23, 1682, etc.

³⁹ Possibly son of John Fayerweather, who was put in command of the Castle at the Revolution of 1689.

⁴⁰ Of Muddy River and Roxbury. Freeman, 1677. Was a lieutenant. He married Elizabeth, eldest daughter of Elder John Bowles.

⁴¹ Stepson of Giles Dyer. See n. 18.

⁴² Nathaniel Nudigate, or Newgate. Grandson of John, merchant, who was in Boston 1632.

⁴³ Of Boston, 1695. A physician of whom nothing is known, but that he married, May 6, 1708, widow Catherine Child. He died Sept. 17, 1715. In his will he gave her all his estate. Savage presumes "it was a doubt in the mind of the widow whether the estate would amount to the few shillings of expense. His gravestone was lately found in the cemetery of King's Chapel."

⁴⁴ Provost-Marshal and Sheriff of New Hampshire, 1681. He married, at Woburn, April 6, 1685, Sarah Osborn.

⁴⁵ Of Boston, son of Simon (Boston, 1650, born in London, June, 1624; returned to London after several years in Boston), a merchant and freeman, 1690. He died December, 1697.

⁴⁶ Of Boston, 1685, a bookseller from Scotland. Artillery Company, 1686. Under commission from home, he "was made postmaster for our side of the world." Dunton says of him: "He is very industrious, dresses all *a mode*, and, I am told, a young lady of a great fortune is fallen in love with him."

⁴⁷ John Coney, of Boston, cooper. Artillery Company, 1662, freeman, 1069. He was a neighbour of Sewall and of the Church. See p. 83.

⁴⁸ (Munford or Mumford). Warden, 1690, Boston. Merchant at the Town Dock and at "Mountfort Corner," now 'Change Avenue. He came, it is said, in the "Dove" from London, 1675, æt. 30. Artillery Company, 1679. Died 1714. He married Rebecca Foster, daughter of an English lawyer of Dorchester. His will says: "I give and recommend my soul into the hands of God that gave it, and my body I recommend to the Earth to be buryed in decent and Christian manner at the discretion of my executrix, nothing doubting but at the general Resurrection I shall receive the same again by the Almighty Power of God. And as touching such worldly Estate wherewith it hath pleased God to bless me in this life, I give, demise, and dispose of the same . . . unto my Dearly beloved Wife." He had been preceded in the ship "Providence," 1656, by his brothers Edmund, who married Elizabeth Carwithy, daughter of Deacon John Farnham, and is the ancestor of numerous descendants, — died 1690; and Henry, married Ruth Wiswall, of Dorchester, and died March 29, 1691.

⁴⁹ Or Goodridge. Kept a coffee-house in Boston on the Main, now Washington, Street. He died Nov. 4, 1717, aged 72.

⁵⁰ Boston. Permitted to teach fencing 1686 (3 Mass. Hist. Coll., vii. 157). He married Sarah, youngest daughter of Rev. John Wheelwright.

⁵¹ Boston, 1671. Mariner. By wife Dorothy had Elizabeth, born Sept. 21, 1672, and eight others. Perhaps from Guernsey, or other Jersey Island.

⁵² Warden 1691, 1697, 1706–1708.

⁵³ R. Durdent is on the tax list of 1687.

⁵⁴ Captain George, Commander of the "Rose" frigate.

⁵⁵ Taverner. Probably brother of Stephen. "Administration was granted on his estate Aug. 12, 1690, to Thomas Walter, at the request of the creditors, his wife and relations did not wish it." Sewall, i. 133 n.

⁵⁶ Boston, 1664. Mariner. Died April 12, 1714, in his 90th year.

⁵⁷ Boston, 1685. Agent of Joseph Thompson, of London, merchant.

⁵⁸ Of Boston. Cordwainer and merchant, 1675. He died January, 1693.
⁵⁹ Of Dorchester. Son of Thomas; probably born in England, freeman 1654. He married (1) Hannah Heath, (2) Mary Bass. He died before Dec. 6, 1699.
⁶⁰ Probably the physician, of Boston. He was representative Sept. 16, 1693, and died Nov. 7, 1693.
⁶¹ Thomas Mallett is on the tax lists of 1687-91. See p. 49.
⁶² Of Boston. One of the founders of Brattle-Square Church, 1698. Probably a son of Abraham Blish or Blush, of Barnstable.
⁶³ Of Charlestown. Married Tamazin Elson. He was a mariner in 1695. His oldest child, Joseph, was born Oct. 14, 1679.
⁶⁴ Of Boston, 1670. A merchant, perhaps not a permanent resident.
⁶⁵ Or Mears, of Boston, felt-maker. He was son of Robert, (of Boston, tailor, who came in the "Abigail," 1635, from London). He was baptized March 31, 1644. He was father of nine children. In 1704 he sold the land on which the French Chapel on School Street was soon built.
⁶⁶ Thomas Shepscoat, perhaps a relative, is on the tax lists in 1674 and 1688.
⁶⁷ Of Boston, son of Robert; turner; baptized Oct. 9, 1659.
⁶⁸ (Or Tolley, or Taulley), of Dorchester, but earlier of Boston, where some of his children were baptized in the South Church. He died Dec. 8, 1717, aged 66.
⁶⁹ On the tax list of 1691.

⁷⁰ Or Wissendunk. Later, agent of King's Chapel in London. He probably married, before 1693, Sarah, widow of Robert Sedgwick, Jr.

NOTE. — Of Captain Hamilton, whose escutcheon was the first to hang on the church walls, the following notice may be added here: Thomas, fourth son by Mary Butler (daughter of Walter Viscount Thurles and sister of the first Duke of Ormond), of Sir George Hamilton (fourth son of James, first Earl of Abercorn), was bred to the sea-service. His father had served Charles I. and Charles II. in Ireland. The son commanded in 1668 the Deptford Ketch and the Nightingale; in 1671/2 the Mermaid and the Constant Warwick; in 1673 the Mary rose of 50 guns, which he commanded in the action with the Dutch, where his brother was killed; in 1675 the Margaret galley, and in 1677 the Charles, in which he captured a large Algerine galley after a desperate fight. In 1681/2 he was appointed to the Dragon, and March 23, 1684/5, to the Kingfisher, in which he captured the Scottish castle of Ellengreg from the Duke of Argyle, whose ship is also said to have taken in the West Indies. See Lodge's "Peerage of Scotland," v. 118, and Charnock's "Biographia Navalis," i. 310, which fails to record his death, and also confounds him with his elder brother James, who lost his leg in the action with the Dutch May 28, 1673, and is buried in Westminster Abbey. See Chester's "Westminster Abbey Registers," p. 180.

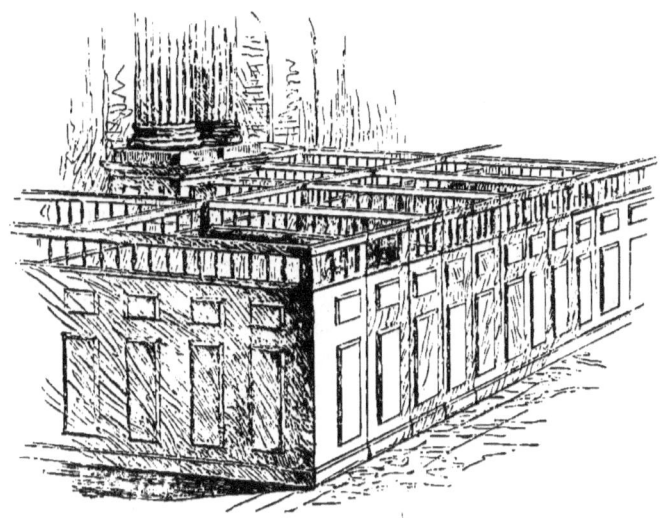

RAILED PEWS. 1694.

CHAPTER IV.

THE CHURCH TAKES ROOT.[1]

HE penalty was a natural one which the church paid for its exaltation under Andros, in that it suffered in his fall. Its adversaries exulted: —

"Surely they are such *Harsh fruits* of which we have had a Taste, and may still be seen in the *Faction* there, who wear the Name of the *Church of England*, that there is no great fear of many *New-Englanders* to be *united to their Assembly*. Alas, poor souls! many of them upon the Rising *Light* of Sir *Edmund's* glory did in a Huff run thereunto; and now upon his Setting they are left in the Dark how to get fairly off without damage to their Reputation."[2] This was harshly expressed in a later controversy:[3] "From this Time the Episcopal cause declined in the Country. Those who had not gone too far to think of recovering their Credit now deserted it. Those who had, continued in

---

[1] The illustration, representing the pews erected in 1694, is taken from a photograph of similar pews in the old Hingham meeting-house, built in 1680.

[2] Andros Tracts, ii. 68.

[3] Hobart's "Second Address," etc., Boston, 1751, p. 26.

a Body, but were generally looked upon as the Betrayers of their Country; and though no Body molested them, yet almost every Body despised them."

At this time, when the air was thick with passion, the publication of a trenchant attack on the English Liturgy urged the popular feeling to a keener height. In this, also, the masterful hand of Increase Mather was apparent. The "Discourse" condemned the Liturgy as being derived from the Popish Mass, and therefore idolatrous; and dwelt in detail on the matters in it most objectionable to Puritans, — "those broken Responds and shreds of Prayer which the Priests and People toss between them like Tennis Balls;" "odd and senseless Translations of the Holy Scriptures found therein;" the use of the Apocrypha; "some things enjoined in it as cannot be practised without sin," — as the communion at marriage, the hopeful phrases of the burial-service, the use of the ring in marriage, "Popish Holy days," the Surplice, and the cross, "the greatest Devil among all the Idols of Rome." "Publick Liturgies of humane Composure are an innovation," it said, "from primitive Antiquity, and it's an Apostacy in this Age of Light to countenance or comply with the Common Prayer-Book worship. A stinted Liturgy is opposite to the Spirit of Prayer." This was the first shot in a pamphlet war which continued at intervals till the Revolution.[2]

The unexpected overthrow of the government of Andros appears to have moved Mr. Ratcliffe to return to England. He waited before doing so, however, faithful to his charge of the nursling church, for three months, — probably until the arrival

[2] "I have to add," wrote Randolph from gaol to the Archbishop, May 28, 1689, "that Mr Mather has published here a booke called the Idolatry of ye Common-prayer worship, which renders all of vs of that church obnoxious to the common people, who account vs Popish, and treat vs accordingly. Mr Ratcliffe can say more of it." This pamphlet, ascribed at the time to Cotton Mather, whose prosecution for it seems doubtful (Andros Tracts, ii. 47), was recognized in later controversy to be by his father. It was published without name or date, as "A Brief Discourse Concerning the unlawfulness of the Common-Prayer Worship; And Of Laying the Hand on, and Kissing the Booke in Swearing. By a Reverend and Learned Divine. 2 Kings, xviii. 4. '. . . . for unto those dayes the Children of Israel did burn Incense to it: and hee called it Nehushtan.'" Printed in the year, [1689], etc. Some Puritan doctrines are hinted at when it says: "I have omitted the mentioning of many particulars contained in the Liturgy, which *as to the Doctrine of them are False* and corrupt. E. g.: It is there affirmed that *Children Baptized have all things Necessary to Salvation and are undoubtedly saved.* Yea, that *it is Certain from God's word that if a Baptized child dye before actuall Sin, 'tis saved.* This savours of *Pelagianisme.* . . . And the Booke sayth that . . . Christ has Redeemed *all Mankind.*"

of his successor and the completion of the modest little wooden
building insured the permanence of the work which he had
begun in a climate that must have chilled his soul. The record
of July 1, 1689, shows that Mr. Myles officiated on that day,
and that for July 27 records the disbursements for Mr. Ratcliffe's voyage home. Before his departure,[1] he transferred to
responsible care the modest offering which was in his hands:

> Rec^d of Mr Robert Ratcliffe twenty-two shillings in money which
> was Given him By Capt John Goory towards buying of Communion
> plate, and one shilling of Mrs Wallett for the same use, — in all 23l.
>
> p THADDEUS MACKARTY.
>
> June 5th 1689.

The successor to Mr. Ratcliffe was the Rev. Samuel Myles,
who was destined to be the Rector of King's Chapel for nearly
thirty-nine years. He was American born, and had grown up
under religious influences at variance with the established Congregationalism, among a body of Christians whose existence was
a protest in favor of religious freedom. His father was Elder
John Myles, a Baptist preacher, who emigrated from Swansey,
in Wales, and was settled over a Baptist church in Rehoboth, in
1663. He returned to England, and came again in 1665, accompanied by a colony. Grants of lands south of Rehoboth
had been early obtained from the Indians; and in 1667 Mr.
Myles " and others, their neighbors at Wannamoiset and parts
adjacent, were confirmed in their title to those lands, and erected
into the township of Swansey, by the General Court at Plymouth. In that town the religious profession of a Baptist never
worked any forfeiture of civil rights."[2] The father was a man
of catholic temper and spirit. Hutchinson says: " I have seen
a letter, dated not many years after this time (1665), from Mr.
Miles, the baptist minister at Swanzey, to one of the congregational ministers at Boston, which breathes the true spirit of the

---

[1] Mr. Ratcliffe carried with him a note of introduction from Randolph to the Archbishop of Canterbury (Perry, Church Docs. Mass. p. 656) : —

" BOSTON, in New England,
May 28th, 1689.

"*May it please Your Grace:*

" I humbly recommend to Your Grace by the bearer hereof, Mr. Ratcliffe, our Minister above 3 years. The sad and distracted condition of this territory of New England is occasioned by a discontented party, who on ye 18 of April last tooke armes, seized upon the ffort, castle, and Rose frigott at anchor in the Harbour in Boston. They haue imprisoned ye gou^r in the fort under a strong gard; they keep me in the common goal, giuing out he is a Papist, and that I have committed treason. Their printed papers, which Mr Ratcliffe will present to Your Grace, will giue account of their actions; but nothing therein that's justly charged."

[2] N. E. Hist. and Geneal. Reg., xviii. 246.

gospel and urges Christian concord, charity, and love, although they did not agree in every point."[1]

Samuel Myles graduated at Harvard College[2] in the Class of 1684. "Samuel Mylesius Mr." stands fifth in a class of nine.[3] After graduation, he taught school at Charlestown for a time, where the town records show that he received the schoolmaster's salary from July 17, 1684, to April 17, 1687, — £25 for each half year, besides £3 for house rent.[4] He must have taught there at least as late as October, 1687, as the town was later obliged to pay him to that date, but he evidently had a controversy at the time of leaving the place, probably on account of his becoming an Episcopalian under the influence of Mr. Ratcliffe. His demands against the town were not granted till after twelve years had elapsed. There is an interval of more than a year between his leaving Charlestown in 1687 and his connection with King's Chapel, in which he may have gone to England for ordination, unless, indeed, he began to preach for the church before receiving orders, — an irregularity which is perhaps implied in the attacks upon him, and which may have been justified by the difficulty of otherwise keeping the church alive, in its present straits.[5] This is rendered more probable by an examination of the weekly record of collections during

---

[1] Cotton Mather mentions him among those who "deserve to live in our *Book for their Piety*," as having "a respectful Character in these Churches of this Wilderness." — *Magnalia*, iii. 7. Rev. John Myles commanded a company in King Philip's war, which began in Swansea in 1675. A descendant, Daniel, served with three brothers in the Revolutionary war, and at its close had such faith in the new government that he converted his whole property into Continental money, losing his all by its repudiation. General Nelson A. Miles, U. S. A., a distinguished soldier, is his grandson.

[2] Mass. Hist. Proc., 1864-65, p. 28. Ibid. 1866-67, p. 252. At this period, and until shortly before the Revolution, the names of graduates were printed in the order of their families' social rank.

[3] He is probably one of the students mentioned in the curious Diary of Noahdiah Russell, Tutor at Harvard College. (March 23, 1682). ". . . Dannforth, Myles, and Watson were publickly admonished for speaking irreverently before ye Corporation," — at a meeting where the "abusing of ye freshmen" was considered. — *N. E. Hist. and Geneal. Reg.*, vii. 53.

[4] Charlestown Archives, 36.

[5] In this case, his visit to England in 1692 must have been to receive orders. But obscurity rests on his transition from schoolmaster to rector. It is clear that hard feeling denied him his just dues in Charlestown, where the town records show (as I am informed by Mr. H. H. Edes) that a committee was appointed in 1699, to settle with Mr. Miles for the arrears due him for keeping the school. In his receipt, March 27, 1699, for £28, he says: "I remise, release, and forever quitclaim . . . all and all manner of actions, suits, cause and causes of actions and suits, bills, bonds, writings, accounts, debts, duties, reckonings, sum and sums of money, controversies and demands whatsoever, which I . . . ever had, or which my executors or administrators or any of us in time to come can or may have, to, for, or against the said Town . . . for or by reason of any matter, cause, or thing whatsoever, from the beginning of the world to the day of the date hereof."

THE CHURCH TAKES ROOT. 99

the period from the departure of Mr. Ratcliffe to that of Mr. Myles in July, 1692. No mention is here made of the purchase of sacramental bread and wine; and though there is every Sunday a record "By Cash receved," the first entry, "Gathered at yᵉ Sacramᵗ," is after Rev. Mr. Smith had taken Mr. Myles's place. There is no indication that the Communion Office was celebrated during the three intervening years. The inference is strong that Mr. Myles had not then received holy orders. The "Vindication," etc., before alluded to, shows the irritation with which old-fashioned New Englanders regarded a son of the College who had thus changed his faith: —

". . . A *Parson* (or a *Piece of one*) *Subscribing to Lyes*. This Youth is an Unfledged Bird who thus defiles the Neast in which he was Hatcht. . . . 'Tis but Yesterday that his *M. A.* had recommended him to the School of a Neighbour-Town for which he was pretty well Qualified (for he writt a good hand and made good pens, and was able to Construe a sentence in *Corderius*). We most readily own a good School Master to be one of the most Honourable and Valuable sights in a Country, and wish *New-England* fuller of them. But if any of them after a while swaggering amongst Boys comes out into the World, and will be Domineering amongst men and prescribing them *Scheams* and *Representations of Government*, and take up and *Lash* whole Countreys, bring that Lad's Fingers to the *Ferula* and let the calling go free." [1]

The same pamphlet says: —

"We must confess there was One who had the Impudence to preach before he was Baptized; his name was *Samuel Myles, M.A.*: but this was none of the Country's fault, — 'twas because of his Descent." [2]

And again: —

"Twas therefore a brave and happy thought that first pitched upon this *Colledge;* tho' at some times it has been unhappy in this, that it has bestowed its favours (its A. M.'s) on some ungrateful persons, who would now undermine that Government upon which its foundations were laid, and by which for so long a time its superstructure has been always sustained." [3]

Soon after Mr. Myles's accession to the ministry he, with the church wardens, drew up and sent to England an earnest remonstrance to the Crown against the recent revolution in New

---

[1] Andros Tracts, ii. 72.   [2] Ibid. p. 39.   [3] Ibid. p. 25.

England and its leaders. This document does not appear on the church records. In some way a copy of it must have been procured by the agents of the colony in England, for its contents were made known on this side of the water, occasioning much angry feeling. To the publication of this document are probably to be ascribed the above contemptuous references to Mr. Myles, as well as the attacks upon the church. The patriot party even endeavored to point out a treasonable ambiguity in the address of the "venomous"[1] petition, as if "the King's Most Excellent Majesty" might refer to James rather than William.[2]

The humble Address of Your Majesty's most loyal and dutiful Subjects of the Church of England in Boston in Your Majesty's Territory and Dominion of New England.

MOST GRACIOUS SOVERAIGNE:

There has been but few years past over our heads, since by the grace and favour of Your Majesty's royal predecessors wee were delivered from the slavery and thraldome of a most extravagant and arbitrary government which had long been exercised over us and many others of Your Majesty's subjects, under colour and pretence of a Charter (wherein no part thereof but the name was ever made use of or regarded), and by that means have been soe happy to enjoy the freedome of divine service and worship after the manner of the Church of England, — which was never, until the vacating of the said Charter, admitted or allowed to any, but all were forced by their penal laws to frequent their meetings and be deprived of the benefit of the Holy Sacraments and other sacred rights, none being admitted thereto but such as are in Church government and fellowship with them and their children, which does not include the 10th part of Your Majesty's subjects in these parts, to the great shame and scandall of the Christian Religion and hinderance of the propagation thereof.

That though, since wee have had the liberty of our religion, wee have

---

[1] Palfrey, iii. 584.
[2] The address of the petition seems to show that it was drafted before the partnership of Mary and William in the crown was known in Boston. This important paper is erroneously described as the "Episcopal Ministers' Address to King William," in 3 Mass. Hist. Coll., vii., 102-103. It was first printed in A VINDICATION OF NEW-ENGLAND FROM THE VILE Aspersions Cast upon that COUNTRY By a Late ADDRESS of a Faction there, Who Denominate themselves of the *Church of England* IN BOSTON.
Printed with Allowance." This was undoubtedly written by Increase Mather. Its pungent sarcasms begin: "Poor N:n-England! Thou hast always been the eye-sore of Squinting malignity."

Another Address "of divers of the Gentry, Merchants, and others to the King's most Excellent Majesty," signed by many Episcopalians, was caustically criticised in "The Humble Address of the Publicans of New England. To which King you p'ease; with some Remarks upon it. London: 1691." Both are printed in Andros Tracts, ii.

endeavored to carry ourselves void of offence to those that dissent from us, and have at our own charge built and erected a convenient Church for the publique worship and service of God, yet such is the malice of our dissenting neighbours that wee are become the object of their scorn, and forced to take many affronts and indignityes by them frequently offered to our persons and Religion, which some of their principall Teachers have lately in a printed treaty[1] charged to be idolatry and Popery.

We have lately, to our great horrour and amazement, been forced to behold a well-established and orderly government here subverted and overthrown; the Governour, several of the Councill, and other principall officers and persons, by force of armes seized and kept under long and hard imprisonment: Your Majesty's forts and garrisons forced out of the hands of those appointed to command them; Your Majesty's standing forces and others, raised and employed for the defence of the Country against our Indian and other enemies, disbanded, and their Officers cruelly seized and imprisoned, and by that means an advantage given to our enemies, who have since destroyed and laid waste a very considerable and goodly part of this Your Majesty's territory, with the loss of some hundreds of your subjects, and many forts and garrisons in those parts of considerable force and service, which, by the disbanding of the souldiers, were left and defeited; Your Majesty's Frigott here, ordered for the defence and security of the coasts against pyrates and other enemies, dismantled and made wholly unserviceable, whilst pyrates infested the same; Your Majesty's revenue, which amounted to about £12,000 per annum, wholly lost;—and all this by a party of pretended zealous and godly men, moved upon no other grounds or reasons but their owne ill principles, malice, and envy, being more fond and regardful of their former Charter-government (famous for nothing but their Male-administrations and cruel prosecutions of all persons differing from them in matters of Religion only) than of their duty and allegiance to Your Majesty, who have since taken upon them to sett up and exercise their said former Government, and to put in execution the pretended laws made under the same, which are wholly contrary and repugnant to the laws and government of Your Majesty's realm of England, and to the great grievance and oppression of some thousands of Your Majesty's loyall subjects, but more particularly to those who now humbly address Your Majesty, who have bin thereby injured and abused both in their civil and religious concernments: our Church by their rage and fury having been greatly hurt and damnified, and daily threatened to be pulled downe and destroyed; our Minister hindered and obstructed in the discharge of his duty and office, and wee now put under the burthen of most excessive rates and taxes to support the interest of a disloyal prevailing party amongst us, who, under pretence of the publique good, designe nothing but ruin

[1] Treatise.

and destruction to us and the whole countrey. And as we cannot but from the bottom of our hearts declare our utter abhorrence and dislike of these and all other their seditious and rebellious actings and proceedings, so wee are resolved with patience to undergoe and 'suffer whatsoever shall be imposed upon us, and to maintaine our duty and allegiance to Your Majesty, not doubting that by Your Majesty's gracious favour and protection wee shall be relieved and delivered from the same.

Amongst these our sufferings, wee were greatly comforted, when to our abundant joy and satisfaction wee received that joyful news of Your Majesty's most great and glorious enterprise for the defence and maintenance of the Protestant Religion and interest, and of Your Majesty's happy accession to the Crowne. And since Your Majesty has bin graciously pleased to have particular regard to the religion of the Church of England, so wee hope that small branch thereof which hath but lately sprung forth in this remote part of the world will not want Your Majesty's favour and countenance, that it may (as no doubt but by God's blessing it will) grow up and flourish, and bring fruites of religion and loyalty, to the honour of Almighty God, and the promotion and increase of Your Majesty's interest and service. And to that end we humbly beseech Your Majesty that we may not be left under the anarchy and confusion of government, under which this country hath so long groaned, but that the same may be ruled and governed by a Governour and Councill to be appointed by Your Majesty, with the advice of an assembly of the people in matters proper for their cognizance, as others Your Majesty's plantations are ruled and governed; with such other libertyes and privileges as Your Majesty shall thinke most proper and conducing to Your Majesty's service, and the generall good and welfare of your subjects in the severall parts of this your territory and dominion of New England.

That the great God of Heaven would continue to bless Your Majesty with a glorious success in all your undertakings, enable you to vanquish and overcome all your enemies, and give you a long, peaceable, and prosperous raigne over us and all your subjects throughout your realm and dominions; and that they may never be wanting to show forth their duty and obedience to Your Majesty, — is and shall be the hearty and continued prayers of Your Majesty's dutyfull and loyall subjects, in the name and at the desire of the whole Church.

SAMUELL MYLES, M.A.,
FRA. FOXCROFT, } Church Wardens.
SAML. RAUENSCROFT,

Perhaps there was nothing in this document which went beyond the proper expression of political opinion by the losing party in an unexpected revolution. It certainly expressed the views of a minority numerous enough to give anxiety to the patriot leaders, and likely to have great influence with the English Court.[1]

The handful of Churchmen here must have shared the confusion which vexed their English brethren. They had just been praying for King James, that "his seed might endure for ever," and "be set up after him, and his house and kingdom be established," that their "gracious King might be prospered in all his undertakings," and that "the princely infant might excel in all virtues becoming to the royal dignity to which God had ordained him." Now they offered public prayers that their late monarch, as one of the enemies of the new king, might be "vanquished and overcome," and that not James, but William, might be "protected in person and his hands strengthened."[2]

The convention which recognized the Prince and Princess of Orange as king and queen had passed the Toleration Act, May 24, 1689, which allowed Trinitarian dissenters to attend their own conventicles instead of church, provided that their preachers should subscribe the doctrinal articles of the Church of England. Efforts for comprehension were again revived, and the more liberal Churchmen proposed many concessions, such as the leaving it to the minister's option to substitute the Apostles' for the Athanasian creed, the change of objectionable phrases in the liturgy, and generous dealing in regard to the baptismal and the ordination service. It has been estimated

---

[1] Queen Mary told Increase Mather: "I wish all good men were of one mind; however, in the mean time I would have them live peaceably, and love one another." — *Cotton Mather's Parentator, in Andros Tracts*, iii. 161. Cotton Mather characteristically adds: "*O mentis Aureæ Verba bracteata!* My *ink*, Too Vile a Liquor art thou, to write so *Divine a Sentence!*" But only time could bring about such a spirit in New England. Cotton Mather himself in his Election Sermon, "The Serviceable Man," 1690, p. 53, said: "*Let us not so much as Touch the Unclean Thing, nor hide so much as a Rag or Pin of a* Babylonish *Garment* with us. For the Children of this Countrey to maintain any part of the *Romish worship* would indeed be not only a wild *Indiscretion*, but also a vile *Apostasie*; and those persons are far from *discerning the Signs of the Times*, who think it worth the while for them now to forego that Great Antipapal Principle, *That no party of men whatever, calling themselves The Church, have any just Authority to appoint any parts or means of Divine Worship which the Lord Jesus Christ has not in the Sacred Bible Instituted.* Let us keep the *Second Commandment*, and our God will *show Mercy* to us, for more than one Generation. If we cannot find that any *Forms of Prayer* were used in any part of the Church until about Four Hundred years after Christ, nor any made for more than some single Province until *six hundred* years, nor any *imposed* until *Eight hundred*, when all manner of Abominations were introduced, — surely it becomes *us* to be particularly Averse unto *such* as may have somewhat worse than their *Novelty* to Create our suspicion of them; and it becomes us much more to be *Non Conformists* unto such other *Church Rites* therein advised, as were not so much as conceived until the *Man of Sin* was born."

[2] Church of England in the Eighteenth Century, i. 141.

that such an Act, drawn up in James II.'s reign, in a statesmanlike spirit, and with due respect for proper scruples, "would have brought over two thirds of the dissenters of the time;"[1] nor was it yet too late. But the narrow spirit in the Church continued to rule, and the little church in Boston must represent that spirit. A noticeable effect of the Toleration Act in England was a decided falling-off in attendance on public worship; but this did not reach to New England.[2]

At the opposite end of the old folio from that which contains the record of the first meetings are entered the financial records of the church, mixed from time to time with other entries. Some of these are important, and many of them are curious.[3]

Boston in New England, anno 1689.

Memorandum that wee, Samuel Ravenscroft and Francis Foxcroft, was appointed p sundry of the members of the Church of England, at a meeting held June 29th, '89, in Boston, to collect the contribution money for the service of the Church officers, and otherwayse to act as Church wardens for the remainder of this yeare /, for what wee receive as aboue s^d, wee forme an acco^t, and make ourselves D^{rs}.

		£	s.	d.
Vizt Mr Maccarty when he deliv^d us this Booke made due to the Church stock rec^d this day, June the last		3.	1.	7
June ult° To Cash rec^d this day		3.	3.	5
„ To Ditto rec^d from Mr Ratcliffe p FF, wch is Capt Nicholson's gift To the Church		25.	0.	0
July 7	By Cash received [4]	2.	15.	7
Augt 4	By Cash Collected att ye request of Mr Miles for tho Paine an Easteran man	2.	6.	9
	By Cash Received p Mr Foxcroft from his Excelentcy Sr Edmond Andross as a gift to ye Church ye sum of	30.	0.	0

---

[1] Church of England in the Eighteenth Century, i. 381.

[2] The laws requiring such attendance continued in force in England through the century, being confirmed in George III.'s reign, and not formally repealed until 9, 10 Victoria. Ibid. ii. 457.

[3] I have copied these nearly in full, except the records of the weekly contributions, which are more briefly indicated by adding up their total annual amounts. See pp. 124, 125.

[4] The weekly contributions run at about this amount, never below £1. 7. 6.

			£	s.	d.
Augt. 8	By Cash from Mr Thomas Pemberton his gift to the Church.		1.	0.	0
1689.	p Contra	Cr.			
July 1	By Cash paid Mr Miles 20 / and the Clerke 5 /		1.	5.	0
ye 5	By Cash pade M^r Wm. Smith for clenishing ye Church.		1.	15.	0
ye 22	By Cash paid Mr Miles and Clarke [1]		1.	5.	0
	and to old goody, a poore woman		0.	5.	0
ye 27	By disbursements for ye acommodation of Mr Ratcliffe for his voy^n home as appeares by severall Bills on file		11.	4.	8
ye 19	to fenceing and other worke about the Church and yard as p acompt		1.	19.	8
23	By Cash paid for our Church Bell to Mr John Baker by Mr Foxcroft		13.	5.	0
ye 30	By Cash paid for work dun in ye steeple and hangin ye Bell as p a Comp^t		4.	4.	9

Of the new wardens, Mr. Foxcroft was a man of note.[2]

---

[1] This payment is repeated weekly.

[2] Son of Daniel Foxcroft, mayor of Leeds, in Co. York, in 1666. Artillery Company, 1679; was Colonel, and imprisoned in April, 1689, as an adherent of Andros, "yet does not seem to have suffered permanent unpopularity." Cotton Mather doubtless alludes to him when he says, "Then *Foxes* were made the Administrators of Justice to the *Poultry*." An "Appeal to the Men of New England" (1689) asks "whether when 't was argu'd, that it would be a very unfair thing to punish the *Noncon's* in this Countrey for not using the Service of the Church of *England*, while the Countrey had scarce any but *Noncon's* in it; and so every man almost in the Land must pay at least 12d. a day (besides other far greater penalties), which with Sundayes and Holy dayes would amount to four pounds a man by the year, for not being present at the *Common Prayer* Worship,—that Justice had not more of the *Wolf* than the *Fox* in him, who reply'd, *We are in a way to bring it to that extremity*." Washburn marks as "worthy of notice, that in the action of Nathaniel Byfield et al. *vs.* Charles Lidget and Fra. Foxcroft, exec'rs of the last will of Heywood, each of which parties, before or afterwards, held high judicial offices, the writ commands the Marshal to attach the goods or estate of the deceased in their hands, and for want thereof *the bodies of the Executors*." It was a suit to recover "£8. 10s. 6d. due for cordage sold and delivered to said Heywood in the year 1689."

A letter from Foxcroft to Charles Lidget in London, Jan. 10, 1690-91, says: "Ravenscroft talks of removing to Virginia; White, West Indies; the Royal Exch^a Tavern shut up; next night was ye Signe blowne downe." He married Elizabeth, daughter of Governor Danforth, Oct. 3, 1682. She died July, 1721. Their children were: Francis, born Jan. 26, 1685, Harvard College, 1712; Thomas, born Feb. 26, 1697, Harvard College, 1714. A touching account of Mrs. Foxcroft is contained in "A Sermon preached at Cambridge after the Funeral of Mrs. Elizabeth Foxcroft, late Wife of Francis Foxcroft, Esq., who died there July 4th, 1721, In the 57th year of her age. With an Addition, chiefly referring to her Death: Also a Funeral Poem of the Reverend Mr. *John Danforth*. By T. F. [Thomas Foxcroft] One of the bereaved Sons. Boston: 1721." The author, minister of the First Church, was intended

The angry feeling on funeral occasions was again revived.

FOXCROFT ARMS.

Randolph wrote from the jail to the Bishop of London, Oct. 26, 1689, of the death of Major Howard and "the refusal of his wife, with advice of Mr. Moode, an independent preacher, to let him be buried in the burying-place of the Church of England, though wished in his will and the grave ready; word sent by Moode that he would have men enough ready in the streets to show [the executors] the place of his burial, and he was buried as Moode directed."[1]

The Episcopalians found themselves barely tolerated, after the brief sunshine of power, and made energetic representations in England.[2]

by his father "for an Episcopal clergyman," but followed the Puritan tendencies of his mother's family.

Governor Dudley "rewarded" Colonel Foxcroft for signing the address to King William, "with a place on the bench of Common Pleas, which he held till 1719." He died at Cambridge, Dec. 31, 1729, having removed to the homestead there on the death of his father-in-law. Henry Flynt wrote, in a preface to the funeral sermon on him by Rev. Nathaniel Appleton: ". . . He lived and died in firm adherence to the Constitution of England in Church as well as State; and yet attended with satisfaction and devotion on all the public administrations of divine worship in Cambridge, where he spent the latter part of his life; and was far from the unchristian opinion, which confines the true ministry and ordinances of Christ to one particular denomination or persuasion of Christians." See Andros Tracts, iii. 200; N. E. Hist. and Geneal. Reg., vii. 306; viii. 171, 364; xxv. 123; xxix. 62; xxxiii. 406; Washburn's Judicial History of Mass., pp. 135, 340.

[1] I am indebted to the kindness of Dr. Palfrey for this abstract from Randolph's letter.

[2] An Impartial Account of the State of New England, etc. By John Palmer. London: 1690. Andros Tracts, i. 53. The same representation is made in a pamphlet ascribed to Dudley: "By the Actings and Proceedings of these *New England* Reformers, it is easily to be seen what regard they had to religion, Liberty, and Property, having now had the opportunity to make themselves Persecutors of the Church of *England*, as they had before been of all others that did not comply with their Independency, whom they punished with Fines, Imprisonment, Stripes, Banishment, and Death; and all for matters of meer Conscience and Religion only. The Church of *England*, altho' commanded to be particularly countenanced and encouraged, was wholly destitute of a place to perform Divine Service in until Sir *E. A.*, by advice of the Council, borrowed the new Meeting-house in Boston for them, at such times when others made no use of it, and afterwards promoted and encouraged the building of a New Church for that Congregation, to avoid all manner of Offence to their dissenting Neighbors, which was soon compleated and finished at the particular charge of those of the Church of *England*, whose number daily increasing they became the envy as well as hatred of their Adversaries, who by all ways and means possible, as well in their Pulpits as private Discourse, endeavour'd to asperse, calumniate, and defame them; and so far did their malice and bigotry prevail, that some of them openly and publickly hindered and obstructed the Minister in the performance of the funeral Rites to such as had lived and dyed in the Communion of the Church of *England*; and a most scan-

" 'Tis the *Church of England* that hath most reason to complain ; ... For at Sir *Edmond's* Arrival they were the only People destitute of a Place to Worship in, until, by Advice and Consent of the Council, the New Meeting-House in *Boston* was borrowed and made use of by them, but at inconvenient Hours,—in the Morning after Eleven, and sometimes, as their Service was prolong'd, at Twelve, and after Four in the Afternoon,—which with patience was endured, tho' the Enmity of that People to the Church of *England* was such that they grudged them that small Accomodation, and shewed their uneasiness therein ; which was soon removed by the Governour's encouraging a Church to be built and compleated in *Boston*, at the Charge of those of that Communion, where the Publick Worship and Service of God hath been attended, until the late Insurrection, when the Minister was forced to leave the Countrey and Church for his own safety. And has not the Minister been before this publickly affronted and hindred from doing of his Duty? What scandalous Pamphlets have been Printed to villifie the Liturgy ! And are not all of that Communion daily called *Papist Doggs and Rogues* to their Faces? How often has the plucking down the Church been threatened ! One while it was to be converted to a School, and anon 'twas to be given to the *French Protestants*. And whoso will but take the Pains to survey the Glass Windows will easily discover the Marks of a Malice not common ; I believe 'tis the first National Church that ever lay under such great Disadvantages, in a Place where those that dissent from her ought to expect all things from her Grace and Favour."

"An ingenious merchant of Boston " wrote to England, May, 1690: "If they should have their charter, all the superstitious party, as they reckon the Church-of-England men, must move to New York" and elsewhere.[1] In the new charter, 1691, "the religious element was eliminated from the government; the qualification of a voter was no longer to be membership of a church, but the possession of a freehold worth £2 a year, or of personal property to the amount of £40 stg."[2]

The reviving life of the little church gave animation to warning voices which the Puritan teachers lifted up against it.

dalous Pamphlet was soon after Printed and Published by *Cotton Mather* [a mistake; it was probably *Increase* Mather], son of the aforesaid I. M., intituled 'the unlawfulness of the Common-prayer Worship,' wherein he affirms and labours to prove the same to be both Popery and Idolatry; and several scandalous Libels both against the Church and Government were spread and scattered up and down the Country, insinuating into the Common People that the Governor and all of the Church of *England* were Papists and Idolaters."—*New England's Faction Discovered ; or, a Brief and True Account of their Persecution of the Church of England. Being an answer to a Pamphlet entituled News from New England, etc. By C. D.* London: 1690. Andros Tracts, ii. 210.

[1] Palfrey, iv. 69, qu. Brit. Col. Papers.
[2] Ibid. iv. 78.

The preachers who had been so steadfast even to obstinacy in passive resistance to the impositions of Andros, and had cautiously yet firmly encouraged their congregations and the whole people in holding fast to their Puritan traditions, now spoke with unrestrained freedom and boldness. Nor is it uncharitable to suppose that some of the renewed attacks on Their Majesties' Chapel in 1691 were due to sermons preached in the First and the South Churches, and sent broadcast in print. Rev. Joshua Moodey's discourse was entitled: "The Great Sin of Formality in Christian Worship;" and Rev. Mr. Willard spoke with equal plainness of "The Sinfulness of Worshipping God with Men's Institutions." Mr. Willard said: —

"A Divine Precept is necessary to warrant every part of Religious Worship. . . . Avoid this sin. . . . Except we thus do, we shall directly vacate our Fathers' design in Planting of this Wilderness. It is certain that their Errand hither was to sequester themselves into a quiet corner of the world, where they *might enjoy Christ's unmixed Institutions, and leave them uncorrupted to their Posterity;* and if this design of theirs were unworthy of them and reproachful to their names, let it then be buried with them and forgotten, and no more mention made of it to stain their memories withal; but if it were worth their parting with so many comforts and conveniences of a pleasant Land," etc., . . . "let us not cast this reproach upon it and them, which we shall certainly do if we depart from the strict avoidance of whatsoever Worship doth not derive from the Precept of God and Appointment of Jesus Christ. In every such act we call them fools; and this will rise up in judgment against us another day. . . . This will be an *Apostasy* in that very thing which is the *Test* upon which God tries the *Churches* in *New England.*"

It cannot be doubted that the indignation of these spiritual teachers burned with less consecrated flame in the mind of the populace.

Thirty years must elapse before Cotton Mather could write, in a gentler mood, in his

"Manuductio ad Ministerium; or, *Angels preparing to Sound the Trumpets.*"

" And let the *Table* of the Lord have no *Rails* about it that shall hinder a Godly *Independent*, and *Presbyterian*, and *Episcopalian*, and *Antipedobaptist*, and *Lutheran* from sitting down together there. *Corinthian Brass* would not be so bright a *Composition* as the People of God in such a *Coalition*, feasting together on His *Holy Mountain*. . . . Tho' in the church that I serve, I have seen the grateful Spectacle!"

THE CHURCH TAKES ROOT. 109

That the popular dislike of the church took active modes of expression is abundantly manifest from the entries in the Records, which refer to "a Colecktion for mendin' y⁰ church winders" on Nov. 5, 1691; to "mendin' The Church winders" a week later; and on the 24th of the same month, "Paid Mr. Tho. Messinger for winder shuters, £1. 7s. 8d.;" and yet again on the 26th of the following March, "Paid Mr. Wheeler for 24 Squ: glas £00. 06s. 00d." The Christmas services in 1695 seem to have roused the old antagonism again, as the Record of that date reads, "pd for mending windous to Coningham 18s.," and the following April again "Mr. Maccarty" was paid £2. 0s. 6d.

In 1698 in February and in April, and in January, 1699, the windows were "mended" again. As late as April, 1700, there seem to have been two distinct attacks upon them.[1]

[1] The Puritan party endeavored to make ridiculous the Episcopal complaints. "We had almost slipt the *Notice* of a *Bawl* or *two* these Libellers make about *Damnifying their Church* (as they call it), and Obstructing their *Minister in his Office*. As to their *Church*, all the mischeifs done is the breaking of a few Quarels of glass by idle Boys, who if discover'd had been chastiz'd by their own Parents; but the late School-Master of *Charles-Town* is of opinion that the *whole Country* must be *Lashed* for it. In the mean time do not these (for a few Quarels) Love to be *picking of Quarels* think ye?

"But to give a fuller account of this *Tragical tale* thus carried to *White-Hall*: They have built their Chapel in a Publick burying-place, next adjoining to a great Free Schooll, where the Boyes (having gotten to play) may some by *Accident*, some in *Frolick*, and some perhaps in *Revenge* for disturbing their Relations' Graves by the Foundation of that building, have broken a few Quarels of the Windows (and how should the contrary be imagined possible)? Other Meeting-Houses in the Toun, neer which the Children use to play, we suppose are at more than twice the charge yearly for Repairing their Windows; nor ever yet have any one of those unruly Children been discovered or complained of. Would not these people deserve here to be called Old Boyes, for so highly resenting Boyes-Play? What! must not a Boy in *New-England* throw a stone or a Ball amiss but the *King* shall hear of it?... Suppose we now His Majesty in Council (and long may we have *that* happiness to glory in!): there he is Exactly considering the several profound Methods that must be taken to unite *England*, Settle *Scotland*, Reduce *Ireland*, preserve *Holland*, Assist *Savoy*, content *Sweden* and *Denmark*, rescue the *Empire*, and subdue *France* (now in the high Ruff), and so render all *Europe* quiet and happy, — when suddenly His Majesty is told there is a matter of *greater Importance* than all these that calls for His Majesties most weighty and Royall consideration; for that some of his Loyal Subjects are come 1,000 Leagues about their business, and that they have brought an Address, — which may be this :—

"*May it please Your Majesty*, — We, Your Majesty's most Loyal Subjects, knowing well that you are managing glorious undertakings against the Enemies of the English *Nation* in General, and of the *Church* of England in particular, thought it needful to Represent to Your Majesty that there is a number of *Boston Boyes* who, having got loose from the *Tyranny* of their School, have *Routously, Riotously, and with force of Armes* (that is to say), with *Balls* and *Stones*, Violently Assaulted our Church Windows to our unaccountable damage, and to the *Terrour of Your Majesties Leige People*. We therefore implore Your Majesties utmost Assistance against these Unlucky Boyes." — *A Vindication, etc., Andros Tracts,* ii. 63.

110   ANNALS OF KING'S CHAPEL.

Mr. Myles was, however, able to sustain himself in Boston for near thirty-nine years, and saw the Church of England prosper greatly under his care. We have to reconstruct the fragmentary history of the early years largely from the financial records.

Contra Cr.

			£ s. d.
8br.	yᵉ 14	By Cash for Bell Brasses	0. 11. 00
9br.	yᵉ 2	By Cash paid for mending Church windows .	5. 10. 00
Xbr.	yᵉ 23	By Cash paid to yᵉ Charge of yᵉ Bell not being paid on yᵉ former acompᵗ	1. 12. 06
Januⁿ	yᵉ 9	By Cash spent at an arbytratione Church worke	0. 05. 00
Feb.	yᵉ 10	By Cash for old goody Tomlin for prison fees	2. 00. 00

Sam. Ravenscroft and Francis Foxcroft, Church Wardens, Dr.

1690			
Aprill	yᵉ 17	By Cash from Benja Bullyfant, Esqʳ, his charity to the poore	3. 00. 00
	yᵉ 20	By Cash recᵈ for poore and Church being easter Sunday	4. 06. 02

p Contra Cr.

1689/0			
Feb.	yᵉ 15	By Cash paid mʳ Bullyvant for Larkin's wife passage for England	5. 00. 00
	yᵉ 17	By Cash paid for yᵉ Church adress to yᵉ King	0. 05. 00
Aprill	yᵉ 20	By Cash for one and twenty weekes for mʳ Miles att 12 ℔ weeke for meattᵉ, drinke, washing, Lodging, fire, and Candle . . .	12. 12. 00
1690			
July 10		Being a day of Humiliation Recᵈ for the poore	3. 05. 00

p Contra.

1690		
August 2	Paid for the buriall of a poore man named Joh Carter	2. 07. 06
	Paid for boards, and raising the pulpit etc. .	0. 12. 00
Sept. 16	For mending the Cushon	0. 10. 00
Octob. 13	Paid mʳ Clarke for mʳ Miles Boarding[1] . .	2. 00. 00

[1] This was Harry Clarke, Church-warden in 1691, who furnished Mr. Myles board at the rate of £½ weekly.

THE CHURCH TAKES ROOT.

Benjamin Mountfort and Giles Dyer,
Church wardens, Dr.

1691			£ s. d.
Aprill 13	By Allowance for advance on 16s. English money recd this year		0. 04. 00

Pr Contra Cred.

1690			
Janu. 8	In Gratitude for occasionall sermons to Mr Miles in a hatt		1. 10. 00
Janu. 12	Paid the minister Mr. Slade		1. 00. 00
Febru. 16	Paid Samuell Checkly for plaisters and phisick for widow Evans		0. 15. 00
1691			
Septemb. 21	Sr Robart Robinson Knite Gave to the Church of England hangings And a Cushin for the Pulpit		

Savill Simpson and Harry Clerke, Church wardens, Dr.

1691			
November 5	By a Colecktion for mendin' ye Church winders		8. 07. 08
December 25	Mr. Thomas Gowlde and Mr. William Weaver gave to ye Church of England The Bras Standard for ye ouer-glass [1]		

p *Contra.*

1691			
Novemb. 5	Gave Mr. Miles for that Sarmon [2]		1. 00. 00
Novemb. 12	Paid for mendin The Church winders		7. 00. 00
Novemb. 24	Paid Mr. Tho. Mesinger for winder shuters		1. 07. 08
Decemb. 25	Paid for 2 Loades of wood for Mr. Miles		0. 12. 00
Decemb. 30	Paid Harry Clerke for a Cage for ye Standard		0. 05. 00
Janeway 25	Lent Mr. Miles if moneys fall short		3. 00. 00
1691/2			
March 26	Paid Mr Wheeler for : 24 : Squ: glas		0. 06. 00

---

[1] The "History of the English Church in the Eighteenth Century" records that in England, "During the earlier part of the century, an hour-glass, in a wooden or iron frame, was still the not unfrequent appendage to the pulpit. . . . As they wore out, they were not often replaced. Bp. Kennet, in the 3d decade of the century, spoke of them as already beginning to be uncommon."

[2] It is to be regretted that no further record exists of the sermon thus signalized. From the date we may conjecture that it was a loyal discourse on the Gunpowder Treason of Guy Fawkes. The date is the same as that of the first "Colecktion for mendin' ye Church winders." We may perhaps imagine that the "sarmon" had something to do with provoking the breakage.

Mingled promiscuously with these financial records are other entries : —

Septr 21st 1691. And it must not be forgott that Sir Robert Robbinson gave a new silk damask cushion and cloth pulpit-cover.

January 9,3. Governor Nicholson sent Ff'oxcroft a bill for £15 sterling, and ordered the disposall thus : £5 to the minister, £5 to the poor at Xmas, and £5 to buy bibles, wth Com̃on prayer and singing psalms for the poorer sort of the Church.

June ye 29th 1689. Mr Francis Foxcroft and Saml Ravenscroft was Chousen wardens for ye Church.

Mem^d. At a meeting after prayers on Easter munday being the 21st Aprill, '90, Mr Benjn Mountfort and Mr Giles Dyer were elected Church Wardens for the Yeare ensueing, who accepted of the same.

1692. Boston, March ye 28th Being Easter monday, Mr Nicholas Tippit and Mr Edw. Goudge was Eleckted Church wardins and Accpted of y^2 Place.

Nicholas Tippett and Edward Gouge, Church wardens, Dr.

		£	s.	d.
1692	Rec'd on Easter day moore y^n then given away	2.	14.	10

p *Contra Cr.*

Aprill 3^d, 92.	Payd Mr Miles and Mr Hill 14 Sabbath dayes thirty-five shillings	24.	10.	00
	Payd old Bowden 2 / p weeke 15 weekes is	1.	10.	00
	Payd a poore woman p Mr Miles request	0.	14.	00
	Payd for Greene boughs against White Suntide	0.	01.	04
	Payd Mr Miles for the thanksgiven Sermon	1.	00.	00
	Payd Mr Miles the £16. 15s. geithered for him alsoe the Church Stocke as was pmist him	29.	04.	08

BOSTON, July 17, 1692.

Received of Mr Tippet and Mr Gouge ye Sum of Twenty-nine pound, etc., in full of all moneys resting in their hands Collected for ye Servise of ye Church of England of ye members thereof I say received by me.

SAMUEL MYLES.

.This receipt is the last given by Mr. Myles before a prolonged absence from his people. He had waited regularly on his office for about four years when he went to England, probably, in part at least, for the purpose of appealing for aid to the struggling church from the high authorities at home. During his absence the care of the church was undertaken by a Mr. Smith, who officiated till July 16, 1693; and from that time till the return of Mr. Myles, July 27, 1696, the pulpit was filled by Mr. George Hatton. Of the former of these gentlemen, unfortunately, no particulars are recorded. Of Mr. Hatton we have an account, perhaps not by an unprejudiced witness, in Captain Thomas Coram. He says: —

" . . . That in the years 1693 and 1694, and some time after, there was but one Minister of the Church of England in all ye Inhabited part of ye English Empire in America, settled by ten or more different Colonies, contiguous but under different sorts of Government, 600 or 700 miles in length or more on the Sea Coast, from Virginia Northward to the utmost extent of the then settled and Inhabited English Country on the Main Land of America. The said Minister, whose Name was Mr Hatton, was a very worthless Man; he resided at Boston, and was utterly unfit to Gaine or Reconcile to the Church such Descentors so strongly inveterate against it; but he was far from ever attempting to do so, for he would frequently on Saturday Nights set up and play at Cards all or the greatest part of the Night in company with an Irish Butcher and an Irish Barber, and another or more of such his acquaintance, whereby he was usually so much disordered wh. prevented him from officiating next day at Church, wh. gave its numerous Enemies great opportunities to ridicule against it; and those few Inhabitants of ye large Town of Boston who were desirous to go to Church were very often disappointed and greatly discouraged." [1]

The law passed Nov. 4, 1692, "for Justices and Ministers Marrying persons," restored to these clergymen a privilege which had been lost in the downfall of Andros.

One of the wardens at this time is described in Dunton's saucy pages: —

"Mr. Gouge, a linen draper from London, son to the charitable divine of that name. He is owner of a deal of wit; his brain is a quiver of smart jests. He pretends to live a bachelor, but is no enemy to a pretty woman. He is High Church, yet so great a lover of his father's 'Christian Directions,' that he bought two hundred of me to give away, that

---

[1] Captain Coram's Petition to the Archbishop of Canterbury, in "Church Documents, Massachusetts," edited by Bishop Perry, p. 66. Captain Coram proposed to the archbishop that a college be endowed at our Cambridge to be called "The King's College," for the purpose of teaching Church principles. Captain Coram was the benevolent founder of the Foundlings' Hospital in London. He had resided in Boston at the time to which he refers, and had given King's Chapel a parcel of land situated in Taunton; but, taking bitter offence at what he considered the careless treatment of his gift, he flatly refused to contribute anything to the rebuilding of the church in 1754. See pp. 185, 365.

he might, as he used to say, 'make the Bostonians godly.' And this was a noted quality in him that he would always tell the truth, which is a

Edward Gouge
Nicholas Lyppett

practice so uncommon in New England, that I could not but value his friendship." [1]

During Mr. Myles's absence the records proceed: —

	£ s. d.
25th Sunday, Gathered att ye Sacramt	2. 04. 08
Soe thatt the whole Sume mr Smith has recd for 40 Sundays is	71. 07. 00
which Comes Short of 40 [shillings] p Sunday the Sume of	8. 13. 00
	80. 00. 00

the last Sunday aboue mentioned was ye 16th Apr., 1693.

1693.
2 July	To Cash received	2. 16. 05
9 ditto	To Cash received	3. 11. 04
16 Ditto	To Cash received	3. 12. 11
23 Ditto	To Cash received	2. 17. 11

[The contributions then fell back again to the old average, except that the amount reached, on the 10th September, was £3. 3. 4.]

Contra.

16 July	Paid mr Smith for this day [2]	2. 00. 00
23 Ditto	Paid mr Hatton	2. 00. 00

Wednesday, 8th April, 1694, being Easter week, at a meeting then held Mr Thaddeus Mackarty and Francis Foxcroft were elected Church Wardens for the yeare ensuing.

---

[1] 2 Mass. Hist. Coll., ii. 106. He was probably son of the Rev. Thomas Gouge or Gooch, who died in 1681, whose funeral sermon was preached by Tillotson. A note in Dunton's Letters, p. 96, says of the son: "He was probably unfortunate in his business. Administration was granted on his estate 6 March, 1704-5, and 11 June, 1708, his widow, Frances Gouge, paid 4s. in the £ to his various creditors." Sewall's record of his funeral, Jan. 26, 1704-5, is more pungent than polite: "The poor Man Liv'd Undesired, and died Unlamented."

[2] This was the last payment to him.

1694, Aprill 15 day, Sabbath. Collected for m^r Hatton,   £   s.   d.
   of wch p 5/ a week to Clerk[1] 1. 16. 08

[At the end of the year the receipts are summed up, amounting to £126. 7. 10.]

of the above receipts, vizt: £126. 7. 10   £   s.   d.
   the poore have had 20. 03. 06
   m^r Hatton our Minister 93. 14. 04
   m^r Hill our Clerk 12. 10. 00

The townspeople were reminded that the little church represented the empire, when after his attempt against Martinique in the West Indies, which had failed from the loss of three fifths of his men by pestilence, in 1693, Admiral Wheeler rendezvoused at Boston for the attack on Quebec. No attempt being made, by Governor Phips's advice, the admiral remarked, "That the real want of early notice furnished an insincere people with a fine excuse for declining what they had no real intention to perform."[2] The officers of the fleet brightened the church with their uniforms, the first glimpse of such sunshine which it had enjoyed since the fall of Andros, and a foregleam of what was to follow whenever the military or naval power of Great Britain should be represented here. They also enriched it with their gifts.

1695.
June 16 | 12 | Sr Fra: Wheeler's and Sea Capt's benevo-   £   s.   d.
   lense in 93 . . . . 24. 00. 00
   left wth m^r Hatton towards Compleating a
   silv^r Cup 1. 10. 00

              Contra.
   pd Shelston last yeare for something he ought
      to doe, nescio 1. 00. 00
   pd Cross for makeing 2 ps plate 3. 00. 00

The preceding record is entered elsewhere more fully.

In the yeare 1693 Sir Francis Wheeler, putting in here to recruite his Fleet returning from an unsuccessfull attempt
   upon Marteneco, gave 10. 00. 00
Capt. Vickers 3. 00. 00
Capt Deane 4. 00. 00
Capt. Hawkins 4. 00. 00
Capt. Greenaway 3. 00. 00
                                                    24. 00. 00

---

[1] After this, Mr. Hatton received whatever was collected over the 5s. for the clerk.   [2] N. Y. Hist. Coll., 1868, p. 114.

The Gentlem land officers gave, I think . . . . . . £32. 00. 00.
Mr John Mills, a Barbadoes Gentleman, gave a plate and Cup.

The early usage in New England meeting-houses was to provide benches for the congregation to sit upon. These were succeeded by pews which privileged persons were allowed to enclose at their own expense,[1] except that the town paid for building a pew near the pulpit for the minister's family, and sometimes provided one also for the elders' families. In accordance with this usage of their Congregational neighbors, the "formes" which had been made for the first services of the church were probably the only seats provided for the worshippers till —

. . . in the yeare 94 an agreement was made to John Cunnabel, of Boston, Joyner, to build pews, etc., by the last of July the same yeare, for which he's to have £85; a second agreement was made wth the said Cunnabell to make a floore for £32. 10, he haveing the old sleepers and timber under the floore, and time given him untill November next.

In this change, the church fell in with a growing custom in the mother country, where even in the reign of Charles II., pews had been exceptional. We are told that Sir Christopher Wren objected to their introduction into his London churches, but with the luxury that came in with the Restoration, " private pews of all sorts and shapes" came into use. " Before Queen Anne's reign was over, they had become so regular a part of the ordinary furniture of a church, that in the regulations approved in 1712 by both Houses of Convocation for the consecrating of churches and chapels, it is specially enjoined that the church be previously pewed. High Churchmen, however, sometimes had their jest at the special love of the opposite party for 'their own Protestant pews.'"[2]

---

[1] "In the old Mortlake (Conn.) meeting-house, soon after the wolf adventure, Israel Putnam and others, on condition that they would reset the squares of glass that were broken out of the meeting-house windows, were granted the privilege of building pews for their own private use in the hinder side of the house, provided that 'they spile not above two seats on a side.' But a while after, the glass having got broken out again, and no ambitious young men appearing who were willing to buy the privilege of building themselves pews by resetting the glass, it was voted by this parish 'to board up the meeting-house windows,' *i.e.*, those which were broken." — *Tarbox's Life of Israel Putnam*, p. 48.

[2] See "The English Church in the Eighteenth Century," ii. 422–424. It is related that sometimes "between prayers and sermon, a livery servant" came in "with sherry and light refreshments." As late as 1790, Mrs. Barbauld wrote: "I would reprobate those little gloomy solitary cells, planned by the spirit of aristocracy, which deform the building no less to the eye of taste than to the eye of benevolence, and insulating each family within its separate enclosure, favoring at once the pride of rank and the laziness of indulgence."

THE CHURCH TAKES ROOT.

The first partial list of parishioners may be drawn up from the following: —

May, 1694. A list of the contributors towards pews; begun May, 1694: —

	£ s. d.		£ s. d.
John Bishop	2. 00. 00	George Rassen [1]	2. 02. 00
Walter Willett	1. 10. 00	William Hill	2. 00. 00
Henry Watkins	1. 04. 00	John Walker	2. 02. 00
Henry Gibbs	3. 00. 00	Mrs. Bayley	1. 12. 00
Henry Charloe	3. 00. 00	Thomas Field	2. 02. 00
Wm. Hobby [1]	2. 00. 00	Richard Ely [10]	2. 00. 00
Benjamin Mountfort [1]	2. 00. 00	Joseph Cowell [11]	0. 09. 00
Thomas Grafford [2]	2. 00. 00	Francis Marshall	0. 10. 04
Savill Simpson [3]	2. 00. 00	Jeremiah Gibson	1. 10. 00
Thaddeus Mackarty [4]	2. 00. 00	Chaddock	0. 12. 00
Francis Foxcroft [5]	2. 00. 00	Thomas Walker	1. 04. 00
Nicholas Tippett [6]	5. 00. 00	Shackbolt	0. 16. 00
Capt. Fox	5. 00. 00	Wm. Lacey	0. 12. 00
Richard Harris [1]	2. 00. 00	Childerston	0. 12. 00
Doct Almond	2. 00. 00	John Cole [12]	0. 18. 00
Giles Dyer [1]	2. 00. 00	Mrs. Garland, purcer	3. 00. 00
Doct Crafford	1. 00. 00	Mrs. Wakefield	0. 07. 00
Thomas Gold [1]	2. 00. 00	Mrs. Squire	2. 02. 00
Doct Lake [1]	2. 00. 00	Thomas Seele	1. 00. 00
Thomas Child	1. 10. 00	Thomas Eyres	1. 00. 00
Mrs. W. Buckley	1. 10. 00	Joshua Barnes	3. 00. 00
Thomas Mackarty [7]	2. 00. 00	John Hooper [13]	1. 10. 00
Spenser	1. 00. 00	John Cutler [14]	1. 04. 00
Elisha Bennett	2. 00. 00	George Turphrey [4]	2. 00. 00
Thomas Newton [8]	3. 00. 00		
Robert Bengeer	3. 00. 00		96. 06. 04
Matthew Cary	2. 06. 00	John Williams [15]	0. 12. 00
Henry Franklin [9]	2. 02. 00		

[1] See the list of subscribers for building the church, July, 1689, pp. 89-94.

[2] Thomas Grafford. Portsmouth. Married, Dec. 11, 1684, Bridget, widow of Thomas Daniel, daughter of Richard Cutts. Was a counsellor of the Province, 1692. Removed to Boston before 1695. Died Aug. 6, 1697.

[3] Warden, 1691, 1697, 1706-8. See p. 183.

[4] See p. 48.

[5] Warden, 1689, 1695. See p. 105.

[6] Warden, 1692.

[7] Thomas Maccarty. Harvard College, 1691. Died in 1698. (Hutchinson, i. 392, 393.)

[8] Warden, 1704, 1709. See p. 182.

[9] Merchant, of Boston. He died in 1713, leaving widow Margaret, and son Henry, who was warden, 1719-21, and died in July, 1725. See Sewall, iii. 361, n.

[10] Perhaps the son of Richard, of Saybrook, who had been a merchant of Boston, 1664, and there married Elizabeth, widow of John Cullick, and sister of Colonel Fenwick. By a former wife he had, perhaps not born on our side of the water, William and Richard. He died Nov. 24, 1684.

[11] Of Boston; cooper; married, about 1673, Mary, daughter of Richard Carter,

---

NOTE. — For continuation of the notes referred to above, see next page.

With the members of King's Chapel at this time should be reckoned Judge Graves of Charlestown, whose bold protest with the Cutlers, against the "Inter-charter" government, had been imperiously punished.[1] Sewall writes of him: —

"June 1, 1697. I goe to the Funeral of my Tutor, Mr. Tho. Graves. . . . Mr. Graves was a godly learned Man, a good Tutor, and solid preacher: His obstinat adherence to some superstitious conceipts of the Coṁon-Prayerbook, bred himself and others a great deal of Trouble: yet I think he kept to the Church at Charlestoun as to his most constant attendance; especially on the Lords Day."

The watchful Puritan, whose diary supplies so many important links in our early history, records at this time: —

"1694. Tuesday, Decr 25. — Shops are open, men at work; Carts of Pork, Hay, Coal, Wood, come to Town as on other days. Mr. Maccarty's shop is open."[2]

The records continue: —

Tuesday, 26th of March, 1695. — At a meeting then of the members of the Church of Engl^d, upon notice given by m^r Hatton the Lord's Day foregoing, m^r Thaddeus Mackarty and Francis Foxcroft were elected Church wardens for the ensueing yeare.

June 9 pd m^r Hatton and Clerk Hill £2. 5.[3]

---

[1] See Andros Tracts, ii. 110.
[2] A Church of England man.
[3] The payments go on afterward at the same rate.

and widow of William Hunter. He was son of Edward, Boston, 1645, cordwainer.

[12] Of Boston. Married Mary, daughter of the brave John Gallop, killed in the decisive battle of Philip's War. Had Samuel, born Sept. 16, 1684, and two other children.

[13] Perhaps the person of this name at Marblehead, who married, Jan. 27, 1691, Mary Litchfield, at Boston.

[14] This may have been Dr. John Cutler, father of the member of the Vestry at intervals from 1719 to 1749, or his namesake of Charlestown (grandson of Robert, Charlestown, 1637), who, by his wife, Martha, had John, baptized July 18, 1680, and five other children (among them, Timothy, born June 1, 1684, Harvard College, 1701, Rector of Christ Church, Boston). He was Major, and died Aug. 12, 1708. He and his father were sympathizers with Andros, signing the petition to the King against the succeeding government, and were imprisoned and fined. The Mass. Archives, xxxv., contain a petition dated Charlestown, Dec. 12, 1689, signed by John Cutler, Senr, to the Honorable Governor and Council, saying: "let an almost three months Confinement to our Houses and many other damages attending the same together with this our Serious promise . . . to demeane ourselves for the future as good subjects to their Maj^{ties} and their Government here . . . expiate for the faults you Judge we have Committed." The same volume has a beautiful letter from Rev. Charles Morton, March 11, 1689-90, in behalf of John Cutler, Jr. A further petition from the two Cutlers, later, was necessary before they could get absolution from the new government here.

[15] Perhaps the person of this name, Boston, 1670, who styles himself of Camberwell, Co. Surrey, late of London. Merchant in Boston.

THE CHURCH TAKES ROOT. 119

One of the most urgent forms of charity was the redemption of white slaves from captivity in Barbary, Morocco, and elsewhere. It is pleasant to find that the little congregation could spare money from its own needs for such a purpose.

```
1695.
Aug! 18th  Collected towards the redemption of Anthony
           Heywood, Thatcher, and Bull from captivity on   £   s.   d.
           galley . . . . . . . . . . . . . . .          24. 01. 02
Dec 25     being Xmas day (40) for poore . . . . . .      5. 00. 00
May        a legacey of nicholas Boare of Maddagasker re-
           ceived of J. Johnston . . . . . . . . .       44. 00. 00
           pd mr Sam: Sewell Nov. 6º day the Collection
           for Haywood, etc. . . . . . . . . . .         24. 01. 02
Dec. 25    pd for mending windows to Coningham . . .      00. 18. 00
[1696.]
Apr. 5     pd mr Maccarty for mending windows, forme, etc.  2. 00. 06
☞ Mr Hatton hath had 40/ p week one wth another, and 4/ over.
```

Capt Thomas Tew gave 600 ps 8/8 currant money of this Provence wh made wth overweight cutt off one hundred and eighty Three pounds, and ordered by him to be imployed for the service of the Church as Francis Foxcroft thought meet and lyes in my hands. June 3rd, 96 ; given about 18 mo past.   Fra. Foxcroft.

Nicholas Beare who deceased at Maddagasker, gave fifty pounds, six pounds wherof was pd to the person that pd it as a gratuity, and made rec⁺ in the Church accº.   F. F.
June, 96.

These were years of great distress in New England. In December, 1690, Massachusetts had emitted the first paper money issued within the English dominions, and found it immediately depreciate in value. The witchcraft delusion threw its shadow of gigantic horror over the land in 1692.[1] The quarrel between England and France, on account of the deposition of James II., brought in its train woe and desolation to this poor and struggling people for a whole generation. There was only a brief respite at the peace of Ryswick in 1697. "For twenty-five years preceding the peace of Utrecht this country was kept in the commotion of war. It is estimated that not less than eight

---

[1] Perhaps the reaction from this brought some strength to the Episcopal cause. Anderson (Col. Ch., ii. 451) absurdly ascribes the evils which ensued from the witchcraft delusion to the New England Theocracy. In the administrators of it "a lordly intolerance was engendered;" in the subjects of it, "a superstitious fear." But the prominence of Parris and the Mathers in the persecution was injurious to Congregationalism.

thousand of the young men of New England and New York fell by the sword or by disease."[1]

Mr. Myles had been the first graduate of the College to enter the Episcopal ministry in this country, but his return coincided with the "apostacy" of another, who was destined to hold a prominent place.[2] Sewall records, July 26, 1696: —

"Mr. Veisy preach'd at the Ch. of Engl'd; had many Auditors. He was spoken to to preach for Mr. Willard; but am told this will procure him a discharge."

"Sept! 8. Mr. I. Mather gave the Right Hand of Fellowship [to Mr. Wadsworth, at 1st Ch.] : Spake notably of some young men who had apostatized from New England principles, contrary to the Light of their education : was glad that he was of another spirit."

During his absence, Mr. Myles had received the degree of M.A. from Oxford, in 1693.[3]

After long waiting for him, the church had been obliged to write to the bishop, urging Mr. Myles's return from his protracted absence in England on July 26, 1696, when Sewall records that Mr. Bullivant and Mr. Myles reached Nantasket and came to town next day. We have no knowledge why this absence was extended over the space of four whole years, nor how he was occupied during that time, — whether in study, or in the cure of souls in the mother country. He had, however, accomplished the object of obtaining aid for the struggling church. It is

---

[1] McKenzie, "First Church in Cambridge," p. 145, well sums up this period.

[2] Rev. William Vesey (H. C., 1693), was born in Braintree, in 1674. Previous to this time he had officiated at Hempstead, Queen's Co., N. Y., in 1695, and had preached in New York city. A charter being granted by Governor Fletcher to Trinity Church, New York, Mr. Vesey received the following invitation from the Vestry : —

This Board " having read a certificate under the hands of the Rev. Mr. Samuel Myles, Minister of the Church of England in Boston, in New England, and Mr. Gyles Dyer, and Mr. Benjamin Mountfort, Church-wardens of the said church, of the learning and education, and of the pious, sober, and religious behaviour and conversation of Mr. William Vesey, and of his often being a communicant — the receiving of the most holy sacrament — in said church, have called " him " to officiate and have the care of souls in New York." He accordingly went to England for orders in 1697, and on his return was inducted by the Dutch ministers, with a Latin service, in the Dutch church, by command of the Governor. He had a violent controversy with Lord Bellomont, and having been made commissary for the Bishop of London in 1712, had another with Governor Burnet. His long and respected ministry closed July 18, 1746. See " Sprague's Annals of the American Pulpit," v. 13, 14.

[3] His writing these letters after his signature to the Address in 1689, may therefore have been one cause of the sarcasm against him quoted on p. 99, as at this time he had not the English degree of M.A., but only the Harvard one of A. M., at that time a less distinguished dignity.

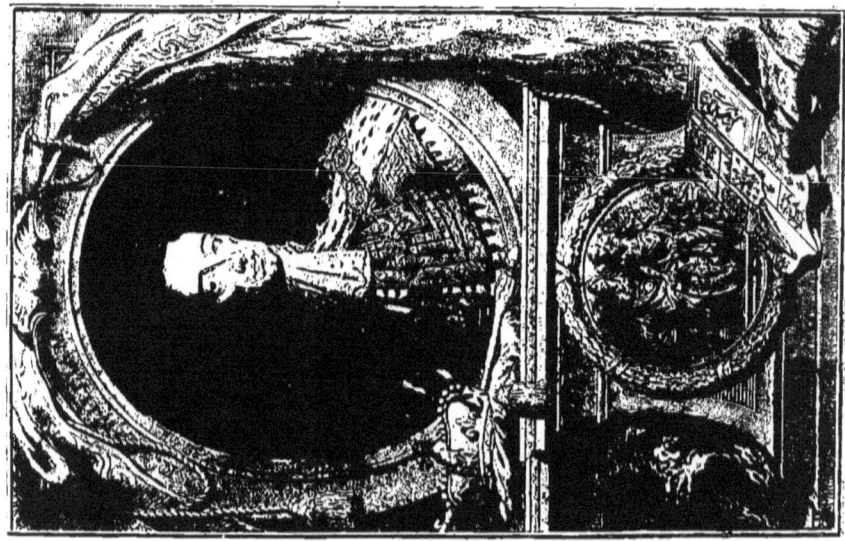

probable that, through the influence of the Bishop of London, he had been presented to Queen Mary, who was a sincere member of the Church of England. King William III. also was too acute a statesman to fail of seeing the political advantage to be derived from strengthening this outpost of the State Church. They extended to the church their personal protection and patronage, and, though Queen Mary died while he was in London, William III. continued to perform what she had engaged to do on her part for the adherents to the English establishment in these distant dominions. Mr. Myles brought back with him the substantial proofs of their bounty, — cushions and carpets, Bible and prayer-books, altar-cloth and surplices; soon after came a very rich gift of communion plate.

Boston, 1696. — This year M? Samuell Myles, Pastor of this Church, Returned ffrom England. Hee Arrived July 4th and Brought with him part of the gift of Quene Mary, performed By King William After her Decease, viz: the Church Furniture, which were A Cushion and Cloth for the Pulpit, two Cushions for the Reading Deske, A Carpet for the Allter, All of Crimson Damask with Silke Fringe, one Large Bible, two Large Common-prayer Books, Twelve Lesser Common-prayer Bookes, Linen for the Allter; Also two Surplises, Alter tabell, 20 y^{des} fine damask.

Boston, Septr 4th, 1696. — Then Att a Meeting of the members of this Church being present M? Myles, Capt^t Foxcroft, Capt. Fox, Mr? Turfrey, M? Hobby, M? Craford, M? Simson, Benja. Mountfort, and others, The Church Gave M? Samu. Myles one hundred and Fourty pounds towards his Charge in England; this was paid, seventy pounds by Capt. Francis Foxcroft and seventy pounds by M? Thaddeus Mackarty, out of the Church Stock.

Boston, October 16th. — M? Nicholas Tippit, when hee dyed in the Island of Neuis, Gave Five pounds to this Church which was paid for white-washing of it, And Five pounds to the poor of Boston, which was Distributed to them.

Boston, October 28th. — M? George Hatton who had preached here in the Absence of M? Myles for about three years, at his going home to the Island of Providence the Church presented him with twenty pounds, which was paid him, Tenn pounds by M? Thaddeus Mackarty, and Tenn pounds by Capt. Fra. Foxcroft out of the Church stock.

Boston, March prime, 1696-97. — Docter Benjamin Bullivant Gave ffifteen pounds for the use of this Church, which was received by M? Myles as in foregoing Accompt.

Boston, March 23, 169$\frac{6}{7}$. — Capt. William Higgins, Comander of his Majestyes Ship the Arundell, Gave six pounds for the use of this Church, and is pased in the Acompt.

The Decalouge, viz., thee tenn Comandments, the Lord's Prayer, and the Creed were drawne in England and Brought over By M.[r] Samuell Myles in July, 1696.[1]

The most substantial fruits of the rector's visit to England followed him later.

Boston, 1697. — Then Received of M.[r] Myles too great silver Flagons, and one silver basen, and one sallver, and one boul, and one Civer, all of Sillver, which was given to the Church by the King and Queen, and brought over by Cap.[tt] John Foye. Received by me, Giles Dyer, Church Warden.

1698. Boston, Aprill. — Received of Giles Dyer and M.[r] Savill Simpson, Late Church Wardens, too great Silver Flagons and one bason, and too Sallvers, and too boules, and too Civers, all of silver; one tabell Cloth, and one napkin, fine Damask ... too Sarplous Fine Hooland, which was given by y.[e] King and Queen; and Eighten Napkines, and one Tabell Cloath, and one pece of Fine Damask which was all of one pece measuring twenty yards, which was Cut by M.[rs] Myles. Reseved by me,

JOHN INDECOTT.

BASE OF COMMUNION FLAGON.

This silver plate was used in the church for about seventy years, when Governor Bernard, bringing over a new communion service, the gift of King George

Giles Dyer Church Warden

III. to the church, took away the older plate and gave it to other churches. A flagon and chalice with paten are now in the possession of Christ Church, Cambridge, inscribed: "The gift of K. William and Q. Mary to y.[e] Reve.[d] Sam.[ll] Myles for y.[e] use of their Maj.[ties] Chappell in N. England: 1694."[2]

---

[1] These memorials of the first wooden King's Chapel are preserved in the chancel of the present church.

[2] See Hoppin's "History of Christ Church, Cambridge." The illustrations are copied from these pieces by the courtesy of the rector and wardens of Christ Church. The corresponding pieces of silver are now in the possession of St. Paul's Church, Newburyport.

To my Labour for Making the Wather Cock and Spindel, to Duing the Commandements and allter rome and the Pulpet, to Duing the Church and Winders, mor to Duing the gallercy and the King's Armes, fortey pounds, which I Frely Give.[1]

G. DYER.

Mr. Myles also brought a more doubtful benefit, in the gift from the King of £100 yearly for supporting an assistant minister at the Chapel, — the chief result of which seems to have been that the assistant was a "thorn in the flesh" to the rector, as is abundantly shown by the records. In establishing this lectureship, the King followed an English custom, as "to nearly every one of the London churches in Queen Anne's time a Lecturer was attached, independent in most cases of the incumbent."[2] Another munificent gift from King William III. arrived with the new royal Governor in 1698, — a very fine theological library for the minister's use, — which was partly scattered and injured in the Revolution.

COMMUNION FLAGON. 1694.

Benjamin Mountfort

MOUNTFORT ARMS.

[1] Greenwood says: "It is no stretch of charity to believe that the honest warden who made this memorandum knew better how to keep the Decalogue than he did to describe or to spell it. Mr. Giles Dyer seems to have had a generous soul, which was inflamed with the desire of imitating the royal benefactors of the Chapel, as his own records may witness. In return for these benefactions the church should have taught Mr. Dyer the useful science and accomplishment of orthography. 'Duing' probably means painting, which was Mr. Dyer's business." Colonel Dyer's later military rank, and his prominence in our church records, show him to have been a man of mark. His shortcomings in spelling were shared by no less distinguished a benefactor of the church than Queen Mary herself, who wrote on the fly-leaf of a Bible, "This book was given the King and I at our crownation."

[2] "A great many of these foundations were an inheritance from Puritan times, . . . men who could not enter the ministry could take a lectureship." — *English Church in the Eighteenth Century*, ii. 495.

This Library, to which reference is made in the letter to Bishop Compton, July 25, 1698, as his gift, was really the gift of the King, and the covers were so stamped.

<table>
<tr><td>SVB</td><td>DE</td></tr>
<tr><td>AVSPICIIS</td><td>BIBLIOTHECA</td></tr>
<tr><td>WILHELMI</td><td>DE</td></tr>
<tr><td>III</td><td>BOSTON</td></tr>
</table>

A complete catalogue of the books is preserved in the book of records. This was the only collection of books not of private ownership in New England at this time, with the single excep-

COMMUNION PLATE GIVEN BY KING WILLIAM AND QUEEN MARY.

tion of the library of Harvard College, and was therefore valuable from the scarcity of books; but it had a greater value in itself, being an admirable collection of the best books for the use of a scholarly theologian of the Church of England. It contained ninety-two folios, eighteen quartos, and ninety smaller works, including Walton's great Biblia Polyglotta, lexicons, and commentaries, fine editions of the Church Fathers, Bodies of Divinity, works on Doctrine and Duty, the sermons of the great preachers of the English Church, historical works (among them such sound histories as Sir William Dugdal's "View of the Late Troubles"), Controversial and Philological Treatises.[1]

The return of Mr. Myles evidently brought strength and some popularity to the church. The wardens testify to the bishop in November, 1698, that he "is well liked of all of us, . . . a good liver, and a painfull preacher." It is evident from the following record of Judge Sewall that the church was emerging from the cloud under which for a time it had lain: —

"Seventh-day, Decemb^r 25, 97. — Snowy day; Shops are open, and Carts and sleds come to Town with Wood and Fagots as formerly, save what abatem^t may be allowed on account of the Wether. This morning we read in Course ye 14, 15, and 16th Psalms. From ye 4th v. of ye 16th Ps. I took occasion to dehort mine frō Christmas-keeping, and charged y^m to forbear. . . . Joseph tells me that tho' most of ye Boys went to ye Ch yet he went not."[2]

The receipts are recorded each Sunday and other church days. It is interesting to note the amounts from year to year.[3]

	£ s. d.		£ s. d.
1686.		1686–7.	
June 20–Oct. 17 . .	48. 08. 04	Jan. 2–Mar. 20 . . .	26. 13. 00
Oct. 24–Dec. 26 . .	26. 16. 02		

There is no record for the year 1688, or the early part of 1689 (in which the Revolution took place). From the resumption of the record on the last day of June, 1689, we infer that the first service in the new church was held on that day.

We group together here the sums annually raised during the period covered by this chapter.

	£ s. d.		£ s. d.
1689.		1690–91	111. 01. 00
June ultimo to 1690,		1691–2	133. 01. 05
Apr. 20	173. 18. 11	1692–3	85. 00. 04
" Church stock " . .	3. 01. 07	1693–4	112. 07. 06
		1694–5	126. 07. 10
Total of contributions and benevolences from one Easter to another . . .	170. 17. 04	1695–6	106. 01. 09
		1696–7. Contributions, etc. .	219. 04. 05

[1] See the catalogue in Mass. Hist. Proc., 1881. In 1824, the considerable remnant of this library was deposited in the Boston Athenæum. See Vol. II.

[2] "Joseph" subsequently became minister of the Old South Church, 1713–1769.

[3] The total amounts only are added up and given here, as the detail of the weekly contributions, which are noted in the records, would occupy too much space.

	£	s.	d.		£	s.	d.
1697–8	150.	19.	08	1705–6[2]	167.	15.	00
1698–9.				1706–7	166.	00.	10
Contributions, etc.[1]	224.	10.	10	1707–8	158.	11.	06
1699–1700 (including				1708–9	139.	03.	03
the sale of pews, etc.)	308.	07.	02	1709–10	164.	11.	9½
1700–1701	177.	07.	03	1710–11	175.	08.	07
1701–2	83.	03.	10	1711–12	231.	13.	03
1702–3	163.	19.	10	1712–13	157.	09.	02
1703–4	172.	10.	05	1713–14	234.	13.	05
1704–5	154.	07.	05	1714–15	266.	05.	03

It is evident from these sums that the church had substantial support from the very beginning; and the decided increase, on the whole, in the amount of the contributions also indicates a steady gain in the number of its supporters. This is shown, too, by other facts which will be mentioned in their proper place.

The receipts for the days preceding and following Mr. Myles's arrival on July 26, are as follows: —

1696.   £ s. d.
July   12   was an Alaram ; no Contribution 0. 00. 00
        19   Recd 4. 06. 06
        26   Recd 4. 15. 04
August   2   Mr. Myles Preached ; we Recd 5. 05. 05
         9   Recd 4. 15. 04
        16   Recd 2. 13. 07
        23   Recd 4. 00. 08
        30   Recd 5. 09. 05
Sept.   6   Recd[3] 4. 01. 01
November prime   By Erer in misplacing first, viz., the two
                     first Recaits 6. 08. 09
Recd March prime, 1696–97, for Mr. Myles 15. 00. 00
Recd March 23rd the Gift of Capt. William Higgins . . .   6. 00. 00

CR.

July   27   pd mr Phesy [Vesey] for sermon[4] 1. 00. 00
August   paid Mr Myles and Clark 8 Aug. 2. 05. 00
             Paid Mr Gouge for 12 weeks board of Mrs. Dansy 6. 00. 00

---

[1] In 1699 the contributions average from £3 to over £5 weekly, but they fell off again later.

[2] A collection to pay debts to sundry workmen amounted to £56 18s. 8d.

[3] The weekly amounts at this period range from £4 to £2 4s. 10d.

[4] Mr. "Phesy" reappears till October, at intervals.

THE CHURCH TAKES ROOT. 127

Boston, May 29th, 1697.

		£ s. d.
1696.	Paid Mr Levingsworth for Lime and Plastering the Church to Keep out the Snow as pr his Note	5. 08. 00
	Paid Mr Godard towards Bulding the Galarey	12. 00. 00
1698. April 29.	Paid Thomas Whiller for Mending formerly the Church winders	0. 12. 00
96.	By Cash pd Mr Simon Smith as a Gratuity	5. 00. 00
	Paid Mr Hatton	10. 00. 00
	Paid Mr Miles	70. 00. 00
98.	Pd for boxes for King's Library	3. 00. 00
1697.	the first Sundey after Easter Received and paied as Folooeth by G. Dyer : —	

Receved the 21 Sunday, being August ye 29	3. 07. 02
paid	3. 05. 00
Paid Mr Coneyball for buying and Carting Poses and hanginge the Doares	0. 08. 00
Whit sunday paid for Bread and wine at the Sacrament	0. 11. 00
November Paid for too Pllates for the youse of the Church	0. 04. 00
Paid for feching the Tabell and seeting up	0. 04. 00
December to A great Chest for the youse of the Church	1. 05. 00
Paid for A Stone Gug Clark Hill broak	0. 06. 00
Crismas day paid for Bread and Wine at the Sacramant	0. 12. 00
Paid for A Cask to put Wine in	0. 02. 00
January Paid Mr Shelson for his Loucking After the Boyes	1. 00. 00
June 4, 1696, Receved of Mr Mountfort Towards the King's Arms	18. 00. 00
May 29 Receved of Mrs Mary Bowdin for the ould Bibell	2. 00. 00
1698.	
Aprill ye 29, Then Receved of Capt Foxcroft . . . . . . which is Money belonging to the Church Stock, Eight pound of it, and Eleven Pound Fifteen Shillings Which is Intrest Money Paid by said Foxcroft.	19. 15. 00
1698.	
Octob. 16 Recd of Mr Richd Williams, purser of the Deptford, Benevolence	6. 00. 00
June 30 Paid Mr Sam Cook, Jamaica minister, a Gratuity	5. 00. 00
Octob. 2 Paid Mr Miles, to pay for the Chests or boxes for the King's library	3. 00. 00
9 ber 20 Paid Richd Knight, carver, for work to my Lord's pew	9. 00. 00
Paid Mr Goddard and Were, Carpents, 15l, and Turner's work and ye for said	16. 12. 00
27 Paid Mr Miles for more chests for the King's library, in all 12 boxes	0. 15. 00
feb. 26 Paid Tho. Whieler mending ten windous, and for an hour Glas	1. 02. 06

128   ANNALS OF KING'S CHAPEL.

The first assistant appointed by the Bishop of London was a Mr. Dansy, who died on his passage to Boston.¹ The next was ²a Mr. White, who was sent with Lord Bellomont, when that nobleman came out to succeed Sir William Phips in the government of New England.³ The man-of-war in which they sailed was blown off to Barbadoes, where Mr. White died. Thus twice deprived of their expected minister, the church applied for another, in a letter to the bishop, May 2, 1698.

At a Meeting of the Congregation of the Church of England in the King's Chappell at Boston, on Easter Munday, the 25 April, 1698, —

Agreed: That the window Shutters of the Church on the outside be painted by Thomas Child, as the Gates are.

John Giles, chosen Clerk, who accepted, upon such sallary as the Church should find him deserve.

Edward Hill, Late Clerk, was Chosen Sexton, and to have 5/ a week sallary.

Mr. White, who was comming over to be assistant to Mr. Myles, by the appointment of the Bishop of London, being deceased in his passage hither, —

Ordered: That the Church Wardens send an Address to Him, in the Name of this Congregation, to returne him Thanks for the care of this

---

[1] The widow of Mr. Dansy appears to have arrived in February, 1697, and was for a time a charge upon the church, to whom her helpless condition, "a stranger in a strange land," must have been perplexing. Before April, 1698, however, Mr. Myles married her and went to housekeeping, his salary being increased in consequence from £2 to £3 weekly.

[2] There were two persons of this name. The warden was probably the one whose gravestone is in the Chapel burying-ground, John Indicott, cooper, who died Dec. 7, 1711, æt. 70. The name was sometimes written like Gov. Endicott's, but there is no evidence of relationship. A list of descendants of John Indicott, who died May 26, 1757, is given in N. E. Hist. and Geneal. Reg., xxxiii. 245.

[3] Sir William Phips arrived with the new charter May 14, 1692. He returned to England in 1694, and died there Feb. 18, 1695. Richard, Earl of Bellomont, arrived in New York May, 1698, and in Boston May 26, 1699.

Dr. Increase Mather had returned to Boston with Governor Phips, and received a vote of thanks and the proverbial ingratitude of those whom he had served so ably. His son expresses the family disappointment in his " Further Quæries upon the Present State of New-English Affairs," — probably A.D. 1690: "Whether great Sect of *Grumbletonians* in the Countrey, whom nothing will satisfie, been't the worst Enemies which this Countrey can have?

. . . . . .

Whether the Country will not shortly deserve that goodly Epitaph, *A People which died to save Charges?*" — *Andros Tracts,* i. 207. Mr. Whitmore's note quotes Cotton Mather's sermon on "The Present State of New England, etc.," Mar. 20, 1689-90: "You are perhaps the most Querimonious and Outrageous of all People in your Discontents."

Church, and to pray him to send another suitable Minister to be assistant to M[r] Myles, and to use his Intrest for the Continuance of His Maj[ty's] Bounty for his Support :—

Right Honorable and Right Reverend Father in God:

May it please your Lord[p],— In our last in October, 96, Wee acquainted your Lord[p] That We had rec[d] the Effect of our former address[1] by the appearance of our Minister, M[r] Sam. Miles, amongst us.

And since Wee have experienced the continuation of y[r] Lord[ps] favours in sending Mr. Dansy, and since M[r] White, who both deceased before they arrived to officiate.

Now by the Providence of God being destitute of an Assistant to M[r] Miles, Wee further intreat your Lord[ps] kindness in sending another proper for us (a single man will suit best), and that your Lord[p] (according to your wonted great bounty and goodness to us, w[ch] we have in continuall remembrance wth all thankfulness) would be pleased to persist in using your Intrest for the continuance of His Majestie's bounty for his Maintenance ; for we are very unwilling to venture the being of Our Church in these parts, so farr advanced to the Glory of God and the bennifitt on Mankind upon the life or humour of one person.

We gave M[r] Myles upon his arrivall £140, in consideration of the Extraordinary Expence he had been at in England ; and soon after augmented his salary for one yeare, in consideration of his marrying the widow Dansey and going to housekeeping, from 40/ to £3 a week. And are and shall be ready to proceed as farr as is or may be in our power for the Ends aforesaid.

So, Committing Your Lord[p] to Divine protection, Wee crave Leave to remaine

Your most obedient Sonns,

In the Name and by the appointment of the Congregation of His Majesties Chappell at Boston in New England,

GEORGE TURFREY, } Wardens.
JOHN INDICOTT,

2 May, 1698.
By John Phillips.

Mr. Stephen Wesendunck:

S[r],— After our hearty Commendations, Wee pray you to peruse, seal, and deliver the inclosed, and give us your assistance to gett the Thing effected ; and withall to discours His Lord[p] That His Majesties Bounty of £100 p Ann., which hath been rec[d] by M[r] Myles, and M[r] Dansey, and M[r] White (the last Minister sent wth my Lord Bellomont), who dyed at Barbadoes in his passage, hath been disposed off by the receivers at their pleasure. Hereafter, if His Lord[p] pleas to cause it to be paid unto you, you will transmit it to us, which we pray you to do, in proper Goods.

[1] No copy has been preserved of either of these letters to the Bishop.

And Wee will pay 40/ a week to the Minister His Lord? shall send; also shall keep a fair Record of it in our Church books which hath been hitherto omitted (tho' not by our fault), for such bennefitts ought to be had in everlasting remembrance. If you can, procure us a Coppy of the Warrant, by virtue of which s.^{d} £100 p Ann. is paid out of our Gracious King's privy purse. We promise our selves your dilligent compliance, wch will be kindly accepted by

The Congregation of the Church of England in Boston.

GEORGE TURFREY, } Wardens.
JOHN INDICOTT,

It appears from the record of March 16, 1698–99, that, in the beginning at any rate, the royal bounty was transmitted through the Bishop of London, who paid it in money to the business agent of the church at London. The best mode of remitting it appears to have been in goods, which were sent to the wardens and sold again by them at a considerable profit. In the first instance, nearly fifty per cent was realized on the goods; the articles (kersey, cottons, and serges), which cost £86 11s. 8d., being sold for £126 2s. 8d., after deducting charges. Out of this the wardens made a weekly payment of £2 to "his Majesties Chaplin." It does not appear from the records that this mode of remittance, which must have involved the possibility of pecuniary loss to the church thus assuming the responsibility for the payment of the salary, was long continued.

Mr Stephen Wesendunck writes from London 19 Octob^r, 1698, That he had rec^d from my Lord of London £78 —od money for accompt of the Church, whereof wee are Wardens, and had sent in Goods y^e Vallue of £86. 11. 8. for the supply of his Majestie's Chaplin, Mr Bridg, to whom we have obliged Our selves to pay 40/ aweeke.

The said Goods delivered into Mr Fran. Foxcroft's hands, to sell and be accomptable unto the Church, 16 March, 169$\frac{8}{9}$.

The goods — consisting of "20 packages kersey, 10 packages large cottons at 25s., 10 packages small cottons at 16s. 6d., 10 packages plain serges at 40s." — were "sold for £126 2s. 8d., after deducting custome and charges, £4 8s. 2d."

Right Honorable and Right Reverend Father in God, Henry, Lord Bishop of London:

May it please Your Lord^p, — In our last address to Your Lord^p, dated 2.^{d} May last, We gave Y^r Lord^p accompt of the death of Mr White, and prayed Y^r Lord^{ps} favour in sending another in his stead to be Assistant to

M.* Samuell Myles, and in still improoving y.* Intrest for the continuance of His Majesties bounty for his maintenance, We being unwilling to venture the Wellbeing of Our Church so farr advanced in these parts on one person. The aforesaid bounty We pray Y.* Lord.** to permit M.* Stephen Wesendunck to receive, who will be carefull in conveying it to Us, and We promise to pay the said Assistant 40 shillings weekly.

Since We have received another experience of Y.* Lord.** care and kindness in sending Us a Library, which we have received in good Condition, and having this Oportunity of a Worthy Gent.*, Coll. Andrew Hammilton, Late Governour of the Jerseys,[1] may not omit to render Y.* Lord.* our most hearty thanks, and shall see them improoved to the true Intent; for the present have lodged them in M.* Myles, his study, for the use of him, the Assistant, when he comes, and his or their successors, and take care that no abuse or imbecilment be made of them.

So, Committing Y.* Lord.* to the Divine Protection, We crave leave to remaine

Your Lord.** Most obedient Sons,

In the name of the Congregation of His Majestie's Chappell at Boston, N. Engl.*,

     GEORGE TURFREY, } Wardens for the time
     JOHN INDICOTT,   } being.

25 July, 1698.

Coll: Andrew Hammilton:

Hon.*** S.*, — We intreat the favour of Y.* Hon.* to present to His Lord.* Henry, Bishop of London, the inclosed address, and to improve your owne Intrest in promoting whatsoever may fall in y.* way for the benefit of the Church of England in these remote parts.

We shall be alwaies thankfull, and in the meantime not wanting in our prayers for y.* Hon.** safe arrivall and prosperity. Subscribing our selves

     Y.* Hon.** most humble Servants,

In the name (as above).

25 July, 1698.

The request of the wardens in their letter of November, 1698, again applying for an assistant to Mr. Myles, was anticipated by Bishop Compton before receiving it: —

---

[1] He was made Governor of New Jersey, 1699–1701; and was Deputy Governor of Pennsylvania, 1701–1709. In 1692 he had been appointed Deputy postmaster for America, for Thomas Neale, who had that office by royal patent. Duncan Campbell was his deputy for Boston.

Right Honorable and Right Reverend Father in God, Henry, Lord, Bishop of London :

May it please Your Lordship, — In our former Addresses to your Lord^p of 2^d May and 25 July last, Which we have reason to believe are safely come to Y^r Lord^{ps} hands, We besought Y^r Lord^{ps} continuance of your favours, in sending us an Assistant to Mr Samuell Miles ; for should any sickness or distemper happen to him, we should run adventure of being dispersed, which would overthrow in an instant what we have been this ten years endeavouring, — The firm Establishment of a Church of England Congregation in this place.

We further intreat Your Lord^p not in the least to admit of Mr Miles's remooval, for he is well liked by all of us, a good liver and painfull preacher ; and, as we have formerly hinted, We hope Your Lord^p is well satisfied with our provision for him.

If Your Lord^p would be pleased to procure a part of the *fides propagandi* money, to be transmitted to us, We question not but to improove it to as good or better advantage Than hitherto the others have done ; for the french, our neighbours at the Eastward, are very sedulous in proseliting Indians that way, and never anything was yet done, by those to whom the money is here remitted, in those parts.

Itt will much add to our present satisfaction to receive the favour of a line from Your Lord^p. Assuring Your Lord^p we are very Zealous in promoting our Increas and are intended (finding it will be needful) to inlarge Our Chappell.

We conclude with our prayers for Your Lordship's prosperity, and crave Leave to subscribe Our selves

Your Lord^{ps} Most obedient Sonns,
In the Name of the Congregation of the King's Chappel at Boston in New England,

GEORGE TURFREY, } Wardens.
JOHN INDICOT,

21 November, 1698.

This letter was " sent by the Mast Shipps from Piscataqua," under cover to Mr. Stephen Wesendunck, in whose " prudent management of our affaires " the wardens expressed their satisfaction.

The arrival of Rev. Christopher Bridge, after a long winter passage, is recorded by Sewall : —

" March 4. 1698/9. Foy arrives, came out of Faymouth in November, in him comes an Assistant to Mr. Myles who preaches March 5."

Right Honble and Right Reverend Father in God :

May it please Your Lords^p, — We have gladly received the effect of our formers, by the appearance of Mr Christopher Bridge amongst us,

THE CHURCH TAKES ROOT. 133

Which favour of Y^r Lordship we acknowledge wth all thankfulness, and doubt not but he will be to satisfaction. We shall constantly pay him 40 shillings a week, wch we began the 5th Instant, the first day of his arrival. Also We continue unto Mr Myles his 3 pounds a week, besides his Perquisites, and shall not be wanting in our due respects to both of them. We have rec^d the Goods from Mr Wesendunck, and pray the continuance of Y^r Lord^{ps} favour. We shall allwaies endeavour to approve ourselves

Y^r Lord^{ps} Most Obedient Sons,

GEORGE TURFREY, } Wardens of the King's Chappell
JOHN INDICOT, } in Boston in New England.

20 March, 169⅞, by In^o Alden.

1698. March 5. P^d Mr Bridge His first Sermon . . . 2. 00. 00.

The church was now fully equipped, and proceeded to organize itself more completely.

At a Meeting of the Congregation of the Church of England in the King's Chappel at Boston in New England, on Easter Munday, April 10th, 1699.

PRESENT.

Samuel Miles } Minist^{rs}	Richard Hancock.
Christopher Bridge }	Mr Conyers.
John Indecott, Warden.	Thomas Gold.
Thaddeus Mackarty.	David Johnson.
Giles Dyer.	Thomas Hayes.
William Hobby.	William Tailer.
Thomas Newton.	Roger Judd.
Benj^a Mountford.	Thomas Sandford.
Savil Simpson.	Mr Apthought.
Giles Silvester.	—— Dolbear.
John Cooke.	John Giles.
Mr Goulding.	Edward Hill.
John Cleverly.	—— Peterson.
Sam^{ll} Checkley.	Robin Scrivener.
Jeremiah Gibson.	Edwd Turfrey.

Mr John Indicott } were chosen Wardens for the Yeare ensueing.
Mr Edward Lyde }

Voted and *Agreed:* That John Giles, for his Service as Clerk, be allowed Fifteen pounds for the yeare past, and also Fifteen pounds for the yeare ensueing, to be paid as the Same becomes due.

Voted: That a Select number of the Congregation be chosen as a Vestry to-morrow morning after Prayers.

At a Meeting of the Congregation of the Church of England in the King's Chappel at Boston in New England, on Easter Tuesday, April 11th, 1699,—

M.ʳ Edward Lyde not accepting of the place of Warden, M.ʳ William Hobby was chosen Warden in his roome for yᵉ ensueing year.

Voted: That Francis Foxcroft, Thaddeus Mackarty, Thomas Newton, Giles Dyer, Benjᵃ Mountfort, John Cooke, Savil Simpson, Edward Lyde, and Edward Turfrey be a Vestry of this Congregaĉon for one year ensueing, to advise and Consult with yᵉ Ministers and Wardens upon and concerning all matters and things as shall by them be from time to time thought necessary to be done and performed relating to the s.ᵈ Church, and yᵉ placing and seating of persons therein, and to represent the whole Congregation in all matters and things whereunto yᵉ consent of yᵉ same is necessary; and that whatsoever yᵉ Wardens, wᵗʰ yᵉ advice of s.ᵈ Vestry, or Major p.ᵗ of yᵐ, shall do in yᵉ premices be accounted yᵉ act of yᵉ whole Congregation. Provided, that this shall not be understood so as to hinder yᵉ Wardens from paying yᵉ weekly allowance of 3ˡᵇ to M.ʳ Miles, 2ˡᵇ to M.ʳ Bridge, 5/ to Edward Hill, Sexton, and 15ˡᵇ a year to John Giles, Clerk, without yᵉ consent of the s.ᵈ Vestry, but that they pay the Same as has been accustomed.

Voted also: That a Vestry be alike annually chosen.

The Puritan dislike of the Church continued to find expression in Sewall's Diary: —

"Fourth-day, Jan.ʸ 4th [1698/9] . . . This day I spake with Mr Newman about his partaking with the French church on the 25. December on account of its being Christmas-day, as they abusively call it. He stoutly defended the Holy-days and Church of England."

"4ᵗʰ day, Jan.ʸ 4 [1698/9]. Roger Judd comes into my house this morning, and talking about Mr. Willards sending for him yesterday, I ask'd him, if Mr. Myles should send for him, whether he would not reckon it his duty to go to him. At first, he said yes; but presently after said, If I please. I told him that he made himself his own Judge. He said, If should now call a church-Meeting and send for him, he would not go to them; for he was none of them. Said he came not into church but [by] the importunity of Deacon Eliot and others; told him then he was for the church of England. And told me now 'twas his Conscience to go to the church of England, and he had sin'd in staying away from it so long. If he was persecuted for it, he could not help it." [1]

"Sabbath-day Jan.ʸ 22 [1698/9]. Bro' Roger Judd is cast out of the Church for his contumacy in refusing to hear the Church, and his contemptuous behaviour against the same, and Mr. Willard the Pastor. Refus'd to be there."

"Apr. 6. 1699 . . . It seems a day or two ago there was a great Funeral of a Barbados Gentleman; Usher, Foster, Dyer, Maccarty, Harris, Newton, Bearers. Funeral Sermon, and great crowding too."

---

[1] Roger Judd was made sexton of King's Chapel, to succeed Edward Hill, in 1701.

THE CHURCH TAKES ROOT.

The records proceed: —

			£	s.	d.
1699.					
January 23.	Paid Tho. Wheeler for mendinge the Church Windowes		1.	00.	00
	By Loss in brass Mony		0.	13.	02
1700.					
Aprill 28.	Paid for an hour Glass		0.	01.	03
Octo' 7.	P⁴ the Carpenter for the Church Porch		2.	00.	00
Aprill 16.	Paid Wheeler for mendeing yᵉ Windous		1.	04.	00
	Paid the Carpenter for Church Porch		2.	05.	00
Aprill· 21.	Paid Mʳ Goddard for mending yᵉ Church Windows		0.	10.	00
1701.					
May 26.	Lost by brass money¹		0.	99.	06
Augᵗ 4.	Paid for Scouring yᵉ brass frame for yᵉ hour Glass		0.	10.	00
	Paid for broom, and brush, and Pail		0.	03.	00
Augˢᵗ 5.	Recd of Majʳ Charles Hobby six pounds, yᵉ Gift of Col. Nicolson		6.	00.	00
	Recd of Majʳ Charles Hobby six pounds, yᵉ Gift of Coll. Nicolson for Piscatuqua, wᶜʰ I dᵈ to Mʳ Samˡ Miles		6.	00.	00
1701/2.					
Febʸ 16.	Pᵈ for mending the Church Windows		0.	12.	04
March 23.	Pᵈ Giles Godward For work done for the Church		2.	04.	00

In refreshing contrast to the confused mass of entries which we have been disentangling, the accounts in the old Record Book are methodically and clearly kept, when kept by the pen of "Ed. Lyde, Churchwarden." A few interesting items stand out in the long record of weekly contributions: —

		£	s.	d.
1702.²				
June prᵒ.	Pᵈ Miles and Judd³	3.	00.	00
July.	Paid for an hour glass	0.	00.	12
Octobʳ 3.	Pᵈ Salter for a wheel	0.	07.	00
Novbʳ 2.	Pᵈ Mʳ Barton for a bell rope	0.	06.	06
Novbʳ 22.	Pᵈ mʳ Childe painting yᵉ hour Glass	0.	03.	00

---

¹ One of the constant sources of loss in the contributions was from "brass money,"—a cheap and delusive form of charity which has afflicted the contribution box from that day to this. With entire impartiality, the bad money afflicted other churches as well as King's Chapel. The records of *Christ Church* Vestry, Oct. 20, 1729, contain a vote: "That Mr. Monk be desired to take in all the broken contribution money to gett it changed."

² Payments vary from £2 10s. to £3.

³ The receipts this year vary from £2 16s. to £6 16s., only once reaching the latter sum.

1702/3.   £ s. d.
Jan⁽ʸ⁾.   Pᵈ for spruce, epine, and nailes 3/6 . . . . } 0. 08. 06
             Pᵈ Everard for putting up the mourning, 5 . }
March 28.   Recᵈ from Doctʳ Checkley,[1] being most part   } 1. 05. 08
             bad money . . . .   }

                              Contra.
             By bad money to be returned 0. 14. 04
1703.
April 17.   Recᵈ for a Seat in yᵉ Gallery of Capᵗ Dobbins . . 0. 06. 00
             To a Bill of Exchᵃ of Colⁿ Nicholson's for £15
             sterl. at 36 pᶜᵗ exchⁿ is this money[2] 20. 08. 00

The increasing relaxation of the earlier severity of doctrine and practice in New England Puritanism has been related in a former chapter, but it received yet more marked illustration before the close of the century, in the formation of what was commonly known as "the Manifesto Church." Besides the controversy respecting the proper subjects for baptism, which had agitated the churches,[3] there were other questions of order and worship on which the community was warmly divided. Of these the most important related to the qualifications for voting in the choice of ministers and in parish affairs. In this, as in civil matters, the franchise had originally been confined to communicants, — a restriction free from objection in either case so long as the great body of the community in Church and State were thus qualified; but which wrought injustice, ever increasing, when, as a new generation grew to manhood, the number of those thus qualified decreased, often to a mere minority. Long after this condition of things had compelled a widening of the elective franchise in civil affairs, the members of the church clung to their exclusive privilege in religious matters, so that a large proportion of those who paid taxes for the support of religious worship had no voice in its administration. Even after the body of the congregation were admitted to this privilege, the church retained the right of the initiative, especially in the choice of a pastor. There had been several instances of joint action by the church and the town, as in Salem and Dedham, but these were exceptional cases.

A further difficulty which pressed on not a few of the most devout and sensitive religious worshippers in the churches was

---

[1] Checkley was junior warden, and this was probably money from contributions.

[2] In 1704 the contributions range from £3 19s. to £1 19s. 8d., once reaching £4 5s. The payments to Mr. Myles vary accordingly.

[3] See p. 33.

the usage of requiring a public "relation of religious experience" from candidates for admission to the church. The stalwart piety of the early Puritans had exacted and rejoiced in this laying bare of the most sacred privacies of the soul's relations with God, and the practice was regarded by many as vital to the well-being of the churches. On the other hand, it was felt that the steady diminution of the number of communicants was largely due to this cause.

To these reasons, which operated to produce dissatisfaction with the established order of the churches, must be added discontent with the rigid bareness of their order of worship. In the reaction from the ritual of the English Church which had used them so harshly, the Puritans had discarded everything which could remind them of its formalism. For this reason the reading of the Scriptures was not practised in the public worship, though they were bountifully expounded in the sermon, an hour or more in length, which was the chief part of the service. Even the use of the Lord's Prayer was discountenanced, on account of its repetition in the English liturgy. In place of the alternations of prayers and singing, which give variety to that stately order of public worship, the Puritans allowed only a single prayer of protracted length, and a solitary psalm, so devoid of instrumental aid, and sung by voices so untaught, as to be free from any musical snares for the unregenerate spirit.

It is possible that if the Church of England had come in more gracious guise, it would have won to its fold a large part of the numerous body of persons who for these reasons were dissatisfied with the established order of the churches. But the manner of its introduction in Boston intensified the inherited antipathy to it which had been transmitted from the first generation of religious exiles, and which had in some cases survived any vital religion in their descendants; so that comparatively few families of the primitive New England stock joined what was regarded as an alien church.[1] The undertakers of "the New Church" in "Brattle Close" had no mind to sever themselves thus from the bulk of New England Christians. A considerable number of influential persons joined in this new organization, which, on the

[1] Of the twenty "Undertakers" of Brattle Square Church, six had been subscribers for building King's Chapel in 1689, viz. Clark, Cooper, Davis, Minot, Blush, Meers, besides John George, one of the first church members of Brattle Square. The son of Addington Davenport, another "Undertaker," became our Assistant Minister in 1737; and Thomas Brattle had sympathies that way. But the fall of Andros seems to have changed their minds.

approach to completion of their house of worship, issued "A Manifesto or Declaration, set forth by the Undertakers of the New Church now Erected in *Boston* in *New England, November* 17th, 1699, . . . for preventing all Misapprehensions and Jealousies." In this interesting document they state that they —

"approve and substitute the Confession of Faith put forth by the Assembly of Divines at Westminister," and "design only the true and pure worship of God, according to the rules appearing plainly in his word." They "judge it, therefore, most suitable and convenient that in Public Worship some part of the Holy Scripture be read by the Minister at his discretion." They profess their "sincere desire and intention to hold communion with the Churches here as true Churches;" and "further declare, that we allow of baptism to those only who profess their faith in Christ and obedience to him, and to the children of such: yet we dare not refuse it to any child offered to us by any professed Christian, upon his engagement to see it educated, if God give life and ability, in the Christian religion. But this being a ministerial act, we think it the Pastor's province to receive such professions and engagements. We judge it, therefore, fitting and expedient that whoever would be admitted to partake with us in the Holy Sacrament be accountable to the Pastor, to whom it belongs to inquire into their knowledge and spiritual state, and to require the renewal of their baptismal covenant. But we assume not to ourselves to impose upon any a public relation of their experiences; however, if any one think himself bound in conscience to make such a relation, let him do it. For we conceive it sufficient if the Pastor publicly declare himself satisfied in the person offered to our communion, and seasonably propound him. Finally, we cannot confine the right of choosing a Minister to the communicants alone; but we think that every baptized adult person who contributes to the maintenance should have a vote in electing."[1]

The new church was fortunate in securing as its first minister Rev. Benjamin Colman, a native of Boston, but then and for four years previous preaching in England, whose gifts and character soon established the church in public favor. A period of controversy, however, intervened. The ministers of the other churches, indeed, united with it in keeping a day of public prayer before its first communion service in January, 1700; but a succession of attacks and rejoinders in print followed through the ensuing year.[2]

[1] A further innovation was made by the new society, Dec. 20, 1699, when they voted "that the Psalms in our Public Worship be sung without reading line by line."

[2] The first shot was fired in March, 1700, in the form of a general treatise: "The Order of the Gospel Professed and Practised by the Churches of Christ in New England Justified, etc.," by Increase

The government of the province, although no longer under the new charter elective from the people, had been practically administered by the representatives of the old system since the overthrow of Andros. It was only by the vigilance of Increase Mather, indeed, then resident as agent of Massachusetts in London, that the re-appointment of Andros was prevented from meeting King William's approval. But Mather was allowed to name his successor, and chose his own parishioner, Sir William Phips, who had risen by a rough force of character from the rank of an illiterate ship-carpenter, had fished up treasures from the Spanish main, and achieved wealth and fame. His rude and incompetent administration, distinguished by a disastrous attempt to frighten Count Frontenac into the surrender of Quebec, was soon ended by his summons to England in disgrace. The parishioner of the Mathers was not likely to smile upon the Royal Chapel, nor did it bask in more sunshine when, on his departure, the old magistrate, Stoughton, lieutenant-governor by name from the King, assumed the chair, and occupied it for nearly four years. The memory of the official dignity of the church during Governor Andros's rule must have been regretfully cherished by

Mather. The Epistle Dedicatory states the principles of the Manifesto, and controverts them in answers to seventeen questions. In the same year appeared "Gospel Order Revived, being an Answer to a Book lately set forth by the Rev. Mr. Increase Mather, President of Harvard College, etc., by sundry Ministers of the Gospel in New England." This was considered to be by Rev. Messrs. Colman, Bradstreet of Charlestown, and Woodbridge of West Springfield, and was printed in New York, because "the Press in Boston is so much under the aw of the Reverend Author whom we answer, and his Friends, that we could not obtain of the Printer there to Print the following Sheets, etc." It says of reading the Bible in public without exposition: "He brands it with a hard, uncouth Name, and twice tells us that some call it *Dumb Reading*. We wish he had named those that so term it. There is so much Venom in the Epithite, and so complicated a Malignity in the Phrase, that we fear it's infectious, and may propagate a Spirit of Pride and contempt of his Neighbours and irreverence to his Maker. The Author well thought so odious a Mark on the Front would give all honest People a disgust to so villanous and stigmatiz'd a Practice. But his Policy has failed him, for it raises a just Indignation in all sensible and ingenuous Christians. We will for once inform the Reverend Author that the Scriptures are read in Churches audibly and intelligibly. Nor can we guess what Dumb reading should mean, unless when men sleep over their Books; and in charity to the Author we wish he had been asleep when this unlucky word dropt from his Pen." Bartholomew Green, the printer, vindicated himself, and was answered by Thomas Brattle caustically; and to this Green replied. Early in 1701 the Mathers published: "A Collection of some of the many Offensive Matters contained in a Pamphlet entitled The Order of the Gospel Revived," with the motto, *Recitasse est Refutasse.* In this President Mather styles Colman "a little thing," whose "impotent *Allatrations*" are beneath his notice. "At *Mocking* he has outdone *Ishmael*, For *Ishmael* Mock'd his Brother only; but this Youth has not feared to Mock his *Fathers.*" See the memoir of Colman in N. E. Hist. and Geneal. Reg., iii. 220, etc.

its more worldly members; and Church and State were so closely bound together in those days, that even the religious worshippers must have felt that it would be strengthened in the best sense if an Episcopalian should be sent over as governor.

Great, therefore, was the rejoicing when, on May 26, 1699, Richard Coote, Earl of Bellomont, arrived at Boston as Governor of Massachusetts and New Hampshire, as well as of New York and New Jersey. He had been commissioned in September, 1697, but, being driven by stress of weather to the West Indies, had been seven or eight months in reaching New York, where he arrived in April, 1698. There he had soon received the following address: —

To His Excellency Richard, Earle of Bellomont, Cap! Generall and Governour in Chief of His Majesties Provinces of the Massachusetts Bay, New York, and New Hampshire:

The humble address of the Congregation of the Church of England, settled at Boston, in the Province of the Massathusetts Bay.

May it please Y^r Exc^y, — As the Inhabitants of these His Majesties Provinces in Generall are highly sensible, as well as of His Maj^{tys} favour in appointing Your Exc^y (every way so noble and worthy a person) to be their Capt. Generall and Governour in Chief, As of Your Exc^{ys} great condescention in undertaking that Station, that you might promote the Welfare and prosperity of His Majesties subjects in these remote Territoryes, —

So this Congregation in particular do wth hearty Thankfulness and Gratitude acknowledge His Majesties Grace in choosing a Governour for us whose Religion and Piety shine forth wth an Eminency no wayes inferiour to those other sublime Endowments wch possess Your Excellency's noble and generous Soule.

And We are thereby encouraged to hope (as we do earnestly pray) That, as well by Your Exc^{ys} countenance and Patronage as by the Example of yor Great Piety, This Congregation may flourish and increase, both in number and Virtue, to the Glory of Almighty God.

With our most humble and fervent supplications to the Throne of Grace for Y^r Excellency's health and felicity, and that (so soon as the Affaires of His Majesties Service will admit) We may be made happy by Your Excellency's presence amongst us, We Subscribe, wth all dutyfull Submission,

Your Excellencyes most humble and Most obedient Servants,

SAMUELL MYLES, Presbiter.
GEORGE TURFREY, } Wardens.
JOHN INDICOTT,

In the name and by the appointment of the above-said Congregation.

Boston, 2 May, 1698.
Sent to Mr. Graham, at New York.

Richard, second Baron Coote,[1] had been M. P. for Dwitwich, and the services of his family had made him welcome at the court of the restored monarch; but on the accession of James II. he retired for some years to the Continent, only returning on the peremptory command of the King, Nov. 22, 1687. A leading Whig and Protestant, he was one of the first to welcome the Prince of Orange, and was soon appointed Treasurer and Receiver-General to Queen Mary, being in consequence attainted by the Irish Parliament of James II. This, however, only increased the favor of King William, to whom, " pleasing in person and manner, sensible and honest," he had become "a warm personal friend," and who created him Earl of Bellomont, Nov. 2, 1689. He was named Governor of New York early in 1695, although his commission was not received until 1697, and it was the spring of 1698 when he arrived in his province. In selecting him for this position, which was one of peculiar difficulty and importance, King William paid a high tribute to his character, saying, when notifying him of the appointment, that " he thought him a Man of Resolution and Integrity, and with those qualifications more likely than any he could think of to put a stop to that illegal Trade and to the growth of Piracy, for which reason he made choice of him for the Government, and for the same reason intended to put the Government of *New England* into his hands."

ARMS OF BELLOMONT.[2]

In this position at New York he displayed resolution and honor. "An unflinching foe to dishonesty," he refused the opportunities to enrich himself by collusion with frauds, and made

---

[1] He was born in 1636, and was descended from (1) Francis Coote, a gentleman of Queen Elizabeth, whose son, Sir Nicholas Coote, had two sons, of whom the elder, (2) Charles, a soldier of fortune in the Irish wars, was created an Irish baronet in 1621, and was killed after gallant services in the Irish Rebellion of 1641. His son (3) Charles succeeded to the title, and held high office on the Parliamentary side in the civil war; but was active in the recall of Charles II., and was rewarded, Sept. 6, 1660, by the title of Earl of Montrath, while his younger brother, Richard, having been active in the cause, was on the same day raised to the peerage as Baron Coote, of Colooney, Co. Sligo, Ireland. Richard had previously married Mary, second daughter of Sir George St. George, Bart. of Carricksdrumruske, Co. Leitrim, by whom he had four sons, the second and eldest surviving, Richard inheriting the title, July 10, 1683.

[2] This escutcheon was hung in the church. The *coots* in this coat-of-arms are in allusion to Bellomont's family name.

many enemies by his resolute efforts to enforce the Acts of Parliament, and to reclaim the illegal grants by which Governor

BELLOMONT.[1]

Fletcher had impoverished the province;[2] while he was "the first actual friend of the people and sympathizer with honest demo-

[1] See the interesting sketch of his life in F. De Peyster's "Address before the N. Y. Historical Society, Nov. 18, 1879." The portrait is taken, by the kindness of the publishers of the "Memorial History of Boston," from this source.

[2] Three fourths of the land in the province had been granted to eleven persons.

THE CHURCH TAKES ROOT. 143

cratic forms of government who administered the affairs of " New York "under the English crown," and incurred the enmity of those who had favored the judicial murder of Leisler and Milburne by his indignation at the wrong and endeavors to right their memory. He was unfortunate in his connection with William Kidd, who had been fitted out by himself and a few friends with a vessel to catch pirates, but could not resist the temptation to become one; and though the governor apprehended and sent him to England for punishment, on his appearance in Boston in July, 1699, he was censured in the debates in Parliament for this connection.[1] The same qualities which commended him on his arrival in Boston won the favor of the people of New York. " Tall, good looking, and graceful, he bore his sixty-two years as lightly as though they were but fifty. No less pleasing in manners than appearance, agreeable in conversation, affable in demeanor, and extremely stylish in dress, he became at first sight a prime favorite with all classes." This regard continued unabated on the part of the Dutch; but the hostility of the "anti-Leislerians," and of the merchants who had evaded the Acts of Navigation and Plantations, was soon roused against the " upright, courageous, and independent" man.[2] He succeeded with difficulty in getting a bill " for vacating Fletcher's land-grants " through his Council and Assembly; its approval by the home government was delayed by the strong influences which were brought to bear by interested parties. A Dutch minister, Godfrey Dellius, who had obtained an enormous tract of land, went abroad as their agent, and prejudiced the ministers in Holland and the Bishop of London against him. The wardens and vestry of Trinity Church in New York petitioned the bishop to save it from the destruction with which they accused him of threatening it; the real grievance being his recall of a lease of land which Governor Fletcher had made to that church. Mr. Vesey, the minister, refused to pray for the governor, and prayed instead for the safe passage of Dellius; and Lord Bellomont was compelled in self-respect to abstain from going to church in New York. The contrast in his reception at Boston must have been as grateful to him religiously as in other points of view.[3]

[1] It is evident to Macaulay that the opprobrium with which Lord Bellomont was visited was due to political reasons.
[2] Macaulay, v. 246.
[5] He died in New York of gout, March 5, 1701. He had married Catherine, daughter of Bridges Nanfan, Esq., of Bridgemorton, Co. Worcester, Eng-

The governor hesitated in which province to reside. He stayed in Massachusetts only fourteen months. But the arrival of a nobleman — even an Irish one — as the head of the government was a great event, and he was received with much show of respect and ceremony. The church fitted up a state pew for him.[1] They also, at the Easter meeting, 1700, placed him first upon the list of vestrymen.

But he strove too hard to please the people, and especially to ingratiate himself with "the stiffer religionists of the old stock" to satisfy his fellow-churchmen. He was "condescending, affable, and courteous upon all occasions. He professed to be of the most moderate principles in religion and government; although a churchman, yet far from high church; and he attended the weekly lecture at Boston with great reverence, and professed great regard and esteem for the preachers."[2] The General Court was wont to adjourn to attend the Thursday Lecture. On one such occasion Hutchinson relates this anecdote of the governor: "Among the more liberal was one Bullivant, an apothecary, who had been a justice of peace under Andros. Lord Bellomont, going from the Lecture to his house, with a great crowd round him, passed by Bullivant standing at his shop door loitering. 'Doctor,' says his lordship with an audible voice, 'you have lost a precious sermon to-day.' Bullivant whispered to one of his companions who stood by him, 'If I could have got as much by being there as his lordship will, I would have been there too.'"[3] The earl was popular here, and, though he could not persuade the General Court to fix a settled salary for the governor, they voted him in grants, during little more than a year, £1,875 sterling, — more than any other governor ever received, and half as much again as he had calculated upon.

It is highly probable that Captain Kidd, during the few days when he braved it in the streets of Boston, before his sinister fame as a pirate had emblazoned his name in the shuddering memory of New England, went with the worshippers to the governor's church, and seemed to say his prayers.

In the Sergeant Mansion, which was later to be famous as the Province House, the Governor was hospitable alike to

---

land, by whom he had two sons, Nanfan and Richard. She lived in New York for some years after his death; but, returning to England, married Samuel Pytts, and died in 1737.

[1] "1699. Augᵗ 30. Recd of Capt. Foxcroft to pay mʳ Everard for my Lord's Pew £13." — *Church Records.*
[2] Hutchinson's History, ii. 112.
[3] Ibid.

THE CHURCH TAKES ROOT. 145

churchman and to puritan. The social place which Lady Andros had held was now filled by a charming person, who softened the spirit even of Judge Sewall: —

"July. 25 [1699]. Between 6 and 7, I have my Lady [Bellomont] up upon Cotton Hill, and shew her the Town. . . . As came down again through the Gate I ask'd my Lady's Leave that now I might call it Bellomont Gate. My Lady laugh'd, and said, What a Complement he puts on me! With pleasancy."

Still, her lord could not have avoided trouble in enforcing the authority which he had come to exercise. His commission commanded him "to allow no printing press to be kept nor any book to be printed without his leave." [1] In July, 1699, the General Court passed an Act giving the power of visitation of Harvard College to the King "and his governor," and excluding from the office of President, Vice-president, or Fellow, all "but such as shall declare and continue their adherence unto the principles of reformation which were espoused and intended by those who first settled this country and founded the College, and have hitherto been the profession and practice of the generality of the churches of Christ in New England." But the Governor arrested the Act, on account of "the exclusion of members of the English establishment from the academical government." [2]

Lord Bellomont, "wrote to the Lords of Trade that some persons in New England desired 'a Church of England minister,' and expressed his hope that they would 'patronize so good a design.'" The Board "interested themselves with the Bishop of London to obtain for the colonists the advantage of ecclesiastical supervision." [3] The governor was not over urgent, however, in presenting the wishes of the church to the home authorities: —

"Last session of the Assembly at Boston, the Petition was deliver'd me and the Council by the Ministers of the Church of England and Vestry Men. Your Lordships upon perusal of it will best judge whether the prayer thereof was reasonable. The Council would give it no countenance; they said the Act against incestuous marriages was found to be good and usefull, and that the King had been pleas'd to approve and confirm it in England, and they did not see cause for breaking in upon a

---

[1] N. Y. Hist. Col., 1868, p. 166.
[2] Palfrey, iv. 195.
[3] Journals of Board of Trade, Feb. 2, 1700, quoted in Palfrey, iv. 189. Palfrey is inexact, iv. 188, about the dispersion of the church at Andros's fall and Lord Bellomont's attempts "to revive it."

good law to please the humours of a few men. The truth is, as I have been informed, some loose people have sometimes come from England and married in New England, though they had left wifes behind them in England; and this law was calculated chiefly for prevention of such marriages. If a Minister of the Church of England will be at the pains of going to any town or place to marry people, nobody will hinder him." [1]

But the death of "the noble governor and vestryman" [2] in New York, soon ended both the hopes and the disappointments of the church.

[1] N. Y. Col. Mss., iv. 793. Earl of Bellomont to the Lords of the Treasury, New York, Nov. 28, 1700.

[2] The disposition to place a name of dignity at the head of the Vestry was later carried so far in Salem, that in 1744 Arthur Onslow, Speaker of the House of Commons in England, was chosen Warden of St. Peter's Church; Benjamin Gerrish, Jr., being appointed his proxy. Felt's Salem, ii., 597.

CHAPTER V.

GOVERNOR DUDLEY AND THE CHURCH.

ND now another royal governor was to excite the hopes and the disappointed wrath of the Boston churchmen. He came as the representative of a new monarch on the English throne. The passing away, March 8, 1702, of the great ruler whose name was the pride of Protestant Europe, which closes Macaulay's stately history as with a funeral march, cast its shadow across the Atlantic.

In May, 1702, "the awful Tidings of the death of our late Soveraign Lord King William, of everglorious memory," was "confirmed, . . . and, together therewith, the Intelligence of the happy Accession of the high and mighty Princess Anne of Denmark to the Throne."[1] There was mourning in the little church. The year was dark, too, at home; for it was one of great sickness in Boston and New York. The pestilence struck down a vestryman of the church: —

---

[1] Mass. Hist. Proc., 1866–67, p. 483. The official announcement from the Council of Massachusetts to Governor Winthrop of Connecticut.

"Jan. 8, 1702/3. Mr. Edward Turfrey dies of the Small Pocks. . . . He was a person of great Abilities. His death is a great Loss to the Town and Province: but more especially to Mr. Addington,[1] to whom Mr. Turfrey was extraordinarily Serviceable, having liv'd with him above Ten years. If real Worth and Serviceableness and Youth wont give a discharge in this warfare, what shall? He is universally Lamented."[2]

The accession of Queen Anne rallied to the throne the disaffected churchmen. The religious convictions of Queen Mary had been well known, but since her death, in 1694, it was felt that her husband's "early training quite incapacitated him for appreciating . . . the position of the Church as guardian of primitive and Catholic truth, while sympathizing with its negative character . . . as against corruptions of Rome." With him "had come from Holland a colder and more sceptical Latitudinarianism than the older type, as represented by the Cambridge divines. This school, as well as the Low Churchmen and Dissenters, had been Whigs, while the High Churchmen were in favor of the previous dynasty, but greatly weakened by the Nonjuring secession of many of their best men." In the speech at the close of her first Parliament, in 1702, the new Queen said: "My own principles must always keep me entirely firm to the interests and religion of the Church of England, and will incline me to countenance those who have the truest zeal to support it."[3] A *régime* of High-Church and Tory principles had begun, whose influence was felt in the spirit and temper of much that was done in the Queen's Chapel in Boston.

Before the decease of King William, Colonel Joseph Dudley had succeeded in obtaining his long-coveted appointment to the high office of Governor. Hated for his desertion of the popular party, a sharer in the downfall of Andros, as in all his most oppressive measures, ten years had passed since he went from the prison which he shared with the companions of Andros to a varied life in English employment. But his heart yearned for his native New England, and perhaps he hoped to efface men's blame of him by a worthy administration. He may have had hard measure in judgment from his contemporaries, which has also been repeated by our historians. But it is to be remembered that he came back from England as governor to enforce the very measures which, as agent of Massachusetts, he had been sent there to thwart. "His townsmen and former friends

[1] Secretary of the Province.
[2] Sewall's Diary.
[3] English Church in the Eighteenth Century, i. 59, 62, 277.

could not find an explanation for his course consistent with simplicity, unselfishness, and integrity. The providence was a dark one, as some one said, requiring, like the Hebrew letters, to be read backwards."[1] Of him Randolph had written in 1682: "If he finds things resolutely managed, he will cringe and bow to anything. He hath his fortune to make in the world."[2] No man was thought by the people here to have been more trusted, or more treacherous. Hitherto in New England he had been a Congregationalist, but now his attitude was to be more dubious. As Governor of the Isle of Wight, and member of parliament, Dudley must have conformed to the Church of England. His uncertain relation to its representative chapel here will appear as our narrative proceeds.

DUDLEY ARMS.

Increase Mather significantly preached: —

"There is more of the Divine Glory in *New England* than in all *America* besides; we have the greater cause not to be high-minded, but to fear.... That which our Great *Hooker* long since predicted, that *the People of* New England *would be punished with the want of Eminent Men to manage Publick affairs, both in Church and State*, is in part sadly verified."[3]

He was, however, received with all outward respect. Sewall describes the official welcome to Governor Dudley on board his ship, the "Centurion": —

"1702. June 11. — I was startled at 2 or 3 things, viz: ... I saw an ancient Minister; enquiring who it was, Gov' sd 'twas G— Keith; had converted many in Engl⁴, and now Bp. London had sent him hether

---

[1] Dr. G. E. Ellis, in "Memorial History of Boston," ii., 49.

[2] Hutchinson's Ch. Coll., ii. 271.

[3] "Ichabod; or, A Discourse showing what Cause there is to Fear that the Glory of the Lord is Departing from New England." Two Sermons, etc. Boston: 1702. The sermon consists of a lament on the Degeneracy of the land. The reverse of the title quotes Herbert's lines: —

"Religion stands on tiptoe in our Land,
Readie to passe to the American strand."

The popular suspicion of Dudley is shown by an order to a constable, Boston, Aug. 29, 1702, in the Mass. Archives, signed by Isaac Addington, summoning "Mr. John Boult, Merch', to appear before Her Maj's Justices of yᵉ Peace at yᵉ Townhouse in Boston to answer to what shall be Objected against him for makeing, publishing, or spreading a lybel or false report concerning his Excellency the Governour, in Saying That the Governour had demanded or askt of Mʳ Walter, viz', the Minister of Roxbury, his Pulpit for a Church of England Minister to preach in one part of the day on Lord's Days, with intent to make the Queen's Governour Uneasy and obnoxious to the People."

Dudley[1]

wth Salary of 200 Guineys p añum. I looked on him as Helena aboard. This man cravd a Blessing and returnd Thanks, tho' there was the Chaplain of y^e Ship and another Minister on board. Govr has a very large Wigg.[2] . . . He rode in Major Hobby's Coach, drawn with Six Horses richly harnessed.

[1] This portrait, given here by the courtesy of the publishers of the "Memorial History of Boston," perhaps represents Dudley as he appeared when President of Massachusetts in 1686. A portrait in the gallery of the Historical Society, giving him more gross and worldly traits, and with a huge wig, probably belongs to this later period in his life.

[2] The text, 1 Cor. xi. 14, led our ancestors to abhor the wearing of long hair.

"June 28. — Govr partakes of ye Lord's Sup̄er at Roxbury. In ye Afternoon goes to Boston to hear Mr. Myles, who inveighed vehemently agt Scism."

Dudley was a consummate politician, in the baser sense, and nowhere was this more evident than in his ecclesiastical relations. His conduct on this early Sunday after his arrival indicated the plan of ingratiation on both sides, of which he sought to avail himself. He retained his membership of the church in Roxbury, which he had joined in his youth, and before which he had preached, yet took an official place in the congregation of the "Queen's Chapel," as it was called after the accession of Queen Anne; and his name appears constantly on the list of vestrymen, with that of the lieut.-governor, it having been voted that these two magistrates should belong to the vestry from their office. He used the church to promote his interests; but, as will appear later, when the smouldering disaffection to him burst into flame, the church gave him little help.

The world must have seemed upside down to the Puritans, when they not only saw Joseph Dudley coming back to govern them, but the Quaker preacher who had bearded the Boston ministers in 1688, wearing the surplice. He came as a missionary from the Society for Propagating the Gospel in Foreign Parts,[1] to make personal examination of the state of religion in

---

Hutchinson (i. 152) says: "The rule in New-England was, that none should wear their hair below their ears. In a clergyman it was said to be the greater offence; they were in an especial manner required to go *patentibus auribus*." Sewall followed close after the fathers in his profound dislike to artificial hair. It was almost a conclusive test with him of a man's vital piety, whether he fell into the fashion then coming in. When Ezekiel Cheever, the renowned master of the Latin School, who had taught for 70 years, died, the Judge recorded of him: "A rare instance of Piety, Health, Strength, Serviceableness. The Wellfare of the Province was much upon his Spirit. He abominated Perriwiggs."

He wrote to his friend, Mr. Nathaniel Walter: "I thank you for bearing me company as far as you can in the fashion of your Head Dress. The Truth is, a Great Person has furnished me with Perukes, *gratis*, these Two and Fifty Years, and I cānt yet find in my heart to go to another." — *Sewall Letter Book*. The Judge records his fruitless expostulation with a young minister, June 10, 1701, and the result. "Sabbath, Novr 30 [1701]. I spent this Sabbath at Mr. Colman's, partly out of dislike to Mr. Josiah Willard's cutting off his Hair, and wearing a Wigg: He preach'd for Mr. Pemberton in the morning; He that contemns the Law of Nature is not fit to be a publisher of the Law of Grace: Partly to give an Example of my holding Com̄union with that Church who renounce the Cross in Baptisme, Humane Holydays, &c., as other New-english Churches doe."

[1] His selection for this duty was one of the first acts of the Society after its incorporation. Keith was born at Aberdeen, though not of Quaker parents. "He was well educated, and his talents were of a high order. His mind was acute and logical, and his temper fearless. In truth, the greatest defects in his character resulted from the indul-

the English Colonies in America. His travelling companion, whom he had chosen by the advice of Governor Dudley and other friends, was Rev. John Talbot.[1]

His interesting Journal[2] gives an animated picture of King's

gence of his temper. . . . He was honest, though scarcely amiable." He was in East Jersey, 1682, then a Quaker and surveyor-general. In 1688 he visited Boston and challenged the ministers to discuss publicly their doctrines, as being "false and pernicious to the Souls of People in many things." Their answer was brief and to the point: —

"Having received a Blasphemous and Heretical Paper, subscribed by one George Keith, our answer to it and him is, — If he desires Conference to instruct us, let him give us his Arguments in writing, as well as his Assertions: If to inform himself, let him write his Doubts: If to cavil and disturb the Peace of our Churches (which we have cause to suspect), we have neither list nor leasure to attend his Motions: If he would have a Publick Audience, let him Print: If a private Discourse, though he may know where we dwell, yet we forget not what the Apostle John saith, Ep. ii. 10."

He replied in a second letter. In 1689 he went to Philadelphia as a tutor, and won a high place as a Quaker preacher. "In 1691 he was again in Penn?., and now commenced his dispute with the Quakers. Their writers charged him with ambition, and he them with departure from the original doctrines held by the Society. Twenty-eight leading members issued against him 'A testimony of disownment' in 1692. He replied with a similar testimony against *them*, signed by himself and 'a considerable party' of adherents. He and his friends were called Christian Quakers; he charged his opponents with Deism. In 1694 he went to England and took holy orders. In April, 1702, he sailed for America. In August, 1704, he reached England and became Rector of Edburton, Sussex, where he ended his days." — *Prot. Episc. Hist. Soc. Coll.*, 1851, p. ix.

Mr. Bancroft (ii. 215, Centennial ed.) is severe upon Keith: "Keith was soon left without a faction, and made a true exposition of his part in the strife by accepting an Anglican benefice." These passages from "Two SERMONS Preach'd at the PARISH-CHURCH of St. *George Botolph-Lane*, LONDON, May the 12th, 1700. By GEORGE KEITH, Being his first Preaching after Ordination," are certainly surprising from so fresh a convert from his rooted Quakerism. He argues "That holy and righteous Persons may and ought to remain in a Church, and not separate from it. . . . This I the rather insist upon, because of divers I know are here, who are not of the Church of *England*; some of whom God hath made me instrumental in his great Mercy, to bring off from the vile Errours of Quakerism; yet it remains a Scruple with them to join with the Church of *England*, because, as is affirmed by many, she is Corrupt, at least with respect to the Practice of many, called her Members. . . . I freely confess I have been so prejudiced my self against all Set-Forms of Prayer, having the same Conceit that I find others now have; but I bless God I not only have seen the Errour of that, but have found by true Experience that to join with the Faithful in the Publick Prayers, in Set-Forms of sound Words, is so far from being any hurt, or cause to kill and extinguish spiritual Life in the Soul, that I have found my very Heart and Soul spiritually Refreshed and Comforted in joining therewith." Sprague, "Annals of the American Pulpit," v. 25, has a full notice of Keith.

[1] Afterward missionary at Burlington, N. J., a Nonjuror, and consecrated by Dr. Welton as a bishop. See Rev. Dr. Hills' "History of the Church in Burlington," and monograph, "John Talbot, The first Bishop in North America." On the monumental tablet to Talbot in St. Mary's Church, Burlington, N. J., is a fac-simile of his Episcopal seal, and the inscription, "A Bishop by Nonjuror Consecration, 1722. Died in Burlington, Nov. 29th, 1727. Beloved and Lamented." Sprague, "Annals of the American Pulpit," v. 30, has a notice of Talbot.

[2] Republished in Prot. Episc. Hist. Soc. Coll., i.

Chapel, and of Mr. Myles's interest in Keith's controversy with his former brethren, the Quakers: —

"At my Arrival the Reverend Mr. *Samuel Miles*, and the Reverend Mr. *Christopher Bridge*, both Ministers of the Church of *England* Congregation at *Boston*, did kindly receive me and the *two ministers* in company with me; and we lodg'd, and were kindly entertained in their Houses, during our abode at Boston.

"*June* 14, 1702, being *Sunday*, at the request of the above-named Ministers of the Church of *England*, I Preached in the Queen's Chappel

THE DOCTRINE
OF THE HOLY
Apoſtles & Prophets the Foundation
OF THE
Church of Chriſt,
As it was Delivered in a
SERMON
At Her Majeſties Chappel, at Boſton in New-England, the 14th. of June 1702.

By George Keith, M. A.

BOSTON.

Printed for *Samuel Phillips* at the Brick Shop, 1702.

at *Boston*, on Eph. ii. 20, 21, 22, where was a large Auditory, not only of Church People, but of many others.

"Soon after, at the request of the Ministers and Vestry, and others of the Auditory, my Sermon was Printed at *Boston*.[1] It contained in it,

---

[1] Keith's sermon, whose title we give in facsimile, is the earliest extant sermon preached in the church, although the Prince Manuscript records that Mr. Myles published in 1698 a funeral discourse on Mrs. Elizabeth Riscarrick.

towards the conclusion, Six plain brief Rules, which I told my Auditory did well agree to the Holy Scriptures; and they being well observed and put in Practice would bring all to the Church of *England* who dissented from her.[1] This did greatly Alarm the Independent Preachers at *Boston*. Whereupon Mr. *Increase Mather*, one of the chief of them, was set on Work to Print against my Sermon, as accordingly he did, and Published a small Treatise against the said six Rules, wherein he labored to prove them all false and contrary to Scripture, but did not say any thing against the Body of my Sermon."

Mather's reply was entitled: "Some Remarks on George Keith's sermon, Showing that his pretended good rules in Divinity are not built on the foundation of the Apostles and Prophets." Boston: 1702. He answers each of the six rules in turn, and proceeds:—

"It is not our opinion that all Forms are unlawful. . . . Indeed, we look upon the *Imposition* of Forms as sinful, but not all use of them.

---

[1] This important sermon contained the following points: "1. (Against the Church of Rome and the Quakers), The *Scriptures* the foundation; 2. Jesus Xt the principal foundation; 3. The unity of the Church of Christ." Under this head he speaks of the evil of divisions, and particularly says:—

"Many born and bred in the Church of *England*, denying her to be a true Church of Christ, which God hath so eminently owned to be his. . . . The which Church began the Reformation from Popery in the English Nation, and in that respect is the Mother Protestant Church of them all. And whoever denys or disowns her, as too many do of various sorts, do show themselves to be undutiful Children, unless they can prove her to be degenerate, which I am well persuaded they can never do.

"And for my part, I freely acknowledge my great error and sin in my uncharitable censures of her, and separation from her some time ago; and I pray God to open the eyes of others, as he hath in his great mercy open'd mine, to see their error and sin of uncharitableness and separation, that they may confess it and return into the bosom of their Mother, which is open to receive them, as it hath been open to receive me and many others, upon our repentance and amendment." In order to "heal up the *breach* if possible," he lays down six "good Rules in Divinity," viz.:

1. Obedience to Superiors, where it is not contrary to God's commands in Holy Scripture. 2. "Whatever Church holds the fundamentals of Christian Religion, and has the Word of God duly Preached, and the Sacraments of Baptism and the Lord's Supper duly administered," is a true Church of Christ, and separation from it is Schism, only excusable "when anything is enjoyned to persons that is really sinful and contrary to God's Commands given us in the Holy Scriptures; not what men by prejudice of Education or by wrong information say is sin, but what really is so, and can be clearly proved to be so out of the Holy Scriptures: And if they cannot joyn in one or some external acts of Worship, because sinful, yet in other acts they ought to joyn that are not sinful." 3. Defects of individuals are not to be charged upon the whole Church, unless the Church justifies them. 4. "To joyn in external acts of publick Worship where the matter is sound, though there be a great mixture of unsound members with the sound, is no sin, but our duty." 5. Whatever was commanded or practised under the Old Testament (except the Ceremonial Law and things peculiar to the Jewish Polity) is still binding. 6. "Set Forms of Prayer and Thanksgiving (where the people pray vocally with the Minister) are a duty as well under the New Testament as the Old."

It were much better for men that have not the *gift* of Prayer to use a *Form* in their Families, than not to pray at all. . . . *George Keith* wrote a very wicked Book in the year 1689, full fraught with Heeresies and Blasphemies, and with Revilings and Slanderings of the Ministers and Churches of Christ. Had he made a penetent acknowledgment of his great sin therein, and published to the world his detestation of that Book of Blasphemies, that would have been a better evidence of the sincerity of his *Conversion* than this *Sermon*, which strikes at the most Reformed Churches on Earth. He has reason to walk softly all his days, from the consideration of the hurt he has done to the Souls of men, not a few having been either perverted or confirmed by him in the damnable Heresies of *Quakerism*. . . . For him who has himself been as great *Schismatick* as ever was any *Donatist* in the world, *now* to insinuate that all the holy churches of *Non-Conformists* are *Schismaticks*, and yet at the same time to scatter his Sermon up and down, with a *Schismatical Design* to make Divisions (if he could) in the churches of *New England*, by seducing and *corrupting them from the simplicity that is in Christ* to another mode of Worship never taught nor practised by the Apostles, deserves severe reproof. . . . So careful were those *Men of God* who laid the foundation here, to keep exactly to *Scripture Pattern*. . . . *Conformists* are in *New England Dissenters*, there being but one or two *Conformist* Congregations in all *New England*, and those not the greatest; but more than one hundred congregations of *Non-Conformists*. Since our Churches, notwithstanding his making them *Schismatics and Sinners*, are built on the true Foundation, it is to be hoped that if an hundred *George Keiths* should come to seduce them, and to *pervert the right wayes of the Lord* among them, they will not forsake that *pure Religion* which their Fathers have left them in the possession of. The *little Foxes* who have sought to *spoil these Vines* have not hitherto prospered. . . . If Mr. *Keith* and those that abett him would follow my (or rather *Gamaliel's*) advice, they should refrain and let these Churches alone, *lest haply they be found even to fight against God.*"

Keith's rejoinder was entitled: "A Reply to Mr. Increase Mather's Printed Remarks on a Sermon Preached by G. K. at Her Majesty's Chapel in Boston the 14th of June, 1702, in vindication of the six good Rules in Divinity there delivered, which he hath attempted (though very Feebly and Unsuccessfully) to refute." New York: 1703.

"This I had Printed at *New York*, the Printer at *Boston* not daring to Print it, lest he should give offence to the Independent preachers there. . . .

"*June* 21. I preached a second Sermon at the Queen's Chappell, on *Rom.* x. 6, 7, 8, 9.

"*June* 28. The Reverend Mr. *John Talbot*, who had been chaplain in the *Centurion*, Preached there."

Keith also had a controversy in print with President Willard about doctrines asserted by him at Commencement, — as " That the Fall of *Adam*, by virtue of God's Decree, was necessary."[1] He went to Lynn, Salem, and elsewhere, and returned to Boston.

"*August* 2. I Preached again at the Queen's Chappel there on *Philip.* ii. 13, and next day set out from *Boston* accompanied with the Reverend Mr. *Samuel Myles*, one of the Ministers of the Church of *England* Congregation there, and we arrived at *Newport* in *Rhod-Island* the next day, where we were kindly received. Mr. *Lockyer*, the Church of *England* Minister there and diverse others of the Church came from *Newport* and met us at the Ferry, and conducted us to the Toun and place of our Lodging. Mr. *Talbot* stayed at *Boston* to officiate in the Church there for Mr. *Myles*, until his return.

"*August* 6. I went to the Quakers' Meeting at *Newport* on *Rhod-Island*, accompanied with Mr. *Myles*, Mr. *Lockyer*, and many People belonging to the Church there. . . .

"After one of their Preachers had spoke a long time, and came to an end, having perverted many Texts of Scripture, . . . I began to speak, standing up in a Gallery opposite to the Gallery where their Teachers were placed, who were many. . . . But I was instantly interrupted by them very rudely, and they were very abusive to me with their ill-Language, calling me Apostate, etc., and they threatened me with being guilty of the breach of the Act of Tolleration, by which they said their Meetings were Authorized.

". . . Mr. *Myles* said I ought to be heard, I being a Missionary into these *American* parts, by the *Society for Propagating the Gospel in Foreign Parts*, sent on purpose to endeavour to reduce the Quakers from their Errors, the which Society hath a Patent from the Crown of *England*, and not to hear me, nor suffer me to Speak, was a Contempt of Supream Authority."

Keith then appealed to Governor Cranston, who was present, but who avoided the difficulty.

---

[1] This was entitled "Refutation of a dangerous and hurtful opinion maintained by Mr. Samuel Willard, an Independent Minister, etc., and President, etc. New York: 1702." It was answered by the President in "A Brief REPLY to Mr. *Geo. Keith*, in ANSWER to a Script of his *Entituled A Refutation* of a *Dangerous* and *Hurtfull* Opinion, Maintained by Mr. *Samuel Willard*, etc." Boston: 1703. The thesis was, "That the Immutability of God's Decree doth not take away the liberty of the Creature." The answer is a very able statement of the Calvinistic Doctrine of the Divine Decrees. An Appendix shows clearly that the "Truths maintained are agreeable to the Established Doctrine of the Church of England."

"The Governor at this went away, and Civilly said to me he thought I had done better to have stayed till they had done. I told him then they would be gone, as they had served me at *Lynn*, at *Hampton*, and at *Dover*." [Then] " one of their Speakers, who was the Deputy-Governour, . . . took out of his Pocket a Printed abusive Paper full of Lies, having no Name to it, and began to read it in the Meeting on purpose to drown my Voice, that I might not be heard. The Title of it was, ' *One Wonder more: or George Keith the* eighth Wonder of the World.' . . . Mr. *Myles* said it was an Infamous Libel, without a Name to it, and it was a shame for such a man as he, being Lieutenant-Governour in the Place, to read such an Infamous Libel against any Man, on purpose vilely to defame him. After he had done, another Quaker Preacher, who had been formerly their Governour, began to preach. . . .

"At last the first Speaker made a long rambling Prayer, full of Tautoligies and vain Repetitions and presumptuous Boastings, as their manner is. . . .

[Then] " All their Preachers went away, and many of the Quaker Hearers, but many of them also stayed. . . . I had now full liberty without any interruption to speak, perceiving the Auditory generally desirous to hear me."

So he went into the Quaker meetings everywhere, though Mr. Myles appears not to have accompanied him further.[1]

We now come to a painful episode in the history of the church. It has already been related that the Rev. Christopher Bridge was sent by the Bishop of London to be Mr. Myles's assistant. He was an educated English clergyman, a graduate of St. John's, Cambridge, where he is entered on the books as " Cestrensis." He was born at Tillington, Essex, son of the Rev. Robert Bridge, educated at Chester School under Mr. Hancock, and was admitted Sizar of St. John's College for Mr. Stillingfleet, June 4, 1689, æt. 17, Tutor, Mr. Wigley. He took his B.A. in 1692–93, and never proceeded M.A., which is accounted for by his going to America.[2] He was at first cordially welcomed, but in the long run brought no edification to the church.

The Earl of Bellomont wrote to the Bishop of London: —

"Mr Myles and Mr Bridge are good Preachers; I will give them all the countenance and encouragement I can. Our church here is very

---

[1] After arriving at Philadelphia, he had a controversy with his former brethren, the Quakers, one of whom, C. Pusey, published " Proteus Ecclesiasticus; or, G. Keith varied in fundamentalls, etc., and proved an apostate." Philadelphia: 1703. Keith answered in "The Spirit of Railing Shimei, and of Baal's four hundred lying prophets entered into C. Pusey, etc." New York: 1703.

[2] I am indebted to Rev. J. E. B. Mayor, of St. John's College, for these facts.

neat and convenient, but 'tis too small; and Mr Myles tells me a great many more people would come to our church if there were room for 'em."[1]

From the Records: —

>At the Kings Chappell in Boston
>Munday the 9th of October 1699.
>Present
>Mr. Christopher Bridge, Minister.
>William Hobby, Warden, etc.

It being proposed on the behalfe of Mr Christopher Bridge, that he should be allowed for the Tyme by him expended in London and on his passage hither in order to his cominge over to be assistant to Mr Miles, he havinge ben ingaged upon that service for the space of six monthes before his arrivell hear, att which Tyme his allowance of forty shillings p weeke began.

Agreed. That the said Mr Bridge, in Consideration above said, be paid Twenty-five pounds, and that the Wardens accordingly pay the same unto him out of the proceeds of the Goods rec^d from England for the Use of this Church.

>Tuesday, March the 24th, 1701.

At a meeting of the Vestry at ye Exchange Tavern kept by David Johnstone.

>Agreed. That Mr Bridge have the £100 p Ann. Ster^g. that is allowed by the King, he running all risques, Beginning the s^d Annuity at Easter next.
>Orderd. That Mr Foxcroft brings in his acc^o.
>Aprill 21th 1701. It is ordered by the Vestry that if the King's bounty mony be withdrawn,[2] the Church is to allow Mr Bridge his Sallary of 40/ p Week.

Mr. Bridge took part in the vestry meetings, as well as the rector.

July 24th 1701. By a Vestry met at Mr John Walker's.
P^{r}Sent Mr Saml Myles, Mr Chris: Bridge, etc.
Order'd, That Clerk Hill shall wash ye Church once in a month during the Summer; Sweep it twice in Every week, and brush the dust off the Seats, Shelves, and tops of ye pews; Shall go out and appease ye boys and Negros and any disorderly Persons; to provide a seat for Strangers according as they appear; to ring the bell, Open the doors and windows and Shut them as formerly, and take care of the books, etc'.

---

[1] N. Y. Col. Docs., iv. 582.
[2] In consequence of the death of King William.

Memorandum   Boston, Decemb: 20ᵗʰ 1703.
          Att a meeting of the Vestry,[1]
P'Sent   his Excellency, Joseph Dudley, Esq'. Governour.
         his Honour, Thomas Povey, Esq'. Lieu' Governour.
         M'. Samuel Miles, Minister.
         M'. Christopher Bridge, Minister.
              Coll Foxcroft. | M'. Jnᵒ Nelson.
              M'. Edwᵈ Loyd. | M'. Giles Dyer.
              M'. East. Apthorp. | M'. Nich'. Roberts.

Then Ordered That the Church Wardens for the time being within ten dayes after Easter day reckon with M'. Myles, and at his direction call a vestry and give us Notice of what is wanting of three pounds a Weeke, which wee promise for ourselves and the Auditory Shall be made up within ten days after./.

Then Ordered that the repairs of the Church from time to time be at the discretion of the Ministers and Church Wardens, Saveing in any Great Article./.

But the cloud soon gathered. George Keith had written, —

"At Boston . . . the Ministers live very regularly and are in good esteem, and the Churches in good order, and the people generally devout and well affected to the Word and the publick worship of God."[2]

But Mr. Talbot spoke more plainly:—

". . . To begin then where we began our Travells, at Boston, New England. There is one Church, and there were two ministers, both sober and discreet men in the main, and I believe would have done good service at a distance. They were both our Friends, and I could wish they had been so to one another, or that those representations were true that are now gone to his Grace and to the Right Reverend Bishops of the Corporation, which say they parted good Friends; but to say the Truth as it is, there is such a variance that the Church can't flourish between them."

The misunderstanding between the two evidently began early. Governor Nicholson wrote from Virginia to the Archbishop of Canterbury, May 27, 1700: —

"I am heartily sorry . . . that there is no very good understanding between the Revᵈ Mr. Miles, of Boston, and Mr. Bridge, about Rhode

---

[1] The names of those present at the meetings are always recorded, but will be hereafter omitted for lack of space.

[2] Prot. Episc. Hist. Soc. Coll., i. pp. xxiii., xli.; Keith to Dr. Bray, Feb. 24, 1703-4, and Talbot to the Secretary of the Venerable Society, April 7, 1704.

Island; but I am not troubled that there are like to be divisions amongst the N. Englanders, especially at Boston and Charlestown." [1]

At the close of 1703 Mr. Bridge went to England, partly to solicit subscriptions for the church, bearing credentials from

"*The Governour of New England and other the Members of the Church at Boston to his Grace the Lord ARCHBISHOP of CANTERBURY.*

BOSTON, 23ᵈ December, 1703.

May it Please Your Grace, — The Reverend Mʳ Bridge, one of the ministers of our congregation, who hath faithfully served his cure and station among us, has obtained the consent of the Reverend Mʳ Myles and the vestry to take a voyage into England to wait on Your Grace; and we should be wanting to our duty to Religion and to him, if we should not recommend him to Your Grace's favor, having in all things in his doctrine and manners been an honor to the Church. Our hopes are by Your Grace's favour to him and ourselves, that Your Grace will obtain for him a good establishment of his maintenance here. Mʳ Myles we hope will be well supported by the contribution; and if Mʳ Bridge, by the Queen's Bounty might be well assured of his support, they would with great honour carry on the service here.

We have further to pray of Your Grace, that since our congregation is increased in number (tho' not so much in estate) that our church is too little for us, we may obtain assistance for the building a new one. The French congregation here have no convenient place to meet in, and if we might be assisted with what may be necessary for a new stone church, ours would be of convenient use for them.[2]

In all other things relating to an account of our Present State, we humbly refer Your Grace to his attendance. And we humbly ask Yoʳ Grace's Favour for him and for ourselves, and are,

My Lord, Your Grace's most obedient Servᵗˢ

J. NELSON. J. DUDLEY.
THOS. NEWTON. THOMAS POVEY, etc."

Mr. Myles followed this action of his vestry with the following letter to Dr. Beveridge: —

BOSTON, N. E., 4 Janʸ 1703-4.

"*Revᵈ Sʳ,* — I formerly wrote by Mʳ Honyman (who is since returned hither) to forward the sending ministers to several towns in this Country,

---

[1] Hist. Coll. Church in Va., p. 121.

[2] The Huguenot colony established by Andros at Oxford had been broken up by the Indians in 1695, and its members coming to Boston formed the French church, which gradually declined in consequence of their intermarriage in other churches. January 1704-5 they bought land, but being refused permission to build, it was delayed for ten years or more. See Mr. C. C. Smith's chap., viii., in Memorial History, ii.

and I hope you will be mindfull and concerned about the same. My Lord of London and D[r] Bray can inform what pains I have taken not only where I am settled, but in many places in this Country, and I bless God with very good success. But the Dissenters are so busie and indefatigable, that I fear the delay in sending ministers according to the Petitions may be Prejudicial. And, therefore, I do now agen renew my request, having this opportunity by a very worthy person of our church and vestry, the Hon[ble] Col[l] Charles Hobby, who has exercised the power and authority he has been invested with, both civil and military, with great integrity, justice, and prudence. And as he has been enabled by a very plentifull fortune, so has his charity and beneficence been very large on all proper occasions to the poor and needy, and his behaviour and deportment so affable, Gentle, Corteous, and obliging to all, as has purchased him a fair esteem and reputation, respect and honor, especially from all affairs of his regiment, and as on the account of his personall worth and desert. I take myself obliged on this occasion to do him this justice so to express my gratefull sense of his great and constant Kindness and Friendship to me. I can do no less than earnestly intreat all Favour and respects to be showed to him, and that he may be brought acquainted with such as may assist in any of his Interests and concerns, he being altogether a stranger in England.

And because M[r] Bridge, my assistant, is now coming for England without my Lord of London's Orders, Leave, or knowledge, and has left the whole work on me without my consent, he not complying with the conditions I proposed, nor allowing time to provide any other assistant, and during his stay here has caused much trouble and uneasiness among us to the prejudice of our Church and Interest, — I do humbly and earnestly pray you would use your interest with my Lord of London to send some other worthy person in his room and to supply his place, who may go on unanimously with me in all our undertakings and performances, be a comfort to me, and maintain and set forward Love and peace among our people, instead of encouraging any that have pique or disaffection, and so make parties and cause division among us to the great prejudice of our Publick Interest. If I obtain these my requests, you will highly oblige your

Most humble Servant,
And most Faithful Friend,
SAMUEL MYLES.

P. S. I humbly intreat you to be vigorously concerned about these matters, and, if possible, to prevent M[r] Bridge's coming here again, who has been full of Falsehood and Dissimulation, and has done us more mischief than our open enemies." [1]

---

[1] This letter was fortified by one from Mr. Brown of Swansea, to the Archbishop of Canterbury, Feb. 23, 1703: "M[r] Myles of Boston has been very diligent and much concerned for our good settlem[t]; and to inform our people in the Way of the Church has not only several times preached among us, but put such

How long Mr. Bridge's absence lasted is not recorded, but he must have returned before August of the following year. Meantime, Mr. Myles did the duty alone, and, though nominally receiving £3 weekly, obtained only what the contributions afforded, — the amounts sometimes going as low as £1 or even less, so that his salary was heavily in arrears.

At a Vestry 27th Sept.r 1704.
Made up acc.ts w.th M.r Miles for the yeares 1702 and 1703, viz.t :

Paid him by E. Lyde for the yeare 1702	£135. 05. 00
Paid him by D.r Checkley for the yeare 1703	139. 14. 04
To a Bill of Exch.a of Col.o Nicholson's for £15 sterl. at 36 p c.t exch.a is this money.	20. 08. 00
To a Bill of Exch.a of Col.o Nicholson's for £10 sterl. at 36 p c.t exch.a is	13. 13. 00
To so much Col.o Nicholson ordred him this money	3. 00. 00
	£312. 00. 00 [1]

Mr. Myles's uneasiness was justified by his assistant's conduct; for the latter, having this estrangement, broke open a letter of Mr. Myles (perhaps the one just given, which may have been entrusted to him in his voyage), and sent it to the Archbishop of Canterbury and to the Bishop of London, thinking to injure Mr. Myles by disclosing its contents. Hereupon, the Bishop of London sent an order for Mr. Bridge's removal, and depriving the church of part of its allowance of £100 from the royal treasury for the support of an assistant. In consequence of this turn of affairs, a vestry meeting was held, to draw up articles of peace between the discordant ministers. All this history is written in the stained and venerable parchment-book of records, where the autograph signatures of the two ministers are still clearly to be read.

Books as Bishop King's and D.r Beveridge's 'Usefulness of the common Prayer,' etc., into the hands of the people in our Town; and having sent a considerable quantity of Books to me, I Lent them severally according to his direction and my direction, so that many among us are better informed than formerly by M.r Myle's assistance, who has likewise been unwearied in his endeavours for the good of the people in severall towns; and being of a kind and condescending temper is ready to embrace all occasions that may present to oblige people, and has this advantage to recommend him above some others, — that he has never been under the imputation of any scandal in the country (I have known him from his childhood)." This and the two preceding letters are taken from Perry's Church Documents, Mass., pp. 73-75.

[1] The provincial currency had heavily depreciated.

By an adjournment of the Vestry from Thursday the 16th of August to Saturday the 18th, and from thence to Sunday after evening service, being the 19th

Voted, that the Church Wardens do draw up such Heads, as relate to a settlement and agreement between the Reverend Mr. Samll. Myles and the Reverend Mr. Christopher Bridge.

And that a Letter be writ to the Lord Bishop of London relating thereto, and signed by them in behalf of the Vestry and Congregation of the Church of England.

BOSTON, NEW ENGD. Augst 22 : 1705.

Whereas, through misunderstandings, there has been Sundry differences risen between the Reverend Mr. Samuel Myles and the Reverend Mr. Christopher Bridge, and has been of very ill consequence, tending to the Dissolution of the Congregation of The Church of England in these remote Parts, to prevent which very great and earnest endeavours have been Used by His Excellency The Governour, The Honourable Lieutenant-Governour, the Church-Wardens and Vestry, for accommodating and Reconciling all Matters and affaires, to which they have solemnly and happily consented, Viz!

1st. That they mutually promise not to take part with (or in the least contrive or abett) any Persons in doing, saying, or reporting anything that shall tend to the Damage or dishonour of either, or give any adheerance to any such reports, or by anyways endeavour to alienate the affections and esteem of the People from each other.

2. That they shall as much as lies in their Powers promote the peace and wellfare of the Church, and at all times use their utmost endeavour to secure and advance the just Interest and Satisfaction of each other.

3. That they shall not undertake to officiate in any other place then the Church where the Reverend Mr. Samuel Myles is constituted Minister, and the Reverend Mr. Christopher Bridge Assistant, without the full concurrance and approbation of each other, and to their equal advantage and benifitt.

4. That the Reverend Mr. Christopher Bridge shall never pretend to or take any perquisites by Marriages, or any otherwise, belonging to the Reverend Mr. Samuell Myles, as Minister of the Church, and appropriated to him by the Bishop's especiall order.

5. That if for the future any offence shall unhappily rise between them, the Party aggreived shall truely and ffreely discover and discourse the other ; and if the offence be of such nature that they cannot overcome and Compose the differences themselves, that then they shall represent it to the Governour of this Province for the time being, and Church Wardens and such other Persons as Mr. Myles

and Mr Bridge shall mutually agree upon; and then, if not composed before, to be represented to the Ordinary at the Liberty of them both.

6. That the Reverend Mr Samuel Myles as Minister of this Church, and the Reverend Mr Christopher Bridge Assistant, shall never without the concurrance of each other (much less in opposition) at any time, or on any account, give orders to Warn any Vestry, or give any countenance or approbation to it, without knowledge and consent of each other.

7. That what allowance the Reverend Mr Samuel Myles ought to have for performing the whole work during the absence of the Reverend Mr Christopher Bridge be referred to His Excellency the Governour, the Lieutenant-Governour, Church Wardens, and Vestry of said Church.

8. I, Samuell Myles, in Testimony of my full and hearty reconciliation unto or with the Reverend Mr Christopher Bridge, my assistant, do concurr with the Prayers and desires from this Church to My Lord Bishop of London for the continuance of said Mr Bridge as formerly.

Samuel Myles

Chris: Bridge

Witness,

N. ROBERTS, } Church Wardens.
J.^o NELSON,

May it Please Your Lordship, — Whereas we have been informed that some of our former proceedings have been by ill-minded men rendred clandestine, we cannot omitt noteing to Your Lordship, that it is now and always has been composed of men of the best Reputation, and from whom the Church receives both Countenance and Support.

BOSTON, Augt 24, 1705.

May it Please Your Lordship, — Att a meeting of the Vestry on Thursday the 16th Ins.^t, Coll^o Francis Foxcraft communicated a Letter to us, which Your L^dShip was pleas'd to Send him, which to our great Surprise and Astonishm.^t imported your L^dShip's displeasure w.th Mr Bridge, wth His removall from us and part of the Sallary from this Church, wch Wee presume is Ocasion'd by Sundry misinformations to Your Lordship of His Carryage.

After some Discourse Wee adjourned to Sunday Evening, being the 19th Inst., where in the Church were His Excellency Our Governour, the L̃t Goṽr, Mr Myles, Mr Bridge; where, after some Debate, it was voted that wee, the Church Wardens for the present Yeare, should Draw up some heads that should Tend to the thorrough good Understanding, Peace, and Satisfaction of them both. And upon their agreeing and Signing sd Articles, *Voted*, that Wee Should Inclose them to Yr Lordship, giveing You an Accot of the State of the Church as it now Stands relating to this Affaire.

1. The first wee have done; and when presented to them they very willingly and Chearfully Signed it, to the great comfort and satisfaction of us all. And now wee are bound in Duty to represent Mr Chris. Bridge to Your Lordship, as his carryage has been to us eversince His first arrivll — that it has not been Proud, Lofty, and Haughty, but of a Courteous, agreable Deportment to Us all, as becomes His Proffession and the Gospell, and so very acceptable to Us.

2. On the 20th of Decr 1703: at a Vestry Present the Goṽr., Lieutt Govr, the two Ministers, and many of the Cheife of the Church, — some few that were Absent haveing had timely Notice, — in the Conclusion it was thought Proper for the Interest and Advantage of the Church that Mr Bridge should go to England in Order to obtaine Subscriptions for the enlargeing Our Church, and what Other advantages Your Lordship should be pleased to favour Us with. Our Governour was the Last consenting to it, but comply'd with it seeing the Gentlemen of the Church so Desirous of it, and being ready at all times to Gratifie us in anything that can be thought to tend to the Promotion and Growth of the Church here.

3. Wee perceive Your Lordship is highly Displeas'd with Mr Bridge his intercepting and breaking Open a Letter, which if true would very Justly Deserve your Resentment, which Wee need not parraphrase upon since nothing can be said more than the Inclosed Affidavitt,[1] which clears him of that aspersion. The Vestry, haveing throughly examin'd and acquainted themselves with all the Originall Causes and Reasons of the Differences between Our Ministers, find them to proceed from Ill offices, Lying Reports, and misrepresentations; and those so triviall and frivolous that, since Seriously considered, is not nor ever was worth while to Mention, and much more to trouble Your Lordship. Whoever it is that has been so bussie has done neither Service to God, Honr to himselfe, or Studied the Peace and tranquility of the Church in these remote Parts.

Wee are very sencible, and have great Reason as in Duty bound, to express all possible Gratitude for Your Lordship's great care of us in promoteing of the Church here, and presume to conclude that the removall of Mr Bridge was intended and Designed for the benifitt and advance-

---

[1] The affidavit is missing from the Records, as is also the Bishop's letter to Colonel Foxcroft.

ment of the Church, — Your Lordship thinking him Guilty of such Crimes and misdemeanours as would be justly thought a Calumny and Reflection to the Church here to continue him amongst Us.

Since Wee have sufficiently cleared Up to Your Lordship that it is quite Otherwise than has been represented, Wee make bold humbly to begg the continuance both of the Sallary and of Mr Bridge's Stay with Us, especially since there is so good an accommodation between him and Mr Myles, and will be for the promotion and establishment of Us, which otherwise might have proved of fatall consequence by the Dissolution of the Church here, there being many who wait for and would greatly rejoice at Our halting and Destruction.

Finding the Evill misrepresentation of matters to Your Lordship, if not proved to the Contrary would be of fatall Consequence to the Church by the removall of either of our Ministers which are both in all respects worthy of our esteeme whether in regard of their Doctrine, Life, or Conversation, which is as becomes the Gospell, — therefore wee humbly Pray to Your Lordship not to adhere to any private insinuations that may be made, assuring Your Lordship that from time to time a true State and Condition of the Church shall be Laid before You from the Church Wardens by order of the Vestry.

Wee are truely and Deeply sencible of Your Lordship's especiall protection and Care hitherto towards Us which emboldens Us in this Plaine and free manner to offer our Prayers and informations, hopeing Your Lords^p will accept of it as a Performance of our Duty, haveing with all Sencerity sett forth the truth of matters. Wee are with all Submission

To the R^t Reve^d Father in God,   Your Lordship's
Henry Ld Bishop of London.   Most humble
                                   Most Dufull and
                                   Most Obedient
                                      Servants,
                          NICH^o ROBERTS } Church
                          JOHN NELSON } Wardens.

But the Bishop of London had made up his mind, as was to be expected from so strong and decided a prelate. The see was at this time occupied by Henry Compton, youngest son of the Earl of Northampton, who had been translated from Oxford to London, Dec. 18, 1675. He died July 7, 1713, aged 81 years. With statesmanlike grasp of his difficult duties, he governed the colonial church. His administration of the see of London is memorable for the rebuilding of St. Paul's cathedral, which "was commenced by Sir Christopher Wren about the time of his induction, and he lived just about long enough to see its completion. He was wise, energetic, moderate, and munificent. 'The princesses Mary and Anne (both successively queens of

England) were educated, confirmed, and married by him, and he also crowned the former, together with her husband, William III." He was suspended from his episcopal functions by James II. Sept. 6, 1686, for refusing to suspend Dr. Sharpe for his sermons against popery, but was restored on the apprehended approach of the Prince of Orange, Sept. 23, 1688. "He warmly interested himself to bring about the revolution of 1688, and was afterward one of the commissioners for the reform of the liturgy, in which enterprise his own liberal and tolerant intentions were unhappily defeated." His spirit of moderation is said to have rendered him less popular with the clergy, and to have probably hindered his advancement to Canterbury.

"From such a bishop, it was to be expected that whatever demanded attention in the way of duty, however distant it might be from the place of his residence, would be attended to in a proper manner. In answer to the representations of the church here he sent a letter, which is marked throughout by a practical good sense, joined with good feeling, which show that he was well fitted for his responsible office. It is to be clearly seen from it that he was not a man to be trifled with, and that having authority, he was determined to exercise it in a steady and decided manner, and as much for the real benefit of the church as possible."[1]

"The Copie of my Lord of London's Letter," say the records, "is as ffolloweth:"—

GENTLEMEN,—I am sorry with all my heart you have so little concerned yourselves for the peace of ye church, as to uphold a Controversy which may so easily be laid asleep ; and whilst those two gentlemen are together upon the same place I doe not see how it euer will be effected. As to y^r imagining that I might too easily blame Mr. Bridge concerning the letter of Mr. Myles wch was broken open, I can assure you the first copy I saw of it was sent up in triumph to London, either by Mr. Bridge or his Order, from Plymouth or Portsmouth, soe that I took it not at second hand ; though I blame Mr. Nicholls Extremely for promoting that which he must needs know could produce nothing but Animositie, but can by noe means Excuse Mr. Bridge ; and, indeed, I hope there is none among you that can approve of that malitious practice of spreading about Copies of this letter, wch must needs breed very ill bloud among you. But I say this rather for my own Justification, than that I would quarrell any further wth Mr. Bridge on that account ; and therefore I shall not be soe earnest for his remouall, otherwise than that I am con-

---

[1] Greenwood, History, pp. 63, 64.

vinced it is impossible for him and Mr. Myles to live togeather in peace. I know his spirit is too high to submitt to that Subordination which it is absolutely necessarie he should comply wth whilst he stayes at Boston; soe that I would by all means advise him to goe to Narragansetts, where he may have an hundred pounds per añum sterling, besides what perquisites he may make upon the place; and there he will be his owne Master.

You must likewise give me leave to tell you that I think you have made a great mistake in one of the articles of reconciliation wch you have drawn up, where you have in a manner sett Mr. Bridge upon an Equall foot wth Mr. Myles, by making the call of a Vestry depend upon their Joynt Consent, whereas Mr. Bridge hath nothing more to doe in the Church than that Mr. Myles shall direct him, as he is the Curate and Assistant; wherefore you must pardon me if, affter all the due regard I have for you, I must deale soe plainly with you as to tell you that you have been carried on too far in this matter by some that have more respect of persons than for the reall good and peace of the church. I know I shall be forced at last to recall Mr. Bridge, and therefore I wish you would persuade him to make it his owne Choice to retire to some other place, where he shall find me his Sincere freind, notwithstanding all that has been said.

I pray God direct you for the best, and desire you would beleive me, Gentlemen,

· Your most assured friend and servant,

H. LONDON.

Postscript. — I forgot to give you a more particular account in the inclosed of Mr. Bridge's proceedings in that letter of Mr. Myles; that he writt from the Port in England, before he went away, to Mr. Wessendunck, to take care to communicate that same letter, or the Copie, to my Ld Archbp. of Canterbery and myselfe; wch I think is evidence enough of his concerne in it.

H. LONDON.

Fulham: feb: 12: 1705-6.

The effect produced by this letter may be seen from the following record, which precedes the copy of it: —

Boston, Sept. 23, 1706. — Att a meeting of the Vestry at Mr. Paule Dudley's,[1] his Excellency being present, my Lord of London's letter was read relating to Mr. Bridge his removall to the Narrowgansetts etc.; to which he complied, and wished me, Savill Simpson,[2] to tell Mr. Myles that he left the Charge of the Church wholly to his care, and intended to goe to Narragansetts in three days.

---

[1] Later, chief-justice, founder of the Dudleian Lectures at Harvard College, one of which vindicated congregational ordination.

[2] Junior warden this year.

"Thus was this very disagreeable affair terminated, affording, most probably, some matter of triumph to the many who, as the wardens in their letter to the bishop express it, waited for and would have greatly rejoiced at the halting and destruction of the Episcopal church."[1]

Mr. Bridge's heart sank at the prospect before him in the rude region of Narragansett, "not capable of providing any comfortable Habitation for a Family, . . . but especially on the account of whom I shall have to do with, when by means of lewd and illiterate fellows that have set themselves up for Teachers, and, undervaluing the Holy Scriptures, have propagated only their own unaccountable notions, are overrun with the grossest errors and heresies, and sunck into the depth of wickedness. To reduce such will be a work to which I know myself very unequal, and should be very glad to see one of better abilities employed in it."[2]

Mr. Bridge now took up his abode in Kingston, R. I., where he again became entangled in difficulties with his brethren, having apparently appropriated the ground to himself for missionary purposes without regard to their rights, first at Narragansett and then at Newport.

"Poor Mr. Honyman is much disturbed at Rhode Island by Mr. Bridge, who says he has a letter from my Lord of London to take his place; if so, he will ruin two Churches at once. Pray help your Countryman what you can, for he is worthy."[3]

Mr. Honeyman was a missionary of the Society for Propagating the Gospel in Foreign Parts, who had gathered a church at Narragansett, and had been appointed to Trinity Church, Newport, in 1704. He "returned to England upon his private affairs in 1708," doubtless to seek redress against the invader of his peace, but came back to Newport, and had a long ministry there.[4]

---

[1] Greenwood, p. 67. In the difficulty between Mr. Myles and Mr. Bridge, it is probable that the fault did not lie wholly on one side. Mr. Myles seems to have been of an irascible temper. At the very period of this controversy, Judge Sewall records: —

"Aug. 24, 1705. Mr. Samuel Myles came with his Bro⁁ before me; I bid him Sam. sit down: but he quickly fell upon Nichols the complainant ag⁁ his Bro⁁, and said by his Looks one might see the Gallows groan'd for him. I check'd him, and said it did not become a Minister so to speak." Perhaps "Nicholls" was the person by that name mentioned in "My Lord of London's Letter."

[2] Church Docs. Mass., p. 79.

[3] Rev. Mr. Talbot to Mr. Keith, Westchester, Feb. 14, 1707-oS, in Conn. Church Docs., i. 37.

[4] See Anderson, Col. Ch., iii., 446, 457. Rhode Island offered a field to the church missionary. Mr. Pigot wrote in

To Mr. Honeyman's visit home, it is probably due that the strong hand of the Bishop of London reached across the sea and compelled Mr. Bridge to remove again to Rye, N. Y., in January, 1710. Here Episcopacy was so recognized by law that he was practically the minister of the town. "The number of those who profess themselves of the Church of England" was 313 out of 799 inhabitants of the parish, 43 being communicants. "Many of the Dissenters come sometimes to church." He reported to the venerable Society in 1710 that there were "seven families of Quakers in his parish, and four or five families inclining." These were probably Keithians.[1] In 1712 he recorded his success in a disputation with some whom he calls "ranting Quakers;" "they have never since held a public meeting in these parts." There were many Friends in the "Purchase." One of their preachers was convinced by the rector's arguments, and came sometimes to church; "but it pleased God, soon after, to take him out of the world." The Quakers kept Mr. Bridge busy, coming over in great numbers from Long Island to hold their meetings near him. "It is my constant care to watch their motions, to prevent their seducing any of my parishioners."[2]

Mr. Bridge "finished his uneasy pilgrimage" at Rye, Friday, May 22, 1719, and, like his excellent predecessor, Mr. Muirson, was buried in the parish church.[3] His former parishioner, Dun-

---

1724: "The inhabitants here are generally well inclined to the Church of England, but not so much out of principle as out of opposition to the Massachusetts profession. For these Providence people, by bordering upon them, having formerly felt the lash of their resentments, are now utterly estranged to their persuasion." — *Conn. Church Docs.*, i. 87.

[1] Members of the party that, under George Keith's lead, separated from the Friends in Pennsylvania in 1691, but retained many of their peculiarities.

[2] Baird's "History of Rye" states that the records of the Vestry of Rye begin Jan. 9, 1710-11. Until Mr. Bridge's time, the justices and vestry appear to have held their sessions without the presence of the minister. July 29, 1712, came an order from the Government that "every Orthodox minister be one of the vestry in his parish." The building was known as "Grace Church" as early as 1736; its legal designation, however, was "The Parish Church of Rye." The town had been settled in 1660. A church was built by the town in 1705, under Rev. Mr. Muirson. The people were too poor to "maintain two differing ministers," but on Mr. Bridge's death the Presbyterians attempted to get possession of the church, regarding themselves, as the more numerous party, as having at least an equal claim to the property. They apparently succeeded, and met in it until another rector was inducted three years later. After this the Presbyterians maintained separate worship, and resisted taxation for the support of English rectors. See Baird's "History of Rye," pp. 310-322.

[3] Mr. Bridge had married Elizabeth Foxcroft. If she was daughter of Colonel Francis Foxcroft, this may explain the strong hold of her husband upon his parish. Letters were granted Oct. 8, 1706, appointing him guardian of his two children, Christopher and Thomas, who were then under fourteen years of age, and had received a bequest from their mother's great-uncle, Henry Layton, of

can Campbell, said in his obituary of him: "He was formerly for many years together one of the Ministers of the Church of England in Boston, a Religious and Worthy Man, a very good Scholar, and a fine, grave Preacher; his performances in the Pulpit were Solid, Judicious, and Profitable; his Conversation very agreeable and improving; and, though a strict Church Man in his principles, yet of great Respect and Charity to Dissenters, and much esteemed by them. He was bred at the University of Cambridge in England, and was about 48 years of Age when he Died. Very much lamented."[1]

An important factor in our history is the close connection between the Bishop of London and the church, whose salutary effect has been noted in the discipline of Rev. Mr. Bridge. It is difficult to trace clearly the whole course of this "accidental connection" of the incumbent of the great metropolitan and commercial see with the church in the American colonies. It began, however, in Virginia, where, in pursuance of the first royal grant by King James in 1606, it had been ordered that "the true word of God should be preached, planted, and used, according to the rites and doctrines of the Church of England. In 1620, the number of clergymen there being less, by one half, than the number of parishes, it was the duty of the 'Virginia Council,' which sat in London, to supply the deficiency. The Bishop of London, Dr. King, had taken a deep interest in the prosperity of the plantations." He was accordingly asked to assist in providing "pious, learned, and powerful Ministers," and was made a member of the Council. Thus grew up this jurisdiction, which was resumed without question after the Restoration. "At length, in 1675, the Committee of Trade and Plantations 'desired that inquiry be made touching the jurisdiction which the Bishop of London hath over the foreign plantations.' What caused the inquiry is unknown, but no return was made to it. In 1679, however, the instruction given to Lord Culpepper, at that time appointed governor, clearly shows that the Bishop of London was not supposed to have any *jurisdiction*, for he had nothing but a mere ministerial office assigned him; the Governor had the power to prefer to ecclesiastical benefices in the colony, and the only notice taken of the Bishop of Lon-

Leeds. Mrs. Bridge married Rev. Thos. Poyer, of Jamaica, L.I., about 1720. In October, 1736, Dr. Cutler recommended for Orders "Christopher Bridge, son of a late worthy Missionary in these parts. He has been an orphan for many years, educated by Dissenting friends, and graduated M.A. at Harvard College; and is now, upon conviction, recovered into the bosom of our church, . . . a man of abilities and very good life."

[1] Boston News-Letter, June 1–8, 1719.

don was in requiring of the person preferred a certificate from that prelate that the candidate is 'conformable to the doctrine of the Church of England.' In 1681 the Governor of Jamaica was instructed to report to the Bishop of London all ministers who officiated in the island without 'being in due orders.'

"In 1685 the Bishop of London proposed to the Committee of Trade that he should have all ecclesiastical jurisdiction in the West Indies, except the *disposition of parishes, licenses for marriage, and probate of wills*. This was approved of, and the governor was directed to give all countenance and encouragement to the exercise of ecclesiastical jurisdiction in the island by the Bishop of London, except in the particulars enumerated, as to which the power was conferred on the governor.

"Similar instructions were given to all the other colonial governors; and under this authority Bishops Compton and Robinson, and for a few years Bishop Gibson, exercised jurisdiction in the plantations. But in 1725 Bishop Gibson desired more explicit authority and direction, and for that purpose applied by petition to the king in council. The petition was referred to the attorney and solicitor-general, who stated it as their opinion that the Bishops of London had all acted by an authority which was insufficient, and that the ecclesiastical jurisdiction of the colonies did not rightfully belong to any bishop in England, and that the most proper mode of conferring on any person the right to exercise such jurisdiction was by *patent*.

"A patent was accordingly granted to Dr. Gibson, but it was to him personally, and not as Bishop of London. His successors were not named in it, so that the patent expired with his life; nor did any of his successors ever obtain another, but acted without one."[1]

---

[1] "Efforts to obtain the Episcopate before the Revolution, by Francis L. Hawks." Prot. Episc. Hist. Soc. Coll. i. 136-157. See also Conn. Church Docs. i. 31. Even during the Commonwealth it was provided in Virginia that ministers should be of the Church of England, and "in the direction of Church affairs to be admitted into the respective vestries. The method of obtaining a living there was by a license from the Bishop of London, and collation by the governor. Vestrymen erroneously think themselves the *Masters* of their parson." — *Church Docs.*, Va., p. 3, *et al.*

The paternal supervision from abroad of American Christians was not peculiar to those of the English Church. "The Dutch congregations in America were ruled by the Classis of Amsterdam in the same manner. Candidates for the ministry, in the one church as in the other, were obliged to go to the mother country for ordination." — *Mag. of Amer. Hist*, Oct. 1879, p. 625.

The petition of some inhabitants of Boston in 1679 (see p. 36 *ante*), that a church might be allowed, is said by Dr. Hawks to have called the attention of Dr. Compton more particularly to the state of the Church in the colonies, and resulted in his proposing to various parts of America to supply them with clergymen; and on his application to the king,

Thus Fulham became to the American Episcopal clergy "the seat of their ecclesiastical allegiance," although the bond was a frail one to stretch three thousand miles; and the need of an American Bishop, which early began to be felt, as is shown in the subsequent chapter, grew and was pressed on the Home Government, urgently but vainly, till the very eve of the Revolution.

To the Puritans, with Dudley's coming, all seemed given over to the hostile cause.[1]

"Thorsday, Octr 1, 1702. — The Govr and Council agree that Thorsday, Octr 22, be a Fast-day. Govr moved that it might be Friday, saying, Let us be Englishmen. I spake agt making any distinction in ye Days of the Week; Desired the Same Day of ye Week might be for Fasts and Thanks-giving. Boston and Ipswich Lecture Led us to Thursday. Our Brethren at Connecticut had Wednesday, wch we aplauded.

"X^r 19. — Heard ye Ch. Bell ring for Capt. Crofte. He dyed last night. X^r 19. Is buried in ye New burying-place in Capt. Hamilton's Tomb. Corps was first had into ye Ch. and a Funeral Sermon preachd. For Debauchery and Irreligion he was one of ye vilest Men y^t has set foot in Boston. 'Tis sd he refused to have any Minister calld to pray with him during his Sickness, which was above a fortnight.

Dies Capt. Crofts, A vile man.

[1704.] "Lord's Day, Apr. 23. There is great Firing at the Town, Ships, Castle, upon account of its being the Coronation-day, which gives offence to many; see the Lord's-day so profan'd. Down Sabbath, Up St George!"[2]

The supremacy of the Queen in matters of religion was brought home afresh to New England in October, 1705, by a Rescript disallowing an Act of the Colony of Connecticut, entitled "Hereticks," which had enacted fines against Quakers and "all who shall Entertain any Quakers, Ranters, Adamites," etc.[3]

In 1704 a member of the Queen's Chapel, Postmaster Campbell, began to publish the first newspaper issued in Boston; but it records nothing of the dissensions here.

Governor Dudley soon found himself in angry waters. In July, 1704, he wrote to the Lords of Trade: "The election of Counsellors is scandalously used . . . to affront every loyal and

---

[1] Cotton Mather, ever vigilant, published "Seasonable Testimony to the Doctrines of Grace, fetched out of the Articles and Homilies of the Church of England." Boston: 1702.

his majesty granted a bounty of £20 to each minister who would go over to the colonies, and instructed the governors to permit none authoritatively to serve any cure of souls "unless he was licensed to do so *by the Bishop of London.*"

[2] Sewall's Diary.
[3] Mass. Hist. Proc., 1866–67, p. 501.

good man that loves the Church of England and dependence on her Majesty's government." No grant was voted him by the House. He wrote, Nov. 27, 1704, to the Secretary of State: "I humbly ask your Honor's favor and patronage for me in my difficult part with an angry people that can hardly bear the government nor Church of England amongst them, and, while my care is to keep them steady to Acts of Parliament, will make me as uneasy as they can."[1]

Lieut.-Governor Povey went home to England weary of his position here, and was followed by a memorial from members of the Queen's Chapel in February, 1706, praying that he might be sent back "with a good establishment, both for the governor and himself, to put them beyond the power of a difficult and ungrateful people."[2] At the same time, the senior warden, John Nelson, wrote to the Secretary of the Board of Trade, Feb. 11, 1706, that he was "informed of the endeavors of a faction who are busy to reinstate themselves into the government." There was no reasonable "complaint against him [Dudley]; but that which displeases is his care and attendance on the Church of England," and his fidelity to the Home Government.[3] Governor Dudley held communication with the venerable Society in regard to "the encouragem' of young Scholars to enter into Holy Orders" in October, 1706, promising to give it. "I pray

---

[1] British Colonial Papers, quoted in Palfrey, iv. 292. In November, 1705, Governor Dudley, hoping for "promotion to the extensive government enjoyed by Andros, charged Connecticut with many maladministrations; among them, with obstructing members of the Church of England as to their freedom of worship." Ibid., iv. 367.

[2] British Colonial Papers, quoted in Palfrey, iv. 299. It is possible that Rev. Thorowgood Moore, a victim to Lord Cornbury's brutality, may have preached for Mr. Myles at this time. That Tory governor of New York and the Jerseys presumed on the fact that he was cousin to Queen Anne to browbeat the Episcopal missionaries in his jurisdiction, churchman though he was.

Dr. Hills, in his "History of the Church in Burlington, N. J.," p. 74, relates that Rev. Thorowgood Moore and Mr. Brooke, who had been imprisoned by him, after escaping, sailed for England from Boston, where Rev. John Talbot met him in November, 1707. Mr. Talbot remonstrated against their taking a winter passage, "but poor Thorowgood said if they were sunk in the sea they did no doubt but God would receive them, since they were persecuted for doing their duty to the best of their knowledge." Mr. Moore's will, witnessed by Rev. Samuel Myles and others, is given by Dr. Hills.

Lord Cornbury denied that the Act of Toleration extended to the Plantations, and was equally despotic to the Presbyterians. See Force's Tracts, vol. iv. "A Narrative of a New and Unusual American Imprisonment of Two Presbyterian Ministers, and Prosecution of Mr. Francis Makemie, One of them for Preaching One Sermon at the City of NEW YORK. *By a Learner of Law and Lover of Liberty.* Printed for the Publisher, 1707." Makemie was found not guilty, but had to pay costs, £81 4s. 9d. He was the founder of Presbyterianism in America, in 1684.

[3] British Colonial Papers, quoted in Palfrey, iv. 299.

you," he wrote, "to assure My Lord Archbishop and that Reverend Society that I truly desire by all methods of their Directions, as well as by a good example personally, to put forward Religion and the Church of England as I ought."[1]

Dudley's name appears at the head of subscribers to various letters of the church, but his connection with it was evidently regarded as doubtful by the best churchmen, while he himself made much or little of it as might suit his own interests.[2] In 1706 the deep grudges against him burst forth, and a strong effort was made to secure his displacement by the appointment of Sir Charles Hobby. The governor was accused of being responsible for the failure of the Port Royal expedition, and of complicity with Vetch and others in the illegal trade with the French; but he succeeded in weathering the storm. Feeling in the church was evidently divided in the matter. Mr. Myles was probably a friend to Hobby; Nelson, to the governor, — while Thomas Newton, another prominent churchman, was censured by Dudley for signing the charges against him.

Sir Charles Hobby " had been knighted, as some said, for fortitude and resolution at the time of the earthquake in Jamaica; others, for the further consideration of £800 sterling . . . Hobby was a gay man, a free liver, and of very different behaviour from what one would have expected should have recommended him to the clergy of New England."[3]

Charles Hobby (signature)

---

[1] Church Documents, Massachusetts, p. 80. Mr. Bridge at the same time expressed his pleasure that the Society was willing to encourage "the Young Students of this College, knowing some of them to have very good parts, sound principles, and to be well affected both to the Government and Worship of our church, . . . and only kept back from offering themselves by the censures and reproaches of some few leading men." Ibid., p. 79. Mr. Bridge and the governor also agreed in recommending Mr. Daillé, the minister of the French congregation, who was "Episcopally ordained, and many years past sent into these parts by the Bishop of London," for a grant from the Society.

[2] Dr. Colman, in his funeral sermon on the governor, "Ossa Josephi," says: "He was in principle a Calvinist, according to the manifest doctrine of the Church of England in her Articles. He preferred the way of worship in our churches, and was wont frequently to say that he loved a great deal of ceremony in the government, but as little as might be in the church."

[3] Hutchinson's History, ii. 153. Sir Charles failed to displace Dudley, however. He was warden of King's Chapel 1713-15, and died in 1715, but not in Boston. His estate was insolvent. Of his inventory, April 23, 1716, "deeds for half the Province of New Hampshire" (bought of Thomas Allen, Esq., in 1706) is one of the latest items, but, as in derision, put down at nothing. Seven slaves are at the head, whose aggregate is £300. His widow was buried Nov. 17, 1716. In 1711 Sir Charles was appointed deputy-governor of Annapolis, Nova Scotia, and he accompanied Colonel Nicholson on his expedition to Canada. He was son of William Hobby, warden of King's Chapel in 1693 and 1699-1701.

Yet he was recommended by the Mathers and other pious ministers.

At a later period, when a fresh effort to displace the governor was to be made, the ministers of the Queen's Chapel would put on record their distrust of him and their favor to Hobby.[1] At present, however, the church lent its powerful aid to retain Dudley in his place, as its records show: —

BOSTON, NEW ENGL? Febru. 4, 1705/6.

May it Please Your Lordship, — The constant Experience Wee have of Your Lordship's fatherly care over Us encourageth Us freely to adress Your Lordship, being sencible of your great regard and esteem for His Excellency Our Governour.

Therefore Wee are humbly Bold to Informe Your Lordship that he has been very Successfull in His Government for the Security of the Country from the Indians, to the Observation of all Her Majestie's Good Subjects, the Enimie haveing been often Defeated and the Frontiers preserved more than in any former Trouble.

That notwithstanding the Taxes have been and are very Burthensome to Support and Carry on the Warr Wee are engaged in against the French and Indians, who in conjunction have done us much mischief, yet through the noted Prudence and good Conduct of His Excellencie the Enimie have not only been repulsed but are now constrained to abandon their own Countries and Places of retreate, unto some hundreds of miles Distance from these Parts. The Administration of the Governm! and Expence of the Revenue is and has been such as gives a Gen" Satisfaction, and makes us Easie and thankfull unto God for Her Majestie's Wisedome and good Grace to us in appointing such an one over us, who by his Long experience in Government and knowledge of the Country in Particular renders him (as we humbly conceive) the most proper Person to promote and maintaine the Hon! and Interest of the Crowne here. Everything proceeding well, except the Gov? own Sallary, which is by no means Sufficient, notwithstanding Her Majestie's repeated Comands in the matter.

That His Constant attendance and Care for the Peace of the Church and Support and Hon! thereof is apparent to all men, as well as His Example of Justice and Vertue. Upon all which Acco! Wee are humbly Bold to Informe Your Lordship that His continuance in the Government will be most Acceptable to all Her Majestie's Good Subjects, Merchants and Planters, that have their Dependance on the Government of England as well as the Churche here ; and therefore Humbly Pray Your Lordship's favourable Acceptance and Representation of this Our Adress as need be for Coll° Dudley's Continuance in the Governm!, which we are well assured will be to Her Majestie's Honour, the Peace and Satisfaction of this Province, and most Particularly of Our Selves and the Congregation

---

[1] See the letters of Messrs. Myles and Harris in chapter vii.

of the Church of England. Under Your Lordship's care and Patronage here We are

My Lord,
With all Submission,
Your Lordship's
Most Humble,
Most Dutifull,
And Most Obedient
Servants.

Gyles Dyer.	Sam.ᴸᴸ Myles.
Sam.ᴸᴸ Checkley.	Chris Bridge.
Antho: Blount.	Nich⁰ Roberts, ⎱ Church
John Devin.	John Nelson, ⎰ Wardens.
Thomas Child.	
John Eastwick.	
Cyprian Southack.	John Endicott.
John Redknap.	Edw.ᴰ Lyde.
Peter Hawksworth.	Easte. Apthorpe.
John Oulton.	Samu.ᴸᴸ Baker.
Ra: Harrison.	Savill Simpson.
Benja: Mountfort.	Henry Francklyn.

Wee have avoyded troubling Your Lordship with a number of names, These being the Chiefe of the Church.

To The Right Rev.ᵈ Father in God,
Henry Lord Bishop of London and one
of Her Majestie's most Hon.ᵇˡᵉ Privy Councill.

At the same time the following letter was sent: —

To The Most Rev.ᵈ Father in God, His Grace, Thomas Lord Archbishop
of Canterbury, and one of Her Majestie's Most Hon.ᵇˡᵉ Privy Councill.

Boston, N. E., Feb. 7, 1705 6.

May it Please Your Grace, — Wee are humbly Bold to address Your Grace, being the Ministers, Church Wardens, and Communicants of the Church of England in Boston in New Engld, to acknowledge your fatherly care of Us at all times and to pray the Continuance thereof, being the only setled Church in this Province, and to assure Your Grace that Wee Shall continue Stedfast in our Profession and Obedience as Wee Ought. And it is Our Duty humbly to Informe Your Grace Wee have been allways assisted and encourag'd by Collo: Dudley Our Present Govern.ʳ, who by His Constant attendance an Good Example has eversince His being in the Governm.ᵗ put Us forward; and haveing been informed of Your Grace's favour to Him in Her Majestie's Appointm.ᵗ of Him to this Governm.ᵗ, Wee pray that Your Grace will please to be assured from Us that nothing will tend more to the Satisfaction and encrease of the Profession of the Church of England, as well as trade and Other benifitts to all Her Majestie's Good Subjects here resideing, than his continuance in the Governm!, which Wee humbly pray Your Grace will please also on Our behalfe to represent to Her Majestie as need be.

And Wee shall ever Pray for Your Grace's Long continuance in the Governm! and Service of the Church.

Wee are Your Grace's
Most Humble,
Most Dutifull,
and Most Obedient
Servants. [1]

Such urgent pleading was successful, and Dudley retained his place till another monarch ascended the throne.

The Queen's Chapel congregation did not decline in numbers notwithstanding the unfortunate dissension between its minister and his assistant.

At a meeting of the Vestry and Congregation of the Church of England at the Queen's Chappel in Boston in New England, on Easter munday, Ap^r 9th, 1705.

Nicholas Roberts, continued, } Church Wardens.
and John Nelson, Esqr.,

His Excell^y Joseph Dudley, Esqr, Capt Gener^l and Gove^{nr} in Cheif, His Honour Thomas Povey, Esqr, Lieu^t Governour [and nineteen others], were Chosen Vestrymen for the year Ensuing.

It being offered at the Vestry that the Gentlemen and principal persons be new Seated and Pews Assigned them, the Minister and Church wardens are desired further to take Care that ye Pews be So Disposed that all persons may have their Places, and may have Liberty to put Locks upon their Doors, and that what is So done may be of Effect.

The cause of the church was strengthened by the character of its vestry and wardens,[2] among whom Messrs. Lyde, Checkley, Nelson, Newton, Simpson, and Tailer gave it distinction.

---

[1] This letter is subscribed in the same manner and with the same names, omitting J. Rednap and J. Endicott, and adding Wm. Tayler.

[2] Edward Lyde, Warden 1701, 1702, 1703. Son of Edward Lyde, who married, 1660, Mary, daughter of Rev. John Wheelwright, and died 1663. The son married (1) 29 Nov., 1694, Susanna, daughter of Capt. George Curwen; (2) 22 Oct., 1696, Deborah, daughter of Hon. Nathaniel Byfield, by whom he had a son, Byfield Lyde, H. C., 1722; and (3) Catherine Brinley. His daughters married Francis Brinley and George Cradock, both of whom were prominent in King's Chapel. He died May 11, 1724, having been judge C. C. P. for Suffolk from Dec. 9, 1715, to March 20, 1722-23. See Sewall, iii., 337.

S. Checkley. This is not the deacon of the South Church, of whom an obitu-

GOVERNOR DUDLEY AND THE CHURCH. 179

In the long roll of wardens, no name is more worthy of honor than that of John Nelson (1705-1707), who had now returned from his long captivity.

Soon after taking prominent part in the overthrow of Andros, being in Nova Scotia on mercantile business, he was taken prisoner and carried to Quebec, where, obtaining intelligence of an important expedition preparing in Canada against the Penobscot and Piscataqua settlements, at the great risk of his life he communicated the designs of the French to the government of Massachusetts by procuring two Frenchmen to bear the information, who, after doing so, were retaken, carried to Canada, and executed as deserters. Mr. Nelson was led out with them, in expectation of sharing their fate. They were shot before his eyes; but he was remanded to prison, and soon after sent to France; and succeeding, when on his passage, in prevailing on a fellow-passenger to carry information of a second project of the French against the English colonies.

In France he was confined[1] in a small dungeon for two years, without being permitted to see any one except the person who gave him food through a grate. At the expiration of this time, a gentleman who had noticed these daily supplies had the curiosity to inquire who the prisoner was, and to speak to him and offer his services. Mr. Nelson desired no other favor than the transmission of a letter from him to his friends in England; in consequence of which a demand was soon after made for his exchange. This gave him some importance, so that he was removed to the Bastile; where he remained until shortly before the close of the war, when he was allowed to go to England on

CHECKLEY ARMS.

ary notice is found in the "Boston News-Letter," 4 Jan., 1739, who was born Oct. 14, 1753, and died January, 1739; was town clerk of Boston and father of Rev. Samuel Checkley (b. Dec. 27, 1723, H. C., 1743, successor of the Mathers as minister of the Second Church). The warden of King's Chapel is thought by Savage to be cousin of the deacon, nephew of Anthony (p. 91, *n.* 14), and son of John, who was in Boston 1645.

[1] I am indebted to Mr. S. A. Drake for a copy from the French records of the order of the Minister of War enjoining his close confinement : —

"à Versailles, le 28 Jan., 1693.

"Monsieur, — M. de Marcagnel m' ayant donné advis de l'arrivée du Sr Nelson prisonnier Anglois qu'il est important de garder soigneusement et m'ayant fait sçavoir qu'il n'a pu le faire mettre que dans les prisons Royalles Je vous envoye pour le faire transferer au château d'Angoulême. Il est nécessaire que vous recommandie a celuy qui y commande de le garder surement et d'empêcher qu'il n' ait aucun communication surtout avec les nouveaux convertys parceque c'est un homme dangereux."

his parole, a French gentleman giving bonds in £20,000 for his return. Soon after, the peace of Ryswick was concluded; and, his situation and conduct having excited attention, he was pre-

JOHN NELSON.[1]

sented to King William, who asked if he intended returning to France, saying that as the war was ended he need not do it. Mr. Nelson replied that it was his intention to return, and mentioned the security which had been given for him. The king, with warmth, repeated that it was unnecessary, and forbade him

[1] The portrait, from the "Memorial History of Boston," ii., by the kindness of the publishers, represents Nelson in his old age.

to do it. "Will your Majesty then pay my bonds?" was asked. "No!" said the king. "Then," Nelson replied, "please God I live, I'll go!" and go he did. After delivering himself up in France he was discharged, and returned to England, where he was brought into trouble for going back to France contrary to the king's order; but at length returned to his family, after ten or eleven years' absence. His private concerns had suffered extremely, nor did he receive any compensation from the royal or the provincial government. Probably his manly honesty prevented it from the one, and his religious opinions from the other.[1]

A pleasing picture was drawn of the old age of such a man, by Dr. Timothy Cutler, in a sermon on the death of John Nelson, Esq., Nov. 15, 1734, and of Mrs. Elizabeth Nelson, his consort, Oct. 25, 1734, entitled: "The Final Peace, Security, and Happiness of the Upright."

"He was always a profess'd Member of Church of England; Her Admirer, Friend, and Advocate, in Times and Places the least favourable to Her.

"With a very good understanding, improved by Education and Travel, the Spirit and Temper of an ancient and worthy Family appeared in him; Genteel, Enlarged, Liberal, contemning mean and sordid Actions. He passed through many Changes and Events of Life, remarkable in their own nature, and though troublesome and dangerous in *Themselves*, and detrimental to his *Family*, yet neither dishonourable in the *Occasion* or the *Improvement* of them. He was unmoveably attach'd to what he tho't just and right, couragious in bearing Witness against and reproving Vice, a Despised of this World, a Lover of his Country, acceptable to his Family, . . . universally affable, courteous, and hospitable. . . . He had a true Regard to Religion and Religious Men, and reverenced the Mysteries and the Demands of it; . . . and with this Temper he closed a Life of fourscore and one Years, fearing GOD, and calmly and quietly trusting in his Mercy.

"And this, after the Example of his worthy Consort, who a few Days before him passed to a happy Immortality. She was the *Virtuous Woman; whom*, etc. This is but a *due* Acknowlegement to her prudent, handsome, frugal Management of her Family; Her patient, submissive going

---

[1] This account is condensed from a letter from Senator James Lloyd to Samuel Breck, 1817, in Mass. Hist. Proc., 1863-64, p. 370-372. Nelson's life is the subject of the picturesque romance "Captain Nelson," by Mr. S. A. Drake. In right of his wife Elizabeth, he was heir and executor with others of Lieut.-Governor Stoughton. He was son of William, to whom Sir Thomas Temple, whom he calls his uncle, had made lease of his patent rights in Nova Scotia.

through the Troubles of this Life, whereof God saw meet to allot her no *small* Share; Her open Heart and open Hands to the Necessitous; Her industrious seeking and cheerful embracing all Opportunities to Good; her Contempt of the World; Her great care to instruct and Counsel her Children in what was good, and to set them a bright Example of it.

"A Person adorned with Innocency and so many Vertues is prepared to quit the World in the peaceable manner that she did; not so much concern'd for the Success of the Physician, as for the Salvation of God, — Which she prepared for by the humblest Addresses to Him, an entire Reliance on the Merits of our Savior, and closing up all in a joint Communion with her beloved Consort in the Body and Blood of Christ. Shortly after which she *slept in Jesus;* and all such as do so, God will bring with Him."

Another warden is commemorated by a tablet placed on the walls of the church in 1853.

SACRED TO THE MEMORY OF
THOMAS NEWTON, ESQUIRE,
One of the
Original Founders of this Church,
A member of its first Vestry,
In 1699,
And a Warden,
In 1704,
And afterwards;
Who died on the 18th June, 1721,
Aged 61 years.

"He was many years one of the
Principal Lawyers in the Province,
And filled various places
Of honour and trust here;
And at the time of his death
Was Attorney-General,
Comptroller of the Customs,
And had been
A Judge of the Admiralty Court.
He was a Gentleman of exalted virtues,
And greatly beloved,
And respected,
Both in this Country,
And in England,
Where he was born and educated."[1]

---

[1] The inscription concludes:—
This Monument is erected by his great-grandson,
EDWARD AUGUSTUS NEWTON, Esquire,
Of Pittsfield in this State;
Under a sense of obligation to the
Memory of a distinguished Relative,
And eminently worthy Man.

Mr. Newton came from New Hampshire, and was secretary of that Province until 1690. Savage says: "His opinion as Attorney-General in the witchcraft prosecution must have led to the cure of the infernal delusion, for in January, 1693, he wrote to Sir Wm. Phips, the Governor, that, of the fifty-two charged at

An obituary notice of Mr. Newton says: —

"He was a Gentleman born in *England* the 10th of *June*, 1660, being *Whitsunday*, and Died on the Lord's Day the 28th past, being also Whitsunday, in the 61 Year of his Age. He was Educated there, and intirely beloved both there and here by all that knew him; one who carryed himself very handsomly, just, and well in every Station and Post which he sustained, being Affable and Courteous, of a Circumspect Walk and Deportment and inoffensive Conversation, of Strict Devotion towards GOD, exemplarly for Family Government, as well as Humanity to all his Fellow Creatures. A Lover of all Good Men, and therefore the more Lamented at his Death."[1]

Savil Simpson was warden, 1691, 1706–8. Of his early history little is known; his place of birth does not appear. He resided in Boston as late as 1708. July 4, 1687, he bought the land granted to Colonel William Crown, which was included in Framingham and Hopkinton. He was rated in Framingham in 1710, and made justice of the peace in Hopkinton, where he probably took up the first land for farming purposes in that town.[2]

Prominent in serving the church was Colonel William Tailer,

Salem, the three convicts should have been acquitted like the rest."

Lord Bellomont wrote, on appointing him King's Advocate in the Admiralty Courts, 1699: "An Englishman born, which I confess is one quality I shall always desire to meet with in men that I recommend to employment in these plantations." He signed the petition for Dudley's removal in 1707, for which he was "convented before the Council." See Palfrey, iv. 177, 303; Sewall, ii. 55, 131; N. E. Hist. and Geneal. Reg. xxxi. 59.

[1] News-Letter, May 29–June 5, 1725.

[2] A plantation of 631 acres eastward of "Magunco Hill" (Magunkaquog) was surveyed for him in 1689. This land now comprises the centre and western portion of the town of Ashland. He died Aug. 22, 1725. His will made June, 1716, proved January, 1725–26, mentions his sons-in-law Anthony Blount and John Jones, and grandchildren Thomas Eyre, Anne and Sarah Lawson, Mary and Elizabeth Jones. His descendants are numerous in the towns of Framingham, Hopkinton, and Ashland. Of his children can be traced: Jane, born Sept. 13, 1680, married (1)

Anthony Blount, (2) in 1730 Stephen Arnold of Warwick, R. I., brother or nephew of a Benedict Arnold.

Savil, born Oct. 15, 1681.

Samuel, born February, 1682.

Elizabeth, born March 5, 1684; married May 12, 1713, Col. John Jones of Boston. He was received from the church in Boston to the church in Hopkinton, Mass., 1727, where he removed with his family, and died there Feb. 7, 1773, aged 82 years. He was the first representative from Hopkinton to the General Court, and was prominent both in Boston and Hopkinton. He was thrice married, and left a large family and much property in lands, money, slaves, and mills.

Deborah, married Thomas Eyre of Boston, who belonged to an old family in England.

Another daughter married John Lawson, of Boston, of whose daughters Annie married Roger Dench, of Boston, and Sarah married Joseph Buckminster, of Framingham. (Hence comes the name of Lawson in the Dench, Buckminster, Valentine, and Nourse families.)

who was chosen warden on assuming the place of Lieut.-Governor in 1711. His honorable service and high character, and his freedom from bigotry, received at his death public eulogy from the minister of Brattle Square, who spoke of —

"The prudence, justice, and moderation of his administration [while for a time Commander-in-Chief of the Province]; his love to his country, and zeal for his prince, express'd in his often exposing himself in difficult and dangerous expeditions, by sea and land, against the enemies of both; the courage, fidelity, and honour, with which he discharged his public trusts; the candour, sincerity, and obliging condescension of his private friendships; the uncommon love of his people while he liv'd, and their universal lamentation at his death; his catholic temper and principles, which led him to esteem all good men, and frequently to join in religious exercises with christians of a different denomination; his tender regards to these churches, tho' not of their communion; his respectful treatment of the ministers of them upon all occasions, and his reverend devout attendance upon *the word and prayer* in this assembly, when he was in *Town* on our lecture days: These things call upon us to mourn his decease in *this* place. . . . His dust will mingle with the precious dust of honourable STOUGHTON and venerable DANFORTH laid up there before." [1]

Wm Tailer

[1] Rev. William Cooper (his nephew), "MAN *humbled* by being compar'd to a WORM. A Sermon Preach'd at the Publick Lecture in BOSTON, March 9th, 1731-32. The Day after the Funeral of the Honourable William Tailer, Esq.; Late Lieutenant-Governour [etc.]. Boston: 1732." Text: Job xxv. 6. In the *dedication* "to the Honourable Mrs. Abigail Tailer, The Sorrowful Relict," Mr. Cooper says: "You and many others are Witnesses to his grave Deportment in his Family, his Care to keep up Religious Worship in it, and his constant reverend Regard to GOD's Day and House. In these Things I hope his Sons will be Followers of him; as also in his moderate, pacific Temper and Principles as to religious Matters. Colonel Tailer was indeed an Enemy to Bigotry and Uncharitableness. Of this his Attendance on the public worship in Dorchester so frequently on the Lord's Days, and his Countenance to and Friendship with the worthy Pastor of the Church there, was a conspicuous proof."

To his shining qualities a notice in the "News-Letter" (March 9-16, 1732) adds: . . . He "died as bewailed as he lived desired by a People duly sensible of his great Merits. . . . Every one acknowledged and admired his quickness of Apprehension and liveliness of Fancy, with his ready Invention and Active Genius. Every one esteemed him as an uncommon Instance of Good Nature, Tenderness, Affability, and Friendship; nor was he less amiable for his Catholick Principles in Religion. And if the most valuable Personal Qualities are worthy of Esteem, if the most obliging Husband and tenderest Parent, if the devout attender upon Divine Service, the sincere Friend, the affectionate Neighbour, and the steady Patriot should be endeared to us, he was all these in a Superior Degree. We have, therefore, all imaginable reason to expect from this Government some distinguishing Marks of their Esteem for his Name and Memory, and of their thankfulness for his Meritorious Actions."

Col. Tailer was son of William Tailer, or Taylor, a Boston merchant. His mother was sister and co-heiress of William Stoughton. He married (1) a

After Mr. Bridge's exodus from Boston, Mr. Myles remained in sole charge of the church for about two years. For a funeral office in his own family he seems to have required the aid of his Congregational neighbor. Sewall records: —

"Apr. 9 [1707]. Some think he [Mr. Willard] took cold at the Funeral of Mr. Myles's child, the evening before."

The remaining half of his ministry includes important interests, both within and outside of the church. At this time the church received a gift on which it looked dubiously. Of Captain Coram and his farm Baylies, in his history of the Old Colony, says: —

"There is reason to believe that he was settled at Taunton previous to 1692; it is certain he was there but a short time afterward. He owned a farm on the river, a little below the Weir Bridge, where he constructed vessels probably for the Newfoundland fisheries. He left Taunton in 1703. The disposition which he made of his farm exhibits a striking and characteristic trait of his benevolence and of his prejudices: he conveyed it to the vestrymen of the Church of England in Boston; namely, 'His Excy Joseph Dudley, his Honor Thomas Povey, etc., their successors, etc., in trust; that if ever hereafter the inhabitants of the town of Taunton should be more civilized than they now are, and if they should incline to have a Church of England built among them or in that town, then upon the explanation of the inhabitants of said town, — that is to say, forty rateable men of honor, — upon their application or petition to the said vestry or their successors, for any suitable part of said land to build a Church of England, or a school-house for the use and service of said church,' the vestry was authorized to convey the whole or a part 'as they should see good for their purpose.' This misanthropical philanthropist before his death had the gratification to know that the people of Taunton 'had become so far civilized' as to build a 'Church of England;' and many valuable books (now, alas! scattered in every direction), bearing in red letters the name of T. Coram, attest his generosity to this church in the wilderness."

The records proceed: —

Att a Vestry held the 17th of August, 1705, at the House of Mr Nicholas Roberts, . . .

daughter of Nathaniel Byfield; (2) Abigail, widow of Thomas Dudley and daughter of Benjamin Gillam. (See Sewall, i. 163, *n*.) He "probably owed his advancement to approved military service at the capture of Port Royal." He was Lieut.-Governor 1711-16 and 1730-32, having held the Naval Office during part of the interval. Eliot says: "His funeral was splendid; the bells in Boston all tolled from 11 A.M. til 5 o'clock, though he was buried in Dorchester, and a greater number of carriages had never been exhibited."

186   ANNALS OF KING'S CHAPEL.

1. Ordered that the Deed of Land given by Coram, Lying at Taunton, be recorded; that the Church Wardens enquire into the Value of the Land, and to Deliver their Opinions to the Vestry at their next meeting.[1]

2. That the Bill of Nine Pounds 2ˢ 4ᵈ, drawn by Mʳ Stephen Wizendunck in favour of Coll. Foxcroft, on the Church Wardens for the time being, being ballance of acc. due to him from the Church, shall be accepted by the Church Wardens, and paid by them when in Cash for the Church, with the Usuall and customary exchange being at 40 per ct., amᵍ to 12. 15. 3.

Occasionally a financial entry is of interest: —

1705.[2]   £ s. d.
Apʳ 22   To Contribution from Colᵒ Romer[3] 6. 00. 00
          A Collection amongst the Congregation of the Church of England to Supply the Last Year's Deficiency, and for payment of the Debts due from the Church to Sundry workmen.
          [Forty persons contributed £57. 01. 00, among whom were:]
          His Excellʸ Jos: Dudley, Capᵗ Genˡˡ and Governʳ in Cheif 6. 00. 00
          Mʳ Add: Davenport 1. 00. 00
1706.
May 12   To the Collection for Sᵗ Xtophers[4] 21. 01. 06
          [pd to Capt. Belcher.]
1707.
August yᵉ 8 Recd of mʳ funill [Faneuil] for breaking ground in yᵘ Church 12. 00. 00
Janeway 3 Recd of Capt. paxto 3. 00. 00
           Recd of mʳ Apthorp 1. 00. 00
March yᵉ 28 Mʳ hearn, ½ year 1. 10. 00

Easter munday, March the 25, 1706. . . . It is agreed that there shall be twelve, besides his Excellency, Left.-Governor, ministers, and Church wardens, in the Vestry, as is Above whose names are Sett doune.[5]

[1] The church gave Mr. Coram bitter offence by its treatment of this gift, as he showed on a later occasion. He had great virtues, but is well described in a letter from Jer. Dummer, London, Apr. 8, 1720: "Mr. Coram . . . is a man of that obstinate, persevering temper as never to desist from his first enterprise, whatever obstacles lie in his way; So that I expect a good deal more trouble and expense, though I don't doubt of continuing to defeat him [about the eastern lands]." — 3 *Mass. Hist. Coll.*, i. 142.

[2] The Sunday contributions in 1705 vary from £1 2s. 4d. to £5 5s. 0d.

[3] Colonel William Wolfgang Römer, "chief military engineer to their royal majesties in North America," rebuilt Castle William in 1701-3.

[4] The church contributed for aid of fellow-believers elsewhere. Among the "Benefactors" of the church in Burlington, N. J., is named [1705] "Mr. Myls, Minister of Boston, £12 10s."

[5] In 1700 the Vestry had been increased from nine to eleven; in 1701 to

The year 1707 saw in the Puritan church the method of the half-way covenant[1] carried to its logical conclusion, in a sermon published by the Rev. Solomon Stoddard, of Northampton, in which he maintained that "unregenerate persons ought to partake of the Lord's Supper," having already taught that this ordinance should be considered a means of regeneration.[2] In the same year Parliament passed the Act of Union, which was to have an important bearing on the later Episcopal discussion, when it would be assumed to extend the Church of England to the American Plantations. Now also Boston began to be the mustering ground of the forces which were to operate in great military movements against Canada; and though those operations resulted disastrously, they filled the little church with the reflection of the military and naval pageant, and gave it a new social and local prestige.

Meantime the congregation steadily increased.

Easter munday, April 5th, 1708. It is agreed that on Whitsunmunday there be a meeting of the Congregation about enlarging the Queen's Chappell; and Mr Miles is desired to give notice thereof on some Sunday after divine service is Ended.

In 1708 the "Saybrook Platform" was accepted by the Connecticut churches, re-affirming the Confession of Faith adopted by the Reforming Synod in Boston in 1680, and constituting a more stringent system than had hitherto existed of Congregational church government by consociations of churches. This has since constituted a point of difference between the Congregationalism of Massachusetts and that of Connecticut.

The Puritan current still ran deep and strong beside the Episcopal church in Boston. Sewall writes: —

"1703. Dec. 26. — The Christmas Keepers had a very pleasant day; Govr and Mr. Dudley at Church, and Mr. Dudley made a pretty large Entertainmt after.

"1704. Decr 25th.[3] — Monday a storm of Snow, yet many Sleds come to Town with Wood, Hoops, Coal, etc., as is usual. [1705.] Tuesday, Decr 25. — Very Cold Day, but Serene Morning; Sleds, Slays, and Horses pass as usually, and Shops open. [1706.] Midweek, Decr 25. — Shops open; Carts come to Town with Wood, Fagots, Hay; and Horses with Provisions as usually.

thirteen; in 1702 to twenty. Afterwards the number varied.
[1] See p. 33, *ante*.
[2] The reaction against this relaxation of Calvinism was led by Stoddard's grandson and successor, the eminent Jonathan Edwards, in 1735.
[3] Judge Sewall made annual entries recognizing the Church and the Puritan view of Christmas.

"1706. Tuesday, Apr. 23. — Gov' comes to Town guarded p the Troops wth y[r] swords drawn; dines at the Dragon, from thence proceeds to ye Townhouse; Illuminations at night. Capt. Belsham tells me several wore Crosses in y[r] Hats, wch made me resolve to stay at home, thô Maxwell was at my House and spake to me to be at the Council-Chamber at 4 p. m. Because to drinking Healths, now the keeping of a Day to fictitious S[t.] George is plainly set on foot. It seems Capt. Dudley's Men wore Crosses. Somebody had fastened a Cross to a Dog's head; Capt. Dudley's Boatswain seeing him struck the Dog, and then went into y[e] Shop next where y[e] Dog was and struck down a Carpenter, one Davis, as he was at work not thinking anything. Boatswain and y[e] other with him were find 10[s] each for breach of y[e] peace p Jer. Dumer, Esqr. Pretty much blood was shed by means of y[e] bloody Cross, and y[e] poor Dog a Sufferer.

There is a certain injustice to the memory of a good man in these extracts from the private record, where his prejudices leave as deep a mark as his convictions. Judge Sewall is deservedly held in honor. Every thorn that irritated him had its root in the ancient troubles of the Puritan conscience; and the necessity of living amicably with churchmen probably drove him to sharper expressions in these whispered self-communings. The sole test which he applied was the Scriptures. Whatever was not written there was abhorred as an "invention of man" in the worship for which the Divine Word gave sufficient rules.

"July 3 [1707]. . . . Mr. Stoddard preached excellently. . . . Said he could see no reason why a Papist might not *cross himself* Ten times a day, as well as Minister cross a child once.
"1708. Feria quarta, Augt 18. Yesterday the Govr comitted Mr. Holyoke's Almanack to me; and looking it over this morning I blotted out ag[t] Febr. 14th, *Valentine;* March 25, *Annunciation of the B. Virgin;* Apr. 24, *Easter;* Sept[r.] 29, *Michælmas;* Dec[r.] 25, *Christmas;* and no more. [K. C. Mart] was lined out before I saw it; I touch'd it not.
"Aug[t] 23, *mane*. At Council, A Petition for building a Quaker Meeting-house with Wood, pass[d] by the Select-men and Justices of the Town, was now offered to the Gov[r] and Council. I oppos'd it; Said I would not have a hand in setting up yr Devil Worship.
"Aug[t] 26. Mr. Henry Flint, in y[e] way from Lecture, came to me and mention'd my Letter. . . . He argued y[t] saying *Saint* Luke was an indifferent thing; and 'twas comonly used, and therefore he might use it. Mr. Brattle used it. I argued that 'twas not Scriptural; that 'twas absurd and partial to *Saint* Matthew, etc., and Not to say *Saint* Moses, *Saint* Samuel, etc. And if we said *Saint*, we might goe thorough and keep the Holy-days apointed for them, and turnd to the Order in the Comon-prayer Book.

"Dec.! 5, 1708. Mr. Nathaniel Gookin preaches in the forenoon; I think every time he mention'd *James*, 'twas with prefixing *Saint;* about 4 or 5 times that I took notice of. I suppose he did it to confront me, and to assert his own Liberty.

"Feria Septima, Aug.! 28, 1708. Mrs. Taylor[1] is buried in Mr. Stoughton's Tomb. . . . There was no Prayer at the House; and at the Grave Mr. Myles read Common-Prayer, which I reckon an Indignity and affront done to Mr. Stoughton and his Friends. There appears much Ingratitude and Baseness in it, bec. 'twas Mr. Danforth's Parish, and Mr. Danforth's Wife is Cousin German to Col. Taylor, and Col. Byfield and his deceased daughter dissenters, as I suppose. I was much surprised and grieved at it, and went not into the burying-place. Majr.-Genl. said, Mr. Stoughton heard them not. . . . The Govr. seemed to haste into ye burying-place when Mr. Myles's voice was heard.

"Sept.! 2. At 3 p. m. the Council meets; frō thence they goe to the Funeral of Mrs. Lyde, Col. Byfield's eldest daughter. Remembring what I had met with at her sister's Burial at Dorchester last Satterday, I slipt from ye Company up to my daughter's, and so went home and avoided the Funeral. The Office for burial is a Lying, very bad office; makes no difference between the precious and the vile. They ought to return to us, and not we go to them by sinfull compliances."

In 1708 the Vestry sent an address to their bishop, asking for aid to Mr. Myles from the Queen's bounty in place of an assistant:[2] —

"*To the Right Reverend Father in God, Henry, Lord Bishop of London:*
The humble address of the Vestry and Church wardens of Her Majesty's Chappell in Boston, New England.

May it please Your Lordship, — We most humbly crave Your Lordship's acceptance of our unfeigned and grateful acknowledgements for all your expressions of favour and kindness, and your tender care and concern for our peace and welfare; and our hopes and prayers are that according to our exigencies we shall ever experience the continuance thereof.

And with all submission we are humbly of opinion that our remaining as we are by the prudent and diligent performances of our Minister, with whom we are well contented and satisfied, and only occasional assistances from our neighbouring Ministers, our peace and welfare will be best continued and secured; and humbly pray that such part of the Queen's Bounty as to your Lordship shall seem meet may be allowed him, for that his Salary is very precarious, depending upon the unsteady humour of the congregation, some of which (as we find by experience) upon the least ungrounded disgust withdraw their contribution.

---

[1] Colonel William Tailer's first wife.   [2] Church Docs., Mass., p. 82.

And we crave leave to assure your Lordship that it shall be our utmost care and endeavour to give all the assistance and encouragement we are able to our present Minister, and inasmuch as in us lies efface all feuds and animosities, and concert such measures as may preserve our quiet, and engage and unite in mutual love and friendship; and in confident assurance of your Lordship's paternal care and kindness, and hearty prayers for your Lordship's good health and happiness, are

    Your Lordship's
      Most Obed^t and dutiful Serv^{ts}
        J. DUDLEY and others."

Mr. Myles himself wrote in the same strain to the Secretary of the Venerable Society: —

"My Lord of London writes me that the Society press him to send an Assistant here, but I trust that the addresses late sent will satisfy that it will be more for our advantage to remain as we are; and then if some part of the Salary as £70 be allowed, the product whereof is here near £200, or if I may not have £20 or £30 (which, indeed, will be a great help to me, since the last Sabbath I had not 40s., and many times far less), rather than have an assistant I would desire that a Minister sent to Braintree or Swansey should have the whole £100, who might be ordered occasionally to assist here. . . . Then two churches will be supplied, and the other I hope be as we are now, in peace and very good order. . . .

P. S. . . . I pray if my Lord will not let me be easy here, I must come to England."[1]

But the order for a successor to Mr. Bridge had already gone forth.

When the rector thus wrote, Dec. 8, 1708, the Rev. Henry Harris was probably beginning his winter voyage to succeed to the place of Lecturer at the Queen's Chapel. The arrival of Mr. Harris practically marks the beginning of a new era in the growth and prosperity, not only of the parish, but of the Church of England in this Province. Notwithstanding the reluctance with which the arrival of another assistant had been anticipated, which was not strange if we remember the recent discords from which the Vestry and Mr. Myles had suffered, the new Lecturer evidently had the gift of winning friends and the faculty of remaining on good terms with the senior minister. Even the persons in the parish who advocated a diversion of the Royal bounty to lighten their own contributions, must have felt the advantage of the strength and graciousness which Mr. Harris brought to the ministrations of the church. In later years, his

[1] Church Docs. Mass. p. 83.

ministry was to be shadowed by bitter oppositions and shortened by disappointment, but at first all was bright. The active spirit of the young, vigorous English clergyman found scope in trying to plant nurslings of the Church at various places along the rocky coast of Massachusetts. While happily confident that the cause which he represented had a superior claim upon the meek obedience of the children of the Puritans, he was yet on cordial terms with his neighbors; and after a severe rebuff in controversy from Dr. Increase Mather, he seems to have become still more friendly with them. Before his ministry should close, he was to find this friendliness made an article of complaint against him by angry party spirit, inflamed with the double venom of political and ecclesiastical disputes in a period of peculiar virulence; but at the beginning none of these clouds darkened the serene sky.

FIRST COMMUNION TABLE.[1] 1686.

CHAPTER VI.

THE CHURCH ENLARGED. — A BISHOP SOUGHT.

HE period on which our narrative now enters begins in sunshine. The records which note the arrival of the new lecturer also mention one of the earlier steps in that system of occupancy of seats which gradually took permanent shape in the present pew system.

1709. April 24, Easter Munday, the Vestry and Congregation Voted that M{r} Roger Pattenson and his wife are to sitt in the seat with M{r} Edw{d} Mills.

Voted, that a Letter of thanks be sent to my Lord Bishop of London, for sending M{r} Harris to assist M{r} Miles.

Capt Walter Riddle, Comand{t} of her Maj{ties} Ship the Falmouth, p{r}sented Thirty pounds to the Church.

Voted, that after the paym{t} of some small debts due to severall persons for work done to the Church, the remaind{r} of the above Thirty pounds given by Capt. Riddell be paid to M{r} Myles, towards the paym{t} of the arrears of his salary.

The seating of families was a complicated business in those punctilious days of marked distinctions of rank and of social form. The order in which the prayers in the Liturgy are ar-

[1] This Communion table is still in use.

THE CHURCH ENLARGED.

ranged was practically followed, — although, of course, with no such intent on the part of the Puritans, — beginning with the patricians and ending by giving such seats as were left "to all sorts and conditions of men," in the belief that such distinctions were divinely ordained.[1]

1707: nouember: 25: Receiued of Cap^{tn} Southack £4: which is for The: 3: pue on the South Side ye Church, to be paid to wido Smith for hir Right in it which M^r hancock: Sold hir and I paid the s^d fower Poundes to the s^d wido Smith on ye 26 day of Fbruarey, by me Sauill: Simpson.

1707: nouember 25: Recd of M^r hall thirty shillings for ye pue Cap^{tn} Southack formerly Sat in, and paide it to the Church youse as by y^e: accompt: by me Sauill Simpson.

[1708] Memorandu that on the 12th day of Decemb^r 1708, Capt Paxton and his family was placed by us in Coll Foxcroft's Pew, by his leave and permission, not debarring him of his Right therein.

[Feb. 16, 1708–9. At a vestry meeting.] *Voted*, That Sr Charles Hobby's pew be enlarged to the Westward at his charge, and that the rest of the pews on that Isle be lessened and made into five at the charge of the Congregation.

That Edward Lyde and Wm Tailer Esq^{rs} have that pew formerly called Mr Maccarty's pew, for them and their familyes; and that they may (if they see cause) at their own charge lengthen the same to the comunion railes, so that the Comunicants may kneel there, as now, on Comunion days; and also that they may line and raile the s^d pew.

That Capt Daniel Wyborne and his family have that pew that belonged to Edward Lyde and Wm Tailer Esq^{rs}, and that he may line and raile the same at his own charge, if he thinks meet.

[1709. April 22.] The Vestry *Voted*, That the Church wardens take out of the two adjacent pews (at the East End of the Church) to the Govern^r for a pew for Mr Edward Mills and his family, and such other person as the Church wardens shall see meet.

---

[1] See Rev. G. E. Ellis, D.D., on "Seating the Meeting-House," in *Unitarian Review*, Jan. 1877. Dr. Ellis shows how the fathers sought "to follow the divine rule of 'honor to whom honor.' Touching evidences are on record of regard for the feelings of individuals and families who were 'decayed in fortune,' who 'had seen better days,' and for those impracticable attendants on public preaching, 'the stone deaf.' It was found best, on the whole, to keep up a standing truce with 'boys,' not forbearing watching or threatening, but sometimes turning only half an eye upon them." A sort of private ownership in pews was sometimes recognized, leading to practical inconvenience. One of those who separated from the North Church in 1720 said "there should always be one pew empty, and nailed his pew up, claiming a part of the house as his property. It remained in this situation until 1727, when some persons went into the meeting-house at night and sawed out the pew through the floor, and placed the whole at his shop door, which stood conspicuously, exciting much mirth in the populace, and equal rage in the old gentleman." — *Eliot's Historical Notices of the New North Church.*

The latter half of Mr. Myles's ministry was by no means free from contentions, though it was much prospered in signs of outward success. After two years of solitary ministering he received another assistant, who seemed to come with fair auspices. Early in 1709 arrived Rev. Henry Harris, with authority from the Bishop of London to succeed Mr. Bridge. He was a graduate of Jesus College, Oxford, where "Henry Harrys" was entered in 1704 as a "Battelar," and took his B.A. degree on Oct. 24, 1707. He became Fellow of the College on Sir Leoline Jenkins's foundation on Dec. 19, 1707. He was born in the parish of Langwm, in the county of Monmouth.[1]

The college fellowship held by Mr. Harris was itself an interesting memorial of the English loyalty which survived the Great Rebellion, and of the devotion to the Stuarts which played so large a part in the foundation of King's Chapel. Sir Leoline Jenkins[2] had been conspicuous in Jesus College and in the State

---

[1] I am indebted to Rev. W. S. Bartlet for the above facts communicated to him by Rev. H. D. Harper, D.D., Principal of Jesus College, who adds: "In April 21, 1730, there is an entry of a Fellowship being vacant 'per mortem naturalem Henrici Harris.' The value of a Fellowship was £20, and the Sir L. Jenkins Fellows received an additional £20. He was accordingly paid £40 a year by the College. Ordinary resident Fellows received £20 a year and a share of a sum of £80 (divided between all the Fellows in residence), according to length of residence, — possibly £5 or £6." Mr. Harris thus received a salary of £140 sterling, including the King's grant.

[2] This distinguished Welshman was born in Glamorganshire, and, "having entered Jesus College in 1641, took up arms in favour of the King's cause." After its overthrow, he retired to Wales as a teacher, but being indicted "for keeping a seminary of rebellion and sedition," withdrew in 1651, first to Oxford and then beyond sea, returning privately to England before Cromwell's death. After the Restoration he became a Fellow of Jesus College, and was its Principal 1671-73. He had been admitted an advocate in Doctors' Commons, and in 1664 was made Judge of the High Court of Admiralty. He was also "Sheldon's Commissary and official for the diocese of Canterbury. The early resignation of the headship of his college was caused by his appointment as Ambassador at Cologne." In 1676 he was one of the plenipotentiaries for the treaty of Nimeguen. Succeeding Sir William Coventry, he was Secretary of State 1680-84. He died Sept. 1, 1685. In these high offices he had been led to see the need of such spiritual aid as he sought to secure by these fellowships. Anderson's "Col. Church," ii. 359. See also Hawkins's "Historical Notices of the Missions of the Church of England," p. 12, who says: "It is much to be lamented that the colonies have hitherto derived little if any benefit from this noble endowment. The election, indeed, of one Fellow — namely, the Rev. Henry Nicholls, B.A., in 1703 — was formally notified by the Principal and Fellows of Jesus College to the Society for the Propagation of the Gospel; and it appears that he was sent as a Missionary to Chester, in Pennsylvania. Since then, successive 'scholars of King Charles II. and King James II.' have been allowed (by whose neglect it were useless to inquire) to escape the responsibility attached to their foundation. It is, however, gratifying to be able to state, that within the last year the Bishop of London, — whose exertions in behalf of the Church in the Colonies equal at least those of the most active of his predecessors, — having at first ascertained

THE CHURCH ENLARGED.

as a devoted servant of the King, and at his death in 1685 he endowed two Fellowships, thus described in his will: —

"Since he owed (under God) all that he was and all that he had to the Royal goodness and bounty of His late Majesty, and His Majesty that then was, he humbly besought that the first of those Fellows, and his successors, may be known and distinguished by the name of the Scholar and Alumnus of King Charles II.; the other, and his successors, by the name of the Scholar and Alumnus of King James II.; and that they may be under an indispensable obligation to take upon them Holy Orders of Priesthood, so soon as, by the Constitutions of this Church and the laws of this Realm, they shall be capable of them; and afterwards that they go out to sea, in His Majesty's Fleet, when they, or either of them, are thereunto summoned by the Lord High Admiral. If they refuse to take orders, or refuse or delay to obey such summons, then their places to be *ipso facto* void, and others to be chosen in their room, as if they were naturally dead. And in case there be no use of their service at sea, and they be called by the Lord Bishop of London for the time being to go into any of His Majesty's foreign Plantations, there to take upon them a cure of souls, and exercise the ministerial function under his Lordship's direction and obedience, and they refuse or delay to go, then their place or places to be immediately void, and supply'd by a new election."

Mr. Harris brought a letter from Bishop Compton, which was evidently designed to prevent such disagreements as had arisen with his predecessor. It bears the marks of the same strong hand which penned the former one already copied. At a vestry meeting on the 1st of April, this year, it was ordered, upon the reading of these instructions, "that the same be entered verbatim as followeth, viz'." : —

Having appointed Mr. Harris to go over assistant to the Minister at Boston, for his better satisfaction I have thought fit to declare, that, as he is not to go under the absolute command of Mr. Myles, yet is he to pay a respect to him in all reasonable things, and take an equall share with him in supplying the Church, but not to meddle in anything that relates to perquisites, whether for marriages, buryalls, or Christenings, and to be contented with what is alloted him from home; and by all means to avoid the insinuation of any that shall attempt to make matters uneasy betwixt him and Mr. Myles, whom I do likewise require to receive this his assistant with all fair and good usage, and that they both conspire into so good an understanding that nothing may creep in to make a

---

that the Board of Admiralty had at present no intention of preferring their claim, has given notice to the College that he feels himself called upon to exercise the privilege accorded to him in the will of Sir L. Jenkyns, of sending out the two Fellows elected on his foundation to some one or other of the foreign plantations."

breach between them: And that they do agree to relate all storyes, that shall be whispered to them, publickly in the next vestry, — that such little make-bates may be discouraged and made ashamed of such base behaviour. And, therefore, I desire likewise that this paper may be read in a full vestry, that they may be witnesses of your sincere conformity to what is appointed. I do also declare that Mr. Harris shall have the full allowance of the appointed bounty, by Midsummer next come twelve month at furthest, as not being yet fully informed to what degree, and upon what grounds, Mr. Bridge hath committed that insolent Riott upon the Church of Road Island; which so soon as I am ascertained of, I intend the full allowance shall commence from that time.

Given under my hand this Twenty-eighth day of May, 1708.

H: LONDON.

It is probable, however, that the difficulties which had arisen between Mr. Myles and his former assistant, and which were now to be repeated in a more aggravated and persistent form, never, indeed, entirely abating until the Revolution terminated the office of "King's Chaplain," were inherent in the nature of the situation. It was impossible to define the duties of the assistant so accurately as to preclude friction between the two ministers. The assistant was an English college graduate, paid directly from the royal bounty, holding a semi-independent position, subordinate in a certain sense and yet *quasi* co-ordinate with the minister of the church, in whom (in the case of Mr. Myles and of Dr. Caner) he saw one, American born and bred, without what he conceived to be his own marks of superior culture. Even if the place had been frankly accepted as "a curacy on the same terms of inferiority on which hundreds of his brethren took curacies at home," which by the bishop's definition of its duties it in no wise was, the aspect of the case in New England would have been wholly altered. As Greenwood says: "When he began his duties at her Majesty's Chapel, and, instead of being kept contented by the customs of the place and the example of those about him, saw that in every Congregational church which supported two ministers they were regarded as colleagues, having equal rights, privileges, and duties, his own subordinate situation must have grown every day more irksome to him, and the task of obedience to his superior every day more difficult. It is not in human nature to rest satisfied with such a condition. It certainly was not in Mr. Bridge's nature, and in the sequel we may have cause to believe that it was not in Mr. Harris's." Any form of subordination and inferiority, such as the lower English clergy had to accept at home, seemed stifling in this free air. Yet, on the other hand, it might well have seemed intolerable, both to Mr. Myles and to his parishioners, to have to divide on equal terms his duties and their affections with a stranger sent by a bishop who could know little of their needs, and in whose selection they had had neither part nor lot.

A glimpse into the minister's domestic economy is afforded by an advertisement in the "News-Letter," of Sept. 17–24, 1711: —

"Ran away from their Masters at Boston on Friday last, the 14th of this instant September, the following Indians, viz.: From the Reverend Mr. Samuel Myles, a Carolina Indian man nam'd Toby, Aged about 20 years, of a middle stature; hath with him a light colour'd Suite edg'd with black, a dark homespun Suite, edg'd and fac'd with black, a Hat edg'd with Silver lace, several Shirts and other cloathing. . . . Whoever shall apprehend the said Runaways . . . shall be sufficiently rewarded, besides all necessary Charges paid."[1]

The story of such events as occurred in the church is best outlined by the records. These state that Mr. Myles was paid £3 a week regularly from May 1, 1709.[2] Our citations proceed:

1709	[Cash]	£	s.	d.
Decr 13	To ditto for opening the Church for Mr Milleney	5.	00.	00
1710	Dr.			
Feb^{ry} 11	To Ball^{ce} of Mr Langharne's Acc^t	48.	08.	09
April 6	To Cash of Mr Langharne £2			
	To ditto from Mr Ranndle for opening Capt }	6.	00.	00
	Apreeces grave £4			
1711				
7^{br} 14	To p^d at Meeting of Com^{tee} at Dragon	0.	04.	02
X^{br}: 21	To p^d at Meeting of Com^{tee}: at Ex^{ch}:	0.	04.	08

[1] This means of grace for the enslaved was deemed peculiarly suitable for religious households. "Even the gentle and humane James Harvey gave to Whitefield, as a parting gift, a slave. 'When you please to demand,' he wrote, 'my brother will pay you 30*l*. for the purchase of a negro. And may the Lord Jesus Christ give you, or rather take for himself, the precious soul of the poor slave!' The Society for Propagating the Gospel in Foreign Parts was itself a slaveholder." — *Church of England in the Eighteenth Century*, ii. 107. A notice in the "News-Letter," March 3–10, 1718, of burials within the Town of Boston, 1717, among which were "80 Indians and Negro's," adds this "*Note:* Reckoning each Indian and Negro at £30, the loss amounts to £2,400, whereas if they had been White Servants at £15 a head, the Town had sav'd £1,200; so that White Servants are better than Negro's. A man can easily procure £12 or £15 to purchase a white Servant, that cannot advance £30, £40, or £50, for a Negro or Indian. The Whites Strengthens and Peoples the Country, that the others do not."

[2] In 1710 the weekly contributions vary from £2. 1*s*. 6*d*. to £7. 1*s*. 0*d*. In 1713 several contributions exceed £7, and one, on March 28, amounts to £9. 18*s*. 9*d*.

	1710	Contra.		
	7br 30	By cash of Andr: Fanuil for Intering the body of	£ s. d.	
		Jnº: Busby in the Church porch	5. 00. 00	
	1711			
	May 8	By Dº of Colⁿ Tho: Savage for Laying the body of		
		Mr Mackentash in the Church	5. 00. 00	
	Feb. 25	By Dº of Tho: Steel for Laying the body of James		
		Allexander, in the Church	2. 00. 00	

The plans against Canada had suffered a check in the failure of the expedition against Port Royal in 1707; but Colonel Nicholson, who had gone to England to urge their renewal, arrived at Boston July 1, 1710, in the "Dragon," as General and Commander-in-Chief of the expedition, which sailed again September 18, and reduced Nova Scotia to a British province. The subscription for enlarging the church, which had lain in abeyance for two years, was generously assisted by the General and his officers; and Sewall's Diary shows that Sir Francis gave friendly aid in a yet more important way: —

"Monday, Augt 14, 1710. At a Town-Meeting, warn'd for that purpose, Fifteen feet of the old burying-place Northward, and Ten feet Eastward, are granted to enlarge the church. Samuel Lynde, esqr., was chosen Moderator; Col. Nicholson made a Speech before, And came in afterward and gave the Town Thanks for their Vote. Mr. Prout, the Toun-Clerk, made some Oposition, because the Graves of his Ancestors would be thereby hidden."[1]

The Town Records (ii. 317) state that, —

Grant of part of the Burying-place for Enlargmt of the Church. "A motion or Request in writing being presented and distinctly read at this meeting, and is as followeth, viz.: 'The Request of the Honble Coll. Francis Nicholson, together with the Ministers, Church Wardens, and others of the Church of England in Boston, sheweth — That the Church being too small to accommodate the congregation and Strangers that dayly Increase, And are desirous to Enlarge the same with the Approbation of the Selectmen and Inhabitants, but wanting Ground on the North side and East end, Re-

---

[1] Among the papers of the Overseers of the Poor is "Mr. Prout's Query Read at yᵉ Town Meeting yᵉ 14th of Aug: 1710.

"In as much as the first Planters and Inhabitants of this Town, who then had in themselves the Sole Propriety thereof, did at their first Settlement here Assign and Sett apart that Peice or parcell of Ground, now known by the name of the Old burying-place in Boston, to be a burying-place for themselves and their Successors, and the Same haveing heitherto since been improved to that use, —

Query, Whether the present Inhabitants of the sᵈ Town can in Justice and Equity Grant the Same, or any part thereof, to be improved to any other use then According to the first Intentions thereof."

quest that they may have a Grant of fifteen foot wide on the North side and Seventy-four foot in length, And ten foot on the East end of the Church in Length, which is included in the said Seventy-four foot, Reserving the same Liberty to all persons who have had any friends buryed in said ground which they enjoyed heretofore; Which Request being granted shall be ever acknowledged, etc.'

"*Voted*, a grant to the said Gentlemen of this above said Request."

The list of subscribers is recorded, and shows how much the church was indebted to its visitors.[1]

In the expedition of 1710, among these subscribers, besides General Nicholson, Colonel Vetch was adjutant-general. There were four regiments raised in New England, the colonels commissioned by the Queen, of whom two were Colonel Reading and Sir Charles Hobby, whose contribution was paid on the day the expedition sailed. Colonel Tailer of the vestry commanded another regiment. Colonel Rednap, Engineer Forbes, Captain Southack of the Province Galley, Captain Bartlett, Captains Mascareen and Davison in command of grenadiers, are prominent in Niles's account of the capture.[2] Captain Pigeon and " Capt. Forbis the engineer" were killed in 1711, in an attack by the French upon Port Royal.

The subscription was aided still further by many of those engaged in the larger expedition against Quebec which mustered in Boston in the following year. The news that this movement was preparing came on June 8, 1711, when Nicholson arrived again in Boston, being followed on the 25th by the arrival of a magnificent fleet, of which the brother of the Queen's favorite Mrs. Masham, Brigadier Hill, was commander-in-chief. Sir Hovenden Walker was admiral of the fleet, "which consisted of fifteen men-of-war and forty transports, one battalion of marines, and seven regiments, — under Colonel Kirk, Colonel Seymore, Brigadier Hill, Colonel Desire, Colonel Windress, Colonel Clayton, and Colonel Kaine, — with upwards of 5,000 men, who arrived safe, in health, and encamped on Noddle's Island, below Boston, where they made the finest appearance that ever had been seen or known in America, the land forces being as fine regimental troops as any that belonged to the Duke of Marlborough's army, and the fleet as serviceable ships as any in the whole navy of England."

---

[1] The weekly contributions, which otherwise follow the average of previous years, range in 1710, on most of the Sundays from June 18 to Sept. 10, from £5 to £7. 01. 10. In 1711 they reach, June 10, £6. 14. 01; June 17, £8. 05, 06; July 22, £7. 01. 00; Oct. 28, £8. 11. 06; Nov. 4, £6. 06. 06.

[2] French and Indian Wars, 4 Mass. Hist. Coll. v. 320, 331.

In the five weeks that this brilliant but ill-fated expedition filled the town with excitements, the church must have been crowded to excess. Sewall records: —

July 4 [1711]. "Went to the Commencem't by Water in a Sloop.... Mr. Shepard, Mr. Myles, Chaplain of the Humber ... had them to my Son's chamber."

And of a Thursday Lecture: —

July 12. "Dr. Cotton Mather preached on the Rainbow, from Rev. x. 1. Many Chaplains at Meeting."

Some of these army and navy chaplains doubtless preached and read prayers in the Queen's Chapel, while the uniforms of Her Majesty's Service made the pews glow with bright color. The subscription for the church reached assured success with this new accession of worshippers. A special sorrow for the disaster which smote the fleet in the St. Lawrence and compelled General Nicholson to abandon his movement by way of the lakes, while the whole costly expedition was brought to nought, must have darkened the church with the sense of the loss of personal friends.[1]

Among the payments for enlarging the Church are the following:[2] —

1710-11.	*Her Majest^s: Chappell in Boston, D^r.*	£ s. d.
Jan^{ry} 5	To Jno Brewer for 1130 ft. Slitt Timber @ 5/6^d	3. 02. 00
1711		
June 5	To Thomas Verin for 12,000 ft. of board	36. 00. 00
June 11	To ditto p^d two of the Chesters Men, for Cleaning the Church, and carrying away ye Rubbish, 2 days	0. 16. 00
	for drinck for them 2/8^d To Judd for Brooms 1^s	0. 03. 08
June 16	To p^d Jno Cary for beer for the Workemen	1. 10. 00
20	To p^d for bread and Chees for Do.	1. 02. 06
July 3	To Robert Howard for Shingles	21. 00. 00
Augst	To Charges p^d goeing to Nantaskett on board the Flagg	0. 13. 04
Sep^{br} 1st	To p^d Samuel Pratt for 1500 Clabboards	4. 14. 06
14	To p^d Jno Parker for a Sparr	0. 15. 00
Octo^r 13	To ditto cash p^d John Keary for 5 ha : Bar^{ll} Bear for ye workmen p Bd	0. 15. 00

[1] See the full list of subscribers, with personal notes, at the end of this chapter.

[2] I have given only a few of the items of payments for laths, lime, timber, stone, etc. The total expended in the enlargement, from Aug. 25, 1710, to April 15, 1712, amounted to £554. 9s. 5d.

THE CHURCH ENLARGED.

		£ s. d.
	To ditto p^d Mr Rayton for mending ye Chair in Sr Charles's pew	0. 05. 00
Dec. 22	To ditto p^d Judd for drinck for ye workmen for 3 weeks past [1]	0. 10. 06

Contra.

1712

May 30.	By Cash Rece^d of Mr John Vallantine Towards inlarging ye Church	5. 00. 00
June 3.	By ditto, of Mrs Mico by ye hands of Mad^m Myles	0. 05. 00
28.	By Cash Rece^d of Mr Henry Francklin, £ 31. 05. 07 ; Paid him by Capt Rouse Comander of her Maj^{ties} Ship Saphire and Comp^a : viz. : —	
	Of the Capt 10. 00. 00	
	The Lev^t 5. 00. 00	
	The Master 5. 00. 00	
	The 7 Warrant Officers 7. 00. 00	
	The rest of ye Company 4. 05. 07	
		31. 05. 07
July 28	By ditto Rece^d of John Jekell, Esqr 10. 00. 00	
	[And from 18 others,[2] from £ 10 to 10^d each]	
	In all	£119. 00. 07
Decr 29	By Cash Rece^d of Capt. Wintworth Paxton . . .	10. 00. 00
Decr and Janu^{ry}.	[From 15 others, in all] [2]	44. 15. 00

May the 26th, 1712. At a meeting of the Vestry at the House of Mr Johns at ye Royall Exchange this Evening,[3] present

              The Rever^d Mr Myles,
           Wm Melross, Church Warden,

Coll Giles Dyer,	Mr John Vallantine,
Ed : Lydd Esqr,	Mr Giles Dyer, Junr,
Thos Newton, Esqr,	Mr Anth Blunt.

Mr Blunt, Late Church Warden, delivered in his Acco^{ts} from ye Tradesmen y^t Worked on ye Church, &c^a which was ordered to be delivered to ye Comitty of acco^{ts} to Ex^n and to make their Report to ye Vestry of ye Same.

---

[1] Similar entries are repeated.

[2] See the list of subscribers at the end of this chapter.

[3] Similar entries occur in August, October, November, and December. It seems at this time to have been the questionable custom to hold the vestry meetings at a place of public entertainment, as has been already noted, March 24, 1701.

Boyle's Episcopal Charitable Society states that, "Apr. 1, 1731. An agreement was made 'with Mr. Vardy (Exchange Tavern, King St.) for a dinner on Easter Monday, at 8s. a head, exclusive of wine. . . . Several of the gentlemen of the Society complained that the agreement was so dear that they would not be at it. . . . Mr. Vardy . . . said he could not nor would not do it under; and then they went to Mrs. Wardell at the Orange Tree, and agreed with her for 7s. a head, and to have half a pint of wine each man.'"

Voted, Y^t Coll Dyer, Esqr. Lyde, Esqr. Newton and ye Church Wardens should on Friday Morning with Brewer the Carpenter vieu ye Church to see what was to be done towards finishing ye work, and ye Severall Small Jobbs wch was to be done should be Compleated by ye Said Brewer, and that ye Glazier should Compleat his work.

June the 17th, 1712. At a meeting of ye Comitty of Acco^{ts} at the above said House of M^r. Johns, present

      Wm Melross, Ch. Warden,
      M^r. Apthorpe,
      M^r. Giles Dyer, Junr.

The Acco^{ts} were produced, Ex^d, and it was agreed ye Vestry should be called, and ye Comitty of acco^{ts} to give in their Report.

June 19th, 1712. At a meeting of the Vestry at the aforesaid House of M^r. Johns, &c^a, the Tradesmen's Acco^{ts} were Laid before them, Brewer ye Carpenter present; the objections made by ye Comitty. Brewer said Litle in his own defence; it was proposed to give him Six pound, wch he said was to Litle, and desired Eight Pound, wch was agreed on, and paid by the Church Warden, Brewer giving a full Discharge for all his demands for work done on ye Church to this Time, he allowing Six Pound towards altering the Church, wch was first deducted out of his Acco^t.

Voted, that ye other Tradesmen's acco^{ts} for worke done on ye Church before Easter Last y^t Remained unpaid, vizt ye Smiths, Glaziers, Carters, &c^a Should be Ex^d by the Comitty of Acco^{ts}, and upon their approbation should be paid by ye Church Wardens.

That ye Church Wardens should Receive of M^r. Henry Francklin £31. 5*s*. 7*d*, wch lay in his hands given to ye Church by Capt Rouse Comand^r. of her Maj^{ties} Shipp Saphire, his Officers and Company.

That what Remained at any tyme in Banck of Contribution Money should be Imployed when there was Occation in Carrying on the Church work.

Augst 27th, 1712. At a meeting of the vestry at ye House of M^r. Johns at ye Royall Exchange this Evening, —

1. It was agreed that the Pulpit be Removed to the next Piller at ye East, being near the Center of ye Church.

2. That the Pews be Built in one forme without Banisters.

August the 28th, 1712. At a Meeting at the Church all ye above-named Gentlemen present, Edward Lyde, Esqr, M^r. John Oulton, and M^r. Thos. Banister proposed that the Gentlemen of the Vestry Should Build the Pews, and they would each of them advance Fifty Pound Towards Building them, to be repaid them as the Pews was disposed off, wch was agreed upon and Thanks Returned the said Gentlemen. Upon wch workemen were Immediatly sent for, and treated with abo^t it; but not agreeing, the Gentlemen of the Vestry pray'd Coll. Dyer he would please to agree with any Workemen he should think fitt to Build the same.

October the 24th, 1712. At a meeting of the Vestry at ye House of M^r. Johns at ye Roy^{ll} Exch^a. This Evening, —

THE CHURCH ENLARGED. 203

It was then agreed that places should be appointed for every Gentleman of the Church (that wanted) to Build their pews, and that they should Build them at their owne Charge, the above order being made void.

October 25th. This Morning the Vestry mett at the Church and Numbered out the Pews, and appointed every Person his place as p List.

Decmbr 20: Att a Meeting at ye Church, all ye Gentlemen here present of ye Vestry agreed that Solomon Clackston should make A flatt Plaine in Order for Laveting and Plastering. The said Solomon Clackston To have Thirty Pounds for his Laber was agreed on.

		£ s. d.
1712/3		
March 7	By Cash Reced of Mrs Neadam for oppening ye Ground to Bury the Body of Mr John Cutton of Barbads for wch she was to pay £5. Reced now in parte 40s.	2. 00. 00
23	By ditto of Doctor John Cutler for oppening ye Ground to Bury the Body of Capt John Keston of Barbads	5. 00. 00
[March] 30	By ditto of Mr Anto Blunt for oppening ye Ground to Bury the Body of Capt Wm Sulliman	2. 00. 00

	The Queen's Chapell.	Dr.
1712		
May 26th	To Cash pd at a Meeting of ye Vestry at Mr John's at ye Excha	0. 04. 00
1713		
May ye 18th	To Cash pd Mr Whitcomb for Mending ye Lt-Gor Chaire	0. 07. 00
Augt 3	To Mr Phillips for Casing the Church Bible	0. 06. 00
11	To Cash pd Mess Samll Whitwill and Hercules Brasford for Pewen the Church in full	2. 10. 00
13	To Cash payd for Bringin the Orgins	0. 10. 00
March 29	To James Barry for looking after the Boys for one year	1. 06. 00
June 7	To Judd for washing the Surplices	0. 04. 00
July 13	To Henry Caner — in part	10. 00. 00
	Contra.	Cr.
June 16	By Do Recd of Mr John Geroul for a Peww	6. 00. 00
Augt 7	By Do Recd of Capt Wybort for the peww behind the Pulpit	10. 00. 00
	[Etc., etc., making with sale of some pews and gifts . . . . . . 124. 02. 00]	
	[Additional on next page . . 77. 05. 03	
		201. 07. 03
1715		
Feby 6	By Henry Caner in full	12. 00. 00

Att a meeting of the Vestry and Congregation of the Church of England at the Queen's Chappel, in Boston, in New England, on Wensday the 15t.h Aprell, 1713.

Continued ye Present Yeare

M.r John Giles, Clark; M.r Rod: Judd, Sexton; James Berry Chosen to Look after the Boys, and is to have 26/ p yeare for the Same.

Voted, that there Shall be 20 Vestree Men beside the Go.r and Lef.t Gou.r, Church Wardens and Minister; that whare as Judd had 5^s p week he shall have 6^s, the last Bell to Ring at 10 of the Clock in the Morning the whole Yeare, and 3 a Clock in the After Noone, from the 10t.h of March too the 10th September, and at 2 the other Months; the Bread and Wine at the Communion to be pay'^{d} out of the Contribution Mony; the Psalmes of Tate and Brady to be sung in the Church. Every Sunday the Commandments are to be Read at the Communion Table. . . .

At a Vestry met at Boston, Wednesday the 12th of August, 1713.

Voted, y.t the Pillers, Capitalls, and Cornish of the Church be painted wainscott Colur, before the Scaffalold be Tacking Doune.

Voted, y.t Unles Doc.r Lake imediatly pay to the Church Wardens the sum of five pounds towards the Repair of the Church, y^t thay dispose of the pew he Sitts in to Sutch persons as they shall See Convenant; and also any other p'son or p'sons y^t shall Refuse to pay ther quotas, paying him or them ther money that was disbursed for that Use.

At a meeting of the Vestry of the Church of England at the Queen's Chappell In Boston in New England this 15th June, 1713.

It was agreed that the Church Wardins shuld agre with Some Workmen for the Lathing and plastering of the Church, and the finishing of the same.

[Easter-Monday meeting, Mar. 29, 1714.]

[List of] Persons Appointed to Sitt in the Fore Seats In the Gallery [beginning with] Capt Turfrey. [29 in all, paying 10^s.] M.r Frogly and M.r Reading In the Box in the Gallery.

1714

[Vestry meeting, August 18th.]

Voted, that thanks be given to the Gent.n of the Brittish Society for their Present of A Clock and y^t M.r Jekyll acquaint y^m of itt.

That A Shell be put over the South Door. And that M.r Price be p^d Seven p^{ds} Ten Shills for one Q^{rs} Sallary due at Midsummer 1714, and Seven p^{ds} Ten shills more for w^t Work he has done ab^t the Organ.

From these records it appears that the action at Easter, 1708, "about enlarging the Queen's Chappell," had gone into effect after the subscription of 1710. The loyalty of British officers to their Church as to their colors ensured success. More than half of the amount subscribed was their gift; so that the renewed building was almost their memorial.

THE CHURCH ENLARGED. 205

These were exciting years. Not only did the noises of the great expeditions resound around the church's enlarging walls, but the echo of the "drum ecclesiastick" came across the water. The year 1710 saw the Sacheverell riots in London, provoked by the preaching of London clergy against the Dissenters. The church was threatened by the terrible fire of Oct. 2, 1711, which "laid the heart of Boston in ashes, reducing Cornhill into miserable ruins, making its impressions on King St. and Queen St., and losing a great part of Pudding Lane,"[1] as well as the First Church and the Town House.

Nor was the enlargement finished without disaster.

"Octob^r 26 [1711] a Man falls from a Scaffold at the Church of Engl'd into the Street, and is stricken dead."[2]

Great things had been done in beautifying the little wooden church without and within. It was enlarged to twice its original size, and the pillars, capitals, and cornice were painted. Places were assigned anew to the proprietors, and each person paid for the building of his own pew. And whereas the pews had been built before, according to the usual fashion, with little rails or banisters running round the top, it was now voted that they should "be built in one forme without banisters." The pulpit was removed from its former situation "to the next pillar at the East, being near the Centre of the Church." The two long pews fronting the pulpit were made into two square pews, one for Colonel Tailer, Lieut.-Governor, the other for Mr. Jekyll, and the two pews behind them were made into one, for the use of masters of vessels; and the pew behind that was appropriated to the accommodation of eight old men. A shell was placed over the south door. The clock given by "the Gentlemen of the British Society" took the place of the great brass mounted hour-glass which used to stand by the preacher's hand, to be turned by him when its sands had run out, in admonition to him and his congregation. We can see the church, as it appeared after these alterations, in a small view of Boston published in 1720,[3] in which may be deciphered the King's Chapel, a little wooden building, with three windows on each side and three at the flat back of the church. It has a tower about as high as the present one, surmounted by a tall mast, at whose top is a weather-cock, and half way up a large gilt

---

[1] Cotton Mather's Sermon on the Great Fire of 1711. See 1 Mass. Hist. Coll. v. 52.

[2] Sewall's Diary.

[3] See p. 58, and also Mass. Hist. Proc. 1880, p. 69.

crown. Beyond it rises aloft the bare crest of Beacon Hill, then much higher than now, with a flag-staff at the summit.

These improvements did not pass without admonitory words from the Puritan side. Rev. Cotton Mather took the occasion of the Thursday Lecture falling on Christmas Day, to preach from Jude, 4, — " Ungodly Men, turning the Grace of our God into Wantonness."

After a general discussion of the theme, he made a special application after his manner: —

" 'Tis an Evident Affront unto the *Grace of God*, for Men to make the Birth of Our *Holy Saviour* an Encouragment and an Occasion for very *Unholy Enormities*. . . . Can you in your *Conscience* think that our *Holy Saviour* is honoured by *Mad Mirth*, by long *Eating*, by hard *Drinking*, by lewd *Gaming*, by rude Revelling, by a *Mass* fit for none but a *Saturn* or a *Bacchus*, or the Night of a *Mahometan Ramadam?* . . . Shall it be said That at the *Birth* of our Saviour, for which we owe as High Praises to God as [the Heavenly Host can do], We take the Time to please the *Hellish Legions*, and to do Actions that have much more of *Hell* than of *Heaven* in them? "[1]

The church wisely replied by publishing without note or comment the Christmas sermon preached by Rev. Mr. Harris on the same day, — a simple religious discourse, well written, and not at all calculated to excite his hearers to the enormities which Mather held up to abhorrence.[2]

At this time Tate and Brady's version of the Psalms was introduced into the worship of the Chapel.[3] In thus improving

---

[1] "Grace Defended. A Censure on the Ungodliness, By which the Glorious Grace of God is too commonly Abused. A Sermon preached Dec. 25, 1712, Boston-Lecture. Boston: 1712." This has been thought to be the first Christmas Sermon from a New England Puritan pulpit.

[2] " A Sermon Preached at the Queen's Chappel in *Boston*, upon Christmas Day, The 25*th* of *December*, 1712. Publish'd at the Request of the Gentlemen of the Vestry. By Mr. Harris, One of the Ministers of the said Chappel, and Fellow of Jesus-College in Oxford. Boston, in *New-England*. Printed by *B. Green*; Sold by *Joanna Perry*, at her Shop in King Street. 1712. St. John, Chap. I. Verse 12."

He says " I 'l (1) consider The Dignity of the Person whom we are to receive. (2) I 'l shew How we are to receive Him. (3) The great advantage of doing so, for thereby we become the Sons of God. (4) I 'l represent the great Sinfulness of not receiving Jesus Christ.

" And in the *Last Place* Draw Some Inferences from the whole." The sermon amplifies these points, but has nothing quotable.

[3] The title was : " Brady and Tate's Psalms for the Use of His Majesty's Chappell of America. Boston: 1713."

The objections to anything except versions of the Psalms in the Church of England itself were stated by Romaine : " I blame nobody for singing human compositions. My complaint is against preferring men's poems to the good word of God, and preferring them to it in the Church. I have no quarrel with Dr. Watts, or with any living or dead versifier. I would not have all their poems burnt. My concern is to see Christian

this part of the service and discarding the Old Version by Sternhold and Hopkins, the English fashion was followed. That version had in London "fallen into general contempt," although in many churches in England it held its place against the New Version and later hymns "well into the present century." The New Version had been allowed "by the Court at Kensington" — the only authority upon which it rests — in 1696, and soon made its way.[1]

It is not difficult to reconstruct, from the hints that remain, the method of music which had prevailed in the church. As in a parish church in England, it was the duty of the clerk to "give out the Psalm, to lead it, very commonly to read it out line by line, and frequently to select what was to be sung," — a "shameful mode of psalmody almost confined to the wretched solo of a parish clerk, or to a few persons huddled together in one corner of the church, who sung to the praise and glory of themselves, for the entertainment and often to the weariness of the congregation." The organ now gave solemn beauty to the service, yet without depriving the clerk of his precentor's function; and it is probable that one of the noblest features of liturgical worship was still lacking, as in England, where during most of the century "chanting was almost unknown in parish churches, being regarded as distinctively belonging to Cathedral worship."[2]

Inadequate as the music still was to the rich capacities of the public order of worship, it was far beyond anything in the surrounding Puritan community. Our forefathers had brought with them from England five tunes; and these, perpetuated not by written notes but by tradition, continued for a long time the

congregations shut out divinely inspired Psalms, and take in Dr. Watts's flights of fancy, as if the words of a poet were better than those of a prophet." Later, Romaine expunged his severe animadversions on modern hymns. "We no longer read," said Toplady, "of Watts's hymns being Watts's whims." See "Church of England in Eighteenth Century," ii. 271.

[1] It has been justly said: "The Old Version, with the exception of that of the C_{th} psalm, which was not by Sternhold and Hopkins at all, nor by their regular coadjutors, but by Kethe, an exile with Knox at Geneva in 1555, has very few real merits."— *Church of England in Eighteenth Century*, ii. 268. The authors of the New Version were men of

no elevation of character, as may be inferred from most of their work. *Nahum Tate* (1652-1715) in 1698 succeeded Shadwell as Court Poet, — "a good-natured, fuddling companion, and his latter days were spent in the Mint as a refuge from his creditors." *Nicholas Brady* (1659-1716) had been an active promoter of the Revolution, and was basking in royal favor as chaplain to the King and Queen; he was also rector of the two benefices of Clapham and Richmond. A few of their compositions have excellence, notably Tate's Christmas hymn, written in 1712, "As shepherds watched their flocks by night."

[2] Church of England in the Eighteenth Century, ii. 481, 484, 485.

only ones in use. It is probable that the stir produced by the music of the Queen's Chapel stimulated the whole community. In 1714 Rev. John Tufts of Newbury published a collection of twenty-eight tunes, which was received with disfavor by the purists as a needless variety in public worship. Cotton Mather described the Puritan music. He says: —

"It has been found in some of our congregations, that in length of time their singing has degenerated into an odd noise that has had more of what we want a name for than any regular singing in it; whereby the Celestial Exercise is dishonoured, and indeed the Third Commandment is trespassed upon." [1]

At this time also the church received a noteworthy gift. The acquisition of an organ was a great event; it was the first ever heard in New England, and was a most dangerous innovation in the eyes of the good townspeople. This was the bequest of Thomas Brattle, Esq., a successful merchant of Boston, the treasurer of Harvard College, and the principal founder of the church in Brattle Square, he having been the owner of the lot of land in Brattle Close on which it was erected.[2] His prominence in this brought him in collision with President Mather.

He had the courage to write (though he held back his paper) in defence of the victims of the witchcraft delusion in 1692. He was a man of wealth and public spirit, greatly skilled in

[1] Cotton Mather: "The Accomplished Singer," etc., 1721. He also published "Psalterium Americanum. . . . Which Pure Offering is accompanied with Illustrations, digging for Hidden Treasures in it, And Rules to Employ it upon the Glorious and Various Intentions of it. Whereto are added Some other Portions of the Sacred Scripture, to Enrich the Cantional. 1718." He says in it that in the "twice seven versions," which he has seen, the authors "put in as large an Heap of poor Things, which are intirely their own, meerly for the sake of preserving the *Clink* of the *Rhyme*, Which after all is of small consequence unto a Generous Poem, and none at all unto the Melody of Singing."

Judge Sewall had a musical gift and used to "set the tune." He records his mishap on one occasion: "I intended Windsor, and fell into High Dutch; and then essaying to set another Tune, went into a Key much too high. The Lord humble me and Instruct me that I should be occasion of any Interruption in the Worship of God." Notwithstanding such drawbacks to devotion, the good Puritan abhorred the æsthetic ways into which the children of the Puritans had fallen: "I heard a sermon [at Oxford] at St. Mary's. . . . I am a lover of Musick to a fault; yet I was uneasy there; and the justling out the Institution of Singing Psalms by the boisterous Organ is that can never be answered to the great Master of Religious Ceremonies. 'Twere a kindness if he that stands up like a Scare Crow to mock the Psalm would spare his pains." — *Mass. Hist. Proc.* 1873, p. 360.

[2] He was born in Boston June 20, 1658, son of Thomas and Elizabeth (Tyng) Brattle; graduated at Harvard College 1676, and May 8, 1693, was chosen its Treasurer, and "Continu^d in that Post 20 years and ten days," more than doubling the property of the College, which, when received by his successor, amounted to "nearly £3,800 of personal estate, and a real estate yielding £280." He died May 18, 1713.

THE CHURCH ENLARGED.

mathematics; "and in the Church He was known and valued for his Catholic Charity to all of the reformed Religion, but more especialy his gr⁺ Veneration for the Ch. of Engl⁴ althô his gen! and more constant comũnion was with the Nonconformists, and both w! Witnesses of his gr! Piety, Strict Justice, and his Exemplary Temperance, even to Austerity. . . . He dyed a Bachelor about 55 years of Age."[1]

"His independence of the strong prejudice universal in New England against the use of instrumental music in public worship," as well as his sympathy with liturgical forms, is indicated by the clause of his will in which he made this bequest: —

"I give, dedicate, and Devote my Organ to the praise and glory of God in the s⁴ Church [in Brattle Square], if they shall accept thereof, and within a year after my decease procure a Sober person that can play skilfully thereon with a loud noise. Otherwise to y⁰ Church of England in this towne on y⁰ same terms and conditions; and on their Non-acceptance or discontinuance as before I give the same to my Nephew William Brattle."

The record of Brattle-Square Church reads thus: —

"July 24, 1713. The Rev. Mr. William Brattle, pastor of the church in Cambridge, signified by a letter the legacy of his brother, Thomas Brattle, Esq., late deceased, of a pair of organs, which he dedicated and devoted to the praise and glory of God with us, if we should accept thereof, and within a year after his decease procure a sober person skilful to play thereon. The church, with all possible respect to the memory of our deceased Friend and Benefactor, *Voted*, that they did not think it proper to use the same in the publick worship of God."[2]

There was a special fitness in the burial of this benefactor of the church in the Brattle tomb in the King's Chapel burying-ground, within sound of the noble instrument which thenceforward enriched the services of the church.[3]

---

[1] Boston News-Letter, quoted in the interesting notice of Brattle in Sibley's "Harvard Graduates," ii. 494.

[2] In 1790 that Society changed their minds and introduced an organ, though for years objection was made to its being played except as an accompaniment to the singing of psalms. There is a tradition that a wealthy parishioner, on the arrival of this instrument from England, offered to give for the poor the sum which it had cost, provided the boxes containing it might be thrown overboard.

[3] It is worthy of note that this handsome gift to the church came through the hands of a Congregational minister. Rev. William Brattle, of Cambridge, who died Feb. 15, 1716–17, in the 55th year of his age and 21st of his ministry, was "a man of marked politeness and courtesy, of compassion and charity. He had a very large estate, and he scattered his gifts with a liberal hand, yet without ostentation. He was patient and pacific in his temper, and 'seemed to have equal respect to good men of all denominations. . . . With humility he united mag-

At a meeting of the Gentlem of the Church this 3ᵈ day of Augᵗ 1713, Refering to the Orgains Giveing them by Thomas Brattle, Esq: Deceᵈ,

nanimity.'... He was thoroughly of the Puritan school in theology, yet in ecclesiastical usages he was liberal." He favored the movement of the Manifesto Church. See McKenzie's " First Church in Cambridge," p. 141; 1 Mass. Hist. Coll. vii. 55.

The first reference to this organ is in the Rev. Joseph Green's Diary : "1711, May 29 [Boston]. I was at Mr. Thomas Brattle's: heard yᵉ organs and saw strange things in a microscope." — *Essex Inst. Proc.* x. 96.

At that time it was still disputed, even in England, " whether organs were to be considered superstitious and Popish. They had been destroyed or silenced in the time of the Commonwealth; and it was not without much misgiving on the part of timid Protestants that, after the Restoration, one London church after another admitted the suspected instruments. . . . It was noted, as one of the signs of High Church reaction in Queen Anne's time, that churches without organs had thinner congregations."

The reasons for the Congregational objection to the use of organs were stated by Cotton Mather. He argues that the instrumental music used in the old church of Israel was an institution of God, the instruments being explicitly called His instruments; but that as not one word of institution is to be found in the Gospel for instrumental music in the worship of God, and that because He "rejects all He does not command in His worship, He now, therefore, in effect, says to us, *I will not hear the melody of thy organs.*" He asks, " If we admit instrumental music in the worship of God, how can we resist the Imposition of all the Instruments used among the ancient Jews? Yea, Dancing as well as Playing, and several other Judaic actions."

The subject was discussed in various Theses at Cambridge Commencements:

" Do organs excite a devotional spirit in divine worship? Negative, 1730.

" Does music promote salvation ? Affirmative, 1762.

" Does the recent reformation in vocal music contribute greatly toward promoting the perfection of divine worship? Affirmative, 1767."

The next organ introduced into Massachusetts may have been in 1743, when John Clark had leave to put up his organ in St. Peter's Church, Salem. In 1728, after Dean Berkeley's return to England, he sent an organ to the town here bearing his name. The gift, not being welcomed, went to Trinity Church, Newport, where it now is. " Stiles's diary informs us that on the Sabbath before July 10, 1770, an organ was played in the Congregational church at Providence, R. I., and that this was the first instance of such music in any dissenting church in all British America. It further relates that an English gentleman had offered £500 to any such church as would set up an organ and have it used in their worship."

As lately as 1786 was published in London " A Tractate of Church Music ; being an Extract from the Reverend and Learned Mr. Peirce's Vindication of the Dissenters," with the motto, " The Christian religion shines brightest in its own dress ; and to paint it is but to deform it;" maintaining that " Instrumental music is not fit and proper for the public worship of God." This Tractate on Church Music is inscribed "to the Reverend Doctor Chauncy and the Reverend Mr. John Clark, The Ministers ; and to the Several Members of the First Congregational Dissenting Church in Boston in America." Mr. H. Stevens (Catalogue, London, 1881) states that, " In 1786 the First Church felt the want of an Organ, and as their Pastor had received large sums of money from Mr. Thomas Brande Hollis for Harvard College, they prevailed upon him to write to this gentleman in London and endeavour to extract from him £500 for the said organ. Instead of granting this extraordinary request, Mr. Hollis caused 500 copies of this Tractate to be printed and sent over to the Pastor, Deacons, and Members of the ' Old First,' endeavouring thereby to inculcate in them that modesty and simplicity in their public worship which was formerly Bostonian, but which they were now apparently outgrowing. Never before or since, probably, was so much pious sarcasm concealed in so small a book. What became of the 500 copies is not known. The tract is now scarce, only two or three copies being known."

THE CHURCH ENLARGED.

Voted, that the Orgins be Accepted by the Church, and that M{r} Miles answer M{r} William Brattle's Letter concerning the Same.

At a Vestry held at Boston Feb{y}, 1713–14, *Voted*; that the Church Wardens write to Coll. Redknap and desire him to go to M{r} Edw{d} Enston, who lives next Door to M{r} Master's on Tower Hill, and discourse him as to his Inclination and Ability to come over to be Organist here, We being willing to allow him Thirty p{ds} p Annum this money, which with other Advantages as to Dancing, Musick, etc., we doubt not will be sufficient Encouregement.

March 2{d}, 1713–14, *Voted*, that the Organs be forthwith put up.[1]

See "Church of England in the Eighteenth Century," ii. 484; Mather's "Magnalia," v. 56; Rev. E. J. Young on "Subjects for Master's Degree," 1655–1791, in Mass. Hist. Proc. 1880, p. 144; Felt's "Salem," ii 634.

[1] 1713. A List of all those well Disspossed Gentlemen and other Persons that Contributed Towards the maintainance and Suport of the Orgins Given by Thomas Brattle, Esq{r} for the Vse of the Church of England in Boston. Viz.:—

	£	s.	d.
M{r} Chris Cornelson	1.	00.	00
M{r} Charles Bruce	1.	00.	00
M{r} John Blore	1.	00.	00
M{r} Sear Mathews	1.	00.	00
Cap{t} David Pigon	1.	00.	00
Cap{t} John Corney	0.	10.	00
M{r} Thomas Coffen	1.	00.	00
Doc{t} Stewart	1.	00.	00
M{r} John Arburtnet	1.	00.	00
M{r} Richard Hall	1.	00.	00
Cap{t} Sypron Southack	1.	00.	00
M{r} Richard Pullin	0.	10.	00
M{r} Henry Sharpe	0.	10.	00
M{r} John Powell	1.	00.	00
M{r} James Iuers	0.	10.	00
M{r} Humprey Hutchenson	1.	00.	00
M{rs} Christian Macarty	0.	10.	00
Cap{t} Mat: Wybert	0.	10.	00
M{r} Iames Lindell	1.	00.	00
M{r} Daniall Stevens	0.	10.	00
M{r} Georg Cabbot	0.	10.	00
M{r} Iames Smith	1.	00.	00
M{r} Will Iones	0.	03.	00
	£18.	03.	00
M{r} Edward Weaver	0.	10.	00
M{r} John Briggs	0.	10.	00
Peter Walton	0.	10.	00
M{r} William Vickers	1.	00.	00
M{r} Eben{r} Mountfort	1.	00.	00
Cap{t} George Morris	1.	00.	00
	£4.	10.	00

	£	s.	d.
Maj{r} Mascaren	1.	00.	00
Maj{r} George Lee	1.	00.	00
M{r} Henry Franklin	0.	10.	00
M{r} Benj. Brumley	0.	10.	00
M{r} Nich{s} Robarts	1.	00.	00
M{r} George Emott	0.	10.	00
M{r} Rob{t} Fowler	0.	10.	00
M{r} Roland Dicke	0.	10.	00
M{r} Benj. Iohns	0.	10.	00
M{r} Tho: Silby	0.	10.	00
M{r} Thomas Shipard	1.	00.	00
M{r} Iobe Bull	0.	10.	00
M{r} Thomas Lichmere	1.	00.	00
M{r} Iob Lewis	1.	00.	00
M{r} Easte Hatch	0.	10.	00
M{r} Thomas Creess	1.	00.	00
M{r} John Oulton	1.	00.	00
M{r} Thomas Banester	1.	00.	00
M{r} Roger Patterson	0.	10.	00
M{r} Ed Mills	0.	10.	00
M{r} Benj Carter	0.	10.	00
M{r} Adam Bathe	0.	10.	00
M{r} Jos: Hearne	1.	00.	00
	£16.	10.	00
Brought from y{e} other side To August 31, £1. 13s. 00d.	£18.	03.	00
	£34.	13.	00
M{r} East Apthorp	1.	00.	00
M{r} Joseph Lloyd	1.	00.	00
M{r} Rob{t} Skelton	1.	00.	00
Tho: Dunklin	0.	10.	00
Cor: Jackson	0.	10.	00
Rob{t} Rudgate	0.	10.	00
	£39.	03.	00
	4.	10.	00
	£43.	13.	00

Voted, that the Two long Pews fronting the Pulpit be made into Two Square Pews, One for Coll. Tailer, the other for M.[r] Jekyll, and that the Two Pews behind them be made into one for the use of Masters of Vessells, And that the Pew behind be for Eight old men as shall be there placed.

Ordered, that M.[r] James Baker be Clark in the Room of M.[r] Gyles. M.[r] Gyles to be p.[d] Ten p.[ds] p Ann. and Baker all other Profitts.

Easter Monday, April 18, 1715. *Voted*, M.[r] James Baker chosen Clerk for the Year Ensuing: he behaving himself as he Ought to Do.

M.[r] Roger Judd, Sexton.

It must have been the greatest musical sensation ever known in Boston when this sound was first heard here. Many a younger Puritan doubtless ventured within the doors of the church to hear it, — and perhaps the organ may share a part of the credit with Mr. Myles of the numerous accessions to his Society, — but to the older generation it must have seemed " an awfu' thing to mak' sic a noise on the Sabbath day."

There was no one thoroughly competent to play the instrument nearer than England, though a temporary supply — Mr. Price — was found, till negotiations with Mr. Edward Enstone persuaded him to cross the Atlantic, and by Christmas, 1714, to assume the duties of organist.

LONDON, July y.[e] 24.th 1714.

Gentlemen, — M.[r] Harrison and my selfe waited on M.[r] Newman the other day, relating to an address sent from the Church Wardens and Vestry, above two years since, which address I know was designed for D.[r] Smalldrige's perusal and delivery; but through what mistake I know not it came into M.[r] Newman's hands, who does protest it was directed to him without one word from any body for his further directions. He gave me the inclosed Coppy which I saw compared with the Original, which is all the acco.[t] he can give of that affair.

I likewise send you a Coppy of the Articles of Agreem.[t] made with M.[r] Enston the Organist. He would come over with Cap.[t] Lethered, but could not possibly get ready; so that it will be late in y.[e] fall before he can be with you.

The Society is not as yet come to any resolution ab.[t] M.[r] Miles's affairs.

I have nothing more to add, but that I am with all respect
Yo.[r] most humble and Obed.[t] Serv.[t]
J. REDKNAP

To S.[r] Charles Hobby }
To John Jekyll.　　　 }

Articles of Agreem.[t] made, had, and concluded upon the 29.th day of Iune, Anno Domine 1714, and in the Thirteenth year of the Reign of Our Sovereign Lady Ann, by the Grace of God of Great Brittain, France, and Ireland Queen, Defender of the Faith, &c.[a], Between Edward In-

THE CHURCH ENLARGED. 213

stone of the Citty of London, Gent., of the one part, and Coll° Iohn Redknap, of Boston in North America, Gent. (for and on behalfe of the Churchwardens and Vestrymen now and for the time being of the Queen's Chappel in Boston aforesaid) of the other part, in manner and forme following, vizt: Whereas, the said Coll° Iohn Redknap was authorized by ye Churchwardens and Vestrymen of the Queen's Chappel in Boston aforesaid, to procure, contract, and agree for them and in their names with a person well qualifyed and would undertake to be Organist in the said Chappel; And if said Edward Instone being a person fitly qualifyed for the said Imploym^t and willing to undertake ye same: It is therefore mutually covenanted, Concluded, and agreed vpon by and between ye said parties, and the said Edward Instone doth agree to ye same, That he the said Edward shall and will by or before the 25th day of October next insueing, Wind and Weather permitting, be at Boston in North America aforesaid; and being there, shall and will at all proper and usuall times of Divine service Officiate as Organist in the said Chappell for and during the space of Three years certain, to be computed from the day that the said Edward Instone shall arive at Boston aforesaid, and afterwards for such terme or time as the Church Wardens and Vestry men of the said Chappel now and for ye time being and the said Edward Instone shall think fit and agree upon. In consideration of which voyage so to be performed by the said Edward Instone, he, the said Collⁿ In^o Redknap, hath this day pay^d unto ye said Edward Instone the sume of £10 of lawful money of great Brittain, the Rec^t whereof is hereby acknowledged; and the said Coll° Jno Redknap (for and on the part and behalfe of the Church Wardens and Vestrymen of the Queen's Chappel in Boston aforesaid now and for the time being) Doth Covenant, promise, and agree to and with ye said Edward Instone, his Exc^{rs} and Adm^{rs}, That the Church Wardens and Vestry men of the said Chappel now and for the time being shall and will from time to time and at all times well and truely pay or cause to be paid unto the said Edward Instone the sume of £7 10s. p Quarter imediately after each Quarter day, Current money of New England, for every Quarter of a year that the said Edward Instone shall officiate as Organist in ye said Chappel. And to ye true performance and keeping of all and singular ye Covenants and agreements herein before contained, each of ye said partys bindeth himselfe, his Exc^{rs} and Adm^{rs}, unto the other of them, his Exc^{rs}, Adm^{rs}, and assignes, in ye penal sume of £20 of lawful money of Great Brittain by these presents to be paid recovered. In Wittness whereof the said partys to these presents have interchangeably set their hands and seals the day and year first above written.

EDWARD ENSTONE [L.S.]

Sealed and Delivered in ye p̄sence of
Jona : Gawthorne,
Stephen Bellas, —
Gentlemen.

1714

		£ s. d.
Augt 20th	P^d Mr Wm Price organist One Qr Sallary due at Mids^r 1714	7. 10. 00
Jany 18	P^l Henry Caner[1] in Full	19. 10. 00
24	P^d Rog^r Judd for Henry Redin for Carving 2 Cantileaners	1. 15. 00
Feby 24	P^d Mrs Rupert Lord for the curtain agst the Pulpitt	1. 14. 00
March 12	P^d to Coll Redknap[2] for Expenses he p^d for Mr Enston In Eng^d £10 12s. st.	17. 00. 00
Aprill 1st	P^d Mr Edwd Enston Organist a Q^r due March 25th last	7. 10. 00
	Contra.	*Cr.*
Augt 30	Rec^d of Mr Judd for Five Seats in the Gallery .	2. 10. 00

LONDON, Septr 7th 1714.

Gentlemen, — According to yor former Request and Directions I now send you over Mr Edward Enstone as Organist to ye King's Chappel in Boston. I sent you in July last by Capt Lethered a Copy of Articles of Agreement between him and my selfe. What I have to say further upon that head is, That he is said to be a person of a sober life and Conversation, and well qualifyed for what he hath undertaken ; and I doubt not but he will approve himselfe as such, which will merit yor assistance in other matters relating to his profession. I am, Gentl^n, with all respects,

Yo^r very humble Servant,   J. REDKNAP.

The organist brought with him not only sacred music to these silent shores, but also secular and profane notes which had been unwonted before. Sewall records: —

"1716 [Nov.] 29. 5. After Lecture Mr. Welsteed and Capt. Wadsworth acquainted Mr. Bromfield and me that a Ball was designed at Enston's in the evening ; pray'd us to prevent the Govr being there. . . . At last his Excel^{ly} promised us not to be there."

There is a tradition, that on account of the public prejudice the organ remained in the church porch, in the boxes in which it was packed, for seven months. In 1756, when a superior instrument took its place in the new stone church, the organ was sold to St. Paul's Church, Newburyport, where it remained in use eighty years, and in 1836 was purchased for the chapel of St. John's Church, Portsmouth, N. H., for about $450, and put up in a new case, and has been in regular use ever since.

"The original pipes and wind chest remain in perfect order. And this time-honored instrument, which certainly was the first introduced into

---

[1] Perhaps father of Rev. Henry Caner, rector of King's Chapel, 1747-76.

[2] The diarist notes that Decr 24, 1716, news comes that Redknap and David Jeffries were lost in the wreck of the "Amity" off Dungeness.

New England, and probably the first erected in the colonies, bids fair to last another century. Could it speak its history, and describe the scenes with which it has been surrounded, in a sweet harmonious tone, as it sounds forth in obedience to the touch, how full of interest would be its narration! It could tell of the reign of Queen Anne, and the interesting events of the reign of five British kings before Victoria ascended the throne. It could tell that when it commenced its notes in Boston, but one newspaper was published in the colony to proclaim its arrival. It could tell you of the little boy who came to listen, and to wonder — that same individual who afterwards harnessed the lightning. It could tell you of all the stirring events of the Revolution, and of its wonderful duty at the age of 84 to sound the Dirge of Washington. Sacred, however, to holy purposes for which it was erected, it has been a looker on rather than a participator in the secular events of the world." [1]

This stage of our narrative opened with the mission of Keith [2] to these shores by the Society for Propagating the Gospel: it closes with the appearance of a lay missionary of not less controversial temper. A more aggressive period in church affairs began with the return once more of Nicholson from England armed with large and special powers, ecclesiastical as well as civil and military. On his arrival, Oct. 12, 1713, he dined with the Governor and Council, and his presence at once braced Dudley's dubious churchmanship. Judge Sewall records: —

"At my motion Mr. Colman was sent for, and crav'd a Blessing. Mr. Myles came in, and the Gov.' desired him to return Thanks."

"Nov.' 19. A Council is call'd; Sit round the Fire. Gen. Nicholson blames the observing a Fast without the order of Authority; the Queen was Head of the Church: seem'd to be Warm. The Lieut.-Governour seem'd to intimat that their Church, the members of it, were Treated as if they were Heathen. Gen' Nicholson mention'd it as graviminous that the Shops were shut up. The Governour said 'Twas voluntary; none was order'd to shut up his Shop; Country-men brought wares to Town as on other days; that he himself came to Town as supposing the Episcopal Church had observ'd the Fast; when he saw they did not, he went to Mr. Colman's. I was surpris'd with this uncomfortable Talk, and said Nothing. At length a Motion was made, I think by Gen' Nicholson,

---

[1] This flight of fancy is by the late Rev. Charles Burroughs, D.D., rector of St. John's from 1810 to 1857. "The organ was put in its new case and repaired in 1836, by Mr. Morse, of Newburyport." An expert states that (in 1876) "the tone is beautiful and clear, though of not much body, owing to so many shrill stops. The stops are open diapason, stopped diapason, principal, twelfth, fifteenth, and sesquialtra. The old organs were deficient in the bass: sub-bass pipes were unknown, and are a modern invention." G Herrick in Lowell "Vox Populi," April 1, 1876.

[2] See Chapter V.

that there might be a Gen¹ Fast. I was of Opinion there was great need of it, and readily voted for it." [1]

The Church Records not only contain important action which was evidently suggested by this distinguished representative of the church militant, but his commission is formally entered there.

The Society's Instrument to the Honble Francis Nicholson, Esqr.

Whereas, her most Sacred Majesty Our Sovereigne Lady Anne by the Grace of God Queen of Great Brittaine, France, and Ireland hath been graciously pleased by Commission under the Great Seal of Great Brittaine bearing Date the Fourteenth day of this Instant October to nominat, constitute, and Appoint the Honble Francis Nicholson, Esqr., her Majesty's Commissioner in North America for several purposes therein mentioned. And Whereas, the Society for the Propogation of the Gospel in Foreign parts have for Just and good Reasons them thereunto moving, desired and Requested the said Francis Nicholson (being a Worthy Member of the same) to make Enquiry of and concerning Such of the Society's Missionaries, Schoolmasters, and Catechists as also of the Present State of the Churches, Glebes, Parsonage-Houses, and Libraries (sent by the Society) in the Plantations for the better Information of the Society concerning them, To which Desire and Request the said Francis Nicholson hath been pleased to consent. Now know all men by these Presents that the said Society Have and by these presents Do (as much as in them is and ought to be in most humble Submission to her Majesty's Royal Prerogative and Power and the Jurisdiction of the R! Rev^d the Lord Bishop of London) Request and Desire the said Francis Nicholson to make Enquiry in the best manner and by such Ways and Means as to him shall be thought fitt and requisite of and concerning such of the Society's Missionaries, Schoolmasters, and Catechists, with respect to the good Purposes and Designs of the Society relating to them, And of the present State of the Churches, Glebes, Parsonage-Houses, and Libraries (Sent by the Society) within all and every Such Part and Parts of Her Majesty's Dominions and Countries as are comprised in the Commission now Granted to the said Francis Nichol-

---

[1] Sewall records a characteristic scene with Nicholson. The Judge had broken up a Health-drinking party on the Queen's birthday, Feb. 6, 1713-4, being Saturday evening, at which "Mr. Brinley put on his hat to affront me. I made him take it off." Several were fined, and Nicholson's secretary was imprisoned. When the Council met, March 9, General Nicholson was present and "asked whether did not know that he was here with the Broad Seal of England? . . . Then with a Roaring Noise the Gen¹ said, I demand JUSTICE against Mr. Sewall and Bromfield for sending my Secretary to prison without acquainting me with it! And hastily rose up, and went down and walk'd the Exchange, where he was so furiously Loud, that the Noise was plainly heard in the Council-Chamber, the door being shut." The governor and a majority of the council released Netmaker the General's secretary.

son from her Majesty for the purposes therein mentioned. To the end the said Francis Nicholson May Give and Transmit to the said Society a full Particular and Impartial account thereof. That the said Society may be the better enabled to Discharge the Great trust reposed in them to the Advancement of the Glory of God the Honour of her Majesty and Spiritual good and Welfare of her Subjects in those Parts. In Wittness whereof the said Society have hereunto caused to be affixed their Common Seal this Seventeenth day of October, in the Eleventh year of her said Majesty's Reigne Annoq Domini 1712.
By Order of the Society,
W. TAYLOR,
Secretary.

In the long story of the efforts of the Church of England to root itself in America, the Society for the Propagation of the Gospel in Foreign Parts has a conspicuous place. King's Chapel, indeed, was founded fifteen years before that Society was organized, and was never aided from its funds; but this was the only exception of a self-supporting church among a group of struggling episcopal parishes which depended on the money, and were in missionary relations to what was known as "the Venerable Society." And even King's Chapel and its ministers, though not in any relation of dependence, were, as the Records here given show, in close correspondence and accord with the Secretary of the Society. Nor does it seem doubtful that in the early years the Queen's Chapel, as was natural with the only parish that had given proof of independent vigor, was informally constituted adviser and deputy of that powerful organization. The origin of this Society is to be traced principally to the wise and Christian spirit of one man, Dr. Thomas Bray; and his inspiration is due to the indomitable Blair, who went to Virginia as a missionary in 1685, and who perhaps did more as Commissary there than any other man to save religion in that colony from utter decay, and to Bishop Compton, who had chosen Blair for his work, and in 1695 appointed Bray his commissary for Maryland. Dr. Bray had a genius for organizing religious philanthropy, and his plans extended far beyond his province. He began by obtaining contributions for libraries for the clergy engaged in foreign service. In this task, which may have been suggested to him by conversation with Mr. Myles and by King William's gift to King's Chapel in 1694, as his appointment fell at that very time, he was successful, establishing thirty-nine valuable libraries in America.[1]

---

[1] The Revolution is said to have scattered them all.

But his enduring monument was in two Societies, so sagaciously planned that they still exist in large vigor and usefulness, — that "for Promoting Christian Knowledge," and that "for the Propagation of the Gospel in Foreign Parts." The latter was chartered June 16, 1701, and although in its incorporation the two Archbishops and ninety-two others — the most conspicuous dignitaries and other Christian people in the kingdom — were named, and although also it was warmly favored by Archbishop Tenison and Bishop Compton, Dr. Bray was pre-eminently its founder.[1] In this Society met in friendly counsel representatives of the most opposed sections of the Church of England, from Bishop Burnet to Robert Nelson, the typical Christian layman of his time.[2] Nelson and Sir Francis Nicholson were both admitted to the Society Nov. 21, 1701.

The objects of the Society are best stated in its charter: —

WILLIAM the THIRD, *by the Grace of* GOD, *of* ENGLAND, SCOTLAND, FRANCE, *and* IRELAND, *King, Defender of the Faith, etc. To all Christian People to whom these Presents shall come, Greeting:*

I. Whereas, We are credibly Informed, That in many of Our Plantations, Colonies, and Factories beyond the Seas, belonging to Our Kingdom of *England*, the Provision for Ministers is very mean, and many others of our said Plantations, Colonies, and Factories are wholly Destitute and Unprovided of a Maintenance for Ministers, and the Publick Worship of God; and for lack of Support and Maintenance for such, many of our Loving Subjects do want the Administration of God's Word and Sacraments, and seem to be abandoned to Atheism and Infidelity; and also for want of Learned and Orthodox Ministers to instruct our said Loving Subjects in the Principles of True Religion, divers Romish Priests and Jesuits are the more encouraged to pervert and draw over Our said Loving Subjects to Popish Superstition and Idolatry.

II. And whereas We think it our Duty, as much as in Us lies, to promote the Glory of God, by the Instruction of Our People in the Christian Religion; and that it will be highly conducive for accomplishing

---

[1] See Sprague, Annals, etc., v. 19.

[2] He was the author of "Practice of True Devotion," and "Festivals and Fasts." His active philanthropy was inspired by a genial and serene religion, yet his sympathies were warmly with the High Church party. He was in 1710 "commissioner for the erection of new churches in London," and labored "for advancing Christian teaching in grammar schools, for improving prisons, for helping French Protestants and Eastern Christians. His thoughts were engaged on hospitals, ragged schools, penitentiaries, homes for destitute infants, associations of gentlewomen for charitable and religious purposes; theological, training, and missionary colleges; houses for temporary religious retirement and retreat," etc. Among his friends were Kew, Kettlewell, Dodwell, Hickes, and other Non-jurors, Bull, Beveridge, and Bray. See the interesting chapter on "Robert Nelson: his Friends and Church Principles," in "History of the English Church in the Eighteenth Century."

those Ends, that a sufficient Maintenance be provided for an Orthodox Clergy to live amongst them, and that such other Provision be made as may be necessary for the Propagation of the Gospel in those Parts.

III. And whereas, we have been well assured That if We would be graciously pleased to erect and settle a Corporation for the receiving, managing, and disposing of the Charity of Our loving Subjects, divers Persons would be Induced to extend their Charity to the Uses and Purposes aforesaid.

IV. Know ye, therefore, That We have, etc.[1]

If this preamble is interpreted simply according to its wording and in harmony with "its mild and gentle spirit," it would seem that the Society "was incorporated in the interests of a common and generous Christian charity" without sectarian or proselyting design, being intended to benefit places destitute of Protestant and civilizing influences. It contains no specific reference to special interests of the Church of England; "so that charitable persons among the English dissenters might not only have been donors to the fund, as they were, but also managers of the Corporation." The Society, however, early took a different view of their duty, and deemed it important not only to send missionaries to such places as the preamble indicates, but to encourage Episcopal missions in New England itself, — the one part of America which was adequately provided with an established clergy of character. This soon led to a series of controversies, which lasted until the Revolution and were highly detrimental to the Christian temper of the country.[2]

Nicholson probably stirred the Queen's Chapel to co-operate in urging a plan which the Society had greatly at heart. The missionaries sent by the Society to all the colonies except Maryland and Virginia (where the church, being established, was provided for) continued to be licensed, as had earlier been the custom, by the Bishop of London. But the manifest imperfec-

---

[1] "An Historical Account of the Incorporated Society for the *Propagation of the Gospel* in Foreign Parts. By David Humphreys, D.D., Secretary to the Honorable Society. London, 1730."

[2] This subject has been ably treated by Rev. George E. Ellis, D.D., in lectures before the Lowell Institute, from which the above sentences are quoted. The device on the Society's seal, adopted in 1701, represents a ship under sail, making toward a point of land; upon the prow standing a minister in gown and bands, with an open Bible in his hand; people standing on the shore in a posture of expectation, and using the Macedonian cry: *Transiens adjuva nos.* A facsimile is given on page 147, *ante*. The instructions to missionaries, adopted in 1702, direct "That they frequently visit their respective Parishioners; those of our own communion, to keep them steady in the profession and practice of Religion, as taught in the Church of England; those that oppose us, or dissent from us, to convince and reclaim them with a spirit of meekness and gentleness."

tion of a system of episcopacy in which the diocesan was three thousand miles distant from his flock, at once stimulated the Society to efforts for a more efficient administration. It is one of the strongest illustrations of the spiritual torpor in which the Church of England lay during the eighteenth century, and of the lack of far-seeing counsels among those who should have been its leaders, that the episcopalians in the colonies were left without the benefits of a complete episcopal organization so long as America was connected with the mother-country. There were, indeed, three attempts to establish bishoprics in the colonies; but the history of each justifies the statement that on the part of the government they were rather political measures for holding the colonies in better subjection, than a religious provision for spiritual needs; and, for this reason perhaps, each failed to be carried through, notwithstanding the urgent representations of earnest churchmen on both sides of the water.

An American Episcopate had originally been proposed during the reign of Charles II., when, about 1672, the King in Council decided to send a bishop to Virginia.[1] A charter was drawn up by the Lord Keeper, Sir Orlando Bridgman, but his displacement through the Cabal ministry defeated the plan. His proposed commission reads thus: —

"Proeterea Volentes Reliquas omnes alias nostras Regiones et plantationes Americanas, sub uno eademq ordine ac Regimine, et sub eadem doctrina et disciplina Authoritate et Jurisdictione Constituere et stabilire: Decrevimus, eas omnes cum ipsarum Ecclesiis presentibus et futuris, adjungere et Unire prædictæ *Ecclesiæ* et *Diocæsi* Virg : Sicuti per presentes, eas omnes et singulas Viz. Singulas Ditiones seu plantationes nostras, versus Borean a Virginia : sive Nova Anglia sive Novum Eboracum aut aliqua alia intermedia loca : . . . adjunctas et unitas esse prædictæ Diocœsi Virg. . . . Volumas tamen et . . . Declaramus quod dictus — et successores sui Episcopi Virginiæ Episcopalem Jurisdictionem et Authoritatem suam Novam Angliam nullo modo exerceant, sed subditos nostros infra Novam Angliam inhabitantes ab omni Episcopali Regimine et Authoritate Immunes liberos et totaliter exemptos esse Volumus, donec aliter a nobis ordinatum fuerit."

It is not surprising that at this early time the rumor of a coming bishop filled the minds of New Englanders with dark thoughts. They did not know that the charter by which he was

---

[1] Dr. Alexander Murray, a companion of the King's exile, was selected. The draught of the proposed charter, found a few years ago among Sir Leoline Jenkins's papers in the library of All Soul's College, Oxford, is printed in Church Papers, Virginia, p. 536.

A BISHOP SOUGHT.

to be created declared them to be "free and totally exempted from all Episcopal rule and authority," or if they had known it, they would have detected Charles Stuart's ulterior purpose in the elastic phrase "till we shall otherwise determine."

The first step taken by the Society had been to send Rev. George Keith on his mission through the northern colonies. Stimulated by his presence, perhaps, addresses were sent to the Society in 1703, "from divers parts of the continent and islands adjacent, for a suffragan to visit the several churches, ordain some, confirm others, and bless all,"[1] in consequence of which the Society addressed a memorial to the Queen, proposing that two bishops be sent to America. What part King's Chapel had taken in this earlier movement does not appear from the Records, but it cannot be doubted that Mr. Myles must have shared in these earnest representations. When the efforts of the Society were directed to the definite point of urging such a measure, neither he nor his church were lacking.

In 1707, Bishop Compton pressed the appointment of a suffragan in a carefully considered statement which was submitted to the Queen's Attorney-General for his opinion.

"The present disorders now arising in some of the Plantations, and likely to increase to an entire discouragement of the Clergy there already Established, doe, I presume, fully convince the necessity of having a Bishop Established in those parts.

"The only question therefore is, what sort of Bishop will be most proper first to settle there. An absolute Bishop . . . will not be so proper, at least to begin with. . . . Besides, all over the Plantations they frequently take other men's wives, are guilty of Bigamy and Incest, which they are apprehensive would be more strictly enquired into, had they a Bishop to inspect over them.

"Now a Suffragan would come among them with all necessary power to restrain vice and keep good order, without any noise or clamour. . . . It will be the safest way to take at first for a proof how it will take amongst them, and all faults and defects may more Easily be corrected and amended."[2]

There can be little doubt that if the Society had moved more rapidly the object would have been gained. The air was full of rumors that such a plan would be carried out. The greatest writer of Queen Anne's time was hopeful of obtaining this transatlantic see. Swift writes to a friend in 1709: —

[1] Abstract of Proceedings, 1703.
[2] Observations of the Bishop of London regarding a Suffragan for America, December, 1707. N. Y. Col. Docs. v. 29.

"I shall go to Ireland some time in summer, being not able to make my friends in the ministry consider my merits, or their promises, enough to keep me here; so that all my hopes now terminate in my bishoprick of Virginia."[1]

The warm interest of Queen Anne in the plan was known, and seemed to insure its success. Her death before its consummation alone prevented the establishment of bishops of the Church of England in America, when in 1713 the Society followed a previous memorial in 1709 by addressing an urgent representation to the Queen, which is entered on our Records, together with Nicholson's commission given above.

The Society's Representation to her Majesty for the Sending Bishops Into America.

To Her Most Excellent Majesty Anne, by the Grace of God of Great Brittaine, France, and Ireland, Queen Defender of the Faith, etc.:

The Representation of the Society for the Propogation of the Gospel In Foreign Parts. Most humbly Sheweth

That as it hath pleased the Divine Goodness to dispose Y^r Majesties Royall Heart for the Establishing of Bishops and Bishopricks within Y^r Majesties Plantations or Colonies and other Y^r Majesties Dominions of America in like manner as the Church of Christ is settled for Ecclesiastical Governm^t In England and Ireland, pursuant to the Apostolical form and Order in all Christian Nations where Bishops have been deemed the true Successors of the Apostles, and as is most agreable to the Inclinations of many of the present Inhabitants of those places, whence there have been made for these Eleven years past Earnest Application for such Bishops to preside amongst them that they may Ordain some, Confirm more, and Bless all by the most Orderly Administration of the Holy Word and Sacrement.

The Society for the Propagation of the Gospel in Foreign Parts Established by the Royall Charter of Y^r Majesties Predecessor, and hereunto Encouraged by Y^r Majesties Gracious Resolution of Promoting so good a Work do as above in all Humility beg leave to lay itt before Y^r Majesty as their Opinion after the most Mature Deliberation That it is Highly Expedient That four Bishops be sent thither as soon as Conveniently may be to forward the Great Work of Converting Infidels to the Saveing Faith of Our Blessed Redeemer and for the Regulating such Christians in their Faith and Practise, as are already Converted thereunto; That is to say, Two for the care and Superintendancy of the Islands and as many for the Continent with the Appointments of Fifteen hund^d pounds p Annum for Each of the Former and one Thousand pounds p Annum for Each of the Latter as the Nature of their Dioceses seem to require in

---

[1] Swift to Hunter, quoted in Anderson, Col. Ch. iii. 127.

Case the Sees of the Former be Settled as is Humbly Proposed by the said Society, The one of them at Barbados for it self and the Leward Islands; The other at Jamaica for it self with the Bahama and Bermuda Islands; Those for the Continent The one of them at Burlington, in New Jersey, where the Society has been at Six hund⁴ pounds Charge and Upwards to purchase a very Convenient House and Land for his Residence, for a District Extending from the East side of Delaware River, to the Utmost Bounds of Y^r Majesties Dominions Eastward Including Newfoundland; The other Williamsburg in Virginia for a District Extending from the West Side of Delaware River to the Utmost Bounds of Y^r Majesties Dominions Westward.

The said Society Humbly beggs Leave farther to Represent That the Appointments for the Bishops of the Islands may be raised from the Best Rectory in the Capital Seat of Each Bishop from the Ordinary Jurisdiction and from the Tenth Parts of all Future Grants and Escheats to the Crown if Y^r Majesty shall so please with such Local Revenues as shall be thought fitt to be made by the Respective Assemblies: The Bishop of Barbadoes to have moreover the Presidentship of Genl Codrington's Colledge to be erected within that Island by the Society therewith Intrusted Under Y^r Majesties Royall Lycence (an Equivolent to which may be found for the Bishop of Jamaica in the Church Lands of St. Christophers, formerly belonging to the Jesuits and Carmelites if Y^r Majesty shall be so pleased to Grant them to the use of the said Society for Propogation of the Gospell in Foreign Parts for the purpose mentioned at the Conclution of the Peace, They being now Granted only in Custodiam) And the Appointments of the Bishops of the Continent, besides what shall be expected from St. Christophers as aforesaid, May unless other proper means be found out for their Maintenance and Support by Y^r Majesties Great Wisdom with that of Y^r Councill and High Court of Parliam^t be made up out of the Ordinary Jurisdiction of their Respective Dioceses, some Lands which may be purchased in those Dominions at Easy Rates, others which may be Granted by the Favour of Y^r Majesties Donation with a Tenth part Clear out of all Future Grants and Escheats, if Y^r Majesty shall be so pleased, and such proportion of the Local Revenues as shall be Sufficient to make up the Amount or In Lieu of such appointments, which shall not be Judged Practicable, That Either a Prebend of Y^r Majesties Guift be annexed to each of the Bishops of the Continent or the Master Ship of the Savoy and that of St. Catharines as Y^r Majesty shall think fitt.

And the Society as in Duty bound shall Ever Pray, etc.

The rumor of such a purpose again stirred up anger and fear in New England; yet it has been truly said that in the papers of King's Chapel asking for Bishops: "There is nothing that could reasonably be objected to in the scheme there proposed for their functions and maintenance. No threats or even ill feeling are manifested towards other communions, and no arbitrary methods are proposed as to the sources or the means of obtaining the funds. The Bishops are asked simply in the service of Episcopalians."[1]

The religious conditions in New England had greatly changed since the charter for a bishop in Charles II.'s time was so easily given and so lightly withheld. There was now here a considerable class of more recent English emigrants, many of them persons of wealth or official rank. They loved their church, and felt the grave inconvenience of the distant supervision of the Bishop of London. It was fitting that the Queen's Chapel, which represented this class in New England, should add its voice to the representation of the Society.

At a meeting of the Vestry of her Majesties Chappell In Boston, New Eng^d Decr 8th 1713.

To the Honble Society for the Propagation of the Gospel in Foreign Parts:

The Representation and Request of the Ministers and Church-Wardens and Vestry of the Church of England In Boston.

We are Informed by the Honble Genl Nicholson, A most Worthy Member of Y^r Honble Society and a most Generous Benefactor to the Church in these Parts that Y^r Honble Society have laid before her Majesty A Particular Scheme for Getting Bishops in these American Parts, and as nothing can contribute more to the Flourishing State of Religion among us, we have made our Humble Address to her Most Sacred Majesty upon that Head, and would Humbly Intreat Some of the Members of Y^r Honble Society to be our Remembrancers to her Majesty on that behalf. And that Almighty God would bless and Prosper all Y^r Pious Endeavours for the Good of his Church, and bless you for those Endeavours, is the hearty Prayer of Y^r Most Obedient and most Devoted humble Serv^{ts},
J. DUDLEY, Govr,
JN^o NELSON,
BOSTON, Decr 8th, 1713. Etc.

At the same time the following address to the Queen was adopted : —

To the Queen's most Excellent Majesty. The humble Address of the Ministers, Church Wardens, and Vestry of the Church of England in Boston, New England.

May it please y^r Majesty, —Your Royall goodness being extended to all, even the Remotest parts of Y^r Majesties Dominions, we take this opportunity of expressing our humble tho' Imperfect Thanks to Y^r Maj-

---

[1] Rev. G. E. Ellis, D.D., in an unpublished Lowell Lecture.

esty for the many Blessings we have enjoyed in the Course of y'r Glorious Reign: Such was Y'r Majestys care of us during the War, that our ease was in a measure Secured by the happy Reduction of the Important fortress of Port Royall under the Auspicious Conduct of General Nicholson, and now that Honble and Advantagious Peace which Y'r Majesty has concluded close mightily Increase our Happiness, by delivering us from the violence of Barbarous Savages who continually infested our country, and acted unheard of Cruelties: To compleat our Felicity, we humbly Entreat of Y'r Majesty to provide for our Spiritual concerns, and to Establish Bishops and Bishopricks within Y'r Majestys Plantations in America.

Wee are informed by Gen'l Nicholson, whose Piety, Generosity, and Zeal for the Church, we cannot sufficiently commend, that the Honble Society for Propagating the Gospel in Foreign Parts, have laid before Y'r Majesty the particular Manner of the Bishop's Respective Settlements. Since nothing can tend more to make Religion Flourish amongst us, we promise ourselves that Y'r Majesty will take this Affair into y'r Royal Consideration. And that it may please Almighty God to grant Y'r Majesty a long and happy Reign over us, and Advance you to Immortal Glory hereafter is the constant and fervent Prayer of Y'r Majestys most Loyall, most Dutifull, and most obedient Subjects.[1]

Bishop Compton had died, at a good old age, in July, 1713, and had been succeeded by John Robinson, Bishop of Bristol.[2] The new prelate was a man of ability, and one of the last to exercise a combination of ecclesiastical and political functions such as had formerly been common in English history. He had earlier been envoy in Sweden, and after his elevation to the See of Bristol he had been Lord Privy Seal, and had for a time left his episcopal office in commission while absent " as chief plenipotentiary to conduct the treaty of Utrecht."[3]

Accordingly, a letter to Bishop Robinson was added: —

May it please y'r Lordship, — The Episcopal Congregation at Boston in New England haveing been favoured with many repeated Instances of their late Diocesan's love and kindness towards them, Humbly presume to lay before Y'r Lordship the State and Circumstances of our Church,

---

[1] It is a striking proof of the success of what may thus early be called the "patriot" party in watching adverse movements in England, that somehow a copy of these papers was obtained and circulated here in a "broad-side," of which a copy is in the library of the Massachusetts Historical Society (572, 6). Only the initials of the signers are printed, but the names have been filled out in ink. "[1715], S'r, 18. Now about," writes Sewall, "Dr. Mather shews me a Copy of Gov'r Dudley's Signing a Petition for a Bishop as the only means to promote Religion here."

[2] Bishop Robinson was translated from Bristol to London, August, 1713. He died April 11, 1723, aged 73 years.

[3] Anderson, Col. Church, ii. 544.

not doubting of an Equal Regard from Y' Lordship's known Goodness, and Consummate Prudences, the Influences whereof we hope to Enjoy in these Remote Parts.

About Twenty years since, a handsome Chappell was built in this place by the Subscriptions of Sir Edmund Andros, and other well disposed Gentlemen, particularly by the Benefactions of the Hon[ble] Francis Nicholson. Esqr (whose Eminent services to his Queen and countrey, and Affectionate Concern for the Church of England, will render his name ever precious amongst us, and famous to Posterity) and has since been adorn'd by the Bounty of the late Queen Mary of Glorious Memory; Our Ministers are supported in the same manner: One by the Voluntary Contributions of the People; the other, by a Sallary of One hundred pounds per Annum paid out of the Privey Purse; and entered in her Majesty's Books; Our Congregation is very much increased, and consists of about Eight Hundred persons; and the Chappell has lately been enlarged into twice its former dimentions: This Additional Building has put us to a very considerable Expense, and therefore we humbly entreat Y' Lordship's good offices in our behalf, That the money from the privey purse may be Constantly and Regularly paid. Thus we shall be enabled to Finish the Work we have begun, and may reasonably expect to be in a flourishing Condition: We will not trespass any longer on Y' Lordship's Time, but beg leave to Subscribe Ourselves, etc.

BOSTON, Dec. 8th, 1713.

Signed by the Governor and Lieut.-Governor, Ministers, Wardens, and Vestry.

To the Rt. Revd Father in God John Ld. Bishop of London.

The records contain references to the business of these letters:—

At a Vestry held at Boston, Dec' 10th, 1713. It is requested that the Rev[d] M[r] Harrison and Coll. Jn[o] Redknap do Take care to Deliver the Packett Directed to the Society for Propagating of the Gospell in Foreign Parts, and take a Receipt for the Same.

And also to Enquire how M[r] Henry Newman came to the knowledge of a Former Packett of which he gives an Acc[tt] to M[r] Sam[ll] Myles by his Letter of the 26th of Sept[r], 1713. And that a coppy of said Letter as far as it relates to the Church be Delivered to the Rev[d] M[r] Harrison and Coll. Redknap. And it is farther Requested of Coll. Redknap that he will Inform the Bishop of London of our Pres[t] Circumstances and recommend us to his L[d]ship's Favour and that he will give us an Acc[tt] of his Proceedings therein.

LONDON, Apr[ll] 27th, 1714.

Gentlemen,—The papers M[r] Harrison and my selfe were intrusted with to y[e] society were faithfully delivered. Those Gentlemen being fully perswaded of the necessity of having bishops sent to America, are resolved to joyne Theire address to those of New York, New England, and Rhode Island to her Ma^{ty} y^t she would be pleased to appoint some proper Person for that worke so soon as possible. I did speak to sev^ll of ye members of ye Society, perticularly to my Lord of London and Clarendon, That they would be pleased to consider of our northern parts before Jamaica or Barbados, there being a greater necessity for having One amongst us — Where Whigs and fanaticks swarme then in those parts.

I have not talked with Mr Newman[1] as yet Mr Harrison being in the Country. I waite his return. Mr Miller's[2] affair has been read before the Society, who are perswaded of ye great advantage an early education in ye principalls of ye Church has upon people's future lives and manners, so that I do not doubt but there will be a Consideration had to Mr Miller's prayer and an incouragement for the instructing a Certain Number of Children in the principalls of ye Church.

I design to move ye Society for some books, not only for ye school, but prayer books for ye Church.

I have been sev^ll times with Mr Enston the Organist who appears to me a good man, I have told him ye Circumstances of ye Church and ye nature of the Country, as well as I could, and have agreed with him for £30 a year New-England Money, and have promised him ten poundes sterling for his and wife's passage over. I could not prevail with him upon other Terms. I reckon about ye end of July he will be able to saile from hence. In the mean time he is to acquaint himselfe with the manner how to keep an organ in repair in case of any accident.

Mr Harrison's[3] agent has received one year and halfe of his Sallary. I hope it will be perticularly pay'd for the future, which he will have over in the next ship, as likewise part of Mr Newman's Debt.

I need not tell you the noise Coll^o Hunter's prosecution of the Church at New York made there, but can assure you it made much more here. Her Ma^{ty} being informed of ye same, immediately ordered all prosecution to be stopt, A copy of which I send inclosed.

What I have to add is to assure you y^t I am with all respect, Gentlemen, Yo^r most Obedient Servt,

J. REDKNAP.

To Sr Charles Hobby, Kn^t, and Jno Jekyll, Esqr.

In the "Abstract of Proceedings for 1715," it is stated that "her Majesty was pleased to give a most gracious answer, highly satisfactory to the Society, and a draught of a bill was ordered,

---

[1] Henry Newman was of counsel for the Province of Massachusetts in London, 1725. See also Hutchinson, i. 187.

[2] Perhaps Edward Mills is intended, later a schoolmaster in Boston under the auspices of the Society. See p. 234, n. 49.

[3] It would seem that this name is an error of the copyist in the records for Harris. Perhaps the assistant minister is intended in the other references to "Mr. Harrison." In that case, the dates given in the record relating to Rev. Mr. Harris's departure for England (see p. 241), are also erroneous.

proper to be offered to the Parliament, for establishing bishops and bishoprics in America." The scheme for completing the organization of the Church of England on this continent was on the very verge of full success, and would have introduced a new and modifying element into the political quite as much as into the religious history of New England.

But that which had been prevented, forty years before, by the fall of the "cabal" ministry, now failed of accomplishment, through the sudden death of the Queen. Though limited in capacity and violent in her prejudices, she loved her family and her Church; and the same sudden stroke dashed the hopes of the Jacobite and of the High Church party. With the accession of the Elector vanished the last illusions of loyalty, as a middle-aged foreigner, ignorant of the habits, the language, and the religious life of England, became the head of her national Church.

A foundation was laid for the desired establishment by the bequest of Archbishop Tenison who, in December, 1715, bequeathed to the Society £1000 " towards the settlement of two Bishops, one for the Continent, the other for the Isles of America." In the preceding June, the Society had addressed to King George I. a similar memorial to that which had been laid before Queen Anne. But the Church of England touched its lowest point of spiritual life during the reign of the first two Georges. It was not to be expected that any plan for its religious quickening or growth would meet with more than a careless reception from the Laodicean powers in Church or State. There was, indeed, a steadily growing urgency on the part of American churchmen, that they needed the complete organization of their Church. This was especially pressed by those who, like Cutler and Johnson, after first being Congregational clergymen, had become Church of England missionaries, — even to a degree which to those clergymen here who were English born and bred seemed obtrusive and lacking in respect to the Bishop of London. "The fountain of all our misery is the want of a Bishop, for whom there are many thousands of souls in this country that do impatiently long and pray, and for want of whom do extremely suffer."[1]

As will be related in due course, earnest efforts were still made from time to time, and an angry controversy concerning the introduction of bishops in America took place, only a few

---

[1] Rev. Mr. Johnson to the Bishop of London. Stratford, Jan. 18, 1723-4. Church Docs. Conn. i. 93.

years before the Revolution, which is memorable as having helped to fan the rising flame. But it was without avail. It was reserved for the "Non-jurors,"—that party in the English Church which, having refused to take the oaths acknowledging King William III., now claimed to be the only true Church of England,—to endeavor to meet the want. But the Non-Juring Episcopate in America, which was hardly known to exist here at all, died out with the departure of Welton and the death of Talbot. "Thus ended the only effectual attempt to provide anything like a Protestant Episcopate for America, until the Revolution having, under the Providence of God, opened a new door, England finally granted to those whom she regarded as successful rebels what she had previously refused to give to obedient children."[1]

The list of subscribers for enlarging the church fitly belongs here. In it, the generosity of gentlemen in "Her Majesty's Service" is to be particularly noted, and is striking evidence of the estimation in which they held the Queen's Chapel as a sort of ecclesiastical outpost. Of the £765. 04. 03 contributed, £403. 07. 03 was given by military and naval officers and crews, besides the gifts of those officers like Sir Charles Hobby and Captain Southack, who were Massachusetts men and also regular members of the parish.

The reader will observe this early connection with our Annals of British regiments, then welcomed in Boston as friends, which will appear again in the army that occupied the town and fought in the battle of Bunker's Hill.

A List of ye well Disposed Gentlemen and other Persons that Contributed their assistance for ye Enlarging of Church of England as by Law Established. Boston, New England.

		£	s.	d.
Augst 21	Maj^r. Maskeren [1]	3.	00.	00
	Capt. Powell	6.	08.	00
	Maj^r. Pegion [2]	3.	00.	00
	Capt. Bartleet [3]	3.	00.	00
31	Generall Nicholson [4]	25.	00.	00
	Capt. George Martin [5]	5.	00.	00
	Coll: Reddin [6]	6.	00.	00
	Capt. Riddle [7]	5.	00.	00
7ber 6	David Woodmerton	3.	00.	00
11	Capt. Holltt	3.	00.	00
	Leiv^t. James Linsey	1.	10.	00
13	Coll: Samuell Vetch [8]	6.	00.	00

[1] Prot. Episc. Hist. Soc. Coll. i. 87–98. See also *n*. on Talbot, *ante*, p. 152.

		£	s.	d.
7ber 15	Mess.[rs] Cookwheathy and Williams	3.	15.	00
18	S.[r] Charles Hobby [9]	12.	00.	00
	John Hamilton	5.	00.	00
20	Cap.[tn] Richard Mullin [10]	1.	12.	00
	Cap.[tn] Rowland Cockrom [11]	1.	12.	00
	Cap.[tn] Forbus [12]	1.	12.	00
	Cap.[tn] Davison [13]	1.	12.	00
	M.[r] Buckley [14]	3.	00.	00
	Phillip Briton	3.	00.	00
	John Jerrett	1.	00.	00
Decb.[r] 11	Cap.[tn] Cyprian Southack [15]	8.	00.	00
14	M.[r] Peters	2.	00.	00
23	Cap.[tn] Tom.[s] Mathews [16]	10.	00.	00
29	M.[r] Benj.[a] Roswell	50.	00.	00
Jan.[ry] 12	William Dowrich	1.	05.	00
1711				
26	Coll John Rednap [17]	10.	00.	00
March 31	Tho.[s] Buckfield, Esq.[r]	10.	00.	00
	Nathaniell Green [18]	4.	00.	00
	William Gould	4.	00.	00
	John Pereson	2.	00.	00
	Stephen North	4.	00.	00
	Cap.[tn] Wills	1.	12.	00
May 10	John Corney	5.	00.	00
	William Lean	0.	12.	00
	Richard Metcalfe	2.	00.	00
June 20	His Exc.[ll] Gov.[r] Dudley	12.	00.	00
	Arthur Jefrey	3.	00.	00
July 20	Cap.[tn] George Paddon [19]	20.	00.	00
	Cap.[tn] Jsaack Cook [20]	5.	00.	00
	Phillip Mathews	2.	00.	00
	Liv.[tn] Tomithy Brett [21]	50.	00.	00
July 25	Generall Hill [22]	50.	00.	00
	Coll. Kirk [23]	5.	00.	00
	Coll Churchill [24]	5.	00.	00
	Coll Cane [25]	5.	00.	00
	Coll Clayton [26]	5.	00.	00
	Coll Windress [27]	5.	00.	00
	Coll Disney [28]	5.	00.	00
	Coll Kempenfield [29]	4.	08.	00
	Coll King [29]	5.	00.	00
	Not Knowne	5.	00.	00
	Maj.[r] Carpfield	1.	00.	00
	Maj.[r] Onby	1.	00.	00
	Maj.[r] Allan	1.	00.	00
	Coll: Arnott [29]	3.	00.	00
	Cap.[tn] Hartt	1.	00.	00
	Doctor Denoon	2.	10.	00
Aug.[t] 10	Thomas Heys	1.	00.	00
	Cap.[tn] Robart Arriss [30]	6.	00.	00
	Cap.[tn] John Bridger [31]	2.	00.	00

THE CHURCH ENLARGED.   231

		£	s.	d.
Augt 10	John Greenough [32]	3.	00.	00
	East Apthorp [33]	10.	00.	00
	John Oulton [34]	20.	00.	00
	The Revd Samuell Myles	10.	00.	00
	James Smith [35]	10.	00.	00
	Sr Hovenden Walker [36]	34.	08.	08
Sept^r	Nath^ll Skanoner	3.	00.	00
	Savill Sampson [37]	5.	00.	00
	Elizebath Walker	5.	00.	00
Oct^r	Anthony Blount [38]	6.	00.	00
Nov^t	Capt Robart Hadley	3.	00.	00
1712				
Jan^y	Edward Lyde, Esqr [39]	10.	00.	00
	Nicholas Robarts [40]	12.	16.	00
	Thomas Coffin	1.	00.	00
	Florance Maccarty [41]	6.	00.	00
March	Liv^{tt} Robart Grigory	5.	00.	00
May 30	John Valintine [42]	5.	00.	00
June 3	Mrs Mico [43] by Mrs Myles	0.	05.	00
28	Capt Rouse [44] and Company Capt	10.	00.	00
	Liv^t of her Maj^ts Ship Seaphire	5.	00.	00
June 28	Master of Said Ship	5.	00.	00
	Warrant officers of Said Ship	7.	00.	00
	The Rest of the Company	4.	05.	07
July 28	John Jeakell, Esqr [45]	10.	00.	00
	Thomas Leachmore [46]	10.	00.	00
	Thomas Crease [47]	5.	00.	00
	John Powell	3.	00.	00
	Jobb Lewis [48]	3.	00.	00
	William Meinzie	3.	00.	00
	Edwd Mills [49]	3.	00.	00
	Benj^a Jones	5.	00.	00
Augst 1	John Gibbs	3.	00.	00
	Person UnKnowne	0.	10.	00
25	Gorge Steward	3.	00.	00
	Ambrose Vincent	6.	00.	00
	Richard Pullin [50]	5.	00.	00
	Adam Baith	5.	00.	00
7ber 3	John Barnett	3.	00.	00
Octo^r 9	Roger Paterson	5.	00.	00
Decm^r 1	Thomas Aubone	3.	00.	00
	John Showers	1.	00.	00
	John Codner [51]	1.	00.	00
	Robert Winter	3.	00.	00
	Winters Seaman	4.	05.	00
Capt	Thomas Lillivred	2.	00.	00
	John Thompson	3.	00.	00
	Nicholas Andreson	3.	00.	00
	John Peassie	1.	00.	00
	William Everton [52]	1.	00.	00
	John Brewer	6.	00.	00

		£	s.	d.
Decmr 1	John Phillips and Compy	5.	00.	00
	Capt Wentworth Paxton [53]	10.	00.	00
	Peter Butler	2.	10.	00
	Wth orders for £10. 00. 00 in Nails out of his Shipp	10.	00.	00
Xber 23	Christian McKarty [54]	4.	00.	00
1713				
Jany 9	Obadiah Procter	5.	00.	00
10	Henry Sharpe	6.	00.	00
22	Benjn Davis	5.	00.	00
Math 25	Elizt Sadler	0.	10.	00
30	Anto Blunt [36]	2.	00.	00
Apl 3	Mary Leeky	0.	05.	00
	Wm Melross [55]	5.	00.	00
	Sarah Robertson	0.	10.	00
	Sarah Giles	0.	10.	00
	Mrs Cowell	0.	10.	00
	Mary Rowleson	0.	10.	00
	Mrs Lee	0.	10.	00
	Mrs Lamb	0.	05.	00
	Elizt Price	0.	05.	00
		765.	04.	03

[1] Jean Paul Mascarene, born near Castras, Languedoc, 1684. His father's sufferings as a Huguenot confessor are related in N. E. Hist. and Geneal. Reg., ix. 239. He was naturalized in England, 1706; "was made lieutenant in the same year and rose in the army to the rank of Lieut.-Colonel to Lieut.-General Philipps' regiment (Foot). 1743-1750 he was also Lieut.-Governor of Annapolis Royall, and in the absence of the Governor, commander-in-chief over the Province of Nova Scotia; when, being aged and infirm, he obtained His Majesty's leave to resign, and His Majesty was graciously pleased to give him a Commission of Colonel of Foot, to hold his rank as such in the Army." Governor Belcher had recommended him as successor to Lieut.-Governor Tailer, April, 1732. In 1735, the Governor asked that he might have leave of absence from Nova Scotia, to repair the fortifications in Massachusetts Bay. While residing much of the time in Nova Scotia, Boston was his home. He married Elizabeth Perry. His son John was Comptroller of Customs, and died 1778. His daughters married Thomas Perkins, James Perkins, and Foster Hutchinson. He was in the Vestry of King's Chapel at intervals from 1715 to 1728, and again 1752-57.

[2] Probably Captain Pigeon, who was killed by French and Indians near Port Royal in 1711.

[3] Captain Bartlett. One of the five captains who took possession of the fort on the surrender of Port Royal.

[4] Nicholson was at this time Colonel of Marines. His regiment afterward became the 31st Foot.

[5] Captain George Martin commanded the "Dragon" in the expedition of 1710.

[6] Colonel Reading commanded one of the five New England regiments in the expedition against Port Royal.

[7] Captain Walter Riddle had been captain of the "Mermaid" 1703; took command of the "Falmouth," 50 guns, 1707. On his passage home from New England in May, 1709, convoying the mast-ships, he was attacked by a French ship of war of 60 guns, and showed great gallantry, being himself wounded. In 1710, in the same ship, he accompanied Captain Martin against Port Royal. In 1712, in the same, he had a spirited engagement with two French ships of war off the coast of Guinea.

[8] Adjutant-General of the expedition of 1710, and Colonel of a New England regiment in 1711. He had been fined for illegal trading with the French in

1706, but on returning with the Queen's Commission in 1709, the fine was annulled. He sought later to be made Governor of Massachusetts.

[9] See p. 175. He had the Queen's Commission as colonel of one of the five New England regiments in 1710.

[10] Probably Major Mullins, who commanded a detachment in the siege of Port Royal.

[11] Possibly Captain Cockburn of the "Sapphire," in 1711.

[12] "Captain Forbis, the engineer," was killed at the same time with Captain Pigeon. *n.* 2.

[13] Captain Davison "marched first with 50 grenadiers," to take possession of Port Royal, Oct. 5, 1710.

[14] Joseph Buckley. Boston merchant. Married Joanna, daughter of Richard Shute, and widow of Nathaniel Nicholls, perhaps in 1688. His will was probated March 19, 1702.

[15] Captain Southack, commander of the "Province" galley in the expedition of 1710. He was warden in 1711.

[16] Thomas Mathews. Of an ancient Welsh family. In 1703 he was captain of the "Yarmouth;" in 1707, of the "Dover;" 1707, of the "Chester," 50 guns, and captured the "Glorieux," March, 1708/9. In the "Chester," in 1710, he joined the expedition against Port Royal; 1711, joined Sir H. Walker's fleet, but was sent back before they reached the St. Lawrence, his vessel being much shaken in a gale of wind. In 1718, he captured the Spanish "St. Carlos" of 60 guns. In 1742 he was made vice-admiral of the red, and commander-in-chief in the Mediterranean; admiral of the blue, 1743; rear-admiral, February, 1743-44. He was deprived of his place in the public service in consequence of failure in the battle of Toulon, March, 1743-44.

[17] Colonel John Redknap. In 1706 is styled "Her Majesty's Engineer for the Continent of America." — *Mass Archives*, lxxi. Was in the Vestry, 1713-15. Procured the organist for the church in London, 1714. His letters show his interest in the church affairs. He was lost at sea, 1716.

[18] Boston. Born April 10, 1679. Son of Thomas, of Providence, and grandson of John, Providence, 1636 (perhaps that surgeon who came from Southampton, in the "James," and arrived at Boston June 3, 1635; had been of Salisbury in Wilts, was one of Gorton's party, and negotiated in London in 1644, for "Narragansett"). He married, Feb. 27, 1703, Ann, daughter of Thomas Gould; had five sons; died Aug. 8, 1714. His widow died Jan. 16, 1728, aged 43.

[19] George Paddon. In 1693, second lieutenant of the "Archangel;" 1703, commanded the "Vesuvius," which was wrecked; 1711, commanded the "Windsor" on the New England station, bringing into Boston the French 42-gun ship "Thetis;" August, 1711, put in command of the "Edgar," 70 guns, the admiral's flag-ship. For his conduct in the disaster on the St. Lawrence, he was court-martialled after George I.'s accession. Meantime, he had served in the West Indies; and in 1713, was commodore and plenipotentiary to the Emperor of Morocco.

[20] Isaac Cook. First lieutenant of the "Archangel," 48 guns, 1692. Commanded the "Terror" bomb-ketch, which was destroyed at Gibraltar. In 1708, captain of the "Garland;" 1711, commanded the "Leopard," 54 guns, and was sent home to England with news of the failure of the expedition. Died Dec. 18, 1712.

[21] Timothy Brett. May 4, 1727, captain of the "Deal Castle" frigate. Died in England 1739, being captain of the "William and Mary" yacht.

[22] Brig.-General Hill, brother of Mrs. Masham, was also colonel of the 11th Foot, or North Devon regiment, which was formed in 1685. They had served at the Boyne and Malplaquet. They wore a scarlet uniform, with tawny facings.

[23] Major-General Piercy Kirke was colonel of the Tangier, or Queen's Own regiment, now the 2d Foot, which had been raised to guard Queen Catherine's dowry. The uniform was sea-green, the Queen's favorite color, with, as badge, the "Paschal Lamb," the crest of the house of Braganza. They were nicknamed "Kirke's Lambs" at the time of their bloody part in the campaign against Monmouth.

[24] Lieut.-Colonel Josiah Churchill commanded Churchill's Marines, formed 1702, ordered to be disbanded, but incorporated in the line as the 31st Foot,

1714. They were engaged against Port Royal, 1709. Their flag bears the names of Spain, Sheriffmuir, Dettingen, West Indies, Ticonderoga, Egypt, Waterloo. They were captured at Saratoga with Burgoyne.

²⁵ Colonel Kane's regiment was disbanded 1713.

²⁶ Lieut.-Colonel Clayton, of General Hill's Regiment, the 11th Foot.

²⁷ Windress's regiment, raised in Ireland 1702, became the 37th Foot. They had served at Blenheim, Ramillies, Malplaquet, etc.

²⁸ Colonel Desney's regiment, raised in Ireland 1701, became the 36th Foot, and wore a scarlet uniform. Their flag bears the motto: "Firm," and the names of Almanza, Montevideo, Spain.

²⁹ Colonels Kempenfield, King, and Arnott were probably lieut.-colonels in some regiment already named, or in Colonel Seymour's, the only colonel who did not personally contribute. This was the Queen's Marines, now the Fourth, or Queen's Own Regiment of Foot. The uniform was scarlet with blue facings; originally the Second Tanjier Regiment. It served at Sedgemoor, Battle of Boyne, Steenkirk, Siege of Namur (1690), Vigo, 1702, Capture and defence of Gibraltar, 1704. Lost about two hundred officers and men by wreck in St. Lawrence, 1711. The flag bears also the later names of Culloden, Concord, Lexington, Bunker's Hill, Ciudad Rodrigo, St. Sebastian, Capture of Washington, Waterloo.

³⁰ Robert Arris. In 1692, First Lieutenant in the "St. Andrew;" 1696, commander of the "Mermaid;" 1703, commander of the "Tartar" in the Mediterranean, under Sir C. Shovel. In 1711 he commanded the "Devonshire," 80 guns; but as she was too large to go up the St. Lawrence, and the general was going in the "Windsor," Captain Arris was transferred to the latter. He died Jan. 7, 1719.

³¹ John Bridger had been commissioned in 1696 to inspect naval productions, etc., in New England; and in 1705 had the Queen's commission "to be Surveyor-General of Woods in America, and to instruct the inhabitants in making pitch and tar, curing hemp, etc." He suggested the formation of the Episcopal Church in Newbury. He was in the Vestry of King's Chapel 1701, 1709-15, 1718-20. In 1718 he was superseded: "After twenty-two years faithful service to this country, I am turned out and obliged to beg my bread."— *Palfrey*, iv. 396–402.

³² Of Boston, son of William (Boston, shipwright; born in England; freeman, 1673); married, Oct. 18, 1693, Elizabeth Grosse, and had eleven children. He died 1732. He was progenitor, says Savage, of most of the name in recent times, including the distinguished artist, Horatio, Harvard College, 1825.

Capt Apthorp

³³ Warden, 1700-1702. For an account of the Apthorp family, see Vol. II.

³⁴ Warden, 1716.

³⁵ Warden, 1722.

³⁶ Sir Hovenden Walker. In 1692 commander of the "Vulture," fireship; soon after, of the "Sapphire," a 32-gun frigate; 1695, the "Foresight," 50 guns. In 1696, the "Foresight" being with the "Sheerness," he had a gallant action with two French ships of 70 and 60 guns. On the recommencement of war with France he was captain of the "Burford," 70 guns. He was commodore of a squadron of six ships of the line in expedition against St. Kitts. He was rear-admiral of the blue 1709, and was knighted and made rear-admiral of the white 1711. In the spring of 1712 he commanded a squadron for the West Indies. On the accession of George I., he was struck out of the list and deprived of half pay for the failure of the Canada expedition,— being a friend of Lord Bolingbroke.

³⁷ Savill Simpson. See p. 190.

³⁸ A. Blount. Warden, 1710-12.

³⁹ See p. 178.

⁴⁰ N. Roberts. Warden, 1704-1706.

⁴¹ Florence Maccarty, of Boston, 1686. Butcher. By his wife Elizabeth he had three children; by his wife Sarah, two. He died June 13, 1712, at Roxbury, leaving a third wife, Christian, and a competent estate.

⁴² Boston; freeman, 1675. Warden, 1715-17. See p. 247, *post*.

⁴³ The wife of John Mico, of Boston; 1689, merchant. He married, Aug. 20, 1689, Mary, daughter of Thomas Brattle. He died October, 1718. His widow died Dec. 22, 1733.

⁴⁴ Augustus Rouse. June 27, 1711, he was captain of the "Dunkirk," 60 guns. He died Oct. 5, 1714, being then captain of the "Sapphire."

⁴⁵ John Jekyll. See p. 244, *post*.

⁴⁶ Thomas Lechmere. In the Vestry, 1722, and later. Lechmere's Point, Cambridge, was his property, and is named for him. He died 1765, at an advanced age. He was for many years "Surveyor General of His Majesty's Customs for the Northern District of America." His wife Ann died 1746. He was brother of Nicholas, who was ennobled Aug. 25, 1721, by the title of Baron Lechmere, of Evesham, in the County of Worcester, but died 1727 without issue.

⁴⁷ Thomas Creese. In the Vestry, 1702, and later. His son married a niece of Rev. Mr. Myles. See Vol. II.

⁴⁸ Job Lewis. Warden, 1730-32.

⁴⁹ Edward Mills. Savage says he was of Dorchester, grandson of John, of Braintree (who probably came to Boston in the fleet with Winthrop, but soon removed to Braintree. In his will he charged his only son John to bring up one of his sons "unto learning, that he may be fit for the ministry," which was, he says, "the employment of my predecessors to third, if not fourth generation"). The grandson, Edward, Harvard College, 1685, seems not to have obeyed the will of his ancestor. Married Mehitable, daughter of Stephen Minot, widow of the younger Henry Messenger, who died Aug. 16, 1690, aged 25. He taught the school in Dorchester, 1687-92, and afterward a school in Boston, partly under the patronage of the London Society for Propagating the Gospel. Dr. Cutler writes in 1724, in answer to the question, "Have you in your Parish any public School for the Instruction of Youth? If you have, is it endowed? And who is the Master?" "In this Town Mr. Miles, the Society's Schoolmaster, a worthy Communicant of the other Church, hath £15 a year for that service."— *Church Docs.*, Mass. p. 149. He died Nov. 7, 1732. Warden, 1717-1719.

⁵⁰ R. Pulling.

⁵¹ Captain John Codner was appointed to the "Deal Castle," and ordered to the West Indies, where, while in command of her, he died April 23, 1714.

⁵² Oldest son of William (Manchester, 1648, Charlestown, 1665) and Sarah, his wife, who was admitted to church in Charlestown Sept. 2, 1677 (at which date six of her children were baptized), licensed to sell spirit May 9, 1690, and married (2) Thomas Bligh, 1691.

⁵³ He is supposed by Charnock to have been a native of New England, and entering into the royal navy was, Jan. 22, 1694, appointed commander of the "Newport." He never obtained the command of anything larger than a sixth rate; and, retiring altogether from the service, returned to New England, where he died, 1736.

⁵⁴ Christian Maccarty, third wife of Florence Maccarty. See *n.* 41.

⁵⁵ William Melross. Warden, 1712.

CHAPTER VII.

FIGHTINGS WITHOUT AND FEUDS WITHIN.

PULPIT, 1717.[1]

BUT the disappointments were still hid in the future, when, on Aug. 1, 1714, Queen Anne died. From the steps of the Old Town House was read the proclamation: "That the High and Mighty Prince George Elector of Brunswick-Lunenburg is now, by the Death of our Late Sovereign, of Happy Memory, become our only

[1] This pulpit, which is still in use, though hidden by drapery, followed the English fashion. "The great three-decked pulpit of the Georgian age is still familiar to our memories. To the next generation it will be at length a curiosity of the past. Nor must the mighty sounding-board be forgotten, impending with almost threatening bulk over the preacher's head. . . . The pul-

Lawful and Rightful Liege Lord, George, by the Grace of God King, etc. ... To whom we do Acknowledge all Faith and constant Obedience, with all hearty and humble Affection; Beseeching God, by whom Kings and Queens do Reign, to Bless the Royal King George with Long and Happy Years to Reign over us."[1] Again the wooden church was hung in mourning and changed its name from "Queen's" to King's Chapel, and the loyal rejoicing of its members at the safe accession of the Protestant House of Hanover found expression in a dutiful address: —

> *To the King's most Excellent Majesty. The humble address of the Ministers, Vestry, Gentlemen, and others of yor Ma^{ts} Chappel in Boston in New England.*
>
> MAY IT PLEASE YOUR MA^{TY}, — Wee your Ma^{ts} most dutyfull and Loyall subjects in this place of the Church of England as by law Established humbly approach your Ma^{ty} with the most sincere and hearty Joy for your peacefull accession to the Crown, — yours by superiour Right and Merit, — A Blessing so great as mitigates our sorrows for the demise of your Royall predecessor of happy Memory, who was always to Us a Gratious and Bountifull Sovereign.
>
> It's Our Misfortune to be removed to so great a distance from yor Ma^{ts} Royall Person whose comfortable Influencys fall with directer Rays upon your more happy subjects in Great Brittain. It behoves Us, therefore, to be constant in our Solicitations, As We doubt not to approve ourselves in our Obedience, Loyalty, and Zeal for yor service. Thô distance may make Us late with our addresses, Yet none of your Ma^{ts} Subjects shall appear more early and dilligent with their Lives and Fortunes in defence of your sacred person and Government. Extend, therefore, most gratious Sovereigne, your princely care towards Us, that whilst the hearts of those Subjects who more immediately share ye blessings of your Auspitious Reign Overflow with joy, we may participate in your Royall Favours.

pit had supplanted the old portable box-desk at the time of the Reformation. In rich London parishes much rare workmanship was often expended upon it." — *Church of England in the Eighteenth Century*, ii. 426.

The old New England pulpit is described as "an inverted bell, in which the minister stood for the clapper. . . . The sounding-board over it hung like an extinguisher, ready to drop and put out the light if it should burn too long, — say beyond two or three hours. An hour-glass stood upon the desk . . . to warn his hearers that the sands of life

were fast running out." — *E. P. Tenney's Agamenticus*, p. 52.

Among the "Articles of Enquiry . . . in the Visitation of Rev. Jacob Henderson, Commissary to the Rt. Rev. Father in God, John, Lord Bishop of London, 1717," are these: " Have you a convenient pew for your Minister to read Divine Service in ? a pulpit with a decent Cloth and Cushion ? a large Bible and the Book of Common Prayer ? " — *Church Documents*, Maryland, p. 97.

[1] Printed in "American Historical Record," March, 1872, p. 104.

That your Ma'ty may long wear the Imperiall Crown of yo' great ancestors and the glorys of yo' Reign increase with yⁱ number of your days, and every day accompanied with an Affluence of all y' can make a monarch great and happy, is yᵉ hearty prayer of yo' Maⁱˢ most dutyfull and most loyall Subjects.

Signed by the members of the Church at Boston, Newberry, and Marblehead.

There is something pathetic in this idealization of the heavy, vulgar German prince who represented the cause of Protestant liberty; and the extremists in the Church had still less reason to rejoice, since Queen Anne had been a sincere though narrow-minded churchwoman, heartily in accord with the measures of religious intolerance which cast an ominous shadow over the last years of her reign.[1]

During all this period Joseph Dudley had continued Governor of the Province, notwithstanding the strong enmities which surrounded him. Twice had determined efforts been made to obtain his removal from office by representations to the English Government. The first time he had called to his aid all the friendly offices of the *Queen's Chapel*, which represented the Established Church of England in Boston. The danger had passed by in 1706; but a more serious peril came upon him in 1713–14, when Colonel Vetch strove to obtain the place. The good offices of the Queen's Chapel in behalf of the Governor do not now seem to have been called in requisition, but Sir Charles Hobby appeared in London with a letter from the two ministers, which would do little good to either Dudley or Vetch:[2] —

"That no representations may prejudice the interests of our Church in these parts, I have thought it expedient for me, at this juncture, to certify, that we have a very considerable number of people belonging to the Church in this town of Boston; and that I am humbly of opinion, the Church here and also in other parts of this province would increase much more under a Governor that was a constant Communicant thereof, from whom we might reasonably expect all requisite protection and encouragement.

---

[1] In 1711 had been passed the Occasional Conformity Act; in 1714, the Schism Act, — the one aimed at dissenters, who purchased office by taking the communion at the parish church; the other making it illegal for them to keep even a private school. Sewall notes, Aug. 29, 1714, the arrival of Heard, bringing the latter Act, "which ordains that no Catechism shall be taught in Schools, but that in the Comon prayer Book." It was, however, suspended in the same year and repealed 1719.

[2] Printed in 1 Mass. Hist. Coll., vii. 216, immediately after the letters, already given, of Dec. 8, 1713, to the Society and to the Queen, asking for Bishops. See p. 224, *ante*.

"This present Governor, Joseph Dudley, Esq., is a member of an independent church at Roxbury, where his dwelling is, and has communicated there from his first coming to be Governor, and never communicated with us since the Rev. Mr. Harris's arrival here (as he can inform), nor, to my certain knowledge, many years before; only this 25th of December last past he was at the Communion, his Excellency General Nicholson then present.

"I do also certify, that Colonel Vetch never received the Communion with us here; and since his arrival from Annapolis Royal has been but once at church, and that in the morning only. This is all true to a tittle, and attested by   SAMUEL MYLES,
"Presbyter of the Church of England.
"BOSTON, NEW ENGLAND, Feb. 17, 1713-14."

"Having served the Church in this place these five years last past, in conjunction with the Reverend Mr. Myles, I can certify the truth of the above-made relation ever since the time of my arrival here. In witness whereof I set my hand.

"HENRY HARRIS."

"A Representation of several Officers in the Province of the Massachusetts Bay in New England, not belonging to the Church of England; and a List of the Names of the Gentlemen that do belong to said Church.

Officers in Public Post.

Members of her Majesty's Council; Judges of the Superior and Inferior Court; Secretary of the Province; Attorney-General; Treasurer of the Province; Commissary-General for the War; Judges of Probate; High Sheriffs; Receiver of the Impost; Naval Officer; Clerks of Courts; House of Representatives; Officers of the Militia; Deputy Post-Master; Officers of the College.

Names of the Gentlemen of the Church.

The Hon. William Taylor, Esq., Lieut.-Governor, communicant, and served as church-warden; Sir Charles Hobby, communicant and church-warden for the time being; John Nelson; Francis Foxcroft; Edward Lloyd, communicant and church-warden; John Jeckyl, Esq., communicant and church-warden for time being; Thomas Newton, communicant and church-warden; John Bridger, communicant; Henry MacKentosh, communicant; Charles Bleckenden, communicant; Mr. Thomas Banister, communicant; Capt. Cyprian Southack, communicant and church-warden; Capt. Wentworth Paxton; Mr. John Oulton, communicant; Mr. Savil Sympson, communicant and church-warden; Mr. Giles Dyer, communicant; Mr. Joseph Hearn; Mr. John Valentine, communicant; Ebenezer Mountforth; James Lyndall; Francis Brinly; Edward Mills; George Turfry, communicant and church-warden; James Smith; Job Lewis; John Tresor, communicant; William Rouse; Anthony Blunt, communicant and church-warden; Edward Weaver, communicant; George Stuart; Thomas Letchmore; John Arbuthnot; Thomas Sheapard; Joseph Lloyd; John Newdicate; Daniel Weyburn; John Powel; John Bearnard; Thomas Creese; George Tarrant; Henry Franklyn, communicant; Eustace Hatch; John Chickley; William Patridge; Samuel Hill; Peter Butler; Richard Pullen; Thomas Selby, communicant; Richard Hall, communicant; Stephen North; Rowland Dyke; Henry Sharpe; John Gibbs; Mr. Renner; Ambrose Vincent, communicant; Roger Patisson, communicant; Stephen Labbie; John Johns.

Mr. Brown, Mr. Bartlett, Mr. Sawyers, Mr. Merrill, *Newbury*.

We have omitted setting down a considerable number of our communicants, because of small though good families in the town.

An account of the number of our congregation we have sent to my Lord Bishop of London, viz., 800; wherein we are well assured we have not exceeded."[1]

Still the Governor held his own, and whatever hopes might be entertained of obtaining a better churchman in his stead were postponed.

If the church had depended on no more strenuous supporters than Governor Dudley, it would hardly have had life enough to alarm its neighbors. But Mr. Myles had in his congregation not a few faithful and zealous persons, whose character and position gave them much weight.

The Queen's death, however, soon closed Dudley's public career. It was a gain for the church when he gave place temporarily to Lieut.-Governor Tailer. Colonel Samuel Shute obtained the position from the new monarch; and in 1715 Dudley retired to his seat in Roxbury, where he died April 2, 1720, aged 73 years. In him disappeared from the scene the most conspicuous political person in New England. To his friends he seemed "a Singular Honour to his Country, and in many Respects the Glory of it; early its Darling, always its Ornament, and in his Age its Crown;"[2] but the distrust excited in the Puritan party by his selfish use of brilliant gifts was shared at last by the church, whose displeasure he incurred, while serving it much, by not serving it wholly. The succession of royal governors who followed were each to give a certain splendor to it, and to be the object of alternate hopes and discontents.

In the winter of 1714, Mr. Harris went to England, partly on private business, and partly to make arrangements with the So-

---

[1] "These petitions were intercepted, but not delivered; said to be found among Sir Charles Hobby's papers, by Mr. Mason, his administrator, and by him transmitted to the Mathers in Boston." — 1 *Mass. Hist. Coll.*, vii. 216.

[2] Boston "Weekly News-Letter," April 11-18, 1729.

ciety for Propagating the Gospel in Foreign Parts to send Episcopal missionaries to Newbury and Marblehead. His people parted from him with regret, and urged his speedy return.

GENTLEMEN, — Being of Opinion that the Churches Interest in these parts of the world may be much promoted by seasonable and proper applications at home, I think it necessary to acquaint you that I am willing to undertake a Winter Voyage in this service ; and in order to obtain yor Concurrence, I beg leave to lay before you the following Particulars : It is well known that many places in this province would have readily embraced the Doctrine and Worship of Our Church had they been in due time provided with Ministers, but for want of such a supply they have fallen off from us. The Inhabitants of Newberry and Marblehead are now ye only considerable body of People (accepting the members of this Church) who express an affection for our Excellent Constitution ; the importance of both these places is very visible, the one being seated in the center of the Countrey, the other being a Town of the most Universall and Beneficiall Trade : It is therefore of the last consequence that faithfull and able Missionaries be sent to them before their patience is tired out with delays as have been the Case of others ; and since letters and addresses to the honorable Society for propagating the Gospel in Foreign parts very often prove ineffectuall by reason of the multiplicity of business which occurs to them, it may be necessary for me to waite upon the Society in Person and urge this affair with the strongest arguments and represent it in the clearest light. Another thing that requires my presence in England is the heavy Tax laid upon my Salary, which I have reason to believe may be taken off by my own solicitation, and cannot possibly hope to succeed any other way. The necessary charges of my Family are so excessive that I can ill bear so large a deduction out of the Royall bounty, — tho' the adjusting of this particular will be not only for my owne private Benefit, but for the publick honour of the Church which depends in a great measure upon the handsome and Liberall maintenance assigned to its Ministers. His Excellency Gen^{ll} Nicholson has already honoured me with his approbation, and indeed he deserves ye praise of his design, since he was pleased first to propose it to me ; there is nothing wanting but yor consent to put it in practice, which I dont doubt your Zeal for the prosperity of the Church will incline you to grant. And the Experience of yor Kindness to me imboldens me to ask this farther favour of you, vizt that you would be pleased to allow the Reverend Mr Myles Twenty shillings p week Extraordinary during my absence, that my Salary may be kept intire for my selfe and my Family, wch will be no more then is needfull to defray my expences. I conclude with assuring you that I shall upon all occasions study to serve the Church in generall and you in particular, and so approve myselfe Yo.^r faithfull friend and most humble Servt,

HENRY HARRIS.

At the meeting at the Vestry at the Exchange Tavern Nov? 16th 1714, Voted by y⁰ Vestry (with M! Myles approbation) that M! Harris may go home, he proposing to return by Mids! next and that M! Myles be allowed 20s. more p week during M! Harris's absence.

BOSTON, Nov! 18th, 1714.

The Reverend M! Henry Harris has now Resided among us about six years, officiating as One of the Ministers of his Ma¹!⁵ Chappel, in all which time Wee have observed him faithfull in the discharge of his Duty and Regular and Inoffensive in his life and Conversation, by which he has gained y⁰ Esteem and love of the whole Church; and because he is now going to expose himselfe to the Difficultyes of a Winter passage to Great Brittain for the service of the Church in generall in these parts and of his Ma¹!⁵ Chappel in particular, We think ourselves Obliged as Friends and Christians to give him this publick Testimoniall that he may be the better enabled to effect a work so good and Beneficial.

SAMUEL MYLES, Minister.

JOHN JEKYLL, } Churchwardens.
THO!⁵ NEWTON,

WILLIAM TAILER,   THO!⁵ CREESE,
E. LYDE,   J: OULTON,
CYPRIAN SOUTHACK, DAN¹!ᴸ WYDORNE,
EDW? MILLS,   G: DYER,   } Vestrymen.
THO!⁵ BANISTER,   JO: HEARNE,
JN? VALENTINE,   ANTH? BLUNT,

BOSTON, Nov! 18th, 1714.

May it please your Lord?, — The affairs of the Church of England in these parts requireing a just and faithfull Representation, we have joined our Endeavours with those of his Excellency Francis Nicholson, Esq!, to prevail with y⁰ Reverend M! Henry Harris (as y⁰ most proper person) to undertake a voyage to London, humbly to lay before Your Lord? the state of these Remote parts of yo! Diocess. He has lived six years among us, in which time an Inoffensive life and Conversation have made him successfull and beloved. And as he is going with the first Oppertunity, We presume to Recommend him to yo! Lord? as such; and as we have no reason to doubt your paternall concern for Us, We beg yo! Lord? will be pleased to favour him with proper seasons for Representing our Case to yo! Lord?, and then to give him a speedy Dismission that he may Return to his charge among Us, Humbly begging yo! Lord!ˢ Blessing and a series of yo! favours, we are

Yo! Lord?ˢ Most Dutyfull sons and most Obed! humble Serv!ˢ,

SAM!ᴸ MYLES, Minister.

[Etc., as above.]   JOHN JEKYLL,   } Churchwardens.
                          THO!⁵ NEWTON,

A return "home" from the provincial life of that period must have been like an escape from prison to an English clergyman.

It is not strange that the congregation were so anxious to secure Mr. Harris's speedy return, that they did not trust to his own homesickness for them, but wrote again to the Bishop: —

May it please yo[r] Lord[p], — We could not omitt so fair an oppertunity by our most bountyfull Patron, Gen[ll] Nicholson, of paying our Duty to yo[r] Lord[p], and intreat yo[r] farther paternal Care of Us; for since the Rev[d] M[r] Henry Harris is gone to solicite Our affairs and to lay the State of the Churches in these parts before your Lord[p], We are aprehensive his stay may be Retarded, or his Inclinations lead him to stay in England some time.

The burthen lying very heavy upon the Reverend M[r] Myles during his absence, and our addition of 20s. a week likewise chargeable, We most humbly intreat yo[r] Lord[p] to order M[r] Harris over as soon as possible, or some Worthy Gentl[n] to supply that vacancy. Wee are the more Sollicitious, in Case M[r] Myles should be sick we should be under an Insuperable inconveniency for want of a Minister amongst Us, and we should be left as sheep without a Sheepard. All which we most humbly lay before yo[r] Lord[p] as becomes, May it Please your Lord[p],

Yo[r] most Dutyfull sons and humble Serv[ts].

It is fair to presume that Mr. Harris was received again with joy after so decided a hint that he had better come back. He did so in the autumn of 1715, some months after the following letter was written by the new Bishop of London: —

Somerset House, June 17th, 1715.

GENTLEMEN, — I take this first opptunity of Sending M[r] Harris Back to you In Compliance wth your request to me on y[r] behalf, tho: he wold have wished to stay some time longer, In order to settle his owne affairs, — His Pension from y[e] Crown not being yet Established anew, and his arrears remaining Still unpaid: I shall however take care y[t] he be no Loser. It is with great Satisfaction I hear M[r] Harris has given so good Content during his Ministry among you, and of y[e] Harmony there is between you. As nothing can Contribute more to y[e] Service of y[e] Church, So I heartily recomend y[e] Continuance of it to you, and am
Gentle: Y[r] Most Assured Friend,   J. L.

BOSTON, Jan[y] 9th, 1715–16.

May it please your Grace, — We, y[e] Church Wardens of His Maj[tys] Chappell in Boston, Humbly presume most gratefully to acknowledge y[r] L[d] Ship's letter and favour by y[e] Returne of the Rev[d] M[r] Harris, and in a more especial manner for those generous expressions, tend[g] to his happy Establishm[t] among us, and y[e] paym[t] of his arrears. The poverty and mean Condition of our Church, as well as his owne pressing Circumstances, Constrain us to be Instant to procure y[r] L[d]ship's good endea[r] to procure his comfortable Settlem!.; w^{ch}, together wth y^r L^{d}Ship's Blessing and Prayers, We in behalf of ye Church most Ardently desire, being with ye greatest Reverence,

Your Grace's Most humb: and Obedient Serv^{ts}, J. O. J. V.[1]

Notwithstanding this joy, however, at his return, troubles were soon to rise between Mr. Harris and Mr. Myles, and between him and a part at least of the congregation. These things, however, must be related a little later in our history.

The parish served by the two ministers was strong in numbers and in men of character. A few of the houses of this period survive in places, to testify to the solid comfort and luxury in which these men lived, and it is less difficult for our generation to picture them, since the most recent taste in architecture aims at their renewal. "There is no revival so little of an affectation on our soil as that of the beautiful work of the Provincial days. Its quiet dignity and quaintness, its cosiness and elegance, always attract us. . . . Any one who in summer drives over the ancient turnpike from Hingham to Plymouth, will not only pass through a beautiful country full of old homesteads, but will find the sunflowers still nodding behind the gambrel-roofed houses that line the road through Queen Anne's Corner."[2] From such homes, long since submerged in the deluge of brick and stone streets, came forth the gentry on their way to join in the prayers which still kept their hearts loyal to the Church and rulers of the mother country where many of them were born.

Among the leading people in the church at this time, besides those heretofore noticed, we may here group together several.

John Jekyll, warden 1713-15, was one of the earliest collectors of the port of Boston, appointed in 1707. He was a nephew of Sir Joseph Jekyll, Master of the Rolls, to whom Butler dedicated his Sermons. A friend of the Faneuils, he was held in general respect. He was perhaps the foremost person in the church, when, twenty years after this time, —

"On Saturday last in the Afternoon died here JOHN JEKYLL, Esq., in the 59th year of his Age, who for the space of about 27 years was Collector of His Majesty's Customs for the Port of *Boston*, and one of His Majesty's Justices of the Peace for the Counties of *Suffolk* and *Middlesex*. He was a very free and hospitable Gentleman, and who discharged his Trusts to good acceptance, and his Death is very much lamented.

---

[1] John Oulton and John Valentine, wardens.

[2] Mr. R. S. Peabody. "A Talk about Queen Anne," in the "American Architect." April 28, 1877.

"Mr. *Jekyll's* Funeral is to go to-Morrow, at Three of the Clock precisely, by reason that there is to be a Funeral Sermon preach'd at the King's Chappel."[1]

An elaborate notice of him was given in the next "News-Letter": —

"Last Friday was interred *John Jekyll*, Esq., Collector of the Customs for the Port of *Boston*, and Justice of the Peace for the Counties of *Suffolk and Middlesex* in *New England*. The Corpse was attended by the Governour, Council, Judges, Justices, Merchants, and other Gentlemen of Note in *Boston*. A suitable *Funeral Sermon was* delivered by the Commissary, and the Solemnity was honoured by *half-minute Guns* from the Merchants Ships.

"Mr. *Jekyll* was born in *England*, Son of *Thomas Jekyll*, D.D., and Nephew to that *Patriot* (in all Administrations unbiassed) the Hon. Sir *Joseph Jekyll*, Master of the Rolls. In his younger Years he travelled into several Countries in *Europe*, and resided for some time at the *Imperial Court* in the Retinue of My Lord *Paget*, British Ambassador at that time. He was appointed *Collector* of the Customs for the Port of *Boston* in *New England*, *A.* 1707, and continued in that Office till Death. He was twice *married*, — first to a Daughter of Mr. *Thomas Clark* of *New York;*[2] the second Marriage was with the widow of *Archibald Cumming*, Esq., Late Surveyor and Searcher for this Port, and Agent for the Perquisites of Admiralty in *New England*. His surviving *Issue* are five Sons and two Daughters.

"His exemplary *Character* in a Domestick Life, — as a very loving Husband, most affectionate Father, etc., — is too confined and private to be mentioned here. He was publickly conspicuous in his Office as *Collector*, for his faithfulness and application in his *Duty to the Crown;*[3] by his courteous Behaviour to the Merchant, he became the *Darling of all fair Traders;* he was not of an avaricious, sordid Temper, but with much Humanity took pleasure in *directing Masters of Vessels* how they ought to avoid the Breach of the *Acts of Trade*. His Religion was tempered with much *Moderation*, no narrow-soul'd, ill-natured Bigotry; no licentious Libertine free-thinking; no cant and hypocrisy of an affected Devotee. He excelléd in *Charity* to the Poor, *Compassion* towards the

---

[1] Boston "Weekly News-Letter," Dec. 21-28, 1733. See also p. 502, *post*.

[2] Mrs. Hannah Jekyll had died Jan. 22, 1726, very suddenly, in the 37th year of her age. "She was a fine Gentlewoman, of a comely Form, courteous and affable to all that knew her, a good Neighbour, a faithful Wife, a tender Mother, and managed her Family with excellent Œconomy: And was Yesterday honourably Inter'd: much lamented by all that knew her."— *Boston Weekly News-Letter*, Jan. 20-27, 1726.

[3] Mr. Jekyll's fidelity to the Crown led him to report to the Lords of Trade, in 1720, that the Council "have their dear idol, the charter, much at heart, and great love for independency."— *British Colonial Papers*, quoted by *Palfrey*, iv. 397. A collision between him and Mr. Mun is duly recorded by Sewall. For his funeral sermon, see p. 502, *post*.

Distressed, *Hospitality* to Strangers, and *Benevolence* to all Mankind. To sum up his Character, *He was much esteemed by our late Governour, Mr. Burnett, who was universally allowed to have been a competent Judge of Men.*

"About ten years ago, Mr. *Jekyll* was seized with a violent *pulmonary* Indisposition and subsequent *Hectick*. He obtain'd special Leave from the Commissioners of the Customs of *Great Britain* to reside in the Country during the Summer Seasons, for the recovery and continuance of his Health: His Country Seat at *Stow*, with the Benefit of Riding had the desired Effect for some Years. The severity and long continuance of last Winter conduced to an *Oedematous* swelling of his Legs and *spurious Asthmatick* disorder, by the Country Air and Exercise last Summer he became much better, but lost his *en bon point*. In the Autumn, being seized with that *Epidemical* Illness with the Symptoms of a common Cold, which prevailed at that Time all over our Northern Colonies, it gave a *fatal* shock to his weak *Habit*, he became *Anasarcous* in his lower Extremities, afterwards gradually in his Thighs and *Teguments* of the Belly, and at last *Ascitical*. Whilst his Physicians were endeavouring by easy Methods to assist *Nature* in the prolonging of Life for some Weeks or Months longer, unluckily over-perswaded, upon the Merit of some chance Cure, performed upon some *Athletick* Rustick Constitution, he made use of an inconsiderate Pretender, who without any regard to his Age, Constitution, and extremest Infirmity, by a *cabaline Dose of a Nostrum*, did precipitate his *Exit*." [1]

Seafaring men found the church more hospitable than the stricter Congregationalism around it. Captain Cyprian Southack served under Colonel Benjamin Church against the French and Indians in 1704, commanding the "Province Snow," of fourteen guns. When Admiral Walker arrived in Boston in 1711, he resided with Captain Southack in Tremont Street. The Captain was to lead the van in the expedition against Quebec. "In 1717 the pirate ship 'Whidah,' commanded by the notorious Samuel Bellamy, was wrecked on the rocks of that part of Eastham, now Wellfleet. The council despatched Captain Southack to the scene of the disaster. Bellamy's ship was purposely run on shore by the captain of a small vessel he had captured the day before. A storm arose, and the pirate's fleet, thrown into confusion, all shared the fate of their commander. Captain Southack buried one hundred and two bodies. A few that escaped were brought

---

[1] Boston "Weekly News-Letter," Dec. 28-Jan. 4, 1733-34.

to Boston and executed."[1] This gallant sailor and noted chart-maker was warden 1711, and vestryman at intervals, 1702–39.

Probably of a rougher type than this honored commander was Captain William Rouse, whose name is prominent in the charges against Dudley in 1706.[2] He commanded the vessel then sent to Nova Scotia to bring back prisoners of war, and was accused, with Vetch and others, of furnishing the French with military stores. He was imprisoned for sedition, but this penalty was remitted and he was excused from "sitting an hour upon the gallows with a rope about his neck;" but he was fined £1200 and "declared incapable of sustaining any public trust." The Queen in Council, however, annulled the punishment and repaid the fine. The stout seaman later commanded the "King of Spain," and had on board four men who were impressed by Captain James Campbell, of the "Squirrell," at Boston, Jan. 9, 1711–12. He was vestryman, 1715–21. His burial, Jan. 12, 1721, is entered in the King's Chapel Register of Burials. The town paid "Madam Rous" for her husband's services, July 4, 1721.[3]

The lawyers also favored the church. John Valentine, warden 1715–17, was descended from an ancient family in the parish of Eccles, Lancaster Co., England, where they owned an estate, Bencliffe Hall.[4] "His argument in the case of Matson *vs.* Thomas, in which he was opposed by Auchmuty, Reed, and Littles, is preserved, manifesting great familiarity with legal principles, as well as ability as an advocate. He is also said to have been an agreeable and expressive speaker."

"Boston, Feby 1st, 1724. On Tuesday, the 4th Instant, the Corps of John Valentine, Esq., His Majestie's Advocate-General for the Provinces of Massachusetts Bay, New Hampshire, and Colony of Rhode Island, was decently Interred. He was a Gentleman for his Knowledge and Integrity, most eminent in his Profession, Clear in his Conceptions, and Distinguishable happy in his Expressions. It pleased God, some

---

[1] 1 Mass. Hist. Coll., iii. 120.
[2] See p. 175, *ante*.
[3] Wyman's Charlestown, p. 824. Palfrey, iv. 301.
[4] It was in the family before and after 1500, and descended to John Valentine's son Samuel. He was son of John Valentine, who was baptized in Eccles, April 25, 1653, and made freeman in Boston May 12, 1675. The son was a lawyer and Advocate-General. He married, April 16, 1702, Mary, only surviving child of Samuel Lynde and granddaughter of Simon Lynde, of Boston, whose descendants are among the best families in New England. Washburn, "Judicial History of Massachusetts," says: "John Valentine, of Boston, held the office (Advocate-General) at the time of his death in 1724, and may have been the immediate successor of Mr. Benjamin Lynde, who was appointed to the office in 1697," the uncle of Mary Lynde who afterwards became the wife of Mr. Valentine. Benjamin Lynde subsequently became a Judge of the Superior Court.

short time before his Death, to deprive him of these Excellent Endowments by afflicting him with deep Melancholy which brought on him the loss of his Reason, and was the cause of his much Lamented Death."[1]

Sewall mentions his death by his own act: —

"Persons and Bearers were invited, and the Bells Tol'd as customarily at Funerals. Judge Davenport and Colonel Fitch were invited to be Bearers, and came. But when they saw Mr. Myles refused to read the office of Burial, they ask'd excuse, and went away."

Mr. Myles's assistant, however, had a gentler spirit: —

"Mr. Harris, minister, and Mr. Auchmutty, giving oath of his distraction, he had a funerall, and was buryed in ye Church yard."[2]

Colonel Francis Brinley, warden, 1723, was grandson of Francis Brinley, of Newport, R. I. (the first of his name who came to this country). He was born in England, 1690, son of Thomas Brinley, and educated at Eton. He came to New England in 1710, by invitation of his grandfather, who made him heir to his large possessions. He was admitted a freeman of Newport July 29, 1713, but did not remain there, building a wooden house in Roxbury, after the model of the stone family mansion, in Datchet, England, on a smaller scale.[3] On the 18th of April, 1719, Colonel Brinley married Deborah Lyde, daughter of Edward and Catharine Lyde, and granddaughter of Judge Nathaniel Byfield. He died Nov. 27, 1765. He had five sons and two daughters. His family were scattered

---

[1] "News-Letter," February, 1723-24. In his will, May 8, 1722, he leaves £30 sterling to his mother, if she survives him, while his legacies to others are in "Province Bills," which indicates that she was then living in England. The usual confusion of him with his father may be due to the return of the elder John Valentine to that country before his death. The Advocate-General had children, — Samuel, born Dec. 28, 1702, died March 14, 1781; married (1), June 25, 1729, Abigail Durfee; (2) October, 1766, Rebecca Hall: he was ancestor of the Freetown and Fall River families of the same name. Elizabeth, born Feb. 22, 1703, married, 1724, James, son of Capt. James and Hester Gooch, of Boston; John, born Nov. 8, 1706, died at Portsmouth, England, 1711, while his parents were visiting that country; Edmond, born Jan. 16, 1709, died Jan. 30, 1710-11; Thomas, born Aug. 3, 1713, married Elizabeth, daughter of Capt. James and Hester Gooch, — settling in Hopkinton, where a portion of his farm is still in the family; Mary, born March 23, 1714, married —— Durfee; Edmond, born Oct. 22, 1717, died July 4, 1730.

[2] Diary of Jeremiah Bumstead, in N. E. Hist. and Geneal. Reg., xv. 200.

[3] It is still standing, and was recently owned and occupied by John Bumstead, Esq., formerly of Boston, and before him by the Generals Dearborn, father and son. Sewall mentions Colonel Brinley, July 21, 1719.

at the time of the Revolution. He was commissioned Justice of the Peace by Governor Shirley, June 27, 1743, and was also colonel of the Roxbury regiment. He was not anxious for office, but preferred the quiet life of a wealthy and loyal gentleman. He was of a liberal and hospitable nature, and had children and grandchildren about him. He was a member of the Boston Episcopal Charitable Society, 1724.

His brother-in-law, George Cradock, warden, 1719-21, 1744-1746, was a merchant in London, descended, according to his statement,[1] from Matthew Cradock, the first governor of the Plymouth Company. *George Cradock* Having established himself in Boston, he married, May 8, 1718, Mary, daughter of Edward and Catharine Lyde, and granddaughter of Judge Nathaniel Byfield.[2] He was appointed Deputy Judge of the Admiralty "of the Provinces and Colonies of the Massachusetts Bay, New Hampshire, and Providence Plantations and the Narragansett Country or King's Province in America," by Judge Robert Auchmuty, Nov. 2, 1736. He received another commission as Deputy Judge from the Hon. Chambers Russell, Judge, May 17, 1762.[3] He was a member of the Boston Episcopal Charitable Society in 1724. Judge Cradock lived for years in Tremont Street, opposite to the "King's Chapel," and next to the house then standing at the corner of Tremont and Beacon streets, and for a time in School Street, a few doors above the "old corner bookstore."[4] "The Boston Post-Boy

---

[1] Doubt has been thrown on this point. See N. E. Hist. and Geneal. Reg., x. 152.

[2] They had only one son, George; he died quite young, a youth of great promise. Of their five daughters, Mary married Joseph Gerrish, Esq. The "Boston Gazette and Country Journal," No. 706, for Monday, Oct. 10, 1768, says:—

"Halifax, September 8. Saturday last was married Hon. Joseph Gerrish, Esq., to Miss Mary Cradock, of Boston, a lady possessed of every agreeable accomplishment necessary to make the married state happy." After his death, she married the Rev. Dr. John Breynton, Rector of St. Paul's Church, Halifax. They died in London, *sine prole*. Deborah Cradock married Robert Auchmuty, Jr., of Boston, Judge of Admiralty. He died in London, *sine prole*. Elizabeth Cradock married Thomas Brinley, of Boston, Jan. 25, 1749. Both died in London, having survived their children. Catharine Cradock married Nathaniel Brinley, of Boston, subsequently of Tyngsborough, Mass. Their only surviving child was the late venerable Robert Brinley, of Tyngsborough. Sarah Cradock died in Boston unmarried.

[3] Both of these commissions are in the possession of his descendant, Francis Brinley, Esq., of Newport, R. I., to whom I am indebted for this and other family notices.

[4] A letter to him from Gov. Andrew Belcher is extant, dated Milton, June 2, 1769, and addressed "To George Cradock, Esq., at the next House to the Sign of the *black and white horse*, South End, Boston,"—*i.e.*, The *Black Horse Tavern*, which was in Newbury Street, near the present Boston Theatre.

and Advertiser," No. 122, for Monday, Dec. 17, 1759, states: "We hear that George Cradock, Esq., is appointed Collector of the Customs for the Port of Boston, in the room of Benjamin Pollard, Esq., and that the Custom House is removed to the house of John Wendell, Esq." "The Boston Gazette and Country Journal," No. 847, for July 1, 1771, records the death of "The Honourable George Cradock, Esq., aged 87 years. A Gentleman of an unblemished character. His funeral is to be attended this afternoon."[1]

There were others, too, whose official position in the church at a later period makes it more proper to mention them hereafter. Such men as these were not extremists: still, they were Englishmen rather than New Englanders, and their church stood in active antagonism to the vigorous provincial life around it.

The bitterness and distrust toward the Church of England which had been implanted and nourished by ancient sufferings had become ingrained in the New England character to an extent now difficult to comprehend. This intense aversion to that Church was due not only to a dislike of her practices, but far more to the sensitive feeling that she was an aggressive presence among them; not only seeking to feed the spiritual life of her own members, but aiming to proselytize from their churches and really desiring nothing less than the same supremacy in a colony which was peopled by non-conformists, that she exercised in the mother country. This jealousy was unfortunately fostered by much that was said and done by the representatives of the Episcopal cause. As it was expressed: "If the church can be settled in New England, it pulls up schisme in America by the roots, that being the fountain that supplyes with infectious streams the rest of America."[2]

Every Episcopal minister within the borders of New England

---

[1] His widow was buried May 24, 1783, in the tomb of Judge Byfield, in the Granary Burying-ground, Boston. The pall-bearers were the Hon. Colonel Powell, Hon. John Pitts, Joseph Dowse, Esq., Major Phillips (of the Castle), John Rowe, Esq., and Mr. James Perkins, all of them prominent gentlemen. It may be added that the name of Cradock, certainly in this branch of the family, is extinct. It is of Welsh origin, Caradoque.

[2] Church Docs., Mass. p. 73: Col. Lewis Morris to Archdeacon Beveridge, Boston, July 27, 1702: The Maryland clergy wrote to the Lord Bishop of London: "When ... Gov. Nicholson came into the Country in 1694, there were but three Clergymen in Episcopal Orders. ... There was also a sort of wandering pretenders to preaching that came from New England and other places, which deluded not only the Protestant Dissenters from our Church, but many of the Churchmen themselves, by their extemporary prayers and preachments, for which they were admitted by the people and got money of them."—*Church Docs.*, Maryland, p. 8.

looked on himself, or was thought to do so, as a solitary representative of the true Church amid a company of schismatics. There were, indeed, those of a wiser spirit, such as was well expressed by Dr. Bray: —

"Nor do I think myself obliged to speak here of New England, where Independancy seems to be the Religion of the Country. True it is, since a Church was opened at Boston about fifteen years agoe for the English Service, the Congregation of Church People are become very numerous; and the young Students of the College are sayd upon the Reading of our Episcopal Authors (against which they are narrowly watched by Mr. Mathers) to become not so ill affected to us, but that some of them would gladly receive their orders from the hands of Bishops if they could; and two of them have lately come over hither to be accordingly ordained. But my Design is not to intermeddle where Christianity under any form has obtained possession of the Country, but to represent rather the deplorable fate of the English Colonies, where they have been in a manner abandoned to Atheism, or, which is much as one, to Quakerism, for want of a Clergy settled amongst them." [1]

The standing grievance, however, between the two parties, was in the fact that each really claimed supremacy of the same kind. Congregationalism was practically the Established Church of Massachusetts,[2] intertwined with the State, recognized by its laws; the town church and the parish were an integral part of society itself.[3] Face to face with this institution, to which the

---

[1] Prot. Episc. Hist. Coll., i. 101. "Communication [near 1700] from Dr. (Commissary) Bray to the Archbishop of Canterbury, the Lord Bishop of London, and the other Bishops, Representing the present State of Religion in the Several Provinces of the Continent of North America." But the same Dr. Bray wrote earlier: "The Plantations growing now into populous and powerfull Provinces . . . ought not to be so neglected as that it should be indifferent to us, whether they be made True Sons of our Church or the most soure leavened of all its Enemies, Independants, Ana-Baptists, and Quakers." — Prot. Episc. Hist. Coll., i. 103.

[2] This view was stated by the Scotch Presbyterian traveller, Oldmixon, in his Description of Boston, 1708: "There are three parish churches, a French church, and two meeting-houses in the city. The Old Church, North Church, and South Church belong to the Presbyterians, who are the Church of England as by law established; the French church belongs to the French Protestants; and the meeting-houses to a congregation of Church of England men and Anabaptists."

[3] An illustration of the power of the Established Congregational Church and of the method of discipline which would have been administered, if practicable, to the setters-up of new ways of worship, is given in the proceedings of "A Council of Fourteen Churches convened at Watertown, Tuesday, 1, 1712. Upon the Desire of the Two Churches there, Complaining of Disorderly Proceedings among several People in the Town. After Solemn Invocation of the Glorious God, and thorough Examination of the Matters laid before us, . . . 1. We Apprehend that the Neighbours who have of late been Combined, and have subscribed to form a Third Congregation in the middle of Watertown, have done

great majority of the people still belonged, while even those who had become indifferent to its best things shared its prejudices and distrusts, now stood a few members of the powerful establishment of the mother country, denying that any other institution could exist by English law except by sufferance, — some of them even denying all validity to Christian ordinances as administered in New England. The question was, Which was the Established Church, and which were the Dissenters? — a question whose only possible solution came in consequence of the long quarrel, but in a way which neither party either desired or dreamed. The highest idea of Christians in the eighteenth century was still that of an Established Religion, in one form or another, which was exclusive in its possession; the practical solution by Christians in the nineteenth century is in a tolerance which is inclusive in its sympathy. But of this there was no vision yet.

For nearly thirty years the Royal Chapel had continued to be the only place for Church of England worship within the Province of Massachusetts. The time had now arrived for a determined effort to establish Episcopal churches in other places, — partly where there was a demand for them from more recent settlers from England, who were attached to the church of their fathers; partly, also, as missionary stations, with a view to proselytize from the stubborn New England stock. But, in either case, the expense of such an enterprise was too considerable to be borne by the Episcopalians of New England.

It was with difficulty, indeed, that these could do very much even in supporting their churches after they were established. King's Chapel is the solitary instance of a self-supporting Epis-

what has a tendency to Defeat the Good Intentions of our nursing Fathers in the Civill Government; . . . and their attempts that way are therefore to be blamed, and such may not expect Countenance from the People of God. 3. It Appears that Mr. Robert Sturgeon, to qualify himself for purposes which he had frequently promised not to prosecute without due advice and Direction, obtained for himself Private Ordination at an House of Boston, from the hands of Three Ministers Lately arrived from, and Two of them returning to, Ireland; And this, without the Advice or Knowledge of any of the United Ministers of Boston, or any other Pastors or Churches that we can learn of in the Province, . . . and that afterwards in a Private House, from the single Hand of Mr. McGregory, Minister of Nutfield, He received an Installment with a pastorall charge of a few of the said Brethren at a Church in Watertown. . . . These proceedings We Judge to be full of Irregularitys. . . . A Rebuke is particularly due to Mr. McGregory, whose Conduct has Expresst so much Temerity, Presumption, and Intrusion as is greatly Offensive unto us. Nor may he Expect the regard of a minister in our Churches untill we have received suitable satisfaction from Him, for the Insult he has made upon that good order of our Churches." — *N. E. Hist. and Geneal. Reg.*, xiii. 113.

copal church in New England previous to the Revolution.[1] Every other church eked out the salary of its minister by the aid of the Society for Propagating the Gospel in Foreign Parts.[2] A bitter controversy arose in time between the friends of the old New England church polity and the Episcopalians, on the question whether it was in accord with the pious intention of the benefactors of this Society, or in harmony with the provisions of its charter, to establish or support churches in places already provided with a gospel ministry and the ordinances and institutions of religion. Be that as it may, we cannot state too strongly the importance of the aid which "the Venerable Society" bestowed on the churches under its protection. It is hardly too much to say that without this the Episcopal Church in New England would have perished in the Revolution.[3]

A speedy result of the arrival of Sir Francis Nicholson in 1713, with large powers from the Society,[4] was that these movements immediately gained force and effectiveness. The churches in Braintree, Newbury, and Marblehead date from this period. Their establishment was attended with much ill-feeling throughout the province.

The history of the origin of the movement in Newbury illustrates how even in sacred things the foibles and passions of human nature are potent forces. Often in the older towns, when the necessity arose for building a new meeting-house, the growth of population in parts remote from the original settlement caused serious controversy as to its proper location, in which those who lived near the old site were obstinately conservative, while those at a distance were fierce innovators. The division of the town into parishes, as in Salem, arose largely from this cause. But in Newbury the difficulty took a more extreme form.[5] The controversy was a long one between the people on

---

[1] This church met all its expenses and supported its minister in the same manner as the Congregational churches around it. The Royal Bounty which provided a salary for "the King's Lecturer" was an addition, not of necessity, but of dignity, to the place. It relieved the regular minister of half of his preaching duty, but was not paid into the treasury of King's Chapel, to relieve it in any way.

[2] The difficulty of raising means for supporting churches was otherwise met in some Southern colonies. The Assembly of South Carolina passed, in 1698, an act for the maintenance of a minister of the Church of England in Charleston. It appropriated the yearly salary of £150, and "directed that a negro man and woman, and four cows and calves, be purchased for his use, and paid for out of the public treasury." — *Anderson, Col. Church*, ii. 463.

[3] "A Sermon delivered in Trinity Church, etc., on the 150th Anniversary of the Incorporation of the Venerable Society for Propagating the Gospel in Foreign Parts. By the Right Rev. Manton Eastburn, D.D. Boston: 1851," commemorates the debt which the Episcopal Church here owed to this nursing care.

[4] See p. 216, *ante*.

[5] See Coffin's "History of Newbury."

"the plains," at the west end of the town, and the others, respecting accommodation for worship. The town insisted that "Pipe-Stave Hill shall be the place for the meeting-house": the minority finally, in 1711, began a house on the plains. The controversy had begun in 1685. Nov. 2, 1711, the majority obtained an order from the General Court forbidding further progress with "the house lately pretended to be raised for the publick worship of God," etc. A petition was drawn, Nov. 4, 1711, signed by sixty-seven persons, but (probably owing to this peremptory order) was not presented, asking permission to finish the meeting-house, "and to call some Orthodox well-approved person." It was at this stage, according to an old account of the precinct, that Mr. John Bridger wrote from Portsmouth, advising them to come under the Church of England, and that he would protect them. In March, 1712, Mr. Bridger wrote to Rev. Mr. Harris, —

"desiring him to give his assistance to these people at Newbury, which he immediately did, and stayed with them 14 days the first time. After this he made them many visits, and took a great deal of pains in instructing them in ye doctrine and worship of God in the Church of England. He gave them a dozen common-prayer Books at his own expence; many more was given them, and the church at Boston reprinted Dr. King's Book of the Inventions of men in the worship of God, and Dr. Williams's defence of the Common Prayer, — one hundred copies whereof were disposed of amongst them at first, and more since. These methods succeeded so well, that when Mr Harris preached at Newbury the number of his hearers often amounted to three hundred persons and upwards. So considerable a body of people was thought worth the Church's care and the Gov^{nt} protection."[1]

Sewall records the next step: —

"Feb. 27th, 1711–12. Joseph Bailey of Newbury, introduced by Mr. Myles, Mr. Harris, and Mr. Bridger, presented a petition to the governor signed by Abraham Merrill, etc., . . . declaring they were of the pure episcopal church of England; would no longer persist with their mistaken dissenting brethren; had sent to their diocesan, the bishop of London, for a minister, and desired protection."

Elsewhere he says: —

"I saw the certainty of what I could not believe before; namely, deacon Merrill and deacon Brown and twenty-two others and so forth.

[1] Church Docs. Mass., p. 105. Mr. Bridger wrote to Lord Dartmouth: "This is a thing without precedent, I presume, to have a body of people to leave their schism at once; and if it meets with your Lordship's favour will be an effectual way to draw that Schismatical curtain from before those people's eyes. But the greatest fear is that the Church was never known to flourish under a dissenting Governour." — *Ibid.*, p. 102.

Now though it is well enough known what was the spring of y^r motion, and notwithstanding their aprons of fig leaves, they walk naked." [1]

Rev. John Lambton (1712-15) was the first missionary at Queen Ann's Chapel, Newbury, being appointed by Governor Nicholson. The observant Puritans around noticed every sign of laxness in the new converts to Episcopacy: —

"Perceiving that some of the ceremonies were camels too big for them to swallow, he [Mr. Lambton] told them they should be left to their liberty as to kneeling at the sacrament, baptizing with the sign of the cross, and so forth. This has been wonderfully taking with them, and a great means to encourage them in their factious proceedings." [2]

Nor did that church easily establish itself. John Merrill, their leader, was imprisoned for church rates; but Governor Nicholson interfered, retaining lawyers to defend such cases.

The Rev. Henry Lucas soon succeeded to this thorny cure. A letter from him to the secretary of "the Venerable Society" only too well justifies the unfriendly observers: [3] —

"NEWBURY, June 19th, 1720.

"When my family came they promised great matters, as a house, glebe, etc.; but I found it quite contrary, being put into a house a mile from the church, to which belongs no manner of conveniency for the keeping any creature, and it is but two habitable rooms. I have not so much as conveniency for anything. They seemed mighty churchmen till I asked them for a house. And the church lyeth in the same condition I found it, which is very miserable. They can never agree when they meet together to do anything but to quarrel one with another. Godfather and Godmother and the sign of the cross they utterly abominate, and sure and certain hopes in the office for the burial of the dead are looked upon by them to be very wicked. True churchmen we have very few, not above six. The canons of the church have frightened them very much, and severall saying they could not join with such a church that owned them, separated, so that what by their withdrawing them, others removing them from hence, and by the death of some of our numbers, there are not now above 25 Communicants. No person could

---

[1] Coffin gives their petition to Governor Dudley: "We are convinced that the church of England is a pure orthodox church, and so are resolved to continue no longer in that separation which has so unhappily prevailed among the mistaken and prejudiced inhabitants of this country." The Governor's reply is given: ". . . I am also informed by the reverend Mr. Harris, one of the ministers of the church of England in this place, that at their desire he has visited and preached to that new congregation, and had a very considerable auditory; and that he shall continue so to do, until their said address to the lord bishop of London shall be considered, and orders given thereon."

[2] Rev. Christopher Toppan to Rev. Cotton Mather, Nov. 28, 1712, quoted in Coffin's "Newbury."

[3] Church Docs. Mass. p. 133.

endeavour more than I have done to persuade them to bring their children to be catechized. I could not get above three or four to be sent, altho' I read them lectures thereon seven weeks to encourage them. I have baptised three, — only one adult."[1]

The death of Mr. Lucas was caused by his disappointments. Under his successor, Mr. Plant, the Newbury church struggled on for thirty years. He described it in 1724 as having one hundred and twenty hearers, thirty-eight communicants, and no surplice. He had sore difficulties, but left it moderately prosperous. We shall later have occasional glimpses of the missionaries to this church; but although its origin was thus due to a vestryman and a minister of King's Chapel, its history thenceforward pursues an independent course.[2]

At Braintree an earlier effort had been made, in 1702, to establish the Episcopal Church, perhaps with the intent of bringing its ministrations within reach of the old Plymouth Colony and of Rhode Island. At the request of Colonel Morris of New Jersey, a petition also having been sent by some inhabitants of the town, the Rev. William Barclay, their first missionary in New England, was appointed by the Society for the Propagation of the Gospel "the Church of England minister" there, with "an Annual Encouragement of £50, and a Gratuity of £25 for present Occasions." Mr. Myles is said to have refused to countenance the application of the Braintree people at this time.[3] Mr. Barclay, returning to England about 1704, was followed, 1711-12, by the Rev. Thomas Eager as "missionary to Braintree, Swanzy, and Little Compton," on a salary of £50

---

[1] Mr. Lucas wrote: "Several of them no more designed to be Churchmen than I intend to be a Pagan, for they thought the Society would never send a Missionary over to them; and if so in time they by making friends could turn Queen Ann's chapel into a Meeting-House." — *Church Docs.* Mass. p. 127.

Mr. Lucas was succeeded (1722-1753) by Rev. Matthias Plant, who graduated at Jesus College, Cambridge, 1712. He was followed (1752-1803) by Edward Bass, D.D., afterward bishop of the Protestant Episcopal Church in Massachusetts, 1796-1804. He was born in Dorchester, Mass., and graduated at Harvard College 1744. "In 1738 St. Paul's Church was erected in what is now Newburyport. During the latter part of Mr. Plant's ministry, and the former part of Bishop Bass's, both churches were used; but in 1766 Queen Ann's Chapel was abandoned, as both congregations could more conveniently assemble in St. Paul's church."

[2] An outline of it is given in Morss's Sermon on the Episcopal Church in Newburyport.

[3] Dr. Coleman's letter to Dean Kennett, *Life*, etc., p. 124. "An Ans^r of the Church of England in Braintree, to a Charge against them, to my Lord our Reverend Father in God, Lord Bishop of London," September, 1710, enumerates their hardships. It says: "Mr Vesey, Minister of the Church of N. York, when he was a youth can say that he with his parents and many more were communicants of the Church of Eng^d, and that in their Family at Braintree Divine Service was daily read." — *Church Docs.* Mass. p. 84.

and an allowance of books. Mr. Eager soon gave a sorrowful account of the difficulties of his situation: —

"I have had a very hard way of living since my abode in this place, provisions being very scarce, and people generally very poor. The whole province has been very much disturbed on the account of my coming to this place, and accordingly have not failed to affront and abuse me wherever they meet me, — 'atheist and papist,' the best language I can get from them. The people are Independents, and have a perfect odium to those of our Communion. Those few which adhere to our church are taxed and rated most extravagantly to support the dissenting clergy. Had this province been called New Creet instead of New England it had better suited, for the people are very great strangers to truth, and I do really believe that I have not passed one day since my arrival without one false report or other raised upon me. Thus you see my case is very pitiful; yet by the assistance of God's grace I shall have constancy and resolution enough to put forward the good work that I was sent about."[1]

The following entry in the old Records of the Queen's Chapel shows the exercise of Nicholson's authority, and is also evidence of the value which he attached to the advice of the officers of this church. It may be that his collisions with the clergy in Maryland had taught him the importance of not assuming too dictatorial a tone even toward an unworthy clergyman: —

To His Excellency Francis Nicholson, Esq.
The Humble Petition of Thomas Eager, Clerk, Sheweth —

That Whereas y.^r Petition.^r was appointed by the Honble the Society for Propogating the Gospell to Officiate as Minist.^r at Braintree, in New England, where y.^r Petition.^r has remained some time, but finding himself very uneasy there w.th the People, and y.^r Exc.^y being Commissionated to Enquire into the State of the Church in these Parts, — there being now a Quart.^r of a year's Salary due to y.^r Petition.^r of his Allowance by the Society (viz: Sixty pounds p Annum), and it being y.^r Excel^{ys} mind y.^t y.^r Petition.^r can be no longer servisable at Braintree, —

Y.^r Petition.^r humbly prays the Favour of y.^r Exc.^y that he may be allowed and have his Sallary paid him untill the 25.th day of March next, to Enable him to pay his Debts and remove elsewhere.

And ye Petit.^r shall pray, etc.

BOSTON, Decemb.^r 4.th, 1713. THOMAS EAGER.

I have Read this Petition, and refer itt to the Gent.ⁿ of the Vestry.

FR: NICHOLSON.

[1] Mr. Eager to the Secretary, Aug. 12, 1713. Church Docs. Mass. p. 92.

The Petition thus refer'd to us by the Honble Francis Nicholson, Esqr, we have considered; and so far as Respects Mr Eager's Dismission we are of opinion that it will be for the Service of the Church that he be Accordingly dismissed.

Signed by the Advice and Consent of ye Vestry.

CHARLES HOBBY,
JOHN JEKYLL,

BOSTON, Decr 8th, 1713.   Church Wardens.

The real difficulty was evidently in Mr. Eager himself, as is clear from a letter of Governor Dudley to the Secretary, dated May 1, 1714: —

"There has been some trouble at Braintree ab^t the arrear, which I hope is over also; but I have heard a sorrowful account from everybody referring to Mr Eager. I had heard of his rude life in his passage hither, being frequently disguised in drink and fighting with ye saylors, even to wounds and taring his cloaths; and during the few months of his stay here he was frequently in quarrels and fighting, and sending challenges for duells, that at length the auditory at Brantry were quite ashamed and discouraged; and he is gone to Barbadoes without any direction or order, and the Congregation without any Minister. General Nicholson has been here and seen ye process of the affair as above." [1]

Rev. Henry Lucas succeeded him for a short time, but was soon transferred to Newbury.

Twelve years elapsed before the Braintree Church was revived under more favorable circumstances, by the Rev. Ebenezer Miller, who remained its rector for thirty-six years, until his death in 1763.[2] His salary was £60 a year from "the Venerable Society."

[1] Church Docs. Mass. p. 97.

[2] He was born in Milton, Mass., June 20, 1703; son of Samuel and Rebecca (Belcher) Miller; graduated, H. C. 1723; ordained by the Bishop of London; deacon June 29, 1726, and priest July 9, 1727; July 16, 1727, received the degree of M. A. at Oxford; Aug. 26, 1727, was appointed missionary of the Society for the Propagation of the Gospel to Braintree, etc., where he began his duties Dec. 25, 1727. (Sept. 28, 1727, he had become domestic chaplain to the Duke of Bolton.) Visiting England in 1746–47, he received at Oxford the degree of S.T.D. Dec. 8, 1747. He died Feb. 11, 1763. He had married, Nov. 16, 1726, Martha, daughter of Thomas Mottram, of Addlethorp, Lincoln County, England. She died Oct. 28, 1755, aged fifty-two. Their descendants still hold a pew in King's Chapel. Mr. Miller has been said to be "the first native of the Puritan colonies authorized to preach under the Episcopal form." ("Address at the Two Hundredth Anniversary of the Settlement of Milton, by the Hon. James M. Robbins, 1862.") This, however, is an error, as the Revs. Samuel Myles, William Vesey, and Dudley Bradstreet take precedence of him. But that his religious antecedents were esteemed important by the English Church is shown by the significant language of his degree of M.A., Oxford, 1726, still preserved in his family. It reads: "Permultis quidem

Sewall notes the beginning of his ministry: —

"1727. Monday, Decʳ 25. — Shops open, and people come to Town with Hoop-poles, Hay, Wood, etc. Mr. Millar keeps the day in his New Ch. at Braintrey; people flock thither."

Dr. Miller was "well versed in the history and doctrines of his Church, and not afraid to meet in public polemic discussion Parson Dunbar of the First Church, who accused him of having been sent by his superiors to 'foment disturbances' and 'cause divisions' among the churches of New England, and 'by promoting Episcopacy, to increase the political influence of the Crown.'"[1]

Dr. Miller had the great advantage of being a native New Englander and belonging to a family known and respected at Braintree; yet even he found scanty gleaning in the field, leaving at his death but fifty families and fifty communicants in his church.

King's Chapel had a close connection in the beginning with these churches. The few gentlemen belonging to them were still interested in that as their metropolitan church, and its ministers took a peculiar interest in their affairs. But that in Marblehead seems to have been in the most intimate relations with the mother church. This is now the oldest parish church of the Episcopal denomination in New England. In 1649 Marblehead was set off from Salem, and it soon became a very important "fishing station," and commanded a large and profitable trade with foreign ports, especially Bilboa, Spain; so that at the beginning of the Revolutionary War the town had become "the second in the colony, both in population and wealth, having forty vessels engaged in the foreign trade." "A great number of these people desired to have the Church of England Service settled there. In 1707 they made subscriptions for building a church, amounting to £416,"[2] and in 1714 they asked the Society to send them a missionary: —

Nominibus commendatum, de Ecclesiâ Anglicanâ ideo optime mereri, quod a præpotenti Schismaticorum Cœtu dissentire ausus oppressæ Hierarchiæ Strenuus Vindex extiterit, honestiqᵘ adeo Propositi tenax a Regionibus dissitissimis ad Angliam nostram appulerit ut Sacris Ordinibus per Manum Episcopalem administratis initiatus ad Suos reverteretur — Sacerdotale munus auspicatiore cum Autoritate et Fructu executurus; ne Viri optimi dignissimiqᵉ Pietas laudabilis nos- tri Judicii Testimonio et Commendatione destituatur 'Sciatis quod Nos.," etc. Dr. Miller was succeeded, July 13, 1764, by the Rev. Edward Winslow, who left at the Revolution, which the church with difficulty survived. It is now Christ Church, Quincy. See "Sermon on Completing a Century since its Formation, by the Rev. Benjamin C. Cutler, 1828."

[1] N. E. Hist. and Geneal. Reg., xxix. 76.

[2] Humphreys, p. 328.

"Of what consideration your petitioners are, will be seen by the number of their names and the value of their subscriptions underwritten. . . . By the blessing of God, we have a certain prospect that the Church here will be every day increased and flourish more and more."

The Records of King's Chapel contain the following: —

We the Subscribers do firmly bind and oblidge our Selves, our Heirs, and Assigns for the Payment of Severall Sumns Subscribed in Order to the Building and Erecting a Handsom Church in the Town of Marblehead, and the maintaining of a Minister to carry on the service of God in the Ways and Methods of the Church of Great Brittain or Church of England; promising hereby to Espouse and Maintain its Articles, and Defend its Doctrine, which are Agreable to the Word of God. And this We are Obliged to Perform as soon as may be, as Witness our hands this 31st day of March, Annoq Domini, 1714.

	£ s. d.		£ s. d.
George Jackson, Senr.	20. 00. 00	Bt forwd	293. 00. 00
John Calley, Senr.	20. 00. 00	Robt. Martin	5. 00. 00
James Calley	20. 00. 00	John Allin	5. 00. 00
Barth : Jackson	20. 00. 00	John Hine	5. 00. 00
Tho : Sarle	20. 00. 00	John Wegar	5. 00. 00
John Yabsley	20. 00. 00	John Lecraw	5. 00. 00
John Palmer, Senr.	20. 00. 00	James Wegar	5. 00. 00
Wm Webber	10. 00. 00	Josiah Sikes	5. 00. 00
Rebecca Norman	10. 00. 00	Hen : Humphreys	5. 00. 00
Tho Candish	10. 00. 00	John Rounday	5. 00. 00
Geo : Slocum	16. 00. 00	John Savidge	5. 00. 00
Peter Fenaly	16. 00. 00	John Walker	5. 00. 00
Ambrose Bowden, Senr.	10. 00. 00	John Cheywell	5. 00. 00
Jacob Phillips	15. 00. 00	Jonan Bowden	5. 00. 00
Nicholas Andrews	10. 00. 00	Geo : Girdler	5. 00. 00
John Calley, Junr.	10. 00. 00	Richd Glass	5. 00. 00
Benjn Calley	10. 00. 00	Tho : Colle	3. 00. 00
John Chapman	10. 00. 00	John Bird	2. 10. 00
Joseph Andrews	5. 00. 00		£373. 10. 00
Joseph Doliber	5. 00. 00		
John Foster	5. 00. 00		
Tho : Candish, Junr.	6. 00. 00		
John Russell	5. 00. 00		
	293. 00. 00		

Note. — Rev. J. W. Leek's "Historical Sermons," etc., gives a list of thirty-four "Benefactors" of that church, from its records in 1716; but no name there given is found on the above list.

Thus St. Michael's Church in Marblehead was built in 1715. Of the thirty-four names preserved in its records as benefactors, twenty-nine were sea-captains, — a class of men naturally restive under the strict New England discipline, — and General Francis Nicholson heads the list. He was asked to name the church, after he removed to South Carolina, in 1722. The first minister was the Rev. William Shaw.[1] Soon after, a second

---

[1] The second minister, the Rev. David Mossom, after a service of nine years, removed to St. Peter's Church, New Kent County, Virginia, where he

Congregational church was built, and the rector wrote home that the Congregationalists had built it "in Damnable spite and Malice against our church, as some of their chief members have openly declared."

Our Records show the nursing care of King's Chapel for this its foster child: —

          Marblehead, Augst 19th, 1717.

Reverend S^r. Upon the sixth of this Ins^t our Vestry and I met and mutually agreed y^t the Reverend Mr. Myles, if he pleased to be so kind, might, upon my relinquishing of the Cure of Souls, in the Church of England in Marblehead, supply, or cause to be supply'd, the Vacancy during my absence, or the Determination of the Venerable Society. S^r upon y^r arrival at Marblehead, which the Church Wardens, Vestry, I humbly beg may be as soon as you conveniently can, I will give you as much Power as I am Capacitated to do. I am,

Superscribed   Reverend S^r,
 To the Reverend   Y^r Affectionate
  M^r. Myles, in Boston.   Humble Servt.,
               Wm. Shaw.
     Church Wardens: Barth?. Jackson,
              Charles Wheeden.

At a Vestry Held at His Majestyes Chappel in Boston, the Twenty-fifth of August, 1717, upon reading the above Letter, it was considered y^t it was proper and very Expedient y^t for the Service of the Church of England in Marblehead y^t the Rev. Mr. Myles should, on the Sunday next, officiate there as Cure, and as long as he should think proper; and, in case of his absence, the Reverend M^r. Harris, as they Shall agree.   G. Dyer, } Church Wardens.
            E. Mills, }

In Marblehead the establishment of this church stirred bitter feelings. Sewall notes: —

became the pastor of Washington, whom he afterward united in marriage to Mrs. Custis. The next missionaries were the Revs. George Pigot, during whose ministry, in 1738, a fearful epidemic (the small-pox) broke out in Marblehead, carrying off about four hundred of its inhabitants, including four of Mr. Pigot's children; Alexander Malcolm, 1740; Peter Bours, 1753; Joshua Wingate Weeks, 1762. "For many years after the Revolution the history of the parish is one of sad struggles and sorrowful experiences." The Rev. Thomas Fitch Oliver was the first rector after the Revolution. In 1813 the Rev. John Prentiss Kewley Henshaw, afterward Bishop of Rhode Island, was settled on a salary of $500. In 1818 Rev. Benjamin Bosworth Smith, now presiding Bishop of the Episcopal Church in the United States, became rector at a salary of $400 and the use of the glebe. The church was deserted and shut up for some years, and in 1822 an attempt was made to transfer it to Congregational worship; but the effort was unsuccessful, and in 1831 the Episcopal worship was resumed. See the "Historical Sermon by the Rev. John W. Leek, rector of St. Michael's Church, Marblehead, at its one hundred and fifty-eighth anniversary, on St. Michael's Day, September 29, 1872."

"March, 5. 1718-19. This morning Bows, a young man, tells me he is fin'd 20ˢ for saying that the new Church of England minister of Marblehead inveigh'd in his Sermon against Extempore Prayers, affirm'd the Dissenters in doing it broach'd damnable Blasphemies."

But even in this, the most hopeful of the newly founded churches, the promise hardly held good.

Mr. Mossom writes, April 28, 1724: —

"More than 50 communicants. Our Church is plain but neat. We have neither Pulpit Cloth, nor communion table-cloth, only one small silver cup for distributing the wine at the Sacrament; the people are so poor that they are not able to purchase more, the Church being still in debt near £200.

"The value of my living is uncertain. I receive nothing from the people but the contributions collected after Divine service on the Lord's days at the Church, most of which depends upon Strangers; taken one with another they are computed between 20 and 30 Shillings this money, which is the most extended value and that does not amount to 10 Shillings Sterling. I have neither house nor Glebe, but am obliged to hire a house myself, for which I pay out of my own pocket £25 per ann., the Parish contributing nothing towards it." [1]

This gentleman "began by declaiming upon all occasions against the Dissenters," but soon changed his course. To the Rev. John Barnard he said: "Why, sir, before I came over to you, I was filled with the conception of you as an heathenish, irreligious people, full of spleen and rancour against the Church of England; but when I had been among you some time, I found you a virtuous, religious, civilized people, and of moderate temper towards the Church; and therefore I thought proper to alter my conduct." His successor, Mr. Pigot, besides grave personal misfortunes, was engaged in a pamphlet controversy with Mr. Barnard. He was followed by a Scotchman who "retained some fondness for the Kirk and was no bigot," and after him by two native New Englanders. The church was large. Almost all the young people of any note in the town flocked to it.[2] But the Revolution brought this to nought.[3]

The establishment of these churches by the aid of "the Venerable Society" was the beginning of a sense of deep grievance in the New England church. As Dr. Colman expressed it, in writing to Dean Kennett, it was felt that —

[1] Church Docs. Mass. p. 150.
[2] Mr. Weeks to the Secretary, 1778.
[3] The curious autobiography of Rev. John Barnard, of Marblehead, a leading Congregational clergyman, (ordained 1716, died 1770, aged 89), is full of information concerning the church history of the period, though alloyed by prejudices and flavored with high self-esteem. It is printed in 5 Mass. Hist. Coll., iii.

"There is one *sordid Motive* which will find you Beggars enough for your Charity in our Country Towns, if you will *free them* from *Rates* to any ministry and *maintain* it for them. A more noble Charity never was projected than your sending the *Gospel* among the *Heathen* here, and into *Heathenish* Places. . . . This *vast* and *waste* Space, desolate and perishing, cries aloud to you for your charitable Care." [1]

The new missions provoked Cotton Mather to say: [2] —

"*Societies for the Propagation of Religion* which, for *Laborers in the Harvest of God*, send forth Men that are *alienated from this Life of God*, and that, instead of Preaching the *more weighty Matters* of the Gospel, Preach up the *lesser Matters* and meer Accidentals of Christianity, and such things as it is not certain that God has ever Instituted, — these do for the most part but serve the *Empire of Satan* under the *Banner of our Saviour;* and by these Cheats a vast disservice is done unto the Interest of the Gospel in the World."

Yet more sharply was this expressed later by Noah Hobart:

"At least in my Way of thinking there is a Difference between the *Church of England* and the *Episcopal Separation in New England*. The former is an ancient and venerable Society, which, though in many Instances not so perfect as the Reformers intended it should be, and as many of its present Members and Ornaments wish it was, . . . yet has a proper legal Establishment. The latter is an *inconsiderable* Sect of late Standing, built upon the Foundations of uncharitable Principles and Schismatical Practices ; and though supported by Money given to a better Use, wholly destitute of all reasonable Pretences to a legal establishment." [3]

Great expectations were excited both in England and among the more ardent Episcopalians here, by the planting of these shoots from the Church of England vine. But the sanguine hopes breathed in the letters of the missionaries on their first arrival uniformly give place to disappointment on finding the true state of the ground. Among native New Englanders a Church could not hope to flourish which took an arrogant and supercilious tone and temper toward the principles and even the prejudices of those among whom it was set, and which prided itself on having no flavor of Americanism. Although thus a little group of churches was formed in Massachusetts at this early date, they continued rather as feeble exotics on the New England soil, until the Revolution, while seeming to destroy

---

[1] Turell's Colman, p. 123.
[2] "*The Stone cut out of the Mountain,* And the KINGDOM OF GOD, In Those MAXIMS of it, that *cannot be shaken:* Rev. xiv. 7. Exhibited in the Year Seventeen hundred and Sixteen," p. 12.
[3] Second Address, etc., p. 21.

them, really gave a chance for independent life. Somewhat later, to these three whose origin was so largely due to Sir Francis Nicholson and his commission from "the Venerable Society," were added others which will appear in our narrative; but none of them had such intimate connection with King's Chapel. Their ministers, however, gathered on occasion in this as their metropolitan church, whose rectors held a primacy among them,— Mr. Price officially, as the Bishop's Commissary, and Dr. Caner by general recognition of his age and character, and of his position at the head of the Royal Governor's Church.

But the closest relation which "His Majesty's Chapel" sustained to these churches and to the scattered members of the same communion was in active endeavors for their protection from the laws taxing churchmen for the support of the dominant faith established in Massachusetts. These efforts were happily successful, but their story belongs at a later period.

The Records of King's Chapel continue to deal chiefly with the internal affairs of the church: —

Rev. S^r,— Having rec^d ye knowledge of your good-will to serve ye Church of this Towne, By Capt Danl Wyborne's Information, we take the Freedom, In behalf of the Whole Congregation, to beg Yo^r friendship, in endeavouring to obtain from ye gentlemen of your Island their Charitable Assistance of our small Number, belonging to the Church afores^d, who hath been at a Great Expense in enlarging the same, which is not yet finished for want of a sufficient Stock to goe on.

Whatever you gather for this Service we pray you will pay to Capt Wyborne, who hath promised to lay out ye same to the best Advantage for the said use. Your Charity and friendship herein shall forever be acknowledged by,

	Rev^d S^r,
To the Rev^d. W^m. Gorden	Y^r Most Obedient &
of	Most humble Serv^{ts}.
Barbadoes.[1]	
Boston, Jany 9th, 1715."	

1716		£	s.	d.
	To Exch^a of Broken Bills other pap^s and Silver .	2.	13.	01
Novr 12th	By Henry Caner in full	5.	02.	06
1717				
Aprill 20.	By J. Gibbs for paint^g ye Gov^{rs} Coat of Armes[2] .	4.	00.	00

[1] The contributions of Barbadoes gentlemen seem rather to have favored Christ Church, perhaps because that was more attended by seafaring folk.

[2] Governor Shute arrived October, 1716.

1718 £ s. d.
March 30. By M'. Kenton the Clerk in full to this day . . 20. 12. 00
By W'" Bennit &ca looking after the Boyes . . 1. 10. 00
By M'. Bagnall looking after the Watch . . . 2. 00. 00
By Wheeler & Cunningham for mending the
Windo 5. 09. 00
By M'. Gyles for officiating when Baker was dis-
miss'd 0. 06. 00
For Altering the Long Seats and Making Pews
as p Acco'.'. 73. 13. 11

Easter Monday, April 22ᵈ 1717, *Voted*, That the Revᵈ M'. Sam'l Myles have Three pound Ten Shillings p week, in Consideration of yᵉ value of our Bills of Credit being Lower'd p Exchange.

Voted, That there be a New Gallery Erected on the North Side of the Church and That the Present Church Wardens do Agree with Suitable Persons for the Same.[1]

A List of the Well disposed Gentlemen and other Persons that Contributed their assistance for the Building a Gallery, a New Pulpit, and adorning the Kings Chappel in Boston, and the Paving before it in the Year 1718.

	£ s. d.		£ s. d.
His Excellency Samuel Shute Esq'. Governo'.	40. 00. 00	M'. Peter Luce	3. 00. 00
Lieu'. Gov'. Dummer	2. 00. 00	M'. John Perrier	5. 00. 00
John Jekyl Esq'.	5. 00. 00	M'. Jobe Lewis	5. 00. 00
Cap'. Cayley	6. 00. 00	Cap'. Thomas Chichester . .	6. 00. 00
Cap'. James Sterling	5. 00. 00	M'. George Craddock Dawlings	5. 00. 00
M'. James Clarke	3. 00. 00	John Boydell	5. 00. 00
John Valentine Esq'. . . .	4. 00. 00	Henry Francklyn	6. 00. 00
Tho'. Newton Esq.	3. 00. 00	Cap'. Rich'.d Quick & J : Franklyn	10. 00. 00
John Nelson Esq	2. 00. 00		
Cap'. David Mackdowell . .	4. 00. 00	M'. Davis, Widdow	5. 00. 00
M'. William Randoll	3. 00. 00	Doctor Mathew Nassaro . .	7. 00. 00
Cap'. W'" Wood	1. 00. 00	Lazzaras Hubbard	10. 00. 00
Cap'. John Cox	2. 00. 00	James King & Comp'ª . . .	10. 00. 00
M'. Girot	1. 00. 00	M'. George Shores	0. 10. 00
M'. Tho'. Selby	2. 00. 00	James Palin	5. 00. 00
M'⁵ Green, Widdow	1. 10. 00	Skinner	5. 00. 00
M'. John Arbuthnot	1. 00. 00	William Spikeman	5. 00. 00
M'. Tho'. Phillips	2. 00. 00	Doctor John Gibbins . . .	10. 00. 00
M'. Ambrose Vincent . . .	2. 00. 00	Cap'. Maxwell & Watts . . .	10. 00. 00
		M'. Thomas Loyd	10. 00. 00
Collected by John Jekyl Esq'. as follows Viz'. :—		M'. Fisher & Davis	10. 00. 00
		M'. Robert Kenton	10. 00. 00
Cap'. Victorious Loobey . .	1. 00. 00	Cap John Cox	8. 00. 00
Jon'ª Shrine	0. 07. 06	Doctor Nassaro	1. 00. 00
Cap'. Tho'. Lithered	1. 00. 00	John Vallentine Esq'. . . .	6. 00. 00
Henry Foster	2. 00. 00	Doctor John Cutler . . .	5. 00. 00
M'. Francis Wilks	5. 00. 00		£167. 10. 00
M'. Verplank	1. 10. 00		103. 07. 06
M'. Tho'. Wroe	3. 00. 00		£270. 17. 06
Carryed to y'ᵉ other side £103. 07. 06		Carried over leafe to the C'.	

[1] In 1718 the cost of the new gallery and pulpit is stated to be £300. 11s. 1d. The new gallery cost £80, and the pulpit £36. 13. 00. The church was white-

At a Vestry held at His Maj^ties Chappel in Boston July 10, 1717:—

Upon reading an agreement of the Neighbourhood of School Street relating to the Paving of the same,— It was then and there agreed that the Present Church Wardens Should agree with Sutable Persons to Pave the Churches Proportion in Said Street, and to pay for the same out of the Church Stock: If they cannot obtaine Subscriptions for the same.

[Do.] December ye 6th 1717. It was then and there *Voted*, That there be a New Pulpit forthwith Built, and that it stand against the Pillar in the Officers Pew.

[Do.] January 17th It was then and there *Voted*, That Mr Edward Enstone be continued as Organist, and that he be paid as heretofore.

At a publick Vestry and Congregation of the Church of England at his Majesties Chappel in Boston, in New England, on Easter Munday, Aprill the 22^d, 1717:—

Voted, That his Excelency Samuel Shute, Esqre, Be of the Vestrey, as being Capt Generall And Commander in Cheife in and Over this Province.

[Do.] April 14th 1718. *Voted*, That Mr Mills and Mr Francklin have Liberty to Build a Tomb under the East End of the Church.

[Do.] Easter Monday, 18 April, 1720. *Voted*, That those that have the possesion of Pews and Dont pay contribution, to have them taken away and sold to others that will: notice being first publickly given the Church Wardens being empowered to dispose of them.

Those pews that are not disposed of or p^d for by them that has them in Possesion to be Sold by the Church Wardens.

That D. Rutley Be appointed to keep good order amongst the Boys, and that for his trouble he be allowed 12^d p Sunday. Left to the Church Wardens to have the Church kept in repair. That a Minute be made p Desire of Mr Jno Checkley that the reason of his being left out of the Vestry was for his refuseing taking the oaths.[1]

Easter Monday, ye 10 April, 1721. *Voted*, The Clark continued and to be allowed 7/ p week. The Sexton continued and to be allowed 7/ p week. That the Revd Mr Samuel Miles be allowed and paid him out of the Church Stock £12 for paving before his house.

Easter, 1722. *Voted*, That the Revd Mr Samuel Miles have £30 paid him out of the Church Stock in full of All Demands for his past charges and servise in London, at £10 a year for 3 Years.

washed, in this year, for £10, and Thomas Fitch was paid £1. 17. 00 for "curtains to ye Gov^rs Pew."

[1] This brief record opens a window for us into the bitter political strife which almost rent the church asunder. A full account of Mr. Checkley and his opinions will be found in subsequent pages. The Maryland Assembly sought to provide for similar cases of conscientious scruple, by passing an Act "for the Service of Almighty God." "If any Person so chosen Vestryman, shal refuse to serve and take the Oaths aforesaid, he shal be fined one thousand pounds of Tobacco to his Majesty."—*Church Docs.* Maryland, p. 44.

FIGHTINGS WITHOUT AND FEUDS WITHIN.   267

That the Revd Mr Henry Harris have 10/ a week for the following Year out of the Church Stock.

That Messrs Thos Selby, Anthony Blount, and North Ingham and Thomas Philips are chose a Committy to make enquiry w^t Pews are unpaid for.

The new Governor did not promise much aid to the interests of the church in its militant relations to the surrounding community. Colonel Samuel Shute[1] (1716-1727) was a grandson of the Presbyterian divine, Joseph Caryl; but his service in Spanish campaigns had not added to his Nonconformist zeal. He was nominally a Dissenter, however, and was welcomed by the ministers of the Province, headed by Dr. Cotton Mather, who told him that his appointment was "An Happiness whereinto we have been indeed most agreeably Surprised, by the Providence of our Glorious LORD;" while King's Chapel does not appear by its records to have presented him any formal address. After he had been in Boston a few months, his coat of arms was set up in the church (it can hardly have been without his approval), and in 1718 he headed with a handsome sum the subscription for a new gallery. It became more and more clear that he did not intend to wear a Congregational yoke. Already when he had landed and taken

ARMS OF SHUTE.

---

[1] Governor Samuel Shute was of Norman descent. His ancestor, Christopher Shute, of Hollington, Cambridgeshire, was father of Robert, Recorder of Cambridge, one of the twelve judges in Queen Elizabeth's reign, second Baron of the Exchequer, 1579, and Justice of the King's Bench, 1585, who married Thomasine, daughter of Christopher Burgoine, Esq., of Long-Stanton, Cambridgeshire. Their eldest son, Francis, married Frances, daughter of Hercules Mewlas, Esq., of Westham, Essex (who married (2) Robert Ratcliffe, Earl of Sussex). Their eldest son, Francis, of Upton, Leicestershire, had three sons: (1) James, whose only child, James, died without issue; (2) Samuel, whose three sons died young and of whose two daughters, Elizabeth married Francis Barrington, Esq., and died without issue; (3) Benjamin, married Elizabeth Caryl, and died 1683. They had three sons: (1) Samuel, the Governor, Lieut.-Colonel of Horse, with brevet of Colonel, severely wounded at Blenheim. He died unmarried, aged 80, in 1742. (2) Benjamin, died unmarried, 1714; (3) John, adopted by his cousin Elizabeth's husband, and took the name of Barrington. He was created Viscount Barrington, of Ardglass, and Baron of Newcastle, 1720. Of his six sons, John, Major-General, married Elizabeth, daughter of Florentius Vassal, Esq.; Samuel was a distinguished Vice-Admiral, and the youngest was the noted Shute Barrington, Bishop of Salisbury, 1782.—*The New Peerage*, iii. 244. London, 1784: The arms are from the "Visitation of Cambridgeshire, 1619."

the oath, on Oct. 5, 1716, he went to "the Church of England" on the 7th, though attending the Thursday lecture following.[1] Sewall records in 1722, Dec. 21, that the Governor urged adjournment of the General Court over Christmas: —

"I said the Dissenters came a great way for their Liberties, and now the Church had theirs; yet they could not be contented, except they might Tread all others down. Govr said he was of the Church of England. I told Mr. Belcher of his Letter to me. He answer'd, He thought he had been a Dissenter then."

In spite of objections, he adjourned the Court to December 26. His name heads the Vestry of King's Chapel, 1717–1720.

The Governor showed his leanings by stretching his prerogative in defence of the members of the Church of England who complained of taxation. His administration was a prolonged wrangle, as the King's representative, with a refractory people, in a contest for a fixed salary and concerning the establishment of a public or a private bank. For the Province suffered much from a depreciated paper currency, and had not learned the heroic remedy. The contribution-box and the minister's salary in King's Chapel felt the evil of this flimsy substitute for the King's coin.

At last, in 1723, the Governor withdrew privily from his endless frettings and went to lay his grievances before the Home Government. Lieut.-Governor William Dummer, a native New Englander, but with wide experience, filled his place 1723-29. He was a Congregationalist, but dealt justly and kindly by the Church of England here. Still, he was not what they coveted in that high place; and they felt wronged when he was appealed to in their intestine strife, although he was the King's lieutenant.

[1] Governor Shute wrote in May, 1721, that "he has visited the Church at *Newbury*, of which the Reverend Mr. *Plant* is Minister, who seems to be a sober and ingenious Man; that he staid there all the Sabbath Day, as did Lieutenant-Governor *Wentworth*, and some other Gentlemen, which he hopes will give him a good Countenance, and assured the Society that he shall want no due Encouragement from him, and the like Encouragement he has promis'd to the several Missionaries in his Government." — 2 *Anniversary Sermon*, 1721-22, p. 44.

April 1, 1723. At a meeting of the Congregation with the Vestry, *Voted*, That the Revd Mr Samuel Miles be paid weekly Ten Shillings out of the Church Stock more than his former Sallary, which makes Four Pounds p week.

Easter, April 15, 1723.

Voted,

That Robt Auchmuty Esqr at the Relinquishing of his Pew in the Gallery, Together with John Overing Esqr, they Paying £20 to the Church, to have the Pew commonly knowne by the name of St Charles Hobbyes.

That Mr Thos Amory and William Coffine, upon their paying £10 each for the pew in the Gallery Formerly Mr Auchmuty's, shall enjoy the same.

That Mr James Smith, paying £20 for the enlargement of his pew and Five pounds four shillings for his arrears of Contribution, Shal Enjoy the said pew as it now is.

That Mr John Powell, Paying £10 for one half of the Pew called Mrs Wibournes Pew, shall enjoy the same.

That Mr James Gordon, paying £15 for the pew formerly Mr Tunly's, shall enjoy the same.

That the Widow Boucher, paying 40/ for the pew formerly Mr Rous's, shall enjoy the same.

That the Widow English, paying £10, shall have the pew that Mr Hays family did sit in, giveing liberty to Mr Brock and his Son to sitt there.

That every Person that has any property in a pew shall pay 52/ p annum, or else forfeit the same. And if any person through misfortunes shall be unable to pay the same, by making application to the Church Wardens and Vestry, shall be By them Relieved; as also all those who have not paid for their Pews and their arrears in Contribution are desired in this month to pay the same to the Church Wardens, on penalty of forfeiting their Pews, which shall then be at the disposall of the said Church Wardens and Vestry.

That Messrs Jno Barnes, George Craddock, and Joshua Wroe be Auditors of the last years acc.^{ts}

Novr 8, *Voted*, by the Church wardens and Vestry, that Mr Edwd Enston deliver the key of the Organs to Messrs Price and Gifford, that they may practise on the Organ in order to quallify one of them to be Organist, as shall be best approved of by ye said Church Wardens and Vestry.

Also *Voted*, That Mr Hays the Sexton have an augmentation of 2/ p week till next Easter.

Jan.^{ry} 10, *Voted*, by the Church Wardens and Vestry, that Mr Baker serve as Sexton to the Church in the room of Thos Hayes dec.^d untill Easter next, provided he continue sober and of a good behaviour untill that time.

The Puritan diarist continues to indicate some of the relations of the Royal Chapel, and of the opinions which it represented, to the surrounding community. Thus he notes, August, 1714, the arrival of news that the Rev. Dudley Bradstreet, "quickly after he had received Orders, dy'd of the Small Pocks."[1]

April 28. [1713.] "Mr. Pemberton spake very fiercely against the Gov' and Council's meddling with suspension of Laws, respecting Church of England men not paying Taxes to the dissenting Ministers.

Oct. 20. [1714.] Capt. Turfrey was buried this Afternoon. I was not there because the Gov' made his speech by Candle-light.[2]

Dec. 27. My Son tells me that Thomas Sewall went to the Church of England last Satterday [25th]. He expostulated with him about it.

[March] 31. 3. 1719. Mr. Belcher says Passion-week was kept last week. Vessels were deny'd clearing for 2 or 3 days."

Worst of all, the Puritan Sabbath was sometimes broken by strange sounds, for which the Church of England was held responsible.

"[1714] Lord's Day, Decemb' 26. Mr. Bromfield and I go and keep the Sabbath with Mr. John Webb, and sit down with that Ch. at the Lord's Table. I did it to hold communion with that Church; and, so far as in me lay, to put Respect upon that affronted, despised Lord's Day. For the Ch. of Engld had the Lord's Super yesterday, the last day of the Week; but will not have it to-day, the day that the Lord has made. And Genl Nicholson, who kept Satterday, was this Lord's Day Rumaging and Chittering with Wheelbarrows etc. to get aboard at the long Wharf, and Firing Guns at Setting Sail. I thank God I heard not, saw not, anything of it, but was quiet at the New North."[3]

It must not fail to be noted, however, that while the Puritan convictions of which Sewall stands as the type continued steadfast, their central principle was reverence for Christianity as they

---

[1] This grandson of Simon Bradstreet and Ann Dudley, H. C. 1698, had been ordained at Groton June 16, 1706, but dismissed probably on account of his Episcopal sympathies, and had gone to England for orders in that church.

[2] One point in which the church services gained by comparison is hinted at in a Memorial among the papers of the Overseers of the Poor, signed by Cotton Mather in behalf of his brethren, dated "24th iv th 1717. Upon an uneasy Experience of a grievous Misuse of Time which we suffer on a long attendance at Funerals (an occasion than which there is none that more powerfully admonishes to a wise redeeming of Time)," the ministers ask the Selectmen to regulate the matter.

[3] This disturbance was really in violation of the reverent custom of Old England, where, through the eighteenth century, "the Puritan Sabbath, in all its principal characteristics, remained firmly established. . . . Amid all the laxity of the Restoration period, the partial triumph of Laudean ideas which marked the reign of Queen Anne, the indifference and sluggishness in religious matters which soon afterward set in, reverence for the sanctity of the Lord's Day and a fixed purpose that its general character of sedate quietness should not be broken into, grew . . . into a tradition."—*Church of England in the Eighteenth Century*, ii. 513.

found it in the Scriptures. The same diarist writes of a debate in the Board of Overseers of Harvard College upon the proposed endowment of the Hollis professorship, to be held, according to the stipulation of the founder, by a professor "In Communion with a Church of Congregational, Presbyterian, or Baptists":—

"Jan. 10. [1721-22.] I objected against it, as chusing rather to lose the Donation than to Accept it. In the Afternoon I finally said, One great end for which the first Planters came over into New England was to fly from the Cross in Baptisme. For my part, I had rather have Baptisme admistered with the incumbrances of the Cross, than not to have it Administered at all."

Thus far, the presence of the Church of England had only indirectly been felt through the Province at large. The people had come to acquiesce in the existence of a representative chapel at the Royal Governor's place of residence, and the irritating consciousness of the presence of a scattered missionary or two was hardly diffused through the body politic. But now a period of controversy was to begin, which would rouse the whole disputatious passion of a people with whom theology was an inherited instinct. It is a strange illustration of the provincialism of New England thought, indeed, that the echo of many of the questions debated in England seems hardly to have crossed the Atlantic. Of the Puritan and the Papal controversies which had so shaken the mother country, New England was itself a living monument; but her people neither knew nor cared much about "the Deistic, the Non-juring, the Bangorian, the Trinitarian, the various ethical controversies," which filled the reigns of Queen Anne and George I. with a succession of disputes.[1]

Though "whole bales of Woolston's Discourses on the Miracles were sent to America," not one of the sixty adversaries who wrote against him, or of the one hundred and fifteen who answered Tindal, was a New Englander. The schism which took place among the Dissenters in England in 1719, on the doctrine of the Trinity, seems to have roused little general attention here, although Cotton Mather lifted a warning voice against it to his English brethren:—

"Yea, Sirs, to be yet more free with you, there is an *Horror of Great Darkness*, which comes upon the Minds of many Good Men in these *Goings down of the Sun*, from an Apprehension that there is a strong

[1] See "Church of England in the Eighteenth Century," ii. 48.

and deep *conspiracy* in our very sinful Nation to dethrone the Eternal Son of God." [1]

Dr. Cutler wrote to the Secretary, April 5, 1731: —

"Some have lately asserted that Hell torments will have an end, and that wicked men and devils will at last be saved thro' the goodness of God and the merits of Christ. I have privately borne witness against this corrupt doctrine, but as yet do not find it to spread so as to make it necessary I should oppose it in the pulpit." [2]

But on any point which touched the principles on which New England was founded the sensitive feeling was still ready to burst into flame if a spark should fall. The persistent advance of the English Church can be traced through the warnings which from time to time were raised against it. Dr. Increase Mather's "Discourse," etc., has been already noted.[3] In 1700 his son had published in England a letter of advice to Nonconformists: [4] —

"But there is the True CHRISTIAN CHURCH of *England*, which would have the *Reformation of Religion* carried on according to the *Direction* of the Sacred *Scriptures* and the *Intention* of the first *Reformers*, and counts not *Christianity* to lye in vain *Ceremony;* which looks on *Diocesan Bishops* as made such by the *King* and the *National Church-Government*, as an *human*, tho' *useful*, Policy; which owns the rest of the sound *Protestants* in the World for *Brethren*, and would have the Qualifications for the *Pastoral office*, and for *Communion* in special Ordinances, to be no other than what the Lord Jesus Christ hath instituted; which, in fine, is against bringing a Yoke of *Slavery* upon the brave English Nation in

---

[1] "Three Letters from New England, Relating to the Controversy of the Present Time." A royal proclamation enjoining the preaching of the doctrine of the Trinity is published in the "News-Letter," April 18, 1715. The question was made public in England by the Salters'-Hall debate in London. An Exeter Dissenting minister having become an Arian, and his congregation being divided, the London ministers were appealed to for a decision on the question of his remaining with his people. "The Independents urged that all ministers must sign a declaration of belief in the Trinity; the Presbyterians mostly voted against any subscription or confession of faith, though most of them still believed in the doctrine. They set up as their only rule the authority of Scripture, to be interpreted by each man for himself." — Herford, *Story of Religion in England*, p. 322.

[2] Church Docs. Mass., p. 263. An illustration of the rank food which was consumed by the coarser stratum of society at this time is afforded by the publication of "A Sure Guide to Hell, etc. By Belzebub. London: 4th ed. Reprinted at Boston."

[3] See p. 96, *ante*.

[4] "A Letter of Advice to the CHURCHES of the Nonconformists in the English Nation; endeavouring their Satisfaction in that POINT, *Who are the True Church of* England?" London: 1700. In 1702 the same active pen sent out "Seasonable testimony to the doctrines of Grace, fetched out of the articles and homilies of the Church of England. Boston, 1702."

Spirituals or *Temporals.* And *of this Church ye are.* God, and the King, and the Parliament, and all sober Men will reckon you a valuable Part of this *Church;* while a certain *Hectoring* sort of People in the World, that would be thought the only *Church of England,* deserve to be counted rather the *Wens* than any *Parts* of it, and indeed *know not what it is.* I beseech you, Sirs, let not the CHURCH OF ENGLAND become a Name of such a *Treasonable Importance,* that it must belong to none but that Faction, whose Religion lyes in *Sainting* their Martyr, Charles I. . . .

" And now, *my Brethren,* if any go to seduce you from your own RE-FORMED CONGREGATIONS into the more CEREMONIOUS ASSEMBLIES in the *Church of England,* you are furnished with an *Answer.* Let your *Answer* be, That you are of the *Church of England,* and that you cannot better express your being *so* than by keeping with your own REFORMED CONGREGATIONS. If the Bishop of *London* should be offended at the Governours of *Barbadoes,* or *Bermudas,* or *Carolina,* for worshipping of God in the Meetings of the *Nonconformists* there, the Gentlemen may truly say in their defence, that they worshipped God with the *truest part of the Church of England* in those Parts of *America.*"

While the Chapel was enlarging its walls the same restless sentinel sounded the trumpet again, in a statement of the strictest Calvinism, in the language of the Articles and Homilies:

"It is to be hoped, that if *Books* are dispersed any where, under a pretence of *Propagating the Christian Religion,* wherein men are either Led away from the Acknowledging of the *Sovereign Grace* that shines in the whole of our Salvation, or at least kept upon Design unmindful of it, the Fine-spun *Devices of Satan* against the Church of GOD therein may be duely Observed and Avoided."

"How the Men who Deny and Oppose these *Doctrines* can pretend to be of *The Church of England* is a little Wonderful! But it is needful to Demonstrate that these *Doctrines* are Built on a Greater Authority than the *Church of* England. The *Pelagian* and *Arminian* Errors prevailing at this Day, are to be struck with more awful *Thunderbolts.*"

[He closes with] "*Supplies from the Tower of David:* by which the *Doctrines of Grace* are to be Defended and Maintained." [1]

The occasion of the Newbury schism was taken to reprint an English pamphlet in the same view, with an introduction by Dr. Increase Mather: —

[1] He asks: "Quest. *Has the Great God, with a Decree* of REPROBATION, *left any to Perish in their Sins?*

"*Answ.* Since it is contrary to all Sense that *All* should be *Elected,* it is plain there must be Some REPROBATES. And since it is Evident that many are never Saved out of their Sins, we may conclude that God never *Decreed* their *Salvation.*" — ROM. ix. 18. These extracts are taken from Cotton Mather's "𝕿𝖍𝖊 𝕺𝖑𝖉 𝕻𝖆𝖙𝖍𝖘 𝕽𝖊𝖘𝖙𝖔𝖗𝖊𝖉. In a

"Did our Nonconformists believe (as their Conforming Brethren do) That the Ceremonies are indifferent things, they would easily comply with them; but they are perswaded that they are transgressions of the Second Commandment, and as long as they so judge, it is their duty rather to Suffer than to Sin against their light. . . . New England differs from the other Outgoings of the English Nation in that our Fathers came into this Land when it was a Land not Sowen, purely on the account of Religion; and this not as to Doctrine, but Discipline. . . . I am hastening out of the World. May my dying Advice be of any weight, I would say to the dear People of New England, Remember how you have received and heard, and hold fast. If Conformity be a Sin, I am sure that it will in New England be a greater Sin than in any Place under Heaven."[1]

And now the battle thickened more and more. Whether inspired by the zeal of the younger minister, Mr. Harris, or by the general enlivenment of their cause, the Episcopal party began in their turn to print. Mr. Harris printed a preface to Archbishop King's "Inventions of Men in the Worship of God," with personal allusions to Dr. Mather such as had never before been breathed above a whisper in Boston:[2] —

"Since the mixture of Humane Inventions in Divine Worship is made the great Subject of Complaints by our Dissenting Brethren, It will be Brief Demonstration that the Doctrines of Grace hitherto Preserved in the Churches of the Nonconformists are not only Asserted in the Sacred Scriptures, but also in the ARTICLES and HOMILIES of the *CHURCH OF ENGLAND;* And That the General Departure from those *DOCTRINES,* Especially in those who have Subscribed them, is a Most Unaccountable APOSTACY. Extracted from some things formerly Published: And Contrived into a single Sheet, for the Use of some that want and ask for the *Armour of Christianity,* against the Seducers of this Evil Time. pp. 12, 24. Sm. 8°, Boston: T. Green, 1711. And Reprinted at London, 1712. With a Preface by Will. Whiston, A.M."

[1] "A LETTER from Some Aged Nonconforming Ministers to their Christian Friends, Touching the REASONS of their PRACTICE. August 24, 1701. Boston: reprinted, 1712."

The Letter begins: "Above Forty Years since, we were removed from our Publick Ministrations, you have now Affectionately adhered to us. . . . Before we die you require our riper Thoughts of the *Way* we continue in." It states the objections against Lay Conformity. "We dare not by Practice violate our Consciences." These objections are to the forms and ceremonies, an imposed Ministry, and the Church discipline. A special defence is made against the charge of Schism. It also states the special objections against Ministers' Conformity: —

"We cannot acknowledge the Prelate or *Lord Bishop* as a Superior Officer in the Church, and swear obedience to him, as if Presbyters were his Subjects and Vassals."

The objections are to Episcopal authority, patronage, a declaration, and subscription. It gives the history of Dissenting. An appendix contains practical advice concerning conscientious application of the religion in practice.

[2] "A DISCOURSE concerning *The Inventions of Men* in the WORSHIP of GOD. By the Right Reverend Dr. *WILLIAM KING,* LORD BISHOP of *London-Derry. The Fifth Edition.* London: MDCCIV. Re-printed at *Boston* in *N. E.,* 1712."

an act of Charity towards them, and a piece of Justice to our Excellent Constitution, to rectifie their Judgments in a matter of so much Importance; this being the most plausible pretence which has been ever used to excuse a Separation from the National Establish'd Church. Now one would think it very natural and reasonable, that those who leave Our Communion upon this account, should be careful not to offend in the same point themselves; but so it happen'd, that in the hurry of their Zeal, they split upon this Rock, and 'tis easy to convince all persons who do not resolve before-hand that they will never be convinced, that the Dissenters alone are blame-worthy in this particular, and the Church of England free from the guilt of Superstition or Popery: The practice of the former being full of Innovations in the Essential Parts of Religious Service; the latter following the Apostle's Rule of doing all things decently and in order. . . . An Eminent Nonconformist Writer should have consider'd this, and corrected what is amiss in the Congregational Scheme of Government, and Method of Worship, before he laid his Charge against the most perfect Church upon Earth; then as his Charity begins and ends at home, so would his Reformation too. But though he is so much wanting in Charity to us, we'll have so much for him as to suppose, that forgetfulness, one of the Infirmities incident to Old Age, is the cause of his renewing this Controversy; otherwise he must needs be sensible that his Objections . . . have long ago receiv'd a most rational and solid Answer. . . . We are by no means displeas'd with him for assigning the Reasons of his Persuasion in Matters of Religion: But a Great man having condescended to answer those Reasons, if his Interest permits him not to acknowledge the strength of his Antagonist's Arguments, we might expect that his Modesty at least should hinder him from repeating the old Slanders and Calumnies, unless we imagine, that though he is vanquish'd himself, yet still he thinks his Cause is good, and triumphs in the performances of others, which he says, as far as he can understand were never answer'd; but if he 'll take the pains to read the Books writ by the Divines of Our Church upon this Subject, he will find his mistake, and his Understanding will be better inform'd; I must confess he is extreamly right in his Notion, that the Letter which he has lately Reprinted is adapted to vulgar Capacities, such as cannot distinguish betwixt Truth and Falshood, and have neither inclination nor leisure to consider the Reasons of the opposite side; but what good it can do is difficult to conceive, unless it be a good to harden People in their Hatred and Animosities which they have unjustly entertained against the best Protestant Church in the World. This is plainly that Writer's intention. . . .

"'Tis the Duty of the People of New-England, as well as of those of other places, to forsake their Errors, and return to their Obedience to Our Spiritual Governours, whose Lawful Authority they have so long rejected and disowned. . . . I will . . . no longer detain the Reader, than just to caution him against Mr. Mather's popular tho' weak Insinuation, that the Fathers of the present Generation were Nonconformists, and their Dissent from the Mode of Worship in the Church of England was the cause of their Coming Over and Settling this Plantation; tho' it would be a sufficient answer to say, that Our Brethren have no more reason to continue in their Separation upon this score, than the Original inhabitants of the Country have for their brutish and savage way of living, viz., because they are accustomed to it."

He concludes with apt quotations from the "Humble Request" of Winthrop's company, and from the "Gospel Order Revived,"[1] in answer to Dr. Mather's insinuation. It must be confessed, even by those who agree with Mr. Harris, that his tone in these remarks is adapted rather to enrage than to convince his adversaries. Nor does the book thus introduced differ in this quality; it speaks in the superior tone of a high dignitary of the Church of England in Ireland addressing his inferiors, comparing the practice of his own church and of the Irish Dissenters in the "Praises, Prayers, Hearing, Bodily Worship, and Celebration of the Holy Sacraments of the Body and Blood of Christ," — in all of which he finds his own method wholly right and the opposite method utterly wrong, both by the test of Scripture and of reason. An answer by Bishop John Williams, of Chichester (the "Great Man" alluded to by Mr. Harris), to Increase Mather's discourse was also reprinted.[2]

This answer to Mather's "Brief Discourse" shows a less sinewy grasp than belonged to that veteran controversialist, yet meets his points forcibly and justly,[3] not without some indignant heat:

[1] See pp. 5, 138, *ante*.

[2] Cotton Mather wrote to Wait Winthrop: "Boston, 19! 11ᵐ 1712. Our Reprinting of the *Letter of the Aged N. C. Ministers* putt our High-fliers into a Strange Ferment. You know what followed, — namely, Dʳ *Williams's* virulent Vindication of the C[ommon] P[rayer] Worship, and Dʳ *King's* heap of Sophistries and Calumnies. My Aged parent's *Remarks* hereupon did not produce a hundredth part of the clamour he Expected. Our people are generally gratified, edified, established.

"The Church of England party resolve to publish no more. *Harris* is under some Attrition for his *unhappiness* (that 's the word) in writing his *Preface*, which was indeed almost universally decried. Our *Newbury* Faction are coming off, and putting themselves under the conduct of one of our Ministers. For the rest, I know nothing but all peace and Quietness." — 4 *Mass. Hist. Coll.*, viii. 414.

It was at this stage that Cotton Mather preached the "Christmas Sermon" already referred to, which doubtless derived its point from the general excitement. See p. 206, *ante*.

[3] For an outline of Mather's statement see p. 96, *ante*. The answer, which had been published anonymously in England nineteen years before its reprint here, but understood to be by Bishop Williams, was entitled: "A Brief Discourse Concerning the Lawfulness of Worshipping God by the Common Prayer. Being in answer to a Book entitled *A Brief Discourse*, etc. London: 1693. *Boston:* 1712." It closes with an answer to the appendix: "The Book is kissed 'in token of Reverence, as it 's the Book of God.'"

"Would any man of a truly Christian Temper alledge these things now against the Common-Prayers, which were alter'd or expunged above thirty years before he published his Brief Discourse? or charge us with violating the Word of God because we change the word Sabbath for the Seventh Day? or say that we sacrilegiously steal from it because Hallelujah, or Praise the Lord, is sometimes left out in the Reading-Psalms? or that we equal the Apocrypha to, and set it up above, the Canonical Scriptures, because it's read on the Highest Holy-days (as he saith, but not very truly), tho' the Articles of our Church expressly declare them to be only of humane composition."

The answer shows that the Popish parts of the Missal are left out, and what is the same with the Roman Liturgy is mostly taken out of the ancient Offices of the Christian Church; it denies the "Idolatry of the Mass-Book," or that, if it were admitted, it defiles what is extracted from it. It proceeds to speak of the matter of the Common-prayer Book. Here it shows that all but one of Mather's instances of mistranslations in it were taken from the book before its last revisal: —

1. "There may be many things that are a reason against Ministerial Conformity, which will not be a reason against communion with the Church.

2. Many of his Objections are only directed against the occasional Offices.

3. Things inconvenient, if not unlawful, are no reason for a Separation, because then there would be no Communion with any Church, since no Church is without them."

As to the charge that liturgies are an innovation, after demonstrating from history their antiquity, the reply closes: "But I can tell *what is an Innovation;* and that is, To hold Liturgies unlawful." As to the apostasy of compliance with this form of worship, it answers that good people have been *for* as well as *against* it; and if "a stinted liturgy" chokes the spirit of prayer, then have most churches been without it.

Dr. Mather's reply soon followed, in the tone of one who was confident that the public would be on his side.[1] As is usual in such controversies, he adds little, except in reiteration, to his

---

[1] "Some REMARKS on a Pretended ANSWER To a Discourse concerning the Common-Prayer *Worship*. With An EXHORTATION to the Churches in *New-England*, to hold fast the Profession of their Faith without Wavering. Phil. i. 17,—*Knowing that I am set for the Defence of the Gospel.* ——— Necessarium est, ut qui falsis dicendis assueti sunt audiant vera, et qui quod volunt effutiunt, etiam quæ nollent intelligant. *Rivetj Jesuita vapulans.*" [London and Boston: 1712.]

first statement, save by correcting here and there a misstatement of his views by his antagonist, — as that the unlawfulness to which he objects is in the imposition of forms, and not "the bare use of them." The charge that he "never compared the English with the Roman Liturgy" he pronounces "Base and Scandalous, altho' he did not think it worth the while to read over every Word in both Liturgies; nor did he ever give the least hint as if he had so misspent his Time."

"Concerning the Name of this *Anonymous Answerer*, I list not to Enquire. Some say he is a Bishop. If he is a Bishop, I doubt not but that there have been many better Bishops in *New England* than he; and I hope there are such still. But I cannot easily Believe that he is one. It is beneath the Gravity and Learning which become a Bishop to Write in such a petulant Style. I should rather by his Book take him to be some High Flyer, who hopes for Preferment by his Bigottry to the Liturgy and Ceremonies. No Man of Honour could act so Mean or so Rude a part as appears in the Answer from first to last. . . . Many serious Men begin to think whether they who thus renounce Communion with all the Reformed Churches in the World (tho' very liberal in calling others by the name of *Schismaticks*) are not guilty of a *Schism*, wherein they shut themselves out of the True Visible *Catholick Church* of Christ.

"And now, O you Churches of Christ in *New England! Hold fast the Profession of your Faith without Wavering.* Be stedfast in your Religion, both as to the Faith and as to the Order of the Gospel. . . . Remember what it was your Fathers came into this Wilderness to see. They did not (as *Conformists* now do) come into a fruitful Land to get Estates; but they ventured their own Lives and the Lives of their Children over a vast Ocean to Encounter with the Straits and Difficulties of a Barren, Howling Wilderness, . . . for no other reason but that so *they and their Posterity* might be freed from the Superstitions of the Common-Prayer Book."

The next year saw the warfare continued from the neighboring pulpits by Cotton Mather and Pemberton. The former said: —

"One Main End of our Predecessors Coming hither was to keep their Children unacquainted with such *Foolish Customs*. To introduce them can be no *Kindness* to us. . . . *Christmas-Revels* begin to be taken up among some vainer Young People here and there in some of our Towns. . . . The *Shroves-Tuesday Vanities* of making *Cakes to the Queen of Heaven*, etc." [1]

[1] "*Advice from the Watchtower*, In a Testimony against Evil Customes, etc., Boston, 1713." "A Discourse had By the late Reverend and Learned Mr. Ebenezer Pemberton, Previous to the *Ordination* of the Reverend Mr. *Joseph Sewall*, at Boston, September 16, 1713. Affirming and proving the *Validity* of *Presby-*

In 1716 Dr. Increase Mather issued one of the several "dying testimonies" which he gave on this subject, while his son followed by a characteristic fulmination[1] on —

"The point of unpolluted Administrations in the *House of God*. . . . If anything be obtruded on the *Worship* of GOD, which His *Word* will not Support, let a *Quo Warranto* be served upon it. This is thy *Crown*, O NEW-ENGLAND!"[2]

Nor was the active part in the controversy confined to Boston ministers. The Rev. John Wise, of Ipswich, minister of the nearest town to Newbury, — one of the strongest men in New England, who had been a chosen subject of persecution under Andros's government, — published his vindication of the church polity of the land.[3]

He quotes: —

"These Weighty and Solemn Words of the Learned and Famous Mr. Oakes, Præsident of the Colledge, in his Election Sermon. . . . *I profess*

---

terial ORDINATION, Boston: 1718." (Published with T. Prince's sermon at his ordination, October 1, 1718.)

Prince's sermon has some interesting statements concerning the South Church and its ministers: "The Church was founded on the 12 May, 1669; and since that Time to this, which is not yet Fifty Years, to 700 communicants, and near as many more that have owned the covenant, there have been about 5,000 Baptized Persons." Of Mr. Willard he says: "I must ever Remember him with peculiar Esteem and Gratitude for the Heavenly Gravity, Condescention, and melting Affection wherewith he treated me in my tender Years, when he took me aside at Colledge to incourage and direct me in the Affairs of my Soul." Of Mr. Pemberton "methought he spake like a flaming Seraph."

[1] I. Mather: "Two Discourses, shewing (1) That the Lord's Ears are open to the Prayers of the Righteous; (2) The Dignity and Duty of Aged Servants of the Lord. Also A Preface in which the Congregational Discipline of the Churches in New England is Vindicated, with the Author's Dying Testimony thereunto. Boston: 1716."

C. Mather: "*Icono-clastes*. An Essay upon the Idolatry too often committed under the Profession of the most Reformed Christianity, etc. Boston: 1717."

[2] The old feeling had by no means died out, though the Petition of Pastors of Churches of Christ in New England to the King, 1716, said: "At the same Time we have but one single Congregation among us of the Worship of the Church of *England*, who are treated by us with all that Christian Respect and brotherly Esteem and Regard they can reasonably expect and desire." — *Turell's Life of Colman*, p. 84.

[3] "A VINDICATION of the Government of *New England* CHURCHES. Drawn from Antiquity; the Light of Nature; Holy Scripture; its Noble Nature; and from the Dignity Divine Providence has put upon it. By *John Wise*, A. M., Pastor to a Church in *Ipswich*. Isa. 51, 18; Hos. 2, 1. BOSTON, Printed by *J. Allen*, for *N. Boone*, at the sign of the BIBLE, in Cornhill, 1717."

To which is appended —

"A TESTIMONY To the *Order of the Gospel*, in the Churches of *New-England:* Left in the Hands of the Churches, by the two most Aged Ministers of the Gospel yet surviving in the Countrey."

The same year was published "The Sameness of Bishops and Presbyters. . . . That Laymen are as essentially the Church as Clergymen, having as much authority, etc. 1717."

that *I look upon the Discovery and Settlement of the Congregational Way as the Boon, the Gratuity, the largess of Divine Bounty, which the Lord graciously bestowed on this People, that followed him into this Wilderness, and who were separated from their Brethren.*"

The testimony appended adds the voice of the revered John Higginson and William Hubbard to the same purport, with grave warning: —

"It is too observable that the *Power of Godliness* is exceedingly Decaying and Expiring in the Country; and one great point in the Decay of the *Power of Godliness* is men's growing weary of the Congregational *Church-Discipline*, which is evidently Calculated for to maintain it. . . . But if this *Church-Discipline* come to be given up, we think it our Duty to leave this *Warning* with the Churches, that probably the *Apostasy* will not *Stop there;* for the same Spirit that will dispose the next Generation to *change their* way in one point will dispose them to more and more *changes* (even in *Doctrine* and *Worship*, as well as in *Manners*), until, it may be feared, *the Candlestick will quickly be removed out of its place.*"

It is probably an indication of the aroused temper of the people that the Legislature took a marked step in 1720. "There had been no public notaries in the province, except such as derived their authority from the Archbishop of Canterbury," in whose Court of Faculties they were enrolled; but the House observed that a notary public was a civil officer, and proceeded to choose them, the Council afterwards concurring.[1]

But the most solemn appeal was published in 1722, under the shadow of the events transpiring in Yale College:[2] —

"Hence also those among us that desire to set up in this Country any of the *Ways of Men's Invention* (as *Prelacy*, stinted *Liturgies*, Humane *Ceremonies* in Worship), they will bid Defiance to the CAUSE and Interest of CHRIST, and of His People in these Ends of the Earth; and will, I persuade myself, but *lay themselves as Potters' Vessels under the Iron Rod*, for CHRIST who has taken this *possession of these uttermost parts*

---

[1] Hutchinson's History, ii. 238. Sewall's records, however: —

"June, 14, 1725. Mr. Giffard, the Organist [of King's Chapel], is made a publick Notary by the Archbishop of Canterbury. Cost of his Comission £80 Sterling, or more."

[2] "ELIJAH'S MANTLE. — A Faithful TESTIMONY to the CAUSE and WORK of GOD in the CHURCHES of NEW ENG-LAND, and The GREAT END and INTEREST of these Plantations, Dropt and Left by FOUR Servants of GOD, Famous in the Service of the Churches; Highly SEASONABLE to be offered unto the People, now Succeeding in the NEW ENGLISH Colonies, for their serious consideration. Jer. vi. 16; Psalm 78, 6, 7. Boston: Printed by *S. Kneeland*, for *S. Gerrish*, at his Shop in Cornhill, 1722."

of the Earth will not endure it. Let us *Go forward* to any of those Things of CHRIST that we are wanting in. But to Go *backward* unto those Things which we know, and have openly Testified to be not of GOD, and which we departed from, will be such a *Wickedness* as the Lord's JEALOUSY will not bear withal." . . .

It quotes William Stoughton (1668): —

"How is our *Wine Mixed with Water?* Many, as we may justly fear, would but too *soon* and too EASILY entertain a *lie* in the Worship of God, and return to the *Onions and Garlick of Egypt again.*"

A plea is added by Dr. Increase Mather, now eighty-four years of age, and venerated as the father as well as the leader of the Congregational clergy: —

"Indeed, I cannot but go away Rejoycing in it That the Means which are indefatigably used for the drawing of *unwary People* into the *Things that will not profit* them have had so little Success; and that the Body of the *Sober People* throughout the Country, so far as I understand, generally continue to discover such a conspicuous Aversion to the Things from the *Face whereof* their Fathers *fled into the Wilderness;* tho' at the same time a too general Decay of that Real and vital Godliness, which is to be the *main Intention* of all, is greatly to be bewailed. But there may be danger of *Another Generation arising* which will not *Know* the *Lord,* nor the *Works* done by *Him,* and for Him, among His People here.

And therefore from the Suburbs of that Glorious World into which I am now entring, I earnestly Testify unto the *Rising Generation* That if they sinfully forsake the GOD and the Hope and the Religious Ways of their pious Ancestors, the glorious LORD will severely punish their *Apostacy*, and be *Terrible from His Holy Places* upon them."

The antistrophe in the same chorus was again sounded by Cotton Mather:[1] —

He speaks of "The Sad and Strange Occurrences of This Day," and asks twenty-four pungent questions on the Scripture use of the word *Bishop,* and the Divine Right of that Order, etc.

An allusion to Checkley is clear in xvii: "Has not that High-flyer,

---

[1] "Some Seasonable Enquiries [concerning Episcopacy], And for the Establishment of the Reformed Churches; Lest being *Led away with the Error of* This Day *they fall from their own Stedfastness.* 1723."
Text: "Enquire for the old Paths," etc. — Jer. vi. 16.
In "A Brief MEMORIAL of Matters and Methods for *Pastoral Visits.* Boston: 1723," the younger Mather exhorted his brethren: "FINALLY, Take this Opportunity to inculcate upon them the Importance of Adhearing to the *Pure Worship* of GOD Prescribed in His Word; and Preserving the *Faith and Order of the Gospel,* which has hitherto been the Profession, *Beauty,* and *Safety* of our Churches."

who has Consigned his Memory over to Everlasting Ridicule and Infamy?" etc.

xxi: "In Fine, *O Vain Men, What are you doing?* Who, after the WORD of GOD in the *Sacred Scriptures* doth so Plainly and Loudly Condemn the Usurpation of a *Diocesan Episcopacy*, will for the Sake thereof Renounce the *Ministry* and *Communion* of all the *Protestant Churches* in the World, Except a very little party on Two Islands?"

xxiv: "Whether the Churches, which have their Beauty and Safety in keeping the *Second Commandment*, and were Planted on the very Design of withdrawing from the *Episcopal Impositions*, will not, as they would Avoid the Jealous Wrath of the Glorious LORD, . . . with much Unanimity Concur to Express their Displeasure against such an *Unaccountable Apostasy?*"

But the controversy in whose early stages Mr. Harris had played so large a part was now to pass into a second period, where he would be placed in a very different attitude. It had begun by being an ecclesiastical dispute between two antagonistic churches: it was now to be colored profoundly by the political dissensions which agitated Church and State in the mother country. The chapter now about to open can be understood only by reference to these exciting questions, which soon brought the statute book to bear upon the Church.

"An Act in addition to an Act entituled 'An Act requiring the taking the Oaths appointed to be taken instead of the Oaths of Allegiance and Supremacy,' made in the fourth year of the Reign of the late King William and Queen Mary, of Blessed Memory," was passed at the second session of the Legislature, 1719-20,[1] requiring all the magistrates and "all and every other person or persons" within the province, "when required by two of His Majesty's justices of the peace," to take and subscribe the oaths prescribed by Act of Parliament, George I., chapter xiii. Quakers were allowed to "make and subscribe the effect of the abjuration oath."

Of these oaths the first swore allegiance to King George, and abjured "as impious and heretical, that damnable doctrine and position that princes excommunicated or deprived by the pope" can be deposed or murdered, and declared that no foreign authority "hath or ought to have any jurisdiction . . . or authority, ecclesiastical or spiritual," within the realm. The second declared "that I do believe in my conscience that the person . . . pretending to be . . . King of England, by the name of James the Third, . . . hath not any right or title." It swore in

[1] Province Laws, ii. 153.

the most solemn language "faith and true allegiance" to King George, to defend him "against all traitorous conspiracies," and to defend the Hanoverian succession to the Crown "against the said James and all others;" "and I do make this recognition, acknowledg^{mt}, abjuration, renunciation, and promise heartily, willingly and truly, upon the true faith of a Christian. So help me God." We are now to see how this law entered into the fightings without and feuds within the Church.

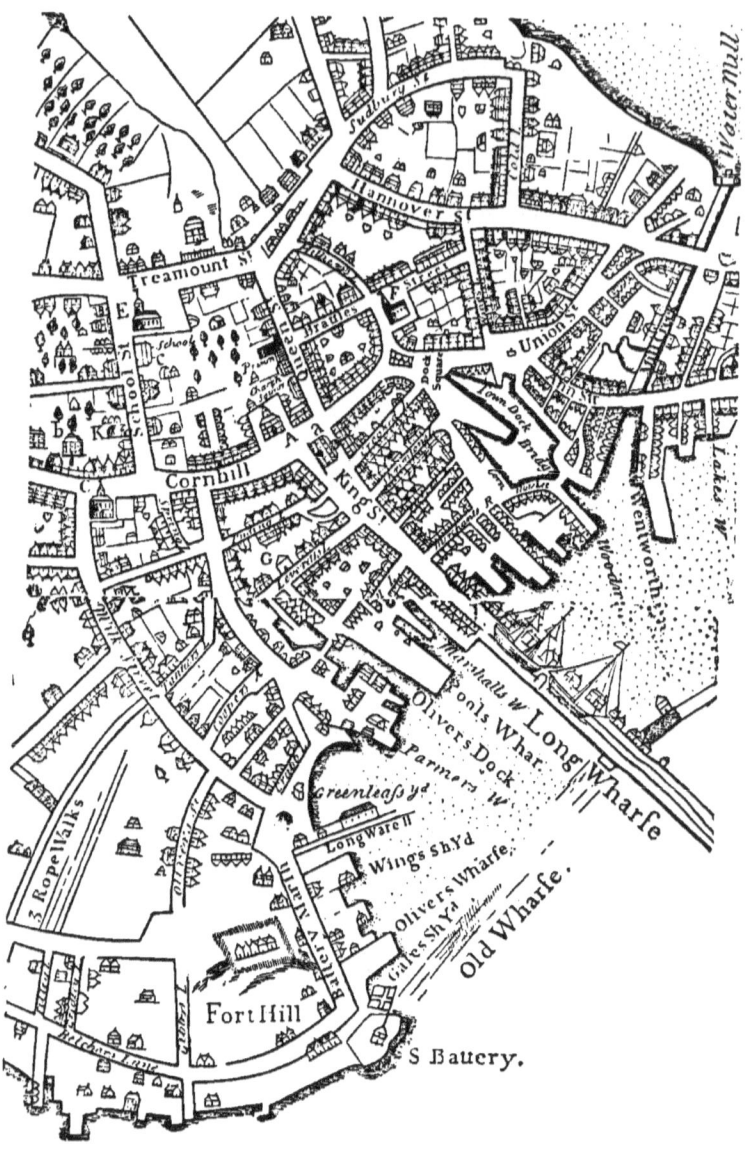

MAP OF 1722, SHOWING KING'S CHAPEL.

CHAPTER VIII.

THE CONTROVERSY WAXES. CHRIST CHURCH.

UT the prince of controversialists and a man of indomitable spirit was Mr. John Checkley, — a member of the King's Chapel congregation, and the representative of the most extreme opinions of the High Church party, both in Church and State. Born in Boston in 1680,[1] and educated there, he is said to have afterward gone to the University of Oxford; he then travelled for some time upon the Continent, and on his return to Boston took a special interest in the study of subjects connected with the doctrine and discipline of the Church to which he belonged. He had a trenchant wit, and made strong enemies and friends.

After Checkley's return to Boston he had become intimate with Thomas Walter (H. C. 1713), son of the Roxbury minister, and grandson of Dr. Increase Mather, to the alarm of Walter's relatives. The younger man was his equal in wit, and, notwithstanding the friendship, was ardently loyal to the New England church polity. In 1715 Checkley published a tract against the

---

[1] He does not seem to have been connected with the family to which the warden of King's Chapel in 1702, and the Rev. Samuel Checkley, the first minister of the New South Church, belonged. He was married to Rebecca, sister of the Rev. E. Miller, of Braintree, by the Rev. Peter Thacher, of Milton, May 28, 1703. They had two children, John and Rebecca.

A vivacious account of him and his controversies is given in Updike's "Narragansett Church," pp. 206-211. Tyler, "American Literature," ii. 49, records an anecdote of him, which illustrates the friendly frankness of the period. He was a member of a club of good fellows, of which Joseph Green, the humorist (born in Boston, 1706; H. C., a successful merchant, and a loyalist exile, who died in England, 1780), was chief. The club called on Checkley after a dangerous illness. "This gentleman was noted for the ugliness of his countenance, at that time rendered still more forbidding by the ravages of disease. The club agreed that his portrait should be painted by Smibert; and Green was appointed to write a few verses to be inscribed beneath it," which he did on the spot: —

"But now, redeemed by Smibert's faithful hand,
Of immortality secure you stand :
When Nature into ruin shall be hurled,
And the last conflagration burn the world,
This piece shall then survive the general evil,
For flames, we know, cannot consume the devil."

favorite doctrine of Calvinism, — "*Choice Dialogues* Between a *Godly Minister* and an Honest *Country-Man*, concerning *Election* and *Predestination*," — to which Walter, then studying theology with his father, published an "Answer by a Stripling," in 1720.[1]

In 1719 he published the first edition of a tract, which made much stir.[2]

The controversy which ensued soon drew the leading theologians of New England into its vortex, whose whirling centre must have been in King's Chapel itself, distracting it with feuds. Remote as it is from us in time, and obsolete as are the political doctrines which envenomed the contest, the story deserves to be told, as showing how the passions which raged in Great Britain during the reign of George I. were also felt in New England. Mingled with ecclesiastical pretensions was the dogma of unconditional loyalty to the Stuarts in Church and State, harmless enough now; but when Scotch fugitives, after the Pretender's defeat, were crowding into New England, it was felt to be like a mine of gunpowder under men's feet.[3]

In all this, Checkley and his party had no more earnest opponent than the Rev. Henry Harris, who, though a loyal member of his church, had no sympathy with their extreme opinions or their extravagant methods. The line of division was as sharp between the two parties in the King's Chapel as it was between either of them and the churches around them. Unfortunately, in Mr. Harris's mind his catholic convictions were mingled with an alloy of feeling against Dr. Cutler, which in the end wrought him great unhappiness. But in his attitude toward Checkley and his opinions he was in accord with his bishop and with the dominant voice of the English Church; and, although Checkley

---

[1] "A Choice Dialogue Between John Faustus, A Conjurer, and Jack Tory His Friend. Occasioned by some *Choice Dialogues* lately Published. . . . By a Young Strippling. Boston: 1720."

[2] It is a reprint from the Non-juror Leslie. "*The* RELIGION *of* JESUS CHRIST *the only True* RELIGION; OR, A Short and Easie METHOD WITH THE DEISTS, Wherein the CERTAINTY OF THE Christian Religion Is demonstrated by *Infallible Proof* from FOUR RULES, WHICH ARE *Incompatible* to any *Imposture* that ever yet has been, or that can *possibly* be. *In a* LETTER *to a* Friend. *The Seventh Edition.* BOSTON: Printed by *T. Fleet*, and are to be Sold by *John Checkley*, at the Sign of the *Crown* and *Blue Gate*, over against the *West* End of the Town-House, 1719." ["The Preface," by Leslie, pp. i-xii; text 51 pp. "Epistle to the Trallians" pp. 7.]

[3] In a memorial of the minister, wardens, and vestry of Trinity Church, Newport, June 1, 1724, they assured the king: "The religious and loyal principles of passive obedience and non-resistance are upon all suitable occasions strongly asserted and inculcated upon your Majesty's good subjects of this church." — *British Colonial Papers*, quoted in *Palfrey*, iv. 470.

seems to have carried the majority in King's Chapel for the time, a reaction appears to have come later against that restless and arrogant spirit.

Mr. Harris wrote a long letter to Bishop Gibson, June 22, 1724, which supplies such important links in the story that it demands a place in our pages: [1] —

". . . The Hon'ble the Lieut Governor, Willm Dummer, Esqre, who has on all occasions employed his authority and influence in protecting our excellent Church and its Ministers from open enemies and pretended friends, from non-jurors and Jacobites, who under color of advancing religion have given it a wound which can't easily be healed, and taken the most effectual method to prevent the growth of the Church in these parts of the world. . . . 'Twould be too long to recount by what steps a defection from the present happy constitution and protestant interest has of late so much prevailed here. In general, 'tis to be ascribed to Scotch Highlanders and other strangers, who, flocking over into this country in great numbers, have fomented divisions and propogated their seditious principles among the inhabitants. But none did they so egregiously pervert as one John Checkley, who keeps a Toy shop in this place; him they found to be an instrument as fit for their purpose as ever Jetzer was for the Monks of Bern in Switzerland. . . . Mr Lesley's rehearsals and other works falling into this man's hands, they work'd so powerfully upon his distempered brain that he was very impatient till he had communicated his discoveries to the rest of mankind, . . . tho' I don't suppose there is one Deist in New England, excepting those of his own party. . . . The doctrine of predestination grew more into reputation than it had done before, and the Dissenters' cause suffered nothing from such feeble attacks. Being thus unsuccessful in print, he resolved to try what he could do another way, and having some acquaintance with Mr Timothy Cutler, then a Dissenting Minister in the neighboring province of Connecticut, he plyed him with such irresistable arguments as compelled him to declare for the Church of England upon Jacobite principles, namely, the invalidity or nullity of the Baptism and other ordinances administered by the Dissenters. I had a great deal of reason to believe that the chief motive of this person's conversion was the prospect of a new Church in this Town, and sent to your Lordship's predecessor an account of that whole affair. . . .

"Checkley valued himself so much upon the above mentioned Proselyte, that he followed him . . . to England, where he appeared as a Candidate for Holy Orders, applying himself to the Honble Society *de propagando Evangelio* for a mission in their service,[2] and insinuating himself by his lies into the favor of several members of that Ven^{ble} body, that

---

[1] Church Docs. Mass. p. 156.
[2] On his visit to England in 1722, Mr. Checkley petitioned the Society that they "would employ an Itinerant Missionary in New England," and "would send over a Library of proper Books . . . to be lent to the poor deluded people of that Country." — *Church Docs* Mass. p. 138.

in all probability he would have obtained his ends, had not His Excellency Col¹ Shute, our worthy Govr, laid open his villany by informing the Honble Society that he had refused to take the oath of abjuration when tendered to him in New England, and that he had also embarrass'd His Excellency's Administration by his factious and turbulent behavior. After this repulse he pursued his old schemes and adhered to his old principles, reprinting while he was in London Lesley's Discourse concerning Episcopacy, intermixing some scurrilous stuff of his own, with many positions of dangerous consequence to the Governm^t. After his return to New England he, in an audacious manner, exposed to sale the said treatise, for which offence the Honble the Lieu^t Govr and His Majesty's Council ordered the Attorney General and another Counsel learned in the law to draw up an Indictment, and the Grand Jury found the Bill against him." [1]

This second book of Checkley's, referred to in Mr. Harris's letter, was a reprint, in 1723, of the "Short and Easie Method," with the addition of "A Discourse concerning Episcopacy," eighty-six pages, also taken from Leslie without acknowledgment, interpolating sharp allusions to New England belief.

[1] Robert Auchmuty, Esq., a member of King's Chapel, was the counsel associated with the Attorney-General. The Council adopted this order, March 19, 1723: "Observing in the s^d Volume many vile and scandalous passages not only reflecting on the Ministers of the Gospel established in this Province, and denying their sacred Function and ye holy Ordināces of Religion as administered by them, but also sundry vile insinuations against His Majesty's rightfull and lawfull authority and the constitution of the Governm^t of Great Britain." — *Council Records*. This is also printed in Church Docs. Mass. p. 142.

At this stage appeared the following: "*Whereas public notice was given, some time ago, in this Weekly Paper, that there was just going to the Press An Answer to the Author of* the Snake in the Grass, *his Discourse of Episcopacy; with seasonable Remarks upon all the Interpolations of the late Edition of it. This is to give as publick notice, that the Author of the Answer hath hitherto supprest what he had prepared, because at present he could not encounter the Interpolator upon even Ground. He leaves others to act for themselves; but for his part he thinks it ungenerous to attack one who must not have* the Liberty of defending himself. *Besides, some may secretly repine (and say they have reason for it) at his assaulting the Interpolator just at such a time, when he knew* they *were under* an incapacity *to do any thing, and* must not make a return. *And this will also lose the effect he promises to his endeavours, by prejudicing by-standers against the Author, and moving their pity to the Interpolator. They may complain that it was no trial of the Cause; and that they could not tell how the Interpolator would have defended himself unless* he had been permitted *the free use of his Weapon. His party will certainly say so; and, inraged at his ill usage, will aver to others that he could have* managed to some purpose, *and attribute the whole of the Author's good success, not to the Interpolator's weakness or want of skill,* which never was tryed, *but to some other thing* which kept it from being tryed. *Upon these considerations the Author desists, and lets the matter drop, till* both *have the liberty of* fairly and handsomely *trying it out* on equal terms. *The Author longs for such a time as much as the Interpolator can do, and* hopes it will be granted." — *The Boston News-Letter*, May 21, 1724.

It begins with the assumption that it is "absolutely necessary that a lineal and uninterrupted succession of the Ministers of Jesus Christ should be preserved."

He cites Pemberton's posthumous Sermon in support. Christ received his Commission from the Father, the Apostles from him, and "the succession from the Apostles is preserved and derived only in the Bishops."

He then "examines historically the Presbyterian Argument for the parity of the Ministry, vindicates the Episcopal Succession in England, and cites the Cambridge Platform to show that the N. E. Churches 'allow Laymen to ordain,' so that their Ordination must be invalid ;" and "our Koralites of several sizes" are bidden to "take a view of the Heinousness of their Schism, and not think their crime to be nothing because they have been taught with their mother's milk to have the utmost Abhorrence to the very name of Bishop, tho' they could not tell why."

"Church government is next argued from its necessity. The faultiness of rulers does not necessarily vacate their authority ; and some of the foreign churches claimed that when they withdrew from Rome her ordination was still valid. The 'Dissenters' also are reminded that they are few in number. The great mass of the Christian world is Episcopal."

A citation of authorities for 450 yrs after Christ is given, including the Fathers and decrees of Councils. Calvin, Beza, and "the rest of the learned Reformers of their part" are asserted to have given their testimony for Episcopacy as much as any.

"Our Dissenters of all denominations imitate the hardness of the Jews, who built the 'Sepulchres of those prophets whom their fathers slew ; while at the same time they adhered to and outdid the wickedness of their Fathers in persecuting the Successors of those prophets.'"

He next argues that no date of its original can be fixed short of the times of the Apostles. The change to Episcopacy would at any time have been noticed and recorded. Hence, the ordinations of Dissenters "in opposition to it are not only *invalid*, but *Sacrilege*, and *Rebellion* against *Christ*, who did institute this *Society* and gave them their *Charter ;* and if their *Ordinations* are null, then their *Baptisms* are so too, and all their *Ordinances*. They are out of the *Visible Church*, and have no *Right* to any of the Promises in the *Gospel.* . . .

"When they receive (what they call) the *Sacraments* of Baptism and the *Lord's Supper* in their *congregations*, they receive no Sacraments, nor are their children baptized any more than if a midwife had done it."

"The argument against Episcopacy, drawn from the interchangeable use of *Bishop* and *Presbyter*, is next considered, and illustrated by the use of the Roman word *Imperator*. He endeavors also to meet the objection that this form of Church Government was gradually introduced.

"'If I was a *dissenter*, till I could give an answer to . . . these papers, I would never go to a *meeting*, lest I perished in their sin ; I would not receive their *sacraments*, lest I offered their *provocations ;* and should think myself *guilty* of the blood of my *child* if I brought it to their baptism. . . . The *Apostles* call themselves *ambassadors* of Christ. And now every *Tag*, *Rag*, and *Long-tail* call themselves his *ambassadors* too, by a call from the people!'"[1]

"Conscious of his misdemeanors, he absconded and fled out of the province," adds Mr. Harris, who proceeds to relate his own course at this time: —

[Checkley's flight] "being a demonstrat" of his guilt, and the passages in the book being very flagrant, I thought it my duty to animadvert in a Sermon upon tenets of such pernicious tendency, the indefeasible hereditary right of princes being expressly asserted in Checkley's libels, and all Magistrates who derive their power in any measure from the consent of the people stigmatized with the title of usurpers. As a good subject, I could not suffer such things to pass without reproof from the pulpit. And as the divine of the Established Church I deemed it incumbent on me to condemn another doctrinal error maintained in that book, namely, the invalidity of the Baptism administered by Protestant Dissenters;[2] . . . and this I am well assured of, that the introducing these notions into this Country has so incensed and exasperated the minds of the people, that it is morally impossible they should ever be brought over to the Church upon the terms of being re-baptized, now so violently urged upon them. On the other hand, the Jacobite party were to that degree enraged against me for preaching in derogation of their favorite book, that they held a consultation, wherein they devoted me as a sacrifice to their revenge; and for the effecting of it they contrived that the people who compose our vestry should call me to account for abusing them, and representing them as disaffected to the Governm'. They met at a tavern, and I had not then the least notion of their designs against me, but, being indisposed, was absent from that meeting; so they sent one of the Church wardens with a message or summons for me to attend at the next vestry, which I declined, as being informed by several honest Gent", whose words I could depend upon, that my enemies had already prejudged my sermon, and charged me with saying things that I did not, and had been likewise guilty of much insolence and ill manners, which sort of treatment I had not deserved at their hands, and might, for aught I know,

---

[1] This outline of Checkley's argument follows Dr. Gillett. See p. 297, *post*.

[2] In this, Mr. Harris had the authority of the upper House of Convocation on his side, the Bishops having made a declaration against the extreme view broached in the reign of Queen Anne.

proceed from their being intoxicated with the fumes of tobacco and wine (two things always offensive to me). I judged it necessary to present a memorial to " the Lieut.-Governor and Council.

The Council Records give the next step: —

"At a Council held at ye Council Chamber in Boston

Thursday April 30th 1724.

" Present

The Honble Wm Dummer Esqr Lt Govr

Samuel Sewall	Thos Hutchinson	Jon^a Belcher
Penn Townsend Esq^{rs}	Thomas Fitch Esq^{rs}	Jon^a Dowse Esq^{rs}
Edwd Bromfield	Adam Winthrop	

"A Memorial of Mr Henry Harris, one of the Ministers of the King's Chappel in Boston, Shewing that having in a Sermon, preach'd at the said Chappel the twelfth of this instant April, expos'd the pernicious tendency of certain Tenets and Principles which are now under censure of Governm^t and directly strike at our Gracious Sovereigns parlem^{ty} right to the Crown of Great Britain, He finds that the faithfull discharge of his duty to God and ye King had drawn upon him the displeasure of some persons who have expressed themselves with much indecent warmth concerning him, and sent him a Message by Captⁿ James Sterling to meet them at the Exchange Tavern on Thursday next (being this day), at five a clock in the evening, — alledging for a Pretence, that in his s^d Sermon he represented them as disaffected to the present happy establishm^t; That this proceeding is irregular and unjustifiable in many respects, and it being a point wherein ye Governm^t is concerned and undoubtedly belongs to the cognizance of this Board, The Right Rev^d the Ld Bishop of London having been likewise pleased to write a Letter to His Honour the Lieut^t Governour, wherein his Lordship in the most earnest manner desires his Honour to grant his Protection to the Clergy when they labour under any difficulties and hardships, And therefore Praying that this Board will order the Memorialist and the above mentioned persons to appear before them, That so the objections against the s^d Sermon and the Memorialists Defence may be heard with sedate and calm attention by Gentlemen eminent for prudence, integrity, loyalty, and all other qualities becoming their high station. Which Memorial being read, Thereupon

"*Voted*, That a Message be sent to Captⁿ James Sterling that the Lieut^t Gove^r and Council desire to speak with him and the other Gentlemen met with him at the Exchange Tavern, except the Revd Mr Miles.

"Captⁿ Sterling with the other Gentlemen with the Revd Mr Miles and Mr Harris being present, Mr Harris's Memorial was read again; And a Letter from the Right Rev^d the Ld Bishop of London to His Honour the Lieut^t Governour, desiring his Protection of the Church of England and the Ministers thereof in this Province, was likewise read, and

"After some discourse of the Parties on the Subject of the Memorial, M.̣ Harris moved for leave to read such Paragraphs in his Sermon preach.ᵈ at the King's Chappel the twelfth instant, as he understood were excepted against; which being granted he read the same, and solemnly affirmed that they were genuine and as he delivered them in His Majesty's Chappel, and no person present objected against their being truly recited.

"The Parties being withdrawn and yᵉ Board having thereupon taken the sᵈ Paragraphs of M.̣ Harris's Sermon above sᵈ into their mature consideratⁿ —

"Are of opinion that they are not only alltogether unexceptionable, but full of Duty and Loyalty to His most sacred Majesty King George, as well as of Zeal and Affection to the Protestant succession and the Church of England as by law established, and of Honor and respect to His Majesty's Governm.ᵗ of this Province, and do tend to promote Piety, Charity, and Peace among His Majesty's Good Subjects here.

"And therefore His Honour the Lieutenant Governour is desired to recommend the s.ᵈ M.ʳ Harris to the Right Rev.ᵈ Lord Bishop of London, and to the Honᵇˡᵉ the Society for Propagating the Christian Religion in Forreign parts, as a person of great Loyalty and Merit." [1]

The Lieut.-Governor, whom Governor Shute's furtive departure for England had left at the head of the government, wrote to the new Bishop of London on the subject: [2] —

"Sʳ, — I have the honour of Yʳ Lordship's Letter of the 29ᵗʰ Novembʳ, which I Receiv'd not till the Middle of April. I heartily Congratulate Your Lordship upon yʳ Promotion to the See of London, — To which your eminent piety and Learning, Moderation and firm Attachment to his Majesty's Interest and Government and the protestant Succession do So Justly Entitle You; and I do Assure Your Lordship that this Government have a Good part of the Genⁿ Satisfaction in Your Lordsᵖˢ Translation to a place of that Important Trust in the Church of England. I shall always Use my best endeavours to answer Your Lordships Desire and Expectation by Countenancing and Encouraging the Church and the Ministers thereof in their endeavours to promote Piety, Loyalty, and good manners, So long as I have the Hon.ʳ to Serve his Majesty in the Chief Command over this province, and have had very early Occasion to give Your Lordship a proof of the reality of my Intentions herein.

"Some Months Since One J. C., a Shop keeper in this place and a person

---

[1] Mr. Harris's Memorial, and a transcript of the record of this meeting of the Council, are given in Church Docs. Mass. pp. 144-147.

[2] Mass. Archives, li. 403. The Bishop's letter to Dummer was doubtless recorded, but probably perished with the other original records which were destroyed in the fire which consumed the Court-house, Dec. 9, 1747. See Plymouth Colony Records, Mr. Pulsifer's Introduction, ix. p. xi. A letter in the same words, sent to the Society for Propagating the Gospel in Foreign Parts, is given in Church Docs. Mass. p. 146.

of known Disaffection to his Majesty and now under Bonds for Recusancy, publish'd a Book entituled a Short and easy Method with the Deists, to which he added a Discourse Concerning Episcopacy (the most of which Discourses were taken from the Writings of the late M! Lesly), which Book gave great Offence to his Majestys Government of this Province, more especially for that an Indefeazable hereditary Right to the Crown was therein Advanced and a parliamentary right Oppugned and Denied ; and the said Book and publisher were presented by the Grand Jury for the County of Suffolk at the last Gen¹¹ Sessions of the peace, upon which the said C. withdrew and remain'd out of the province till the End of the Session. During the prosecution of this Book the Rev⁴ M! Henry Harris, one of the Ministers of his Majesty's Chappel in this Town, preached a Sermon in the Said Chappel, In which he condemned The Tenets advanced in this Book, and warn'd his Auditors against Incouraging and Abetting the Said Book and Author, upon which he acquainted me that Hee was sent for by the Gentlemen of the Vestry to give answer to the Exceptions they had taken at his Said Discourse. M! Harris looking upon himself under Great Hardships that he Should be called to Acc! by his people for anything he had Deliver'd from the pulpit, especially what was Intended for the Hon! and Support of his Majestys Government, thereupon made application to Me and his Majestys Council, Complaining of his Treatment, and praying that the Matter might be heard at the Board, which was done accordingly. And upon a fair and Impartial hearing, all partys being present, the Board were entirely Satisfied with the Sermon, and passed a Vote wch I herewith inclose, that M! Harris be Recommended to Your Lordship as a person of Great Loyalty and Merit, etc.; which I can do with the Greater freedom, from my personal Knowledge of him to be a Gentleman of that Vertue and Learning, and so Capable of Serving the interest of Religion here, as to deserve Your Lordships protection and Favour. For which Qualities he has had a General Esteem in this Place for the many Years of his Residence among us."

April 20, 1724.

Checkley returned, however, and took the oaths, as was supposed, with a mental reservation; and being tried at the next Sessions, the jury found him guilty, " if the Book . . . be a false and scandalous Libel."

"While these things were transacting," continues Mr. Harris, "the Tories became a little apprehensive of their danger, and procured a vote in the vestry that an address should be presented to His Majesty, the tenor and design of which is to clear every individual person belonging to our communion from the imputation of disloyalty ; which address I refused to sign, for the reasons specified in a remonstrance subscribed by myself and some other Gent^n of honor and veracity, who enjoy considerable posts and bear commissions under the King." [1]

[1] This was sent to Governor Shute in London, to be presented to the Bishop.

[Checkley took] "the oaths about 3 weeks ago, which all discerning people ascribe to the impending penalties of the law. . . . I submit it to Your Lordship, whether I ought not to have warned and cautioned my hearers against such principles and practices; whether by these warnings I have represented them as Jacobites, or have they not rather (I speak only of some of them), by their malignant and froward carriage, represented themselves more effectually than I could possibly do? . . . But that I have reflected upon the whole body of the people belonging to the Church, or treated them ill, I utterly deny. On the contrary, . . . I have shewn a forgiving spirit, even to my most inveterate enemies, being contented with a liberty of differing from 'em in judgment, . . . having during the whole course of my ministry for more than 15 years behaved myself inoffensively, as they have themselves acknowledged upon a thousand occasions."[1]

But the King's Lecturer had given his adversaries a grievous handle against him by thus appealing to the King's representatives. From Rhode Island the complaint was sent to England:[2] —

"Some *remoras* seem now to give a check to the increase of the church in the neighboring province of Boston in that —

"First, The laws that relate to marriages and the maintenance of Dissenting Ministers there, whereby the Missionaries and Members of the Church are much distressed and discouraged, are put in vigorous execution.

"But, secondly, What has given the most deep and sensible wound to the interest of religion in this Country, and whose fatal effects we feel at this distance in the insults and triumphs of the Church's enemies from the unfortunate occasion, is the late unhappy conduct of M![r] Harris assistant to M![r] Myles in Boston, whose vestry he cited to appear before the Lieut.-Governor and Council there (whose members are strangers to the Church's principles and professed enemies to its interest and advancement), to answer his feigned insinuations of their being dissatisfied with him for his zeal to the Government whereunto (so far as we can learn) they are all firmly attached, and would devote their lives and fortunes to its service and support. The intent of his applying to the council (it's plain by the results) was to gain upon their interest and obtain their recommendations, which we know our superiors are too wise to take any notice of, they being the testimonies of the Church's avowed enemies."

During Checkley's trial he "printed by stealth" the first original controversial writing of any importance on the Episcopal

---

[1] Church Docs. Mass. p. 156.
[2] A letter from Rev. Mr. Honeyman, the church-wardens, and vestry of Trinity Church, Newport, June 1, 1724, to the Secretary, in Church Docs. Mass. p. 154.

side in the long debate here. This famous pamphlet is entitled, "A Modest Proof of the Order and Government settled by Christ and his Apostles in the Church." This it does by showing: "1. What offices were instituted by them. 2. How those offices were distinguished, and that there was an imparity between them. 3. That they were to be perpetual and standing in the Church. 4. Who succeed in them and rightly execute them to this day." In this he claims:—

1. That the Ministers of the Church of England who freely own that the Power of Ordination was first derived from the Apostles, and from them, through all Ages since, in a succession of Bishops, from whence they derive their own Ordinations, are to be acknowledged true Ministers of the Gospel.

2. That it is a daring Offence to intrude into the sacred Function without a regular designation to the Exercise of it.

3. That People ought to endeavour after all the Assurance they can attain to, that they have the means of Grace in the Word and Sacraments duly administered and dispensed unto them by Persons fully authorized for those holy offices. For since the Priest's Lips are to preserve Knowledge, the People ought to be satisfied that they are really such at whose mouth they seek the Law.

4. That it is a very criminal Presumption, and an insufferable Intolerance in some, to value their Gifts at so high a rate as to think themselves, by the virtue of them, entituled to the Ministerial office without being admitted by the Imposition of the Hands of those whom Christ has ordered to preside over the affairs of his Church.

5. That since there is no approaching before God's Altar without the appointed Rites of Consecration, nor any medling with his Institutions without his Order and Command, Those invaders of the sacred Services cannot be said to be the Ambassadors of God, or accounted the Stewards of the Mysteries of Christ, who presume to touch those Holy Things with their unhallowed Hands, and, like Saul, would sacrifice without a Call,— 1 Sam. xiii. 9–14. For those who offer strange Fire before the Lord, their Incence must be an Abomination to him,— Levit. x. 12.

Lastly, Christ himself " did not enter upon his Ministry until he was solemnly inaugurated into that Office," and likewise commissioned his Apostles, " from whom the standing Ministry in the Church of England is derived."[1]

Nothing was so offensive to the Puritan feeling as the sacerdotal claim of apostolic succession, not only because they held

[1] At the same time he procured the publication of another tract: "A DISCOURSE Shewing *Who* is a *true Pastor* of the CHURCH of CHRIST. 8vo., pp. 16. Errata 1 p." [without titlepage or imprint]. This contains " The Epistle to the Trallians."

it to be utter formalism, but because of their abhorrence of Roman Catholicism, through which the descent must be derived.[1]

Checkley made a trenchant speech in his own defence; in which he cleared himself, to the satisfaction of the jury, from the first specification, that he had "drawn into Dispute his present Majesty's title to the Crown." His main force was expended on the second, "of scandalizing the Ministers of the Gospel by *Law established* in this Province," maintaining that "the Church of England, and NO OTHER, is established" here; and therefore that his book was "a defence of THEM and their SACRED CHARACTER." He besought the jury " to reflect with yourselves whether *those Gentle methods* of reasoning and perswading, and *those tender* and *compassionate Expostulations* with those Gentlemen, to make them seriously consider with themselves of the Validity of that Commission by which they act, . . . looks like Malice;" and, in his plea for arrest of judgment, he still stoutly maintained that " *Dissenters of all Denominations* are *no Ministers, Schismatics,* and *Excommunicates* by the Laws of the Land."[2] Thereupon —

---

[1] Cotton Mather expressed it thus: "To maintain their Episcopal ordination, they set up that vile, senseless, wretched whimsey of an uninterrupted succession, which our glorious Lord has confuted with such matter of fact that it is amazing the builders of Babel are not ashamed of it; and they will have none owned for Ministers of Christ in the world but such as anti-Christ has ordained for him; such as the paw of the beast hath been laid upon them that they pretend a succession from. Do not those men worship the beast who allow no worship in the Church but by them who have their consecration legitimated by a derivation through the hands of the beast unto them?" — *Church Docs.* Conn. i. 76. This doctrine was strongly stated in "A PERSUASIVE to the People of *Scotland*, In Order to remove their PREJUDICE to the BOOK of *COMMON PRAYER*. Wherein are Answered All OBJECTIONS against the LITURGY of the CHURCH of *ENGLAND*, etc. By P. Barclay, A.M. The Second Edition. London: Printed for JONAH BOWYER, at the *Rose* in St. *Paul's Church-yard*; And sold by the Booksellers in *Edenborough*, *Dublin*, and *Boston* in *New-England*. 1723. 12mo., pp. 172." This was a reprint of "A Letter to the People of Scotland, in order to remove their prejudice to the Book of Common Prayer," etc. 1713. It says: "If you have *no Ordination* you can have *no lawful Ministers*. If you want *lawful Ministers*, you yourselves allow that you can have NO BAPTISM; and without *Baptism*, you have no Title to the *Covenant of Grace*, in God's ordinarily way of dealing with us."

[2] The doughty author published two editions of "The SPEECH of Mr. *John Checkley* upon his TRYAL at *Boston*, in NEW ENGLAND, for publishing the Short and Easy METHOD with the *Deists*, etc. London, 1730, 1738. A SPECIMEN of a True *Dissenting* Catechism, upon right True-Blue Dissenting PRINCIPLES, WITH LEARNED NOTES, By Way of Explication : —

"*Qu.* —Why don't the *Dissenters*, in their Publick Worship, make use of the Creeds?

"*Ans.* — Why? Because *they* are not set down, *Word for Word*, in the Bible.

"*Qu.* — Well, but why don't the *Dissenters*, in their Publick Worship, make use of the *Lord's Prayer*?

Suffolk, ss.: At a Court of Assize, Nov. 27, 1724.

The Court, having maturely advised on this special verdict, are of opinion that the said John Checkley is guilty of publishing and selling of a false and scandalous libel. It is therefore considered by the Court that the said John Checkley shall pay a fine of £50 to the King, and enter into recognizance in the sum of £100, with two sureties in the sum of £50 each, for his good behaviour for six months, and also pay costs of prosecution, standing committed until this sentence be performed.

Checkley advt. Dom. Reg.

Att'd. SAMUEL TYLEY, *Clerk*.

Checkley's political views had never found such extreme expression in New England, and gave quite as much offence as his prelatical opinions.

"And perhaps at the Bottom 't is none of the least prejudices against *Episcopacy*, that they of that Perswasion have generally asserted the *just Rights* and *Prerogatives of Princes* as the surest foundation of a Kingdom's Happiness and Tranquillity; and accordingly have maintained the Doctrines of *Non-resistance* and *Passive Obedience*, etc., whereas its Rival Government hath been thought by some more serviceable for Checking and Curbing the *Power of Princes*."[1]

The school in the English Church to which he belonged began in a devotion to conscience, so illustrated by men like the saintly Ken, that even their mistakes deserve a certain reverence. But the loyalty to the Stuarts, which inspired the early Nonjurors to give up everything rather than take an oath of allegiance to the Prince of Orange against him whom they held to be their anointed king, in the Jacobite opponents of the House of Hanover degenerated into venomous bitterness. During the reign of Anne, most of the laymen of this party had become merged again in the High Church portion of the Church of England, which had gone to a length not surpassed in our own day. Dean Kennett wrote to Dr. Colman, July 28, 1716: —

... "Some would not go to their Seats in the Church till they had kneeled and prayed at the Rails of the Communion-Table; they would not be content to receive the Sacrament there kneeling, but with Pros-

---

"*Ans.* — Oh! because *that* is set down, *word for word*, in the Bible.
"They're so perverse and opposite, as if they worshipped God for Spite."
This was republished with a valuable introduction, by Rev. E. H. Gillett, D.D., in the "Historical Magazine," II. iii. 109.

[1] "Modest Proof," etc., p. 5.

tration and striking of the Breast and kissing of the Ground, as if there were an *Host* to be adored. They began to think the Common-Prayer without a Sermon (at least Afternoon) to be the best way of serving God, and Churches without Organs had the thinner Congregations; *bidding* of Prayer was thought better than praying to God, and even Pictures about the Altar began to be the Books of the Vulgar; the *Meeting-Houses* of Protestant Dissenters were thought to be more defiled Places than Popish Chappels. ... Our greatest deliverance under King *George* will be that of *our being delivered from our selves*, and being restored not only to our Religion and Liberties, but to our Senses." [1]

After the final downfall of the Stuart cause, a lingering remnant adhered to the Non-juring church, until, as Macaulay says, "At length in 1805 the last bishop of that society which had proudly claimed to be the only true Church of England, dropped unnoticed into the grave." In the early years of George I., however, the party was still eager and confident.[2]

But Checkley was not only dealt with by the Court, but by skilful controversialists on the other side. The minister of the

---

[1] Turell's "Life of Colman," p. 132. In England, at this time, the preacher on his entrance to the pulpit showed at once whether he was High or Low Church, by his use of the "bidding" or of an extempore prayer.

"The Bidding Prayer had its origin in pre-Reformation times. ... After the Restoration it was not very much used, and the pulpit prayer, as adopted by Low Churchmen from Puritans and Presbyterians, began in many places to assume a most prominent position. High Churchmen could not endure it. South said: 'It is a long, crude, extempory prayer, in reproach of all the prayers which the Church, with such an admirable prudence, has been making before.' ... In Queen Anne's time, the Bidding Prayer became general."— *Church of England in XVIII*[th] *Century*, ii. 487.

It probably illustrates the political proclivities of a portion of the Church of England here, as well as the Hanoverian loyalty of the New England reading public, that in 1722 there was reprinted in Boston from the London edition "A LETTER to the CLERGY of the *Church of* ENGLAND: on Occasion of the COMMITMENT of the Right Reverend the Lord Bishop of *Rochester* to the TOWER of LONDON. By *a Clergyman of the Church of England*." This is an able statement of the history of Bishop Atterbury's commitment, and an urgent appeal to "the Friends of our Establishment,— with too many men we lie under the Scandal of being a Restless and Ungovernable Body;" and, in view of their interest, "to those who wish for a Change, for Conscience is here out of the Question with You, who have broke thro' the most solemn Oaths."

Checkley was stated by a New England pen to have "printed a pamphlet to maintain that the God whom King William and the churches then prayed unto is the Devil! The church," it was said, "rarely gains a proselyte but King George loses a subject."— 2 *Mass. Hist. Coll.* ii. 139.

[2] In a "Character of the Clergy in Maryland," 1722, their names and parishes are given, and they are characterized. One is "A Tory;" another, "A stickler for the present happy establishment;" and others, "An Idiot and Tory," "A Whig and an excellent scholar and good man," "A Grand Tory and a Rake," "A Whig and a good Christian," "A Whig of the first rank, and reputed a good liver, but a horrid preacher."— *Church Docs.*, Maryland, p. 128.

First Church, himself the son of a prominent early warden of King's Chapel, and the Cambridge Professor of Divinity, each published a reply. Mr. Foxcroft dealt wholly with the Scriptural argument against Episcopacy.[1]

Professor Wigglesworth said:[2] —

"*And there may come an unhappy Juncture when* the Papacy *may come to be thought as* needful as Prelacy. *For alas! If the Truth may be told, 'tis greatly to be fear'd that* the Power of Pastors, and the strict Discipline commonly used in Presbyterial Churches, *is become intolerable to too many carnal Libertines*, whose Language is that, *Come, let us break their Bonds asunder, and cast away their Cords from us!* and that not a few, who with an uncharitable and bitter Zeal contend for the Episcopal Pre-eminence, have too much of the Roman Leaven in them; are too sincere friends to the Papal Supremacy, *and only want a favorable Opportunity to vent their Minds* and throw off the Mask."

The first President of the College of New Jersey, and therefore head of the Presbyterian body, "thought it necessary to hold up the shield."[3]

---

[1] "THE Ruling and Ordaining POWER OF *Congregational* BISHOPS, or PRESBYTERS, *Defended*. Being Remarks on some Part of Mr. *P. Barclay's* PERSUASIVE, lately distributed in *New-England*. By *an Impartial Hand*. [Tho. Foxcroft.] In a *Letter* to a Friend. Boston: Printed for *Samuel Gerrish* and Sold at his Shop near the Brick Meeting-House, in Cornhill. 1724."

The late Bishop Burgess, of Maine (Pages from the Ecclesiastical History of N. E. Boston, 1847), describes Foxcroft as "an Episcopalian by education, but ardent in his love of the Puritan doctrines, and the most attractive preacher of his time, till an early paralysis somewhat shook his powers." His adoption of the church of his mother, a daughter of Lieut.-Governor Thomas Danforth, rather than that of his father, will be understood by readers of his "Sermon on the Death of Mrs. Elizabeth Foxcroft, wife of Hon. Francis Foxcroft; By T. F., One of the bereaved Sons. With a Funeral Poem by Rev. John Danforth. Text: Ps. xxxv. 14. Boston: 1721."

"An Addition" at the close gives an affecting account of her religious character and Christian death, with many utterances of faith and trust.

[2] "*Sober Remarks* on a Book lately reprinted at Boston, Entituled *A Modest Proof* OF THE ORDER AND GOVERNMENT SETTLED BY CHRIST AND HIS APOSTLES IN THE CHURCH. In a Letter to a Friend [by Ed^{wd} Wigglesworth, A.M.] Boston, 1724."

[3] J. Dickinson. "A Defence of Presbyterian Ordination in Answer to . . . *A Modest Proof* etc. Boston: 1724." Tyler, "American Literature," ii. 217, well sums up the life of Jonathan Dickinson: "Born at Hatfield, Mass., 1688; graduated Yale College 1706; in 1708 he went to Elizabethtown, N. J., and there, for 39 years, lived a most energetic life as minister, physician, educator, and author. Leader in ecclesiastical politics; a mighty pulpit-orator; principal founder of the College of N. J., and its first president,—in person he was so saintly and impressive 'that the wicked seemed to tremble in his presence.' 'The memory of his life is still fragrant on the spot where he lived,' and the descendants 'of those who knew and loved him cherish an hereditary reverence for his name and his grave.' He was a protagonist for Calvinism, next to Jonathan Edwards."

"For such a small upstart Sect gravely to attempt, by Arguments a hundred times baffled, to Unchurch all the Protestant World but themselves, and to nullify all their Ordinances, Rather exposes their Bigotry to Contempt, than their Zeal and Charity to the envy of any thinking Person.

"If some Arguments occur in this Dissertation that have been used before in the same Controversy, it must be remembered that Truth is always the same; and that the same Thing must be repeated to those that are dull of hearing."

He states the points in controversy: —

"1. Whether *Bishops* are by Divine Right superiour to *Presbyters*, and have by vertue of that Superiority the sole Power of *Ordination* and *Jurisdiction*.

"2. Whether the English *Diocesan Bishops*, . . . with their *lordly Dignity* and *secular Power*, are the only Scripture *Bishops* on whom our *ministerial Authority* and *sacred Administrations* do necessarily depend."

He then follows Checkley's argument through all its heads, very pungently: —

"And must then the Tradition of the Church be our Rule, to interpret *Scripture* by? An excellent way to find out the Truth doubtless, to bend the Rule to the crooked Stick!"

In conclusion, he makes —

". . . a short *Expostulation* with the *High-Church* Party. Whose Interest, *Gentlemen*, do you think you are driving on, while you are not only *damning* almost all the *Protestant Churches* for want of a *regular Ministry*, but what in you lies bringing a Contempt upon the Persons, and a Blast upon the Labours, of so many of Christ's *faithful Servants?* Is it a light thing to wound the Consciences of the *weak*, to strengthen the Infidelity of the *carnal Libertine*, and to give such matter of Triumph to the *Papists*, by rendring the very *Baptisms*, and all other sacred Institutions in most *reformed Churches*, matter of Question and Debate, and even sapping the *Reformation* at the very Root? Would not *Modesty* oblige you to question your Arguments, since level'd against so considerable a Part of Christ's Mystical Body, so often refuted by the *Presbyterians*, and all of 'em condemned by some or other of the most eminent of your own Party? Is not the condemning of *Presbyterian Ordination* an egregious Reflection upon the *Legislature* of the Nation, who have established *Presbytery* in *North Britain?* Nay, is it not an equal Reflection upon the Fidelity of our *Blessed Saviour*, that he should leave so great a Part of his Church without either *Ministry or Ordinances?* Do you think that our Lord Jesus Christ will disown his faithful Servants, in *the Day of his Kingdom*, for their want of external State and Grandeur, and for not submitting to a Government whereof there is not one Word in the *Scriptures?* Truly, Gentlemen, some small Allay of *Charity* in your Principles would render 'em nothing less amiable to the Protestant World; who maugre all the *Anathemas* of *Rome*, or Imputations of *Schism* from HIGH-CHURCH, will suppose that 'the Opinion which wants *Charity* is not from God, but that the Error is of the damning side.'

"Our Comfort is that we are not to stand or fall by your Judgment; but can chearfully go on in our Work, with a refreshing Expectation that *when the Chief Shepherd shall appear,* we shall receive the promised Crown of Glory that fadeth not away."

Checkley's former friend, Walter, also entered the fray, in a temper which showed his Mather blood: [1] —

"But let us . . . try if we can't beat out the little PERT *Jacobite* from his fancied secure Retreat [i. e. the Ignatian Epistles].

"The *Deists* and *Dissenters* must, I'll warrant ye, in his Book be joined together. A spiteful Numbskul! Where did he ever find a *Deist* in the communion of the *Dissenters?* But GOD knows many such there have been, and are, in the *Episcopal Communion.*

"There can be no such Thing as a *Dissenting Presbyterian* in New England, for we are the Original *Established Church* of this Land; nor can we with good sense be said to *dissent* from the *Established Church of England,* who do not live in England.

"His Argument, in short, amounts to this: The *Episcopalians* esteem themselves the true Church, and you *Presbyterians* allow they are; but we Episcopalians do not allow you Presbyterians to be a true Church; therefore . . . [etc] I may say to him, as Arch-Bishop Tillotson . . . to ten Papists . . . *According to this Argument it is safest for a man to be on the most uncharitable Side.*"

Another answer, of not much force, appeared from the College.[2]

---

[1] "An Essay Upon that Paradox, Infallibility may sometimes Mistake; Or a Reply to a Discourse Concerning Episcopacy. Prefixed some Remarks upon *A Discourse,* [Mr. Checkley's] shewing who is a true Pastor of the Church of Christ, etc. By a son of Martin Manprelate. Boston: 1724."

Walter was recommended by Cotton Mather for the chaplaincy of the Castle, Nov. 7, 1716. He preached the Boston Thursday Lecture, as colleague to his father, in September, 1723, on "The Scriptures the only Rule of Faith and Practice." He died at the age of 28, and was commemorated by his uncle, Cotton Mather, in a sermon, "*Christodulus* . . . [commemorating] 'Mr. Thomas Walter, Lately a Pastor to a Church in Roxbury: Who had an Early Dismission from what of that SERVICE was to be done in THIS WORLD. Jan. 10, 1724-25.' Boston: 1725."

"To Which I must add, That his faithful and steady Adherence to the *Puritan* Principles of *Instituted Worship*— and *What saith the Scripture?* — was very considerable; when Temptations of, I know not what Glory, to desert them, could not seduce him to an Infamous Apostasy."

[2] "An Answer to Lesley and his late Interpolator's Discourse concerning

His doctrine of baptism was met by republishing an English tract,[1] which had been called out by the re-baptism of a Dissenter in that country.

A special answer[2] was addressed to his political heresies: —

"Justice obliges me to say, That the Inhabitants of *New England* in general, and the Civil Rulers, Ministers, and People of *this Province in particular*, have all along, on every proper Occasion, discovered a very peculiar Loyalty and Affection to King GEORGE and His Royal Family. Nor can I, after the strictest inquiry, learn that there is *one single Person* in any Dissenting Church disaffected to the present Establishment. Some there are, indeed, *who went out from us*, tho' they were never *of us;* but their *Hypocrisy* begins *to be manifest to all Men*. And these are but very few in Number, and (whatever Figure some may make) are justly despis'd and slighted by all Good Men."

Episcopacy. By N. P. [Nathan Prince], A.M. and Fellow of Harvard College. 1724." Nathan Prince, H. C. 1718, and afterward Tutor and Fellow there. He was brother of the distinguished minister of the Old South, who was founder of the "Prince Library." He took orders in the Church of England, and died a missionary of the Society in the West Indies, 1748. A long letter from him to the Secretary, Aug. 29, 1745, is printed in Church Docs. Mass. p. 391, arguing against difficulties which had been raised against admitting him to orders: (1) Because in a pamphlet on the Resurrection he had stated "Creeds to be Vain." "I was a Dissenter when I wrote that Piece, and then lived at a Dissenting College, in which (at that Time) The Latitudinarian Scheme prevailed, and accordingly I was then against imposing all Creeds whatever. But This was Twelve years ago, while I was young and had not sufficiently considered the fatal Tendency of such loose Principles. Experience at length convinced me of the Necessity of a Centre of Unity, when the Times of Dessolation were brought on this Country by Whitfield and Company." (2) Because he had been expelled from the College for intemperance. He says that he was only charged "with one or two Acts of Intemperance during fifteen years' run of their lascivious Commencements and other publick Entertainments;" that he could have defended himself against this charge, but that his real offence was his sympathy with the claim of the Episcopal ministers to a seat among the Overseers. (3) Because the Episcopal clergy had refused to recommend him for orders; the fact being that they had simply deferred doing so till the College excitement against him should "blow over."

His early tract against Checkley does not appear to have been brought in judgment against him. He is described as superior in abilities to his distinguished brother.

[1] "*Caveat* against a new set of Anabaptists that are great zealots for Diocese Bishops, yet no Great Friends to the Established Church of England. Boston, 1724."

[2] "The *Madness of the Jacobite Party*, in attempting to set a *Popish Pretender* on the *British Throne*, Demonstrated; In a short View of
1. THE Calamities of former Popish Reigns.
2. THE Present Happy Establishment.
3. THE Miseries which would Ensue should the Pretender come in: With a Word to the Disaffected Party, And to the Friends of the Present Constitution.
What Verse the Blacken'd Party can Expose!
Art sinks as the Infernal Mischief Grows:
No Words the Horrid Principle can tell,
'Tis Born of Crime, and laid too deep for Hell.

BOSTON, in N. E. Printed for D. HENCHMAN, and sold at his Shop. MDCCXXIV."

The atmosphere was heavy with controversy, with the usual results of bitterness on both sides and little edification to either; but Checkley's spirits rose with the turmoil which he had aroused. Before the year was out he published a reply to four of his adversaries at once.[1] Its temper is sufficiently indicated by a single sentence: —

"For however near the Nature of the *Stygian* the waters of *Geneva Lake* may be, and however swift the *Geneva Raven* in its Flight, yet, thanks to the Glorious Head of the Church, it was preserved from being poisoned with their pestiferous Influences."

Speedily followed Dickinson's able rejoinder,[2] in which he keenly points out Checkley's fallacies, and closes: —

"Nor will the World be easily persuaded to believe that the *Infinite Fountain of Love and Mercy* will eternally damn his Creatures for not submitting to an Ecclesiastical *Government*, whereof (by the Confession of the most Considerable of your own Party) there is not one Word in the Divine Oracles."

Checkley hardily rejoined.[3] He spoke of Dickinson's "wild ramble," and charged him with "Defective Reason;" repeats from his "Postscript" that —

"Truth will bear the Test, and stand alone against all the Assaults that are made upon it by impotent Malice, Venom, disordered Brains, Petulance and Ignorance, Empty Skulls, Profane Ribaldry, sawcy, puny Scribblers."

He adds: —

"That the Defence of the *Modest Proof* has given a deep and sensible, nay, a mortal, Wound to your expiring Cause, is demonstrable in that the Supporters of it hideously Roar and Rage at the Smarting of it."

Weapons from the other side of the water were borrowed in this holy war.[4]

[1] "A DEFENCE of a Book lately reprinted at *Boston*, ENTITULED *A Modest Proof of the Order*, etc. In a REPLY to a Book entituled *Sober Remarks on the Modest Proof*, etc. With some Strictures on J. *Dickinson's* Defence of *Presbyterian Ordination*, by way of POSTSCRIPT. Also ANIMADVERSIONS *upon* TWO PAMPHLETS, The one entituled *An Essay upon that Paradox*, Infallibility may sometimes mistake. The other, *The ruling and ordaining Power of Congregational* BISHOPS *or Presbyters defended*, etc. Num. 16.10. *And seek ye the Priesthood also*. Boston: Printed by T. Fleet, 1724."

[2] "Remarks upon the Postscript to the *Defence of . . . a Modest Proof*, etc. In a Letter of Thanks to the Author. By Jonathan Dickinson, M.A., Minister of the Gospel at Elizabethtown, N. Y. Jonah iv. 4., 'Dost thou well to be angry?' Boston: 1724."

[3] Checkley, John, A letter to Jonathan Dickinson, 1725.

[4] The following reprints were issued: "Church of England. Brief account of

Mr. Foxcroft also rejoined in an elaborate and well-reasoned but rather heavy discussion of the arguments from Scripture in favor of "The Ruling and Ordaining Power of Congregational Bishops or Presbyters." "While he [Checkley] dreamt of casting up a mighty Trench for his Security," he said, "in the Defense of an expiring Cause, he was really digging a profound Grave to bury it in."[1]

Mr. Checkley now went to England, in 1728, to apply for holy orders, but he had succeeded in rousing against him the enmity of the whole New England Church; and a letter from two of its ministers to Bishop Gibson led that prelate to refuse him ordination, as being an enemy to the House of Hanover, an enemy to all other Christian denominations, and an uneducated man, — three charges which were all peculiarly offensive to that eminent scholar and catholic Whig bishop. Checkley returned to Boston to busy himself in the affairs of the church, as is indicated by our later records.[2]

But with only a short cessation his strongest antagonist re-

---

the Revenues, Pomp, and State of the Bishops and other Clergy. Boston: 1725."

"Plain Reasons I. for Dissenting from the Church of England. II. Why Dissenters are not nor can be guilty of Schism in peaceable Separating from the Places of Publick Worship in the Church of England. By a true Protestant. [18th ed.]. Boston: 1725."

The largest contribution to the controversy from England was by Samuel, brother of Dr. Increase Mather. "A Testimony from the Scripture against Idolatry and Superstition. In Two Sermons upon the Example of that Great Reformer HEZEKIAH. The *First* Witnessing in general against all the Idols and Inventions of Men in the Worship of GOD. The *Second*, More particularly against the Ceremonies and some other Corruptions of the Church of England. Preached in Dublin, September 1660. [1725]."

The motto is the downfall of Dagon, 1 Sam. v. 3, 4.

"I shall Instance only in these Ten Particulars the Principal Ceremonies and Idols of the Church of England: 1. Do you think that ever Jesus Christ wore a Surplice? 2. The Sign of the Cross, that special mark of the Beast. *Rev.* xiii. 16. 3. Kneeling at the Lord's Supper . . . is a dangerous Symbolizing with the Papists, who Kneel before their Breaden God. 4. Bowing to the Altar, and setting the Communion-Table Altarwise, etc., is . . . a gross Piece of Popish Idolatry. 5. Bowing at the Name of Jesus. A most Vile piece of *Syllabical Idolatry*. . . . We ought to look at the Person and Office of the Lord Jesus, and not to be like Children Playing with Letters and Syllables. 6. Popish Holy Days. As if the Lord Jesus Christ himself were not wise enough to appoint Days and Times Sufficient to keep his own Nativity, etc., in everlasting Remembrance in the Hearts of his Saints, but the Devil and the Pope must help it out. 7. Consecrating of Churches. Inherent Holiness is in Persons, which Places are no way capable of. 8. Organs and Cathedral Musick. Not one word of Institution for them in the Gospel; but on the contrary they are cashiered . . . by that General Rule, 1 Cor. xiv. 26, 15. 9. The Book of Common-Prayer. It is as unreasonable and absurd as to force a Man to go with Crutches when he is not Lame." Etc.

[1] "A Vindication of the Appendix to the *Sober Remarks*. Being a Reply to the *Defense* of the *Modest Proof*, etc. Boston: 1725."

[2] See p. 459, *post*.

turned to the charge with a writing in the form of a dialogue, — a favorite method of controversial statement, in which the adversary is always at disadvantage. In "The Scripture-Bishop," E., who had been brought up in Episcopacy, but had embraced Presbyterianism as more conformable to the Gospel, convinces his clergyman, in two conferences, that there is much to be said on his side.[1] Others followed, on both sides of the argument.[2]

An anonymous hand next launched a feeble reply,[3] in which many of Dickinson's arguments from Scripture are conceded, and some of the strongest of them are quietly ignored. "It will not, I hope, be impertinent to ask . . . if the Dissenters ever did suffer such Persecution from the Church of England as she has suffered from them [in the time of Cromwell]." He affirms that New England has "been notorious for her Barbarities and cruel Persecutions," and still "robs honest and well meaning Christians, members of the true Church, for the support of Schismatical teachers, and yearly imprisons them for refusing to comply." He closes with the argument, that, because bishops alone at the time of the Reformation had the power of ordination, the modern presbyters never were invested with that power. This brought Dickinson once more into the field.[4]

After a tremendous recital of the sufferings of Dissenters from King Edward's time down, he gives a recapitulation, with still greater force, of his former arguments, not failing to note his adversary's concessions, and meets his opponent's closing point with the statement: "If these *Bishops* had the *Power* of *Ordination* themselves, the *Presbyters* ordained by them received *all* the

---

[1] "The Scripture-Bishop; Or, The Divine Right of Presbyterian Ordination and Government. A Dialogue Between Prælaticus and Eleutherius. Boston: 1732."

[2] (1) J. Parsons. "The Validity of Presbyterian Ordination. A Sermon at Newcastle, N. H., Dec. 20, 1732. Boston: 1733." A discussion of the Scriptural argument. In the Application he says: "Shall we do well to go spit in our Fathers' Faces in the Grave, tax their Conduct with profound Ignorance? or, what is worse, with Folly and Frenzy, in taking all this pious Paines to form and establish a Scriptural Constitution for us, which the Churches in this Land have for so many Years been happy in?"

(2) "*The Evangelical Bishop.* A Sermon Preached at Stonington, etc. By Nathaniel Eells, V. D. M., Father to the Ordained; And Pastor of the South Church in Scituate, etc. *N. London:* 1734." The preface by Eliphalet Adams is, "A Nervous and Succinct" Statement of the Controversy. He calls it "a Day when the power of Presbyters to Ordain is frequently Scrupled, and these Scruples made a pretence for returning to the Ancient Bondage."

[3] "The Scripture Bishop, . . . examined in *Two* LETTERS to a *Friend.* 1733." This was by Rev. Arthur Browne, of Providence.

[4] "*Prælaticus Triumphatus.* — The Scripture-Bishop Vindicated A Defence of the *Dialogue between Prælaticus and Eleutherius* against *The Scripture-Bishop Examined.* In a Letter to a Friend, by Eleutherius, V. D. M. *Boston:* 1733."

Authority *appointed by Christ* and *his Apostles* to those of their Order; and consequently had the Power of *Ordination*, according to the original Institution, *inherent* in them, by what *Usurpations* soever they were kept from the *exercise* of it."[1]

While the foregoing was in the press, two of the new converts, Messrs. Johnson and Wetmore, appeared in the fray[2] with a sprightly dialogue, in which Philalethes and Eusebius (on the Episcopal side) meet Eleutherius (on the Presbyterian side) at the house of their friend Attalus; and so easily overthrow him in their arguments from Scripture, that their host is at once reclaimed to his faith in the true church, from which he had begun to stray. This is followed by two letters by Johnson, in defence of the episcopal government of the church, wherein an unwary admission is made: —

"I shall wholly wave the Consideration of the State of Things while Christ was upon Earth, . . . because the Church was then in her Embryo and first Rudiments; and therefore nothing can be so absolutely concluded from thence, as from the State of the Church afterwards when it became more ripe and settled."

This was answered by Foxcroft[3] (in the same volume with *Prælaticus Triumphatus*). "If these Episcopal Advocates," he says, "ever serve Religion or their Cause by the Method and Manner of Writing they've gone into, I shall be one among many that will be very greatly mistaken." He takes up the dialogue and the two letters separately. As he criticises point by point it is impossible, without occupying too much space, to give an outline of his argument. He turns such writers as Hooker, Chillingworth, and Hoadly against his adversary. "Can you upon your professed Principles make out an authentick Claim (foró Ecclesiæ) to the character of *Christian*? . . . Let the Secret come abroad, if you have ever received any *other* than *Lay-Baptism*." This is the most vivacious of Foxcroft's writings in this controversy.[4]

---

[1] His statement will hardly hold (p. 30): "All must acknowledge that *from the Beginning* our Treatment of *Episcopalians* coming into these parts, has been with an exemplary *Candour, Charity*, and *Civility*. Many years passed, indeed, before the *Church of England* Service or Common Prayer was publickly us'd in the Country. But what was the Reason? Not because the Government forbad or hinder'd their setting up the *Episcopal Way*."

[2] "*Eleutherius Enervatus*; Or an Answer to a Pamphlet Intituled *The Divine Right of Presbyterian Ordination*. New York: 1733."

[3] "*Eusebius Inermatus*. Just Remarks on a late Book, Intitled *Eleutherius Enervatus*, etc., done by way of Dialogue, by Phileleuth Bangor, V. E. B. *Boston:* 1733."

[4] It provoked Dr. T. Cutler to call the writer "Tom Foxcroft, a bitter creature, son of a Churchman, and bap-

Mr. Johnson had already published "A Letter from a Minister of the Church of England to his Dissenting Parishioners,"[1] the calm assumption of whose very address called forth a reply by John Graham, whom Cutler contemptuously termed "an Irish teacher[2] in his neighborhood." In answering this reply, Johnson paid his respects to Foxcroft in a postscript to "A Second Letter from a Minister of the Church of England to his Dissenting Parishioners."[3] Here he takes up in detail the citations by Phileleuth Bangor from Church of England writers, his depreciation of the Fathers, and his argument from the identity of meaning of the words "bishop" and "presbyter." "I really wish I could see for what End he could write, at least half this long-winded Pamphlet, unless it were purely to amuse his Readers with a tedious Verbosity."

This "Second Letter" examines "some Remarks made by one J. G.," of whose pamphlet it says: "Malice and Impertinence are the shining Ornaments of his Book." Johnson recapitulates his reasons against the prevalent religion of New England, as given in his first Letter: 1. It is destitute of the episcopal government; 2. In this it is disobedient to authority, both in Church and State; 3. It is unjustifiable separation; 4. It does not read the Holy Scriptures in public worship; 5. It does not use the Lord's Prayer in the same; 6. It is destitute of public forms of prayer; 7. The people do not take part; 8. Neglect of *bodily* worship, especially kneeling at the Sacrament; 9. The teaching, or implying, that God has forcordained sin.

"The Church of *England* does not need such a furious, scolding, delusive Management in defending her; She has stood the test of Time, of Fire and Faggot, of Civil Rage and Tumult, of Popish Tyranny and Enthusiastic Anarchy, and is not to be look'd out of Countenance at this time of Day by the bold Insults and brazen Effrontery of little impertinent Adversaries."

He repeats his calm assertion of having proprietorship in the sturdy Americans whom he addresses: —

"That you are my Parishioners is as true as it is that I am appointed Minister of this Town and the Places adjacent, by the Honourable Society incorporated by Royal Charter for providing Ministers for the Plantations, and by the Bishop of *London* to whom the Ecclesiastical Government of

---

tized in the Church." — *Church Docs.* Mass. p. 673.

[1] Boston, 1732.

[2] This was the usual style by which the Episcopal missionaries who had previously been Congregational ministers designated their former brethren.

[3] Boston, 1734.

them is committed by the Supreme Authority of our Nation: And for this I can produce my Instructions. That you are Dissenters is as true as it is that you dissent from our Church and do not conform to it, as I have proved it your Duty to do. That the Church in this Country are not Dissenters, in his sense of the Word, is as evident as it is false, which he says, that *the Presbyterians are the established Church here;* And that neither they nor any other Persuasion contrary to the Church of *England* are established in this Country is evident from the *Lords Justices Letter to the Lieutenant-Governour of* Boston, in the Year 1725, which declares That there is no regular Establishment *of any National or Provincial Church in these Plantations, nor can there be any without His Majesty's Consent, and that it would be a Contempt of His Royal Prerogative for the Legislature here to undertake to make any Establishment without* Him, etc."

With this lofty claim of a right which to concede would have been to reduce to logical absurdity the history of New England, and to contradict the whole temper and traditions of her people, Johnson closed his part in this stage of the dispute, in which his style of controversy is grave and dignified, with occasional lapses to a much lower level. It is a striking illustration of the honesty of the man, as well as of the arrogant attitude of his party, that he, a native New Englander, should have put forth claims which he must have known would so prejudice the people whom he addressed against the cause which he had at heart.[1]

In this controversy the disputants had now gone over the ground even to weariness. The extreme claims of the High Church had been urged, and had been rebutted by the Puritan arguments from Scripture and reason. But a most important part of the question in debate between the two parties, — the historical discussion of the evidence to be obtained from the Church fathers, — remained substantially untouched. To this one of the ablest of the Boston Congregational ministers now directed his attention.

The "News-Letter" of May 30, 1734, contained: —

"*There is now preparing for the Press A* COMPLEAT VIEW *of the first Two Hundred Years after* CHRIST, *touching* EPISCOPACY; *Wherein is exhibited an Account of the* Writers *within that Time, as to their Characters and* extant *Writings, or* preserved Fragments; *With an Impartial Representation of* ALL *that they say relating to the* Controversy *about* BISHOPS

---

[1] Johnson has an honorable place in early American letters, as well as in the history of the ante-Revolutionary Episcopal Church. Although he bore his part in the whole of the long controversy, his strength was rather "in the still air" of those "delightful studies" to which his intimacy with Dean Berkeley and his own turn of mind invited him.

and PRESBYTERS, *and* Observations *and* Remarks *tending to make it evident that* These *were the* SAME ORDER *in the Primitive Church: Design'd as an* Answer *to the* confident Pretence, *as if it were a* Fact universally handed down even from the Apostles' Days, that Bishops are an Order in the Church superior to Presbyters. *By one that has purposely consulted the* Primitive Records *to be satisfied* what is Truth *in* these Particulars.

"*The Work will be so managed as that the most* Vulgar Reader *may be let into a clear and perfect Idea* of all Antiquity upon this Head, *within the time prescribed.* The Testimonies *from the* Fathers *so far as any stress is laid on them will, for the sake of the learned, be inserted in the very* Words of the Original Authors, *with an* English Translation *for the help of others.*

"*The Peice will contain between* Thirty and Forty *Sheets; and may be afforded handsomely Printed and Bound for about* Twenty Shillings *a Book. If the Design is approv'd and encourag'd, it will soon be made ready for the Press; And those inclin'd to promote it are desired to give in their Names, with the Number of Books they may please to subscribe for, to Capt.* Daniel Henchman, *into whose Hands the Work will be committed.*"

Dr. Cutler wrote: —

"The Proposals are from Charles Chauncy, a Teacher of this Town, who has but a little time ago begun his enquiries, and not above a month before the publication of his Proposals professed himself to a Churchman as but an Enquirer then. . . . I suppose no thinking person will be shocked by the doughty performance of this insidious person. . . . However, I am heartily glad that subscriptions do not come in near enough, for what through the inability and indisposition of the Laity here we should not defray the charge of an Answer, and so our Adversaries would triumph."

There is reason to believe that the saner spirits among the congregation of King's Chapel had no relish for this turmoil, and were aware that it neither aided the cause of their church nor that of "pure religion and undefiled," and the other party perhaps had the same feeling. The studies of Dr. Chauncy remained in manuscript for a generation, when the rising tide of a new interest in the subject floated them into print.

The controversy was reflected at intervals for forty years on the Cambridge Commencement stage, where among "Subjects for the Master's Degree" were these: —

"Is the so-called Apostles' Creed, considered in itself, of any authority? Neg. 1729.

"Is an unbroken apostolic succession necessary to the validity of the ministry? Neg. 1733.

"Does the title of bishop belong to all pastors of churches? Aff. 1765."[1]

It also received what was designed to be a permanent memorial in the foundation, in 1751, by Chief-Justice Paul Dudley, son of the Governor, of "Dudleian Lectures" at Harvard College, in which opposition to the Papacy and a defence of Congregationalism were provided for future ages.[2]

Thus the dispute which began in King's Chapel, but in which, strangely, neither Mr. Myles nor Dr. Cutler appeared as participants, while Mr. Harris came forward to rebuke extremists in his own party, had enlisted the ablest pens in America on both sides, and had ranged over a wide field both of argument and of invective. In this discussion the weight of character and of force in argument predominates on the New England side, whose advocates sound a thoroughly American note in opposition to positions which belong to the Old World rather than to the New.

It is an irksome task to stir the dust which has happily long settled on these ancient controversies; but the course of our narrative cannot be fully understood without thus reviving the memory of discords which may well have disturbed the quiet of the church and filled the community with bitterness. The significance of this pamphlet war was even greater in the State than in the Church; for it is beyond doubt, that, as it continued, it became one of the predisposing causes of the Revolution. Its later phases, however, will be touched upon in a subsequent chapter.

At this time Boston had about eighteen thousand inhabitants, but was and felt like the metropolis of a growing people, whose contracted size raised to greater heat the fever of the disputes which vexed it. The state of angry exacerbation during Governor Shute's administration, partly from political and partly from theological quarrels, is said by Hutchinson to have ex-

---

[1] Rev. E. J. Young, in Mass. Hist. Proc., 1880, p. 144.

[2] The four lectures were to be on Natural and Revealed Religion, on "the idolatry, errors, and superstitions of the Romish Church," and "for maintaining, explaining, and proving the validity of the ordination of ministers or pastors of the churches, and so their administration of the sacraments or ordinances of religion, as the same hath been practised in New England from the first beginning of it, and so continued to this day." In this, his will declares, he does not intend to invalidate Episcopal, Geneva, Scotch, or Dissenters' ordination, all which "I esteem very safe, Scriptural, and valid." — *Quincy, Harvard University*, ii. 141.

ceeded that of any other period since the time of Mrs. Anne Hutchinson. Still, occasional glimpses are opened, which show that social and friendly life continued. Judge Sewall " met Colonel Dyer and gave him one of Mr. Foxcroft's books." All parties met cheerfully at funerals. Men turned from reading these sharp pamphlets to look at " the spinning craze," when the fashion which the Irish emigrants from Londonderry had brought, of making linen thread, was taken up by the women of all degrees, and they mustered on the Common with their humming spinning-wheels, twisting the thread with hands more familiar with English Prayer-book or Puritan Bible.

Coincident with the beginning of this paper strife, were significant movements on the Puritan side. The ministers of the province had always been accustomed to come to Boston at the time of the annual election, when they dined together, — the Governor and other magistrates being guests. Indeed, the connection of the Puritan clergy with the government had been so close that it would hardly have seemed to be inaugurated without their presence. About this time this annual gathering took permanent form, and the " Convention of Congregational Ministers " was organized, voting, in 1720, " that a sermon should be preached annually to the ministers on the day following election," — the two Mathers preaching; the father in 1721, the son in 1722. In 1724, also, the town of Boston voted to open the town-meetings with prayer, Dr. Cotton Mather officiating on the first occasion.

The controversy which we have been describing was undoubtedly fanned to more intense heat by developments in the New England Church, whose successive stages coincide with its progress; for now began a remarkable course of events in Connecticut, which soon had a near connection with the history of King's Chapel. Whether Mr. Harris was right or not in ascribing the credit to Checkley, Episcopal opinions had a most surprising and unlooked for manifestation under the very shadow of an institution which had been established in the interest of the purest and straitest orthodoxy.[1] The Rev. Timothy Cutler,

---

[1] The state of feeling in Connecticut was pithily described about this time by an unfriendly observer: "I really believe that more than half the people in that government think our Church to be little better than the Papist, and they fail not to improve every little thing against us. But I bless God for it, the Society has robbed them of their best argument, which was the ill lives of our clergy that came into these parts; and the truth is, I have not seen many good men but of the Society's sending; and no sooner was that honourable body settled, and those prudent measures taken for carrying on of that good work, but

Rector (or President) of Yale College,[1] had for some time been reading with several other ministers a collection of English theology recently presented to the college; and on the day after Commencement, Sept. 13, 1722, he with two tutors and four other ministers presented to the trustees of the college a written declaration "that some of them doubted the validity, and the rest were fully persuaded of the invalidity, of Presbyterian ordination in distinction from Episcopal."

This event was sufficiently remarkable to have excited much notice at any time; but happening when and where it did, it burst like a terrible bomb-shell in the heart of the New England camp. The Connecticut ministers wrote to those in Boston for advice, and the correspondence shows that it is no new thing now to have a bitter want of charity for men who change their religious opinions.[2] A few sentences will suffice: —

the people of Connecticut, doubting of maintaining their ground without some further support, with great industry went through their colony for subscriptions to build a college at a place called Seabrook; and the Ministers, who are as absolute in their respective parishes as the Pope of Rome, argued, prayed, and preached up the necessity of it, and the passive, obedient people, who dare not do otherwise than obey, gave even beyond their ability. A thing which they call a college was prepared accordingly, wherein, as I am informed, a commencement was made about three or four months ago." — Colonel Heathcote to the Secretary, Nov. 9, 1705, in *Church Docs.* Conn. i. 9.

[1] He was born 1683, son of Major John Cutler, of Charlestown, whose unfriendly treatment by the Massachusetts government in 1689 may have instilled disaffection into the boy's mind. He probably learned his letters from Mr. Myles while the latter was schoolmaster there. He graduated at Harvard College, 1701. Jan. 11, 1710, he was ordained and installed pastor of the Congregational Church in Stratford, Connecticut. He was a prominent preacher in that body. He preached a Connecticut election sermon, May 9, 1717, and a sermon before the General Assembly of Connecticut, October, 1719. The first, while he was minister at Stratford, was entitled "The Firm Union of a People Represented; and a Concern for it urged upon all Orders and Degrees of Men." Psalm cxxii. 3. The second, while he was Rector of Yale College, was a practical religious sermon on "The Depth of the Divine Thoughts: and the Regards due to Them." Psalm xcii. 5. Both are elaborated in the usual style, but less profoundly colored by Calvinism than most sermons of the time. March, 1719, he became Rector of Yale College. After being "excused" from further service there, on his going to England for orders he received them, March, 1723, from Bishop Green, of Norwich, and was licensed as missionary of the Society for the Propagation of the Gospel, in Boston at Christ Church, where his services began Dec. 29, 1723. During the last nine years of his life he was disabled by palsy. He died Aug. 17, 1765, at the good old age of 82 years, and his funeral sermon was preached by the last Royalist rector of King's Chapel. For the relations between the two churches at that period, see Vol. II.

[2] Church Docs. Conn. i. 68. Revs. F. Davenport and S. Buckingham to Rev. Drs. Mather, Stamford, Sept. 25, 1722. The correspondence is printed in 2 Mass. Hist. Coll., ii. 128–140; iv. 297. Dr. Cutler's motives in his change have been variously interpreted. He himself wrote soon after, according to a letter from Thomas Hollis to Dr. Colman: "I have lost all my old friends. I am turned out of all. And if I should do anything now that looked like doubting, it were the

"... how our fountain hoped to have been and continued the repository of truth and the reservoir of pure and sound principles, doctrine, and education, in case of a change in our mother Harvard, shows itself in so little a time so corrupt. How is the gold become dim! Our school gloried and flourished under its first rector, the Rev. Mr. Pierson, a pattern of piety, a man of modest behaviour, of solid learning, and sound principles, free from the least Arminian or Episcopal taint; but it suffered a decay for some years, because of the want of a resident rector. But who could have conjectured, that, its name being raised to *Collegium Yalense* from a Gymnassium Saybrookense, it should groan out Ichabod, in about three years and a half under its second rector, so unlike the first, by an unhappy election set over it."

The step of Mr. Cutler and his associates had not been taken without long and careful deliberation.[1] The Episcopal missionary at Stratford wrote: —

"Those gentlemen who are ordained pastors among the Independents — namely, Mr. Cutler, the President of Yale College, and five more — have held a conference with me, and are determined to declare themselves professors of the Church of England, as soon as they shall understand they will be supported at home. They complain much, both of the necessity of going home for Orders, and of their inability for such an undertaking; they also surmise it to be entirely disserviceable to our Church, because, if they should come to England, they must leave their flocks, and thereby give the vigilant enemy an opportunity to seize their cures and supply them with inveterate schismatics. But if a Bishop could be sent us, they could secure their parishes now and hereafter, because the people here are legally qualified to choose their own ministers as often as a vacancy happens; and this would lighten the Honourable Society's expenses to a wonderful degree. I am informed, also, by these, that there are other gentlemen disposed to renounce their separation, not only in this colony, but also in other provinces of North America, and those a body considerable enough to perfect a general reformation."[2]

way to lose my new friends. ... I was never in judgment heartily with the Dissenters, but bore it patiently until a favorable opportunity offered. This has opened at Boston, and I now declare publicly what I before believed privately." — *Quincy's Harvard University*, i. 365. Dr. Beardsley, however, says: "There is not a particle of evidence coming directly from Cutler to support the charge, and what thus comes from other sources is based chiefly on rumor; so that if at any time he dropped a word which was construed in this way, he probably intended no more by it than that there had long been a struggle between his religious convictions and his temporal prospects." — *Beardsley's Episcopal Church in Connecticut*, i. 41.

[1] See Beardsley's "Episcopal Church in Connecticut," and his "Life of Samuel Johnson, D.D."

[2] Mr. Pigot to the Secretary, Stratford, Aug. 20, 1722, in Church Docs. Conn. i. 57.

The trustees held a conference with the signers of the declaration, and, headed by Governor Saltonstall, — himself a minister, — argued the points of difference, but without result.

" Further Mr. C. then also declared it his firm persuasion that out of the Church of England, ordinarily, there was no salvation. To the last we only say Μὴ γένοιτο ; for we dare not so offend the generation of the righteous, nor disturb the ashes of the myriads that have slept in Jesus, of the Catholick professors of the Orthodox faith in the three kingdoms, yea, and all reformed Christendom, and in New England particularly, who have not been of the communion of the Church of England.

" It has caused some indignation to see the vile indignity cast by these *cudweeds* upon those excellent servants of God who were the leaders of the flock that followed our Saviour into this wilderness. . . . It is a sensible addition unto their honour to see the horrid character of more than one or two who have got themselves qualified with Episcopal Ordination, to fortify little and wretched parties in disturbing the Churches of New-England, and come over as missionaries perhaps to serve scarce twenty families of such people, in a town of several hundred families of Christians, better than themselves." [1]

Perhaps from this point is to be dated a remarkable divergence in the ecclesiastical history of the two colonies. In Connecticut, Episcopacy seems to have become fairly established as a refuge from the prevalent stern Calvinism; while in Massachusetts this relief came in another form, by the gradual adoption of Arminian views by many ministers and their congregations. These again were forced later by the more extreme Calvinistic party into opposition, being at last, during the Unitarian controversy (1815–1820), quite driven out from communion with their associates in the old Congregational body.

The case was difficult, and nothing remained for the trustees except to depose the offending members.[2]

"At a Meeting . . . Oct. 17, 1722, *Voted*, That the Trustees, in faithfulness to the Trust reposed in them, do excuse the Rev. Mr. *Cutler* from all further Service as Rector of *Yale-College*. . . . *Voted*, That all such Persons as shall hereafter be elected to the Office of *Rector* or *Tutor* in this College shall, before they are accepted therein, before the Trustees, declare their Assent to the *Confession of* Faith [the Saybrook Platform], . . . and shall particularly give Satisfaction to them of the sound-

---

[1] 2 Mass. Hist. Coll., ii. 138.
[2] "History of Yale College. By Thomas Clap, A. M., President. New Haven. 1766." p. 32.

ness of their Faith, in Opposition to *Arminian* and Prelatical Corruptions, or any other of dangerous consequence to the Purity and Peace of our Churches. . . .

"*Voted,* That upon just Ground of Suspicion of the Rector or Tutor's Inclination to *Arminian* or Prelatic Principles [the principle that Prelacy or Episcopacy is of Divine Right], a Meeting of the Trustees shall be called, as soon as may be, to examine into the case."

The defection of men holding such a position in the dominant Congregational Church sent a shock throughout New England. Sewall records: —

"7ʳ 25 [1722]. Fast is kept at the old North to pray for the pouring out of God's Spirit on N. E., especially the Rising Generation. . . . Dr. C. Mather preached from Mat. ix. 18, Tabitha Cumi. . . . Dr. I. Mather pray'd; much bewail'd the Coñecticut Apostacie. . . ."

To such a stanch follower of the fathers, what news so grievous as that an Episcopal church had been set up in his family town of Newbury! But now, in his seventieth year, hearing of Mr. Cutler's defection, —

"It quickly brought to my mind Rev. xvi. 15. I apprehend that in this extraordinary and unexpected Alarm we have a Demonstration that the Drying up the Great River Euphrates is near at hand. . . . I am fully of Mr. Cotton's mind that Episcopacy is that upon which the Fifth Vial is poured out, and he will have hard work that shall endeavour to controll that Angel."

On the other hand, extravagant hopes were entertained of a general revolt from the Congregational order and discipline.

Already, as we learn from the "Old Proprietors' Records, Christ Church," probably at the rumor of the impending event in Connecticut, a movement within King's Chapel for a second church in Boston was taking definite form. The first record of Christ Church reads: —

"*Laus Deo: Boston, New England.*

"The second day of September, 1722. At the request of Severall Gentlemen, who had purchased a peice of Ground at the North End of Boston to build a church on, The Reverend Mʳ Samuel Myles ordered his Clerk to give Notice to his Congregation That all those who were willing to Contribute towards Erecting another Church at the North end of Boston were desired to meet at King's Chappel the Wednesday following.

"Agreeable to which Notification Severall Persons assembled, and Chose Mʳ John Barnes Treasurer; Thomas Graves, Esqʳ, Messʳˢ George

Cradock, Anthony Blount, John Gibbons, Thomas Selbey, and George Monk a Committee to receive subscriptions and build a Church on Said Ground at the North end of Boston.

" *The Preamble to the Subscription.*

" Whereas, the Church of England at the South part of Boston is not large enough to contain all the People that would come to it; and Severall well disposed Persons having already bought a piece of ground at the North part of said Town to build a Church on, —

"We, the Subscribers, being willing to forward so good a Work, do accordingly affix to our Names what each of Us will Chearfully Contribute."

This was promptly followed by a letter to —

"*Boston, Ye* 2^d *Octo^r*, 1722.

Mr TIMOTHY CUTLER, — We, the Subscribers, congratulate you and the Gentlemen your Friends on Account of your late Declaration, and we pray to God it may have that happy Influence on this Country which some Men so much dread and deprecate; while others Expect . . . at.

SIR, — We being appointed a Committee . . . for taking in Subscriptions to build a New House for the Worship of God at ye North end of Boston (our present building not being capable to contain the People of the Church), and having the hearty Concurrence and prayers of the Reverend Mr Saml Myles in our undertaking, We have thought proper to acquaint you that we would have you come to Boston; and (by what we have learnt from the Gentlemen of the Church) We take upon us to Assure You that a Passage shall be provided for You, and all things proper to support the Character of a Gentleman during your Stay in London, whither (wth the Approbation of the Rever^d Mr Saml Myles) We Shall Send our humble Petition to Our Right Rever^d Diocesan, My lord Bishop of London, that after the Church which is now design'd to be erected, He would be graciously pleased to grant his license to You to preach in, the People here being willing to Maintain You.

We desire that Mr Brown and Mr Johnson may come down with You in Order to accompany you to London (wch Gentlemen shall likewise be our Care as to procuring them a Passage and doeing them all the Services in our power). . . . ke no Question, but that you will all be very kindly received by the R^t Rev^d the Bishops, both the Universities and the Honble Society; and altho' your Sincerity (Mr Cutler) is called in Question by the Reverend Mr Henry Harris, Yet we hope Your future behaviour will fully Demonstrate Your Integrity. And if that Worthy Gentleman should by some wicked Men be unhappily persuaded to persist in his Opinion, Yet notwithstand^g We assure You S^r that your coming to Boston by the Month . . . will be very gratefull to the Church here, and you all may depend upon a wellcome from the Rever^d Mr Sam^{ll}

Myles, the whole body of the Church, and in a particular Manner from, Gentlemen,

Your Friends and very humble Servants,[1]

JOHN BARNES.   JOHN GIBBINS.
THO^s GREAVES.   THO^s SELBY.
GEO: CRADOCK.   GEO: MONK.
ANTH: BLOUNT.

P.S. We assure you that Care shall be taken of yor Spouse and Children (either here or where else you please till Your Return from Britain). We expect a possitive Answer by the bearer of this Letter."[2]

These promises were kept, as is shown by, —

"BOSTON, Octob: 1722.

"A Subscription for the Subsistence of Mr Tim^o Cutler while at London and paying his and Messrs Browne and John[son's] Passage to England,[3] £58. 10."

To this there are thirty-four subscribers.

The cordial welcome thus extended to Mr. Cutler was dashed, as is here explicitly stated, by the personal disappointment of Mr. Harris, to whom the prospect of the new church must have opened the inviting prospect of a more independent position than he occupied as Lecturer at King's Chapel, and who also had other motives of distrust and disagreement. His mistake was that he did not accept the inevitable with resignation, but, as will be seen, maintained a hostile attitude, which in a few years resulted in a yet more trying disappointment to his hopes.

It would seem as if, in so small a company as was that of the Episcopal ministers, they would have rejoiced in such an accession of strength as was now coming to them; but it is evident that this feeling on the part of the laity was only shared in part by the few clergy then in New England: —

---

[1] Of these signers, some of whom now passed from King's Chapel to the new church, Judge Greaves (H. C. 1703) should be noted here. He was a son of Judge Thomas Greaves (H.C. 1656). He was born Sept. 28, 1683, and, like his father, became a physician, and judge of the Superior Court. An admirable portrait of his character is drawn by Dr. Cutler in "The good and faithful Servant: and the Joy awarded to him. Sermon occasioned by the death of the Hon. Thomas Greaves, Esq., of *Charlestown*. June 19, 1747. Æt. 63. Matt. xxv. 21." "Conscience bore him up against the popular Stream, and against outward Views, into the Church of England, whose Constitution and Worship he ever admired and defended. And this Church we are now in found, from the first, the Benefit of his Heart and Purse, and Counsels and Assistances."

[2] I am indebted to the Rev. Henry Burroughs, D.D., Rector of Christ Church, for the privilege of making extracts from the original records of that church. Dr. Burroughs has printed the above letter in his valuable "Historical Account of Christ Church, Boston, 1873."

[3] Old Proprietors' Records, Christ Church.

"Upon the whole it seems highly probable that upon these gentlemen's fate, we mean their reception and encouragement, depends a grand revolution, if not a general revolt, from schism in these parts."[1]

On the other hand, Rev. Matthias Plant wrote from Newbury to Dr. Bearcroft: —

"Mr. Mossom of Marblehead says there are but three Old England clergymen in these parts, — viz., Mr. Harris, myself, and you [viz., Mr. Plant]; and these fellows are going home for orders, and they will get the best places in the country and take the bread from off our trenchers. There is the new Church in Boston: of right it first belongs to Mr. Harris, — if he refuses, to myself, and next to you; but they make no offer of it to any of us, and we that have served the church must serve the church as we have, and take up with their leavings. We now who have stood the brunt of the battle and laid the foundation of the churches in this country, are not so much as consulted who shall be their minister. Mr. Harris is resolved to write to my Lord Bishop to oppose their ordination, and I'll join with him, and am come up to acquaint you with it; and we would have you join with us, for a three-fold cord is not easily broken."[2]

The excommunicated gentlemen from Connecticut came to Boston to take passage for England, there to obtain holy orders in the English Church, and found in the King's Chapel which had welcomed them so warmly their first experience of the religious privileges of their new church. Mr. Johnson records:[3]

[1] Church Wardens and Vestry of Newport, R. I., to the Secretary, Oct. 29, 1722, in Church Docs. Conn. 1. 91.

[2] Coffin's Newbury, p. 381. The clergymen already in Massachusetts were not the only disappointed persons. Rev. John Urmston writes to the secretary of the Venerable Society from Cecil County, in Maryland, June, 1724 (*Prot. Episc. Hist. Soc. Coll.*, i. 90): —

"I went from London to New England, where I had some hopes of staying, but was prevented by the New Converts, one whereof had the offer if he would go to England and be ordained, and forthwith did, and is now minister of the New Episcopal Church in Boston, the only man that could be thought of; he'll do more good there than any other."

Mr. Urmston would hardly have been content long if he had been invited to the new Church, if we may judge from his account of the place in Philadelphia, from which he was dismissed, or, as he expressed it, "kicked out very dirtily by the Vestry." "I was not sorry for my removal from so precarious and slavish a place, where they require two Sermons every Lord's Day, Prayers all the week, and Homilies on Festivals, besides abundance of Funerals, Christenings at home, and sick to be visited; no settled salary, the Churchwardens go from house to house every six months, every one gives what he pleases."

[3] "Life and Correspondence of Samuel Johnson, D. D. By E. Edwards Beardsley, D.D. New York: 1874." p. 23. Sewall took such comfort as he could in noting: "1722. Tuesday, Decr 25.—The shops were open, and Carts came to Town with Wood, Hoop-poles, Hay, etc., as at other Times. Being a pleasant day, the street was filled with Carts and Horses."

"Being with Cutler and Brown at Boston, on way to England in ship 'Mary.' Last day before sailing. Nov. 4, Sunday. . . . This day by God's grace I first communicated with the Church of England. How devout, grand, and venerable was every part of the administration, every way becoming so awful a mystery! Mr. Cuthbert, of Annapolis Royal, preached."

They carried with them to England an important letter to the diocesan.[1]

MAY IT PLEASE YO^R LORDSHIP, — We, the Minister, Church Wardens, and Vestry of the King's Chappel in Boston in New England, humbly wait on Yo' Lordship, begging leave to lay before You the present State of the Church in this Place.

It hath pleased Almighty God to bless the Vine which his Right hand hath here planted, and committed to Yo' Care, wth a very fruitful Encrease. It has taken deep Root, and now begins to fill ye Land. The Number of Strangers and Converts who are daily added unto the Church are become so Considerable that we are under the Necessity of Erecting another House for the Publick Worship of God in this Town.

In order to Advance the Kingdom of Jesus Christ, by Carrying on a Work so indispensably Necessary for his Service, God hath blest us (we hope) wth Unanimity and a General Disposition to promote and, Under Yo' Lordship's influence and Favour, finish what is so much Wanted and desired here; And We most humbly address our Selves to our Right Reverend Diocesan, that he would be pleas'd in his abundant Love and Care for the Flock over which the Holy Ghost hath made him Overseer, to regard this distant Portion thereof by Continuing His Care and Protection of us in this Undertaking.

Among many who have Return'd to the Bosom of the Church, We in a particular manner Embrace, and wth all due Deference Recommend to Yo' Lordship's Approbation and Favour, Mr Timothy Cutler, late Rector of Yale College, in Connecticut; Mr Daniel Brown, late Tutor in the Same; and Mr Johnson, late a Dissenting Teacher in Connecticut.

These, my Lord, were persons very Considerable in their Stations in these parts, and have signaliz'd themselves in behalf of the Church by Publickly declaring themselves of it, and as publickly asserting its Rights and maintaining its Dignity against all Opposers. They are Persons of an Unblemish'd Character, well Effected to the present Government, and their Publick Declaration was no sudden Emotion, but a Work of Time perfected wth Maturest Deliberation, in Pure Love to the Truth, and against a Visible Worldly Interest.

Of their Qualifications Yo' Lordship is the Great and Consummate Judge; their Sincerity in this affair we have sufficient Reasons to believe Unquestionable, and therefore humbly request Yo' Lordship if so be it

---

[1] This letter, from the files of Christ Church, is now first printed.

may seem good Unto You, y^t You would be pleas'd to grant unto them Holy Orders. And this we move wth the great^r Earnestness, because fully persuaded Yo^r Lordship will put it then into their Power to become Signal Instruments of Reducing Many (whose Eies are Upon them) to ye Obedience and Unity of the Church.

Mr Timothy Cutler is a person so well Esteem'd in this Place that no Encouragem^t will Ever be wanting, Should Yo^r Lordship please to Grant him Yo^r Licence for the Church now to be built in this place, which We most humbly Entreat Yo^r Lordship to do ; and we have no other View herein, no other Motives inducing us thereto, but a firm belief that the Church of God will receive great Benefit thereby, as being the most suitable person, in our humble Opinion, this Country affords to serve it on this Occasion, and to advance its Number and Intrest ; and we make no Question but his maintenance will be suitable to his great Merit.

The Contributions advanced for this Undertaking are about £1,200, and the Ground purchased whereon to Erect the Church, and our Contributions are daily advancing, so desirous are we to see so good a Work begun.

The Church of God has always on such Occasions as these had its Enemys. A Nehemiah never appear'd to Erect a Temple to God but some arose to hinder it, and cause the Work to Cease. Representations may peradventure be made to our Disadvantage upon this Head, which makes us renew our Assurances to Yo^r Lordship that we have no Interest, no other View, but the pure Glory of God and the Advancement of his Kingdom upon Earth, wch Encourage us to believe we shall not be disappointed of our hope.

May it please Almighty God to shower his Blessings down on Your Lordship's head ; may he continue You long an Ornament and Pillar to his Church upon Earth ; and having finisht Yo^r Glorious and appointed Race, May he recieve You into Everlasting Glory, is the constant prayer of, My Lord,

   Yo^r Lordship's most obedient humble Serv^{ts},
       SAMUEL MYLES, Minister.
       JN^o CUTLER, } Church Wardens.
       JAMES SMITH, }
       JOHN JEKYLL.

BOSTON, NEW ENGLAND, Novr 1st, 1722.

Bishop Robinson, to whom this was addressed, was already disabled by his last illness ; and, before they left England on their return, he was succeeded by Dr. Edmund Gibson, one of the most eminent and worthy men who have adorned that venerable See.[1] He was a learned antiquary; but his great work, " Codex Juris Ecclesiastici Anglicani," in two volumes folio, is

---

[1] He was translated from Lincoln to London, April, 1723, and died Aug. 4, 1748, æt. 79.

his chief monument, though he published also a large collection of writings of English divines against Popery, and his own valuable " Pastoral Letters." He was " a strenuous defender of the rights of the Church considered as a political community, but liberal in respect of doctrines," willing to risk the displeasure of the King in rebuking offences, and as a man greatly respected and loved. He was a warm Whig and Hanoverian, and it may perhaps be on that account that Cutler seems not to have had close personal relations with him, though in England at the time of his translation to London. The King's Chapel, also, was then so predominantly swayed by the Tory element that it is not strange to find recorded no message of congratulation to Bishop Gibson, while it shortly assumed an attitude of hostility to his exercise of powers which in his predecessors had not been questioned, though he disarmed the opposition by sagacious good sense. The bishop could hardly have expected cordiality from men of the school which said of Tillotson: "His politics are Leviathan, and his religion Latitudinarianism, which is none."

Of Mr. Cutler's associates, Mr. Brown died soon after landing in England, of small-pox. His associates were received at both Oxford and Cambridge with much warmth and kindness. Each university conferred on Cutler the degree of S.T.D., and that of M.A. on Johnson, —

"And relations of private friendship were then formed between them and many of the leading Heads of Houses and Fellows, which bound the hearts of zealous Churchmen on both sides of the Atlantic in closest brotherhood."[1]

Messrs. Cutler and Johnson returned to America in the summer of 1723, the latter to become Episcopal missionary at Stratford, Connecticut, and one of the influential men of his time; while Dr. Cutler found the North (or Christ) Church nearly ready for his ministry of forty-two years to begin.[2] For the

---

[1] Anderson, Colonial Church, ii. 395. The fatality among those going "home" for orders was extraordinary. Dr. Johnson later said that "out of 51 who had gone from this country, in little more than 40 years, for ordination, ten had died from sickness or been lost at sea." — *Beardsley's Johnson*, p. 301.

[2] The Rev. Samuel Johnson was one of the most eminent representatives of the Episcopal cause in America before the Revolution. Born in Guilford, Connecticut, Oct. 14, 1696, he graduated at Yale College, then at Saybrook, in 1714, and acted as tutor until in 1720 he became minister at West Haven. After two years in the Congregational ministry, he followed his gradually matured convictions and joined in the public declaration of Dr. Cutler and five other tutors and ministers in favor of Episcopacy. On his return from England he was appointed by the Society for the Propagation of the Gospel missionary in Stratford, Connecticut, where he labored through the western part of the province

Church of England in Boston was so prospering that its second church had been built by means of the subscription already mentioned.

"*A List of the Subscribers and Benefactors who contributed towards the building of* CHRIST CHURCH, *at y* North End, Boston,*" is headed by —

	£	s.	d.
"The R! H^{ble} Tho! Earl of Thanet,[1] 30 £ St. @ 200 adv^{ce}	90.	00.	00
"His Ex^{cy} Fr. Nicholson, Esq!, Gov! of S. Carolina, and also five Ceder posts and 65 d? planks, freight free	69.	00.	00
"Doctor Trapp, 2 guyneas	6.	06.	00
Total	£2,184.	14.	00

There were two hundred and fourteen subscribers in all, many of them members of King's Chapel.

The next step is thus recorded: —

Aprill the 15th, A.D. 1723.

"The Reverend Mr Samuel Myles, accompany'd with the Gentlemen of King's Chapel, laid the first Stone in Christ Church, saying these Words, Viz!: *May the Gates of Hell never prevail against it!*"

Another sign of the changes that were coming over New England was the death of Dr. Increase Mather, Aug. 23, 1723. The last survivor of the old theocracy, he passed away full of years, and having retained his powers so as to preach almost to the close of his life. A man who would have been a marked figure in any period of history, and eminent among those who have greatly served their country in critical times, he stands in this narrative chiefly as the leading representative of the old New England principles in opposition to the English Church. He was followed to the grave by such a mourning as befitted

for thirty years. He enjoyed the intimate friendship of Dean Berkeley during his stay in Rhode Island. In 1754 he was chosen president of King's College, New York, which was then founded under Episcopal control (after an animated struggle of the Presbyterians for ascendancy). Dr. Johnson resigned this position in 1763, returning to his church at Stratford, where he died, Jan. 6, 1772.

His son, William Samuel Johnson, LL.D., was president of King's College after it had taken the name "Columbia," after the Revolution. It is a curious fact that " the grandson of this father of Episcopacy in Connecticut married the granddaughter of Jonathan Edwards, the great New England apostle of Calvinism." — *N. E. Hist. and Geneal. Reg.*, xxvii. 47.

[1] Thomas (Tufton), sixth Earl of Thanet and eighteenth Lord De Clifford, died 1729. His chaplain, meeting Cutler and Johnson in London, "counted out to each of them ten guineas," "a present from his noble patron for the purchase of books." — *Beardsley*, i. 45. The Earl's subscription was probably obtained by Cutler at this time.

the father of the churches, by those who must have felt that with him the old era ended. A month later, Sewall records:

"Sept! 29. Dr. Timothy Cutler [his first sermon] : For this Cause left I thee at Creet. Mention'd Forty One. The second Chapt' of Ezekiel was Read."

The new missionaries, accompanied by Rev. James Wetmore, who had shared their course, had landed in Boston, Sept. 24, 1723.

"To the great joy," wrote Cutler, "of our Episcopal Brethren . . . I have preached for the most part every Sunday since I have been here."[1]

The Boston Gazette, Sept. 23–30, 1723, recorded: —

"Yesterday the Reverend Dr. *Timothy Cutler* Preached a Sermon at the King's Chappel from Tit. i. 5. *For this cause . . . appointed thee.* In the Afternoon the Reverend Mr. *James Wetmore* (Missionary for Stratton Island) [2] preached from Matt. xxiv. 46."

The minister of Christ Church was a man of talent and power, of wide general learning, and one of the best Oriental scholars of his time, of imposing presence also, and a strong preacher. He brought a real accession to the Church of England force here, especially in its polemical relations. But the impression made by him in the general community, and his ministerial success, were far less than might have been looked for from such a man. Partly this is due to the stony nature of the ground which he ploughed; but partly it must be ascribed to an imperious temper, and a disposition to some degree soured by such a change of ecclesiastical relations as few men can pass through without some fermentation of spirit.

Dr. Cutler had been able to serve his church while in England.[3] His first sermon in Christ Church was, Dec. 29, 1723, from the

---

[1] Church Docs. Mass. p. 142.
[2] Mr. Wetmore was sent to New York, and later to Rye, N. Y., where he served for nearly thirty-seven years, dying 1760, æt. 65.
[3] This appears from Dr. Cutler's representation to the Hon. Society, etc., "in Conjunction with the Church in Boston, in whose name, as well as in his own, he appears. . . . That the Church now erecting there may have the support and protection of the Honourable Society, there being an apparent and universally allowed necessity of a new Church in that town, the old Church not being capable, in any manner, to accommodate all that are disposed to attend the Communion of the Church of England in that town, and many greatly disadvantaged by their remote situation from it." Among the reasons for aid, this paper mentions: "1. The present slenderness of their number, of whose increase, though a great probability, there is no certainty." — *Church Docs.* Conn. i. 60.

text, "My House shall be called an House of Prayer for all People."

The Mill Creek, flowing where Blackstone Street now is, was considered the dividing line between the two sections of the town. At the North End resided much of the wealth and fashion of the town; but Christ Church seems never to have divided these equally with its mother church. The best account of the new church was given by Dr. Cutler to the Secretary, Oct. 10, 1727:[1] —

"The Rev? M: Myles, Minister of His Majesty's Chapel in this Town, with the whole Body of his Parishioners, finding their Church after a considerable enlargement too small for his Congregation, which was daily growing by the accession of Strangers from Foreign Parts and the Church's daily victories over the prejudices of our Native Dissenters, and observing many to keep from the church purely from want of good accommodations in it, did think it proper to build a new church at a convenient distance from the other, and have prosecuted that design with heart, hand, and purse, and that mutual peace and love wherein they have been very exemplary to the Dissenters, whose intestine quarrels give life to a great number of their new conventicles. We are considerably in debt, and need some hundred pounds to complete our church, and to furnish it with an organ, Bells, Communion Plate et?; and we are Kept back the more by the assistance which other Church's . . . receive from us, and if we were emerged out of these difficulties, it is generally thought there would be soon a third church set up in the Town. The Church is 70 feet long, 50 wide, 35 high, the walls 2 feet and ½ thick, the Steeple's Area is 29 feet square, 80 feet high, the walls of it 2 feet and ½ thick. The whole Building is of Brick, saving that the Spire (not yet begun for want of money) will be of wood. The Church is not endowed at all; the Minister

---

[1] From the Christ Church Records we learn that, April 6, 1724, "Two Church Wardens and 8 vestrymen" were chosen, viz.: —

Thomas Graves, Esq!. } be Church
Anthony Blount,   } Wardens.

Henry Franklyn,
Edward Watts,
John Gibbs,
Gillam Phillips,   } Vestrymen.
John Corney,
George Monk,
North Ingham,
Rob! Temple,

The congregation voted that these should be "allways chosen by a written vote;" "2dly that Thomas Watts be appointed to sett in the Gallerys and keep the boys in order that no Disturbance be in the time of Divine Service, and that Fifty-two Shillings p annum be paid him out of the Contribution."

A question which caused difficulty somewhat later, in King's Chapel, was settled in the new church, April 11, 1726, when the congregation "*Voted*, That it is convenient that the Doct: should nominate one Church warden and the Congregation the other."

The Vestry records of Christ Church indicate some characteristic traits of the North End population at that period:

"Nov. 21, 1726. *Voted*, That for the future the Sexton shall keep y⁶ rails at the Altar clear from Boys and Negroes setting there.

"That no Nailes nor pinns be put in the pillars nor the front of the Gallerys with a design to hang Hatts on."

is paid out of the Weekly Contributions £3 per week of our currency, which is £1 Sterling, to which my People have lately added 10s. per Week of our currency more, my former Salary being found insufficient for my numerous Family of 7 children, in whose maintenance I have been brought a great deal in arrears: and tho my People do for me cheerfully what they are able, I find it very difficult to live decently in this expensive Town.

"At the first opening of my Church I had generally an audience of about 400 persons, which is now encreased to about 700 or 800. The Trade and Business of this Town is better represented than I can in prospect of it, which (with a plan of it) Mr Wm Price, a worthy Member of my Church, presents to the Society by my hands. In this Town are Presbyterians, Independants, Anabaptists, and Quakers, and I fear the principles of Deism, Arianism, and Popery are privately instilled into some; and we also feel the sad effects of such Books as the 'Rights of the Christian Church,' and the 'Independent Whig.' My Church has no parochial bounds, and my Congregation is scattered all over this large Town, and in and beyond Charlestown, parted from this Town by a considerable River, where there are 15 Families, and in some other places separated from us by water or at the distance of many miles from us, besides the parish of Bantry [Braintree] which I have reason to call mine till they are blest with the arrival of a minister. Strangers in the Town, and new Converts to the Church could accommodate themselves with Seats in my Church and could not in the other, so that many who live equally near or nearer to that, resort to mine. Storms, Ice and Snow, which are considerable in this Country, make Winter travelling by Water or Land very difficult, and my visits of my People have a proportionable difficulty from all these considerations. The inhabitants of the Town are now thought to be 20,000, by some 24,000, and the Town is continually growing in Business and Riches." [1]

[1] Church Docs. Mass. p. 229. The ministers of Christ Church have been as follows: —

Rev. Timothy Cutler, D.D., December, 1723-August, 1765; Rev. James Greaton, assistant, 1759-1765, appointed rector 1767, resigned on account of disaffections Aug. 31, 1767; Rev. Mather Byles (then Congregational clergyman at New London, Conn.), chosen Easter Monday, 1768, went to England for ordination, May, 1768, and returned in September; he resigned April, 1775, and accepted an invitation from the church in Portsmouth, N. H. The church was then closed till August, 1778. Rev. Stephen Lewis was rector 1778-1784 or 1785; Mr. Wm. Montague acted as lay-reader for six months; Easter Monday, 1786, the engagement was renewed. June, 1787, Mr. Montague obtained holy orders, and continued with some interruptions till May, 1792, when he declined longer officiating.

In 1789 an act of incorporation from the General Court was obtained.

May 29, 1792, Rev. William Walter, D.D., died Dec. 5, 1800; May, 1801, Rev. Samuel Haskell, resigned September, 1803, going to Gardiner, Me.; Oct. 23, 1803, Rev. Asa Eaton, lay-reader, took orders and charge of the church in the summer of 1805, resigned 1838, died March 24, 1838; May 31, 1839, Rev. William Croswell, D.D., resigned 1840; Rev. John Woart; 1852-September, 1859, Rev. William J. Smith; February, 1860-1868, Rev. John F. Burrill; 1868, Rev. Henry Burroughs, D.D., the present incumbent.

CHRIST CHURCH.

CHAPTER IX.

THE THREE CLERGYMEN.

DR. CUTLER'S relations with Mr. Myles seem to have been friendly, and they were in accord in undertaking an active campaign for full clerical and ecclesiastical recognition in Massachusetts. The records of King's Chapel indicate, however, that everything did not go smoothly with the swarming from the old hive;[1] and the hostility between Dr. Cutler and Mr. Harris had already become the talk of the town: —

"Yesterday the new church at this end of the town was met in, though very much unfinished. People flocked to it in abundance. What made them so hasty to improve it, as I am informed, was because Dr. Cutler's salary was not to begin till he began to preach there. There seems to be a considerable strangeness between Harris and Cutler, as well as a great dislike of one another; and there seems to be a breach among their people."[2]

[1] See p. 334, *post*.
[2] Robbins's "Second Church," p. 313.

Letter of Rev. Mr. Waldron, Dec. 30, 1723.

In the same letter which gave to the Bishop of London the account of Checkley already quoted,[1] June 22, 1724, Mr. Harris frankly laid open his mind on this subject: —

"I am not ignorant that at this juncture I am blamed by some for my conduct towards T. Cutler, the Minister of the new Church in this place, tho' upon the most impartial examination I can't charge myself with the least offence in that respect; . . . for, from the time of his admission into the Hon[ble] Society's service, it has been my particular care not to say or do anything which might tend to his disparagement. But what my opinion of him was when he declared for the Church, your Lordship will perceive by my letter to your Lordship's predecessor; and my present opinion of him is that his behaviour is so imprudent, his notions so wild and extravagant, and his principles so uncharitable, that I may venture to affirm that the Church will never flourish under his care, the affections of the Dissenters being entirely alienated from him, and there is not so much as one person of tolerable note and distinction whom he has brought off from the congregational persuasion. This is what I foresaw would be the issue of his management, and to show my dislike of it I declined having any intimate conversation with him, lest his principles should be thought to be espoused by all of our Communion, and so the whole Church should suffer thro' the indiscretion of one man. I am satisfied that by this means I have promoted the interest and credit of the Established Church, and am favor'd with the approbation of all the King's Officers (one only excepted) and the most intelligent part of the congregation; and the King's Chapel wherein I officiate is throng'd and crowded with a very numerous audience. This it seems is no small grievance to D[r] Cutler's friends, who impute the ill-success of his ministry to my coldness towards him, and as I am informed have sent to your Lordship a complaint against me, which was kept a secret by the persons who were active in it" [petitioning] "for my removal. . . . I am told that some people who belong to the King's Chapel have concurred with those of the New Church, but how far my colleague, the Rev[d] M[r] Myles, is concerned in this dirty work I can't say; only this I am sure of, that he has declared more than once he had no quarrel with me and should not interest himself in the differences betwixt me and my adversaries, since which time he has rec'd large presents from them, which 'tis possible may be attended with the same effects which they had in Solomon's days, viz., of blinding the eyes. However, I am not averse to the substance of the petition, that your L'dship would please to remove me from this place, — I hope not in anger, or by way of punishm[t], but as a reward of my faithful and laborious services in these parts of the world; . . . not that I gained the Dissenters by any sinister arts, or made 'em any concessions, either in doctrine or discipline, but used the

[1] See p. 287, *ante.*

strongest reasons I could think of to convince their understandings, and the softest words with the most affable corteous behaviour to attract their esteem and engage their affections, commending the purity of their morals, and desiring their perfection in a union with our truly primitive and apostolic Church. . . . I confess the scene at present is much altered, and the Church's interest visibly declines, since D! Cutler has tried his new experiments. Thus, tho' he was made a Doctor in the Schools, he proves himself to be a Novice in the Church, and obliges the World with the taste of the first fruits of his Novitiate — in supplanting me, into whose labors he is entered without expressing the least grateful sense of the benefit he reaps from my unwearied patience, toil, and industry."

He concludes by saying that these vexations have thrown him into so ill a state of health that he proposes to go to England during the year, "depending upon your Lordship's goodness in the continuance of my subsistence till I am provided for at home."[1]

This unfortunate misunderstanding led to further and yet more public difficulties. Mr. Harris was a decided Whig, while Dr. Cutler, though not a Jacobite, was a High Tory in politics, in sympathy with the party of Checkley, whose trial occurred a few months after Cutler's arrival, and with whose ecclesiastical doctrines he was in accord.[2] A few months after his settlement at the new church he preached a sermon which made a stir. This seems to have called forth a rejoinder from the pulpit of King's Chapel by Mr. Harris, of so bitter a tone as to justify interference by his church-wardens, who addressed to him the following: [3] —

REVEREND SIR, — Wee the Church Wardens of His Majesty's Chappel, being Impowred by the 53! Cannon of the Ch! of England To take Nottice of all oppositione amongst preachers, and being farther Commanded by one order of King William the third of Glorious memory to See the said Cannon put In Executione. And you Sir, haveing offended against said Cannon and order In your Sermon, the Sunday before last, as wee Conceive, Doe now Desire of you a Copy of the Said Sermon,

---

[1] Church Docs. Mass. p. 156.

[2] "A poor woman of the other Church at Boston," wrote to Dr. Cutler, May 5, 1726: —
"I . . . have been sundry times to hear you, and should go very often, but I find you preach up morality and little of Christ in your Sermons. . . . I pray preach more on true conversion and the life of Christianity, and not so much on passive obedience and non-resistance. Pray, in your little prayer before the Sermon, for King George and Royal Family, as our Ministers do, and I will come often, . . . and I am sure your Church will be full." — *Church Docs.* Mass. p. 667.

[3] From the files of Christ Church papers.

In order that wee May transmitte the Same to Our Right reverend and Right honourable Diocesan, the Bishop of London, That His Lordship may Determine this Matter Equally betwixt you and The Reverend Dr Timothy Cuttler.

JAMES STIRLING.

BOSTON, July 27, 1724.   JOHN BARNES.

In this transaction, it cannot be doubted that the wardens were stirred to the more vigor by the fresh sense of discomfiture in Mr. Harris's appeal to the Lieut.-Governor and Council, when taken to task for his loyal criticism of Checkley from the pulpit, in the preceding April. Dr. Cutler also wrote to the Secretary of "the Venerable Society," asking the Society to mediate in his behalf with the Bishop of London, in his complaint against Mr. Harris:[1] —

"But whatsoever difficulties arise from their disaffection to us they are not equal to the troubles that arise from some of our own members, a late instance whereof, affecting myself in such a manner as I think the canons of the Church and our reputation in general here is injured, I think myself obliged to let the Society know of it at this time; tho' at the same time I do with grief say it is the unhandsome treatment I have received from the Revd Mr Henry Harris, Assistant to the Revd Mr Samuel Myles, Rector of His Majesty's Chapel in Boston.

"Mr Myles on the 18th instant desired of me that we might in the next day on the forenoon exchange pulpits, which I accordingly complied withal, and preached the sermon which for the meanness of it I am ashamed to shew, but for my own vindication am obliged to send over to this Honble Society, trusting in the candor of the Honble Members of it towards a composition of one day, — for being obliged to make two sermons every week I think that the best proportioning of my time to this service. In it I had an eye to the first and fifth head of instruction given to the missionaries with respect to themselves; and tho' perhaps there may appear a little tartness in remarking the spirit of Dissenters with us, yet I humbly conceive, and upon my conscience declare, that I think it necessary, and that I keep within as good bounds as any Missionary here. However, Mr Harris made not this a bone of contention, but in the afternoon of the s^d day took notice in his Sermon of an expression of mine to tax me with Popish principles, as will I presume appear from a true inclosed copy of what he delivered, to which several of the hearers have subscribed their hands in what I have made bold to send to my Lord of London. I chose rather to have gained a copy of his Sermon from him, and after I failed by the private intercession of a friend of his, I went to him with the Churchwardens of His Majesty's chapel, and with all possible civility desired the same; but, instead of

---

[1] July 31, 1724. Church Docs. Mass. p. 163.

gaining that, was very rudely bid to go out of his house, — and so I must be contented with what evidence I can get.

"I have sat down tamely under many injuries and affronts from that Gentleman, and so I should do under this, did I think it supportable; but I look at all my serviceableness to the Church struck at by such insinuations, and do find that some dissenters already build upon his words in representing me as carrying on designs of Popery, and what further ill effects the thing may have to evacuate the ends of my mission God alone knows."

To this letter Mr. Myles and his wardens appended their affidavit that Mr. Harris said these or like words: —

"'For a small skill in chronology may inform any one that the Church at that time was overspread with thick darkness, error, and superstition. One century makes a great difference. If I had been to have expressed it (if I would wish to err), I would have said if I must err, let me err with the Church as it is now or as it was 100 years ago. I think it my indispensible duty to say thus much at this time as a preservative against Popery and superstition.'

"The reason why the above attestation begins so abruptly is because the subscribers are not so positive of the immediately preceding part of the discourse, tho' several of the auditors remember it was introduced in the following words, or words to the same purpose: 'I can not but take notice of a shocking expression from the mouth of a protestant, if he may be called so. If I must err, let me err with the Church as it was 200 years ago; for a small,' etc."[1]

Dr. Cutler was also vindicated by his friend, Rev. Mr. Johnson, writing from Boston, Oct. 30, 1724, to the Bishop of London, to whom the whole strife was referred: —

"'There are indeed a number of very worthy Clergymen here in New England, but yet many things occur from time to time which make it very apparent how extremely unhappy we are for want of an ecclesiastical governor to have an immediate inspection over us. Among other instances of this kind, the conduct of Mr. Harris, of Boston, is a very flagrant one. The malice wherewith he hath all along persecuted good Dr. Cutler is very extraordinary, and for no other reason but because the good people of Boston were desirous, and are so happy as to obtain, that the Doctor should be the incumbent of their new Church, which it seems Mr. Harris had an expectation of. Your Lordship will, I believe, be sufficiently sensible by looking into the Doctor's sermon, how far it is from the least favourable aspect upon Popery; and yet this gentleman would persuade people that the Doctor is a Papist, and that sermon, at the same time, is all he pretends for a foundation for it."[2]

[1] Church Docs. Mass. p. 163.   [2] Ibid. p. 96.

The strength and wisdom of Bishop Gibson were never better indicated than in the letter which these deplorable contentions evoked from him.[1] Being a private letter, it did not find its way into the church records; but it belongs here as an important paper in our history:[2]—

"GOOD SIR,— I am very sorry to find, by the Account which I have received of late from New England, that the differences among the clergy at Boston are grown to such a heigth, and that they have spread themselves into other parts of the government, and are like to spread more and more. The Representations whh come over hither, concerning the true ground and foundation of these unhappy differences, are so various, that I am not able as yet to form any certain judgment about it, nor to see who is most in the blame. But as in cases of this nature there is usually more or less of blame resting on both sides, while passions prevail against reason; so I earnestly entreat and require both sides to lay aside passion and think seriously of peace. They should remember that they belong to one and the same Church, and what is more, a Church that is yet in its infancy, and in the midst of enemies who will take great advantages against it from the unhappy Feuds and Animosities among its ministry and principal members. The letters from thence, both to the Society and myself, are full of the hardships whh the ministers of the Church of England suffer from the independants there, which one would hope should be a lesson to the ministers to unite firmly among themselves to support one another, instead of reproaching and aspersing their own

---

[1] These discords have been perpetuated in letters of Dr. Cutler, on church affairs in New England, to his friend Dr. Zachary Gray. He wrote, April, 2, 1725:—

... "My Church grows faster than I expected, and while it doth so I will not be mortified by all the lies and affronts they pelt me with. My greatest difficulty ariseth from another quarter, and is owing to the covetous and malicious spirit of a clergyman in this town, who, in lying and villany, is a perfect over-match for any Dissenter that I know; and after all the odium that he contracted heretofore among them, is fully reconciled and endeared to them by his falsehood to the Church, and in spite of me. I have a clear conscience towards him, and have tried to gain him, and, for the peace of the Church, have passed over many affronts that everybody would not have thought supportable, and have not stirred till he gave such vent to his furious malice that none but an ass would bear; upon which I have made my complaint, which I need not be particular in, because I doubt not the Dean of Ely hath related it to you."

Dr. Cutler's letters to this correspondent,— Dr. Zachary Gray, of Houghton Conquest, Bedfordshire, printed in Nichols's "Illustrations of Literature," vol. iv.,— though written with a pen dipped in gall, are an entertaining and valuable account of religious and other matters in Boston in the second quarter of the last century. Most of them are reprinted in the appendix to Bishop Perry's Church Docs. Mass., but with omissions of some pungent matter.

[2] This letter, in Mass. Hist. Proc., 1865, p. 226, is said to have been written to Hon. Thomas Graves, of Charlestown; but it is corrected by a more perfect copy, in Mass. Hist. Proc., 1866-67, p. 342, dated "Fulham, Sept ye 3d, 1724," and the address, "To ye Revd Mr Miles, at Boston, New England."

brethren, to enter into the most proper Christian methods of defending y^m selves against the oppressions of their adversaries, and of preserving and, by degrees, enlarging, that poor Chh whh is committed to y^r care.

It is with great concern y^t I write this, arising from a just apprehension of the mischiefs whh are like to accrue from those differences to religion in general, and to the Chh of Engl^d in particular; and I write to you as a person who is not directly concern'd in ye quarrel, and who being upon the place can best judge of the most likely methods to bring both sides to a peaceable disposition, whh I earnestly entreat you to endeavor by all ways possible. One way, and I hope a successful one, may be, to show wh^t I write to both contending parties, and to let them know that I beseech and conjure them to lay aside their animosities, and to forget and forgive ye provocations y^t have passed on both sides, as becomes Christians, and more especially the ministers of the gospel. The ent'ring into a strict examination of all the particulars, in order to see who is most to be blam'd, would be a long work, and I doubt, at this distance, impracticable; but at best it would be a work of much time, and all that [time] the feuds would be kept up and increased, and the Chh would be bleeding of the wounds whh they have already given her, and whh is the earnest wish of all good men, both here and there, to see immediately closed by mutual forbearance and friendly reconciliation.

I have been informed, within these few days, by one of the Bishops who had rec^d a Letter from Boston, that some of the ministers of the government are beginning the dispute about the validity or invalidity of Baptism administered by persons not episcopally ordain'd. This was on foot here in England by the non-jurors some years since, and bred great disturbance among us; and the Arch-Bishop and Bishops, in Convocation, set forth a paper to show that it has been the constant doctrine of the Chh of Eng^d, y^t Baptism wth water, in ye name of ye Father, and of the Son, and of the Holy Ghost, by w^t hand soever administered, is valid in itself, and not to be repeated, however irregular in ye manner of it. Nothing is more certain than that this was ye Doctrine whh the greatest patrons of our Chh maintained against the puritans in the reign of Q. Eliz^th and K. James I^st; and it is easy to see wth w^t views ye contrary doctrine has been advanced and espoused of late years by the enemies of the protestant succession and the present governm^t; and if any missionary shall renew this Controversy, and advance the same doctrine there that the non-jurors have been advancing here, I shall esteem him as a enemy to the Chh of England and to the protestant succession, and shall deal with him accordingly. I earnestly recommend these things to your care, beseeching God to dispose both parties to peace, and to prosper your endeavors for obtaining of it.

I remain, Sir, your Faithful friend and Brother,

EDM^D LONDON."

Mr. Mossom of Marblehead wrote to the Bishop, Dec. 17, 1724, thanking him for his "pathetick exhortations and authoritative injunctions to Peace and amity" in this letter: —

"Such is the flaming zeal of this M!. Checkley and the party which abets him, that, be your Lordship's decisions what they will, except they agree with their ways of thinking, they put 'em behind 'em and take no notice of them; and . . . we . . . the poor inferior Clergy . . . are the Butts of their vehement and ungoverned heat. . . . I conferred with M!. Harris . . . whose Temper and disposition of mind I knew to be naturally peaceable, and he declared himself ready to come into any methods for healing all breaches, in pursuance of which we took the first opportunity of inviting D!. Cutler into the same. We met him at a Gent'ˢ house, in company with another, both of whom were his very good friends; and yet, whatsoever we all could urge, he would not consent to the sealing of a Peace except a good number of the Laity were also resolved to it, whose minds he would first know. I showed him the absurdity of calling in the Laity to close the difference between Clergymen, and probably the unsuccessfull issue it would have, and the event has fully confirmed my judgment. I have, indeed, once and again talked with D!. Cutler upon it, requested him to consider the value of peace itself, as well as the authority of him that enjoins it; but I do not discern anything I can say makes impression upon him.

"And for a close, my Lord, be pleased to give me leave to observe that we are but in this province 3 English Clergymen, — M!. Harris, Plant, and myself. An exceedingly difficult part we have to act, for while we are true to our trusts, and the Laity can't mould us into their tempers and make us as fiery zealous as they are, we are sure to encounter the utmost of their spleen and displeasure. However, I doubt not we each of us shall go on in the faithful and conscientious discharge of our duty; by the Grace of God I will, and M!. Harris has requested me to assure your Lordship of the same for him."[1]

These unfortunate dissensions, in which the wardens and vestry of King's Chapel evidently did not sympathize with their lecturer, will explain several allusions in the records during the next two years.

April 6, 1724. *Voted*, By a vote of the congregation, that M!. Nathaniel Gifford[2] be Organist for the year ensuing, and that he play a Voluntary before the first Lesson, and attend the Church upon all holy Days.

---

[1] Church Docs. Mass. p. 169.

[2] The nuptials of the new organist were soon announced, — in the "Boston Gazette," Dec. 23-30, 1728: "We hear that a Treaty of Marriage is Concluded upon and will soon be Consummated between Mr. Nathanael Gifford and Mrs. Elizabeth Rame, a celebrated Beauty of this Place."

Also the Clark to be continued. That James Baker, the Sexton, be Continued upon his good behaviour.

April 23, 1724. *Voted*, That the Church wardens, for the time being, have liberty to putt out at interest what money shall be in their Hands belonging to the Church, at good Personall Security, not exceeding One Hundred pounds to one person.

Also, That the two Church Wardens, Mr Iekyll, Mr Accmuty, Mr Reed, and Doct.^r Gibbins, or the major part, are desired to assist the Revd Mr Miles in drawing up proper Answers to the Lord of London Queries; also A Letter of thanks. The same Committee draw up a letter of thanks to his Excellency Gen^{ll} Nicholson, and send him a Coppy of the answers to his Lord^{ps} Queries;[1] And to draw up a dutifull and Loyall address to the King.

The Revd Mr Henry Harris was sent for to the Vestry, but sending word he was indisposed, —

Voted, That Capt Sterling be Desired to waite on Mr Harris, to meet the Vestry the next thursday, at 4 o'clock, at this House.

April 30, 1724. *Voted*, That Capt Corny have leave to continue in his Pew, paying Contribution.

Also, that those Gentlemen who are already gone to the North Church shall have a consideration for their Pews, one half of the first cost.

Also, that those Gentlemen who shall for the future go to the North Church shall have no consideration at all for their pews.

Also, that Mr. Thos Selby have a right to three quarters of the N.º 20 of the North Isle, Relinquishing his own pew, N.º 22, in the same Isle; and when the Widow Britton is provided otherwise to her satisfaction, then Mr Selby is to pay to the Church £3. 15, and have a right to the whole Pew.

Also, that Mr Thomas Phillips have the Pew N.º 22, formerly Mr Selby's, paying ten Pounds to the Church, and that he has liberty to give up his pew, N.º 34, on the North Side, to Mr Luke Verdy.[2] The money rec'd.

Also that Mr Valentine's Pew be disposed of.

Also that Mr John Tubee shall have the pew N.º 37 on the North Side formerly in the possesion of Messrs Monk and Warner, Paying ten Pounds, — the Mony Rec^d.

---

[1] One of the questions and answers was as to "Support of Ministers":—

"*Question*. — How is the revenue of church applied which arises during the vacancies?

"*Answer*. — In this Gov.^t the Clergy of the Church have a weekly gathering toward their maintenance, besides what the Missionaries have allowed from the Society."— *Church Docs.* Mass. p. 153.

[2] The Vestry had often met at his house. The Royal Exchange (S. W. corner of State Street and Exchange Place) "was kept by the popular London cook and publican, Luke Vardy, described by Joseph Green in a satire on a masonic celebration in 1749:—

"For them his ample bowls o'erflow'd,
His table groan'd beneath its load;
For them he stretched his utmost art, —
Their honours grateful they impart.
Luke in return is made a *brother*,
As *good* and *true* as any other;
And still, though broke with age and wine,
Preserves the *token* and the *sign*."
Memorial History of Boston, ii. 499.

Also that M#rs# Bath be spoken to; and if she pays the arrears from the Death of her Husband, and security to pay the Contribution for the time to come, then Her Title to be Confirmed if not to be disposed of to M#rs# Britton and Bucher. Answer, Nothing to do with the pew. The title given to her Son, at Present abroad; and when returnes She is to Informe him of the Above Vote.

M#rs# Rows has a Title to one half of the Pew.

M#r# John Arbuthnot title to one half of his pew.

May 7#th# 1724. Pearson pew, N#o# 33, North Side. *Voted*, that Fletcher Whitehead, and Eliza Cox and husband have a title to two thirds of Said Pew, and that they pay each of them Sixpence p Week quarterly.

May 21, 1724. *Voted*, that Major Paul Mascareen and his family, with Coll#o# Tayler's leave, sitt in that Pew; and that no other Person come there untill a Suitable pew be vacant agreeable to the Major and his Lady, and that they have the prefferrence of the Same before any one Whatsoever.

June 4#th# 1724. *Voted*, that M#r# William Randle be sent to the Reverend M#r# Henry Harris to Desire the Letter he promised to give the 30#th# of last April, and answered he had no timely Notice, and that he would have Nothing to say to us.

Voted, That the Minister and Church Wardens of the King's Chappell make a faithful and just representation to My Lord of London of the Rev#d# M#r# Henry Harris's Conducte for the last two Years.

Dec#r# 1, 1724. *Voted*, that the following Certificate and Declaration, in Favour of Doct#r# Timothy Cutler, be entered: —

We, the subscribers, Members of his Majesties Chappel in Boston, do certifie all persons Whom it doth or may Concern, that the Reverend Doctor Timothy Cutler hath to the best of our Knowledge, Ever since his declaring for the Church of England to this Instant, behaved himself after a becomeing and Innofensive manner to all orders and Degrees of Men in this Place, more Especialy towards the Reverend M#r# Henry Harris, and neglected no means proper for a Clergyman and a Christian or a Gentleman to use for gaining the Said M#r# Harris's good will and to Live peaceably with him. In Testimony whereof we have hereunto Set our hands This first Day of Dec#r#, in the Year of Our Lord 1724.

The above certificate Read at the Vestry, the Reverend M#r# Henry Harris being present, and approved of the same. Likewise gave his opinion that the said certificate be registred in the Church Books.

March 29, 1725. *Voted*, M#r# Nathaniel Gifford to continue Organist, and shall have for Sallary forty Pounds for this year. And the Contribution shall be gathered by going round w#th# boxes.

Also the Clark Continued, and that he have for Sallary for the ensuing Year twenty-two Pounds.

Also that James Baker the Sexton be Continued, and is to have for Sallary 8, for the Ensueing Year.

March 30. Also that the Church Wardens wait upon the Honourable Willm Tayler, Esqre, and Desire him to sit in the Governour's pew.

Boston, Jan^{ry} 24, 1725-26. Att a meeting of the Congregation belonging to the King's Chappel in boston, *Voted*, That som of 20/ p week be added to the Sallary of the Reverend Mr Saml Myles, to make it five pounds p week for the time to come; and that £400 be lent him out of the Church Stock the next Easter, without Interest, he paying into the Church Wardens, for the time being, £100 p year untill the whole £400 be paid, his house and land to be security for the said four hundred pounds.

Boston, April 11th, 1726. At a meeting of Congregation on Easter Monday, *Voted*, That Robt Kenton the Clark's Sallary be raised to thirty pounds p annum.

That the Ministers, Church Wardens, and Vestry be impowered to manage the whole affaires of the Church for the ensuing Year.

April 13th. The reverend Mr Saml Miles Informed the Vestry that Mr Charles Apthorpe refused to serve as Church warden, and nominated Mr Thos Selby, who was Chosen by a majority of voices.

May 30, 1726. Whereas the Reverend Mr Samuel Miles, instead of receiving £400 from the Church, agreeable to a vote of the Congregation, Jan^{ry} 24, 1725-26, has taken the same from his honour the Lieu^t Governour, — *Voted*, That the sum of twenty-four Pounds be paid out of the Church Stock to his Honour for the first Year's Interest of the said sum of four hundred Pounds, eighteen Pounds for the second, twelve pounds for the third, and six Pounds for the fourth Year's interest.

Voted, That fourscore pounds be raised within a fortnight from this day, and lent to the Revd Mr Sam^{ll} Miles upon his promissory note payable within six months from the Day of the date hereof.

That Inasmuch as Mr Joseph Hearne has, by Indisposition of Body, been absent from the Church for nigh two Years last past, Major Paul Mascreen be intituled to the pew next to Mr Jno Barnes's, paying for said pew twenty pounds, and reserving a place for Mr Hearne when ever he shall be able to come to Church.

That Mr Nathaniel Gifford be continued organist for the year ensuing, and be paid Forty Pounds Sallary.

March 28, 1727. Ordered that the Sexton ring the bell every Sunday morning from three Quarters after nine to ten of the clock; and in the afternoon, in the Summer, from three Qu^{rs} after two untill 3; but in the Winter from 3 Qu^{rs} after 1 till 2.

Some interesting statistics of King's Chapel and its offshoots are given from the Fulham manuscripts in a —

" List of Parishes or places where Divine Service is performed according to the rites of the Church of England." [1]

---

[1] Taken from the books of the Society for Propagating the Gospel in Foreign Parts, July 1, 1724. Prot. Episc. Hist. Soc. Coll., i.

"NEW ENGLAND. — N. B. No provision is made by Act of Assembly for the Church in this Province.

In *Boston* there are two Churches, one called *The King's Chapel*, of which the Rev. Mr. Myles is the present Minister, who is supported by the voluntary contributions of the people, the amount whereof is not known to the Society. The Rev. Mr. Harris, who is called the King's Chaplain, is afternoon preacher, for which he receives from the Crown £100 sterling, paid in England, and has one of Sir Leoline Jenkins's Fellowships at Jesus College. The Society allow nothing to this Church.

The other, called *Christ Church*, lately built. The present Minister is the Rev. Dr. Cutler; he has an allowance[1] from the Society, which, together with the voluntary contributions of the people, is a comfortable maintenance for him and his family.

Newbury. — There is no house nor glebe yet provided; but the people, by voluntary contributions, pay the minister as much or more than the Dissenting rate was for the maintenance of a Dissenting teacher; besides which he has £60 [from the Society]. The Rev. Mr. Plant present Minister.

Marblehead. — There is no house nor glebe; the voluntary contributions very precarious.[2] The Rev. Mr. Mossom, Minister."

At this time was formed the Boston Episcopal Charitable Society, whose benevolent objects are indicated by its name.[3] It was organized Easter Monday, April 6, 1724, with officers from both churches, John Jekyll being treasurer; and Mr. George Cradock, Robert Auchmuty, Esq., Mr. John Barnes, Thomas Greaves, Esq., Mr. Henry Franklyn, Mr. James Sterling, trustees; and with eighty-three members.

The seal of the society figured "an indigent and wounded man, and a person, representing the Good Samaritan, pouring wine and oil into his wounds, with the motto, " Dare quam accipere; " and the constitution read: —

"We are seldom without real Objects of Charity belonging to that truly Apostolick Church of England in which this great duty is so earnestly recommended, and in which it is so much practised."

Mr. Myles wrote June 1, 1724, that the clergy here "yet never had any convention or visitation in any place," but perhaps at the Bishop's suggestion, and probably stimulated by the returning missionaries, the Episcopal clergy seem as early as at

---

[1] £60. 0. 0 allowance from the Society, sterling.

[2] £60. 0. 0 [from the Society; Voluntary contributions]. About £20 per annum — New England money.

[3] See "An Historical Memoir of the Boston Episcopal Charitable Society," by Isaac Boyle, D.D. Boston: 1840.

this period to have begun the custom of assembling occasionally for mutual advice and sympathy, and took advantage of this opportunity again to urge the necessity of a resident bishop upon the home authorities: [1] —

<blockquote>
NEWPORT, ON RHODE ISLAND, 21st July, 1725.

". . . We humbly conceive nothing can more effectually redress these grievances and protect us from the insults of our adversaries than an Orthodox and Loyal Bishop residing with us; and at this time are awaken'd to such a thought by the coming over of Doctor Welton, late of White Chapel, who has privately received the Episcopal character in England, and from whose influences and industry we have reason to fear very unhappy consequences on the peace of the Church and the affections of this country to our most excellent constitution and his most sacred Majesty's Person and Government. Not only those who profess themselves Churchmen long and pray for this great blessing of a worthy Bishop with us, but also multitudes of those who are well wishers to us, but are kept concealed for want hereof, and immediately appear and form many congregations too. If once this happiness were granted, this would supply us with many useful Ministers from among ourselves, whom the hazards of the seas, and sickness, and the charges of travel discourage from the service of the Church and tempt them to enlist themselves as Members or Ministers of Dissenting Congregations. Our people might receive the great benefit of Confirmation, the usefulness whereof we preach and they are deeply sensible, . . . "
</blockquote>

This was at a meeting of "the New England Clergy" at Newport, R. I., July 21, 1725, which addressed an application to the King "for his Gracious Countenance and Protection," which they begged the Bishop of London to lay before him. They also asked the Bishop to give due consideration to "the Arguments for the Necessity of a Bishop in this Country," arising from the coming over of Dr. Welton, the Nonjuring Bishop. They added: —

"All our Brethren in these Parts have been notified of our Designs to meet and the Reasons of our Assembling together, and have had sufficient time to joyn us. But (Excepting M! Myles, who was not able to undergo the Fatigue of a Journey) we can't account for the absence of Those who now don't Concur in our Representations."

This letter was signed by Messrs. Cutler, Honyman, M'Sparran, Plant, Pigot, and Johnson. Mr. Usher declined to sign it, and "abruptly left the Convention."

Messrs. Harris and Mossom, hearing later of this proceeding,

---

[1] Clergy of New England to the Secretary, in Church Docs. Mass. p. 178.

wrote to the Bishop, Dec. 7, 1725, explaining why they went not to Rhode Island: —

"It arises from a sense of humble duty and modesty that we do not expressly pray a Bishop may be fixt among us, because you and not we are the most competent judge of what will make most for the service of the Church in general, — our being at once cut off or still continued a branch of the See of London." They also objected to "the impropriety of going out of this into a Quaker Governm^t," and to the town whose minister, Mr. Honyman, had "refused the oaths when tendered to him by the Governm^t as a test of his allegiance. Moreover, Mr Checkley we heard was to be there, and the event proved us rightly informed. . . . As Your Lordship has been pleased to observe that you account him a downright Jacobite, we shall not insist how open to censure we had laid ourselves by accompanying with him, but abstracting even from this for our own Peace and Quietness sake, could we not rank or have anything to do with him. In what manner and to what degree he has broke that, only we who sadly feel it can declare; and were it not for the kindly supports and encouragem^{ts} which upon every occasion of applying (and frequent ones we have) his honor our Lieutenant Govr vouchsafes us, we should be borne down by the outrages of the party which he had made. . . . We have experienced enough from his first attempts and practices to get into holy orders, and therefore were not willing to shew anything that had the least face of encourageing those or his publickly associating with the clergy. We have hitherto . . . by our moderation wrought the doctrines and discipline of our Church into the good opinion of many of these people, and we can declare as the strictest truth, that the Church flourished and encreased under our care before these impracticable doctrines of the nullity and invalidity of their administrations were advanced; and the ground we hold, next to the blessing of God, is owing to the mild and gentle methods we pursue."[1]

But personal quarrels still embittered their relations with one another. Cutler wrote: —

"Mr. Harris is a sore mortification to us in every good design. . . . That person refused reading prayers but last Sunday for Miles, who is greatly indisposed; and this is but one out of a thousand instances of the beastliness of the man. A good-for-nothing Clergyman, one of his great abettors, is now, I hope, taking his final leave of us."[2]

---

[1] Church Docs. Mass. p. 200.

[2] To Dr. Z. Gray, Oct. 22, 1726, in Church Docs. Mass. p. 669. The allusion is to Mr. Mossom, of Marblehead, whose worthy ministry here and in Virginia was a sufficient answer to such aspersions. He wrote in 1729, proposing a change. "For my not going into the indefensible doctrine of the absolute invalidity and nullity of the Dissenters' Ordinances and others of an obnoxious tendency which had been advanced and published here by a few hot-headed Men and avowed by a party they had made, I

"The Clergy of New England" met in Boston, July 20, 1727, Dr. Cutler being the only Massachusetts man signing the letter, and wrote to the Secretary again urging the need of a bishop, the repeal of laws taxing churchmen, and their admission to a share in governing the college: —

> "The dreadful schism it is our business to disclaim them from. . . . As to Religion in general and the state of our respective Churches, it is certain that in many places, thro' the prevailing of the Gospel, there is a great reformation in life and manners; and vice and immorality, rampant heretofore, do now begin to disappear; the Lord's Day, free from former profanations, is now observed with commendable strictness, and Swearing, Drinking, and Debauchery are put under proper restraints, more from the awe of Religion than the Laws of Government: and that these things are owing to the settlement of the Church in these parts is not only with joy acknowledged by her friends, but is plainly allowed by her Enemies both in principles and morals, in their grief, envy, and united opposition to it." [1]

Dr. Cutler wrote to General Nicholson, excusing the thinness of this meeting, "encouraged and assisted by your generosity":

> "Mr Usher has a long time sided with Mr Harris against us; . . . and since Your Excellency excused us the trouble of Mr Mossom's company if he remained confederate with Mr Harris, we have presumed Your Excell'y will excuse our not calling Mr Usher for the same reason. As for Mr Plant, . . . he was notified and came to our meeting, but without any provocation from us . . . he left us and went home; and tho' we sent an express to Newbury to recall him to join with us, he could not be persuaded to return. It is with grief of heart that I observe this to Your Excellency." [2]

The imperious spirit of Dr. Cutler made itself felt in asserting the dignity of his church. He went to Scituate, in 1725,[3] to preach at the invitation of Lieutenant Damon (who was at variance with the Rev. Mr. Bourn), during Mr. Bourn's absence, taking possession of the meeting-house for the service, without the consent of any proper authority.

An account of this visit was published in the "Boston Gazette," setting forth the numbers and respectability of the audience. A counter statement, by a Scituate gentleman, appeared in the

drew upon me such a storm of uneasiness as I see no means of ever weathering; and therefore, as our Blessed Saviour has directed His Discourses, I conceive I may unblameably do — If they prosecute you in one city flee into an other." — *Church Docs.* Mass. p. 255.

[1] Church Docs. Mass. p. 224.
[2] Ibid. p. 227.
[3] See Deane's "History of Scituate," 1831, p. 45.

"Boston News-Letter," "by authority," denying that any principal inhabitants of the town had invited the Dr. hither; and asserting "that only three men of Scituate, a number of disappointed men from neighboring towns, and about forty schoolboys were present."

Dr. Cutler addressed to the Council a memorial,[1] complaining of a notice in the "'News-Letter,' No. 1170, published by authority," which said sarcastically:—

"'However, by the way, this shews the Doctor's fervent zeal and indefatigable pains to make Proselytes to ye Cause and promote Ceremonies by destroying substantials in Religion.' And desiring such reparation may be made to his Character, and protection afforded to the Church of England in this as well as all other Instances, as His Honour in his great wisdom and justice shall see fit."

On Dr. Cutler's remonstrance, the newspaper received a rebuke from the Governor and Council for presuming to meddle in the affair; being required to discontinue the words "Published By Authority" from its heading. Dr. Cutler was reported to have declared[2] "that, *ordinarily*, there was no salvation out of the communion of the Episcopal Church; and that none but an episcopally ordained minister could perform any religious offices with validity and effect." All these things made their impression.

The dispute in the Congregational churches concerning the proper mode of psalmody continued at this time to divide with Episcopacy the public attention. In some "Cases of Conscience," 1722, it was asked "Whether you do believe that singing in the worship of God ought to be done skilfully? Whether you do believe that skilfulness in singing may ordinarily be gained in the use of outward means, by the blessing of God? Whether they who purposely sing a tune different from that which is appointed by the pastor or elder to be sung, are not guilty of acting disorderly, and of taking God's name in vain, also by disturbing the order of the Sanctuary?" In 1725 was published in Boston: "An Essay to silence the Outcry that has been made in some places against regular singing, in a Sermon preached at Framingham. By the Rev. Mr. Josiah Dwight, Pastor of the Church of Christ in Woodstock. Acts xvii. 6: 'These that have turned the world upside down are come hither also.'"

---

[1] Council Records, Sept. 2, 1725.
[2] Bradford's "Life of Mayhew," p. 382. See also p. 314, *ante*.

Perhaps if the Orthodox ministers of Boston had been asked their opinion about Dr. Cutler's " becoming and inofensive manner of behaving himself to all orders and degrees of men in this place," they would not have agreed with the " members of his Majesties Chappell; " for he seems to have greatly strengthened Mr. Myles's hands (if, indeed, he did not stir him thereto) in a warfare against the Congregational churches of Boston in two controversies, which it will not be unprofitable to describe.

The first was in relation to a proposed synod of the Massachusetts churches. Under the old charter government, when Massachusetts acted and felt substantially as an independent State, the General Court had more than once authorized such an assembly of what was really the State Church. The ministers and churches assembled under these circumstances had regarded themselves as the State Church organized, and had accordingly on those occasions adopted not a few measures highly significant for the common weal.

Since the new charter of William and Mary, no such synod had been held. Meantime, the very presence and the growing power of the Church of England here were such as to alarm the " Orthodox " clergy, and, among other reasons, to turn their minds to the idea of an imposing assembly which should show that they were still the established church of Massachusetts. Accordingly, the General Convention of Ministers in May, 1725, " considering the great and visible decay of piety in the country, and the growth of many miscarriages, which we fear may have provoked the glorious Lord, in a series of various judgments, wonderfully to distress us; considering also the laudable purpose of our predecessors to recover and establish the faith and order of the gospel in the churches, and provide against what immoralities may threaten to impair them,"— petitioned Lieut.-Governor William Dummer and Council, that the General Court would call such a synod to consider [1] " What are the miscarriages whereof we have reason to think the judgment of Heaven upon us call us to be generally sensible, and what may be the most evangelical and effectual expedients to put a stop unto those or the like miscarriages?" This petition was signed by Cotton Mather in the name of the General Convention, " in hopes that it may be worthy the study of those whom God has made, and we are so happy to enjoy as, the nursing fathers of our churches." [2]

---

[1] These documents are printed in full in Church Docs. Mass. pp. 170-191.

[2] A similar synod had been authorized by the House, but not by the Council, in 1715.

The Council cordially voted in favor of the synod; but before it had been acted on in the lower branch, Dr. Cutler and Mr. Myles filed a memorial against the holding of any such synod: 1. Because the petition respected "the miscarriages of the whole body of the people" here; that is, "comprehending the Churches of England, wherein the petitioners have no right to intermeddle." 2. Because "the tenour of the Petition, which is to revive decaying Piety in conformity to the Faith and order of the Gospel," refers to the last synod held before there was any Church of England here, and therefore it seems likely that the synod, if held, would prejudice the people of the land against that church; "and we have little reason to expect that in such a synod she will be treated with that Tenderness and respect which is due to an established Church." 3. "As the Episcopal ministers in the province are equally concerned with the petitioners for the purity of faith and manners, it is disrespectful to them not to be consulted in this important affair." But even if they had been consulted, they added, it would be very improper to move in this business without the knowledge of the Bishop of London and the consent of King George, "because by Royal Authority the Colonies in America are annexed to the Diocese of London, and inasmuch as nothing can be transacted in ecclesiastical matters without the cognizance of the Bishop." The memorial was dismissed by both bodies as containing "an indecent reflection on the proceedings of this Board, with several Groundless Insinuations;" but it brought the matter to a stand-still in the House and the Council, being referred to the next General Court.

Meantime, Messrs. Cutler and Myles wrote to headquarters at London, with effect. The Lord Bishop of London wrote to the Duke of Newcastle, Aug. 21, 1725: —

"If by this clause the Ministers and people of the Church of England in the Plantations be made the established Church within the several Governments, then all the rest are only tolerated as here in England; and if so, this double ill use may be made of by permitting the Independent Ministers of New England to hold a regular Synod. The established Clergy here may think it hard to be debarred of a liberty which is indulged the Tolerated Ministers there, and the tolerated ministers here may think it equitable that their Privileges should not be less than those of their Brethren in New England."

In October, 1725, was returned a letter from the Lords Justices at Whitehall to Lieut.-Governor Dummer, reproving him sharply for not having transmitted any report of this highly important business. The letter says that the Attorney and Solicitor-General have inquired into the charter and laws of the colony, and "cannot collect that there is any regular establishment of a national or Provincial church there, so as to warrant the holding of convocations or synods of the clergy. But" even if such synods were proper, "it would be a breach of the King's prerogative in matters ecclesiastical to have them authorized by the Provincial authorities, or by any one but the King." Even the innocent purpose of the loyal subjects in New England received a rebuke. "They conceive the above-mentioned application of the said Ministers not to you alone, as representing the King's Persons, but to you and the Council and the House of Representatives, to be contempt of His Majesty's Prerogative." Accordingly, Governor Dummer was ordered to put a stop to any such remarkable proceeding as the sitting of such a pretended synod, and not even to allow them to dissolve formally, in case they had already met, "lest that might be construed to imply they had a right to assemble." This summary forbiddal of an assembly such as had heretofore been held without question, and which was felt by the most earnest Christians to be needed, was a curt sign to the New England Church of what it had lost by the abrogation of the ancient charter. Dr. Colman[1] admirably pleaded its cause: —

"The Catholick Air ... is the very Spirit of our College. ... And such it has continued, till of late a Parcel of *High-flyers* have poisoned and stagnated it by leading us into a Course of angry Controversy, which has alarmed and narrowed us, who before received the Writings and Gentlemen of the Church of *England* with the most open Reverence and Affection. And I am afraid that now the Paper-War here is a little over between some Gentlemen of the Church and others on our Part, the Alienation is like to increase by the Measures taken by Dr. C ——— and others."

He strongly stated the just rights of the New England churches: —

"And whereas it is insinuated that this Synod would have come to some Resolutions to the Prejudice of the Church of *England*, it is only Surmise, and without any Grounds, save what the Objectors may apprehend from the Principles of Nonconformity which we openly profess, and from the late Disputes which they have raised among us about Episcopacy. ... In all the Debates among the Ministers, whether this year or in years past, upon this Head of calling a Synod, I remember

[1] In a letter to Bishop Kennett, of Peterborough, Dec. 17, 1725, in Turell's "Colman," p. 136.

THE THREE CLERGYMEN. 345

not a Word that has dropt among us to give Occasion for such a Suspicion. Or if it be that our Churches are now envied the Reputation of holding Synods as in Times past by Gentlemen lately come among us, and who have been treated by us with all due Respects, they are neither courteous nor just; for it ought in Righteousness and Honour to content them that they receive all kind and brotherly Treatment from us, and enjoy their own Opinion and Persuasion with the greatest Freedom; and they ought not to use Means to grieve and trouble us among whom they are come to sojourn, and where they find a Country filled with Churches, wherein Knowledge, Devotion, and Piety flourish at least equally as in their own Communions."

But the protest was in vain. This time Dr. Cutler and Mr. Myles were victorious, and Cotton Mather must have thought with a gloomy mind how these two renegades from the old New England way had spoiled his well considered plan; but in the next battle, victory perched on the other banners.

The second controversy concerned the right of Dr. Cutler and Mr. Myles, as Boston ministers, to membership in the Board of Overseers of Harvard College. Sewall[1] testifies that Sir Edmund Andros brought Mr. Ratcliffe with him to Commencement in 1687; and that clergyman, by his orders, was seated in the pulpit with the President, who however went his way, unheeding his guest in the religious exercises of the occasion.

The act of 1642, establishing the Board of Overseers, created the "teaching elders" of Boston and five other towns members of that body. Until Mr. Ratcliffe's arrival there had been no "teaching elder" here except in the Congregational ministry, nor was any minister in any other body by this term officially recognized as such for thirty-one years after his departure for England.

In 1720, for the first time, Mr. Harris, who was personally very popular among the non-Episcopalians, was notified to attend the meetings, and for some years Mr. Myles also; but after 1722, the year when Dr. Cutler left Yale College, no such summonses were sent.[2] In 1727, May 18, Dr. Cutler applied to be notified

---

[1] See p. 72, *ante*.
[2] It is probable that Mr. Harris was summoned for a time, under the influence of Governor Shute and Lieut.-Governor Tailer, but that on Cutler's "apostasy" "a rigid inquiry into this right was determined upon," the last record of his presence at the Board being in December, 1722. (Quincy, History, etc., i. 367.) Cutler wrote in 1730: "Upon my first settlem^t in this town, anno 1723, I was cited as a Teaching Elder to sit at that Board, but some particular personal affairs hindered my attendance. At that time, there being a new episcopal church planted in this Town, and the Church lifting up her head everywhere with considerable vigour, it was look't on with jealousy and an evil eye, and it was thought proper to exclude the ministers of the Church of England from the oversight of that College, which they were as

of the meetings; but the Board voted that he was "not entitled thereunto." On June 15 the two ministers sent a written inquiry to the Overseers, to know whether they were not entitled to be present at these meetings, and how they had forfeited the title. The Overseers decided that they had not, nor ever had, such a right.[1] Thereupon Dr. Cutler and Mr. Myles memorialized the General Court, "asking redress from the Legislature for the wrongs they had sustained in being excluded, as ministers of the Church of England, from the inspection and ordering of Harvard College." They aver that "the orthodoxy of that church is questioned by no sound Protestant;" that "its members bear an equal proportion in all public charges to the support" of the college; that "its ministers are equally with any others qualified and disposed to promote the interests of religion, good literature, and good manners;" and that, by their ordination and induction into their respective churches of the town of Boston, they are fairly included within the denomination of "teaching elders," and as such, entitled to a seat at the Board of Overseers of Harvard College.

This petition was supported by another, signed by about seventy Episcopal gentlemen, claiming that the college is "the common nursery of piety and learning" to all parties in New England, and therefore should be in the charge of all; claiming, also, that both Dr. Cutler and Mr. Myles were ordained as teaching elders by the Bishop of London, and were sent to execute that function in Boston, and that their being such had never before been questioned. It is on our records that the wardens were directed to sign this petition, and to provide for half the expenses connected with it.[2]

Aug. 3, 1727. At a meeting of the Vestry at Mr. Thomas Selby's, *Voted*, That the Church Wardens be desired and empowered to sign a certain memorial to the Generall Court, in relation to the ministers of the

much concerned to make a nursery of schism as of learning."—*Church Docs.* Mass. p. 258.

The reply of the Board states that "when they were notified, it was done without the direction of the Overseers."

[1] Colonel Tailer "dissented from the Vote [of the Overseers], and has generally borne their displeasure for appearing in our just cause. . . . A Memorial from Mr. Myles is now prepared to be offered to the General Court which sits by adjournment the next week, and this will be backed by a Memorial of the Ministers and Vestrys of Rhode Island, Providence, Narraganset, the Minister of Stratford, the Vestries of Boston and Marblehead. We expect a repulse, and then the affair must be carried to England, unless we will give up the most valuable interest the Church has here."—*Church Docs.* Mass. p. 228; Cutler to Nicholson, Aug. 10, 1727.

[2] President Quincy states (History, etc. i. 368) that "it appears by the records of King's Chapel that as early as August, 1725, a memorial had been presented." These records, however, contain no reference to the subject except what is here given.

Church of England in Boston being Overseers of the Colledge att Cambridge.

Voted, That the Church wardens shall be impowerd to pay one half of the present Contingent Charge and w^t here after may arise by presenting to Effect a Certain Memorial to the Great and General Court Exhibited, asserting and maintaining of the Right of the Revd Dr Timothy Cutler and Samuel Miles, being rejected as overseers of Harvard Colledge, according to the Original Establishment.

That Thomas Lechmere, John Reed, and Robt Auchmuty Esq^{rs} be Committers to present the Memorial.

Does the following entry indicate that the modern practice of "lobbying" was then in use?

September 1st 1727. Att a meeting of the Ministers, Church wardens, Vestrys, and Congregations of the two Episcopal Churches in Boston, at the Kings Chappel in Boston, —

Voted, That Mr Samuel Grainger for his services done to the said Churches be paid as a Gratuity the Sum of ten Pounds; Viz. Six Pounds part thereof by the Kings Chappel, and Four Pounds Remainder thereof By Christ Church.

On the part of the Overseers, this petition was met with a rebutting answer to the General Court, which defined the words "teaching elders" to be "in this country, from the very beginning, the pastors and teachers of a complete Congregational church, — the very same which the Scriptures call by the name of bishops;[1] who have full power both of teaching and administering the sacraments, and of ruling in the said church." And that "for above fifty years after the settlement of the colony there was no minister, magistrate, or representative in the General Court, professedly of the Church of England; and for above forty years after the act constituting the College there were no other teaching elders, except those of Congregational churches then in being in the country." That "all the insinuations of the memorialists about their being teaching elders are groundless and vain, because no such denomination as 'teaching elder' can ever be found attributed to ministers of the Church of England."

To this Dr. Cutler and Mr. Myles once again replied,[2] maintaining their right on the ground: "1. That Episcopal ministers, by force of ordination, institution, and induction, are in fact proper teaching elders. 2. That these ministers were meant

---

[1] This able paper was prepared by Rev. Dr. Colman.
[2] This reply was drawn by the eminent lawyer, John Read, of King's Chapel. The papers relating to this controversy are given in Quincy's "History," etc., i. 360-374.

and intended to be included in that act, by the plain force of its terms. 3. That they have the same right now as they would have had in case they had applied for it forty years before. 4. That the liberty of individuals to form churches, under the New England ecclesiastical law, did not deny to members of the Church of England the right to have their ministers ordained by bishops, nor intended to refuse ministers so ordained the character of teaching elders." 5. That in New England the right of ordaining, etc., is vested in the body of pastors, no one of whom is any more a bishop, therefore, than one of the ministers of the Church of England, but each equally a "teaching elder."

The final result, however, where the decision rested with a body like the General Court, composed chiefly of the members of New England churches, could be only one way. Mr. Myles and Dr. Cutler were remanded to private life, so far as the Board of Overseers of Harvard College was concerned. Perhaps in remembrance of this stubborn contest the title of "Teaching Elder" has been explicitly given to the ministers of King's Chapel, in the services of their induction, since the Revolution.[1]

From all this strife Mr. Harris had held resolutely aloof, while the senior minister, although he stood by Dr. Cutler, was blamed by him when he could no longer defend himself: —

"The late Revd Mr Myles, tho' cited, never cared much for their Conversation; and by such an Aversion has given them too much an Handle for the lasting Injuries they have done us."[2]

But the former rector of Yale College did not submit without a further struggle: —

"Tho' the Overseers had the space of a quarter of a year to answer our complaint in, . . . we were not allowed the space of two days wherein to make our reply. I know no reason to be passive under such treatment."[3]

Indeed, passivity under supposed wrong was not a trait of which his worst enemy could have accused Dr. Cutler. He urged the Bishop and "the Venerable Society" to interfere in England. To the Secretary of the latter he wrote:[4] —

"We humbly presume it is much more for the public interest of Religion that there should be no Charter for the College or a new one de-

---

[1] See Vol. II.
[2] Dr. Cutler to Bishop of London, June 25, 1730, quoted in Church Docs. Mass. p. 260.
[3] Letter from Cutler, June 11, 1730, in Church Docs. Mass. p. 258.
[4] Feb. 3, 1727-28. Church Docs. Mass. p. 210.

rived immediately from the Crown, than that the Ministers of the Church of England should be debarr'd of their present claims. . . . The college . . . is now only a Battery planted against the grand designs of that worthy Body in Erecting Missions and sending Missionaries into these parts."

Notwithstanding his private sentiments about Governor Burnet, he obtained his promise of an —

"Opportunity of presenting the Case at the Board of Overseers; but His Affairs grew more and more intricate till He dyed; and I tho't it not proper to be very importunate with Him. The late Lieut.-Governor Dummer put Me off with fair promises from one time to another; but no Opportunity presented till the day that His Commission was superseded."

He did not, however, sit down patiently under the decision, but applied to the Overseers for "free liberty of such copies from" their records, as he might "think necessary to set this matter in a just and true light." This request, however, was dismissed, on the ground that the whole matter had already been maturely considered and settled both by the Overseers and the General Court. The memorialist could do nothing more except to urge the Bishop of London to "gain an Order to have all Records here relating to this affair searched, and Affidavits taken of whatever might give further light into it. If any Redress comes to the Injured Ministers and Members of this Church, it must come from that Fountain from whence all Power and Authority here is derived. In all this," however, he added, "and everything else I submit to Your Lordship's Correction," which seems to have disapproved of any further efforts of his "well-meaning Zeal."

It is a marked testimony to the character of the administration of the College, as then conducted, that Dr. Cutler writes, July 18, 1729, to Dr. Z. Gray: —

"Notwithstanding my struggles about it, I have been forced to put my son under Dissenting tuition; but I must do them the justice to say that I know not that he suffers for my sake." [1]

While this question was pending, June 11, 1727, King George

---

[1] Nichols' "Illustrations of Literature," iv. 289. Dr. Cutler had presented his diploma for a doctorate from Oxford University to the President of Harvard College, and demanded to have it recorded, in which was this offensive phrase: "Cumque nobis compertum fuerit egregium hunc virum, apud antiepiscopales nutritum, postmodum agnito errore in ecclesiæ anglicanæ sinum se recipisse, et eadem de causa, a suis multimodis contumeliis et injuriis vexatum esse." — *Bradford's Mayhew*, p. 382.

the First died. He was succeeded by his son, the second George, now thirty-four years old, and beginning a reign which was to last nearly as long, — a sovereign who "had scarcely one kingly quality except personal courage and justice," insignificant, hot-tempered, avaricious, and unfaithful to his best friend, his Queen. And the records duly note the change of rulers with decent sorrow and congratulations, which spoke the truth in their praises of Queen Caroline: —

18th August, 1727. *Voted,* That the Pulpit and Desk of the King's Chappel be put into Mourning, and also the Communion table.

From the character of the new monarch and of his counsellors there must have been small hope of obtaining an American bishop; but efforts were made.

Boston, Augt 21, 1727. Att a meeting of the Congregation of the King's Chappel in Boston, at Mr Vardy's, the Revd Mr Samuel Miles being absent through indisposition, but attended on by Mr Thomas Phillips, Mr Willm Randle, and Mr Robert Skinner, who reported that he approved of the meeting this night, and would sign such Loyall address to his Majesty as the Committee Chosen should draw up, —

Voted, That an address be drawn up accordingly, and that the Revd Mr Samuel Miles and the Revd Mr Harris, wth the Honble Coll^l Taylor, Thos Lechmere, Esqr, and Major Paul Mascarine, be a Committee to Draw up the same;

That the Church wardens do wait upon the Revd Dr Timothy, and desire that his Church may appoint a Committee to join in the drawing up the said address.

Boston, Augt 22, 1727. Att a meeting of the Committees of both Churches at Mr Verdy's for drawing up a dutifull and loyall address to his Majesty, That the Church Wardens of both Churches be aquainted that they have accordingly prepared a Draught of it, and Desire that Warning may be given to both Congregations to meet on Wednesday, the 30th of this Instant, at the King's Chappell, to hear the same read, in Order to Give their Assent for Signing.

Present,		
	The Revd Doctor CUTLER.	PAUL MASCARINE.
	The Revd Mr HARRIS.	THOMAS GREAVES.
	The Honble Coll W^M TAYLOR.	M^r SAM^{LL} WEEKS.
	THOS LECHMERE.	

To the King's most Excellent Majesty. The humble Address of the Ministers and Congregations of the Episcopall Churches in Boston, in the Massachusetts Bay, in New England.[1]

MAY IT PLEASE YOUR MAJESTY, — We, your Majesty's Dutifull and Loyall Subjects, humbly beg leave to condole with your Majesty on the

---

[1] This was written by Dr. Cutler.

Death of your Royall Father, Our late Gracious Soveraign; a Loss only to be repaired by your Majesty's happy and peaceable Accession to the throne of your Ancestors, to which you are intitled by your Vertues as well as by your Birth, it being the united Voice of all your Majesty's Loyall Subjects that the Graces and perfections which adorn your Royall Person reflect a greater Lustre upon the Crowne more than they receive from it, and the Gems in your Imperiall Diadem are not so resplendent as the shining accomplishments of our most Excellent Queen, rendered still more glorious by the beautifull prospect of your Illustrious offspring.

We are, indeed, far removed from the Center of your Majesty's Government, nevertheless, we doubt not but your propitious Influences, like the Rays of the Sun, will be extended to the utmost bounds of your large Dominions. Your Majesty's most Gracious Declaration has already filled our hearts with extraordinary Joy. We are thereby encouraged to hope for your Majesty's Protection and speciall favour to the Episcopall Churches in New England, being in their Infancy and strugling with many Difficulties; and though we are not so capable of serving your Majesty as some of our Fellow Subjects who are placed under your immediate Presence, yet in our inferiour Station We shall embrace all Opportunities of Demonstrating our hearty Zeal and unfeigned Affection for your sacred person and Government. We shall allways esteem it our principall and most Comprehensive Duty to fear God and Honour the King, Our Rightfull and lawfull Sovereign, King George the Second; and pray with the most fervent Devotion that God would be graciously pleased to grant your Majesty a long and happy Reign over us, that He would Crown you and your Royall Consort with everlasting felicity, and make you glad with the Joy of his Countenance, and grant that there never may be wanting princes of your august Family and of your faith, who may transmit the Blessings of your Majesty's Reign to After Ages.

Att a meeting of the Ministers, Church Wardens, Vestrys, and Congregations of the two Episcopal Churches in Boston, at the King's Chappel, in Boston, the 30th August, 1727, An address to his Majesty, prepared by the Committee chosen and appointed to draw up the same from the Ministers, Church wardens, Vestrys, and Congregations of the said two Churches, being read —

Voted, That the said address be accepted and signed by the said Ministers, Church Wardens, Vestrys, and Congregations.

A letter to the bishop of London being presented by ye Revd Doct^r Cutler was read and accepted.

Voted, That the said letter be signed by the Ministers, Church Wardens, and Vestrys of the said Churches in behalf of themselves and the Congregation.

Voted, That an address be made to his Majesty for a Bishop, and that the said address be sent to the Bishop of London in twelve months, and that the persons who signed the address to his Majesty shall likewise sign the address for a Bishop, unless otherwise Determined by the Bishop of London;

That the address to his Majesty be sent to Mr Thos. Sanford, Merch.^t, in London, to be by him presented to Gen^{ll} Nicholson and Govr Shute, in order to be presented to the Bishop of London, and in their absence to present the same himself; and that the Honble William Taylor, Esqr, Major Vassal, and Mr Craddock, Be the persons to forward the same.

This address was signed by two hundred and nine persons.[1] They also wrote to the Bishop of London: —

MAY IT PLEASE YOUR LORDSHIP, — The two Episcopall Congregations of this Town embrace this Opportunity to Express their unfeigned Loyalty to his present Majesty, and their most joyfull Congratulations of his Accession to the throne of his Hereditary Dominions of Great Brittain and Ireland, and we the under written do now in their Names and at their desire tender their Address to your Lord^{ps} Approbation, ambitious of the presentment of it by your hands.

It was, may it Please your Lord^p, the Inclination of several to have now presented to his Majesty our want of a Bishop Resident in these American parts, and humbly to have askd this Blessing as the first Instance of his Princely Care to us, but by others it was thought too early to be so particular. However, We have all concurred to have an Address on this Subject prepared and Signed within the Compass of twelve months, and then to tender it to his Majesty by your Lord^{ps} assistance, unless your Lord^{ps} Wisdom shall direct us better in the mean time.

We do Assure your Lord^p that no part of this motion arises from any Doubt of your Lord^{ps} great Abilities or tender Care of us, but purely from a Sence of our Unhappy Distance from your Eye. For which reasons We remain with humble Expectations of your Lord^{ps} thoughtfullness upon this Affair, and of what ever Instructions your Lord^p shall think proper for us all, and particularly for, may it please your Lordship,

Your Lord^{ps}
Most Dutifull Sons and Servants,

ESTES HATCH.	W^M RANDLE.	SAMUEL MILES.
JOB LEWIS.	SAM WEEKS.	LEONARD VASSALL.
W^M SPEAKMAN.	ROB^T SKINNER.	THO.^S SELBY.
HENRY WHITTON.	GEORGE SHORE.	THO.^S PHILLIPS.
THO.^S CREESE.	HENRY LAUGHTON.	W^M TAYLER.
GEORGE MONK.	JOHN POWELL.	THO.^S LETCHMERE.
THOMAS GREAVES.	THO AMOREY.	CYPRIAN SOUTHACK.
WILL.^M PRICE.	JOSHUA WROE.	JAMES SMITH.
JOHN JEKYLL.	TIMOTHY CUTLER.	WILL LAMBERT.
ED: MILLS.	HENRY HARRIS.	PAUL MASCARINE.
		W^M PATTEN.

[1] See the list, appended to Vol. II.

This was followed, December 12, by "The Humble Address of Several of the Clergy of New England," from Newport, to their new King, representing " the great necessity of a Bishop resident in these parts." " It reached the Board of Trade with an indorsement that 'the Bishop of London desired it might not be inserted in the Gazette.'"[1]

But these loyal assemblies which crowded the church with persons eager to sign their names to an address which might come into the King's own hands were soon succeeded by tumultuous meetings of a more discordant character. In his quest of holy orders, Checkley did not go to England till he had participated in the stormy scenes which attended the close of Mr. Myles's long pastorate.

The embittered feeling between the two parties in the Church, combining as it did political with religious differences, seems to have spread into the community. An anonymous correspondent wrote to the Duke of Newcastle from Boston, Jan. 30, 1727: " Episcopal ministers have been mobbed here, and bonfires made near their houses, mocked and insulted, and forced to keep within doors."[2]

Of this, however, the records take no note. From the "King's Chapel Ledger" we gather such entries as are of interest: —

		£	s.	d.
1719-20	Silver Money @ 12/ pr oz., or Ex? 140 p Cent.			
1721-22				
Sep! 25.	p soo much receiv'd Jos. Bissell for half a pew und' ye new Stairs y^t was Terrant's	5.	00.	00
1722-23				
Mar^h 22.	By Cash of Mary Roe for a Seat and Key in front seat in the Gallery	0.	05.	00
1724				
Apr. 15th	By ye widdow und^r ye Pulpit	1.	00.	00
1725				
Nov. 7.	By Bad Piscataqua Bills[3] Exch?	13.	00.	00
1726				
Sept! 28.	By bad Connect! Bills Exchang^d	6.	13.	00
1719-20	*Contra.*			
Feby 15.	To Ditto p^d Peregrin White Smith for a new Casement	2.	08.	00

[1] Brit. Col. Papers, quoted by Palfrey, iv. 479, who thinks it was suppressed by *Walpolean* influence.

[2] Palfrey, iv. 454. As the Duke was known to be capable of being imposed upon, there may have been exaggeration here.

[3] "Bad Bills" frequently appear "in Exchange" in these accounts.

			£ s. d.
Febʸ 20.		To Ditto pᵈ Jnº Harvey for glayzing and plumber's work p note	2. 09. 06
25.		To Ditto pᵈ Mʳ Pilot in full for building Stares, etc.	8. 11. 00
1722			
Dec. 24.		To pᵈ Benjᵃ Bagnell for mending the Dyall .	0. 15. 00
31.		To pᵈ David Kinsly for Doggs for Church spoutes	0. 18. 00
1723			
Aug. 3ᵈ		To cash pᵈ Capt James Sterling to pay yᵉ workmen for repareing yᵉ Steple. As pʳ their Accoᵗ given in (and allow'd by Cap. Sterling) reference theretoo being had May More fully Appear	80. 14. 08
1723 Novemʳ 18ᵗʰ.		To Cash pᵈ to Bury John Pike	1. 00. 00
1723-24 Janʸ 13 :		To ditto pᵈ Mʳ Hays In Full For winding up the Clock, etc.	1. 04. 00
14 :		To cash pᵈ yᵉ Glaizʳ mendᵍ as pʳ Accoᵗ . .	5. 00. 00
Marʰ 14ᵗʰ		To Cash pᵗ Thoˢ Bennit for making a new weal and hangᵍ yᵉ Bell	1. 10. 00
1726			
April 25.		To pᵈ for a Diñer to Entertain yᵉ Ministʳˢ at Mʳ Myles	25. 01. 00
June 21.		To pᵈ the Town Interest for Mʳ Myles's 320ˡᵇ to this day	1. 06. 08
1726-27		Silver Money @ 15.6 p oz., or Exchᵃ wᵗʰ London 210 p Cent.	
Augˢᵗ 21.		To Cash pᵈ Bᵃ Atkinson for a pᶜᵉ of Black Cloth for the Pulpitt.	28. 14. 00
Nov. 20.		To Dº pᵈ Baker for seiting yᵉ Congregation on Account of the Earthquake	0. 05. 00
Dec. 4ᵗʰ.		To Dº pᵈ Auchmuty, Esqʳ, on Account of the Memoriall to the Genˡˡ Court in behalf of the Revᵈ Mʳ Myles and Dʳ Cutler . .	5. 00. 00
1727-28 Jan. 1.		To Dº pᵈ Mʳ Reed on Accᵗ of the Colledge Affair for the Secretary	0. 10. 00
8.		To dº paid the Secretary more for the Memoriall for our Church and the North . . [Other payments were also made.]	1. 05. 06
March 4.		To dº paid Shores for nursing Mʳ Myles . .	3. 15. 00
1728		To Dº pᵈ Mʳ Harris p Vote of the Congregation	25. 00. 00

		£ s. d.
April 29.	To Cash p⁴ Mʳ Thomas Phillips sundrys for Mʳ Myles's Funerall, et ca as p his Acco͏ᵗˢ and rec͏ᵗˢ	106. 00. 00
	p⁴ James Gordon sundrys supply'd Mʳ Myles's Funeral	44. 06. 01
	Ditto to Jonᵃ Barnard as p his Acco͏ᵗˢ for D°	8. 00. 03
	Ditto p⁴ Henry Laughton as p Ditto . . .	11. 02. 04
May 7	To Cash p⁴ W͏ᵐ Cowell for Mʳ Wats's plate .	25. 05. 10
June 12.	p⁴ Mʳ Stoddard for Crimson damask . . .	28. 14. 00
17.	p⁴ Samᵃ Gifford's Accᵗ for the Govern͏ʳˢ Pew et ca	47. 08. 00
July 1.	To Ditto for a pʳ mourning Shoes for Baker	0. 16. 00
1728-29		
March 3.	To d° paid for Copy of Coram's Deed . .	0. 04. 00

During the later years of Mr. Myles's ministry the sums annually raised were as follows:[1] —

	£ s. d.	
1715-16	311. 01. 10½	
1716-17	267. 10. 05	
1717-18	287. 01. 10	
1718-19	291. 17. 03½	
1719-20	334. 07. 10	
1720-21	353. 00. 08	[54. 00. 00]
1721-22	276. 09. 11	[16. 00. 00]
1722-23	368. 06. 06	[3. 14. 00]
1723-24	497. 14. 02	[105. 12. 00]
1724-25	468. 08. 05	[117. 09. 06]
1725-26	523. 08. 08½	[50. 00. 00]
1726-27	646. 02. 05	[93. 03. 00][2]
1727-28	276. 18. 09	[15. 08. 00]

The Church stock was the accumulated surplus from receipts over expenditures. It was largely lent out at interest to responsible members of the church, and amounted as follows: —

	£ s. d.		£ s. d.
1719-20	70. 07. 04	1724-25 . . .	300. 13. 07
1720-21	18. 19. 03	1725-26 . . .	454. 11. 01½
1721-22	38. 05. 09	1726-27 . . .	657. 11. 04½
1723-24	121. 09. 02	1727-28 . . .	650. 00. 00

[1] The amounts of receipts from contributions and benevolences in previous years are given at p. 124. In the years 1720-28 a considerable sum from sale or rent of pews is included in these receipts, and is here indicated thus [ ].

[2] This year's receipts also include £80 from Mr. Myles in repayment.

The only regular expenses of the church were for the salaries of the minister, clerk, sexton (whose chief duty was that of "looking after the boys"), and organist, and for "washing the surplices." In those stalwart days the only fuel used in church was such warmth as parishioners brought with them. The weekly payments for minister and clerk are as follows: —

		£	s.	d.
1720.	"Miles and Hays"	3.	16.	00
1721.	„ „ „	3.	17.	00
1722.	"Miles, Harris, and Hays"	4.	07.	00
1723–24.	"Miles and Hays"	4.	07.	00
1725.	"Miles and Baker"	3.	08.	00
1726.	„ „ „	4.	08.	00
1727.	„ „ „	5.	08.	00

The story of this period is largely spread out on the records. March 28, 1727, the Vestry —

Voted, That the Paper, relating to the Security of the Church Stock, laid before the Vestry by Dr. George Stewart, be referr'd to the Consideration of the Congregation on monday in Easter Week.

At that meeting: —

BOSTON, April 4.th 1727. *Voted*, That the Minister, Church wardens, and Vestry be impowred to manage the Affaires of the Church for the Year ensuing.

Voted, That Church Wardens for the time being provide a good strong Box with 3 different Locks and Keys, — One of which shall be kept by the Eldest Church Warden; another Key by the other Church Warden for the time being; and the third Key by such Proper person as the Congregation shall apoint, And that the Box containing the Church money shall be Lodged at the Ministers house.

Voted, That Mr Job Lewis be the third person to keep the third key for the year ensuing.

Voted, That the said Church Wardens and s[d] Mr Job Lewis shall meet at the place where the said box is kept on the first Monday in every Month, and make fair Entries in the book, and put into the said strong box such monies as shall be in the eldest Church Wardens hands, and do all other business relating to the stock which is never managed only by the eldest Church Warden, except paying the Weekly Salaries and mending the Windows; And that no sum of money shall be put out to Interest without the Consent of two of the key keepers at least; And in Case any one of the key keepers should want any money upon Interest with Good Security, he shall have the approbation of the other two; And that no person shall have any Sume exceeding one hundred pounds without Land Security.

June 26, 1727. *Voted*, That the Church Wardens pay unto his Honour the Lieu^t-Governour the Sum of twenty-four Pounds for one Years Interest of four hundred pounds ending ye 20th Instant due from the Reverend Mr Samuel Myles.

In the summer of 1727, his increasing illness rendered Mr. Myles unable to discharge his duties at the church, where his portion of the services was performed by a Mr. Watts. This gentleman probably represented him at the funeral of his ancient warden, the father of the controversialist of the First Church, where Sewall also notes that the jarring clergymen walked meekly together: —

"Jan. 4, 1727-28. Col. Francis Foxcroft was inter'd at Cambridge. . . . Dr. Tim Cutler, Mr. Harris, and another Minister went before the Corps; but Mr. Harris read the Office."

As his illness became more serious, the dissensions of his people forced themselves upon the minister: —

"Mr Myles being confined to his house by sickness, he is continually beseiged by that turbulent person Checkley and his adherents, who, tho' they dont exceed ten in number, yet have the confidence to attempt in a clandestine way the supplying Mr Myles's place before his decease. The greatest part of the congregation are not concerned in this irregular proceeding."[1]

Mr. Myles, however, was soon to be called where these strifes, whether for the success of his church or within it, would seem a very small matter to him. Already when the closing steps were taken in the controversy for seats in the body of Overseers of the College, he was a very sick man, and he wrote the following touching letter: —

To the Parishoners of the Kings Chappel at Boston in New England:

GENTLEMEN, — Inasmuch as I am at present in a very low and languishing Condition, and God only knows when I shall recover my health So as to be able to performe the Duties of my Holy Function, I therefore most earnestly Entreat you Speedily to find out some method to procure me a Curate from England, who may Come over as soon as may be. And in so doing you will oblige your (very weak and afflicted but) Faithfull Friend,

SAMUEL MYLES.

BOSTON, N: ENGLAND, Feb^{ry} 2^d 1727-28.

[1] Mr. Harris to the Lord Bishop of London, Boston, Jan. 26, 1727-28, in Church Docs. Mass. p. 245.

Att a Meeting of the Congregation of the Church called Kings Chappel, at Boston in New Eng^d Feby 6, 1727–28, Summon'd by the Reverend Mr Samuel Myles, to send to England for a Curate, Mr Thomas Phillips, Church Warden, having refused to —

1. Enter a vote put up by himself, Viz., Whether the Congregation proceed to Business or not ? which was Carried in the Affirmative by a very great Majority, and then Absenting himself together with the Revd Mr Henry Harris and some others, and Carrying away with him the Church Books, —

The Congregation then proceeded to Business and passed the following Votes, Nemine Contradicente : —

2. That John Jekyll Esqr. be Moderator.
3. That John Gibbins Enter the Votes of this Congregation.
4. That the Revd Mr Sam^{ll} Miles be provided with a Curate according to his Desire.
5. That Gen^{ll} Nicholson and Mr Thomas Sanford, Merch^t in London, be the Persons to whom Application shall be made, or in the Absence of one of them the other be the Person to whom we shall make Application, to procure such a Person, well affected to his Sacred Majesty King George the Second, and the Protestant Succession in his Illustrious Family, and a Sincere Friend to the Church of England as by Law Established.
6. To allow the said Curate for a Salary one Hundred Pounds Sterling p annum, to be paid here, at the Difference of Exchange, and Twenty pounds Sterling to pay his Passage hither.
7. To Encourage some Gentleman Qualified as above, and whose Ability of Performing Divine Service and preaching, as well as Morals, shall Recommend him ; that he shall Succeed the Revd Mr Samuel Myles in this Church, upon the Decease of the Revd Mr Myles.
8. That there be a Committee of five Persons to write to Genl Nicholson and Mr Thos Sandford, Merchant in London, to procure a Person to Come over here Qualified as above.

9. That John Jekyl, Esqr.
Mr George Craddock.
Mr John Eastwicke.
Mr John Barnes.
Mr John Checkley. } are Voted to be ye Comittee.

10. That Mr Thos Phillips, Church Warden, take possesion of the Church Stock, and the Keys of ye Church in Case of the Death of Mr Sam^{ll} Myles, and keep the same till further Order from the Congregation.
11. That the Comittee wait on the rev^d Mr Sam^{ll} Myles, and acquaint Him with Our Proceedings at this Meeting.

A list of ninety-seven names is appended as " Present " with the following note : —

The above Votes are what was passed by the Congregation in King's Chapel; and the above names are those I took down in the said Church at the Request of the Congregation.

JOHN GIBBINS, Scrib. pr° Tempore.

Altho' We, the Subscribers, Members of King's-Chapel, were not present at the passing all the above Votes, yet in Testimony of our Approbation of them We hereunto Sign our Names. [Signed by thirty-nine persons.]

Whereas I was desired to go to the Revd Mr Henry Harris's House to Sign a Paper, which I did thro' Inadvertency, tho' I neither read nor was it read to me; and Since having carefully perused the Votes of the Congregation, in Testimony of my Approbation of them I here Sign my Name.

THOMAS COLLE.

The above is duly recorded by the scribe *pro tempore* to be "a true Copy from the Original in my Hands."

Mr. Myles died in the beginning of March, regretted and beloved by his people, who gave him a costly funeral, and recognized that he had served them faithfully and long, though hardly peaceably in his relations with his assistants, or with the other Christian Churches of Boston. But even while Mr. Myles was waiting for his burial, the flame burst out again: —

Whereas, a vote was passed by the Congregation of the King's Chappel, in Boston, in Easter week last, impowring the Minister (Viz^t, the Revd Mr Sam^{ll} Myles), Church Wardens, and Vestry of said Church to transact the affaires of the Church for the year ensuing, or words to this purpose; and inasmuch as one of the Church wardens (Viz^t, Mr Thos Selby) is since dead, and the Revd Sam^{ll} Mr Myles the Minister being Dead also; And being informed that Thos Baker the Sexton has warned those Persons who were chosen Vestrymen last Easter to meet as a Vestry at Mr Luke Verdy's on Monday, the fourth Instant, at a Eleven a Clock in the forenoon, —

We, therefore, whose Names are under written, Members of said Congregation, do Protest against all and Everything that hath been done Since the Death of the Reverend Mr Samuel Myles, our late Minister, By those Persons chosen last year Vestrymen, or shall hereafter be done by them as a Vestry, they not being that Compleat Organized Body to whom the Power of Transacting the affaires of the Church was devolved by the above recited Vote, March 2^d, 1727-28.

To this were appended one hundred and three names.[1]

[1] From these lists of names we can gather a partial roll of members of King's Chapel at this period. See the list, appended to Vol. II.

Att a meeting of the Vestry of the Kings Chappell in Boston at the Royall Exchange on the fourth day of March, Anno Dm! 1727-28.

Present :[1]

The Reverend Mr Henry Harris, President.

Mr Thomas Phillips,* Sole Church Warden.

The Honble William Tayler, Esq.   Mr James Smith.*
John Jekyll, Esq.   Thomas Lechmere, Esq.
Capt.ⁿ Cyprian Southwaike.*   Maj.^r Paul Masquerine.*
Mr John Powell.*   Mr Job Lewis.*
Coll.ⁿ Estes Hatch.*   William Lambert, Esqr*
Mr George Shore.*   John Read, Esq.^{rs}*

    Mr William Speakman, Non Consenting.
    Mr Robert Skinner, Non Consenting.
    Mr John Cheeckley, Non Consenting.
    Mr Joshua Wroe.
    Mr William Randall, Non Consenting.
    Mr Edward Mills.*
    Mr Thomas Amory.*
    Mr Thomas Creese, Junr,* Non Consenting.

Voted, Being met together at the Place above written, It was put to vote whether It was a Vestry legally met ; it passed in the Affirmative by a great Majority, Every Body Consenting Except five Persons whose Non Consent is above written over against their respective Names.

Voted, That Notice be given to the Congregation to meet at the Kings Chappel to Morrow at Eleven of the Clock, in order to Consult what may be proper in Relation to the Funerall of the Rever.^d Mr Samuel Miles, Dec^d, and upon no other business ; and Also that Notice be given on Sunday next y^t ye Congregation meet on the Wednesday following at the Kings Chappel at three of the Clock, p. m.

A true copy of a paper deliver'd to Rob! Kenton, Clerk of the Kings Chappel in Boston, by the Revd Mr Samuel Miles to be read in the said Chappel : —

"The Congregation are desired to meet here at three of the Clock in the afternoon next tuesday, to Consult proper methods of procureing a Curate from England for the Revd Mr Sam^{ll} Miles.

"SAMUEL MYLES.

"BOSTON, N: ENGLAND, Feb. 4, 1727-28."

BOSTON, March 5th, 1727-28. Att a Meeting of the Congregation at the Kings Chappell in Boston, in Order to Consult what may be proper in Relation to the Funerall of the Rever^d Mr Samuel Miles dec'd,—

---

[1] At this meeting every member of the Vestry chosen at Easter, 1727, was present, except Mr. Thomas Selby, warden, who had died. At the next Easter meeting, March, 1728, the number of vestrymen was reduced to fifteen, those indicated thus * being dropped, and re- placed by Messrs. James Stevens, George Craddock, John Barnes, Francis Brinley, John Gibbins, Samuel Bannister, George Steward, Benjamin Walker, and by John Eastwicke and William Randall as wardens,—a victory for Checkley's party.

Voted, That there be a Committee [of five] chosen to Consider for the said Service.

Voted, That the Charges arising upon the said Funerall be left to the discretion of said Committee.

Voted, That the said Charges be paid out of the Church Stock.

The meeting then adjourned until after the funeral.

Mr. Myles was the first Episcopal clergyman of New England education, and, it is probable also, of New England birth. He had seen the nursling church, which when he took it in charge was drooping from the sudden loss of its official supporters, gain steadily by a natural and healthy growth, till it saw offshoots from it in three other towns of Massachusetts, besides a vigorous one in Boston. He had won for it the favor of King William and Queen Mary; had brought home their noble gifts to it, and saw a perpetual witness of the royal favor to it in the Lecturer whom the royal bounty placed by his side. At the time of his difficulties with Mr. Bridge, he seems to have felt insecure in his tenure of his parish, whose favor to the "Lecturer" was strongly shown by their recommendation of the latter to the Bishop in 1703.[1] The minister's own character then received, perhaps in rebuttal of this, a strong endorsement from what may be called his supplementary parish at Braintree:[2] —

"We most humbly pray the continuance of your Lordship's Favour and kindness unto the Revd Saml Myles, . . . he having been zealous and constant to the Church in the worst of times. His conversation is blameless, so as that the Enemies of the Church cannot reproach him; he hath demeaned himself worthy of his Sacred Function, and hath been very serviceable and industrious in the work he hath been called to."

But after this cloud had passed over he seems to have kept his hold on his people, and to have been busy in the duties of his place, and treated with deference. As in some sort the head of the clergy here, he was desired, in 1724, to answer the questions propounded by Bishop Gibson to the persons who were his predecessor's commissaries. One religious usage which he kept faithfully was later discontinued. In 1747 Governor Shirley wrote : —

"I am inform'd that Mr Miles, the first Episcopal Minister here, did in the beginning of the Church (and I think all his time) Keep up a

---

[1] See p. 160, *ante*.
[2] The Church-wardens and Vestrymen of the church in Braintree to the Bishop of London, April 22, 1704, in Church Docs. Mass. p. 221.

monthly Lecture in the King's Chappel, every Wensday before Sacrament Sunday. How it came to be dropt I can't learn."[1]

"With the exception of his voyage to England, and occasional services rendered to the church at Marblehead," says Greenwood,[2] "he officiated constantly at the Chapel from its opening till within a few months of his decease, — a period of nearly forty years. To judge from the steady increase of his congregation, he must have been a worthy and pious man and an acceptable preacher. His successful mission to England shows him to have been prudent and energetic. He certainly was not very happy with either of his assistants, but the nature of the relation between them sufficiently accounts for this; and though he may have committed no aggression or wrong, he probably maintained all his rights. He lived peaceably and usefully with his congregation, much of whose prosperity was owing to his exertions, and which continued to flourish without intermission under his equable care till he was called, as we may trust, to higher services in a holier temple."

That Mr. Myles was a man of power is shown by the fact that he held his own as a preacher and as a man in a community which knew how to estimate both aright, and where he was surrounded by men of mark in the pulpits of the town. He had come as a very young man to stand by the side of strong men, the representative of the system which they hated; and, outliving them, he was now surrounded by their successors. Dr. Increase Mather and his learned son had been the steady voice of the old faith and ways of New England, at every step of his church lifting up a clarion note of warning. They had outlived the other opponents of Andros; but had died, the father in 1723, and the son in 1728. Colman had begun at Brattle Street almost simultaneously with Myles, — like him in representing ideas which the dominant hierarchy feared, and in a long and wearing opposition; but had won his way to the recognized headship of the Congregational churches, and to a friendship with the heads of the more liberal section of the English Church in England itself.[3]

---

[1] Church Docs. Mass. p. 411.
[2] History, p. 87.
[3] One element in the growth of the church, may have been Mr. Myles's pastoral devotion. There are indications that a very lax standard prevailed in the Congregational churches.

Dr. Colman, in his ordination sermon for Mr. William Cooper, his colleague at Brattle Street, says: "I have already led you through the greatest part of the congregation, but am sensible we have missed many, some of whom we know not where their habitations are, and should be glad to learn them, that we may do our duty to them also." Dr. Col-

Every other Congregational minister in Boston, except Colman, was Mr. Myles's junior by twenty years or more. Their ministries were to run along beside that of his successors, and they were to maintain the high character of the Boston clergy through the time of Whitefield. At the First Church was the Rev. Thomas Foxcroft, son of the early warden of King's Chapel, and himself a strong opponent of Episcopacy; ordained 1717. No minister is said to have been more universally admired. He published an apology for Whitefield in 1745. He died 1769, aged seventy-two. There were also the Rev. Samuel Checkley, first minister of the New South Church: he died 1769, in the fifty-first year of his ministry, aged seventy-three. The Rev. Joshua Gee, colleague of Cotton Mather, 1723, possessed a strong and penetrating mind, but "preferred talking with his friends to everything else." He died 1748, aged fifty. The Rev. John Webb, ordained first minister of the New North, 1714, died 1750, aged sixty-two. His colleague pronounced him "one of the best of Christians and one of the best of ministers." The same company included the Rev. Joseph Sewall, D.D., son of Judge Sewall, ordained at the Old South 1713, died 1769, aged eighty; Rev. William Welsteed at the New Brick, 1728-1753; and the Rev. William Cooper, colleague of Dr. Colman, 1716, who died 1743, four years before that eminent man.[1]

As we read the record of controversies whose very ashes are bitter, it may seem that there could have been no friendly bond between Mr. Myles and these worthy and able advocates of another cause. It is probable, certainly, that the feud between

---

man also extols Cooper in his funeral sermon, as knowing "where to find the poor and sick of the flock, when they sent their notes." Cotton Mather is commended by his biographer for thinking it "his duty to visit the families belonging to his church; taking *one* or sometimes *two* afternoons in a week for that purpose." Nor was it the length of his visits that prevented their greater frequency; for "he could seldom despatch more than *four* or *five* families in an afternoon, and looked on this work as laborious as any in all his ministry." See the note on p. 41 of Dr. Palfrey's "Sermon preached to the church in Brattle Square, July 18, 1824. Boston, 1825."

[1] The formation of new churches on differences of doctrine, or of ecclesiastical practice, had ceased with the church in Brattle Square, being probably checked by the presence of the Church of England. The later Congregational churches arose partly from social discords or grievances, and partly from convenience. The "New North" had been founded in 1714 by "substantial mechanics," who withdrew, not without mutual heart-burnings, from Dr. Mather's parish. In 1720 a dispute in it concerning settling a colleague with Mr. Webb, caused the secession of some of its members and the formation of the "New Brick" church. This was reunited to the "Old North" in 1775. The "New North" ceased to exist in 1869. Its communion plate was subsequently given to King's Chapel. (See Vol. II.) The "New South" had a more peaceful origin in 1716, in the need of accommodating people at the South End.

their church systems hindered him from a free intercourse with them, which would have been only wholesome and catholic; but in the little town of 18,000 inhabitants, where men met daily in the street for twenty years, they cannot always have remained in a state of armed truce.[1] It would have been well for all if they could have found a ground of real brotherhood during life; it was something that they could bury the old animosities in Mr. Myles's grave.

Rev. William Cooper recorded in his interleaved almanac:

"1728, Feb. 19. Dr. [Cotton] Mather buried. I was one of the bearers. Mar. 8, At the funeral of the Rev. Mr Miles."

The Register of Burials of King's Chapel contains the following: —

March 1, 1727-28. Revd Samuel Myles, Minister of King's Chapel. Cœtera desiderantur usq^e ad Annum 1738.

The foregoing faithfully transcribed from the Register of the Revd Samuel Myles.

The "Weekly Journal" recorded: —

"On Friday, March 8th, he was buried with great ceremony. He was the oldest Episcopal minister of the town. The Rev. Mr. Hunneyman of Rhode Island, Mr. Plant of Newbury, Mr. Piggot of Marblehead, Mr. McSparran of Narraganset, Mr. Miller of Braintree, and Mr. Watts were pall-bearers; the Rev. Dr. Cutler led the Widow; the Rev. Mr. Harris walked before the corpse, and buried it. The corpse was also followed by his Honour the Lt.-Governour, and Council, the Justices, and the Dissenting Ministers of the Town, together with a vast number of gentlemen, merchants, etc."[2]

Considering the length of his ministry and his prominent

---

[1] "I speak it knowingly, that the Ministers of the Gospel in those Provinces which go by the name of *New England*, sent and supported at the Expence of this Society, have by their Sobriety of Manners, discreet Behaviour, and a competent Degree of useful Knowledge, shewn themselves worthy the Choice of those who sent them, and particularly in living on a more friendly Foot with their Brethren of the Separation, who, on their Part, are very much come off that Narrowness of Spirit which formerly kept them at such an unamicable Distance from us. And as there is reason to apprehend that Part of *America* could not have been thus distinguished and provided with such a Number of proper Persons, if one half of them had not been supplied out of the dissenting Seminaries of the Country, who, in Proportion as they attain to more liberal Improvements of Learning, are observed to quit their Prejudice towards an Episcopal Church." — *Dean Berkeley's Sermon before the Society for Propagating the Gospel in Foreign Parts*, 1731, p. 21.

[2] "N. E. Weekly Journal," March 11, 1728.

position as the eldest clergyman of the Church of England in these remote parts, it is strange that so few personal traits of Mr. Myles survive to us. While his contemporaries among the Congregational clergy stand forth in vivid outline against the background of their time, he remains a dim and shadowy figure. This is partly due to his abstinence from print, and in part, probably, to his rigid attitude of non-intercourse with his Christian neighbors outside his own communion, which was still in some degree like a foreign colony in an unfriendly community. Such traces of him as we succeed in gleaning portray a man of character and force, devoted to his Church principles; the first graduate of the College to take such open ground against its ecclesiastical basis, and not unlike most converts in an acrid spirit against the Church which he had left. Generous in favoring the formation of Christ Church from his own parish, and in his welcome to Dr. Cutler, he seems to have avoided quarrels with his own people; but the bitter discords which separated him and his two assistants can hardly have been wholly due to the fault of both Mr. Bridge and Mr. Harris. Under all the ashes of more than a century and a half still glow the coals of his hot temper. Of his domestic life almost nothing remains. It was childless, and his will seems to indicate a lack of implicit confidence that his wife of thirty years would always remain his widow. One miniature of them both is etched with a mordant pen by Captain Thomas Coram, who confesses that he liked Mr. Bridge better than the senior minister: [1] —

"There happened about this time an unhappy difference, hurtful to the Church, and prevented many from coming to it. The said Mr Bridge was a sober man, well esteemed, and had married a sober, virtuous, and well-bred young Lady out of one of the best families in that Country, at which the Church were highly pleased, and made her a handsome present of Plate. At which Mrs Miles, the other Minister's Wife, who was not so well respected, was filled with resentment, and she incensed her husband, who was a very fiery man, against Mr Bridge, who came soon after for England for a short time; and then Mr Miles, by his influence with Mr Hall, Sec.^y to Bishop Compton, prevailed with his Lordship to order Mr Bridge to remove from Boston, first to one place, then to another, in some remote parts of the Country, where he and, I think, his Wife died."

[1] Church Docs. Mass. p. 344. In a letter to the Secretary, in 1740, complaining of the course of the Vestry in regard to his gift of land at Taunton, already described (see p. 183, *ante*), Captain Coram attributes their neglect to the fact that he "lodged the deed in the hand of Mr. Bridge," for which reason "Mr. Miles disrespected the said deed of Gift, and prevented the Vestry from taking any notice of it."

That Mr. Myles was a sincere, religious-minded Christian, despite such natural infirmities, is testified by the respect amid which his life closed. Such a spirit seems to breathe in the devout phrases with which his will begins, after the pious usage of the time, — words which, though often formal, doubtless express the essence of the teaching and faith of his long ministry: —

"In the Name of God, Amen! I, Samuel Myles, an unworthy Minister of Jesus Christ and of the King's Chappel in Boston, New England, being very Infirm and weak in body, but, thrô the Goodness of God, of perfect mind and Understanding, do make and ordain this my Last Will and Testament, Revoking all other Wills whatsoever, In manner and form following: Imp^{ris} I Comit my Soul into the hands of God my ffaithful Creator and Merciful Father, which I beseech him mercifully to Look upon, not as it is of it self, infinitely polluted with Sin, but as it is Redeemed and purged with the blood of his only beloved Son and my dear Saviour Jesus Christ, In Confidence of whose merits and mediation alone it is that I Cast myself upon the mercy of God for the pardon of all my Sins and hopes of Eternal Life. As for my Corruptible body, I bequeath it to the Earth whence it was taken, to be decently buried the Third day after my decease, from whence I hope, thrô the mercy of God and merit of my Saviour, to find a Glorious Resurrection at the next Personal Apearance of our Lord Jesus Christ. Item: I Will and ordain That all my Debts y^t I Justly owe to any be paid in Convenient time by my Exec$^{rs.}$ hereafter mentioned. Item: I Give and Bequeath to Ann my Wife, formerly Relict to the Revd Mr Joseph Danzy, all my Plate, Books, Wearing Apparel, Household Goods, of what sort soever; also Two hundred pounds in money, imediately to be paid after my decease; also my Negro man Amboy, and the Rent of my House wherein I now dwell untill it be sold, which my Will is should be sold as soon as may be; and after the Sale of the said House, my Will is that she have the use of Eight Hundred pounds during her natural Life, or untill she marry; and after her decease or Marriage, the said Eight Hundred pounds and all my other Estate to be Equally divided among the Children of my Nephew, John Myles, and my neices Sarah Price and Ann Creese, or their heirs. Item: I Give and bequeath all my Lands and Tenements in South Wales and Carmarthen Shire unto the Children of my two Sisters, Margaret and Katharine, in South Wales, to be Equally divided amongst them or their Heirs. Item: I Give and Bequeath unto the Poor of my Church Ten pounds. Item: I Give and Bequeath to Thomas Palmer, the boy whom I brought up, Fifteen pounds to be paid unto him upon the Expiration of his Apprenticeship. Item: I Nominate and Apoint my Wife Ann, the Revd Dr Timothy Cutler, William Price, and Thomas Creese, Junr, Executors of this my Last Will and Testament. In Witness whereof, I have hereunto affixed my hand

and Seal, this Tenth day of February, Annoq Domini One Thousand Seven hundred and Twenty-Seven–Eight.[1]

SAMUEL MYLES (and seal)."

Geo. Oxenden, }
Martin Brimmer, } *Witnesses.*
James Baker, }

It is sad to relate that the quarrel in the church itself was hardly hushed long enough for those sacred and solemn offices to be rendered to the beloved and honored minister. "The Church at Boston," wrote Mr. Johnson to the Secretary, "has lost a very worthy pastor in Mr. Myles; and I doubt they will break into sad confusion there, unless a very worthy and discreet minister be sent them from England, for I am told above five to one are so greatly disgusted with Mr. Harris that they will never be content under his ministry."[2]

It may occasion some surprise that Mr. Harris should have been anxious to succeed Mr. Myles as rector of the church. The difference of salary was not great, and there would seem to have been more independence and a peculiar dignity in the position which he already held, where he was amenable only to the Bishop of London. But there must have been practical annoyances in the relation to another, in which he was

---

[1] This will (as others hereafter referred to) is on file in the Suffolk Records. The estate in Wales here bequeathed to Mr. Myles's sisters was probably inherited from his father, a native of that country. The inventory, Aug. 30, 1731, mentions : —

	£ s. d.
Cash Rec'd of M'. George Craddock for the House	1,925. 00. 00
Cash Rec'd M'. Brooks	118. 16. 00
Cash Rec'd of M'. Henry Laughton	5. 00. 00
Cash in the House rec'd of Madam Ann Myles	87. 01. 10
Ten pounds Sterling Rec'd from the Hon'ble Society for Propagation of the Gospel, at 250 p C!	35. 00. 00
Cash Rec'd of Mad'm Anne Myles, Deceased	70. 00. 00
	£2,240. 17. 10

The account of the bequests to relatives is as follows:—

	£ s. d.
To Cash p'd M'. Tho' Creese his part	449. 13. 02
To cash p'd M'. Tho' Creese, being one half p'. of the Portion of John Myles Children, viz!	224. 16. 07
To Cash p'd M'. W'm Price his Part	449. 13. 02
To D° p'! s'd Price the other half of Jn° Myles Children's Portion	224. 16. 07

Mrs. Myles did not long survive her husband. Her will, dated May 1, 1731, divides "all my household Linnen" equally between Sarah Price and Ann Creese, and bequeathes £380, "deducing my Funeral Charges," to be divided equally between them; and "in Case the s'd Sarah Price shall die without Issue, Male or female," then the said sum to return immediately to the children of Ann Creese, to be divided equally. To Mrs. Creese she left all her household goods, with her wearing apparel; to her godson Thomas Creese, her silver Tankard and the remainder of her Plate; and to her goddaughter, Anne Creese, £200.

[2] Stratford, April 2, 1728, Church Docs. Conn. i. 127.

really a subordinate, and knew that he was so regarded by the rector and his congregation; and here is probably the explanation.

The rest of the painful story is best told in the words of contemporary letters and records. A remonstrance was sent to the Bishop of London "by the most considerable Gentlemen belonging to the King's Chappel," against "the designs that Mr Checkley and his adherents were forming against the peace of the Church," which Mr. Harris followed, Feb. 16, 1727–28, with a letter:[1] —

"I am sorry that Dr Cutler has given me fresh occasion to complain of injurious treatment, he being not only active in prejudicing the minds of my constant hearers, but also encouraging many of the members of his church to vote in the King's Chapel, which they had no manner of right to do. However, notwithstanding all the efforts that he and his friend Checkley could make, the best part of the congregation which is committed to my care, jointly with Mr Myles, strenuously opposed their unjust designs, and were superior not only in interest but in number, if the members of Dr Cutler's Church be excepted, together with several seamen and officers' servants belonging to the man-of-war which is the stationship for this province. There has not been any outrage of this kind committed here since Bishop Compton, of blessed memory, reprimanded Capt. Stukely for meddling in the difference betwixt Mr Myles and Mr Bridge, about 24 years ago. . . . I have indeed industriously avoided all quarrels, though Dr Cutler and his party are for repeating old differences, which, if they were thoroughly examined, could derive no honour to persons who were proved in the face of the whole country to be turbulent, seditious, and disaffected to the present happy constitution. . . . My enemies, indeed, represent me as not sufficiently zealous for the Church; but if they mean the Church of England as by Law established, they can't be guilty of a greater falsehood. And if your Lordship were here present, I doubt not you would be fully convinced of the great baseness and iniquity of those who load me with vile aspersions, which they themselves know to be false, and which were never cast upon me till I made a stand against the pernicious doctrines which were published here in certain Jacobite books and Libels; but that my zeal for the Governm^t is not inconsistant with my affection to the Church will, I hope, be very evident from the petition humbly offered to your Lordship on my behalf by the prinicipal members of our own Church. It is not wealth or power that I contend for, — my present Pension from the crown, which is the only allowance I have for my service here, being pretty nearly equal to, or

[1] Church Docs. Mass. p. 246. Dr. Colman wrote to the Bishop of London at this time, in warm praise of Mr. Harris, and expressing the hope of the non-episcopal people that he might be appointed to succeed Mr. Myles. Church Docs. Mass. p. 249.

at least contenting me as well as, the Contributions of the people allowed to M.̱ Myles for his service : but it is the earnest desire of persons of the greatest worth and honour in our Church that after M.̱ Myles's death I should be appointed the first minister of the King's Chappel in the place ; and it would be a real grief to them, as well as a prejudice to the Church, should it be governed, as it has been of late, by the counsels and maxims of the disaffected party. This will be prevented if your Lordship pleases to grant the petition of the above mentioned Gentlemen on my behalf, which may be done, either if I retain my present pension, or if I accept the Contributions of the people, supposing that they may be allowed me after M.ʳ Myles's death by the major part of the Congregation when they are regularly convened. I have no thoughts of calling them together till Gov.ʳ Burnet's arrival, here being no Magistrate of our Communion invested with authority to repress the insolence of the mob who lately committed great disorders in the Church. I am unwilling to apply to the L.ᵗ Gov.ʳ or the Justices, who are Dissenters, lest my enemies except against that as an extraordinary method of Proceeding. I hope your Lordship will bear with me if I obviate any objection made by some people who insinuate that I intend to engross the whole church to myself; but your Lordship will perceive by the remonstrance that I have no such intention; and I beg leave to assure your Lordship that I will come into any measures which shall appear just and reasonable when Gov.ʳ Burnet arrives, and matters can be calmly and maturely debated. In the mean time I humbly presume it is reasonable that as M.ʳ Myles rec.ᵈ the pension from the crown as well as the Contributions of the people for some time after M.ʳ Bridge, my immediate predecessor, left this church, and before I was appointed to succeed him, so I ought to be allowed the contributions of the people, as well as my salary from home, during the vacancy of the church ; but if I receive nothing upon this account, I shall make myself easy, and enter into no disputes about it."

But the question was soon closed.

At a meeting of the Congregation of the Kings Chappel in Boston, Wednesday the 13 of March 1727-28 by adjournement, —

The Question was put Whether the Rev.ᵈ M.ʳ Henry Harris has a right to joyn with the Congregation in Church affaires as the Minister of the Kings Chappell for the time being.

Then It was proposed Whether the Question as above written should be put to Vote or not : It passed in the Negative.

The Question was put Whether the Chusing of a Minister should be deferred till Governour Burnett comes or not : It passed that it should not be deferred.

1. If it be your Minds That proper Methods be taken to procure a Clergyman from England well affected to his Sacred Majesty King George the Second, and the Protestant Succession in his Illustrious

Family, a sincere Friend to the Church of England as by Law Established, and whose ability for performing Divine Service and Preaching, as well as Moralls, shall moreover Recommend him to succeed the Late Revd Mr Samuel Myles in this Church? Manifest it, etc. It passed in the Affirmative.

2. If it be your Minds that his Excellency General Nicholson and Mr Thomas Sandford, Merch^t in London, be the persons impowered to, or in the Absence of one of them the other be impowred to, present a Clergyman for Institution qualified as by the foregoing Vote in the name and behalf of this Congregation within six Months from the Death of the late Revd Mr Myles to our Right Reverend Diocesan the Lord B^p of London, to succeed the (late) Reverend Mr Miles in this Church? Manifest it, etc. It passed in the Affirmative.

3. If it be your Minds that One hundred and ten Pounds Sterling be Setled as a yearly Sallary upon the aforesaid Clergyman, to Commence upon his Arrivall here, and to be pd Weekly proportions at the difference of Exchange? Manifest it. It passed in the Affirmative.

4. If it be your Minds that Messrs John Jekyll Esqr, George Craddock, John Eastwicke, John Barnes, and John Checkley be a Committee to acquaint our Right Reverend Diocesan with the Death of the Reverend Mr Samuel Myles, and that they likewise informe Gen^{ll} Nicholson and Mr Sandford of the same and the Votes of this Congregation? Manifest it, etc. It passed in the Affirmative.

5. If it be your Minds that the Vote passed by this Congregation on Feb^{ry} 6th last, Impowering the Church Warden to take possession of the Church Stock etc., be annulled, and that the Box now in the House of our late Incumbent with the Stock etc. in it be forthwith put into the hands of the Committee now chosen, to whom shall be added (for this purpose) Messrs Job Lewis and Thomas Phillips, Church Warden, and that these seven or the Majority of them be hereby impowered to passe a Receipt to Mr Myles's Executors for the same, and that the said Box with the Stock in it etc. be kept in the house of Mr John Barnes, Merchant? Manifest it, etc. It passed in the Affirmative.

6. If it be your Minds that the Church Warden pay unto the Reverend Mr Watts out of the Church Stock twenty-five pounds for having done the Duty of Mr Myles in this Church by Mr Myles's Desire? Manifest it, etc. It passed in ye Affirmative.

7. If it be your Minds that Mrs Myles, the Relict of our late Incumbent, be paid 20/ p Week out of the Contributions untill the Arrivall of a Clergyman to succeed the late Revd Mr Samuel Miles? Manifest it, etc^r It passed in the Affirmative.

8. If it be your Minds that the Committee, or the Majority of them, forthwith remitt 20£ Sterling out of the Church Stock to Mr Thomas Sandford to pay the passage of the Clergyman, who shall be presented by Gen^{ll} Nicholson or Mr Sandford or either of them for Institution, to suc-

ceed the (late) Rev⁴ Mʳ Samuel Miles? Manifest it, etc. It passed in the Affirmative.

9. If it be your Minds that the Committee now chosen, or the Majority of them, be impowered to remit such Sume or Sumes of Money out of the Church Stock, as they or the Majority of them shall find absolutely necessary to Defend our Right of Presentation to this Church against any person and or persons whomsoever shall dispute the same? Manifest it, etc. It passed in the Affirmative.

10. If it be your Minds that Mʳ Kenton the Clerke be allowed his Mourning out of the Church Stock? Manifest it, etc. It passed in the Affirmative.

11. If it be your Minds that this Congregation adjourn themselves untill the twenty-second day of Aprill next at Eleven a Clock in the Forenoon, being Monday in Easter Week? Manifest it, etc. It passed in the Affirmative.

The inner secrets of this grievous contention are revealed by two contemporaneous letters, — the one written by a member of King's Chapel who was in political sympathy with Mr. Harris; the other by Dr. Cutler, who was heartily opposed to him.

"BOSTON, February 13ᵗʰ 172⅞.

"The high church party (being but a few though very noisy) would not delay the choice until Gov. Burnet's arrival, having a prejudice to the name of Bishop Burnet. By some unlucky persuasions, Mr. Jekyll, our collector, was this time (though a loyal man), from some personal pique to Mr. Harris, induced to be of his party; as was also Capt. Cornwall (a loyal officer), perhaps from some disgust two years ago to our government of this Province, who in a slight to him (being unprovided) fitted out a vessel of their own against the pirates: the moderate churchmen, Mr. Burnet's friends, being always in favor of our government, it was thought he resented that affair on them at this juncture. Mr. Burnet's friends, the moderate party, are beyond comparison the most considerable men in the chapel, for estates, etc. The others, though but a handful of leaders, are industrious, noisy, and mobbish."

The same writer continued: —

"18ᵗʰ March, 1727-28.

"As to our Church affairs, which I wrote you were in great confusion, John Checkley's party by a superiority of mob would not defer the affair of another minister until his Excellency's arrival, neither could we prevail that it should be left to the Bishop of London; they have left it to Colonel Nicholson and Mr. Sanford of London to nominate a Parson, and in case we make any stand at home (as we design strenuously to do) against their proceedings, they have voted the church stock (which they have taken into their own hands) to defray all charges in compassing their designs. Mr. Harris and his friends are a sending home remonstrances to the Bishop ; they proposed also to remonstrate to his Excellency in a body, which I prevented, because Mr. Burnet prudently declines meddling with any affair in this Province until his arrival here. A missive letter is too short to let you fully into the merits of the affair. On the one side is Mr. Harris, whose character for learning and correct sermons is known all over our Continent, and who of late years has, by his conduct, rendered himself so agreeable in this Province, that if the presentation were in the Lieut.-Governor, Council, and Lower House or Assembly, he would have it *nemine contradicente*. His friends in the congregation are men of substance generally, and all moderate churchmen. On the other side is John Checkley, a young man, ringleader of the party. His character is notorious ; not long ago in this Government he published paragraphs in a pamphlet reflecting on our present constitution at home and our Government here ; he went twice to England for Ministerial Orders, and was as often refused by the bishops because of his bad character ; he has lately been under bonds for some vile actions under the color of making proselytes of our late hostages from the Eastern Indians, as also of the Narragansetts Indians in Rhode Island government ; lastly to sum up all, as, not affraid to own his principles, he wears a crucifix. His followers (Captain Cornwall, Mr. Jekyll, and a few others excepted) seem generally to be of the same principles ; Cornwall and Jekyll listed I think not so much for any esteem they have to Mr. Checkley the leader of the party, as out of some pique to Mr. Harris : on their conduct I shall not pass any judgment ; but they being engaged in such a party they are obliged to labor the more to vindicate themselves. Pray excuse me to his Excellency for presuming without leave at this critical juncture (last week was the crisis) to encourage Mr. Harris' friends, by acquainting Mr. Harris that his Excellency had a good character of him from good hands, but had no good opinion of violent proceedings."[1]

Dr. Cutler's letter to Dr. Zachary Gray requires to be read with the allowance due to an angry man : —

"Since my last, I think, died the reverend and excellent Mr. Miles ; and Mr. Harris's conduct ever since has been a dreadful tragedy. His sermons have been distracted invectives upon all his opposers. A worthy

[1] Dr. William Douglass to Cadwallader Colden, in 4 Mass. Hist. Coll. ii. 179, 182. Dr. William Douglass was an influential physician in Boston, 1718-1752. He was a Scotchman, educated in Paris and Leyden, "a man of fine intellectual parts and a versatile writer. He understood astronomy and could calculate eclipses; he had a taste for natural history, and was an excellent botanist. It was neatly said of him that he was always positive and sometimes accurate. He had little tact, and it is not surprising that he found himself continually in hot water." He was the only regularly graduated physician in the town at this time, and had vehemently opposed the practice of inoculation in 1721. — *Dr. S. A. Green's Centennial Address before the Massachusetts Medical Society*, 1881.

woman, who with smartness and boldness enough resented his ungrateful and abusive treatment of her character, dying suddenly, he the Sunday after remarked the judgments of God on *that wicked Jezabel, who made it her business to speak against her neighbours;* and accordingly refused her Christian burial. Being displeased at a gentleman of character belonging to his Church and Vestry, he pulled him by the nose, and bad him get out of the Church, and said he would follow him; and, after that, charged him with going to strike him in the Church, whereas every one there were witnesses to that gentleman's meek behaviour. And yet this Monster is a worthy friend to the present Government, and none of those that do oppose him; and we conclude that he has fixed these apprehensions in the true son of Bishop Burnet, who is appointed our Governor, and I understand that somehow or other I am brought in for a scrape; but I hope I can live without Governors, as I have hitherto done, though if Mr. Harris finds the favour with my Lord as he doth with our authority, we must all stand clear." [1]

A month later, in April, 1728, it was voted to pay Mr. Harris for the extra duty which had fallen to him in the lack of a rector, — a state of things which lasted more than a year. But the record darkens again in April, 1729: —

Nov. 25. 1728. Att a meeting of the Vestry at Mr Pattons [the Green Dragon], *Voted,* That the Church wardens Look into the Vault where Mr Myles lyes Interrd, and Consider what may be proper to be done on removeing his Corps, and to Act as they shall think Proper. It Passt in the Affirmative.

April 7th 1729. *Voted,* That the Number of the Vestry shall not exceed twenty.

Voted, That no Money be given to the Revd Mr Harris out of the Weekly Contributions or Church Stock untill the Arrival of a Minister and his being in full possession of this Church, in Consequence of the Votes of this Congregation on the 13th March 1727 8; and that then the Congregation Consider what shall be due to the Revd Mr Henry Harris for his extraordinary Service, and pay him accordingly, But not before.[2]

Voted, That the Church Wardens give out of the Church Stock towards the Relief of Mr James Baker what they shall see necessary.

Voted, That the Church Box be removed to Mr Craddock's, — two Keys of the said box to be kept by the Church Wardens, and the third be in the Possession of Mr Craddock.

So the period of feuds and fightings drew to a close; the controversies which had embittered the relations between the church and the surrounding community being equalled, if not

[1] April 7, 1728. Nichols's "Illustrations of Literature," iv. 258.

[2] Mr. Harris was paid £100, July 12, 1729.

surpassed, in intensity by these internal strifes. Amid these jars and factions, while we listen in vain for the voice of peace, it is something to remember that enemies were compelled, week by week, to a truce of silence, as the "King's Lecturer" bade his "dearly beloved brethren" "The Lord be with you," and they answered, "And with thy spirit!"

---

[1] Part of the titlepage of Rev. Henry Caner's Funeral Sermon on Dr. Cutler, Aug. 20, 1765.

THE PROVINCE HOUSE.

CHAPTER X.

THE BISHOP'S COMMISSARY.

ALTHOUGH he was a churchman and a bishop's son, the transfer of Governor William Burnet from New York to Massachusetts was not received with the enthusiasm with which the Church of England in Boston had greeted Lord Bellomont. That no address of congratulation was presented to him may indeed have been due to the fact that Mr. Myles's recent death had left the King's Chapel without its head; while Mr. Harris could do nothing, in the divided state of feeling, and Dr. Cutler was too hostile, politically, to take the initiative. Yet in any less heated time the arrival of a person so distinguished by birth and breeding, to fill a place at the head of the Vestry which Governor Shute and Lieut.-Governor Dummer had left void so long, would have been marked with triumph.

The strongest proof of the height to which political and party passion had risen within the church may be found in the fact that the matters in dispute were not submitted with one accord to the new Governor. The son of Bishop Burnet might have

GOVERNOR BURNET.

expected that his father's eminence in the Church, and distinction as the friend of William III., would cause the people of the King's Chapel to hail his appointment as a providential way out of their controversies; but the very fact that Mr. Harris's friends looked hopefully to his coming doubtless determined the other party not to make him a court of final appeal. They took due action of respect, however: —

Boston, April 22.d 1728. *Voted*, That the number of the Vestry consist of fifteen. That the account deliver'd in to the Congregation for the funerall of the Rev:d M:r Sam:ll Myles, Amounting to £190, 14s. be paid by the Church wardens.

That the Rev:d M:r Harris be allowed for his past service to this day the sum of Twenty-five Pounds, to be paid out of the Church Stock.

That Painting and beautifying the Governour's pew be left to the Church wardens and Vestry.

Boston, April 29:th 1728. *Voted*, That the Governour's pew be new lind with China, and that the Cusheons and chairs be Covered with Crimson dammask, and the Curtains to the Windows be of the same damask.[1]

Although the above vote was passed, Dr. Cutler had expressed the distrust with which the majority in King's Chapel received the new Governor. To them, however, this feeling may have been alleviated by the prestige which his presence, with that of his little court, would bring to the Chapel, — now "the King's" indeed, since the King's Governor attended it. But outside the Church it was not so.

He had been brought up under "long and frequent religious services at home in his youth," and attributed to that his aversion to regular attendance on public worship. The graver Puritans thought that he went too far the other way: —

"A little more caution and conformity to the different ages, manners, customs, and even prejudices of different companies would have been more politic; but his open, undisguised mind could not submit to it. Being asked to dine with an old charter senator who retained the custom of saying grace sitting, the grave gentleman desired to know which would be more agreeable to His Excellency, that grace should be said

---

[1] The "Governor's pew" remained a unique property of the King's Chapel. The nearest approach to it in the other Episcopal church was an acknowledgment of the gift of a cargo of logwood from Honduras. Christ Church Records, June 9, 1727: "*Voted*, That a Pew be expeditiously built next to the Pulpit and lin'd handsomely For the use of the Gentlemen of y:e Bay of Handoras who have been or shall be Benefactors to this Church." This was "handsomely lin'd with red Chany." (Vestry book). There was a Governor's pew, however, in the First and South meeting-houses.

standing or sitting? The Governor replied, 'Standing or sitting, any way or no way, just as you please.' He sometimes wore a cloth coat lined with velvet; it was said to be expressive of his character. He was a firm believer of the truth of revealed religion, but a bigot to no particular profession among Christians, and laid little stress upon modes and forms. By a clause in his last will he ordered his body to be buried, if he died at New York, by his wife; if in any other part of the world, in the nearest church-yard or burying-ground, all places being alike to God's all-seeing eye." [1]

The watchful Cutler wrote: [2] —

"The poor Church is, in some places, squeezing to death under the weight of the Dissenters' loins; and neither Bishops, nor the son of a Bishop now at the head of us, give us any relief. The latter is vigourously pursuing his own interest to get a fixed salary on a Governor, and our House of Commons as obstinately opposing it. If he carries our compliments home, and the Court be provoked to abolish our charter, he will prove the greatest blessing we ever had. Our only consolation at present is that good may come out of evil. It cannot be otherwise, when our great man shall never come within the walls of a church for a month together, and he shall be so free as to tell two clergymen that he refused Priests' orders because he could not assent to the Athanasian creed; and they so complaisant as to show no uneasiness at such awful conversation. I only wait for a little more openness in such talk, and then my pulpit shall ring; and I believe I shall by that means become popular among the Dissenters, who, as well as the Church, do greatly dislike his principles and practice."

The theological complexion of New England had changed very little since the earlier days. A Calvinism of a strict type still ruled in the churches. Brattle Square Church still stood alone on its somewhat relaxed ground of practice, but doctrinally agreed with its sister churches. The Episcopal churches won their way by the beauty and solemnity of the liturgy, but were not thought to differ, on the Calvinistic points, from their neighbors. One of the earliest traces of the multitude of heresies which have since sprung up in Boston is in a letter of Dr. Cutler to the Secretary: [3] —

"An Heresy has been lately received here, denying the Eternity of Hell Torments; but I hope the infection will not spread."

[1] Hutchinson, ii. 365.
[2] To Dr. Gray, Boston, Oct. 10, 1728, Nichols's "Illustrations," etc., quoted in Church Docs. Mass. p. 671.
[3] April 24, 1732. Church Docs. Mass. p. 274.

Although other seeds of the future divergencies of religious opinion may have lurked here, there was no break in the outward conformity to orthodox belief by all reputable folk; and there can have been little power of understanding the tolerant and free spirit with which Burnet's cosmopolitan training and temper regarded much which was generally held to be beyond question.

If his life had been spared, however, the Governor must have won favor in the church by his manly discharge of his difficult duty as the King's representative among a people resolute against yielding to the King's demands, as well as by his charm of conversation and personal attractions, — notwithstanding his lax churchmanship. Whatever shadow of unbelief may have rested on his youth, he had written a work on theology since his arrival in New York, and had testified to his hostility to the Church of Rome by a letter which aimed to recover a pervert to that faith.[1] As he entered on his official occupation of the Province House, which was henceforward to be the scene of so many vice-regal pageants, and to see the interchange of greetings between the successive governors and the representatives of the Royal Chapel, the proximity of that stately mansion to the church, but a stone's throw away, may well have seemed to betoken a closer connection between their occupants. Here were to enter the processions of clergymen, with their wardens and vestries, to welcome each new occupant of the governor's chair; and from this broad portal such of the governors as were churchmen would descend with a brilliant company of officers and guests through the wide courtyard, when the deep-toned bell of the church summoned them to occupy the pew which held aloft the royal crown.

ARMS OF BURNET.

A fanciful mind might, indeed, have found an ominous significance in the fact, that, though they passed beneath the King's arms as they went out of the porch, the Province House was surmounted, as a weather-vane, by an Indian pointing his bow and arrow, — an emblem surviving from the old colonial seal; so

---

[1] "Letter from a Romish Priest in Canada, To One who was taken Captive in her Infancy, and Instructed in the Romish Faith, but some time ago returned to this her *Native Country*. With an Answer thereto, By a Person to whom it was Communicated. Boston: 1729." The answer by Governor Burnet is sensible and clear, and shows thorough acquaintance with the controversy between the two Churches.

that whenever the northwest wind blew from the "heart of the Commonwealth" with a fresh breath from the free farms, the dusky warrior aimed his weapon at the church![1] Its new occupant brought to this noble residence all the elements of a tragedy, in the swift contrasts of light and shadow.

Governor Burnet had been received, July 19, 1728, "with a Splendour and Magnificence superiour to what has ever been known in these Parts of the World." Besides the customary stately formalities of reading his commission in the presence of the ministers and civic dignitaries, crowds of gentlemen met him as an escort, and salutes resounded as he entered the town.[2]

The Bishop's eldest son, and godson of King William III. for whom he was named, had been born to brilliant prospects. A lover of books, and bred in the atmosphere of the court, " his figure and manners were dignified and engaging. He was intelligent, witty, learned, accomplished, and experienced in business. He had a nice, if arrogant, sense of honor."[3] Straightway this English gentleman found himself entangled in the controversy with the Representatives about the settling of a stated salary on the Governor, which occupied his fourteen months' administration. Soon the Province House saw the minister of the Chapel enter on a sad errand. The King's Chapel register of burials records the Governor's death, the result of being overturned into the water as his carriage approached the ferry in coming

---

[1] The Province House, built with bricks brought from Holland in 1679 for his own mansion, by Peter Sergeant, a wealthy merchant, was bought by the Province for the Governor's residence in 1716. It stood a hundred feet back from Marlborough (now a part of Washington) Street, with trees and lawn and a carriage-way in front, and was occupied by all the succeeding Royal Governors except Hutchinson, who dwelt in his own mansion at the North End. "The English General Howe took French leave of it" in 1776. In 1811, the State gave it to the Massachusetts General Hospital, which leased it in 1817, for ninety-nine years, to David Greenough. It was "put to various mean uses," and finally was destroyed by fire in 1864. The Indian was made by Deacon Shem Drowne, who later made the grasshopper on Faneuil Hall, after the pattern of that on the Royal Exchange, London. See Mass. Hist. Proc., December, 1876, p. 178.

[2] A glowing account is given in the "Weekly News-Letter," July 18-25, 1728. The company dined at the "Bunch of Grapes," when a "poem" was read: —

"Immortal William saved the British Isle,
Groaning in Romish Chains, and Bid it smile;
And when th' infatuate Tribe grew mad again,
And fain would Re-assume the broken Chain,
Great *Sarum's* Eye Pierc'd quick the deep Designs,
Warded the Ruin, Sapp'd the fatal Mines!"

[3] Palfrey, iv. 498. Governor Burnet had been a Fellow Commoner of Trinity College, Cambridge, where he took his M. A. in 1702. A lawyer by profession, he had a place in the Treasury, but obtained the governorship of New York as a means of retrieving his fortune, which was impaired by dabbling in the South Sea stocks. Franklin, in his "Autobiography," gives a charming glimpse of the Governor's love of letters. His removal to the Province of Massachusetts, though a promotion in dignity, was a pecuniary injury, which, with his large family of children, he could ill bear.

from Cambridge, to which place he had adjourned the stubborn House : —

1729. Sept. 7. His Excellency William Burnet, Esq', Governour of the Province of the Massachusets Bay. 42 years.

The burial service which had been read over Lady Andros again sounded its solemn warning of the transiency of man's life and the eternity of God, while the hush of the shadow in which his messenger of death was silently enthroned, fell upon the throng who filled the panelled rooms and corniced halls where comfort and luxury seemed too daintily housed for such a guest to enter. A funeral sermon was preached by Commissary Price, from Ecclesiastes ii. 17; and the Governor's place passed again into Congregational hands.

The story has now been told how the mingled web of Mr. Myles's prosperity within his congregation, and controversy without, and discord with his assistants, was at length unravelled by his death, — only to be tangled again in yet more unhappy disputes.

It may naturally be asked why Mr. Harris remained, and why the congregation retained him in these doubtful and unsatisfactory relations. The answer may be found in the fact that he was really independent of them, being paid by the £100 of King William's grant, which he would lose by departing, while in that case King's Chapel would be without any assistant at all. So he retained his salary, and the church retained its assistant minister; but it may be questioned how much of the best advantage accrued to either party.

Loyalists and churchmen though this congregation were, it proves the power of the free air of America that they should at this time have seriously formed the plan to resist any claim by the Bishop of London to the right of presentation to the rectorship of the church, as indicated by the vote which has been quoted. Perhaps the well known character of the Bishop of London at this time contributed to this purpose on their part. Bishop Edmund Gibson was a very able man, " a laborious student, and also pious," but sometimes intolerant, and zealous for the rights of the Church, — as John Wesley found a little later. Such was his ecclesiastical power, that Sir Robert Walpole was reproached with allowing to him the authority of a pope : " And a very good pope he is," he answered.[1] He did not, however, in this case press his authority too far, but told the agent of King's

[1] Tyerman's " Wesley," i. 207.

Chapel, Mr. Thomas Sandford, at their first interview, that "he did not pretend to the right of presentation, but thought that it was in the congregation who supported the minister; and it was agreed that His Lordship should recommend some fit person as rector," and that Mr. Sandford, as agent of the congregation, should then present this person to him again for license, — a very good way for a "Protestant pope" to give up the semblance while keeping the reality of power. Mr. Sandford had several interviews with the Bishop, in order to bring about this amicable result, in some of which he was accompanied by Mr. Charles Apthorp of the congregation, who was then in England.[1]

A report was published in Boston, a few months after: —

"*London, Septem.* 10. The Rev. Mr. Allen, late Curate of Lavenham in the County of Suffolk, has been presented by Thomas Sanford Esq. to the Living call'd King's-Chappel in Boston in New-England, worth 600*l.* per annum."[2]

Nothing of this, however, is noted in our Records; but it appears that in due time "Mr. Roger Price was recommended, presented, and licensed," in the way suggested by the Bishop.

It is a marked illustration of the inability of the authorities at home to use their opportunity, that the presence in America at this time of a man pre-eminently fitted to consolidate the English Church here and to conciliate its opponents, — the highest dignitary who visited these shores previously to the Revolution, — should not have been utilized by his appointment to some commissarial or episcopal authority. The romantic episode of Dean Berkeley's residence in Newport, while fruitlessly awaiting the planting of his Utopian college in the Bermudas, shed little direct light upon the metropolitan church of New England, although King's Chapel must have shared some quickening influence from the presence of that gentle and luminous intelligence even in a neighboring colony. But though Berkeley landed at Newport in January, 1729, early in the same year in which Mr. Price arrived at Boston, he never visited our town until he came here to sail for England in the autumn of 1731. He can then hardly have failed to preach in King's Chapel; but on this point no record remains, and we are left to imagination to recall in the old pulpit the "gentleman of middle stature, of an agreeable, pleasant, and erect aspect," whose manly courtesy impressed the Newport people. These on their part impressed

[1] Greenwood, p. 88.
[2] N. E. Weekly Journal, Nov. 4, 1728.

the Dean with the conviction that their "many sorts and subdivisions of sects all agree in one point,—that the Church of England is the second best."[1]

But though the halo of a great and sacred reputation thus only dimly touches King's Chapel, this church was more directly indebted to those who came in Berkeley's train,—to the artist Smibert, who found a harvest for his pencil in its velvet-coated or brocaded worshippers, and to the architect Harrison, who furnished the plans of the present church.

The history of the anomalous relation in which the Bishop of London stood to King's Chapel, as well as to all churches of the Church of England in America, has been already traced.[2] The ecclesiastical authority which he exercised over these remote provinces was vague and ill-defined, but had been well used, and by King's Chapel received in a filial spirit. The words of Bishop Compton were not an empty phrase, in which he said: "As the care of your churches, with the rest of the plantations, lies upon me as your diocesan; so, to discharge that trust, I shall omit no occasions of promoting their good and interest." Bishop Robinson inherited from his predecessor, and acted upon this view of his duties. On the appointment of Bishop Gibson, however, to the See of London, he, being learned in ecclesiastical law, sought to know the source of his authority, and was referred to an order in council under Charles II., making the colonies a part of the See of London. "For this order," says Wilberforce, "he, being a careful man, caused a diligent search to be made, when he discovered that none such existed. Finding, therefore, no ground whatever on which to rest his claim of jurisdiction, he declined even to appoint a commissary. Thus the colonies were separated from all episcopal control. But, after a while, having obtained a special commission from the Crown committing this charge to him, and thinking it better under all the circumstances of the case to act under this authority than to abandon them entirely, he began to discharge it with his usual fidelity."

The "Weekly News-Letter," May 4-11, 1727, announced that —

"A Commission impowering the Lord Bishop of London to exercise Ecclesiastical Jurisdiction by himself or sufficient Commissaries in his Majesty's Colonies, Plantations, and Dominions in America, concerning the Visitation of the Churches where Divine Service is celebrated according to the Rites and Liturgy of the Church of England, etc., will soon pass the Seal."

[1] Fraser's Berkeley, p. 160.   [2] See p. 171, *ante*.

Even after obtaining this, however, Bishop Gibson "felt that his hold upon these distant parts was little what it should be, if he were indeed to deem himself their bishop. Every line of his first address to them, in 1724, breathes this spirit."

"Being called," he tells them, "by the providence of God to the government and administration of the diocese of London, by which the care of the churches in the foreign plantations is also devolved upon me, I think it my duty to use all proper means of attaining a competent knowledge of the places, persons, and matters entrusted to my care. And as the plantations, and the constitutions of the churches there, are at a far greater distance and much less known to me than the affairs of my diocese here at home, so it is the more necessary for me to have recourse to the best and most effectual methods of coming to a right knowledge of the state and condition of them,—which knowledge I shall not fail, by the grace of God, faithfully to employ to the service of piety and religion, and to the maintenance of order and regularity in the Church."

He then furnishes a paper of inquiries, which he desired Mr. Myles to answer for New England, and promises his "best advice and assistance in order to the successful and comfortable discharge of their ministerial function."[1]

But even this "shadowy" authority expired with Bishop Gibson, since this commission had been "granted only to himself personally, and not to his successors." So that in appointing Mr. Price his commissary over the Episcopal churches in New England, the bishop conferred that responsible dignity for the sole time that it was borne by any one during the connection of the colonies with Great Britain. The whole exercise of the commissarial function, indeed, at such remoteness from the bishop's possible supervision would seem to have put a severe strain on those duties as properly defined. The name is—

"A title of jurisdiction, appertaining to him that exerciseth ecclesiastical jurisdiction in places of the diocese so far distant from the chief city that the chancellor cannot call the people to the bishop's principal consistory court without great trouble to them. He is called by the canonists *commissarius*, or *officialis foraneus*, and is ordained to this special end, that he should supply the office and jurisdiction of the bishop in the out places of the diocese, or in such parishes as are peculiars of the bishop, and exempted from the archdeacon's jurisdiction."[2]

[1] "A History of the Protestant Episcopal Church in America. By Samuel Wilberforce, M.A. London, 1844."
[2] Burn's Ecclesiastical Law, ii., 8.

The restrictions upon admission to this office, imposed by the canons of the church, were these: that it should be exercised by no one who was not "of the full age of six-and-twenty years at the least, learned in the civil and ecclesiastical laws (at the least a master of arts or batchelor of law), and reasonably well practised in the course thereof, as likewise well affected and zealously bent to religion, touching whose life and manners no evil example is had," — it being likewise required that he should have taken "the oath of the king's supremacy in the presence of the bishop or in the open court, and should subscribe to the thirty-nine articles; and should also swear that he would, to the uttermost of his understanding, deal uprightly and justly in his office, without respect of favour or reward."[1] So eminent a canon lawyer as Bishop Gibson doubtless saw to it that these conditions were carefully fulfilled; and also satisfied himself of Mr. Price's personal qualifications for an office which was not only so delicate, but largely tentative and provisional. But few traces remain of the extent to which he exercised it. The records of King's Chapel are silent on the subject, as it was an office which he held apart from his relation to this church, and which survived his connection therewith; nor do enough of his own papers, or of his communications to the bishop, now survive to enable us to reconstruct that chapter of history. It is obvious, however, that such an authority, even in its shorn and curtailed state, if exercised here during a long period by a succession of able men, might have done much to consolidate English civil as well as ecclesiastical power in the New World; instead of which the rulers of Great Britain seem in this, as in other things, to have steadily shaped the way for the separation of the colonies.

Mr. Price's commission as commissary, in 1730, soon followed his induction as minister of King's Chapel; and it terminated, as was usual with such offices, on the death of the bishop, in 1748.

The commissarial duty devolving upon Mr. Price does not appear to have been very onerous, though it must have increased the efficiency of the Episcopal superintendence of this outlying part of the diocese of London. This dignified office had formerly been filled by Dr. Blair in Virginia, and by Dr. Bray in Maryland, — both commissioned by Bishop Compton.

"The judicial office of Commissary had at first been vested in Governors of Colonies; but in 1695 the Governor and Assembly of Mary-

[1] Burn's Ecclesiastical Law, i. 290.

land agreed in a petition to William and Mary to transfer it, as a purely ecclesiastical office, to the Bishop of London, and wrote to the Bishop requesting him to send over a Clergyman to discharge its duties." [1]

No such officer had been commissioned in New England before Mr. Price, nor did any one succeed him. In the course of his duty he called conventions of the Episcopal clergy of New England. The first of these was held in September, 1738. The vestry records of Christ Church for September 5 contain the following: —

"Whereas the Rever! Gentlemen of the Clergy are to meet at Boston in Convention to be held at Christ Church on Wednesday, the 20th Instant, It is *Voted* That a handsome Dinner be provided for the s^d Rever! Gent^n of the Clergy, and that the Wardens of Each Church and the Treasurer of the Charitable Society be invited, and the Church Wardens do acquaint the Revd Mr Commissary Price therewith.

"£10 to Dr. Cutler for Assistance towards defraying the Expenses he will be at upon this Extraordinary Occasion of Entertaining at his house the Rever! Gent^n of the Clergy."

There had been earlier gatherings of this kind, informally met, in various places. The sermon preached in King's Chapel, by the Rev. Mr. Honeyman, at such a convention in 1726, was printed.[2] But this meeting, in 1738, seems to have been the beginning of a fixed custom. The sermon, by the Rev. Arthur Browne, was printed.[3] Its pith is in the following sentences:

"Let Free-thinkers then riot in the Argument of Divine Goodness; their Notion of this Attribute banishes other Perfections from the Divine Nature, and is palpably inconsistent with Divine Government."

"If any Stray from the Fold by our Fault or Mismanagement, it will not be so easy to avoid the Guilt as some may imagine. It will therefore highly become us to Conduct our Selves so as to give no Offence to our People, by tempting them, by too much Remissness, to Slight our Constitution, or by too much Rigour and Severity, to be afraid of it. Let them see that we make a Conscience of observing our Rules, by which Means we may engage those that Dissent from us to entertain better Opinions both of our Church and Persons, and in all probability, by Degrees, prevail upon and win over many to our Communion. This, and a kind, obliging Behaviour, will go a good way."

---

[1] Anderson, Col. Church, ii. 383.

[2] [J. Honeyman.] A Sermon preached at the King's Chapel in Boston, N. E., at a Convention of Episcopal Ministers. in the year 1726. Boston. [1733.]

[3] "The EXCELLENCY of the Christian Religion. A Sermon before the Episcopal Clergy of New England, Convened at Boston: And Preached at Christ Church, Sept. 20, 1738. By Arthur Browne, A. M., RECTOR of *Portsmouth* in *New-Hampshire*, and Missionary to the SOCIETY for the Propagation of the Gospel, Etc. Boston: 1738."

It was also the commissary's duty to investigate any irregularities in the conduct of his brethren.[1] These duties, however, expired with the office, on the death of Bishop Gibson in 1748. Mr. Price wrote to the Secretary more than a year after: —

"Boston, Oct. 6, 1749. . . . We are very unsettled here in our Ecclesiastical State; it is the current Report that the Bishop of London has refused to concern himself with the American Churches, and I suppose my Commissarial power is now extinct. . . ."[2]

The new minister was of good English family and education.[3]

[1] An animated correspondence in the Life of Rev. S. Johnson is due to this. Mr. Price writes to Johnson: —

BOSTON, June 18, 1742.

REV. SIR, — Mr. Morris [itinerant missionary] made a complaint to me and the clergy convened at Boston relating to your going to the dissenting meeting, and suffering your son to do the same, which gave some uneasiness to our brethren. I hope your prudence will always direct you to avoid anything that may show such a favorable disposition towards the separation as will obstruct the growth of the Episcopal Church.

I am your affectionate brother and humble servant, ROG. PRICE.

Johnson replies, July 5, 1742, that his son is obliged to go as a student in Yale College. . . . "All the foundation of Mr. Morris' complaint is only this: that on Commencement night, when Davenport was raving among the people there, Mr. Wetmore and I went in the dark — no mortal knowing us but our own company — and stood at the edge of the crowd, and heard him rave about five minutes, and then went about our business; this, I humbly conceive, could not be called going to meeting any more than a visit to Bedlam, — for we heard no prayers, nor anything that could be called preaching, any more than the ravings of a man distracted. . . . I look upon the worst part of going to meeting to be, being present and joining with extempore prayers. . . . Upon the whole I can truly say, and thank God for it, my prudence has always directed me, and always shall, to avoid anything that could show the least favorable disposition towards the separation as such, or to obstruct the growth of the Episcopal Church. . . . I believe he [my brother Morris] had better have gone twenty times to meeting, than once have shown such a spirit of ingratitude and malevolence as he has done. But I heartily pity and forgive him, etc., . . ."— *Johnson's Life*, p. 113.

[2] Bishop Sherlock writes to Johnson, 1749, that he will appoint a commissary "as soon as I take a proper authority from the King, which I have hitherto delayed, in hopes of seeing another and better settlement of ecclesiastical affairs in the country. . . . I am persuaded that no bishop residing in England ought to have, or will willingly undertake, the province."— Beardsley's *Johnson*, p. 131.

[3] John Price, of Water Stratford, Bucks, married Isabella Collingwood, from Berwick-upon-Tweed. "Her father was a captain in King Charles I.'s army, and was shot through the thigh at the battle of Edge Hill, of which wound he afterwards died." The family of Collingwood were noted in Berwick and Northumberland. Mrs. Price had several sisters and one brother, Daniel Collingwood, who emigrated to Virginia.

John and Isabella (Collingwood) Price had several sons and daughters. Their son William Price, born March 22, 1663, educated at Oxford and inducted to the living of Whitefield, near Brackley, Northamptonshire, Feb. 27, 1692, married Elizabeth Izard of Beckley, near Oxford. She belonged to an ancient family connected with the Duke of Bedford and the Duchess of Marlborough in 1780. Ralph Izard of South Carolina was her brother. The sons of William and Elizabeth (Izard) Price became clergymen, and the daughters, who married, became the wives of clergymen. William Price possessed a small entailed estate

Roger Price, born Dec. 6, 1696, the eldest son of the Rev. William and Elizabeth (Izard) Price, was educated at Oxford, where he took his B.A. at Balliol College, Feb. 21, 1717. He gives an interesting account of his checkered professional career in a letter written in his later years, when, being in straitened circumstances, he was obliged to apply for aid: [1] —

"Soon after my admission into Priest's Orders I accepted a Chaplainship at Widdaw, a Factory on the Coast of Guinea. In my voyage there

PRICE COAT-OF-ARMS.[2]

I fell into the hands of Pirates, who detained me for some time, and robbed me of the best part of my effects. Upon my release I proceeded to the place of my destination, where I was soon seized with a fever which destroys many there. Sir Challoner Ogle, after taking the same Pirates, came to the Factory of Widdaw; and finding me in a low state of health, in compassion carried me from thence in the 'Swallow' Man-of-War, as Chaplain, to Jamaica, about the time of the Duke of Portland's arrival there; upon whom I waited in order to receive his commands to England, where I then designed to return, but upon his persuasion was prevailed upon to remain on the Island, and was thereupon appointed his chaplain and Minister of St. Ann's Parish.[3] In this station I continued three years, till my health began to be impaired; upon representing which to the Duke of Portland, after some entreaty, he consented to my return home, and favored me with Letters of recommendat[n] to sev[l] of his relations in England, and to D[r] Gibson, the Bishop of London, who soon after presented me to the living of

at Beckley, which eventually came to his eldest son Roger. The Price family "trace their lineage even from royalty." William Price died in 1749. There were eleven children, — Elizabeth, Roger, Thomas, John, Sarah, Mary, William, Susannah, Philadelphia, Catherine, and Cornelius. The family coat-of-arms is sable, lion rampant regardant; or, crest demilion. They quartered Collingwood, Shillingford, Izard, and others.

I am indebted to Mrs. Frances A. Weston, a great-granddaughter of Rev. Roger Price, for most valuable biographical materials. The account of Commissary Price, in Sprague's "Annals of the American Pulpit," v. 69, was furnished by her to the compiler.

[1] "Mr. Price to the Secretary: London, July the 13th, 1762." — *Church Docs. Mass.* p. 470.

[2] From a seal of Roger Price.

[3] The contrast of ecclesiastical methods in some of the English colonies from those of New England is illustrated by the fact, that, in the year 1722, Mr. Price receives a commission from Henry, the Duke of Portland, "Capt. Gener[l] and Commander-in-Chief over his Majestie's Island of Jamaica," etc. "For-as-much as the Parish of St. Ann's in the Island of Jamaica is vacant of an Incumbent," etc., "I do therefore by Vertue of my Authority," etc., "Present and Collate you Roger Price, Cle[r] into said Church and Parish of St. Ann's aforesaid, and to the Rectory, Benefice, and Cure thereof, and to every Right, Profit," etc., "belonging," "according to the Canons of the Church of England. Given under my hand and seal-at-arms, this 3[d]. day of Feby., 1722. PORTLAND."

Leigh, in Essex, with a promise of farther favours. Here I lived, with bad health, abo' 2 years, when a Presentation to the King's Chapel in Boston, in New England, was offered me. My ill state of health, and a desire of being serviceable to the Church in a Country where Ministers are much wanted, inclined me to accept the offer, notwithstanding many fair views of preferment I had at home. Soon after my Admission into the King's Chapel, in Boston, the Bishop of London honor^d me with the Commissarial power over the Churches in New England, which station I continued in until his decease, and I flatter myself not without approbat^n. How faithfully I discharged this trust, the great increase of churches during my presiding there will testify, to most of which I contributed no little assistance both by my labours and benefactions. Advancing in years, and wearied with my publick and private duties in Boston, after a residence of 20 years there, by the favour of the Society for the Propagation of the Gospel, I retired to a mission at Hopkinston, where I spent the remainder of my time in that country. An order from Bishop Sherlock and a desire of seeing my native country brought me home, where I would willingly spend the remainder of my days; but as my income at present is very scanty, and my family large, having a Wife and 6 children, I humbly hope my case may be considered as worthy a favorable notice and recompense."

A touching letter from his father, on his first departure from home for his Guinea chaplaincy, is preserved: [1] —

"You are going into a far country, remote from all your friends: make it, therefore, your first and chief concern to make God your friend, that He may go along with you. Acquaint yourself with Him by constant and fervent prayer; by meditation, reading, and strict duty and obedience, not fashioning yourself to what you see, but setting yourself a pattern of what you are to teach and preach, — considering that you never can appear so much to advantage, or gain so much esteem and reputation to yourself, as when you walk by rule, and study to order your whole conversation as becomes the Gospel of Christ. Think not that you go abroad to get money, and to enrich yourself by merchandise: you have business of more consequence incumbent upon you, — a duty which requires your constant thought and serious attention. Mind the work more than the wages. I had rather you should return with the character of a faithful minister, . . . than to have you return with a different character, though with your weight in gold; and in the end you will be of my mind, whatever you may think at present. . . . Abstain from all things unbecoming your profession. . . . and, if you will take my advice, from all kind of gaming, which can no ways turn to your advantage, only often to your damage and reproach. You will observe the miserable condition of the natives where you go, the slavery, ignorance, and barbarity in which they

[1] Sprague's Annals, v. 69.

live; bless God for the happiness you enjoy, and prize it by your thankful acknowledgments, and by a right use and improvement of it."

The next document among Mr. Price's papers is the following: —

"I do declare, as it is now by law established, I will conforme to the Liturgy of the Church of England. ROG. PRICE."

"This Declaration was made and subscribed before me by the said Rog. Price to be collated and presented to the Rectory of Lee in the County of Essex and my Diocese of London this 22^d day of April, in the year of our Lord 1725, and the third year of our Translation.
"EDM. LONDON."

This living he retained during his life, and there he died and was buried. He also possessed livings at Durrington and Wiltshire, where he employed curates. After his father's death he came into possession of the estate at Beckley. Then comes his appointment to America by the same Bishop of London, in the year 1728-29.

"The account of the new rector's induction is truly," as Dr. Greenwood says, "a tale of old times to us, and must impress every reflecting mind with a sense of the changes which" time has wrought: —

At a meeting of the Vestry in King's Chapel on the 25. June, 1729, Present,

William Randle, } *Church Wardens.*
William Speakman,

James Stevens, Esq.,	John Checkley,
George Cradock,	Benjamin Walker,
Joshua Wroe,	Samuel Grainger,
George Stewart,	Robert Skinner,
Jonathan Pue, Esq.,	Thomas Creese, Jr.,
Thomas Child,	Thomas Holker.
Thomas Wallis,	

About 4 o'clk in the P. M. the Rev. Mr. Roger Price was conducted into King's Chapel by the Rev. Mr. Henry Harris, it being a few hours after the arrival of the Rev. Mr. Price, and a letter from Mr. Thos. Sandford to the Committee was read, importing that the Rev. Mr. Roger Price was the person he had presented to the Lord Bishop of London, by virtue of the power devolved upon him by the votes of the Congregation of the 13th March 1727-28. Whereupon the Rev. Mr. Price produced the following License and Certificate, reading them in the Church, and then delivered them to the Church Wardens to be recorded in the Church Book.

"EDMUNDUS permissione Divina LONDINENSIS Episcopus, Dilecto nobis in Christo Rogero Price Cler. Salutem et Gratiam. Ad peragendum Officium Ministrale.in Provincia de Nova Anglia in America, in Precibus communibus aliisque Ministeriis Ecclesiasticis ad Officium Ministri pertinentibus juxta Formam descriptam in Libro publicarum Precum Authoritate Parliamenti hujus inclyti Regni magnæ Brittanniæ in ea parte edit. et provis. et Canones et Constitutiones in ea parte legitime stabilitas et publicatas, et non aliter neque alio Modo: TIBI cujus Fidelitati, Morum Integritati, Literarum Scientiæ, Sanæ Doctrinæ et Diligentiæ plurimum confidimus (Subscriptis prius et Juratis per Te coram Nobis omnibus et singulis Articulis et Juramentis in hac parte de jure subscribendis et jurandis) LICENTIAM et Facultatem nostras concedimus et impartimus per Præsentes: ad nostrum bene placitum duntaxat duraturas. In cujus Rei Testimonium Sigillum nostrum (quo in hac parte utimur) Præsentibus apponi fecimus. Dat. apud Westmonast. quarto Die Mensis Martis, Anno Dni millesimo septingentesimo vicessimo nono. Nostræque Translationis Anno Sexto.

"I do declare that I will conforme to the Liturgy of the Church of England as it is now by Law Established.

Rog Price

SEAL.

This declaration was made and subscribed before me by the said Roger Price to be lycensed to performe the Ministerial Office in Boston in New England in America this fourth Day of March in the Year of our Lord 1728-29, and in the sixth year of our Translation."

Edm: London:

These above being read, the Rev. Mr. Henry Harris, the Church Wardens, the Vestrymen, and the people who were present, all went out of the Church, the Church Wardens at the door delivering the key of the Church to the Rev. Mr. Price, who, locking himself in the Church, tolled the bell, and then unlocked the door of the Church, receiving the Church Wardens and Vestrymen into the Church again, who wished him joy upon his having possession of the Church. Then the Rev. Mr Price ordered the Clerk to give public warning in the Church upon the Sunday following, that the Congregation meet in the Church next Wednesday, at eleven of the clock in the Forenoon.

"This ceremony," says Greenwood, "was in accordance with the customs of the English Church; but though it was gratifying to many of the Chapel congregation, and met with open opposition from none, there were yet many who did not in the least relish it, for a republican spirit was even now working in this most royal and loyal church. There were many who preferred to come to the King's Chapel, who yet were not thorough English churchmen. They had the congregational notions respecting their property, and could with difficulty agree that Mr. Price should own, even in form, what they had paid for. They had a dislike, also, to the whole proceeding of foreign presentation to the Bishop. These sentiments spread and prevailed in the church more and more." [1]

The new rector was, however, very cordially received.

May 6th 1729. *Voted*, That the Church Wardens and Vestry wait on the Reverend Mr Price upon his arrival, and conduct him to Mr Peter Feurt's for lodging and entertainment till he shall provide for himself.

2nd of July 1729. *Voted*, That the Sum of one hundred pounds be paid to the Reverend Mr Harris for his Extraordinary service. That the Church Wardens and Committe Returne thanks to Mr Thos Sandford, and make him a present of Ten Guineas for his Service done.

Att a meeting of the Congregation in King's Chappel on the 25 Aug. 1729, — The Question was put whether the Revd Mr Price's Sallary should be raised or not. It passed in the affirmative. *Voted*, Thatt the Revd Mr Price's Sallary should be raised to eight Pounds p week.

Dr. Cutler reflected the satisfaction of the people of King's Chapel, at this apparent close of their controversies, in a letter to his English correspondent, July 18, 1729:[2] —

"Mr. Harris has lost his point in the Church in this town, one Mr. Roger Price being placed over him by my Lord of London. His coming has pleased a great many, and composed others; and I think his public performances are generally acceptable. His temper and parts seem to be good. He has travelled much, though, I think, read but little; and he has yet but too slender a value for the Rituals of the Church. I would yet hope that time will rectify and improve him, if he will study, and not rigorously press some demands upon his parish, which are more than they have promised, and more than they can perform, unless Mr. Harris's friends will fall in; but there is the danger. I need not grudge Mr. Price the gaining his point, for this would prove the best of motives to my people to exert themselves in my favour, and it would be no damage if

---

[1] Greenwood, p. 91. See Izaak Walton's description of George Herbert's locking himself in the church at Bemerton, where he was so rapt in prayer as to lose all sense of the flight of time. Mr. Mossom writes from Marblehead, April 28, 1724: "We have no induction in this country, nor has the Govr, as I have heard, any power to induct. We take possession, and hold by the Bishop's Licence." — *Church Docs.* Mass. p. 149.

[2] Nichols's Illustrations, etc. iv. 288.

the Churches in New England would a little more copy after the Churches in Old."

In this final defeat of his hopes Mr. Harris must have suffered in proportion to his expectations, and it is impossible not to be touched with regret for him. He was evidently a man of tolerant sympathies and peaceable spirit, the victim, in some degree, of the fierce political passions of the time. Of his personal and domestic life we can trace but little. There is a tradition about his marriage: —

"'This gentleman was the father of Mr. Benjamin Harris, for whom Harris Street [in Newburyport] is named. At the time of his coming, when a ship arrived from England it was customary for persons expecting friends to go to the wharf to meet them on their landing. Amongst the throng assembled on this occasion was a young lady, whose glance riveted that of the handsome missionary ere the ship reached the landing. This 'love at first sight' was soon followed by the marriage of the youthful pair." [1]

Notwithstanding his marriage Mr. Harris seems, however, to have retained his college fellowship until his death. Another glimpse of him is given by a correspondent of Sewall, May 21, 1716: [2] —

"Your house is now altered into two very convenient tenements. . . . I have let the lower part of the house to Mr. Harris, the minister who comes in this day; he is a Sober man and hath but a small family. The garden I doe not let him, save on pleasure for the use, but keep it for the upper end of the house where I live."

The Burial Register of King's Chapel records the burial of "Thomas, of Henry and Sarah Harris, Dec. 7, 1724."

This family history closes with Mr. Harris's will, Sept. 4, 1729. In this he bequeaths "to Sarah, my well beloved Wife, £120 per annum in lieu of her dower, . . . to be raised by my executors letting out at Interest the Sum of £2000, as soon as they can raise the same out of my Estate." He gives his son Benjamin all his books, and also "my first Lott or division of Land which is laid out in Providence," R. I.; to his daughter Mary and her heirs forever, his "second Lott;" "to Hannah Luger of Boston, spinster, £10, or

---

[1] Reminiscences of a Nonagenarian, Newburyport, 1879, p. 197.
[2] Letter from Chris. Taylor, — Sewall, iii. 96.

a suit of Mourning and a ring;" and all the rest of his estate to his two children.[1]

Poor Mr. Harris did not long survive the arrival of the new rector, but died on the sixth of the following October, it may well be in part of weariness and disappointment. Rev. William Cooper records in his interleaved almanac: "1729, Oct. 10. At the Burial of the Rev. Mr. Harris." The dislike of his opponents followed him, it is to be feared, beyond the grave; for more than a year afterward they voted "that no money should be paid out of the church stock toward defraying the charge of" burying him. (For Mr. Myles's funeral they had paid £200). Well says Dr. Greenwood: "His life, indeed, for the last years of it must have been a 'fitful fever;' and whatever were the exciting causes of it, or whoever was most to blame for it, himself or others, it is enough now to know that 'after it he slept well.' This is the universal termination, and it is a quiet one. And truly, as I turn over the yellow leaves of our records, and read the lines of faded ink, and note the successive variations of orthography and style, and the constant changes of handwriting, and see names, some familiar and some forgotten, of ministers, governors, wardens, and vestrymen, appearing and then disappearing, the representatives of generations which here 'kept holy time,' the fleeting nature of our life, with all its scenes and occupations, is revealed to me with more than a common distinctness, and men and ages seem to melt away before me like the flakes of snow in spring-time, which dissolve as they feel the earth. And truly, when I have perused votes expressive of division or estrangement, and think that the hands which were held up to pass them, and the hands which were employed in recording those, are now turned to dust, and that some of those who were so active and so heated then are now sleeping coldly in the green yard beside us, or beneath this very floor, I seem to hear the voice, the 'still small voice,' of peace. It speaks of love; it speaks from the grave; it speaks to those for whom the grave is waiting, — and alas for us if it speaks in vain!"[2]

As the old generation was now rapidly passing away from the streets of Boston, no more marked figure vanished from among those who had watched with anxious forebodings the rise and

---

[1] The executors are his wife and his brother-in-law, Mr. Benjamin Pemberton, F. Brinley, and Job Lewis. The autograph is copied from the signature to this will. Besides his Christmas Sermon, already mentioned, and his Preface against Dr. Mather, Mr. Harris published a "Sermon at Boston, Aug. 15, 1713, at the Funeral of Giles Dyer, Esq. Boston: 1713."

[2] Greenwood, p. 92.

prosperity of the King's Chapel, than that of Judge Sewall. The pen of the diarist who has walked with us thus far on our journey was laid aside forever with his death on Jan. 8, 1729-30; and one of our most important sources of information is thus closed.

Mr. Price found among his new parishioners many of the persons whose names have been already noted in our narrative; but the changes which soon removed Mr. Jekyll and Colonel Tailer made a sad inroad upon the congregation. There were funeral pageants and sermons, but all this only showed the more how ill such men could be spared.

"Yesterday the Corpse of the Honourable WILLIAM TAILER, Esq., was Inter'd in Dorchester with great Honour and Respect. The Bells of this Town were tolled from Eleven a Clock till Five. The Cannon of His Majesty's Castle William (of which he was the beloved Captain) were discharged at their Funeral Distance, the Flag being half rais'd. The Pall was supported by His Excellency Governour BELCHER, the Honourable WILLIAM DUMMER, *Addington Davenport, Thomas Hutchinson, Elisha Cooke,* and *Adam Winthrop,* Esqrs. The Funeral was attended by a great Number of Gentry in their Coaches, Chaises, etc., and abundance of Spectators." [1]

Brighter events in one of these families were also noted in the public prints: —

"We are informed from Philadelphia, that on the 20th of *October* last, about 9 o'Clock at Night, *John Jekyll,* Esq., Collector of His Majesty's Customs for this Place, was married there to Mrs. *Margeret Shippe,* a beautiful young lady." [2]

"Last Week the Hon. Col. *Saltonstall* was married to Miss *Molly Jekyll,* Eldest Daughter of the late *John Jekyll,* Esq., deceased." [3]

Two members of the Vestry were connected with the not successful attempt to bring up the youth of Boston in sound Church and State principles, by schools under the Church control. Cutler wrote to the Secretary Oct. 10, 1727: —

"There are no Schools belonging to my Parish; but at each end of the Town there is a public Grammar School. At the South End of the Town the School Master has £150 per Ann^m and his House Rent free; his usher has £50 p^r ann^m; the Scholars are about 120. At the North

---

[1] Boston News-Letter, March 2-9, 1732.

[2] N. E. Weekly Journal, Nov. 4, 1734. John Jekyll, Jr., who had succeeded his father in the Customs and in the Vestry, did not long hold either place. He died in 1740, aged twenty-nine years.

[3] Boston Gazette, Feb. 26-March 5, 1739.

end, the School Master has £100 p' ann^m; the Scholars about 90. There are also three public Schools for writing and cyphering; the Masters have each £100 per ann^m, and one an House Rent free: one has about 90 Scholars, another about 80, the other about 50. None of these are Churchmen, saving one Writing School master, Mr Mills, a worthy person, and very forward to serve the Church as the Society's School master, which capacity he also sustains. All these persons are chosen and paid by the Inhabitants of this Town. There is also one Mr Grainger, a Churchman, who is a private writing School Master; has about 100 Scholars, and recommends himself by his distinguishing capacity for that business." [1]

Sewall also notes the arrival in Boston of Mr. Granger, writing-master: —

March 8 [1719-20]. "Never such a person in Boston before. . . . Professes himself of the Church of England."

This is the Samuel Granger who was in the Vestry, 1729-34. He seems to have succeeded to Mr. Mills as school-master for "the Venerable Society." The Trinity Church Vestry Records contain a letter: —

" . . . There is an allowance of £15 p ann. to a School in this Town; ye last y^t injoy^d it was one Grangier, who has been more than a Yeare absent. Besides, this Town is very well supplied with 5 or 6 free schools, to wch we all pay, and ye Mass^r have handsome Suports." [2]

In sympathy with the church by marriage and friendly feeling had been John Menzies, Judge of Admiralty, — a man much respected and an able judge, who had married as his second wife the widow of Dr. Lancelot Lake, an early Vestryman. A long notice of him in the "Boston Gazette," Sept. 30, 1728, concludes: —

"As to his Religion, he was of the Church of *Scotland* as at present by the fundamental act of Union established, but of a Spirit so moderate and charitable that he occasionally joyn'd with the Church of *England* as by Law established, and with the Congregationalists of this place as by Law tolerated."

Among the influential members of the parish at this time Dr. John Cutler, warden 1721-23, and vestryman most of the time between 1719 and 1749, should not fail to be named. He "was the son of John Cutler, and was born Aug. 6, 1676, at Hingham. The father was a 'chirurgeon,' and served in King Philip's War. He came originally from Holland, where his name was

---

[1] Church Docs. Mass. p. 230.   [2] To Mr. Merrett.

written Demesmaker. On coming to this country he adopted the English translation of his Dutch patronymic, and called himself Cutler. The father removed to Boston about 1694, and lived in Marlborough Street near the Old South Meeting-house. He had a large practice, and was the preceptor of Dr. Zabdiel Boylston, who afterward became famous during the time of the small-pox inoculation. He died probably in the winter of 1717, and his son John, Jr., inherited his practice as well as the homestead. The son married the widow Mrs. Joanna (Dodd) Richards; and he was actively connected with the King's Chapel. He died Sept. 23, 1761, having lived a long life of usefulness."[1]

More than a year elapsed before the arrival of a successor to Mr. Harris, during which time the whole duty fell upon Mr. Price.

27 *day Feb.* 1729-30. *Voted,* that Mr. Peter Pellham have the Pew in the North Gallary (formerly M!. Job Lewis's. S.ᵈ Pellham Paying Twenty pound for the Same.

Easter Monday, the 30ᵗʰ *of March*, 1730. *Voted*, that the Reverend M! Rodger Price have one Hundred pounds for His Extraordinary Service untill this day.

The great event of the arrival of a new governor fell in this year. Another native of New England, Jonathan Belcher, he was the grandson of Andrew Belcher, a tavern-keeper at Cambridge in the early days of Harvard College, whose son Andrew became a rich Boston merchant and provincial councillor, and sent the future Governor to that college, where he graduated in 1699. He was handsome, rich, and ambitious, and travelled in Europe with pleasure and success, twice visiting the Court of Hanover, where his future monarch resided. Returning to Boston, he succeeded his father as a merchant and politician, and was long on the side of prerogative, but shifted to the popular party. He had been sent to England by the Representatives to act for them in their quarrel with the Governor, but Burnet's death opened the way for him, by changing sides again, to persuade the Government

ARMS OF BELCHER.

---

[1] Dr. S. A. Green's Centennial Address before the Massachusetts Medical Society, June, 1881.

that, if appointed to the vacant chair, he, as a native New Englander, could bring Massachusetts to yield the disputed point. Our historian has summed up his character: [1] —

"He had not a generous nature, but in traits which attract popular good-will he was not wanting. Though foolishly irritable, and prone to small resentments which he pursued without dignity, he was not troubled, like his predecessor, with pride and obstinacy about points of honor. He loved intrigue and tortuous methods. He brought into politics some habits of trade. If greedy in acquisition, he was no miser. Especially was his purse freely opened when it might buy large returns of praise and consequence."

It was almost an article of a Massachusetts churchman's creed, that the King's governor ought to attend His Most Gracious Majesty's chapel. Dr. Cutler expressed the general disappointment of Episcopalians that the Governor was a rigid Dissenter: [2]

"Very mortifying to the Church here is the Governor, whom we expect every day, Jonathan Belcher, Esq. Not long ago this gentleman married his daughter here to a person baptised and brought up in the Church; but not before he had strictly obliged him entirely to forsake the Church, which the booby has faithfully done."

David Dunbar, Lieut.-Governor of New Hampshire, wrote, also, Feb. 4, 1730, to the Duke of Newcastle, —

"That the rumor of Belcher's appointment occasioned much apprehension and displeasure among the members of the Church of England, to whom Belcher was a known enemy." [3]

---

[1] Palfrey, iv. 531.

[2] May 9, 1730. Church Docs. Mass. p. 671. The son-in-law was Byfield Lyde. See p. 178, *ante*. One of the "revenges of time" was the fact that the Governor's son, Jonathan, was married in King's Chapel, April 8, 1756, to Abigail, daughter of Jeremiah Allen.

It was not unnatural that the Massachusetts Churchmen should be aggrieved by the indifference or hostility of the Royal Governors, when the statute book of England contained —

"*Anno Quinto Georgii Regis.* An Act for Strengthening the Protestant Interest in these Kingdoms.... Provided always, and be it Enacted ... That if any Mayor, Bailiff, or other Magistrate in the part of Great Britain called England, the Dominion of Wales, or the Town of Berwick-upon-Tweed, or the Isles of Jersey or Guernsey, shall knowingly or Wilfully resort to or be present at any publick Meeting for Religious Worship, other than of the Church of England as by Law Established, in the Gown or other peculiar habit, or Attended with the Ensign or Ensigns of or belonging to Such his Office, That every such Mayor, Bailiff, or other Magistrate, being thereof Convicted by due Course of Law, shall be disabled to hold such Office or Offices, Imployment or Imployments, and shall be adjudged incapable to bear any publick Office or Imploym^t whatsoever within that part of Great Britain called England," etc.

[3] Palfrey, iv. 567.

Although a Dissenter, Governor Belcher brought a generous gift from England for the Church: [1] —

Octob[r] 14th 1730. Voted, That the Church Wardens wait on his Excellency the Gov[r] and return him Thanks, in behalf of the Church, for Solliciting his Majesty for his Royal Bounty to Kings-Chapel; and pay the Contingent Charges, as by the acc[ts] deliver'd, to the Satisfaction of his Excellency.[2]

		£ s. d.
1729	[Part of Mr. Thos. Sandford's acco[t].]	
Apr[l] 24.	To Cash paid y[e] Rev[d] Roger Price, passage Over	20. 00. 00
Nov[r] 19.	To P. L. for a peice of Plate as p[r] Letter, 9 July last.	10. 10. 00
Jan[ry] 13.	To Charges of Packett et c[a] about y[e] Presentation	4. 09. 02

1730	D[r] To J. Belcher as foll[o].	
Mar[h] 28.	To Coach to and from the King's Wardrope . .	0. 01. 06
Apr[l] 4.	To Ditto y[e] Jewel Office	0. 02. 00
8.	To Ditto to y[e] Treasurey	0. 01. 06

[1] Belcher's religion manifested itself in unsavory forms. He wrote to Waldron, in 1734, that he had made young Dick Wibird, of New Hampshire, "a half-sheriff, for which I was offered in London 100 guineas." In the same letter he tells Waldron, "I have good reason to believe Mr. Belcher [himself] grows in favor with God and man."

[2] The vigilant care of Dr. Cutler secured with some difficulty a similar gift for Christ Church, whose Vestry, Nov. 18, 1730, "In consideration of late Donation of his present MAJESTY, our most Gracious Sovereign KING GEORGE the Second to his Maj[ty's] Chappel in this Town, at the Desire of his Excellency Jon[a] Belcher Esq[r] our Govern[r], and under the Promising Views of obtaining the like Benevolence from our Said SOVEREIGN, by the good Interest and Encouragement of our Govern[r] afores[d], —
"*Voted,* That the Minister, Church Wardens, and Vestry do Concur with his Excell[y] Jon[a] Belcher Esq[r] in a due Application for getting plate and other Vtensills for y[e] Altar of Christ Church, and for a Bible, prayer book etc., for the Use of the Said Church like as his Majesty's Chappel in this Town as lately been given by the Interest of the said Govern[r].
"*Voted,* That the Church Wardens for the Time being shall pay out of the Church Stock all the Expences of getting the S[d] Utencills out of the proper Offices in Great Britain, amounting to about Seventeen Pounds Sterling.
"*Voted,* That a letter be Sent by the Said Minister, Church Wardens, and Vestry To Edmund Lord Bishop of London to that End."
A vote of thanks to those who had obtained the gift was passed in 1732. I am indebted to Dr. Palfrey for the following, from the Treasury Papers:—
"These are to signify unto your Grace His Maj[ty] pleasure, that you provide and deliver to the Lord Bishop of London one large Bible, two large Common Prayer Books, and twelve small Common Prayer Books, two Cushcons for a Reading Desk, a Cushcon and Cloth for the Pulpit, a carpet for the Altar, and also two Surplices as a Gift from His Maj[ty] to *Christ Church* at *Boston* in *New England*. And for so doing &c. Given under my hand this 18 day of April 1733, in the 6th year of his Ma[tis] reign. GRAFTON.
"To His Grace the Duke of Montagu &c[a].

| The particulars of this Warrant come to £106 or thereabouts. 24 April, 1733. Thos. Dummer. Jn[o] Halls Compr. | Let this Warrant be executed. Whitehall. Treasury Chambers 3[d] day of May, 1733. R. W.(alpole). W. C.(layton). W. Y.(onge)." |

			£ s. d.
Apr¹	13.	To Ditto, Ditto	0. 01. 06
	15.	To D° for yᵉ Warrᵗ for Chapel Necessaries	0. 03. 00
	16.	To Mʳ Lowe, Clerk of yᵉ Treas'ʳʸ for Pulpit Cloth	2. 02. 00
	17.	To Coach for Warrᵗ for yᵉ Plate	0. 01. 06
	20.	To Ditto for D°	0. 01. 06
	23.	To D° to yᵉ Treasury et cᵃ	0. 01. 06
		To Mʳ Lowe, fees for Takeing up yᵉ Warrᵗ for yᵉ Plate	2. 02. 00
	25.	To King's Wardrope, Vizᵗ	
		To yᵉ Deputy	1. 01. 00
		To yᵉ Clerk	0. 10. 06
		To Messengʳ and Porter	0. 05. 00
	28.	To Coach for yᵉ Plate	0. 03. 00
	29.	To D° from yᵉ Jewel house wᵗʰ D°	0. 03. 00
	30.	To a Deal Chest to pack up yᵉ Plate et cᵃ	0. 16. 00
		To packing of Ditto	0. 04. 00
		To a Rope for yᵉ Chest	0. 02. 00
		To porteridge of Ditto	0. 02. 06
		To Lord Chamberlain for 2 Warrants	2. 17. 06
		To Mʳ Brudnell, Master of yᵉ Jewel Office	4. 09. 00
		To Carriage of yᵉ Plate et cᵃ to Portsmouth	0. 15. 06
			£16. 07. 00

1731
July 8. To his Excellency Jonathan Belcher, Esqʳ., for his charges in Procuring and bringing Plate, &c. . 57. 04. 06

1730
Novʳ 11. To paid Mʳ Wright for the Govnrˢ coat of Armes 6. 00. 00
To a Cask of Nailes Sold to Mʳ Joseph Scot at 14. 00. 07
Advance £325 pʳ Cᵗ 45. 11. 10

£59. 12. 05

The last item is explained in: —

A Copia of Mʳ Thoˢ Sandford, Letter of London pʳ Cap: Leatherhed.

LONDON, March 25, 1730.

GENTLEMEN, — I received a Letter signed by the Church Warden of King's Chapel, and likewise by Messˢ Geo: Cradock, John Eastwick, and John Checkley, dated Boston, yᵉ 9 July last, adviseing me of the safe arrival of yᵉ Reverᵈ Mʳ Roger Price at Boston, and of his Being put in full possesion of yᵉ Church without yᵉ least opposition from any quarter, which I was very glad to hear; and I return yourselves and yᵉ Congregation my thanks for yᵉ present of ten Guineas, ordered me as an acknowledgment for my appearance here in order to preserve Your Right et cᵃ: to be laid out in a piece of Plate, which I have accordingly done; and with an addition theretoo, Bought a very handsome peice of Plate, and yᵉ Inscription yᵗ was ordered is Engraven thereon, which I hope will Long remain in family as a lasting Monument of ye gratitude of the Congregation in Respect to myself, and to set forth ye Right of presentation to King's Chapel, and out of which I have often Drank wishing ye prosperity thereof. I was ordred to Remit ye Ballance in my hands, But no mention in w^t; in my opinion Nailes may do as well as anything; so I have Bought some 4^d and 10^d, which are put into a Cask and Shipt Aboard ye Ship Mary, John Leatherhead, Comand^r, and goes Consigned To your Selves, ye Cost whereof, and Charges thereon, amounting too £14. 15, for which ye King's Chappel acc^t Debter, and Inclosed you have ye Account Curr^t, — ye Ballance which remains due from myself being five Shillings and ten pence, which shall pay as y^o shall order. And wth my hearty Service to your Selves and all ye Gentlemen Concerned, I am, Gentlemen,

Yo^r Very Humble Servt   T. S.

To Y^e Church Wardens of King's Chapel, Boston.

Besides this gift of a communion service from King George II., His Majesty sent a supply of prayer books: —

October 18th 1730. *Voted,* one New Common prayer book for the Altar, two for the Desk, one for the Clerk, two New great books for the Govr. pew, and the two Old ones in the Govr. pew for the Church Wardens' pew.

Voted, two New books for the Church Wardens W^m. Speakman and Job Lewis.

Voted, two New Books for Francis Brinley Esqr. and M^r. George Cradock, they returning the old ones and everybody else that have old ones to return 'em.

Voted, two New books to Capt. Cyprian Southack and Col^l. Es. Hatch.

Voted, two New books to Mr. Thos. Phillips and M^r. Geo. Shape.

Voted, M^r. John Chickley to have Capt. Southack's book.

Voted, D^r. Gibbins and D^r. Stewart the two books that are in the Church Wardens' pew.

Voted, M^r. W^m. Randle the book that is the Communion Table.

Voted, Capt. Child to have M^r. Brinley's book.

Voted, M^r. Hall to have M^r. Cradock's book.

Voted, M^r. W^m. Gould to have the Clark's book.

Voted, M^r. Robt. Skinner to have the book in the Desk.

Voted, that the Rev^d. M^r. Roger Price, Minister

W^m. Speakman } Churchwardens
Job Lewis

Robt. Auchmuty Esqr.   D^r. John Gibbins
M^r. George Cradock   M^r. John Checkley

be a Committee to write a letter to Col^l. Shute for the Plate that is now in his hands that was given to King's Chapel by his late Majesty King George the first.

Still further additions to the Church accommodations were needed: —

8th July 1729. *Voted,* That the Church Wardens w^t on his Exc^y the Govern^r, to know his opinion concerning a proposall made in the Vestry about building a gallery on the South and South East sides of the Church, and make a report to the next Vestry.

25. July, 1729. *Voted,* Thatt a Gallery be built on the South and S. East of the Church, Excepting over his Exc^{ys} seat, over which there is only to be a passage.

10th *of Sep:* 1729. *Voted,* That (notwithstanding the vote passed on ye 6th of August last for the Building a Single Gallary on the South Side of S^d Chapel) a Double Gallary Should be Built with the front Pews, Leaveing the Back part of Said Gallary Vacant.[1]

Sept. 23, 1729. *Voted,* That the moving the Pulpit and Desk, and alteration of the Pews between the middle and South Isle, is necessary and advantagious to the Church, Nemine Contradicente. *Voted,* that the above alteration be Left with the Comittee for Building a Gallary, Nemine Contradicente.

Boston, Sept. 19, 1729. I, John Pillet, do Covenant and Agree with Messrs William Speakman and William Randle, Church Wardens, George Craddock, Josh. Wroe, George Stewart, and John Gibbins (a Comitte of Vestry) To build a double Gallery on the South Side of King's Chappel, Consisting of ten Pews in the front, each of them five feet Six Inches deep, and one Single Bench behind, and find all the Boards, Timber, Nails, Iron, Lime, Lathing and Plaistering, and everything also necessary to Compleat the same Workman like. Also take down a large Window over the South door, make two Window-frames and Casements, and fix them, and find Such Clapboard and plaistering as shall be necessary for Inside and Outside work about Said Windows; Move the Pulpit, Reading Desk, etc., and make four Pews In the Place Where the Pulpit, Reading Desk, etc. now Stands. All this I promise to do and Compleat within two months from the Date hereof, Upon consideration that W. Randle and W. Speakman, or either of them, pay me the sum of One hundred and Sixty Pounds Bills of Credit as I shall want the same; and I do further Promise to attend the direction of the above Comitte In the Premises.

31st *Day of Octo:* 1729. The Question was Put whether the South Gallary Should be Built in the Front over the Governour's Seat: it Passed in ye negative. *Voted,* that the West Gallary be altered in to as many Pews as Conveniency will Permit.

August 11th 1730. *Voted,* That His Excellency Govr Belcher's Arms be painted and put over his pew in King's Chapel.

---

[1] "Galleries are often enumerated in Paterson's account of London churches (1714) among recently erected 'ornaments.' It was an object of some ambition to have a front seat in a gallery." — *Church of England in the Eighteenth Century,* ii. 424.

These years saw a renewal of the controversial warfare, which had ceased for a brief space. The observance of Church days by the faithful called forth the spirit of opposition among the learned, and more noisy arguments from the multitude.[1] Now, too, Bishop Beveridge's sermon on the Common Prayer was reprinted in Boston.[2] This is an admirable, clear, practical statement of the edifying character of "the Language, the Substance, the Method, and the Manner of Performing" the Liturgy. The adaptation, however, of such a passage as the following to New-England readers seems doubtful: —

" By what kind of Spirit the *Common-Prayer* was then [in the reign of King Charles I.] cast out you all know, and some of you found by *woful Experience*. All that I shall say of it is only this: that the same *Spirit* that then stirred up People so violently against the *Common-Prayer* stirred them up at the same time to rebel against their *King*, to take away Men's *Estates* and *Lives* contrary to all *Law* and *Justice;* and at last to *murther* one of the most *pious Princes* that ever lived. And whether that was the *Spirit* of *Christ* or *Antichrist, God* or the *Devil*, judge you. . . . Yea, together with the *Liturgy* they laid aside all Distinction betwixt sacred and common things."

In 1730 Mr. Price received from Bishop Gibson his commis-

---

[1] A controversy took place between the minister of Marblehead and the Episcopal missionary there: —

"The Certainty, TIME, and END, of the BIRTH of our Lord and Saviour JESUS CHRIST: with the Accomplishments of several of the *Prophecys*, relating thereto. A SERMON, at the *Lecture*, in *Marblehead, Dec.* 25, 1729. To which is added An APPENDIX, attempting more clearly to State the *true Year* of our Lord's *Nativity*. By *John Barnard*, V. D. M. of *Marblehead. Boston:* Printed for *S. Gerrish*, at the lower end of *Cornhill.* 1731."

"A VINDICATION of the Practice of the Antient *Christians*, As well as the *Church* of *England*, and other *Reformed* Churches, in the Observation of CHRISTMAS DAY: In Answer to the Uncharitable Reflections of THOMAS DE LAUNE, Mr. WHISTON, and Mr. JOHN BARNARD of *Marblehead:* In a Sermon preach'd on the 4th of January, 1729-1730. By *George Pigot*, V. D. M. at *Marblehead*. Published at the Desire of the Church-Wardens and Vestry. Etc. BOSTON, Printed by *T. Fleet* at the *Heart* and *Crown* in *Cornhill*, and sold by *Gillam Phillips* at the *Three Bibles* and *Crown* in *King Street*, 1731."

"I *wish* the same," said Mr. Pigot, "and that the vile Rout and Firing of Guns, at *Marblehead* on *Christmas-Day*, were suppressed by *Authority;* and that the same Respect at least were paid to *that* Day, and the *Thirtieth* of *January*, from his People, as is given by Church-Men to their *Thanksgiving* and *Fast Days*. For *our Festivals* are founded upon as good Authority as *Theirs* can be; and if the *Act* of *Toleration* secures Them from the Penalty of the Law, for not observing 'em, so likewise ought the *Rule* of *Moderation* to secure us from being insulted upon their Account."

[2] [Beveridge, William, Bishop of St. Asaph.] "A Sermon concerning the Excellency and Usefulness of Common Prayer. Text, 1 Cor. xiv. 26. Preached at the Opening of the Parish Church of *St Peter's*, Cornhill, London, Nov. 27, 1681. 29th ed. Boston: 1733." It was first printed by desire of Bishop Compton.

sion as commissary, or superintendent of Episcopal churches in New England, under and as representative of the Bishop,[1] in a letter which was entered on the church records.

At the same time arrived a successor to Mr. Harris, — Rev. Thomas Harward, previously incumbent for many years near Guilford in Surrey.

July 13th, 1730.

GOOD S^R, — I send you the Comission, together with a copy of mine, from the King, wch I believe is entered among the public Records there, Govern^r Belcher having had it particularly in his Instructions to make such entry, as the Secretary to the Comissioners of Trade and Plantations informs me. I also send ye three Copies of the Directions I have drawn for all the Comissarys in the Plantations, in order to their proceeding against Irregular Clergymen, wch I hope you will have no occasion to carry into practice.

Mr. Harward, who comes over to succeed Mr. Harris, is well recomended by the neighbouring Clergy in Surrey, where he has been an Incumbent for many years, near Guilford; and their Recommendation is confirmed by the Bishop of Winchester, their Diocesan, according to the method I use for receiving due Satisfaction Concerning the Characters of Such Persons as offer themselves for Missionaries.

He is directed to behave himself towards you with all due respect as his Superior, and not to intermedle in any matter but what shall appear to belong to him as Lecturer. But its impossible for me to descend to particulars, since I do not know what share of Duty properly belongs to him as Such. If you can fix that matter between your Selves, with the advice and assistance of some discreet and serious persons of the Congregation, I shall be ready to ratify it, that it may be a rule to all future Ministers and Lecturers of that Church; and if any doubt arise concerning the proper bounds, you may refer it to me, and I will consider and determine it according to the best of my Judgm^t etc.

I pray for a Blessing upon y^r Pastorall Labours, and am,

S^r, Y^r assured Friend and Brother,

EDM^D LONDON.

Already, before Mr. Harward's arrival, there is a premonition of troubles to come: —

November 25th, 1730. *Voted*, That the Rev^d Mr. Roger Price have three Pounds p week from Easter to the arrival of the Revd Mr Thomas Harward, the said Mr Price quitting all Pretentions to any part of the Money paid by the Crown to the s^d Mr Harward.

7th *of Dec^r.*, 1730. *Voted*, That no money be payd out this Chh Stock towards defraying the charge of burying ye Reverend Mr Henry Harris.

[1] Greenwood, p. 94.

19ᵗʰ *April*, 1731. *Voted*, That the Number of the Vestry shall not exceed twenty.

Voted, That the Rev. Mr Roger Price be paid three pounds for his extraordinary Service.

Voted. That the Consideration of building a Vestry room be left to the Church-wardens and Vestry for them to make a report to the Congregation at the next meeting.

The old difficulty soon seems again to have risen between the rector and his assistant: —

At a meeting of the Ministers, Church Wardens, and Vestry of King's Chappell at Mr Verdy's, 12 July, 1732, It is mutually agreed between the Reverd Mr Roger Price and the Revd Mr Tho. Harward that the Duty of Reading Prayers and Preaching be equally performed by them.

The Reverd Mr Price put the Question, whether the Revd Mr Tho. Harward has any right to the perquisites that may arise by marrying, Christning, or burying, etc., it was unanimously *Voted* that he had not. It was also agreed that in the absence of Mr Price, by being in the Country for any such length of time as renders him incapeable of performing either marrying, Christning, or buryalls, that Mr Harward, performing either of these Dutys during such absence, shall be intituled to the perquisites, — and likewise unanimously voted by the Vestry.

The primitive state of the times in regard to journeyings is strikingly shown by the following record, in which also sound the first mutterings of a gathering storm between the minister and his people: —

28 September, 1732. Whereas the Reverd Mr Roger Price did, on the 18ᵗʰ day of Septemr, 1732, Set out on a Journey, intended to New York, contrary to the desire of the Cch Wardens, and without consultg the Vestry, and this not being the first time of his absenting from his duty without adviseing with the Vestry or Congregation, to prevent the like for the future, and We being desirous of his constant residence amongst us,

Voted, That the Church Wardens for the time being do not pay the Sᵗ Reverd Mr Price any money for the time of his absence till further Orders from the Vestry or Congregation.

1ˢᵗ Febry, 1732–33. *Voted*, That Mr Nathl Gifford has no power to depute any person to act for him as Organist.

Voted, That twenty-four pounds be paid to the Reverd Mr Price for this time of his being absent.

Mr. Harward is probably the Thomas Harward who took his B. A. at University College, Oxford, Nov. 6, 1721, and his

M. A., July 7, 1724.[1] He had been educated a physician before taking orders, and could not resist the opportunity to try his skill and to propound to the world his remedy for the evils wrought by the east winds of his new home. He published in 1732 a medical treatise entitled "Electuarium Novum Alexipharmacum," describing the composition of a variety of "troches," and in the same year a sermon on "The Fulness of Joy in the Presence of God."[2]

Mr. Harward soon showed that he had an independent mind, and that he did not favor controversy with the prevailing church in Massachusetts, by refusing to join "in drawing up a memo-

---

[1] Another Thomas Harward took his B. A. at the same college, March 27, 1751.

[2] The full title of Dr. Harward's medical treatise is "Electuarium Novum Alexipharmacum, or, A new Cordial, Alexiterial and Restorative ELECTUARY; which may serve for a succedaneum to the grand *Theriaca Andromachi*. The *Theriaca* examined, with reasons humbly offered why the *Troches* should be ejected, as well as a great number of the rest of the Ingredients. A new correction of *Theriaca*, most humbly proposed, and with due Deference submitted, to the superior and impartial judgment of the Royal College of Physicians; and dedicated to the most Honored the President, the justly Honored the Censors, with their most worthy Brethren the Elect, and the rest of the Fellows of that most Honorable society. By the Revd Mr Harward, a Licentiate of the Royal College, and Lecturer of the *Royal Chappel* at *Boston* in *New-England*. *Eo melius, quo communius Bonum*. Boston: Printed by B. Green, 1732. Price, Two Shillings." 8vo. pp. 26.

"If these poor Endeavours of mine . . . are despised, or at least reckoned of little Moment; if the Divine Art of *Physic* must perpetually lie sleeping, and the Wheels of *Medicine* by no Means move on, — I hope I shall have the Liberty of Enjoying my own Thoughts upon any *Medicinal* (tho' Capital) Preparation, as well as of lamenting the Unhappiness of humane Nature, which is owing in too great a Measure to the INDOLENCE OF MANKIND."

Of this Electuarium Dr. S. A. Green says: "The author proposed a much-mixed conglomeration to take the place of mithradate, a still more complicated mass of medicated confusion. He speaks of the electuary as 'my own,' a form of expression which furnished the origin of the word *nostrum*." — *Centennial Address before the Mass. Medical Society, June 7, 1881.*

Dr. Harward, in combining the two professions, continued the early New England tradition. Many of the early ministers practised medicine. "The earliest treatise on a medical subject was written by Rev. Thomas Thacher, first minister of the Old South." Both Increase and Cotton Mather and Dr. Colman also published medical pamphlets. The union of the two professions is called by Cotton Mather an "Angelical Conjunction." Ibid. p. 16.

In the preface to the "Electuary" he says: "I think it is my Duty, as well as Happiness, to submit and dedicate my first Endeavours in Medicine to that most Honourable Society, which, after the most just and candid Examination, have been pleased, with great Goodness, to think me worthy of Practice." The "Boston Gazette," Sept. 9, 1734, contains an advertisement of Dr. Harward's "Account of and Observations on the Reigning Flux, which has lately been so fatal among us."

The full title of Dr. Harward's sermon is "The *Fulness of Joy* in the Presence of GOD, Being the Substance of a DISCOURSE Preach'd lately in the *Royal Chappel* at BOSTON in *New-England*. By the Reverend Mr *Harward*, Lecturer at the *Royal Chappel*. Boston: Printed by *B. Green*. Sold by *Gillam Phillips*, over against the South side of the Town-House, 1732." 8vo. pp. 23. Text, Psalm xvi. verse 11.

rial to the Lord Bishop of London, and a petition to the King's Most Excellent Majesty, respecting the Sufferings of the churchmen in this Province," of which our narrative will presently speak. He also showed that he took a more broad and self-sacrificing view of the duties and opportunities of a king's lecturer than seemed to have been the case with the other clergymen who held that honorable position.

The early efforts of the first generations of Puritan settlers, in New England, to win the aboriginal inhabitants to Christianity seem to have died out in despair. Notwithstanding the saintly memory of the Apostle Eliot, and the multitude of " praying Indians " whose cause Gookin had earnestly pleaded, the next generation hardened into that indifferent policy which has marked their whole later treatment of this question. Nor was it otherwise with the negro slaves, whom the growing wealth of the country had multiplied. Here and there a minister or pious church-member would labor for the soul while enjoying the service of a slave or two; but this method of missionary work, while well approved of, was limited in its scope, and too often these wretched beings were considered more profitable in proportion as they were more brutish. There are tokens that the missionaries of the Church of England sought to rouse the people to a better sense of their duty. Dean Berkeley, whose residence at Newport had made him acquainted with the state of feeling, said of the negroes, in 1731, in a sermon before the Society for Propagating the Gospel in Foreign Parts: —

"The Religion of these People, as is natural to suppose, takes after that of their Masters. Some few are baptized; several frequent the different Assemblies, and far the greater Part none at all. An antient Antipathy to the Indians — whom, it seems, our first Planters (therein, as in certain other Particulars, affecting to imitate Jews rather than Christians) imagined they had a Right to treat on the Foot of *Canaanites* or *Amalekites*, together with an irrational Contempt of the Blacks, as Creatures of another Species, who had no Right to be instructed or admitted to the Sacraments — has proved a main Obstacle to the Conversion of these poor People.

"To this may be added an erroneous Notion that the being baptized is inconsistent with a State of Slavery. To undeceive them in this Particular, which had too much Weight, it seemed a proper Step, if the Opinion of his Majesty's Attorney and Solicitor-General could be procured. This Opinion they charitably sent over, signed with their own Hands, which was accordingly printed in *Rhode-Island*, and dispersed throughout the Plantations."

Bishop Gibson showed a Christian solicitude to stir up to their duty the distant members of his vast diocese, by publishing "A Letter of the Lord Bishop of LONDON to the Masters and Mistresses of Families in the *English* Plantations, Exhorting them to Encourage and Promote the Instruction of their NEGROES in the Christian Faith." (London: 1727.) This is an admirable plea so far as it goes. He thus meets the argument of selfishness against Christianizing slaves: —

"But it is further pleaded that the Instruction of Heathens in the Christian Faith is in order to their Baptism; and that not only the *Time* to be allowed for Instructing them would be an Abatement from the Profits of their Labour, but also that the *Baptizing* them when instructed would destroy both the Property which the Masters have in them, as Slaves bought with their Money, and the Right of selling them again at Pleasure; and that the making them Christians only makes them less diligent and more ungovernable.

"To which it may be very truly reply'd that Christianity, and the embracing of the Gospel, does not make the least Alteration in Civil Property, or in any of the Duties which belong to Civil Relations," etc.

The Bishop also asked aid at home in England to the same end. Mr. Price, in letters to the Secretary, touched the root of the difficulty: [1] —

"REV? SIR, — I rec'd the Favour of your two letters with the Sermons, which I have distributed according to your direction. It is a great satisfaction to the Members of the Church of England in these Provinces to hear that their unjust sufferings are thought worthy the Societies Notice, and have engaged their Compassion. Mr. Arnold is informed of the Societies permission to goe to England, and designs to embrace it unless prevented by the expectation of some preferment in New York Government. The pious design of instructing the Negroes, which you mention'd, will meet with so many Obstructions as is much to be fear'd will render it abortive. The two grand impediments that occur to my Mind is the want of ministers properly qualified for this undertaking by an uncommon share of Humility and Zeal for the Glory of God, and the low Ebb of Christianity at this Day throughout the World, and in this Countrey especially too slight a regard to the use of Baptism, which, among the Dissenters, is frequently omitted upon very trifling Motives. There is better care taken in the Church to Baptize their own Children, but Baptizing of Negroes is too much neglected even there. This evil may, in some measure, be remedied by an order from the Society to their Missionaries often to insist upon this duty with their people, and by distributing a sufficient number of Discourses upon

---

[1] I am indebted to Mrs. F. E. Weston for this and other letters of Mr. Price.

this Subject, — the ministers at the same time enforcing the same by their Public and private admonitions. This is all, in my poor judgment, that can be done purely in a Spiritual Manner, without the concurrence of the Civil Authority by the sanction of rewards and penalties. After all, to declare freely my sentiments, I believe the Societies Bounty may as usefully be dispenc'd by introducing a Regular Worship of God and a rational Religion in some parts of this Countrey where the true Spirit of it is almost lost in form and Profession, and ignorance and infidelity are daily prevailing, as in attempting what the present corruption of Manners and the despised authority of the Church will render almost impracticable. As for the Salaries bestow'd upon the Churches of Boston and Newport, I believe they might be much reduced, and by degrees totally withdrawn without any detrement to the general good; and the Salaries bestow'd upon two Schools in the Collony of Connecticut are entirely needless. I could mention some other impositions upon the Societies Generosity, but I am affraid I have been already to bold in declaring my opinion."

He wrote again: —

"In a former letter I gave you my sentiments relating to the conversion of negro slaves, which, in short, I look upon as an attempt almost impracticable in the present state of religion; and till masters can be persuaded to have a greater value for their own souls, we have but small hopes they will be very anxious about the salvation of their negroes."[1]

The unchristian "Indian policy" of the whites dates from the Pequot War in 1638, which roused a feeling of horror and revenge which adopted methods of savage warfare as barbarous as those used by the red men. When these became not merely the natural reprisals of man in mortal peril, but the recognized expedient of the Government, the sporadic attempts to convert the Indians not only encountered the obstacles inherent in the savage character, but were rendered hopeless by the opposition even of many good men. The English Government stirred the most cruel passions of the Indians for service in its own warfare

---

[1] Mr. Price to the Secretary, July 28, 1740. Church Docs. Mass. p. 341. The contemptuous dislike of the inferior races followed them even to the grave. "Small-pox spread with such fury and fatality during the summer of 1721 that the Legislature passed a resolve, applicable only to the town of Boston, that no bell should be tolled for the burial of persons who had died of the disease, except such as the selectmen of the town should direct." They ordered "That one Bell only shall be made use of for a Funeral, and that to be Tolled but Twice, each Tolling not to exceed the space of Six minutes. Further, that there be but one Tolling of a Bell for the Burial of any *Indian, Negro,* or *Malatto,* and that they be carried the nearest way to the Graves." This was the time when Dr. Boylston and Cotton Mather excited so much hostility by advocating inoculation. — *Dr. S. A. Green's Centennial Address, etc.,* 1881.

with the French, who also had their own Indian allies. At the period of our narrative, the Royal Governor and head of the vestry of the King's Chapel proclaimed —

"That there be granted, to be paid out of the publick Treasury, to any Company, Party, or Person singly, of His Majesty's Subjects belonging to this Province, who shall voluntarily, and at their own proper Cost and Charge, go out and kill a male Indian of the Age of Twelve Years, or upwards, of the Tribe of St. *Johns* or *Cape-Sables*, . . . and produce his Scalp in Evidence of his Death, the Sum of *one Hundred Pounds* in Bills of Credit of this Province of the new Tenor, . . . and the Sum of *Fifty Pounds* in said Bills for Women, and the like Sum for Children under the Age of Twelve Years killed in Fight."[1]

The Government occasionally recognized for a moment that it had a religion to give to the Indians, but in reality only used it as a pawn in the great game of chess which it was playing against France for political supremacy in America. In 1701 the sachems of the Iroquois expressed their hope that the "Squa Sachem," Queen Anne, "would be a good mother, and send some to teach them religion, and establish religion amongst them, that they might be able to purchase a coat, and not go to church in bear-skins." They also sent her "ten beaver-skins to make her fine, and one fur muff to keep her warm." In 1710 four of them were taken by Nicholson to England and presented the Queen with belts of wampum, telling her that they had "hung up the kettle" of peace and "taken up the hatchet" to join Great Britain in the war. "Since we have been in alliance with our great Queen's children we have had some knowledge of the Saviour of the world. . . . If our great Queen will be pleased to send over some persons to instruct us, they shall find a most hearty welcome." But, as might have been expected, this alliance between the tomahawk and the New Testament came to nothing.

Noble efforts were made among the Mohawks by some of the missionaries of "the Venerable Society."[2] In Massachusetts the name of David Brainard, the Congregationalist missionary to the Indians (born April 20, 1718; died Oct. 9, 1747), shines with saintly lustre. An attempt was made

---

[1] "By His *EXCELLENCY WILLIAM SHIRLEY*, Esq'r, Captain-General and Governour in Chief in and over His *MAJESTY'S* Province of the *Massachusetts-Bay* in *NEW ENGLAND*. A PROCLAMATION For the Encouragement of Volunteers *to prosecute the WAR against the St.* John's and Cape-Sable's *Indians*," Nov. 2, 1744.

[2] An outline of their labors is given in Anderson, Col. Church, iii. 286-336.

by the Church of England to win some of the New England Indians to Christianity; but their work among the Indians, difficult at best, was further impeded by the jealousies between Congregationalists and Churchmen. The clergy of New England wrote to the Secretary, July 20, 1727: —

"It is the vehement heat raised against the endeavours and hopes of some of us to bring over Charles Augustus Ninaagret with the Narragansett Indians, of whom he is Sachem, to embrace the Christian Religion. He hath related his case in his letter to yourself, and we humbly beg that credit and countenance may be given to it. The view of bringing him into the Church of England when he is Christianized has already raised many fierce and unnatural resentments against some of us who are instrumental in the affair, and we fear all possible oppositions to us here, and the worst representations of the case before the Society, and wherever else any possible assistance may be expected." [1]

It is a proof of the humanity and Christian zeal of Rev. Thomas Harward, that he was eager to undertake a missionary work among the Indians, notwithstanding Mr. Price's despairing views of such a work. He wrote to the Bishop of London, July 19, 1731, picturing a strange group in the Governor's pew: —

"His Excellency and his Lady and the Lieutenant-Governor Colonel Taylor, who is a very worthy man, were all at the Royal Chapel yesterday in the afternoon, with three Indian Sachems of the Mohock tribes. Tis a pity some care is not taken of those poor creatures, whose souls are as capable of immortality as ours. I declare with great sincerity, if the Society will allow me an assistant for the Chapel, — I mean my Lecture, and some small matter to support me in my travels during the summer season every year, — I will not only spend considerable time among those unhappy Indians, but will likewise go over the several Provinces. I find I could soon master the Indian Language enough to do those poor souls good as to spiritual concerns. If this proposal be agreeable to your Lordship and the Honorable Society, I desire I may go in some capacity or other, — as Commissary General, or what your Lordship shall think proper, — that I may have some respect shown me more than a mere itinerant; otherwise I shall not be willing." [2]

Governor Belcher wrote to the Bishop of London, July 24, 1731, commending the design: —

[1] Church Docs. Mass. p. 225. Sewall notes: "March 27, 1729. — Went to the Comissioners Meeting in the Council Chamber . . . Directed a Letter to be written Concerning Ninnigret the Sachem, — his desiring to have a Church of England set up."

[2] Church Docs. Mass. p. 268.

"Had the Rev.d M.r Harwood some allowance or assistance he might, at proper seasons of the year, greatly serve Religion and the Church not only among some English Plantations at a distance from hence, but also among the Indian natives, who, to the shame of Europe and America, are to this day without the knowledge of the true God and the Saviour of mankind."[1]

From the following letter in our records it appears that the minister, wardens, and vestry did not approve of this plan, in which Mr. Harward and the Governor were in accord, but interposed to prevent him from making acquaintance with the race whom he desired to help: —

July 9th, 1732.

To His Excellency Jon.n Belcher, Esq., Govern.r and Command.r in Chief in and over his Majesties Province of Massachusetts Bay, etc.

The Remonstrance and Representation of the Minister, Cch Warden, and Vestry of King's Chappell in Boston, Humbly Sheweth, —

That with the greatest concern they hear Yo.r Excellency has laid yo.r Comands on the Rev.d Tho. Harward to Attend you in yo.r designed expedition and treaty w.th the Eastern Indians;[2] and that he, without duly Considering his own Duty and the present circumstances of the Church, implicitly obeys them, — and that in opposition to M.r Comissarys Order.

It is with the like concern that We should have this unhappy Occasion of calling in question such Yo.r Excellencys Authority, being desirous always of Distinguishing our Selves, as our Holy Religion does Our Church, in being the most Dutyfull and most Loyall in all things Lawfull. But We must with Submission now Remonstrate That M.r Harward's Duty is Locall, and no Power but the Power that apointed Him for that Duty can dispence therewith.

However, Such is our Attachment to Yo.r Excellency, and the Honour we pay to Yo.r high Station, That we cheerfully would fall into such Yo.r Comands: But as it is well known the absence of the Rever.d M.r Pigot has been the means of many members falling from the Episcopall Church of Marblehead, So M.r Harward's attending you in this Expedition may, We greatly fear, be the means not only of shutting up that Church's Doors but possibly terminate in the Ruin of it, and what probably may be the Secret Views of the Enemies of our Church who advise Yo.r Excellency in this affair.

We therefore beg you to consider if it please God to visit M.r Comissary Price with Sickness, then Two Churches will be without Ministers; and probably from Such Like reasons why Our Ministers have not attended Govern.r on Such Negotiations. As Yo.r Excellency has declared

---

[1] Church Docs. Mass. p. 271.
[2] His Majesty's ship "Scarborough" took Governor Belcher to confer with the Eastward Indians in July, 1734.

in the strongest Terms Yo.^r Readiness to Serve the Church of England, We flatter Our Selves you will now give Demonstration in recalling Orders that inevitably must tend to the hurt thereof. And as in Duty We will ever pray, etc.

The Govern.^r Read it before the Comittee and made Reply: It is very well, Gentlemen.

Whatever thought Mr. Harward may have had of renewing his attempt later, his early death precluded it.

The disagreements between the two clergymen on this and other subjects are preserved for us in letters which each wrote home to England. From these it seems that the appearance here of an Irish clergyman named Christian, without credentials, but winning a following in the church by his plausible speech, aggravated the difficulties. Of this person nothing else is known. Mr. Harward wrote to the Bishop, July 19, 1731:

"Mr Commissary is now determined for England within a Month, as he at present gives out; but he has altered his sentiments several times this Summer, and perhaps may alter them once more. I would advise him by all means to look a little into the state of the Churches in the several Provinces, before he goes for England, that he may be the better able to give Your Lordship some true account of their condition after a regular and impartial examination into things; but in this as well as other things, his sentiments and mine do not always coincide. I could never get him yet to visit Dr Cutler once since I have been at Boston, which gives occasion for our own people to think there is not so good an harmony as there ought to be among us, and to our enemies to laugh at us: for my part I have endeavoured to keep a good correspondence with both, and have served both of them often with a great deal of pleasure. But since this Irish Minister came over whose name is Christian, who tells us he was Curate to Doctor Pearce of St Martin's, and that he waited on Your Lordship, but brought no letter from any person, my unwillingness to join them in encouraging his preaching, without Your Lordship's notice, licence, or approbation (which I thought was by no means right, and would never be allowed of), has occasioned some small dispute between Mr Commissary and myself, which I thought fit to drop, and let them do as they please. As for Mr Christian, he may be a very good man for anything I know; but as to the persons he is fallen in with, and whose councils he likes to follow, they have almost ruined the Church once already by their fiery zeal in poor Mr Harris's time, and 'tis my humble opinion they never will be at rest until they have effected it, or at least occasioned some new confusions. For my part, had I power I would soon (with prudence) put a period to all their power in the Church, for their number is very small, — but three principales for Ringleaders, and Mr Checkley the chief of them (who would never take the Oaths until he was obliged to do it, and who was in London for Orders in Governor Shute's time, and whose character was sent over to prevent his stealing into Orders by his late Excellency and M! Harris) : I suppose Your Lordship knows the man and the rest of his accomplices, one Gibbons an Apothecary, and Steward a Surgeon.[1] These men are so furious and clamarous for the Church that a man dares not preach upon Charity and mutual forbearance on any degree of tenderness towards those of differing sentiments in order to bring them in. No, you are an enemy to the Church; if you pretend to oppose her enemies in the spirit of meekness you are a favorer of the Dissenters, you give up the Church's cause, and don't stand up for the Church at all. For my part I have ever found, and I believe I ever shall, gentleness, meekness, moderation, etc., to be the best and most Christian means to reduce those that are Seperated from the Church, and 'tis my humble opinion will always sooner effect it than all the bitterness and clamour in the world. I wish M! Commissary a good voyage, and hope Your Lordship will find some agreeable preferment for him (for his own sake) elsewhere. If Your Lordship commands me to give my reasons for what I say, I will do it with great truth; otherwise I say no more, but beg leave to be removed if he returns again. I most humbly request a line from Your Lordship's hand, and beg Your Lordship to let me know whether I do well or ill in preaching up charity, tenderness, and moderation. I have filled the Chapel with this spirit, and 'tis my humble Opinion the contrary conduct will soon make it thin."[2]

Governor Belcher's character was a strange mixture of showy and popular qualities with those that were small and sordid. A politician of the school of Walpole and Newcastle, he made office a matter of bargain and sale. An unctuous professor of piety, he used his religion for his political advantage, and thus "made the best of both worlds." He was touchy in regard to real or fancied slights on his personal dignity, and seems to have regarded himself, although a Congregationalist, as in some sense the official head of the King's Chapel. On the other hand, Mr. Price did not recognize this privilege, and used a straightforward method when they came in collision, which the Governor greatly disapproved. A serious difficulty soon arose between them, of which Mr. Price gave a full account to the Bishop of London: —

"MY LORD, — I am much surpris'd that I have receiv'd no Letter from Your Lordship in so long a season, When I understand the affairs of the Church have occasion'd Your Lordship to write to others here present.

---

[1] John Gibbins, warden 1725-27; George Stuart, warden 1732-34.
[2] Church Docs. Mass. p. 266.

I have perplex'd myself in assigning some cause for this Silence; but without coming to any Certainty, I can only fix it upon some Conjectures which I have picked up from Expressions drop'd by Mr. Harward out of a Letter he has lately receiv'd from Your Lordship which he industriously reports to my disadvantage,— as that Your Lordship is displeas'd with my proceedings here, that the State of the Church will be put upon a new footing, that we may expect sudden and great alterations in it, by which he alarms the minds of the People and keeps them in a Ferment. Again it is reported that Your Lordship has receiv'd but one letter from me since I have been in the Countrey, which is represented as a neglect of my Duty. This I can scarce believe, since I have wrote many,— Two especially, soon after the arival of Mr. Harward, for the Miscarriage of which I should be much concern'd, and a third by Mr. Piggot. Another reason might be that Your Lordship expected me in England the last Summer, and indeed I had a design of spending it there if the jealousies and dislike of the Congregation to Mr. Harward had not prevented me, who refused their Consent upon any terms. Perhaps this Expectation might be revived in Mr. Christien's time, when many thought it a more seasonable Opportunity, and Mr. Harward, among others, endeavour'd to persuade me to it by giving hints telling me Your Lordship intended to give me some preferment, and declaring that he was very willing to divide the Duty with Mr Christien. But I was then too well acquainted with his design; and it is now no longer a secret that he was then and still is endeavoring to supplant me in the Church in hopes of succeeding himself, but at present to no other effect than making himself and the manner of his behaviour contemptible, and loosing the good will of almost every Member in it. This may look too much like design and Malice in me, but I make no doubt but time and other accounts will convince Your Lordship of the certainty of it, or I can confirm it by the hands of almost . . .[1]

"I have lately presented to the General Court here two Memorials,[2] which I have sent to Your Lordship with the Governor's speech and the vote of the House in pursuance of it. The first of these Memorials we were excited to draw up under some resentment that the Church was so little taken notice of, notwithstanding our Frequent Complaints when a Bill was preparing by a Committee appointed for that purpose, to releive the Quakers from an Argument used by the Governor in their favour that their Friends were a great body in England. I carried the First of these Memorials to the Governor for his Approbation, who seemed very well pleased with it, and promised his Interest, and we are now expecting the event. About a Day after this Memorial was presented and all things seemed promising, there was trumpt up by the Governor the pretence of an old affront I had put upon him about the Twentieth of March last and has laid dormant till now. The Affair is as follows:

---

[1] The letter is here imperfect.   [2] See p. 454, *post.*

The last Lady-day was appointed by the Governor and Council to be observed as a Fast; this put our Congregation, who are very tenatious of the rules of the Church, under a Dilemma, either of acting contrary to their own Rubrick or giving Offence to the Dissenters by contemning their Authority. This I was desired by them to represent to the Governor; accordingly I went to him and told him the difficulty we were drove to, and that it seem'd to have been done either as a contempt to our Church, or to make us Obnoxious to the Dissenters. The Governour answer'd it was not appointed with any such design. I replied that I did not charge His Excellency with such a design, but it had the appearance of it, for that it was not the first or second time it had been so ordered. The Governor then ask'd somewhat abruptly, How should I know your Festival Days? I returned, it would be an easy matter, when the design of setting apart such a day was on foot, to inquire of some minister of the Church whether it did not interfere with our [ ] Solemnities, if they expected we should take any notice of it. The Governor said he should not consult the Church about what he did in Counsel. I answer'd, I thought such respect was due to it, as it was the Established Church of the Kingdom, from whence the people here derived their Priviledges and His Excellency the Honors he enjoyed. This was all that pass'd between us that was material, and, indeed, all that I can remember, for which I had the thanks of the Church, and for which the Governor now expects I should ask his pardon. He has been urging D! Cutler to relate this conference to Your Lordship, in Obedience to whose Commands the D! prepared a letter; but as it did not give full satisfaction he has threaten'd to put him upon his Oath before the Counsel, which I have desir'd.

"This is a mistery in Politicks which puzzles all people; some think it is designed by the Governor as an excuse in England for not engaging in the service of the Church, which he avoids lest he should give offence to the Dissenters.

"There is no doubt but Mr. Harward is concerned in it, by his constant attendance upon the Governor at this time and their private conferences, and many are of Opinion that it is a Stratagem of his to alienate the affections of the Congregation from me, if this memorial should Fail of its design as the cause of it by not interesting the Governor in it; but if our Church here is to depend upon the Favours of a Presbyterian or Independent Governor we are in a Wooful case. However, the time and Circumstances of this Dispute are a proof of the insincerity of His Excellency's professions for the good of the Church; and the weakness of Mr. Harward's plot appears, if it is his, in that he has only enrag'd the Church more against him, and united them in my Interest, who are averse to the least thought of an acknowledgement where they can perceive no fault: if there be any, let the law take its course; or let the World judge if the Governor has not taken his own satisfaction by his abusive expressions of me since, That I was an Impertinent Fellow, and if it had not been for D! Cutler he would have kick'd me down stairs. This we are sure of, that a Governor here can do us no injury while we have the Laws of England on our side and a Friend in Your Lordship to defend our Title to those Laws, and therefore we are in no terror; and we are as certain that the present Governor has no inclination to serve the Church, and farther, that if he could creep into the management of it, which he is endeavoring, he would soon put it into Confusion. This they have Woful Experience from former Governors, and begin to feel it in this; but have more reason to fear it than from any other, from the bitterness of his malice dead against it before he obtained the Government. Let his own words condemn him: While his daughter was courted by a member of the Church of England, he declared publicly he would rather cut her legs off than see her go into the Church, which was never before or since made an Objection to a good Match, and is the only example we have of a Deserter; another time, when he was asked the reason of his going to Church in England and not here, his answer was that the Churchmen there were a sober and regular People, but here only a loose, disaffected Company. But this I will be bold to affirm, that no congregation in England of our bulk can express more Reverence to their God or Loyalty to their Sovereign; and I believe there will be a time, and it is much hoped for, when there will be few Friends in this Country to the Crown of England but in the Church. I know it is a common practice and the last resort of a malicious design upon an Enemy to represent him as disaffected; if this charge should fall upon me, I can produce sufficient proofs of my Affection to the Royal Family and even the approbation of the Court of Hanover. But to pursue my design. The Governor has indeed been at Church two or three times since his last arival, but it seems to aim rather at the dividing and disturbing it than with any religious design of doing it a service.

"When, Contrary to the Customary design of paying Contributions, which is always appropriated to the Support of the Minister and Church, he has directed his bill in a Paper to Mr. Harward notwithstanding, this has raised more heat in our congregation than anything that has happened in it since I have been Minister; but it will be prevented for the Future by a vote of the Vestry, which I am afraid will be a Fresh Offence to the Governor.

"My Lord! If the Church of England is worth defending, I am certain it cannot be done by prostituting the Doctrine or Government of it to an Enemy in power (which the Governor is, notwithstanding his fair pretences), which is too much attempted, nor by a lukewarmness and indifference in our principles concerning the points in dispute between us, which is with them termed Moderation and Charity, by which they mean a patient, tame submission to all the hardships they shall lay upon us, and an approbation of all their Innovations. If this is to be the Standard of our Doctrine, our Church will soon sink into a meeting and follow the Multitude; for who in these days would bare the oppression of harder taxes, be excluded from all posts of Honour or Profit, and be pointed out for all servile offices, which is the case of Churchmen in this countrey, if all those Sufferings are endured for the sake of trifles only or matters of little Importance. We, who are here upon the spot, can see by what steps they are raising themselves to a power over the Church, and assuming titles of establishment and Orthodoxy, which by the Laws of England they have no right to, and I hope your Lordship will oppose.

. . . .

"And from an unjust character we are told the present Governor gave, when he was Agent in England, of the persons suffering by this and some others of their Laws, when he was charg'd by the Lord Townsend before the King and Counsel with taxing the Churchmen for the support of their dissenting Teachers, he excused himself by saying they were only a disorderly, loose people who. . . ."[1]

The result of this interview appears to have been a chronic irritation in the Governor's mind toward Mr. Price, although with Mr. Harward his relations were very pleasant. That gentleman seems, indeed, to have been more conciliatory toward Congregationalists than stricter Churchmen approved. An animated letter is preserved,[2] in which the Rev. Mr. Plant, one of his brethren, relates a conversation which took place at the Governor's house. The letter gives a vivid glimpse into several things: —

. . . "I can't conclude this long letter without adding one remarkable instance of my hearty affection and zeal, showed in a publick manner for the honour of the church. I happened to be at the house of Governor Belcher, on one of the princesses' birthdays. Several gentlemen being present were invited to dine with the Governor. His Excellency says to Capt. Atkins: 'When did you see my mother Partridge? How does she do?' Capt. A. replyed: 'I saw her on Sunday in the afternoon, at Mr. Lowell's meeting.'[3] Says the Governor, 'You call *ours* the *meeting*, and *yours* the *church;* but you should call *ours* the *church* and *yours* the *meeting*.' He added, 'When I was in England, I waited on Viscount Townsend, and, talking on the state of the church in New England, said his Lordship, I suppose you call the church people Dissenters there, and yours the church, as we here call *ours* the *church*, and *you* the Dissenters ; so that we are the church and *you* are the *Dissenters*,' says the Governor. Dr. Harwood, the assistant at the King's Chapel, being my senior, I waited to see what answer he would return to his Excellency's speech (resolving it should not want an answer). Every person present being silent, and Mr. Harwood and Esqr. Atkins, the only two persons of the church, being seemingly thunderstruck, I thus addressed myself to the

---

[1] The close of this letter is missing.
[2] Coffin's "History of Newbury," p. 381.
[3] Rev. John Lowell, minister of the Third Parish in Newbury, was ancestor of numerous descendants in Boston.

Governor : ' May it please Your Excellency, I do not know what my Lord Townsend may say to you in his chamber, nor what his opinion was in his study, but if he expressed himself in these terms to Your Excellency, his opinion was in direct opposition to the Lords Justices, who, in their letter to Lt.-Gov. Dummer, ordered their Secretary to inform him that they had no regular establishment of any church in this Province ; neither have you,' said I to the Governor, ' any other establishment but what is on the same footing with other sectaries, viz., the act of toleration.' I went on very warmly for 2 or 3 minutes, but the Governor put a stop to me : ' Mr. Plant, I'll not dispute the matter with you.' ' Nor I with Your Excellency.' When Mr. Harwood and myself returned from the Governor's house, I asked him whether he took notice of the affront he attempted to put upon two Clergymen in their habit. He said, ' Yes.' I asked him why he did not give the Gov. an answer? He said to me, ' I do not give myself any trouble about these things ; the Gov. is kind to me, and I dine with him two or three times a week, and when I want a good dinner I always go there. I am always welcome, and you cannot help yourself if they do say so of you. What signifies it for you to show your resentment? They do not in England mind us that are here.' I then said to Mr. Harwood : ' I am sorry you are tyed so fast by the teeth as not to resent such a designed affront as that was. For my own part, I will eat bread and cheese so long as I live before I'll sneak to the Gov. for a dinner, and at his table hear myself called a Dissenter, and my Church represented a Conventicle.'"

Whatever the Governor might say or do, the minister and people of the church which was so identified with the proud power whose representative he was, felt a secure sense of superiority. A shadowy gleam from the peculiar treasures which enriched His Majesty's Chapel shines even upon the pages of the records which tell so little of what we would most like to know, and enables us to see how damask hangings and altarpiece, communion plate which was the gift of kings, and escutcheons which repeated the Old World fashion of bringing the distinctions of men into the House of God, marked its difference from the plainer "meeting-houses" around it: —

An Inventory of Vestments and Ornaments belonging to the Church Called King's Chappel in Boston in New England, Taken by George Steuart and Mr. George Stone, Church Wardens, and Mr. George Craddock, one of the Vestrymen of the said Church, on the nineteenth day of Aprill, 1733.

Impr. Six Surplices of fine Bagg Holland.

It. The Altarpiece, wheron is the Glory painted, the Ten Commandments, The Lord's Prayer, The Creed, and Some Texts of Scripture.

It. A Comunion Cloath of the finest Crimson Genoa Damask.

It. an old Comunion Cloath of silk Damask.

It. Five China Cushions, Given for the Comunicants to kneel upon, without the Rails of the Altar, by Captain James Sterling when he was Church Warden.

It. The pulpit Cloath, Desk Cloath, and Three Cushions of fine Genoa Damask.

It. Two old Cushions of Silk Damask.

It. An old pulpit Cloath of Ditto, and a Cushion Lent the Church at Braintree.

It. Three Table Cloaths of fine Damask Linnen.

It. Seventeen Napkins of Ditto.

It. Two pieces of fine Diaper, ten yards in a piece.

It. The stand for the Hour Glass of Brass, Given by Thomas Gold and Mr. William Weaver.

It. one Bible and fifteen Common Prayer Books, all old.

It. one New Bible and fourteen Common Prayer Books.

It. one large Common Prayer Book, Given by Thomas Lechmere, Esqr.

It. twelve Leather Bucketts given by the Gentlemen of ye Brittish Society.

It. a Clock given by the Same Gentlemen.

It. an Organ Given by Thomas Brattle, Esqr.

It. The King's Coat of Arms.

It. The Arms of Sir Edmund Andross, Knight, and Governour.[1]

It. Do. of Francis Nicholson, Esqr., Lieut.-Governour.

It. Do. of Captain Hamilton of his Majesty's Ship.

It. Do. of Joseph Dudley, Esqr., Governour.

It. Do. of Samuel Shute, Esqr., Governour.

It. Do. of William Burnett, Esqr., Governour.

It. Do. of Jonathan Belcher, Esqr., Governour.

It. The Bell.

An Inventory of the Silver Plate taken by the above persons, on the 19th day of Aprill, 1733.

Impr. four Large Flaggons.

It. three Chalices and their Covers.

It. one Bason.

It. one Receiver.

It. Two Servers.

A few financial items may be added from the King's Chapel Ledger: —

[1] This was a general custom in English churches at this period. "Who does not remember . . . the half-obliterated escutcheons, scarcely less dismal in appearance than the coffin-plates with which the columns of the Welsh churches were so profusely decorated?"— *Church of England in the Eighteenth Century,* ii. 425.

1730-31.   £   s.   d.
Feb. 7. By Cash rec^d for Braking ground und^r Church for
            Mr Stevens 5. 00. 00
     28. By Cash of Mr Hope for a Brick grave etc^a . . 13. 00. 00
1734.
Decr 1. By 1 English Shil^g 0. 05. 00
                               Contra.
1732.
Dec. 18. To p^d for Spruce boughs 1. 00. 00
1735
July 2. To Mr Step^n Dublois, for 1 qu^r Sallery to 25th June 10. 00. 00

More and more it appeared that Mr. Price had the habits of an English gentleman and country rector, and that these were widely divergent from New England ways:[1] —

"Oct 20th 1733, a very serious accident occurred. Mr Commissary Price's horse, a very unruly one attached to a chaise or chair, being left standing in the alley leading from Milk Street to Justice Clark's corner in Summer St., from some affright, started and ran through the alley. One Mrs. Stivens, a 'very ancient woman,' being then in the alley, was run over and so injured that she survived but a few hours. A child was much hurt at the same time."

During these years a second church growing out of King's Chapel, and soon to be known as Trinity Church, was gradually taking shape, as will be related in a subsequent chapter.[2]

A succession of collisions occurred between the will of Mr. Price and that of his congregation, which had the effect of steadily educating them to a more independent ground than they had hitherto maintained. "The short account of them is," as Greenwood remarks, "that he presumed too much on his place and dignity of Commissary, and they were growing jealous of their congregational rights and privileges." The Records indicate the points of difference which arose between them: —

Easter Monday, 10th April, 1732. *Voted*, That the Number of the Vestry shall not exceed twenty.

Easter Monday, 26 March, 1733. *Voted*, That Mr Dublois be Organist for the year ensuing, at Forty pounds Salary.

The Rever^d Mr Roger Price claimed his right of choosing a Cch Warden, but was overruled by the Congregation.

---

[1] A tradition of him survives in a letter from Dr. Belknap to Hazard, May 11, 1795: "At present I am obliged to adopt Roger Price's translation of Paul's advice to Timothy. Instead of 'Give thyself to *reading*,' it should be '*riding*.' Roger was formerly a King's chaplain here, and a great sportsman." — 5 *Mass. Hist. Coll.* iii. 353.

[2] See chap. xii.

Voted, That every person that pays Fifty-two shillings a year Contribution, and has punctually p^d it for the year past to the satisfaction of the Cch Wardens, be allowed to Vote; and no other.

30th of March, 1733. *Voted*, That publick notification be given next Sunday, that all persons that intend to give 52/ a year, or more, are desired to give their names with their money Every time they Contribute, that so ye Churchwardens may know what each person Contributes.

(N° 62). *Voted*, That ye pew that was formerly ye Reverend Mr Samuel Myles, our late minister's, be a Ministeriall pew for Ever.

Aprill 6th, 1733. *Voted*, That a proper Book for Recording Christenings, Marriages, and Burials, as also another Book to Record pews in, be provided by the Church Wardens.[1]

Friday ye 13th of Aprill, 1733. *Voted*, That the Pews be numbered, provided the painter will do it, in Oyl Colours, for sixpence a piece.

Wednesday ye 16th of May, 1733. *Voted*, That the Church Wardens treat with workmen about the Repairs of the Church, and report their doings therein to the Vestry.

Voted, That the number of the pews be entered in a Book Covered with marble papper, called the Book for Registering of Pews, together with the names of their owners.[2]

Sept. 12, 1733. *Voted*, That those persons who have already bought pews, and that do not pay for them in four weeks from this date, shall have them sold to others that will, they being first notifyed of this Vote; and that all pews that shall be sold for the future, the money shall be payed befor they have possession of the same.

Oct. 11, 1733. *Voted*, That the Brass Stand for the hour glass be lent to the Church of Scituate, as also three Diaper napkins, provided the Reverend Mr. Addington. Davenport, their Minister, gives his note to Return the same to the Church wardens of this Church for the time being, whensoever this Church shall see meet to demand them.

May 22, 1734. *Voted*, That the Church Wardens be Impower'd to have a place fixed up in the Belfrey to place the Books in belonging to the Library of King's Chapel; and that the Books be removed from Mr. John Barnes's house to said place in the Belfrey, the Church Wardens taking a Cataloge of the same.[3]

Aprill 7, 1735. *Voted*, That the Church Library be Delivered unto the Rev. Mr. Roger Price for the Use of the Ministers belonging to the Church of England In Boston, he giving a Receit to be Accountable for the Same, and to return the Same to the Church Wardens for the time being, when and So often as desired by the Church.

---

[1] The Registers of the Church are entered in these volumes since the year 1714, but with gaps.

[2] See the list at the close of Vol. II.

[3] "I hope," wrote Mr. Harward, July 19, 1731, "Your Lordship will not forget to give some orders about our library, for in the hands they are in at present I am afraid they will be much damaged, and I am credibly informed their number is much lessened." — *Church Docs. Mass.* p. 269.

June 17, 1737. Whereas, Thomas Child, one of the present Church Wardens, is chose a Juryman for the next Inferior Court of Common Pleas, to be holden at Boston the first Tuesday of July next, *Voted*, that he do not serve, and if he is fined, to appeal to the Seshions and stand tryall, and the Charge to be paid out of the Church Stock.

Although Mr. Price was loyal to the English crown and Church, he found himself so outrun by the extreme party which Checkley represented, as to be uncomfortable in his place. He wrote to the Bishop of London, Nov. 5, 1733: [1] —

"The old spirit of contention still reigns among our people, which I find very difficult to be restrained within the bounds of discretion. . . . To speak my sentiments, it is not any real advantage to the Church, which without any scruple they can trample upon when it interferes with their own interest and humour, but pride and ill-will to the Dissenters, which pushes on a set of men who will dispute as warmly for popery as for the Church of England, and are as great enemies to their own Governm' both in Church and State, when it opposes their schemes, as to Presbytery. But the misfortune is, he that contradicts them falls under the lash of their Evil Tongue. . . . I ment^d to our Vestry my design of going to England with an intention to return, who made so many objections to their being left under the care of Mr Harwood that I have laid it aside, and am now bent upon quitting the place entirely when a proper opportunity offers, not without hopes of being thought worthy your Lordship's care."

In May, 1734, he communicated his intention of leaving the church and returning permanently to England, and apparently no regret was manifested by his people at the prospect of losing him.[2]

15th Aprill, 1734. *Voted*, That ye Vestrie men do not Exceed the number twenty-five, and that any nine of them be a Coram to do Business, provided all of them be Warned.

May 4th 1734. Whereas, I, Roger Price, Rector duly Inducted of ye Church Called King's Chappel, in Boston, in the County of Suffolk, being Nessenated to Quit that parish or Congregation, In consideration Thereof I hereby Volantarily and of my own free will Resign, Release, Disavow, any Right, Title, Intrest, Claim, and Demand I now have, Ever had, Or at any time hereafter might pretend to have to the Rectory or parsonage of that Church, and Relax and Discharge all and Every Contracts, Agreements, Sacred or Civil, between the Congregation and mee as Rector as Aforesaid, and declare it Shall and may be Lawfull for Said Congregation to proceed to the choice of another Rector or Minister for

---

[1] Church Docs. Mass. p. 293.

[2] "The Rev. Mr. Commissary *Price*, Capt. *Tyng*, and several other Gentlemen embark'd on board Capt. *Shepherdson*, for London." — *Boston News-Letter*, May 21, 1734.

said Church, promiseing in nowise to Dispute or Call in Question the Validity of Such Choice, but at all times Execute every thing to Confirm the Same. Rog. Price.

Witness, George Shore, }
          Tho? Greene, } Church Wardens.

But Mr. Price had not anticipated one contingency. Though he set sail for England, he was detained in the harbor by contrary winds, and returned to Boston to pass the Sabbath. Tradition in the family states that he attended divine worship at Trinity Church, and there saw, for the first time, Miss Elizabeth Bull. He was so much pleased with her beauty that he gave up his intention of returning to England, sought her acquaintance, and during the year 1735 she became his wife. She was the daughter of Jonathan Bull, granddaughter of John Bull, and great-granddaughter of the Mayor of St. Edmonsbury of the same name.[1]

Mr. Price now reconsidered his resignation, and wished his people to do so likewise. But he had given them an opportunity for compelling him to release to them all his claims, of which they were not slow to avail themselves: —

Att a meeting of the Vestry of Church called King's Chappel, at M? Luke Vardy's, on Saturday, ye 25 May, 1734. Whereas, ye Rev^d M? Roger Price had taken passage on Board Capt. W^m. Sheppardson, Bound for London, and being detained in Nantasket by Contrary winds, he came up to Boston and desired the Church Wardens to Call a Vestry in Order to Lay before them his Resolutions in Staying with his Church, Accordingly, Wee the Vestry, when mett, *Voted* Robt Auchmuty Esq? and J^{no} Eastwick Esq? to talk with ye Rev^d M? Price Relating to Severall Properties belonging to ye Church, as are mentioned Underneath, which he pretended Some time past to have a Right too ; And upon his giving up his pretentions to them all, he Should be Received again by a Vote of the Congregation. Whereupon ye Rev^d M? Price was Sent for, And Every Article Concerning ye former disputes was Read to him, to which he Consented, Agreed to, and Gave up them all.

1. To have no pretentions to ye Perquisites of ye Monys for burying under ye Church.

---

[1] Her mother's maiden name was Mann; and grandmother's, Perry. She was very beautiful, and possessed considerable property on Marlborough and Summer streets, — the latter known as Bull Tavern and Bull's Wharf. Roger Price's father, in a letter dated March 11, 1729, cautions his son "not to let his love of a pretty face run away with his judgement in choosing a wife," but to "chuse by weight, and then you will be sure of something." The Marriage Record of Christ Church states: "1735, April ye 14th. The Rev^e Mr Roger Price, Mrs Elizabeth Bull."

2. To have no pretentions in Chuseing a Church Warden.
3. To have no pretentions to the Church Stock.
4. To have no pretentions to ye Church Library, Only the use of them.
5. To preach on Sunday Afternoons, when it can be done.
6. To make due Entrys of ye Church Marriages, Christenings, and burials in the book provided for that purpose.

To this is appended, in Mr. Price's own handwriting, with the later date : —

2 July, 1736. I this day freely Consent and agree to the foregoing Articles, particularly explaining the second thus, viz. : That I do not pretend to any right of appointing either of the Church wardens, or nominating him for the Congregation's Election. Witness my hand,

ROG. PRICE.

Att a meeting of the Congregation of King's Chappell, on Sunday, The 26th May, 1734, Boston, N. E. The transactions of the Vestry att Mr Luke Vardy's, on May ye 25, 1734, being Read to the Revd Mr Roger Price and Congregation, and no Objections made, then the Congregation *Voted*, That the Revd Mr Roger Price be Rector and Minister of the Church call'd King's Chappell, as before.

"That Mr. Price should ever have made such pretensions as are here resigned appears singular to us, with our present customs and habits of thinking. But it must be recollected that Mr. Price came over from England and took possession of the Chapel with English notions of a rector's prerogatives, and that some of the concessions which he was obliged to make were extorted by the innovating spirit of the church. With regard to the appointment of wardens, for instance, it would seem that Mr. Myles, the predecessor of Mr. Price, exercised the privilege of nominating to that office; for it is recorded that, in the year 1726, he informed the vestry that Charles Apthorp refused to serve as Church Warden, and nominated Mr. Thomas Selby, who was chosen. I have been told that the English custom is that the Rector nominate one of the wardens, and the Vestry the other. But Mr. Price undoubtedly assumed too much, and, by thus rendering himself unpopular, lost some privileges which by quietness he might have retained."[1]

[1] Greenwood, p. 104. Christ Church was as firm as King's Chapel in resisting a similar claim of its minister at this time. Its Vestry Records state, March 10, 1734: "Whereas The Revd Doc^{tr} Tim^o Cutler has of late disputed the Church Wardens' Right of Calling a Vestry Meeting to manage the Affairs of the Church (Untill leave be first had from him), Although the Church Wardens have by their undoubted Right Called Vestry meetings Ever Since the founding of this Church without any Application to the said Revd Dr Cutler (Not to deprive Nevertheless

The congregation could now afford to treat Mr. Price with consideration: —

Sunday, Mar. 30, 1735. *Voted*, by the Congregation, Y! the Rev? M! Roger Price Shall have all the Contribution that shall be gather'd in Said Chappell the Next Easter Sunday instead of his Weekly Eight pounds.

Easter Monday, April 7, 1735. *Voted*, That the number of Vestrymen exceed not Twenty-Eight; and that any Nine of them be a Quorum to do business, Provided the whole be Warned.

Voted, That the Church Stock be called in and lett out again To the Treasurer and Trustees of Trinity Church, They Giving Good Security for the Payment of the Principal Money and Lawfull Intrest on the Same. Proposed and agreed too that when there Shall be either Prayers or a Sermon on any day Excepting Sunday, that the Prayers shall begin at Eleven of the Clock in the forenoon, Excepting the time Should be alterd by giving Publick notice in the Church the Sunday before.

Friday, April 9, 1736. The Question was putt, If it be your Opinion that there Shall be a meeting of the Congregation In order that the Rev? M! Price may lay before the Congregation his reasons why his Sallery should be Augmented, please to Manifest it. It Passed in the affirmative. [Vestry.]

Wedesday, April 14, 1736. The Question was put, If it be your mind that the Rev? M! Roger Price Shall have One Hundred and Ten Pounds Sterling a year for his Sallary, please to manifest it. It was Voted in the Affirmative.

Voted, That the Rev? M! Roger Price shall have the Contribution that Shall be Gethered on Easter Sunday Next in the afternoon, insted of his Weakly allowance.

Whatever lack of harmony there may have been between the the Rev⁴ Dr Cutler of his Right of Calling a Vestry Meeting upon any Ecclesiastical Affairs), And as this Method Conduces to the Peace and Quiet of this Church, It is now *Voted*, That the Church Wardens (for the Time being) Do Still continue in all the Same Power and RIGHT they have hitherto had of Calling Vestry Meetings so often as they shall think .proper, for the Service of this Church. . . . That the above Vote, and all other Votes Concerning the Right of the Church Wardens and Vestry be allways read by one of the Church Wardens to the Rever⁴ Doct! T. Cutler's Successor or Successors, before he, or they, be presented or Inducted, or any other Minister recommended and Received in this Church."

"It is worth notice that the canons of 1603 do not pretend to give the incumbent the absolute right of appointing a Warden, but only in case he and the parishioners cannot agree in the choice of two. Again, the practice is even now not universal. In the parish of St. Cuthbert, Wells, one Church Warden is chosen by the rate-payers of the rural part of the parish, the other by the Town Council of the city. The Vicar, as Vicar, is thus shut out; so are the rate-payers of the inparish, except so far as the Town Council are their representatives." — *Saturday Review*, Dec. 30, 1871.

commissary and his assistant was soon stilled by the quieting touch of death.[1] Mr. Harward died April 15, 1736, and the vestry next day —

Voted, that Mr John Merrett, Mr James Gordon, and Thos Greene be a Committy to take Care that the Revd Mr Thos Harward be buried in a Decent, Frugall Manner, and in the absence of either of them Mr Saml Banister is to act in his room.

Lord's Day, April 18, 1736. *Voted*, That the Charges that shall arise by burying the Rev.^d Mr. Thos Harward, deceasd, be paid out of the Church Stock.

Voted, That Mr John Merrett, Mr James Gordon, and Thos Greene be a Committy to order the way and manner of the funeral.

1735–36, April. To the Charges of the Funeral of the Revd Doc.^r Harward, deceas.^d, £178. 18*s*. 1*d*.

Doubtless Mr. Harward's friends remembered the doctrine which he had preached, in the argument to show that —

" 1. The Happiness of the other World is in the immediate Presence of God. 2. It is entirely Perfect. 3. It is Perpetual."

Under the second head he had said: —

"It wants nothing to compleat the Joy both of the Body and of the Soul. . . . The *Fourth* Thing necessary to compleat the Bodies Happiness in the celestial Paradice is, That it be free from all manner of Sickness, Infirmity, and Pain. What wou'd a Man give, or rather what wou'd He not give, for so desirable a Priviledge in this present Life? . . . I am apt to believe, if such a Jewell were to be purchased, that almost every Man wou'd be ready — but particularly those who hardly know what Health is, like the Merchant in the Gospel — *to sell all that they have to buy it*. But, alas ! this Privilege is not attainable here. . . . When this Mortal hath put on Immortality it will not be so. . . . It will feel no more the Gripings of Hunger and Thirst. . . . Nay, every Defect of Nature, with the usual Infirmities of Sickness and Old Age, will be supply'd and repair'd in Heaven. . . . No *Gout* or *Stone* will be ever heard of there ; for St. John tells us, *All Tears will be wiped from our Eyes*. . . . The *Last* Thing necessary to compleat the Bodies Happiness in Heaven is, That it be raised as Immortal as the Soul. . . . The very Thoughts of a Dissolution again wou'd undeniably discompose it ; and the fear of being deprived of its ineffable Weight of Glory wou'd render it in some Degree uneasy under it. . . . The Bodies of the Saints,

---

[1] "On Thursday Evening last died here the Rev. Mr. *Thomas Harwood*, Lecturer of the King's Chappel in this Town, and Licentiate of the Royal College of Physicians in *London*, and was decently inter'd on Tuesday last." — *Weekly News-Letter*, April 15-22, 1736.

like the Pictures of the Graces, will be always Florishing in Immortal Youth."

He then had enlarged on "the Happiness of the *Soul*, which, as it exceeds the Body in the Purity of it's Nature, so also it exceeds it in the Purity of it's Joys. . . . More than this, the everlastingness of GOD's Existence is a conspicuous Demonstration that Heaven must endure as long as GOD does. . . . From whence 'tis certain that this Service, or rather Pleasure, of Blessing and Praising GOD will never cease, never have an End, but be the Exercise and Joy of holy Men and Angels to all Eternity."[1]

The King's lecturer left a widow and two sons.[2] His descendants continue in this country. He seems to have had but scanty means. A dim picture of his frugal household and its furnishings is imaged for us as we read the "Inventory of Household Goods and Books belonging to the Estate of the Rev.d Doct.r Thomas Harward, dec̄ed," returned by "Samuel Shipton, Admin.r," May 25, 1736, amounting in total to £383. 15. 1. That modest interior is provided with, —

6 Walnut Chairs, Lea : bottoms, 1 brok, @ 35/ ea.

1 La : Gilt Sconce, brass Arms, £20 ; 1 Couch and Squab Pill.o and Callico Cover, £10.

1 Mohogony Tea Table, 45/; 1 D.o Tea board 10/; 1 brass Fend.r, 40/; 1 Grate, £5.

1 Card Table, Mohogony, 40/; 1 sma : Walnut Table, broke, 25/.

1 p.r brass Doggs, 30/.

1 Silver Watch, £14 ; 2 Silver Salts and 4 Tea Spoons and 1 p.r Tongs, £21. 16s. 11d.

1 Iron Bedstead, £14 : Chints Curtains, Tester, etc., head Cloth Lin'd w.th Greenpeel, £15.

2 Pewter Basons, 6 Do. Plates, 3 Do. Porringers, £1. 15s. 0d.

2 doz. and 5 hard-mettle Plates, 31 @ 4, 6, £6. 19s. 6d.; 9 Pewt.r Dishes.

6 of the Apostles in Frames, 2 Glaz'd, 12/; 1 Dog Collar, 1/; 1 Jugg and Cock, 20/.

---

[1] Mr. Harward concluded this discourse with the ascription, which was later substituted for the "Gloria" in the King's Chapel Liturgy: "*Now to the King Eternal, Immortal, Invisible, the only wise* GOD (*in whose Presence is Fulness of Joy*), *be all Honour and Glory, all Praise and Dominion, for ever and ever.* Amen."

[2] I am indebted to Mrs. C. I. Harward for information that the King's lecturer's son George married in Boston and settled in Brunswick, Me., where he lived many years as a teacher in the town school. The other son, William, went to Jamaica, W. I., and was successful in business, becoming possessed of large estates, which he bequeathed to his brother. A descendant, of pure and interesting character, is commemorated in the "Life of William Eugene Harward, by Rev. Frank E. Clark, Portland, 1879."

There is the usual kitchen furniture; and Mr. Harward's two professions are blended with more secular pleasure: —

1 Tobacco Sifter, 3/.
4 Lancets, 18/.
1 brass blunderbuss, 40/; 1 Saddle and Bridle, 30/.
1 Cloth Gown and Cassock, very much worn, 60/; 1 Prunella Gown, £5. 8. 0.

His library is but scanty, containing in all only ninety works, mostly small and of poor quality. Among them, standing side by side, are Fuller's "Medicinal Gymnastica," one volume, octavo; Sydenham's Works, one volume, fourteen shillings; and Howe's "Blessedness of the Righteous," one volume, eight shillings.

His own publications seem to have been largely left on his hands: "163 'Happiness of Enjoying the Presence of God,' by T. Harward; 410 'Electuarium,' etc., £2. 5. 0."

It is but a gray picture of life's twilight which these scanty hints shadow forth; nor is it brightened by any after-gleams of sympathy and consideration for those whom Mr. Harward left in need.[1] Apparently, the church regarded the King's lecturer, alike living and dead, as foreign to any pecuniary provision by them. Without loss of time they applied for a successor in his place.

1736, April 26, Easter Munday. At a meeting of the Congregation of the King's Chappell in Boston, —

Agreed, that if Dispute ariseth upon any Vote, a scrutiny shall be made, and none be allowed to vote but such as are qualified according to ye Vote of this Congregation to that end made upon Easter Munday, 1733.

That ye Vestrymen for this year be fifteen.

And lastly, that the Minister, Chh Wardens, and Vestry are desired to write home of ye Death of the Revd Mr Harward, and make all such Applications as are proper upon this Occasion.

---

[1] Sept. 20, 1738, his estate is represented to be "Insolvent, or not sufficient to pay his Just Debts. After the Subduction of necessary Implements, his Widow, Charges of Adminačon and other Expenses, there remains but the Sum of £291. 2. 7." — and the claims of the creditors amount to £767. 0. 7.

Among the allowances by the administrator are these: —

"To Letitia Harward, y^e dec$^d's$ Wid^o, p Order of his Hon^r y^e Judge of Prob^t £70. 0. 0.

"p^d 1 Gall^o Wine for the Apprizers, £0. 12. 0.

"p^d Mary Demilde, Wages, £8. 5. 0.

"p^d Luke Vardy, Expen^s on y^e Book Auction and Commiss^rs Meeting, £4. 6. 3."

BOSTON, New England, April 30, 1736.

MAY IT PLEASE YOUR LORDSHIP, — We, the Minister, Church Wardens, and Vestry of King's Chappell in Boston, do humbly beg the favour of Your Lordship to repair the Loss our Church has Sustained by ye Death of ye late Revd Mr Harward, who died y² 15. of this Instant.

Our Infant Church being surrounded with ten dissenting Congregations in this principal Town, which are provided with Ministers the most Esteem'd for Learning and Piety among them, Its prosperity depends much on ye Abilities and good Qualities of our Ministers.

We therefore Rely on your Lordship's Judgement and Goodness in speedily supplying us with a Proper Person.

We are, with all Submission,
Your Lordship's
Most dutiful Sons and Servants.

The Right Rev^d the Lord Bishop of London.

Still there were delays which the church could not at first understand, but which are explained in the following vote and correspondence: —

1736, Nov. 17. *Voted*, That a Committee from this Vestry wait upon Mr Comissary Price and pray him to Write to the Bishop of London, and therein effectually remove those difficultys about ye immediate Settlement of his assistant here, and the powers he is to have, w^h by his Lordship's Letter to Col Williamson Mr Commissary has raised, and now do retard ye coming of an assistant, and pray him to deliver them this letter open, to be inclosed by ye vestry in theirs to his L^dShip to hasten ye matter.

Voted, That a Committee be appointed to write to Mr Sandford and to the Bishop of London (according as Mr Commissary Shall answer the above Committee) to press ye Sending of an assistant to us as Soon as Conveniently may be, and lay these letters before the Vestry at their next meeting.

This record is explained by a letter from Mr. Price to his brother, written in this interval, which is preserved: —

" My assistant, Mr. Harward, is lately dead, and I have wrote to the Bishop of London to confer the place upon me, that I may have the liberty of appointing a Curate under me who may be more dependent and serviceable than the Assistant has hitherto been. The salary is a Hundred Pounds per Annum, paid out of the Treasury, deducting something for taxes, out of which I propose to give the person that shall act under me seventy pounds per annum, certain, and the rest of the Income If he behaves himself orderly, according to his Station. I my request therefore is that you would wait upon the Bishop of London, and to back the request, and know his resolution thereupon; and if he consents to it, first to ask him if he pleases to recommend any person, or leave it to you to provide, and then to use diligence to procure me a proper curate, and to agree with him according to this proposal. I have added a niece to the number of your relations to send over.

I have made a Considerable purchase of a Farm, containing about four hundred Acres of good Land, beautifully situated, and bounded by a Noble River; for the payment of this off will oblige me to draw all my money (as I am uncertain) out of England, near the value of two hundred pounds, in two years' time. . . . I beg the Favour of you to go to him and tell him that I very much depend upon his punctual acceptance of my bills; and if the money in his or my Brother Tom's Hands should be short of my draughts, I hope that you and he will be answerable for twenty or forty pounds if it should be wanted, and you may repay yourselves by my salary as it comes in; but by all means let me know what my present substance is, and how far I can depend upon you.

I should be glad of any one of my Sister's Company here, — I don't mention the particular person, because I don't know their Inclinations; but whichever is disposed to come I will make welcome, and let her bring a Maid servant with her. If you should meet with an ingenious, agreeable young gentlemant to send me as a Curate, he would be an agreeable Companion to her in the voyage. I have added a neice to your relations. My wife is now in her last week of her setting up. She joyns with me in her compliments to your wife, you, and all our Relations. If you will be an adventurer for a bargain of land in this Province, I will endeavour to procure you a pennyworth. Two hundred pounds will go a great way in a Purchase.

I am,   Your L."

Mr. Price wrote to the Bishop of London, Oct. 16, 1736:[1]

"If my assistant is not already appointed, it would be a great pleasure to me to be joined with one of my own Countrymen. I find the New England Ministers too overbearing, and to want some balance."

But the church distrusted any such arrangement as he might propose.

1736, 19 Nov. At a meeting of ye Vestry according to adjournment. *Voted*, That the letters now produced by ye Committee pursuant to the above orders be Copied, and duplicates of them Sent Accordingly, the tenor whereof is this: —

BOSTON, in N. England, Nov. 22, 1736.

MAY IT PLEASE YOUR L^DSHIP, — On the 30th of April last we wrote Y^{or} L^dship of ye death of ye Revd Mr Harward, humbly praying his place might be well and speedily Supplied at y^{or} discretion.

Since that we have casually met with Your L^dsp's letter to Col. Wil-

---

[1] Church Docs. Mass. p. 317.

liamson of ye 11th of August, wherein you say that ye Revd Mr Price raises some difficulties about ye Settlement of His Successor, and ye power he is to have, and you know not how long it may be ere these matters are adjusted.

Upon this we applied our Selves to the Revd Mr Price to let us know what these difficultys are, and to write to Your L^dp effectually to remove those difficultys y^t retard ye Settlement of his assistant, and join with us to hasten ye matter; to which he answerd us, that as he had already, So he would now write y^or L^dp for an Assistant, but praying that he might be oblig'd to perform half the duty of all kinds if Mr Price should require it, but be intitled to no fees; and if Mr Price Should be absent upon any necessary call, then to perform ye whole without any extraordinary reward.

Wherefore we apprehend it necessary to inform y^or L^dp how ye dutys and privileges of our Minister and ye King's Chaplain in this Church have been heretofore Settled, and for y^t purpose send the inclosed Copys and Settlements, whereby we understand they are independent of each other, must take equal Shares in supplying the Chh; and Marriages, Christenings, and burials, with their perquisites, belong to our Minister, but in his occasional absence to ye King's Chaplain.

What his words above, w^h he has given us in writing, may intend, differing from the former settlements, or what may casually drop from his pen more than he has given us, we are not Sollicitous to know; but we humbly pray Y^or L^dp by no means to depart from those Settlements.

For as we are scituated in this Metropolis of New England, where there are many men of good learning and discretion, and surrounded with many dissenting Congregations, who are Generally furnisht with two Ministers each, and those the best for learning and Piety that this land can afford,—So it's absolutely necessary for ye prosperity of this Chh, or even to save it from Contempt, that our Ministers should be equally qualified for their places; and therefore Y^or L^dp must Judge that his Majesty's Chaplain for this place should by no means be Crampt, Subjected, and made an inferiour Curate, because then ye man must be accordingly, and will certainly be, despised.

To Conclude, therefore, We humbly pray Y^or L^dp, as soon as conveniently may be, to send us an assistant to ye Revd Mr Price, the best for solid learning and Exemplary Piety y^t can be procured for us, together with your pastoral blessing upon

Your Lordship's most dutifull Sons and Servants,

To y^t Right R^d y^t Ld Bishop of London.

	Wm SPEAKMAN.	J^no REED, } Church
	JOB LEWIS.	THO. CHILD, } Wardens.
	PETER LUCE.	ROBERT AUCHMUTY.
	THO. GREEN.	W^m. SHIRLEY.
	C. APTHORP.	EDWARD TYNG.
	J^no. MERRETT.	J^no. EASTWICK.
	J^no. GIBBINS.	G. STEWART.
	GEORGE SHORE.	

THE BISHOP'S COMMISSARY.

Boston, in N. England, Nov. 22, 1736.

S^R,—On y^e death of y^e Revd Mr Harward, Mr Comissary Price, in Conjunction with y^e Vestry of King's Chappel, wrote to y^e Bish^p of London, intreating his L$^{dp's}$ interest that an assistant might be imediately sent over to that Ch^h, A Copy of w^h we take the freedom of transmitting to you, and flatterd ourselves we should have succeeded in such our Sollicitation before this time. But y^e affair, Contrary to our expectation, being protracted, put us upon endeavouring, if possible, to discover ye Secret cause, and very fortunately acquired a letter from his L^{dp} directed to Col. Williamson (a copy is also inclosed), which in our Opinion manifests y^e double part acted by our Minister has hitherto been y^e Clogg. This will appear most glaring by comparing y^e letter wrote by y^e Minister and Vestry with his L$^{dp's}$: by y^e one y^e united desire of y^e Minister and Vestry was that an Assistant might imediately be sent; by y^e other his L^{dp} observes y^t Mr Comissary had raised such difficultys as hitherto retarded y^e affair, and that he knew not when the same will be adjusted. This duplicity in Mr Comissary's conduct makes the Stronger impressions on his Congregation, for y^t it's too visible interest and a recess from parochial Duty were at ye bottom; And this is not ye only instance we have against him, as by an Abstract tracing his conduct for some years past (under this cover) will Evidently appear. Good Sir, the pious Zeal to ye growth of our Establisht Ch^h that shines thro' ye whole Conduct of your life, and what (to our happiness) we frequently experienced, encourages us in this explicit manner to lay before you the unhappy Scituation of our Ecclesiastical affairs; and from ye State of ye case, a Gentleman much inferiour to your penetration must discover ye absolute necessity of having an assistant Immediately sent us. And when you Seriously consider his performance is to be in ye first Establisht Ch^h in ye metropolis of New England, amongst an Audience inferiour to very few Congregations for natural and acquired abilitys, encircled with meeting-houses filled with ye most Shining teachers of their persuasion, Surely you and all ingenuous minds truly attached to the propagation of Our holy Religion, must conclude ye person ought to be a Gent in some measure eminent for his learning, a polite and popular preacher, and of an exemplary life; and that a Gent so qualified will not prostitute such distinguishable merit and dwindle down to a Servile curate. So y^t we apprehend a low life man, y^t will render our Minister's Scituation a Sinecure, will best suit ye Comissary, but most effectually hurt not only ours, but all ye Establisht Ch^{hs} in these parts. Therefore, to guard against this, we conceive the regulation of ye Assistant's duty should be as prescribed by our former and present Diocesan, and according to ye Agreem^t Solemnly entred into by Mr Price and Mr Harward in full Vestry; and such reasonable terms will well Comport with y^e Character of y^e Gent we want: and we shall have but a contracted Opinion of one that embraces lower, which regulation and agreem^t we likewise inclose.

By a paragraph in his L$^{dp's}$ Letter, we concieve there is an Opening given us to think his L^dp would not take Umbrage at our recommending a Gent satisfactory to us. We therefore presume to Observe that by y^e Character we have of y^e Revd Mr James Sterling, now a Chaplain to a Regiment, he will be equal to y^e duty and answer our Expectation; and ye rather for y^t he is the Gent his L^dp makes Some Account of in his Letter to Col. Dunbar, tho thrô Mistake he therein gives him ye Sirname of Auchmuty, w^h mistake is easily accounted for, because he is first Cousin to Robert Auchmuty, Esqr, the Judge of ye Admiralty in these parts. Thus we unavoidably have troubled you with the detail of our Ch^h affairs, pointed out the qualifications of ye Gent to be sent, condescended to the nomination of ye person, if, in his L^dp's and your Judgmt, his character answers; therefore upon the whole we earnestly pray you would exert your good Offices in so critical a Juncture, and wait on his L^dp, deliver ye inclosed letter to him, Obviate the difficultys already started, press ye Immediate Sending an Assistant equal to our Expectations, and conduct your Self in all things as may tend to ye best interest of our Ch^h: and all contingent expences shall, with the utmost faithfulness, be paid to you by our Ch^h, and your Singular Services for ever will be acknowledged by, S^r,

    Y^or greatly obliged humble Servt^s,

          J^no READ,   } Ch^h
          THO. CHILD, } Wardens.
          Etc. [as above].

Voted, also, That Robert Auchmuty Esqr be desired to draw up the letter to Mr Sandford touching Mr Price in the above letter, to be inclosed with ye assistance of Mr Read, w^c was accordingly done in the following tenor: —

S^R, — As to an abstract of ye conduct of ye Revd Mr Price among us, we are the more free to disclose it to you, his very good friend, because we trust youl so improve it as may best Serve the advantage of either party, — not hurt that Gent's Character, and at ye same time bar his assistant's being made his Curate.

In June, 1729, the Revd Mr Price came hither, and the next Spring we were visited with the Small pox, always a desolating and mortal disease among us; then Mr Price took a house in ye Countrey, about four miles from Town; and there spent his Summer. Now tho' it was easy for him to resort to his Church for ye performance of publick service, yet it's evident he must be all that time out of the way of performing that most necessary duty of visiting the sick when there was the greatest Occasion for it.

In 1735 he dwelt about four Miles out of Town all the Summer Season, at w^c many people were Uneasy for his neglect of Visiting ye Sick among us as before.

The last Summer, when we had no other Minister, he purchased several lands at Hopkinton, about 27 Miles from Town, and ever since that has frequently resorted to that place, and still must do it as long as he

holds those lands to make any benefit of them. These things are great
retirements from his parochial dutys, and the furnishing of him with a
Curate is not ye properest means to make him the more Steady and laborious in his duty.

He has been urged to keep a just register of the Christenings, Marriages, and burials of this Church, but never could be prevail'd upon to
undertake it till May, 1734, when he solemnly, under his hand in the
Ch^h books, kept by ye Ch^h Wardens, resigned up to ye Ch^h all his right
to the parsonage or Rectory of this Ch^h, intending to proceed directly to
Great Brittain; but in few days changed his mind, and upon his promise, among other things, to make due Entrys of the Ch^h Marriages, Christenings, and Burials in ye book provided for that purpose, was received
by a Majority of ye Ch^h again, — and yet we have reason to doubt he has
never done it still.

We might add that we did not take it kindly when he took a Tour of
about a month to New York to see the Countrey, without giving his
Ch^h any notice of it.

Yet nevertheless during all this time we have been so just to him, as
that for several years we gave him eight pounds a week in our Currency
at his request, which was better than his £110 Sterl a year, w^e we prom-
ist him; and when that came to be worse, we have raised it to eleven
pounds a week of our Currency, of the full value of our first Agreem't.

Wherefore upon ye whole we cant but think we have well performed
our duty, and he ought willingly to attend his duty amongst us, — w^e is
the true intent of our Contract and obligation to him; and that there
will be no reason or Justice in releasing him from his duty, and turning
the King's Chaplain into a Curate for that end and purpose. To all
this we, who were present and perfectly knowing of all these things, subscribe ourselves,

Y^{or} humble Serv^{ts},

    THO. CHILD.   PETER LUCE.
    G. SHORE.   G. STUART.
    THO. GREEN.   JN^o EASTWICK.
    JN^o MERRETT.

*All bound up and d^d Mr Merrit to transmitt by ye Cambridge C^t
Morris and ye duplicate by Capt. White, to Pool this* 29 *Nov.*, 1736.

                    J. READ.

The request of the church was soon answered in harmony
with its wish: —

*A Copy of the Lord Bishop of London^s Letter to ye Church Wardens and
Vestry of the King's Chapel in Boston.*

             WHITEHALL, Feb. 1, 1736-37.

GENTLEMEN, — I Rec^d y^r Application for a new Minister To succeed
Mr Harward, and have now appointed Mr Davenport, a person who has

been Long known to you ; and of whom I Conceive'd a very good Opinion, from his Behaviour and Coversation while he Continued in England. In my Letters to M.' Price and him, wch Come by the same Vessel that brings This, I have Recommended to both of them the Living in peace and good will towards Each Other, and that in Case of Sickness or Necessary absence, which may Equally happen to both, They be Ready to give their Assistance, Mutually, without Expecting any Consideration for it. This I assure my self they will be Ready to do ; and Particularly that M.' Davenport will think it no hardship to take upon him M.' Price's share of Duty when he is called to any other place as my Commissary, tho' that be an Occation of Absence which cannot befall M.' Davenport : these Absences are short and Rarely happen ; and as Long as the Ministers can agree these Matters between themselves, and the whole Duty is Regularly Performed, the Congregation will have no cause to Complain.

I am unwilling to Suppose that any misunderstanding can happen between M.' Price and M.' Davenport ; but if any should happen, — which I shall be truly griev'd at, — I doubt not but you will be ready to interpose your good Offices to Remove it, and to prevent the mischiefs which must unavoidably Ensue upon any breach, or Even coldness, between them. And so commending you all to the Divine blessing and Protection,

I Remain, Gentlemen, your assured Friend,

EDM. LONDON.

Rec.^d by Capt Shepardson, April 18, 1737.

The records also contain : —

A Coppy of the Lord Bishop of London.^s Letter to the Revd Mr Addington Davinport.

WHITEHALL, Jan. 29, 1736-37.

GOOD S^R, — I have appointed you to succeed Mr Harward in the duty at the Kings Chapple, there to be performed by you under the rules and Directions wch have been given by ye Bishop Compton and myself. You will not fail in generall to pay all due respect to Mr Price, both as Chief Paster of ye Congregation and as my Comissary ; and when the duty of this latter station obliges him to be absent from Boston, w^{ch}, as I am Informed, is very seldom, I think it reasonable that you should Perform his duty there without expecting any Gratuity for it : as to other accidental Inabilities or absences on Acc. of health or necessary business, which both of you in your turns may have Occasion for, I hope there is no need to expect either of you to afford mutual assistance to each other. I desire you to Communicate this Letter to Mr Price ; and have no more to add at this time but to commend you to ye divine protection, and to wish you success in your Pastorall Labours, — wch will always be a Great satisfaction to

S^r, your assured fr^d and B^r,

EDM. LONDON.

My intention is that you enter upon the duty as soon as ye 15. of Aprill is over, that being the day wch Mr Harward dy'd, and the society will appoint a Missionary for Situate without Loss of time.

In this appointment, Bishop Gibson had exercised a sagacious judgment of what would be for the best interest of the church; and although Mr. Davenport and Mr. Price did not escape the misunderstandings which the bishop feared, the King's lecturer, before his untimely death, was able to do important service in building up the new church that sprang from the mother church to which he now came.

CHAPTER XI.

THE CHURCH UNDER LAW.

I[1] bringing our annals to the time of Mr. Davenport's appointment to succeed Mr. Harward, we have thus far only alluded to the most important chapter of the ecclesiastical history of this period, in which our narrative again passes out of the limits of a mere local and parish record, and becomes closely involved with great questions of public policy which lie at the foundation of our modern Commonwealth. It has been mentioned that Mr. Harward, soon after his arrival, held aloof from certain action taken by the church in regard to "the sufferings of Churchmen," — a course which doubtless alienated his people from him. The series of events in which his refusal was one link had many years antedated his arrival, and were not concluded until he had passed beyond this earthly scene. In them the Rev. Roger Price, from his official position as representative of the Bishop of London, became the central figure.

Mr. Price's ministry is marked by two controversies, — first, with the Provincial authorities in his capacity as commissary; and also, personally, with his own people.

Under the laws of the Province, all persons living in a town or parish precinct were obliged to pay their share toward the erection of the house of worship of the place and the maintenance of its religious institutions. These laws had been made when the people were of one way of thinking, and were a wise provision of our forefathers for securing the privileges of religion even in the smallest settlements: to their influence are due the best characteristics of New England to this hour. But the laws which had been intended to constrain mean or godless

---

[1] The initial letter is taken from Mr. Harward's sermon on the "Fulness of Joy in the Presence of God."

persons to do their part toward supporting this great public interest were now found to operate hardly on some tender consciences.

The noble idea on which the fathers of Massachusetts founded their State,—that "the order of the churches and of the commonwealth" was identical, — had survived the loss of the original charter, in "a profound conviction of the indissoluble alliance between the spiritual and civil order."[1] The whole course of the legislation on this subject is justly comprehended only when this guiding principle is kept in mind. Religion and education were treated alike as of supreme public concern; and the laws for the support of public worship, which were an inestimable blessing where the people were substantially agreed, were relaxed for the relief of dissenters when and in so far as it could be done, in the judgment of the best part of the community, without endangering religion itself. In William and Mary's charter, as interpreted by Increase Mather,[2] —

"Religion is secured; for liberty is granted to all men to worship God after that manner which, in their consciences, they shall be persuaded is the most scriptural way. The general court may, by laws, encourage and protect that religion which is the general profession of the inhabitants there."

In this sense the statute-book of Massachusetts contains a series of enactments designed to insure the permanent support of religious teaching. These laws made under the new Provincial charter and always subject to revision by the Crown, to whose approval or rejection every law had to be submitted, continued the religious policy of the Colony as it had been shaped under the first charter. The earliest Assembly after the new order of things began, passed in November, 1692, "An Act for the Settlement and Support of Ministers and Schoolmasters,"[3] providing —

"That the inhabitants of each town within this province shall take due care, from time to time, to be constantly provided of an able,

---

[1] This was well stated by Professor Diman: "Before we flout the legislators of Massachusetts for being behind the age, we should ascertain precisely what they sought to do. They were not emptying into the cup of colonial liberty the dregs of an old experiment. The support of religion, not the endowment of any specific church establishment, was what they had in mind." See the remarkable "Study of Religion in America. 1776–1876," by the late Professor J. L. Diman, — a scholar too early lost to the American church.

[2] Account of his negotiations, quoted by Hutchinson, ii. 107.

[3] Province Laws, i. 62.

learned, orthodox minister or ministers of good conversation, to dispense the Word of God to them;" to "be suitably encouraged and sufficiently supported and maintained by the inhabitants of such town;" to be "chosen by the major part of the inhabitants of any town."

"Every town . . . having the number of 50 householders, or upwards, shall be constantly provided with a schoolmaster to teach children and youth to read and write."

The next February "An Act for the Explaining and altering of some clauses," etc., changed part of the above law to read, —

"Each respective gathered church in any town . . . shall have power, according to the directions given in the word of God, to choose their own minister, . . . the major part of such inhabitants as do there usually attend on the publick worship of God concurring with the churche's act; . . . *provided* that nothing herein contained . . . abridge the inhabitants of Boston of their accustomed way and practice as to the choice and maintenance of their ministers."[1]

These early laws were made when King's Chapel alone represented the Church of England in the province; and as that was in Boston, where from the beginning the ministers were maintained by a voluntary contribution, no injustice was done to its members by taxation.

In June, 1696, "An Act in further Addition" to this Act provided that, —

"If the major part of inhabitants disagree with the church in such choice, the church may call a council, and, if they approve, settle him as minister of the town."[2]

In November, 1702, was passed "An Act more effectually providing for the support of Ministers:" —

"Whereas," said the preamble, "in some few towns and districts within this province divers of the inhabitants are Quakers and other irreligious persons, averse and opposite to the publick worship of God and to a learned orthodox ministry, and find out ways to elude the laws provided for the support of such, and pervert the good intentions thereof to the encouragement of irreligion and prophaneness."[3]

The law proceeded to fine delinquent selectmen or assessors, and appointed a special board to collect ministerial rates where they should fail to do so. By this time, however, it had be-

---

[1] Province Laws, i. 102.   [2] Ibid. p. 216.   [3] Ibid. p. 505.

come evident that there were some adherents of the Church of England here and there, who were not disposed to acquiesce in the worship of their neighbors. This law had, therefore, a possible bearing on the interests of the Church of England here, which explains the following action of our diocesan in relation to it: —

"Whitehall, May the 24th, 1704. . . . The Lord Bishop of London desired that an Act passed in Massachusetts Bay entituled [as above], may not be confirmed to Her Majesty 'till he be heard thereupon."[1]

In December, 1715, "An Act for Maintaining and Propagating Religion,"[2] limited to seven years, required the grand jury to present all towns and districts which are destitute of a minister, or neglect to fulfil their contracts and make suitable provision for support of ministers, — the General Assembly to "send an able, learned, orthodox minister, of good conversation, . . . recommended by three or more of the setled ordained ministers, to every such town or district," taxing it accordingly "for his honourable support and maintenance."

In June, 1718, was passed "An Act in Addition to an Act pass'd in the first year of Queen Ann, entituled 'An Act more effectually providing for the Support of Ministers.'"[3] By this, when the majority in a town-meeting have voted money for building meeting-houses, or "any other charge necessary for the support of the worship of God," the assessors were required to raise the same. All these enactments contemplated the unanimity of the inhabitants of each town upon a matter of such supreme public concern as the administration of religion, and were intended to discourage a dissent which might paralyze that vital object.

In the hardships resulting from these laws the members of the Church of England scattered in towns away from Boston were not alone; but they made the great mistake of not associating with themselves the names of the despised and feeble Quakers and Baptists, and thereby constituting themselves the apostles of religious freedom.

A brief digression will suffice to outline the course of legislation with regard to these other Christian bodies, and will show how the religious policy of Massachusetts bore upon them.

Cotton Mather wrote in 1689: —

---

[1] "Trade Papers" (Journals) in Public Record Office, xi. 48, quoted in "Province Laws," i. 508.
[2] Province Laws, ii. 26.   [3] Ibid. p. 99.

"Since our Jerusalem was come to such a consistence that the going up of every fox would not break down our stone walls, whoever meddled with 'em."[1]

Such is not, however, the view which the statute-book bears out. The Baptists did not obtain full relief until the Revolution; and the Quakers were relieved in consequence of a stubborn controversy between the inhabitants of the towns of Dartmouth and Tiverton (which were chiefly inhabited by this sect) and the General Court, "respecting the power of the Legislature to oblige towns to support ministers against the will of a large majority of the inhabitants and legal voters."[2] In 1704 the General Court had authorized Mr. Gardner, a preacher in Dartmouth, to join persons in marriage. In 1708 the court appointed the Rev. Samuel Hunt minister for Dartmouth, — "the necessary Orders . . . not being duly observed, but eluded." No tax lists survive to show whether he was paid from the general province tax or by a special tax on Dartmouth. In 1709 the court ordered "that the Neighbouring Ministers . . . preach in their Turns at Tiverton," being paid twenty shillings each. In July, 1720, the Quakers petitioned the court, "showing that the said People for Years past have suffered the Distraint and Loss of their Goods for the support of the Presbyterian or Independent Ministers, . . . and that too often with much Extortion," and praying for relief. In June, 1721, to relieve them, the court directed that "the Constables . . . take as near as may be the Value of the Sum or Sums assess'd on such Quakers." In June, 1722, the court voted £100 salary to Mr. Hunt at Dartmouth, and voted to provide a minister at Tiverton. In July, 1722, "An Act for Apportioning and Assesing a Tax of £6,232 13s. 11d." was passed, which included £100 for Dartmouth, and £72 11s. 0d. for Tiverton, above their proper proportion of this tax, being intended to meet these provisions for ministers in those towns (where a large majority were Quakers). The inhabitants of Dartmouth resisted by laying in town-meeting the amount of their proportionate tax, exclusive of the charge for the support of the ministry, and by making a protest by agents to the General Court. They also voted to indemnify the selectmen for not complying with the "Act," and to allow them payment "for every day they lay in jail on the town's account." In March, 1723, they chose a Quaker their

---

[1] Late Memorable Providences, etc., Appendix.
[2] See the note, from which these facts are drawn, in "Province Laws," ii. 269.

minister. The law was, however, enforced; and May 25, 1723, the assessors of the two towns were committed to jail for non-compliance with the law. An appeal was now made in their behalf to the Home Government, and was referred by the Lords Justices in Council, Oct. 24, 1723, to the committee for hearing appeals from the Plantations, who requested the Lords Commissioners for Trade and Plantations to report on the Acts complained of, which they did after obtaining Mr. West's opinion on them : —

"We think it our duty to represent, . . . that, by the Charter granted to the Massachusetts Bay, the foundation of this Colony was laid in an absolute and free liberty of conscience for all Christian Inhabitants there, except Papists, But the *Presbyterians*, having absolutely the ascendant in the Assembly of this Province, have assum'd to themselves the authority of an established Church," etc.

June 2, 1724, the King in Council remitted the additional taxes on the two towns, and ordered the release of the assessors from imprisonment.[1] The principles of the "Friends" had now been vindicated, and it was only a question of time how soon their policy of passive resistance would triumph.

"An Act to Exempt Persons commonly called Quakers, within this Province, from being taxed for and towards the Support of Ministers,"[2] was passed in December, 1731, by Governor Belcher's influence, but was limited to five years, — assessors being "certified in writing, under the hands of two principal members of that persuasion," duly appointed by their societies, that such persons are "conscientiously of their persuasion, and that they do frequently and usually attend their meetings for the worship of God on the Lord's day." Persons so exempted were debarred from voting in such affairs in town-meeting. This was the law which, as will presently appear, stirred the wrath of the Church of England people by its discrimination in favor of a sect which they particularly disliked.

Feb. 9, 1735, the committee of council for Plantation affairs took this Act into consideration, and decided that as it only mentioned Quakers, and did not include "all persons whatsoever of the perswasion or denomination of Protestants," it was not proper for the King's approbation; and as it was temporary and near expiring they recommended that the Governor be in-

[1] The statutes granting temporary relief to Dissenters, for a limited term of years, were perhaps framed on the model of similar English enactments at the same period.
[2] Province Laws, ii. 619.

structed not to give assent to any such law, unless conformable to the charter. It was nevertheless re-enacted for ten years in June, 1738.[1]

Already, however, laws had been passed which blended Quakers and Baptists in the same contemptuous toleration. The first act of exemption, June, 1729, said: —

> "Whereas some of the inhabitants of this Province, called Anabaptists (and others called Quakers), refuse to pay any part or proportion of such taxes as are from time to time assessed for the support of the ministry in the several towns whereto they belong, alledging a scruple of conscience for such their refusal; and thereupon frequent application has bin made to this court for their relief."[2]

It therefore provided that if enrolled members of their society regularly attended worship and lived within five miles, they should be exempt from the poll-tax, and from having "their bodys taken in execution to satisfy any such ministerial rate or tax laid upon their estates or faculty." This was for five years and no longer. Quakers were also required by this law to subscribe the declaration of fidelity to George I., and the profession of Christian belief directed by Parliament in the first year of William and Mary. By this Act polls only, and not the estates, were exempted; but in July, 1735,[3] the same persons were exempted from having "their poll or estate, real or personal, in their own hands and under their actual improvement, taxed towards the support of such minister or ministers, or for the building of any meeting-house or place of public worship." A list was required to be made by the assessors and lodged with the town clerk; persons exempted were not to vote in such affairs. This act, to continue for five years, did not "extend to new towns, granted upon condition of settling an orthodox minister and erecting a house for the public worship of God, till such time as those things are accomplished." No penalty, however, being annexed to the neglect or refusal of the assessors to make the required list, they were able practically to nullify the statute; and such a list was prepared in only a few towns. The act, indeed, authorized an Anabaptist, "omitted in such list," to claim exemption by certificates "under the hands of two principal members of that persuasion, appointed thereto by the respective societies;" but this involved trouble and expense. This law was re-enacted in June, 1740, "for the space

---

[1] Province Laws, ii. 876.   [2] Ibid. 494.   [3] Ibid. 714.

of seven years and no longer,"[1] and was subsequently extended ten years further.

In consequence of the "New Light" movement under Whitefield and Tennent, a number of Baptist churches had been formed, which were not yet received in fellowship by the elder churches of that body. In 1752 an amendment was passed, requiring an endorsement from each of three other churches "commonly called Anabaptists in this or the neighbouring Provinces," that they conscientiously believe the persons giving such certificates "to be Anabaptists." This would exclude members of the "New Light" churches from the privileges of the Act, which was further oppressive in that it compelled them to apply to themselves the opprobrious name of "Anabaptist," which was "on principle offensive to these immersed believers." They therefore decided to appeal to the King, sending an agent to England, who, however, first presented a petition to the Assembly, so plain spoken that Governor Shirley had to intervene to protect the signers from punishment; and a committee of conference being appointed by the Assembly, the appeal was delayed. In 1757 was enacted a new statute for the relief of Baptists and Quakers, — relieving from rates for the support of the "Standing Order" such Baptists as were named in a list signed by the minister and three principal members of their Church, that "they are really belonging thereto; that [the attestors] verily believe them to be conscientiously of their persuasion, and that they frequently and usually attend public worship in said church on the Lord's day." This led to various cases of hardship, — as in 1765 at Haverhill, where John White was taxed for the minister's salary, and his goods distrained, notwithstanding his possession of a certificate; and, suing the assessors for the money, finally lost his case on the technical question "whether the law contemplated a baptized church member, or only a steady attendant upon public worship."

In 1770 a new law substituted the designation "Antipedobaptists" for "Anabaptists," and "congregation" for "church," retaining the word "conscientiously" to meet the case of "those avaricious and dissolute persons who get under water to wash away their minister's rates, without any expectation or desire of washing away their sins."[2] The Revolution, which was so largely inspired by resistance to taxation without representa-

---

[1] Province Laws, ii. 1022.
[2] Boston Evening Post, May 17, 1773, quoted in the article on "Disestablishment in New England," in the "British Quarterly Review," January, 1876, to which I am indebted.

tion, carried with it the emancipation of all such religious believers.

The jealousy with which such enactments treated these two religious bodies is explained by their early history as sects. The quiet body of "Friends" could hardly have thought it strange that the extravagances of the early Quakers were long remembered against their spiritual descendants; while the Baptists, in reviving by their name the memory of the fanatics of Munster, depreciating the historical church while emphasizing as a cardinal doctrine a single custom of the primitive church, demanding an unlearned ministry and a marked personal religious experience, were an organized protest against the established order of New England.

To the Church-of-England men nothing could have been more offensive than any implication that their case was in any way parallel with that of these heretical scions of the Christian Church. They would be satisfied with nothing less than an acknowledgment that they were the only Legal Establishment, with all the immunities and dignities appertaining thereto.[1] Here, as in so many political controversies also during the fifty years preceding the Revolution, the question of the degree of subordination of the Province to the English Crown lay close beneath the surface.

The overwhelming majority of the people of the province

---

[1] The two opposing views on this subject were stated by Colman and Checkley. The former wrote to Bishop Kennett, Dec. 17, 1725: "By our present Charter . . . our Churches are here the *Legal Establishment*, and our Ministers, both in respect of their Induction and Maintenance, are the King's Ministers, as much as even the Church of *England* Ministers are in any of the other Provinces; who did not settle as we did on the declared Principles of Non-Conformity, and without the least Charge or Expence to the Crown, as we have done. But when I say that our Churches and Ministers here are established by the King's Laws, I would pray Your *Lordship* not to understand me in Opposition to the Church of *England*, for so they are not; but if any Town will chuse a Gentleman of the Church of *England* for their Pastor or Rector they are at their Liberty, and he is their Minister by the Laws of our Province, as much as any Congregational Minister among us is so. So far is our Establishment from excluding others from the common Rights of Men and Christians, and I hope ever will remain so." — *Turell's Colman*, p. 138.

Checkley's speech at his trial said: "Gov. Shute, in his Order to the Magistrates of Bristol, etc., wherein he prohibits their taxing the Church-men towards the Maintenance of any other Ministers of any other Profession than Episcopal, calls *the Church of England* the *established Church* here. And the late Governour, Col. Dudley (by wise Men deservedly acknowledged the wisest Man that ever was in this Country), in a like Order in favour of the Church at *Newbury*, declares the *Church of England* to be the *established Church*. . . . By the Laws of *England*, the Church of *England, as established in England*, and no OTHER, is positively established in all His Majesty's Plantations."

were of the Congregational way, and the Quaker or Baptist dissentients were few and scattered. Probably fewer still, but of more conspicuous social position, were the adherents of the Church of England here and there. The Assembly certainly moved more sluggishly to relieve Churchmen than it did to exempt Quakers; but an explanation for this is probably to be found in the distrust of the political entanglements of the English Church. The first concession was that by which wherever a church was within reach, the law allowed Episcopalians to declare their wish to belong to it, and so to have their taxes applied to that use. Already in July, 1725, the East Society in Salem stated that several of their principal men had "signed off to Marblehead Episcopal Church . . . to escape large taxes."

Mr. Myles writes, June 1, 1724,[1] in answer to the Bishop's question: —

"Can you suggest anything that may be serviceable to religion, and conduce to the ease of the Clergy and their more substance, which you believe to be fairly practicable, and which will no way interfere with the authority of the Govr, nor be judged an infringement of the rights of the people?

"*Ans^r*. It would tend very much to the advantage of the Church and comfort of the Clergy, if the members of the Chh were freed from any compulsion to pay to the independant ministers, as they are forced to do in many places, particularly in Bristol, where the Church people have been imprisoned for not paying their rates towards the maintainance of Mr Cotton, a Dissenting Minister of that Town."

Instances had earlier occurred of similar hardship, — as in the case of the indomitable Mr. Veazy of Braintree, who was, however, "chiden and let go," as recorded by Sewall.[2] But about 1724 matters reached a crisis.

Dr. Cutler wrote to the Secretary, Nov. 28, 1726:[3] —

---

[1] Church Docs. Mass. p. 154.

[2] June 2, 1713.

The Massachusetts Archives (lii. 134) contain Rev. G. Pigot's (of Bristol) letter relative to imprisonment of men belonging to his church, and Lieut.-Governor Dummer's reply: —

"April 5, 1725.

"S^r, — I received your Letter of the 22^d of March, Concerning three Men of this Government whome you mention to belong to your Church, that are Committed to Prison at Bristol. The Case is very new, as they belong to this Jurisdiction, and your Church being in an^r Government. However, I have, by advice of his Maj^{ts} Councill of this Province, directed the Justices of Sessions at Bristol to give me an Account of the whole proceeding thereon; and you may assure your Selfe that as I am an Enimye to Violent proceedings, so I shall on all occasions, when anything of that nature appears, exert the utmost of my Authority and influence to Suppress it."

[3] Church Docs. Mass. p. 205.

"The Churches in this place would soon be too small for the Parishioners, were we blessed with a resident Bishop, and several from the pressure of the Dissenters Lyons, who are very industrious to blacken our Characters, and to burthen us with Taxes, the only ways to check the advances of our excellent Church."

The Lieut.-Governor, though not an Episcopalian, endeavored to alleviate such hardships, to the discontent of his own party, as Dudley and Shute had formerly done. In answer to an application from Mr. Plant of Newbury, referring to the taxing of his hearers within the town of Amesbury, he wrote, Dec. 12, 1726:[1] —

"My proposal was to have a law made, that the taxes of those belonging to the Church of England be paid by the collectors to the Ministers of the Church of England to whom they severally do belong, which will not only put you upon an equal, just foot, but save you much trouble. . . . I must advise you when you mention the ministers in the Towns, that you give them the character the Laws of this province vest them with, — vizt, Ministers, and not Dissenting Teachers, for that gives offence to the Court."

The Braintree churchmen wrote to General Nicholson, Dec. 28, 1726,[2] asking him to —

"Use his endeavours that what the Independants here call Laws, by which they tax the Churchmen, and force them to pay towards the support of the Congregational Teachers, may be explained; and if they be explained according to the Laws of England, we shall be free from their impositions."

They also wrote to the Secretary, May 27, 1727:[3] —

"One of our Church, Dr Turner, has been lately presented by the Grand Jury for totally absenting himself from the Worship of God; and though he proved himself utterly innocent, yet he was obliged to pay the cost of Court: and many such ways have they to persecute us."

A letter to Colonel Quincy from the Lieut.-Governor, April 7, 1727, in relation to this affair, sets in an honorable light the just purpose of that worthy chief magistrate:[4] —

"Sir, — I have rec'd a Memorial from Some Persons living within the North Precinct in Braintree, who profess themselves of the Chh of England, Complaining of their being taxed for the Settlem^t of your Minister, Of wch you have a Copy enclosed. I am surprized to find this Matter driven to Extremity, especially after the Hopes you had raised in me that

[1] Church Docs. Mass. p. 206.
[2] Ibid. p. 209.
[3] Church Docs. Mass. p. 221.
[4] Mass. Archives, xi. 418.

your People were throughly disposed to make those of ye Church of England amongst them easy in all these Matters.

"I am not inform'd who are the Parish Committee (thô I suppose you are one), And therefore I pray that you would acquaint them with my desire that a Meeting may be called to consider of the Case of these Memorialists, and that you would use your utmost Influence that it may be with good Effect, that so these People may obtain the Relief they look for, and as I think common Justice intitules them to while they contribute to the Settlem^t and Support of their own Minister. These are Matters of that Weight with me (as I take them highly to affect ye Caracter and ye Welfare of ye Governm^t), That I hope they will not be pass'd over slightly by you and the People of Brantrey; And therefore I hope to have some good Acc^t of it from you in a very short time."

But the most conspicuous victim of the law was Philip English, a Salem merchant, who found the ferryman between that town and Marblehead unwilling to carry him across on the Sabbath, while by land the distance exceeded the lawful number of miles. Here again the authorities strove to mitigate the working of the law. The Massachusetts Archives [1] contain a petition and depositions relating to him, February, 1724–25, which state that he was "three weeks since committed Prisoner to his Maj^{ty's} Goal in Salem, . . . for non-payment of an Assessment made for the support of the minister of . . . Salem." He declared "that he was bred and born in the Comunion of the Church of England, and that he would go to no other publick worship willingly."

The Lieut.-Governor and Council desire to "have the Affair speedily compromised, and the Man discharged from his Imprisonment; Wch the Board apprehend of great Consequence to the General Interest of this Province, And that a very ill use will be made of the Proceedings against him unless he have some speedy redress." [2]

These interferences, however, seemed arbitrary to the adherents of the old way. Cotton Mather, in 1726, wrote: [3] —

"In some Churches the Salary of the Minister is raised by a Voluntary Contribution, especially in populous Places, and where many Strangers resort; but in others a Tax is levied for it. . . . In those . . . the Case is thus: The Laws of the Province, having had the Royal Approba-

---

[1] See N. E. Hist. and Geneal. Reg. xxxv. 163.

[2] In 1733 St. Peter's Church was erected in Salem, and consecrated June 25, 1734. "Philip English and his family connections gave £95 worth of the land for it, valued at £120, and for the rest took a pew." The present stone church was built in 1833. The society erroneously stated, in an inscription in the church, to have "owed its establishment, under God," to the intrepidity of the brothers Browne in 1629.

[3] Ratio Disciplinæ, pp. 20–22.

tion to ratify them, they are the King's Laws. By these Laws it is enacted that there shall be a Publick Worship of God in every Plantation; that the Person elected by the Majority of the Inhabitants to be so, shall be looked upon as the Minister of the Place; that the Salary for him, which they shall agree upon, shall be levied by a Rate upon all the Inhabitants. In consequence of this, the Minister thus chosen by the People is (not only Christ's but also) in reality the King's Minister; and the Salary raised for him is raised in the King's Name, and is the King's Allowance to him. If the Most of the Inhabitants in a Plantation are Episcopalians, they will have a Minister of their own Persuasion; and the Dissenters, if there be any in the Place, must pay their Proportion of the Tax for the Support of this Legal Minister. In a few of the Towns a few of the People, — in Hope of being released from the Tax for the Legal Minister, — sometimes profess themselves Episcopalians; but when they plead this for their Exemption, their Neighbours tell them they know in their Conscience they do not do as they would be done unto. And if a Governour go by his arbitrary Power to supersede the Execution of the Law, and require the Justices and Constables to leave the Episcopalians out of the Tax, the People wonder he is not aware that he is all this While forbidding that the King should have His Dues paid unto Him, and forbidding the King's Minister to receive what the King has given him."

At this date there were but three Church of England societies in the province, outside of Boston, and it was supposed that five miles was as great a distance as would be travelled on a Sabbath day's journey to church. The law did not contemplate the excuse of those who preferred the Book of Common Prayer from " going to meeting," when " church " was not to be had. It was not easy for the two parties to understand each other, or for either to do justice to convictions so opposite and so resolute. To the churches of Massachusetts it seemed that the refusal of a few Episcopalians here and there to join in the only worship which had been known since the settlement of the country was factious, and tended to weaken the sanctions of religion: to the members of the Church of England it seemed their duty to disobey the laws of the land, and to go in opposition to the convictions of the best men in it, rather than take any part in the prayers and praises of their neighbors after a fashion which they deemed schismatical. Meantime the measures which they resisted were meted out more abundantly to the Dissenters in England during this whole period. The laws against their holding office sank, indeed, into disuse from the reluctance of their fellow-citizens to enforce them against good men elected by public confidence. In 1728 Parliament passed an act of indemnity, relieving them from penalties, which was annually re-enacted. The Test and Corporation act, however, remained on the statute-book.[1] Dissenters were only tolerated on condition of subscribing the articles, until 1779, when a declaration that they took the Scriptures for the rule of faith and practice was substituted, while no concession about the payment of tithes was proposed or dreamed of.

Notwithstanding their strong conviction of the religious safeguards needed in Massachusetts, the repeated instances of men submitting to imprisonment, for conscience' sake, wrought on the Assembly to pass, in 1727, " An Act in Addition to the Several Acts for the Settlement and Support of Ministers."[2] This act recapitulated that, by the law made under William and Mary, —

"All the inhabitants and ratable estates in a town, etc., obliged to pay in proportion ; . . . and altho' it is found by experience that the said provision for the settlement and support of ministers is of great benefit and necessity for encouragement of ministers of the gospel, and for maintaining peace and good order in the several towns and precincts in this province, yet forasmuch as it may so happen, for want of some limitations and qualifications in the said act, that some persons who conscientiously profess themselves to be of the church of England, and to differ in opinion from the discipline and form of worship used in the respective churches setled by law within the towns . . . where they reside, may be under difficulties by reason of being obliged to pay for the support of the minister setled according to law, altho' they give no attendance on his publick administration, but they and their families usually attend the public worship of God, according to the manner of the church of England."

It relieved them from such taxation if they lived within five miles of an Episcopal church. But the strictness of the " Sunday laws " operated to prevent them from attending church at any distance from their homes.

Mr. Checkley clearly stated the case to the Lord Bishop of London, in 1728 :[3] —

[1] "One exception must be made to the statement that no one liked to enforce that act. The Corporation of London made a bye-law fining all persons who refused to serve as sheriff £400, or if elected by the citizens, £600 ; and then elected Dissenters year after year, devoting the fines to the rebuilding of the Mansion house. . . . When £16,000 had been extorted in this way, however, the bye-law was resisted, and in 1767 the House of Lords finally confirmed the refusal." — *Herford's Story of Religion in England*, p. 369.

[2] Province Laws, ii. 459.

[3] Church Docs. Mass. p. 250. " In all the other colonies, the law lays an obligation to go to some sort of worship on Sunday, but [in Rhode Island] liberty of conscience is carried to an irreligious extreme." — *McSparran's "America Dissected."* [1752.]

"There are but few churches (at great distance from each other) in this great country; and the Churchmen being dispersed throughout the whole territory, they are obliged (some of them) to ride 30 or 40 miles to partake of the Holy Sacrament. It is, moreover, usual for the Church people to walk or ride 6, 8, and 10 miles upon the Saturday evening, or very early on the Sunday morning, to the town where the Church of England is settled, and to return home again on the Sunday evening. But if a stop is not put to this first law, they will be obliged to spend the greatest part of the Saturday and Monday in going (for all are not able to keep horses) and riding to church and returning home. But this would be very hard upon the poor people, who are generally husbandmen, etc."

The result was that, by law, members of that church, unless within easy reach of some one of the few Episcopal churches of the province, were still liable to be distrained or imprisoned for not paying toward the building of Congregational, or what they termed Dissenting, meeting-houses and the support of Dissenting teachers.

It is clear, however, that notwithstanding the strictness of the letter of the law, the ruling powers must have interpreted it with leniency, as in the cases at Braintree and elsewhere just referred to, and also that the number of scattered churchmen must have been less than was claimed on their behalf, from the fact that, after the passage of the act of 1727, as Greenwood expresses it, "only three cases of oppression could be produced before the General Court, and the churches were obliged to pay for hunting up more," as our record will presently show.

But the churchmen watched the General Court with so jealous an eye that they interpreted any enactment which looked toward religion, as if intended to bear hardly upon them. Thus the Sunday law of 1728, with its restrictions upon travel, though intended to guard the strict observance of the Lord's Day, which was "the special Happiness of this Country" as Governor Belcher said, caused earnest protest. Yet this law was really in accord with the forty-first instruction to him: "The Bishop of London having presented a petition to his late Majesty beseeching him to send Instruct^s to Govr's of all Plantat^s to cause all Laws to be vigorously executed against Blasphemy, Prophaneness, Adultery, Fornication, Polygamy, Incest, Prophanation of the Lord's Day, Swearing, and Drunkenness,—those vices to be punished."[1]

---

[1] Governor Belcher, in his speeches to the Assembly, Dec. 2, 1731, and Nov. 2, 1732, recommended to their "Serious Consideration the Reformation of man-

THE CHURCH UNDER LAW. 453

By the timely enactment,[1] as related above, of the Act of Exemption in 1727, the plans of the Episcopal missionaries, inspired by Dr. Cutler, were disconcerted. His controversy with the Overseers of Harvard College was in progress, when, in 1725, a petition was addressed by those clergymen "To the King's Most Excellent Majesty in Council,"[2] complaining that —

"The Independants being more numerous than the people of the Church of England, to whom the Charter allows at least equal rights, . . . have usurped and assumed to themselves the authority of an established Church, . . . and have taken upon themselves to pass Laws tending to the very great prejudice and oppression of the members of the Church of England and the rest of the inhabitants of the said Colony. . . . And the Inhabitants of the said Province, who would otherwise freely embrace the public worship of the Church of England [are] hereby greatly discouraged from openly professing themselves Members thereof; whereas, if these Acts were repealed, and any acts of the like nature prevented from being pass'd for the future, it is very reasonable to believe the Members of the Church of England would receive a daily increase, and that by this means many flourishing Churches would be very soon effectually established among us."

They accordingly prayed His Majesty "to pronounce Your royal Negative and repeal the same and each of them," and to forbid such oppressive acts for the future. The next steps went through the usual leisurely English course. July 14, 1727, in Council, "the Right Hono^ble the Lords of the Committee for hearing Appeales, Complaints, etc., from the Plantations," to whom the petition was referred, ordered that it be "referred to the Lords Commissioners for Trade," with the request to "report their opinion thereupon to this Committee." Nov. 10, 1727, the Commissioners for Trade and Plantations considered the Acts of Massachusetts complained of, and "ordered, that the Lord Bishop of London be acquainted that the Board are desirous of speaking with him thereupon." Nov. 14, 1727,

---

ners by making some other Laws, if it be thought necessary. . . . When We Consider that Our Worthy Ancestors freely professed true Religion to be their Principal End of their Settlement of this Plantation, I hope it will provoke in Us an Emulation, and make us Endeavour to bar up the Flood Gates of Vice and Wickedness."

At the fifth session of 1733-34, was passed an Act in further addition to an Act, entitled "An Act for the Punishing of Criminal Offenders," ordaining fines for swearing and drunkenness. — *Province Laws*, ii. 700.

[1] A similar enactment was made in Connecticut, May 15, 1727.

[2] The petition is given in Church Docs. Mass. p. 191. It was signed by Mr. Myles, but not by Messrs. Harris and Mossom.

the Bishop being present, they "gave directions for writing to M! Attorney and M! Solicitor Gen¹ for their opinion whether the said Acts are repugnant to the Charter of the Massachusetts Bay; and if they are so, whether it be not in the King's power to repeal the same." The law officers of the Crown were, however, in no haste to pronounce on this subject, so that May 21, 1729, it was "ordered, that a letter be written to M' Attorny and Sol' Gen¹ to remind them of the letter . . . for their opinion."¹

Meantime, a second petition, signed by "Timothy Cutler, in behalf of himself and the rest of the Clergy and the severall Congregations of the Church of England in the said Province," was sent to England.² This document (date not given, but received before Oct. 28, 1731) speaks of the delay in reporting on the former petition, —

"Occasioned, as Your Petitioner humbly conceives, by the Assembly of the said Province having, as soon as they were informed of the said application, passed an Act, etc. [1727–28]. Your Pet' humbly conceives it was apprehended this Act would, in a great measure, free the Members of the Church of England in the said Province from the many oppressions brought upon 'em by the severall Acts complained of. . . . But Your Pet' most humbly informs Your Majesty that it is very common for the people of New England to go ten or fifteen miles to Church; so that this last Act, by limiting the exemption to five Miles, is very far from removing the grievance complained of.

"And your Pet' humbly informs Your Majesty that James Ellis of the Town of Cambridge, . . . a Member of the Church of England, and who hath a Pew in your Pet'ʳ church at Boston, where he duly attends the Divine worship of God, and who pays towards the support of the said Church, hath been greatly distressed, and is now actually confined and imprisoned in Cambridge gaol for not paying towards the support of the established Minister of that Town, by reason that his place of residence is upwards of five miles distance from your Pet'ʳ said Church.

"That Your Pet' further humbly submits to Your Majesty's wise consideration whether the said Act, by subjecting the Inhabitants generally (which includes the Members of the Church of England) to make up all Deficiencys to the Established Minister of each Town, Parish, or Pre-

---

[1] See the exhaustive notes on this subject in Messrs. Ames and Goodell's edition of the "Province Laws," ii. 477, 483. A note in this says:—
"It is to be regretted that no opinion upon these acts by the eminent lawyers, Attorney-General Yorke, afterwards Earl of Hardwicke, and Mr. Solicitor, afterwards Lord Chancellor Talbot, to whom these petitions were referred, has been discovered. Neither has any record been found of further action upon this subject by the Privy Council." The opinion is, however, given in full in Church Docs. Mass. p. 274.

[2] Province Laws, ii. 483.

cinct, does not make it the very same thing as if there was no Exemption at all.

"That Your Pet' likewise most humbly submits to Your Majesty's consideration, whether the Governor and Councill of the said Province are warranted by their Charter to pass any Law whereby to tax the Members of the Church of England, or of any other perswasion, to the support and maintenance of the Ministers of what they have taken upon them to establish as the Provincial Church."

He therefore, "for himself and his suffering Brethren," prayed the King "to annull or repeale the said Laws," and to forbid the enactment of similar laws in future. Nov. 1, 1731, the Committee of the Privy Council took into consideration this second petition, and referred it for examination to the Lords Commissioners for Trade.

Meantime, weary of waiting for a decision of the final authority, the churchmen here made a fresh effort to obtain relief. "Xber 1, 1731. Roger Price, Clerk and Commissary of ye Episcopal Churches in New England," addressed a memorial[1] to the Governor, Council, and House of Representatives, in his new official capacity under the Bishop of London. He referred to Governor Belcher's speech to the General Assembly, which recommended,

"As an Act of due Gratitude to the Crown, to make good Protestants of all Denominations easy in their way and manner of worshiping God, and particularly . . . the People called Quakers."

The memorial proceeded: —

"And whereas, a Committee of the Lower House is Ordered to prepare a Draught of a Bill for the Ease of those People, Your Memorialist apprehends he may with equal Justice, and does, with the greatest Humility, Tender to the Compassion of this Honble Assembly the case of the Church of England within this Province; the Members whereof, in Several parts of it, ly under great difficultys and Discouragements from Obedience to their Consciences, in that they are Taxed to the Support of the Congregational or Presbyterian Meetings in their vicinity, and are not Exempted unless they live within five miles of a Church, — nor even then if that Church be out of the bounds of this Province; And for non payment of Such Taxes their Bodies are Imprisoned, or their Goods taken from them by Publick Officers.

"Your Memorialist, therefore, in duty bound to his Publick Character, thinks himself Obliged to lay these Grievances before this Great and General Court, as inconsistent with that Liberty in the Exercise of Reli-

---

[1] See Church Docs. Mass. p. 272. Mr. Price's own account of these transactions is given at p. 415, *ante*.

gion to which, by the Laws of England and Charter of this Province, we think Ourselves Intitled; humbly apprehending the Good Characters bestowed by his Excellency on the Quakers do, in as eminent a manner, belong to the members of the Church of England, — namely, that they are good Protestants, a vertuous and inoffensive People, and good members of the Commonwealth, and as well attached to His Majesty and his Royal House as any the best of his Subjects, and consequently merit the Same Notice and Relief. All of which is humbly submitted to the great Wisdom and Goodness of the Great and General Court."

In this course King's Chapel sustained Commissary Price, the Court being backward about affording redress, and sceptical about the genuineness of the three cases of hardship presented by Dr. Cutler from among his parishioners.

Whereas, the Rev[d] M[r] Roger Price having Presented a Memorial to the General Assembly of this Province, for the Relief of the Members of the Church of England who have Suffered great hardships from some of the Laws of this Province respecting the Exercise of their Religion; and whereas, the General Assembly has appointed a Committee from both houses to consider of the same, which Comittee not being Contented with the Evidence of three Persons who had suffered, Belonging to the Rev[d] D[r] Cutler's Church, but insisting upon more particulars of Persons who had suffered, — the Rev[d] M[r] Price called his Vestry together, who met at M[r] Pattin's, Dec. 17, 1731.

Voted, That two thirds of the Charges which have or shall Arise upon presenting the said Memorial, and procuring a greater Number of Instances of Persons who have suffered by the Laws of this Province respecting the Exercise of their Religion, shall be paid out of the Church Stock.

Jan. 26, 1731–32. *Voted*, That the two Vestrys of this Town of Boston doe Unite as one body or Society, to Consider what is proper to be done further upon the two Memorials lately presented to the General Assembly of this Province, — the one by the Rev[d] M[r] Roger Price, Com[ry], alone, and the other by the Rev[d] Mr. Roger Price and the Rev[d] D[r] Cutler, the Rev[d] M[r] Harward and the Rev[d] M[r] Miller.

Voted, That the Prayers of those Memorials being Rejected by the General Assembly, a Memorial, wherein to lay open the state of the Case to the Lord Bishop of London, and a petition to present to the King in Council, be prepared by the Rev[d] M[r] Com[ry] Price, D[r] Cutler, M[r] Harward, M[r] Miller, and offered to the consideration of the United Vestries of this Town.

The Christ Church Records add: —

"At a Joint Meeting of the Vestry of Christ Church and King's Chappel, the 17th of Decem[r], 1731, *Voted*, That whereas a Memorial has lately been presented to the General Court by the Rever^d Mr Roger Price, to obtain a release of those Gent. who are obliged to pay Rates to the Support of the Dissenting way of Worship, and the Committee appointed by the General Court to consider that Memorial Require there should be produced whatever Instances there are of Church Men who Suffers by those Province Laws affecting this Case, which Calls for considerable Charge, —

"That one third of whatever Charge has risen or may arise in pursuit of this affair Shall be deffray'd by this Church. And tho' three Evidences have already been presented by the Revd Doc^r Cutler to Said Committee of Churchmen, Resorting to the Worship of God in his Church, who Suffer on the Said Acc^t to Comply with, which calls for considerable Charge."

Although he had signed a memorial to the General Court, the assistant minister did not sympathize in this course.

Feb. 3, 1731–32. Whereas the Rev^d Mr. Thos Harward refused to join wth the Committee in drawing up a Memorial to the Lord Bishop of London, and a petition to the Kings most excellent Majesty, respecting the Sufferings of the Church men in this Province, it is now *Voted*, That he be no longer of the said Comittee, but that the Revd Mr Commissary Price, Dr Cutler, and Mr Miller be the Committee; and that the United Vestries be Adjourned to Monday night next at five o clock, being the 7 of this Instant. Passed Nemine Contradicente.

The Christ Church Records note a joint meeting of the two Vestries: —

"Feb. 7, 1731–32. *Voted*, That the Memorial drawn up by the Committee, and Unanimously accepted by both Vestrys, be Sent to the Lord Bishop of London.

"That the Church Wardens of Christ Church and Mr Wm Ridout, and the two Church Wardens of King's Chappel and Mr Thos Green, are desired to Collect the Subscriptions for deffraying the Charges that may arise in defending the Church of England in this Province."

A draught of this memorial has been preserved among the papers of Mr. Price: —

"*May it please, etc.*, — As His Majesty has been graciously pleased to appoint Your Lordship our diocesan and the Guardian of our Religious Rites and Liberties in this Province to our great Satisfaction, we think it our duty to represent to your Lordship the Unhappy Circumstances our Church now Labours under.

We have hitherto, by the Blessing of God, maintain'd our Ground in the midst of different Opinions and Uncharitable Attempts against us;

but when to the goodness of our Cause Your Lordship pleases to joyn your kind patronage and Protection, it will mightily Contribute to fortifie our Resolusions, and defend us from the evils which threaten us.

We beg leave to inform Your Lordship that there are several Laws enacted in this Province which are very prejudicial to the Interest of the Church of England here, and an Infringement upon that Liberty of Conscience which, by the express words of their Charter, is equally the priviledge of all Protestants settled in this Colony, — Particularly that our Brethren of the Church are restrained from Traveling above five miles on the Lord's day to a Church of England, if there be any Publick place of worship nearer, tho' differing from their principles; and the Sabbath here Commencing early on the Saturday Evening Occasions the loss of that Day's Labour to those who live a great distance and attend the service of the Church, which Prevents many people from frequenting our Worship who are otherwise inclined to it, and is a great Inconvenience to those who pay their attendance under this restriction. And altho' we have not regularly made our Complaint of this Law to the Legislature here, Yet forasmuch as the Independants themselves are under a necessity of exceeding these bounds in many parts of the Province by reason of the much greater distance of several of their settlements from any publick place of Worship, this law we presume will be thought no less unreasonable than those we have made the subject of our Complaint, Which we have transmitted at large to Your Lordship, with the Methods which have been taken, and the Memorials presented to the General Court to obtain a redress, Wherein Your Lordship may observe the motive which excited us at this juncture to struggle for our liberty, and be satisfied of the justice of our cause and the necessity of this appeal.

We flatter'd ourselves from the encouragement given us by his Excellency Governor Belcher upon our first attempt, and the repeated assurances we received from his Excellency thro'out the whole Course of our Proceedings (of the Favorable Disposition of the General Court towards us), that our Endeavours would have proved effectual; but to our great surprise and concern our well grounded expectations were in the event deluded by a flat denial to the prayer of both our memorials, and that with a most aggravating Circumstance, when the Quakers, with whom we were levell'd in our sufferings, had Obtained that relief by a Law pass'd in their Favour which we applied for with great pains and expense.

This law we likewise lay before Your Lordship, with the answers we receiv'd soon after, which we conclude will convince Your Lordship of the Necessity of this Appeal.

The Dissenters pretend indeed that these Laws are made for our advantage, yet, by the effects of them and the frequent complaints of our Injured Bretheren, which upon examination have appear'd just, we are sensible they have a different tendency. And the grievances many of them suffer — Submitting rather to Imprisonment and the seizure and sale of their Goods at a publick outcry than comply with these laws — sufficiently Invalidates the strongest Argument they use against us in their answer to our first memorial, and proves beyond doubt that these men act by the impulse of their Consciences in adhering so strictly to the Worship of the Church of England, however some few persons' practices may allow an indifference.

We likewise think it a matter worthy Your Lordship's consideration, and of the utmost importance to the Church of England here, to inquire into their right to those titles of Orthodox Ministry and Established Churches which the Independants assume to themselves as a sanction to all their unjust proceedings against us, but by what Authority we cant learn from their Charter, and which, by the Laws of England and in particular by the Union Act, we apprehend do more justly belong to our Episcopal Churches.

We promise ourselves that the same spirit and zeal which has so eminently appear'd in Your Lordship's Labours, and so much to the advantage of the Christian Religion, will not be slack in defending that particular Church in which Your Lordship is deservedly distinguish'd as a bright Luminary, and that part of it, especially, which more immediately falls under Your Lordship's care and Protection."

The united Vestries, Feb. 24, 1731-32, —

Voted, Thom^s Sandford, Esq., be and hereby is our Agent to prosecute our Petition to his most Sacred Majesty, and one other to our Dioceson the Bishop of London, and to Govern himself therein by his Lordship's directions, and such advices and Acc^{ts} as he shall from time to time Receive from us.

Voted, y^t John Jekyll, Esqr, George Cradock, Robt Auchmuty, Esqr, John Gibbins, Robt Harris, Thos Cannington, and Chas. Apthorp Are Appointed a Committee to Carry on a Correspondence wth our Agent, Thos Sandford, Esqr, Conformable to the Vote afores^d and to the orders to them from time to time Given by us, and also to remit to our S^d Agent such Sums as shall be by them Reced from us to defray the Contingent charges he shall necessarily be at, and that they make fair Entrys of all their proceedings therein, which, wth such advices as they shall receive, are to be laid before us as often as we require the same, and that any four shall be a sufficient number to act in s^d p.misses ; and we hereby reserve to our Selves the power at all times to change or add to the Number of the s^d Committee, and finally to Dissolve the same as we shall see cause.[1]

Voted, That Mr John Checkley be appointed to goe into the Coun-

---

[1] The wardens of both churches, with Thomas Green, of King's Chapel, and Mr. Rideout, of Christ Church, were desired to collect subscriptions for "defending the Church of England in this Province."

try to get the address and petition signed, and his Charges to be paid out of the Money Received ῳ Subscription.[1]

Already, however, Jan. 5, 1731-32, the Commissioners for Trade and Plantations had referred the second petition "to S' Philip York, Kn'., and Charles Talbot, Esq'^e., His Maj^{ys} Attorney and Soll' General," desiring their opinion "in point of Law as soon as conveniently may be." Thereupon, Aug. 16, 1732, the opinion of those gentlemen was at last given.[2] Its pith is in the following sentences: —

"We conceive that, by Vertue of the General power of making Laws, the Legislature of this Province may take care and provide for the Celebration of the Publick Worship of God, and for the Maintenance of Ministers as incident thereto; and the doing of this in a reasonable manner cannot be said to be inconsistent with Liberty of Conscience. Neither doth anything arise upon the construction of the Charter which either forbids the making of such provision in general, or confines them to do it in any particular form. It appears to us that the Constitution of this Province has been thus understood by the Crown, the first three Acts of Assembly complained of having many years ago, and near to the time of granting the Charter, received the Royal Confirmation, and having been acted under ever since. And therefore it seems to us harsh and unreasonable to say that either the Laws thus Confirmed, or the Subsequent Acts which are grounded upon them, are void in themselves as being Repugnant to the Charter.

"If they were really void in themselves on this account, yet no Extrajudicial Declaration that they are so would be conclusive; but the only Method of bringing that Matter to a Determination would be some Judicial Proceeding."

They concluded by pointing out that the objection to the law of 1727, "that it doth not extend far enough in their favour," is "a prudential and not a legal objection to the Act," which, besides, being limited to five years, would expire "in the present year."

"Here," says Greenwood,[3] "was consistency, at least. Dissenters in England were and still are obliged to support the clergy of the Establishment, beside obliging themselves to support their own; and it was but fair that Churchmen, when sur-

---

[1] Among the receipts is the following: —
Boston, January 24, 1731.
Recd! of Job Lewis, Esq'., three pounds four shillings and eight pence, being my Expences (⅔^{db}) in going to Providence, Bristol, etc., to procure Evidence concerning the Sufferings of Churchmen.
JOHN CHECKLEY.
[2] Church Docs. Mass. pp. 274-288.
[3] History of King's Chapel, pp. 95, 97.

rounded abroad by a majority who looked on them as Dissenters, should not be permitted to complain very loudly or effectually of the operation of a principle which was acted on at home. But how defective is the principle itself; and how impossible it is, at least in this case, for an old wrong to grow into a right!

"The sufferings of the Churchmen! What a change, and what a retribution! Think of the days of Archbishop Laud. Think of the 'sufferings' of the old Puritans. And think, and think again, how unjust, how blind are pains and penalties and all kinds of coercion in matters of religion. History teaches nothing more plainly than this; and it teaches nothing more important than this, or more necessary to be learned and got by heart."

A summary of this opinion duly found its way into the records of King's Chapel: [1] —

A Copy of part of The Lord Bishop of London's Letter to the Reverend M^r. Roger Price, dated

WHITEHALL, Febr. 6, 1732-33.

We have at last obtained the Opinion of the Attorney and Sollicitor Generall in Relation to the New-England Charter and the power of the Legislature there to make Laws for rateing the members of the Episcopal Churches to the Independent ministers. I am truly sorry that the opinion comes out so litle in our Favour, but am oblidged to transmitt it you in order to be comunicated to the Clergy, that they may be Satisfyed that we have done all that is in our power. I heartily wish we could have sent over some better prospect of Relief; but the truth is, the Exercise of the power they claim began so early, and continued so long, that I doubt their is litle encouragement to hope that their acts will be declared null and Void, as made by an Incompetent Authority. You see by the Enclosed paper that they make this length of time, and this continued Exercise of the powers they claim, the rule of Interpreting the Charter.

I am oblidged to write in this plain tho' uncomfortable manner, that you may Judge how far it will be advisable for the members of the Church there to make it a cause; and if Judgement be given against them, as it certainly will, to bring it befor the King and Council by way of appeal.   EDM. LONDON.

P. S. — I desire you to accquaint Mr Brown, of Providence, that I have not been unmindfull of his affair, which could not be thoroughly Judged of till we had the Opinion. If they had no power at all, his would be a clear case; and if they have power, you see our Lawers will allow no remedy but in a Judicial way there, and by appeal hither.

[1] The misspelling in this letter may be due to the copyist in our records, rather than to the bishop.

The united Vestries of the two churches now debated what course to adopt: —

26th day of June, 1733. *Voted*, That the Committee be desired to consider the Report of the Attorney and Sollicitor Generall and the Method Chalked out by the Bishop of London for the Relief of Such members of the Church of England within this Province as shall be distrained or imprisoned for not paying rates to the dissenting Teachers, and make report to the United Vestrys of such ways and means as they shall think Expedient for the above said Vestries to govern them selves by, relateing to the premises, for the future; and this is to be done by the Above said Comittee with all Convenient Speed.[1]

On the 19th of October following, the committee reported that they —

Are of Opinion, That it is most agreeable to the above report, and Method chaulked out by my Lord of London, That Robert Auchmuty, Esqr, John Reed, Esqr, and Mr William Bollan be immediatly Retained in order to prosecute Such officers as the Committee shall think proper, who have or shall hereafter distrain or Imprison any members of the Church of England within this Province, for their not paying towards and Building Dissenting meeting-houses, or Supporting Dissenting teachers; and that the Comittee be Impowered to Support and Mentain such prosecutions out of the money already collected for the Relief of the Suffering members of the Church of England within this Province.

The united Vestries —

29th October, 1733. *Voted*, nemine Contradicente, That the Report of the Comittee of the nintenth of this Instant be received, Provided the said Comittee's power shall Extend no farther than only for carrying on and prosecuting the cases of the agrieved Churchmen only in the Courts of this Province.

Voted, That Robert Achmuty, John Reed, John Oberine, William Sherrly, and William Bolan, Esq^{rs}, have each of them a retaining fee of three pounds for the Service of the Suffering members of the Church of England in this Province.

Voted, nemine Contradicente, That the Comittee be Empowered to defend any Churchman That shall be presented for travailling to, or coming from, any Church of England throughout this Province for the worship of God.

Voted, That the Comittee be Empowered to defend the Church of England Ministers, in case they should be prosecuted in any of the Courts of this Province, for Marrying according to the Custom of

---

[1] At this time, George Cradock was added to the committee in place of J. Jekyll, Esq., deceased.

Marrying in the Church of England, Provided the said Ministers do marry according to the usuage in the Common Prayer Book and Canons of the said Church.

Voted, That M.' William Price be added to the Comittee in the room of M.' Thomas Cannington, whose affairs will not permit him to attend ; and that M.' William Speakman be in the room of M.' George Craddock, who is now Speedyly going in a Voyage for England.

Voted, That M.' George Craddock be joined with Thomas Sandford, Esq.' in Prosecuting the affairs of the Church of England in these parts dureing the said M.' Craddocks continuance in England.

All these proceedings did not pass unnoticed by Governor Belcher, who wrote to the Bishop, Oct. 5, 1733 : [1] —

"I am afraid, my Lord, there are people here that affect to make themselves uneasy without reason, and that they are too much encouraged from the superciliousness and Bitterness of some of the Church Clergy, who might be very quiet and happy, and so might their several congregations, if the Clergy would from time to time, as they found occasion, dutifully apply themselves to the Government established here by the Crown ; but instead thereof they seem inclined to ride over it, which I am sure your Lordship will never countenance them in. . . . Would the Clergy here practice the duty of Christian meekness, and duly apply themselves to the Government here, I believe they might generally save themselves and your Lordship a great deal of trouble."

The Commissary was more in accord with the Governor in this matter than his Excellency supposed. Mr. Price wrote to the Bishop, Nov. 5, 1733 : [2] —

"I opposed them in their . . . addressing the House of Commons ; I opposed them in their address to the King, but in vain ; I opposed their defending 2 Dissenters from the penalty of the Law, for withholding their minister's rates, who, altho' they frequented the meeting, had been persuaded to refuse payment by a promise of Protection from the Church. I opposed the leaving the whole management of this affair to two or three men who have no merit but being Lovers of Contention, who, because very inconsiderable in their proper calling, endeavor to get a name and renown of stirring up strife. Mr. Cradock, whose name I suppose your Lordship has met with in the List of wranglers, . . . will represent the case of our churches more fully to your Lordship. But he is to be believed with Caution ; Dissimulation is his noted Talent, and tho' he may talk big for the Church, yet his end is gain. What advantage we shall reap from our success in this undertaking I can't say, but it is certain we shall render ourselves odious to the Dissenters by our Pro-

[1] Church Docs. Mass. p. 292.   [2] Ibid. p. 294.

ceedings, and discover such weakness at home if we should fail in the attempt as will expose us to great contempt and make our condition more deplorable than it was before."

The Bishop's letter was duly acknowledged by him, however, in an official letter: [1] —

"According to your Lordship's advice, the Committee of the United Churches have prepared a Memorial to be laid before the Archbishop, setting forth the grievances the Church labours under from the severity of some laws here, and the partial treatment we, her members, have met with from the present Governor, a copy of which will be presented to your Lordship."

The following appeal was made to the Archbishop of Canterbury: —

"*May it please your Grace*, — I suppose your Grace is not unacquainted with the State of the Church of England in this Province, surrounded with many and powerful enemies who have so unjustly strained their legislative power as to deprive the members of the Church of England, not only of the just priviledge we think ourselves entitled to as a branch of that Church established by the laws of England, but even of the Common priviledge allow'd by their Charter and indeed indulged to protestants of all other denominations here. These hardships we have from time to time represented to our Diocesan, who after many endeavours to procure us a redress has acknowledged his interest at Court too weak to oppose the united attempts of the dissenting party against us, and has advised us to apply to your Grace for relief; by his advice and your Grace's distinguish'd zeal and protection of the Church have embolden'd us to humbly lay our complaint at your Grace's feet, humbly hoping that the great distance from the fountain of Equity will not exclude us from the Patronage and Protection of the General Father of our Church, and from whose favour alone under God we expect a deliverance from the evils we have long struggled with."

The Bishop wrote to Mr. Price:[2] —

"FULHAM, Jan. 28, 1734-35.

GOOD S^R, — I wrote to you Some time since, and hope that my Letter came safe to your hands, and that you are satisfy'd that my not writing to you before was occasion'd by the current report of your intention to come for England. I now acquaint you that I have no thought, nor ever had, of disposing of the Living of Leigh; nor can I conceive upon what ground you could fall into that suspicion. I push

---

[1] From Mr. Price's family papers.   [2] The *lacunæ* are in the original.

on the affair of the Church of England's contributing to the maintenance
of the Independant Ministers as much as I can; but having to take so
                    owise, and to travel thro' so many hands, and   full
of other business, that it is the hardest thing in the world to gain the dis-
patch one desires and presses for.   Papers that came last were lodg'd
in ye hands of Mr.   ye Sollicitor employed by the Society in
this   it will be found true in fact that
England does not warrant the giving disturbance of any kind to any
Denominations of Religion, except Papists; but I find the King's Council, before whom ye case now lies by reference, think it will be a large
step to make such a Declaration now, as shall render all their acts relating to Religion as an Establishment there null and void. So that our
misfortune is that this matter was not enter'd into twenty or thirty years
ago; I mean, that they were not check'd in their first pretensions to act
as an Establish'd Church. This, I foresee, we shall find a weight upon
our Cause; but yet I cannot think It will operate so far as to
the Council to connive at their pressing hards   members of
ye Church of England. I am, S^r

Your assured friend and B^r,

Edm^D London."

The records relate the next stage of this determined contest:

Att a meeting of the Ministers,[1] Church Wardens, and the United Vestrys of King's Chapple and Christ Church in Boston, att the House of Mr Luke Vardys, Boston, August 20th 1734. The Revd Mr Arther Browne[2] being Present at ye above Meeting. *Voted*, That the Comittee that have hitherto Prosecuted Mr Mathew Ellis' Case are hereby impower'd to Send it home to England to Mr Thomas Santford, in Order for prosecuting it to Effect there; and also that Mr George Craddock be added to said Comittee.

Voted, That Mr Mathew Ellis have out of the Money gather'd for Prosecuting the Church Affairs Twenty five pounds, to be p^d to the Revd Mr Browne for Mr Ellis' Use.

Another exciting dispute has left its traces on our records:

At a Meeting of the United Vestrys of Christ Church and King's Chapple at Mr Luke Verdys, Oct. 31st 1735. The Committy for carrying on the affair of the Appeal of Mr Matthew Ellis made their Report that they had Served Mr Richd Sprague[3] with a Coppy, and Shewed him the Original of three Orders of Council Sent to the Committy from Mr Thomas Sanford by Capt Shepherdson, and likewise Read the Letter of Mr Thomas Sanford to the Committy and their answer to Mr Sanford.

---

[1] Mr. Harward was not present.
[2] At this time Episcopal missionary at Providence, but later at Portsmouth.
See the interesting memoir of him in Sprague's Annals, v. 76.
[3] The Medford constable.

And the United Vestrys *Voted* that thanks should be given to the Committy for their Services in this affair.

[Do] Thursday, Nov. 13th 1735. The Question was put whether the Present Controversy Conserning the Ministerial lott in the Pettequomscutt Purchase, between the Rev.d M.r James MacSparrun and M.r Jos.e Torry, should be Carryed on by the United Vestrys, either in Prosecuting an Appeal Against or in answering an appeal of Said Torry, if occasion so require, before his Majesty in Council as the affair of Ellis and Sprague was Carryed on, or not: It was *Voted* in the affirmative.

Voted, That M.r George Craddock have Thanks for his Service to Whilst in England.

The Further Question was put whether Tho.s Sanford Esq. be Intrusted in the Premises aforesaid with the Same Powers and under the Same Restrictions as in the Case of Ellis and Sprague. It was *Voted* in the Affirmative. The Question was also put whether the Present Committy that has the Conduct of the Case of Ellis and Sprague Shall have the like Conduct of the Premises aforesaid, and with the Same Powers and under the like restrictions as in the case of the s.d Ellis and Sprague. *Voted* in the affirmative.

The controversy to which this record alludes, originating in Rhode Island, stirred the feeling of the New England churches to its depths, and drew Congregationalists and Episcopalians into moral and pecuniary sympathy on both sides. It concerned the right to certain ministerial lands, and was justly felt by the Congregationalists to involve the title to lands held for this use in most New England towns. The lands in question were "granted in 1668 by the Proprietors of *Petaquamscut* Purchase, now in *South-Kingston* in *Narraganset*, to be laid out and forever set apart for the Use of an Orthodox Person that should be obtained to preach God's Word to the Inhabitants. These Grantors were five, who all brought up their Children in the Congregational Way, and Three of them were Members in full Communion in our Churches."[1]

There being no preacher there, a Mr. Mumford gained possession of the lands; but when Mr. Torrey was ordained pastor of the Congregational Church in that place he brought an action for them, and his case being carried before the King in Council, judgment was rendered in his favor "as an orthodox minister according to law." Dr. McSparran, the zealous Episcopal missionary in Narragansett, who had formerly himself been a Presbyterian, now brought suit against Mr. Torrey, in 1723, for the possession of these lands, on the ground that no minister could

---

[1] Turell's "Colman," p. 114.

be denominated "orthodox" who was not of the Church of England. This case was also carried up to the King in Council, and was at length, in 1752, decided by the Lords Justices in Whitehall in favor of Mr. Torrey, who was confirmed in possession of the ministerial lands as "the first incumbent of ordination." So important was this case in its relations to nearly every New England church, that the Massachusetts Assembly, notwithstanding the lands were out of the Province, published a brief for a collection in the churches, to assist Mr. Torrey in meeting the expenses of the suit.[1] Dr. Cutler and Mr. Price wrote home in favor of Dr. McSparran;[2] but it is pleasant to record that the Archbishop of Canterbury, Dr. Herring, steadfastly asserted the justice of Mr. Torrey's claim. This, however, could not countervail the effect throughout New England of a case so noted and so protracted, in educating the people to a fresh dislike of the Church of England. Though doubtless stirring much interest in King's Chapel, it is an episode which only on this occasion appears in our records; but it is to be regretted that the Church thus committed itself to the partisan side.

The action above recorded, on Oct. 31, 1734, was the final step in the case of Dr. Cutler's parishioner, Matthew Ellis, of Medford, who having been imprisoned, as related in his rector's second petition, for not paying his ministerial tax, had sued the constable Sprague, but "was cast in the inferior Court, superior Court, and Court of Review, and denied an appeal from these judgments by the Judges of the Superior Court." The King in Council, however, granted an appeal, and the Medford constable was cited to appear before a committee of the Privy Council, to answer for Ellis's imprisonment.

But at this point the resolute attitude of the Massachusetts Churchmen, thus championed by King's Chapel and Christ Church, with the best legal counsel in the Province (all of whom were members of the Vestry or Congregation of His Majesty's Chapel), produced the desired result upon an Assembly who were doubtless already convinced that the laws which they believed important to the religious welfare of the Commonwealth

---

[1] Turell's "Colman" mentions that Samuel Holden, Esqr., of London, the head of the Bank of England, managed, at Dr. Colman's request, the cause of the infant Church at South Kingston, and sent over the order of the King in Council confirming Rev. Mr. Torrey in possession. The Prince Library contains all the documents in this celebrated case.

[2] "There is a tract of land in [McSparran's] parish claimed by the Church of England, in opposition to the Saints here, who would inherit the earth."— *Cutler to Gray, July 2, 1735.*

could not justly be pressed further against stubborn consciences. Without waiting for the matter to be pronounced upon by the final Court of Appeal in England, they yielded of grace rather than by compulsion, as was their wise usage. Before the close of 1735 the earlier Act of Exemption was extended, taking off the limitation of distance, "to all such persons as profess themselves to be of the Church of England . . . that live in the bounds of any town, parish, or precinct throughout the Province," being "excused from paying taxes for the building meeting-houses for the use of the established church within this government." The Episcopalians were thus to be taxed for the support of the ministry, with the other inhabitants; but the town treasurer was required to pay over their ministerial tax to the minister of the church which they attended.[1] The act was at first limited to five years, but under Governor Shirley was made perpetual.

This enactment had hardly been passed when Mr. Harward died, and the protracted negotiations ensued concerning his successor. The same letter from the Bishop to Mr. Price announced who that successor was to be, and closed his part in the controversy about the hardships of American Churchmen: —

"WHITEHALL, Jan. 29th 1736-37.

GOOD S^R, — The same Vessel that brings this Letter will also bring one to Mr Davenport, appointing him to succeed Mr. Harward after the 15th of April next. I have desired him to communicate his Letter to you; and I hope that what I have said to him will be to your Satisfaction, and lay the foundation of a lasting Peace and good understanding between you.

I have urg'd from time to time, as far as I could, the *inconsistency* of the Independents setting themselves up for the National Church, as well with their own principles as with the tenor and meaning of ye Charter; but I find a great unwillingness here to unravel so many Acts of Assembly wch have pass'd there and been confirm'd here, in a style too favourable to that notion. In the late reign they were carrying it so far as to design a National Synod, which I represented to ye Court, and procur'd a stop to be put to it; but as I happen now to be on no good terms with the Court, I dare not promise the like Success in case any future attempt should be made, as I hope there will not.

It is a very laudable part in you to endeavour that all the members of

---

[1] Province Laws, ii. 783. The contest for religious freedom was now left in the hands of the Baptists, who continued to testify by suffering until the year before the first blood of the Revolution was shed at Lexington, when "no less than eighteen members of a Baptist church were imprisoned in Northampton jail for refusing to pay ministerial rates."

the Church of England may have the benefit of our publick Service ; and you cannot be more sincerely desirous to see it done than the Society is. We have had many Petitions from thence, and found our selves obliged to return ye same Answer to all, "That we are not in a condition to help ; " wch must be our Answer, at least for the present.

We are, by degrees, lessening the allowance to our Missionaries in some places where the Inhabitants are well able to contribute to their maintenance more plentifully than they have hitherto done ; but as that order extends only to *future* Missionaries, the benefit arising from thence to other places will not be considerable for the present. We have also an Estate left us in the Island of S! Christopher's ; but it is burden'd with many and large Legacies, and we cannot yet tell how it will come out. Upon ye whole, both you and we must be content to go on as well as we can, under an assurance that both are using their best endeavours to promote the same great end, as far as the condition of things will admit. I am

Your assured friend and Brother,   EDM? LONDON."

Although the laws of the Province were thus modified, its religious constitution remained the same in essentials till long after the Revolution. So deeply fixed were the principles from which such a course of legislation sprang, that John Adams told the Continental Congress in 1775, "a change in the solar system might be expected as soon as a change in the ecclesiastical system of Massachusetts." But the growth of many variant sects, the conscientious scruples entertained by some against any enforcement of religion by the civil authority, and, above all, " the rise of the secular theory of the State," led to the transformation which the last century has witnessed. The last laws for the support of public worship were repealed in Massachusetts in 1833, nor did they long survive elsewhere. Thenceforward, the nation was fully committed to the modern theory of the absolute separation of Church and State.[1]

The wise and catholic Bishop also wrote to Dr. Colman, May 22, 1735 : [2] —

"My Opinion has always been that the Religious State of *New England* is founded in an equal Liberty to all Protestants, none of which can

---

[1] Professor Diman, on "Religion in America," etc., has pointed out that the change from the former theory to the modern idea is clearly indicated in the different religious tone of the Declaration of Independence and the Federal Constitution. See also "Rice's History of the First Parish, Danvers," pp. 131-32, for an excellent statement of the advantages which have resulted to the New England churches from the abandonment of the system of general taxation for the support of preaching.

[2] Hobart's "Second Address," etc., p. 37.

claim the Name of a National Establishment, or any kind of Superiority over the rest."

This point was, however, tenaciously disputed by "Church" writers through the whole controversy which intermittently raged until the Revolution, it being urged by them that "the Act of Union" between England and Scotland in 1707 extended the Church of England to the American Plantations. The knowledge that the laws had been amended so as to give full relief travelled across the Atlantic much more slowly than the complaints had before done. The Society's "Abstract" for 1742 says: —

"The Soc. hath the Pleasure of being . . . informed . . . that the Assembly of the Province of *Mass.-Bay* . . . hath at length . . . past a Law which frees the Members of the Church of *England* in that Province from paying to the Support of what the Independents there call the established Religion." "And yet," said Hobart, caustically, "though they own the 'peculiar Burdens' are removed, they are so far from withdrawing the 'peculiar Assistance' they pretend to have afforded on that Account, that they have since increased the Number of their Missionaries in that Province."[1]

Thus the cause of disturbance occasioned by the early action of the Society for Propagating the Gospel was still present. This subject, among others, is touched upon in a letter from the secretary to Mr. Price: —

"CHARTERHOUSE, Nov. 6th, 1742.

REVD. SR, — My last Letter bore date 27 Febr., 1741; and from that time I am indebted to yrs of the 29 of January, 1741, of 3d of May, and 24th of July, 1742. It is a Pleasure to hear that the Church of England gains ground amidst that Torrent of Enthusiasm wch hath spread itself along the Continent of North America, and that the Books sent

---

[1] Dr. Andrew Eliot pointed out, in 1767, that "Since the grievance was redressed in the Massachusetts, Presbyterian ministers have been punished only for preaching in Virginia. Even the ministers of other denominations who are settled with them are not excused from paying rates to Episcopal ministers. In the province of New York the members of the Church of England are far from being the majority. Governor Fletcher procured the assembly to set out six churches, with allowances for the maintenance of ministers. In several of the towns . . . are Presbyterian churches; but all the Presbyterians, both ministers and people, are obliged to pay to the Episcopal ministers. We shall, it is probable, be told that the Church of England is the established church. The Church of England, then, has an exclusive right to lay burdens on all who dissent from her; . . . but the members of that church must never be taxed for the support of any other minister. Beware, ye colonists, who have not yet submitted to this yoke! . . . Can any wonder that you fear the approach of a bishop?"— 2 *Mass. Hist. Coll.* ii. 208.

thither by the Society have been of service to help People to distinguish true Religion from Rant and a misguided Zeal.

Your House of Representatives have no power by the Charter to make an Establisht Church; but I doubt it is not true that the Church of England is by the Law the Established Church in all the British Dominions Except Scotland. Most of the American Charters, and particularly that of Massachusetts Bay, If I am not very much mistaken, were granted in a general Liberty of Conscience; it was, therefore, very unjust to tax people of other persuasions to the support of Independency there, and the Heighth of insolence to deny to excuse the members of the Established Church of the Mother Country from this Tax, at the same time they excused the Quakers from it without their asking that favour. But I am very glad they are now so far come to their senses as to relieve you from that Imposition.

The now Governour[1] being of our Communion, the society have chosen him into their Corporation, and recommended the Episcopal Churches within his Government to his Protection and Favour, and have made a present of 200 Copies of the Bp of Man's Essay to be given away, as his Excellency shall Judge most beneficial to Religion.

The scheme of having a previous settlement of Glebe Lands to a reasonable Value before the erection of a New Mission is fixed; and therefore if there is any considerable Endowment at Hopkinton of that Nature, upon a Petition to the society setting it forth, and submitting it to be settled according to their Directions, they might, perhaps, begin this new Scheme with that Church. This waits on you with 50 of the last Anniversary Sermon to be disposed of as usual, and a parcell of books to Mr. Usher, of Bristol.

Wishing you, Mr. Commissary, all Success."

To the Revd Mr Commissary Price,
 at Boston in N. England in America.

For a moment, however, the Society for Propagating the Gospel seem to have inclined to reconsider their action on this matter. An earnest protest was made by the Hampshire Association of Congregational Ministers[2] against the sending of missionaries, whose —

"Very uncharitable and unchristian spirit . . . tends to breed disorder and confusion in our Churches, by cherishing a small number of *disaffected persons* in several places, to the ill example of a whole town,

---

[1] Governor Shirley.
[2] Church Docs. Mass. p. 299. It is signed by "Jonathan Edwards, Scribe." Point is given to this protest by the fact that at this stage the constable of Brimfield, in Hampshire County, being himself a Churchman, petitioned the Legislature for information whether he would be liable to the penalties which Sprague, of Medford, had incurred, should he obey a warrant which he had received from his Assessors to distrain or imprison certain churchmen in his town. Church Docs. Mass. p. 311.

... and to lead them to place religion rather in some external *observations and ceremonies* than in love to God and our neighbours, and in a life of Faith, repentance, and Holiness."

By their request this communication was enclosed by Dr. Colman to the Bishop of London, Sept. 13, 1734: —

"Were your *Lordship* and the pious Trustees here on the Spot, I am sure you could not think the professed End of your Charter and the Design of the Donors answered in your supporting Missionaries at *Boston, Braintree* [etc]. Or if the Seaports of great Trade, such as *Boston, Newport, Marblehead,* need to have Ministers of the Church of *England* for the sake of some Inhabitants and Strangers, yet also are they well able to support their own Worship: or did they want some Assistance, there can be no Pretence for it out of a Fund sacred to God for sending the Gospel into dark and ignorant Places of the Earth. They ought to be provided for some other Way, and not by alienating a devoted, confined Charity, which were to run the Danger of Sacrilege and great Unfaithfulness." [1]

Dr. Cutler wrote to Dr. Gray, Nov. 8, 1734: [2] —

"Mr. Davenport ... is just returned, and brings us the sad news of the uncertainty of the Society's countenancing any new missions. When this takes air it will give a sad damp to the Church among us."

But the society's own words spoke more significantly on the other side. The "abstract" annexed to a sermon preached by Dr. Maddox before the society in 1733, says: —

"The Society have this year very much increased the number of their missions upon the earnest petitions of the principal inhabitants of each place, representing ... the rising generation ... as never having seen, nay, scarce heard, any thing of the publick worship of God and administration of the sacraments. ... The Society have, therefore, sent ... the Rev. Mr. Davenport to Situate, in New England," —

where, for a century, there had been an uninterrupted succession of faithful ministers, and were then two Congregational churches, each with a worthy pastor.

Dr. Secker, Bishop of Oxford, preached before the society in 1740, reiterating the ancient charges: [3] —

"The first European inhabitants — too many of them — carried but little sense of Christianity abroad with them. ... No teacher was known, no religious assembly was held; the Lord's day distinguished only by

---

[1] Turell's "Colman," p. 142.
[2] Church Docs. Mass. p. 673.
[3] Dr. Andrew Eliot wrote a forcible review of this sermon. See 2 Mass. Hist. Coll. ii. 190.

more general dissoluteness. . . . Such was the state of things in more of our colonies than one; and where it was a little better it was, however, lamentably bad."

Thus the old grievance of the God-fearing adherents of the early New England system was not appeased, and the way was preparing for the new and more inflamed outbreak of the controversy, by which Jonathan Mayhew was to become one of the forerunners of the Revolution.

If we could bring back the reality of the past, the scanty traces which remain on our records of this long dispute would be vividly alive with intense passion; but we can see only dimly through the fumes of tobacco smoke and wine — to which the Rev. Mr. Harris objected — the animated meetings of the vestry at the Royal Exchange Tavern, and the debates of the Assembly, where doubtless the old feeling of the country against a Church from which their fathers had fled contended against the demand for justice to it as a dissenting form of faith. But in contemplating the slowness in granting their rights, of which the members of the Church of England complained, so that Quaker and Baptist were, as they thought, more kindly dealt with than they, it should not be forgotten that the New England feeling was greatly embittered by the variety of controversies which ran along side by side with this particular demand. The instinct of the country felt that the pamphlet war, the defeat of the proposed synod, the attempt to gain a foothold in the college, and this claim of those who (as it was thought) took the name of Churchmen to escape taxation for the support of the religious institutions deemed vitally necessary to the wellbeing of the land, were all part of a systematic effort to establish here not merely the equality but the supremacy of the Church of England; and they were met by the same policy of resistance — active or passive according to opportunity — which the demands of English authority in civil affairs encountered.

Meantime the pamphlet controversy, which had lulled for a time, broke out again; and, although the writers were remote from Boston, it is a significant proof in what place their readers were found, that most of their productions bear the Boston imprint. In this phase the dispute was largely beween unmodified Calvinism and the Arminian tendencies of the Church of England. It began with a sermon by Dickinson on "The Vanity of Human Institutions in the Worship of God."[1] To

[1] Sermon at Newark, N. J. New York: 1736.

this a rejoinder was made by the Rev. John Beach, formerly a Congregational minister at Newtown, Conn., where he continued as an Episcopal missionary, having shared in Cutler's change of ecclesiastical relations. Dickinson replied,[1] and was followed again by Beach in "An Appeal to the Unprejudiced, in a Supplement to the *Vindication of the Worship of God, according to the Church of England* [Boston: 1737] from the injurious and uncharitable Reflections of *Mr. Jonathan Dickinson.*"

The tone of Mr. Beach in this is often flippant and injurious, while professing affection for his former friend. "The greatest trouble I am like to meet with is the naming your manifold Untruths, Misrepresentations, and Slanders." He begins by defending the Arminianism of the Church of England. "We dare not say that Millions of Infants are tortured in Hell to all Eternity for a Sin that was committed thousands of Years before they were born.... We dare not dress up the infinitely good and merciful God in such a Dress of Horror." He then argues that his opponent requires, as a religious duty, what God has not required. "You have taught People that it is a religious Duty to abstain from a stinted imposed Prayer, when God never required Men to avoid it." "No Church upon Earth can avoid imposing some Things, as Terms of Communion, which God has not injoyned."

He proceeds to defend liturgical forms of prayer, and many points in detail in the English services and in the discipline of the church. There is an affecting passage: —

"I have parted with much of my worldly Satisfactions for my Opinion, and exposed my self to the Ill-Will and hard Words of many of my old Friends, who formerly shewed me more Love, and gave me a better Word than I deserved, — your self for one.

"But I rejoice and am glad that I am worthy to suffer the Persecution of the Tongue for (as I think) Christ and his Truth's Sake."

Dickinson rejoined.[2] This reply is cast in the form of a dialogue, giving Mr. Beach's arguments in his own words. Mr. Dickinson is far the stronger wrestler in this debate. He denies

---

[1] "A Defence of a Sermon preached at Newark, June 2, 1736, entituled *The Vanity of Human Institutions in the Worship of God*, against the exceptions of Mr. John Beach. New York: 1737."

[2] "*The Reasonableness of Nonconformity to the Church of England in Point of* Worship. A Second Defence of A Sermon preach'd at Newark, June 2, 1736, ... Against the Exceptions of Mr. John Beach, in his *Appeal to the Unprejudiced*. By Jonathan Dickinson, M. A. Boston: 1738."

the doctrine imputed to him. "We do all of us leave the future State of *Infants* to the Righteous Determination of that God whose tender Mercies are over all his Works, without such positive and bold Conclusions as you are pleas'd to make." He discusses with much power the enforcement of religious observances and terms of communion which God has not required as such, the restrictions of the English Church, the defects of its prayer-book, its repetitions, the reading of the Apocrypha, the sign of the cross, etc., and the validity of non-Episcopal ordination, showing that Mr. Beach himself, while a Congregational minister, could trace his orders through an undoubted succession from primitive times.[1]

From these grave public agitations and the smoke of controversy our narrative passes again into the quiet though not

---

[1] These old friends and veteran antagonists did not fail to continue their warfare in a controversy which falls beyond our limits. Dickinson published in Boston, in 1741, "Discourses on the Five Points of Calvinism;" in 1743, in Philadelphia, "Dialogues on the Display of God's Special Grace;" and in New York a "Sermon on The Nature and Necessity of Regeneration, with Remarks on Waterland's Discourse." He also printed in Boston, in 1743, a Defence of the "Dialogues" against the exceptions of the Rev. Andrew Croswell. In 1744 Rev. James Wetmore published a "Letter occasioned by Mr. Dickinson's Remarks on Dr. Waterland, etc. Boston." In 1745 Dickinson published "Familiar Letters to a Gentleman on Religious Subjects. Boston;" and in 1746 a "Vindication of God's Sovereign Free Grace. Boston." In 1746 Dr. Samuel Johnson published "Ethices Elementa. . . . By Aristocles. Boston;" and in 1747 Mr. Beach published "God's Sovereignty and Universal Love reconciled, in a Reply to Mr. Jonathan Dickinson's Remarks upon a Sermon on Free Grace. Boston;" and Dr. Johnson, a "Letter to the Rev. Jonathan Dickinson in Defence of Aristocles and Authades, concerning the Sovereignty and Promises of God. Boston."

Dickinson's death did not prevent the posthumous issue of a strong vindication of Calvinism by him, showing that Mr. Beach's opinions are the same with those of Pelagius, in "A Second VINDICATION of GOD'S *Sovereign Free* GRACE, Against The Exceptions made to a former *Vindication*, by Mr. John Beach, in his Discourse intitled GOD'S *Sovereignty and his universal Love to the Souls of Men reconciled*, In a LETTER to that Gentleman, By JONATHAN DICKINSON, A. M., Late Minister of the Gospel at *Elizabeth-Town*, and President of the College of *New-Jersey*, With Some brief Reflections on Dr. Samuel Johnson's Defence of *Aristocles*' Letter to *Authades*, concerning the *Sovereignty* and *Promises* of GOD, Begun in a Letter to the Author from the said Mr. *Dickinson*, left unfinished, And on Occasion of his Decease Continued in a Letter to the Dr. from Moses Dickinson, A. M., Pastor of the first Church in Norwalk. Boston: 1748."

In 1748 Mr. Beach wrote a "Second Vindication of God's Sovereign Free Grace Indeed, in a fair and candid Examination of the last Discourse of the late Mr. Dickinson, entitled 'a Second Vindication, etc.,' with a Preface by Dr. Johnson. Boston." In 1750 Moses Dickinson published "An Inquiry into the Consequences of Calvinistic and Arminian Principles, In Answer to Mr. Beach's Second Reply to Jonathan Dickinson's Second Vindication of God's sovereign free Grace, Occasioned by a Ms. intitled An Inquiry into the Consequences of Calvinistic Principles, in a Letter to Liberius. Boston."

wholly peaceful interior of the church's own affairs. Disputes concerning the ownership and occupancy of pews fill no small space in the records, from which a few selections on this point will suffice: —

[Apr. 13, 1733]. *Voted*, That Elizabeth Smith has a good right to the pew next the South west Stairs, on the North Side of them.

Septemb.^r 10th, 1735. *Voted*, That Mr John Checkley, Doct.^r George Stewart, and Capt Thos Child, With the Church Wardens, be a Committy to View the Church and See what Repairs they shall think is Proper to be done, and Communicate the Same to the Vestry at the next time of their meeting.

[Vestry], April 16, 1736. *Voted*, That Mr Saml Barrister have liberty to Sett in the Pew No. 8, and to place his family in one half of the Same till Further Orders; and that Mad^m Barrister be notified when the Vestry meets the next time that Shee may give in her reasons (If any shee have) why the one half of Said Pew Should not be voted to the use of Mr Saml Barrister.

April 30, 1736. Mr Samuel Bannister and his Sister, M^{dm} Banister, were heard upon their Respective Claims to ye Pew N°. 8. The determination whereof is Adjourned with this Meeting to ye fourth of May next at 6 o'Clock in this Place.

May 4. At a meeting of the Vestry, according to adjournment, Determined the Right of ye Pew N°. 8 is in Mad^m Banister and her children only.

These family questions were sometimes complicated, but the Vestry strove to do justice to conflicting claims.

15 of April, 1739. It being moved to the Vestry that Mrs Wharton was Ordered out of the Pew N°. 15 by Mr Flag, —

Voted, that she continue to Set in the Pew No. 15, reserving a place for the Grandchild of Mr Edward Lock till he comes of age or further order from the Vestry, and continuing to pay her contrabution weekly, and not Inviting any to Set with her but her own Famaly.

Another difficulty had to do with the behavior of the younger members of the congregation.

April 11, 1737. *Voted*, That the Minister, Church Wardens, and Vestry be Desir'd to choose a proper man to Look after the Boys, and give Him a proper allowance for the Year Ensuing.

May 10^h, 1737. *Voted*, That Doc.^t Geo. Steuart and Mr Thos Greene be Joyn'd wth the Church Wardens as a Committe to Inspect Into the Church to See what Repairs is wanted, and to make Report of the same to the Vestry this day Sevennight.

Voted, That Mr Wm Rullow be Requested to keep the Boys and Negroes in Good Order in the time of Divine Service, and be allowed five shillings p Month for that Service.

17!ʰ May, 1737. *Voted*, That the Church Wardens Procure Workmen to repair the Ground Cell at the west end of the Church, and doe what is necessary their, and repair yᵉ Window Frames, Gutters, and shingling of yᵉ Roof so soon as they are in Cash so to doe.

9ᵗʰ August, 1737. *Voted*, That a Bench or Seat be put up on the Back part of the Kings Pew.

Voted, That we are Content that Coll! Wᵐ Barwick and Major Josiah Martin, with their Family, sitt In the Kings Pew till they can be Otherways Provided for, — So it be with the Governers Consent.

Easter Monday, yᵉ 3ᵈ April, 1738. *Voted*, That no Persons are Quallified to vote in this Church unless they pay 52/ p year, and write their names on their mony.

Voted, That Step. Rullow, for takeing care to keep the Church clear of unruly boyes, etc., be allowed £5 for the Ensueing Year.

14ᵗʰ November, 1738. That whereas the Comittee that has veiu'd the State of the Church are of Opinion that Twenty pounds is Absolutely Necessary to be lay'd out in Repairs this fall, —

Voted, That the Report of the Comitte be Received, and that the Church be Repair'd Imediately.

Voted, That £150 of the Church Stock be called in to pay for the Repairs of the Church, and to make good the Deficiency of Mr Commissary Price's Sallary and the other Officers of the Church.

8ᵗʰ Feby, 1738. Uppon some complaints made by severall Gentlemen belonging to the Church That Robᵗ Kenton, by his Irregular behaviour, haveing Render'd himself unworthy of his Office, its the opinion of the Minnester and Vestry he shall be no longer Clark.

And Whereas Mr Commissary Price nominated Powers Marriett to be Clark in his room, The Vestry Unanimously approved of the same.

Easter Monday, April 22, 1739. *Voted*, Stephen Rullow take care to keep the Boys and Negros in good order, and have £5 p annum for his Services.

Easter Munday, April 7, 1740. *Voted*, Stephen Ruleau be continued to take care to keep Boys and Negroes in good order, etc., in time of Divine Service.

Such trivial details fill the pages which take no note of the presence here of a noteworthy guest. There can be little doubt that King's Chapel at this time listened to the accents of that peerless singer of the Christian Church, Charles Wesley, who passed a month in Boston on his return from Georgia in 1736. The Oxford scholar and earnest clergyman, not yet a Methodist, but devout with the spirit which had made him a member of the "Godly Club," received a warm welcome, and notes that he preached in two or three churches, which must have been those of the Church of England, since he would not have entered any other. In later years, his exquisite hymns have often given wings to the devotion of worshippers in King's Chapel,[1] but no record remains of the words which the saintly poet may have spoken from its old pulpit to those who knew not that they "entertained an angel unawares."

This chapter, which has been occupied with the narrative of the struggle of the Church of England as a dissenting form of faith here for larger freedom under the law, closes with the departure of the man who had been a leading spirit in all the controversies. The restless career of Mr. John Checkley and his prominence in the affairs of the church have already been fully noticed. His last appearance in a position of influence is as chairman of a committee on repairs, in September, 1735. But the feeling of his fellow-worshippers toward him seems soon to have undergone a change. He went to England again, seeking ordination, and Mr. Price wrote to the Lord Bishop of London,[2] Dec. 21, 1738: —

"There is some uneasiness at present in my church, from a suspicion that M! Checkley is waiting in England in order to succeed M! Davenport if he quits the Chapel. I think I should be deficient in my duty if I did not inform Your Lordship that his admission into this church would be attended with great inconveniences, upon the account of his troublesome temper and the dislike many of my congregation have to him, some of which have declared to me they would leave the church if he should officiate in it."

This time the resolute Checkley obtained his wish, and was ordained when in his sixtieth year, in 1739, "by Weston, Bishop of Exeter, with the concurrence, of course, of Gibson. The evidences supplied from the records of the Church at Providence prove that even at that advanced age, — nearly the latest at which any man ever entered the ministry, — Checkley did good and valuable service for a period of 14 years. He exercised a remarkable influence among the Indians and Negroes."[3] In this he deserves the more praise, from the neglect with which the religious interests of both these classes of persons had usually been treated.

Mr. Checkley's parting from King's Chapel, on this occasion, was more emphatic than pleasant.

---

[1] He was under the medical care of "Drs. Gibbons and Gardiner" of this church. Among his printed sermons is one from Ps. cxxvi. 6, preached in Christ Church, whose venerable edifice remains unchanged.

[2] Church Docs. Mass. p. 323.

[3] Anderson, Col. Church, iii. 451-452.

April 14th 1740.

The Question being put, Whether the two letters from ye Revd Mr John Checkley, — the one to ye Congregation, and ye other to the Minister, Church-Wardens, and Vestry of ye King's Chappel for ye last year, — concerning ye Sale of his Pew, be now read: It passed in ye Negative.

The question being put, Whether ye Pew Number 39 is become vacant by the Reverd Mr Jno Checkley's removal with his ffamilly to Providence in Rhod-Island Government, and being there settled as a Missionary to ye Church there, — And it not appearing that he has paid Contribution According to ye votes of this Church: It passed in ye Affirmative.

There seems to be an almost dramatic fitness in the disappearance from this scene of action of the veteran controversialist, at a period so nearly coincident with the successful close of the long endeavor to modify the ecclesiastical laws of the province in the interest of scattered churchmen. Henceforward, whatever discords might exist within the church, the animating spirit who had so long given them life and fire was gone.

The special exemption sought by the members of the Church of England had now been accorded, doubtless against the best judgment of many of the best men in the community, who feared a general loosening of the bonds of religion, while, on the other hand, it was received with the sanguine hope of great accessions to the church. As is often the case, however, both parties must have been disappointed. The day of religious indifference had not arrived, and the force of the New England ecclesiastical polity was not spent. The chief gains to Episcopacy were in the town of Boston, which had been outside the operation of the laws complained of, and must have been largely due to social causes which were powerful in the chief town of the province, where the influence of British ideas was felt, but which were weak in the country towns. While the Baptist denomination, being essentially a democratic movement, throve and grew under harsh treatment, the Church of England continued, in a great degree, a stranger in the land.

OLD TRINITY CHURCH.

CHAPTER XII.

TRINITY CHURCH.—A CLOSING EPOCH.

HE struggle for exemption from taxation had passed beyond the church's sphere of action, when, in 1737, the missionary at Scituate was transferred to King's Chapel.[1]

In this appointment the Bishop had not acceded to Mr. Price's request for an English assistant, but had chosen a New England man of the best birth and breeding to be found in the country.[2]

---

[1] As related in Chapter X.

[2] The Rev. Addington Davenport was a grandson of Eleazer Davenport, mariner and sea-captain, who married Rebecca, daughter of Mr. Isaac Addington (admitted member of First Church, Boston, 13th day 4th month, 1640, married Anne Leverett). She was a sister of the Hon. Isaac Addington, Clerk of the Council of Safety after Andros's overthrow in April, 1689, Secretary of the Province from June, 1690, till his death, Judge of the Court of Common Pleas, Chief Justice of the Superior Court, and Judge of the Probate Court of Suffolk; he died March 19, 1714-15, æt 70 years 1 month 27 days.

"Their son, Addington Davenport, born Aug. 3, 1670, graduated H. C., 1689, after which he travelled extensively, and returned to Boston, and was Register of Deeds for the County of Suffolk. Afterwards he sustained some of the most responsible offices in the Government, was Clerk of the House of Representatives, of the Supreme Court, and Court of Common Pleas, a member of the Council, and in 1715 was appointed a Judge of the Supreme Judicial Court, which office he held until his death. He was one of the 'undertakers' of Brattle Street Church. He married, November, 1698, Elizabeth Wainwright, daughter of John Wainwright, of Ipswich, and Elizabeth Norton, his wife. He died April 2, 1736. By his will he gives, upon the Decease of his Wife, 'two fourth parts or a double portion' of his Real Estate in Boston to his 'son Addington Davenport, his Heirs and Assigns, for ever.'"—*N. E. Hist. and Geneal. Reg.* iv. 111.

The Rev. Addington Davenport had grown up in the Brattle Square Church. He was born May 16, 1701, graduated at Harvard College 1719, and was made M. A. at Oxford, by diploma, March 12, 1732. He was the second missionary at St. Andrew's Church, Scituate, 1732–1737, succeeding the Rev. Charles Brockwell, who afterward succeeded him at King's Chapel. He next became assistant minister of King's Chapel, April, 1737, to May, 1740, when he became first rector of Trinity Church, Boston. He was educated for the law and had entered on his profession, when his attention was called to the ministry. In 1728 and 1732 " Addington Davenport, Jr., was chosen Attorney General, but it seems doubtful whether he was permitted to perform the duties of the office."[2] Sewall records: —

"Oct. 13, 1729. Judge Davenport comes to me and speaks to me on behalf of Mr. Addington Davenport, his eldest Son, that he might have Liberty to Wait upon Jane Hirst,[3] now at my House, in way of Courtship. He told me he would deal by him as his eldest Son, and more than so. Inten'd to build a House where his uncle Addington dwelt for him; and that he should have his Pue in the Old Meeting-house."[4]

---

[1] The autograph is taken from Trinity Church Records.

[2] Washburn's Judicial History of Massachusetts, p. 207.

[3] Daughter of Judge Sewall's daughter Elizabeth.

[4] He married (1), Dec. 23, 1729 (by Rev. Joseph Sewall), Jane, fourth daughter of Grove Hirst, merchant of Boston. She died before 1738, and he married (2), May 9, 1738, Ann, daughter of Benjamin Faneuil, deceased. She died Nov. 15, 1744. He died Sept. 8, 1746.

The Christ Church Register of Baptisms contains the following: " 1733, July 8. Jane, daughter to the Revd Mr Addington Davenport and Jane, his Wife."

His will, made Feb. 1, 1744-45, when he was "bound to Sea," contains the following clauses : " First and principally, I commend my Soul to God the Father, Son, and Holy Ghost, humbly beseeching him to pardon all my Sins and prepare me for his heavenly Kingdom, and my Body to the Earth or Seas, as it shall please Almighty God, in a firm faith of its future Resserection by the power of my blessed Lord and Saviour Jesus Christ."

He bequeaths to his daughters Jane and Elizabeth " £2,500 apiece, to be taken out of the Bank of England, if they see cause, when they arrive to the age of Twenty four Years, Severally." All the residue of his Estate, Real and Personal, he bequeaths to his "Only Son Addington Davenport, and his heirs, for ever." He appoints his "worthy Friend" William Price, Cabinet Maker, one of his daughters' guardians. His son Addington, "Merchant," died at Portsmouth, Feb. 24, 1761, in his 29th year. He perhaps went there to live, on account of the neighborhood of his aunt, Lady Mary Pepperell, residing in Kittery. His father's library was bequeathed to him, and was probably sold in Portsmouth, as many books with his autograph were procured there, and are now in the library of the late Rev. Charles Burroughs, D. D. With him

For this pew, however, he soon ceased to have a use.

Mr. Davenport was also a cousin of the Rev. Samuel Cooper. Dr. Chauncy says:[1] —

"Mr. Davenport, who married my first wife's sister, declared for the Church, and went over for Orders upon this pretence, — that it was a certain fact that Episcopacy, in the appropriated sense, was the form of government in the Church from the time of the Apostles, and down along through all successive ages."

Samuel Sewall, Jr., wrote:[2] —

"1730, Nov. 25th. Couz. Addington Davenport Goe on Board Capt. Sheperdson To sale for England. On the 12th Instant I hear he partook at the Church of England in Dr. Cuttler's Church, and on the 19th He and his wife went to church there. It is said he goes to take Orders to be a Church of England Parson."

In 1732 he was appointed by the Society for the Propagation of the Gospel its missionary at Scituate.[3] When he left this place he gave his house and land to the society, in trust, toward the support of the ministers of St. Andrew's Church in perpetuity.[4]

DAVENPORT ARMS.

The growth of population at the south and west ends of the town, at this period, caused the formation of two new Congregational churches, — that in Hollis Street (built on land given by Governor Belcher), in 1732, whose first pastor was Dr. Mather Byles, grandson of Increase Mather, and father of the rector of Christ Church, of the same name, at the date of the Revolution;[5] and the West Church, in Lynde Street, formed in 1736, being the first in that section of the town.

the family name became extinct, in his branch of it. Fuller particulars of the family are given in N. E. Hist. and Geneal. Reg. iv. 111–116. The will of the last Addington Davenport is given in N. E. Hist. and Geneal. Reg. iv. 351. The inventory is such as would belong to a wealthy person. Among the articles are " 2 dozen Silver handled Knives and Forks and Case, 1 Organ, 1 Negro Boy."

[1] Sketch of Eminent Men of New England, in Mass. Hist. Coll. x. 161.

[2] In his interleaved almanac, in N. E. Hist. and Geneal. Reg. xvi. 71.

[3] This mission was established after Dr. Cutler's first preaching at Scituate, in 1725. See the Historical Sermon, 1846, by Rev. Samuel Cutler, rector of St. Andrew's Church, Hanover (formerly a part of Scituate).

[4] The house decaying, the frame was blown down in a storm, in 1804. By act of the Legislature, December, 1816, the land (about seven acres) was sold, the proceeds invested, and the income appropriated according to the donor's intent. "The annual income of the glebe amounted to about $25. It was sold for $463.57, and invested in stock of the State Bank, Boston."

[5] The younger Mather Byles, originally Congregational minister at New London, took orders in the Church of England in 1768.

TRINITY CHURCH.—A CLOSING EPOCH. 483

Mr. Price's ministry also saw the introduction in Boston of Presbyterianism, in the organization of the church on Long Lane, by a body of Irish emigrants, who in 1727 had brought that sturdy form of Calvinism with them from Ulster. It was the fashion with Episcopal writers to apply the name "Presbyterian" to the New England churches; in fact, however, the original repugnance of the Congregational system to that more rigid ecclesiastical polity survived in undiminished force; and the church which afterward gave its lane the name Federal Street, from the assembling within its walls of the convention which ratified the Federal Constitution, in 1787, continued to recruit itself only from the original emigrants and their descendants. No transformation could have seemed more unlikely than that any alliance should be formed between the church of these humble folk and that where the bishop's commissary preached to the congregation of His Majesty's Chapel; yet, in the political and theological changes which were to come in Boston after the Revolution, children whom Mr. Price christened were to live to see a successor of his in accord with Channing, while that lofty religious teacher was to give world-wide fame to the lowly pulpit of Moorhead.[1]

The Church of England also grew. Notwithstanding Christ Church had been built in 1723, and galleries had been added to King's Chapel, there was need of further accommodation. April 25, 1728, "by reason that the Chapel is full, and no pews to be bought by new comers," of whom in this growing period of the town there were many from England, the first steps were taken toward the formation of Trinity Church. A subscription was begun April 6, 1730, it being provided that the subscribers were to be "repaid, in proportion as money arises from the sail of the pews, or any benefactors."[2]

Among the early subscribers to Trinity Church were William Speakman, a warden, Thomas Greene, John Arbuthnott, Peter

---

[1] This society removed to their church on Arlington Street, Dec. 11, 1861. See Dr. E. S. Gannett's Discourse on that occasion, with an Appendix. The Presbyterian body have, at times, sought to obtain possession of this church. See the chapter on "The Price Fund," in Vol. II.

[2] Trinity Church Vestry Records mention among the "Benefactors, January, 1739, the Ld Bishop of Exon, £2. 2, the Dean and Chapter of D?, £5. 3." The Society for Propagating the Gospel gave £50 toward finishing the church. The same records contain a letter "To Mr Nicholas Weber at Exeter," acknowledging "... your Bounty^s to our Infant Church in a part of the World where the Glorious Established Ch: of England is in so low esteem. ..." The Christ Church Burial Record contains the following: "1737, Capt. Abraham Hitchcox, aged —— years. [This man gave the land upon which Trinity Chh was built.]"

Luce, and William Coffin, then members, and William Price and Francis Johonnot, subsequently members, of the Vestry of King's Chapel. These and other prominent names could ill be spared from the church, even if they had retired with entire mutual good-will.

The first wardens of the new church were William Speakman and Joseph Dowse.[1]

April 13, 1730, Leonard Vassall conveyed the land at the corner of Summer Street and Bishop's alley (now Hawley Street) to John Barnes, John Gibbins, and William Speakman, in trust, for £514 7s. 2d., on condition that within five years and five months they should cause to be erected thereon a building, "with all convenient speed," contrived in a manner "most conducing to the decent and regular performance of Divine Service, according to the Rubrick of the Common Prayer Book used by the Church of England as by law established," and for no other use.

There still seems, however, to have been an uncertainty as to the location of the new church. Mr. Harward wrote to the Bishop, July 19, 1731:[2] —

"His Excellency was pleased to tell me he thought an handsome Chapel would be very convenient and soon wanted for the service of the Church of England, at the sound [South] end of Boston, where great buildings are going forwards, and which in a little time will be the beauty of this spacious town. Dr. Cutler's Church stands at the North End, the Royal Chapel in the centre; and I think another at the South will be highly necessary. His Excellency was pleased to add that he had a fine spot of ground there, which he could now sell for £300 in house lots, but he would give it to the Church of England if we would build a Chapel there; and the King's Advocate General being present was pleased to make an offer of £100 towards it. We are not able to raise money sufficient for it here, but if his most gracious Majesty and The Honorable Society would be so good as to assist us with one £500 I will be answerable for the rest, notwithstanding we should have no encouragement from the furious hot-headed bigotry of this place, who would rather oppose it on His Excellency's account, for these men cannot bear to hear of a Dissenter's doing anything for the Church, and I have often heard them say never desire to see them in."

---

[1] The Vestrymen to whom, with Messrs. Speakman and Dowse, and to their successors for ever, the land and building were conveyed in October, 1739, were John Arbuthnot, Philip Dumaresque, Charles Apthorp, Benjamin Faneuil, John Merrit, John Hammond, Thomas Austin, Henry Laughton, Peter Kenwood, Rufus Greene, Lawrence Lutwyche, James Griffin, and William Coffin.

[2] Church Docs. Mass. p. 268.

The Governor's proposal came to nothing, and on April 15, 1734, Mr. Commissary Price laid the corner stone of the new church on the spot designated by Mr. Vassall's conveyance, — two stones, a Connecticut free-stone and a common slate, being deposited with the inscriptions: —

"TRINITY CHURCH.
This Corner stone was laid by the Rev. Mr. Commissary Price, April ye 15th, 1734."

and

"SEMPITERNO TRI-UNI-DEO, GLORIA."

"Trinity Church did not receive any aid from the Society for the Propagation of the Gospel. The proprietors of the pews were the patrons and owners of the living, and elected their clergymen and presented them to the Bishop of London for ordination."[1]

February, 1735, John Gibbins and William Speakman (John Barnes being absent) "conveyed the land with the building thereon, the church edifice being erected but not finished inside, to Peter Luce, Thomas Child, William Price, and Thomas Green, a committee chosen by the proprietors, until they were reimbursed the sums of money advanced for said building, and then by them to 'be conveyed to the Church Wardens and Vestry, for the time being, for the use of the proprietors for ever.'"

The new church was thus described by a visitor:[2] —

". . . This Build is very Plain without, with Large Sash Windows, But within Verry Neat and comodious, the Architect Modren, with a Very Neat little Oargan Pretily Embelished. This Church hav^s no Steeple, looks more like a Prespytarian Meeting-House."

Its wooden exterior, sixty feet broad by ninety long, with no soaring spire, and only three bare doors in front on the lower story, was "of such exemplary plainness as would delight the souls of those who grudge the House of God the touch of beauty. Indeed, its exterior is almost exactly what one sees in multitudes of Pennsylvania Quaker Meeting-Houses."[3] Within, the roof was a great "arch resting on Corinthian pillars, with handsomely carved and gilded capitals. In the chancel were some paintings, considered very beautiful in their day."[4]

Aug. 15, 1735, "the Rev. Mr Thomas Harward read prayers

---

[1] Batchelder's History of the Eastern Diocese, i, 557.

[2] N. E. Hist. and Geneal. Reg. xxiv. 55, Captain Goelet's Journal.

[3] Historical Sermon by Rev. Phillips Brooks, 1877, p. 28.

[4] Drake's Old Landmarks of Boston, p. 386.

according to the rubrick of the Church of England, and the Rev. Roger Price, his lordship's commissary, preached the first sermon at Trinity Church, from Heb. x. 23, — which sermon was preached before a large number of people, His Excellency, Jonathan Belcher, Esq., being present." Here for four years the Commissary and the King's Lecturers officiated alternately, dividing their duty between King's Chapel and Trinity Church, the latter being practically a "chapel of ease." The process of entire separation from the mother church is chiefly preserved for us in the Trinity Church Vestry Records,[1] from which we quote the next links: —

"Apr. 30, 1739, at Mr Verdy's. They take into concideration the Mes'age delivered Yesterday (being ye 29th) in the Church by the Revd Mr Davenport from the Revd Mr Com^y Price, concerning a promise made by the Late Comittee of this Church of paying in behalf of said Church Six pounds p week for the two Ministers (he and Mr Davenport) service there ; and that he will not, nor suffer Mr Davenport to, performe Service any longer without haveing said Six pounds p week.

"*Resolved*, haveing asked the Necessary Questions of . . . the said late Comittee concerning any promise by them made in behalf of s^d Church ab^t paying s^d Six pounds p week, — its our oppinion that they never made any such promise.

"*Voted*, That the Church Wardens with Messrs . . . joined in a Comittee do waite on the Revd Mr Com^y Price to accq^t him of this our resolve ; and that as we have been disapointed in our Expectations of being provided with a Minister by this Time, the Church has now embodied its self for the more Easy and speedy procuring a Minister ; y^t untill they are so provid^d they cannot consistent to ye Intrest of said Church raise money suficient to pay more than four pound p week as formerly voted by the proprietors, — and therefore to Beg and intreat the said Revd Mr Price y^t he with Mr Davenport may continue to performe Divine Service in said Church untill they do provide themselves with a Minister, wch they will do with the Uttmost Expedition.

"*Voted*, That the same Comittee Wait on the Revd Mr Davenport, and desire to know of him Wether he continue in the same mind he was sometime ago (as he accquainted the Late Comitte upon their Application to him in behalfe of the Church), of being Minister of Trinity Church upon securing to him One Hundred pounds a Yeare, Sterling money."

To the above propositions both Commissary Price and Mr. Davenport assented. The latter gentleman consented to become minister of Trinity on certain conditions, which were, in sub-

---

[1] I am indebted to the Wardens of Trinity Church, Messrs. C. H. Parker and S. G. Deblois, for the privilege of quoting from these records.

stance, that joint action of the minister and people should be required in the choice of a clerk, in any alterations in the altar or pulpit, and in the choice of an assistant; and that the minister, if in town, should be present at meetings of the Vestry. The prospect, however, soon clouded over. The records of the new church contain a letter, May 8, 1739, "To Mr Jno. Merrett," then in England, asking him to push forward an application to the Society for Propagating the Gospel for a grant of £30 per annum: —

" . . . We are aprehensive y^t we have been misrepresented and some Cloggs laid to our affairs; we therefore Beg your endeavour to obviate any such . . .
[Minute enclosed to Mr. M.]
The King's Chapell being very full y^t many could not gett Seats, and ye Accesion to ye Church daily increasing and likely to do so could they be accomodated. To incourage this growing prospect many well dispos^d persons (cheifly such as where themselves well accomodated) purposed to build a new Church in this Town."

They mention that Mr. Price and the King's Lecturer had alternated in the care of the pulpit from Oct. 16, 1735. The following letters of Mr. Price to the Bishop of London give more details of the situation at this time: —

"BOSTON, May 17, 1739.

MY LORD, — Being informed of a letter lately sent by the Wardens and Vestry of Trinity Church to your Lordship, requesting the removal of Mr. Davenport to their Church, which he has determined to accept, I have taken the first Opportunity to acquaint you that I can foresee no great inconvenience in his removal, as my congregation is not much averse to it. But the Clandestine manner of transacting this affair, and their not communicating their design till the Ship was sailed that carried their letters, has given some offence to my Congregation, and causes me to suspect that the person employed to Solicit for them at home — whose name is Merrit, well known here for the Oddness of his Opinions and Fractious temper — intends to interfere in recommending to the Lecturer's place Mr Rowe, an Irish Clergyman that pass'd thro' this Town on his way to South Carolina, whose Interest is warmly espoused by Mr. Steward, the greatest enemy I have in my congregation, and the principal fomenter of Strife: Their success, therefore, in this attempt would be very prejudicial to my Interest. If your Lordship but knew the unhappy Circumstances of my Situation here, you would not be surprised that I meet with some enemies, or that I desire to quit it. I am in a State of entire dependance upon the people, who are for the most part very Haughty and very Covetous, and expect more compliance from a Minister than is Consistent with his Character or Comfort, and are ready upon the least disgust to set up the Lecturer for their Idol, — who puts them to no Charge, and from whom no services are expected but what are regular and stated. My Salary, for two years past, has fallen considerably Short of the stipulated Sum, occasioned by many of my Congregation going of to the new Church. This deficiency has hitherto been supplied out of the Church Stock, which is now exhausted; so that I have great reason to apprehend for the future many difficulties in obtaining my just allowance, especially if the people are further encouraged to joyn with the new Church upon the account of their being eased of the expense of a Minister by a Salary from the Society which they expect. Upon these considerations and the great desire I have of spending the remainder of my days in peace and quiet, I have apply'd to the Society for a Mission in Hopkinton, to which I have yet received no answer. If this request should fail, I should be very thankful for the Lecturer's place, for which I would resign my own, provided your Lordship would continue to honour me with the Commissarial power, which I think more consistent with any employment under your Lordship's more immediate direction or the Societie's than what is control'd by the People; and I should, upon this change, desire to receive such instructions as may make both dnties compatible, which may be express'd in a general order that the Commissarial duty shall always take place. But if no alteration be made till next Spring, I shall be better able to give a clearer account of the posture of our Church affairs and my own, which are at present upon a tottering Foundation. Your Lordship may perceive from this imperfect representation of my condition what cause I have of uneasiness; it would be too tedious to express the Hundredth part of what I have felt. I should be highly rejoiced if you would afford me some remedy that shall appear most agreeable to your Wisdom and Goodness.

I am

Your Lordships most dutiful son and obedient Servant,

ROGER PRICE."

"MY LORD, — I have in a late letter mentioned Mr. Davenport's design of quitting the Lectureship for Trinity Church, provided they will come up to his Terms, which at present they seem to be in some doubt about. This, his design, has been communicated to the Vestry of my Church, who have desired me to write to your Lordship, and beg Your Lordship to supply his place, when. vacant, as soon as conveniently may be.

I have been at a considerable charge in carrying a monthly service at Hopkington, and in improving the Ministerial Farm there, which is the greatest donation of this kind that has been made in New England; and by the Blessing of God these labours have not been ineffectual, but have produced the appearance of a very numerous Congregation. But my expense in this affair has been considerably augmented by Mr.

Davenport taking the advantage in my absence of marrying as many as he could persuade to wait for that opportunity, which have been not a few, and withholding the perquisite, which is the only one belonging to my Office; and this whereby he has acted contrary to an agreement between us, in which he declared he would deliver to me all surplice fees he recev'd in my absence, provided I was employed in my Commissarial duty, which he salves by saying that this service is not properly any part of the Commissarial duty. My Lord, If I should lie under this disadvantage in my care of this or any other Church. . . . "[1]

"My Lord, — According to Custom, the Clergy have lately met att Piscataqua, but nothing material then offer'd. Some troublesome People of my Church took the opportunity of my absence privately to hand about a letter to your Lordship, recommending Mr. Rowe to the Lectureship. I hope, your Lordship, such an act of contempt and defiance of me will [have] a suitable reception.

I could make several objections to this Gentleman, which I forbear. If your Lordship pleases to confer the Lectureship on me, my resignation of King's Chapel will give the people of my Church an opportunity of shewing their affection to M! Rowe. My Salary is upon a very precarious footing, and decreases weekly; and it is out of my power to remedy this evil, which may be done in a new choice. I could likewise better discharge my Commissarial duty by being something more at Liberty than I am at present. We are at present something alarmed at the great struggle the dissenters are making to oppose . . .[1]

I hope, tho we can expect little favour or justice here, yet the Church will not be without friends in England to support so important an affair as this is and is condusive to her Interest.

M! Brockwell continues to officiate at Salem, where he has had great success; and I think it would be injurious to the common cause to remove, especially to a place of so little consequence as Situate."

Further correspondence is preserved in the records of Trinity Church: —

BOSTON, June 2ᵈ, 1739.

"*To the Rev! M! Roger Price:*

Rev? Sʀ, — Last Night yᵉ Vestry of Trinity Church, wᵗʰ several others, desired that yᵉ Holy Communion might be administred there on Trinity Sunday; we therefore earnestly desire you'l be so good as to performe the same, — wᶜʰ with your answer p the bearer will very much oblidge, Revᵈ Sʳ, yoᵘ Most Humble Servᵗ,

W. S., J. D., } Ch. Wardens.

N. B. — M! Price desired, by a line, to be excused from the service above desired."

[1] The letter is incomplete.

The " line " was this brief note: —

BOSTON, June 2 [1739].

"GENTLEMEN, — As the time of my officiating at Trinity Church will be but short, I am unwilling to deviate from my accustomed duty, and beg the Gentlemen will excuse my non-complying with their request.
I am Your obedient Humble Servant,
ROGER PRICE."

"Whereupon," the record continues, "wrote to ye Revd Mr Adin: Davenport: —

"REV^D S^R, — The Vestry and others of Trinity Church desire you will administer the Holy Communion there on Trinity Sunday. We think it proper to informe y^o we first applyed to ye Revd Mr Com^y Price, from wch he desired to be excused. Yo^r compliance will be very pleasing to many, as well as to
[signed by the Wardens.]

"Sunday, June 17th, being Trinity Sunday, the Holy Communion, or Sacrement of the Lord's Super, was administered in Trinity Church (being the first time) By ye Revd Mr Adington Davenport. The Revd Mr Saml Seabury assisted.

BOSTON, July ye 8, 1739.

"GENTLEMEN, — Your proceeding in opposition to my declared resolution is not, in my opinion, consistent with that regard which is due to me as minister of that Congregation in which you act as Officers, and confirms me in the suspicion that you are setting out upon principles not agreeable to the Government of the Church of England. This irregularity, together with the loss the King's Chapel sustains by my officiating in your Church, has convinced me of the necessity I am under of declining for the future that part of duty. I therefore give you this notice of it, that you may act accordingly. And am
Your Most Humble Servant,
ROG. PRICE.

"July 8, Mr Com^y Price Sent a line to the Church Wardens accq^t them their proceeding was displeasing to him, and that he would not performe Service any longer in y^r Church; upon which they sent the following Answer: —

BOSTON, July 10, 1739.

"REV^D S$^R_?$, — We rec^d y^{or} leter to us, dated y^e 8th ins^t, and are much concerned and very uneasy y^t you should think we have proceeded in anything in opposition to yor declared resolution, or that we have not payd y^e regard there to you. If we have been guilty of such a Slight we are very Sorry; but assure you we are ignorant of any such thing. Therefore we pray youl be so kind as to explain yor thoughts. What we have done to cause (much less to confirme) a Suspicion of setting out disagreeable to y{e} Government of y{e} Church of England is unknowne to us, and pray youl informe us in what it is, and assure you we will take your advice very kind. We think in promoting Trinity Church we have no other intentions than the Church of England, according to y{e} Rubricks, to the very best of our knowledge.

We pray and beseech you that y{e} Enimies of the Church of Engl{d} may have no cause to boast in any division, but y{t} youl be so kind as to continue your service in our Church. We pray y{r} answer, and y{t} youl be assured we are, with y{e} Greatest regard,

   Rev{d} S{r}, Yr most Ob: Hum. Serv{ts},

           [Etc]. Wardens.

"July 13{th} M{r} Price Answ{d} he would continue his resolution not to officiate any more in Trinity Church; and accordingly, Sunday, July 15{th}, No service was performed there.

         BOSTON, July y{e} 13, 1739.

"GENTLEMEN, — I shall say no more upon this Subject, but that I shall continue in my resolution not to officiate any longer in Trinity Chnrch, and leave it for you to guess at the reasons. I am

  Your Most obedient Humble Servant,

              ROG: PRICE."

The Vestry of Trinity Church then voted, July 17, to ask Mr. Davenport to officiate at an hour *after service at King's Chapel was over;* and thus matters appear to have continued for some months.

         BOSTON, Oct{r}. 26, 1739.

"*To Cap{n} John Thomlinson* [*in London, asking his influence with y{e} Ven. Soc.*]:

 . . . could we be so happy as to succeed w{th} them, and gett the Rev{d} M{r} Davenport our Minister, in a few Years great Accesions would be made to the Church of England in this town (upon w{ch} the State of the Church thro the Country in a great measure depends), especially from amongst our Desenting Brethren, — w{ch} was one of the principall Aims of the first concerned in Erecting this Church, and which, we Bless God, we begin to see y{e} benefitt.

"*To M{r} John Merrett:*   Oct{o} 26, 1739.

 . . . Our Church has grown but little since y{o} left us, by reason of Discouragem{t} we are under, not haveing a setled Minister, and being liable to be shutt up in evry M{r} Com{ys} Humours as we have already Experienced, and wrote you p Cap. Fones, and are again Threatned. . . .

"Nov. 4, 1739, being Sunday, The proprietors Mett in the Church; and being inform{d} y{t} M{r} Com{y} Price had acqu{td} the Church Wardens y{t} unless they would pay him Three pounds p Week he would not permitt Service to be performed any longer here; and if they would comply with this the Church should Continue to have service as now untill May Next. *Voted*, by written votes, that Three pounds p week be paid Each Minister till Easter.

"May 8, 1740. *Voted* [on the conditions formerly recorded], that ye S^d Revd Mr Adington Davenport be Minister of this Church.[1]

". . . That Messrs Peter Kenwood, Benj^a Faneuil, and Thos. Greene be a Comittee to waite on the Revd Mr Davenport and acquaint him of our Vote, and desire he would come to the Church. The Revd Mr Adington Davenport accordingly came with the said Comittee and accepted the Invitation; and thereupon by the proprietors was presented and Inducted into this Church, and invested in all the benefits and perquisits of the same, and accordingly put into possession (wch is the manner of a Donative Church, vid: Clergyman's Vade mecum page 83, Vol: 1.) . . ."

They had already, in 1739, voted that —

"The right of presentation shall be and remain in the proprietors of pews in the Church, conven^d together by a legall warning from the Warden or Wardens, for the time being for that purpose."

The friends of King's Chapel did not all share in the Commissary's feeling towards the new church. Peter Faneuil, brother-in-law of Mr. Davenport, who had a pew in Trinity, and gave £100 towards its organ, but took a generous interest in the mother church, subscribed a large sum toward its rebuilding, which his brother Benjamin, who survived him, refused to pay; and Governor Shirley, who headed the vestry of King's Chapel, placed his name high among the benefactors of Trinity.

---

[1] The ministers of Trinity Church have been —

Rev. Addington Davenport. Inducted May 8, 1740; died Sept. 8, 1746.

Rev. William Hooper. Inducted Aug. 28, 1747; died April 5, 1767.

Rev. William Walter, D. D. Assistant minister, Oct. 17, 1763; Rector, 1767-1775.

Rev. Samuel Parker, D. D. Assistant minister, 1773. Rector, 1779; died Dec. 7, 1804.

Rev. John S. J. Gardiner, D. D. Assistant minister, 1791; Rector, 1805; died, 1830.

Rev. G. W. Doane, D. D. Assistant minister, 1828; Rector, 1830-1833.

Rev. John H. Hopkins. Assistant minister, February, 1831, to Nov. 1832.

Rev. Jonathan M. Wainwright, D. D. Rector, March, 1833, to January, 1838.

Rev. John L. Watson. Assistant minister, 1836-1846.

Rt. Rev. Manton Eastburn, D. D. Rector, 1843-1869.

Rev. Thomas M. Clark. Assistant minister, 1847-1851.

Rev. John Cotton Smith, Assistant minister, 1852-1859.

Rev. A. G. Mercer, D. D. Assistant minister, 1860-1863.

Rev. Henry C. Potter. Assistant minister, 1866-1868.

Rev. Phillips Brooks, D. D. Rector, 1869. Since 1871, the place of Assistant minister has been held by Revs. C. C. Tiffany, C. H. Babcock, L. Bradley, B. B. Killikelly, and F. B. Allen.

"Whereas his Excellency Govⁿ Sherly has been pleased to write for a sett of Plate and furniture for a Church (His Majesty' usual Bounty to his Governours at their receiving their Commission), Which Grant he has been pleased to say he designes for the use of Trinity Church; and as there will be a Duty on the Plate, and some Charges at the several Offices where this afaire must pass thro, We, the Subscribers, for that End cheerfuly pay to the Wardens of s^d Trinity Church the following Sums.

BOSTON, Oct. 8, 1741."

That church also covenanted —

"To return ye s^d Plate to William Lord Abergavenny when ye same shall be required."

May 15, 1739. Mr Commissary Price delivered a Letter from the Revd Mr Davenport, and it being put to vote whether the Letter should be recorded in our Church Books or no, and it passed in the affirmative. The Letter is as follows: —

BOSTON, May 9, 1739.

REVD S^R, — As I have determined to comply with ye repeated desires of the Prop^{rs} of Trinity Church in removing there upon receiving an Equivalent for my present allowance, and our worthy Diocesan not forbidding it, I therefore think it Just and proper to acquaint you and your Vestry herewith, that so what is best and most convenient may be done to Supply the Lecturer's place if it Should be Vacant.

I am, sir, your most obed^t humble Servant,

ADDINGTON DAVENPORT.

At a meeting of the Vestry of King's Chappel at Mr Luke Vardy's ye 19 of June, 1739, *Voted*, That the Vestry write the following Letter to my Lord of London to fill the Lectureship of King's Chappel in case the Revd Mr Davenport removes to Trinity Church, as soon as may be: —

May it please your Lordship, — Wee the church wardens and vestry of King's Chappel in Boston, having lately received notice from the Revd Mr Davenport (a Copy of which we Inclose to your Lordship) that he designs to Quit the Chappell and accept the Cure of Trinity church in this Town upon his being assured of receiving from that congregation an Equivalent for his Present allowance, Provided your Lordship shall not forbid his Removal, humbly beg leave thereupon to Intreat your Lordship in behalf of the Congregation of this Chappel that, in case of that Gentleman's Removal, the Vacancy may be filled up with a minister of Known Learning and Piety, — Such an one as Your Lordship Shall think Proper to Send us. And to prevent any Inconvenience which may arise, not only to this but to other neighbouring churches, from our remaining any time unSupplyed with an Assistant, we take the Liberty further to Beseech your Lordship that Mr Davenport's Successor may be ready to Supply his Place immediately upon his Removal from us, —

which Instance of Your Lordship's Goodness Shall ever be gratefully Acknowledged by
Your Lordship's most Obedient and Dutifull Sons and Servants,
[Signed by the Wardens and Vestry].

A year's delay intervened.

May 23rd, 1740. *Voted*, That ye Revd Mr Roger Price, the Church Wardens, and Jn? Read, Esqr, be a Comitee to draw up a letter to his Grace ye Bishop of London, requesting his Lordship to Send us an assistant to ye King's Chappel in ye room of the Revd Mr Davenport, and to recomend ye Revd Mr Stephen Rowe for such, and to get the Sd letter signed and dispatched.

Voted, That the letter from the Revd Mr Addington Davenport to the Revd Mr Roger Price be recorded. Done as follows, viz. : —

BOSTON, May 9, 1740.

REVD SIR, — I have at length accepted the Cure of Trinity Church; you will not therefore expect any further assistance from me at ye Chappel, and will be so good as to communicate this advice to ye gentlemen of that Church as soon as conveniently may be.

I am, Revd Sir, your most Obedt humble Servt,
ADDINGTON DAVENPORT.

Coppy of a letter to the Bishop of London, drawn up and forwarded agreeable to ye above written Vote.

NEW ENGLAND, BOSTON, May 24, 1740.

May it please your Lordship, — The Revd Mr Davenport hath at length quitted his place in ye King's Chappel for Trinity Church, — a Copy of his letter whereof is here inclos'd. Wherefore we humbly pray yr Lordship to supply his place in ye Chappel wth such a person as yr Ldship shall judge most suitable, by his learning and Piety, to honour the Church in ye Capital town of New Engd, and that as soon as conveniently may be, because in case of Sickness we have no assistance from any casual Lecturer in these parts. And as wee are inform'd that the Revd Mr Stephen Rowe, for want of his health, cannot continue in Carolina, wee begg leave to insinuate that wee once heard him reading Divine Service and preaching among us, well approved his talent therein, and shall be generally gratified in his removeal to this place, for what wee then saw and have otherwise heard of him. Yet finally wee rest ourselves in your Ldship's wisdom and goodness, properly and seasonably to supply us, and wait,

Your Ldships most Dutifull and Obedt Sons and Servts,
ROGER PRICE, Minister.
JAMES GORDON, } Chr Wardens.
Wm SHIRLEY,
[Etc.]

The final settlement of Trinity Church on an independent foundation, and Mr. Davenport's withdrawal from the Chapel, drew away so many of the supporters of the church as to make it difficult to meet the current expenses. The records indicate also that there was hard feeling on both sides: —

10th day of March, 1739-40. It being put to vote that whether a Publick notification from the Desk be a good or a Sufficient warning for a vestry Meeting or no, it passed in the Affirmative.

Voted, That the Church Wardens and Vestry has Power to Proceed to the Sale of any Pews that are forfeited by the known Rules of the church if the minester is not Present, Provided the minester has due notice of the meeting; more especially if he calls the Vestry himself.

Sept. 8, 1740. *Voted*, That the pew N. 56, lately possess'd by Mr. Thos. Green (who has left ye Chappel), be sold, and what money Mr. Green can make appear he paid to ye Church for ye purchase of Said pew be returned to him.[1]

Sept. 18, 1740. *Voted*, That the Church Wardens Order a lock to be put on ye door of ye Pew No. 56, lately Sold to Mr. Thos. Hawding, and to deliver the Key to Mr. Hawding wth Possesion of ye Said pew. At ye Sametime. Agreed by the Vestry (nemine contradicente) that if Mr. Thos. Green should goe into ye aforesd. pew, or Order any person or persons into said pew to intreupt Mr. Hawding in ye quiet possesion, or disturb ye peace of ye Church, that the Church Wardens wh Some of the Vestry Shall goe and warn him or them out; and if he or they are refractory they shall be turned out by force.

Voted, That a Comittee of Six persons of this Church shall be joined wh the Minister and Church Wardens, and shall be chosen to consider of a method of raising a Subscription for the rebuilding the King's Chappel.

Sunday, Oct. 29, 1740, p. m. The Gentlemen of ye Vestry were desired to Stay after Evening Servis, and were acquainted that Mr. Thos. Green had (on Wednesday last) taken of the lock they orderd the Wardens to put on Mr. Thos. Hawding's pew, N. 56, and carried it away.

The Sd. Vestry orderd Mr. Green to be notified to meet them on Wednesday Evening next at ye Sun Tavern.

The Vestry at ye Same time Orderd James Gordon, Chr. Warden, to

---

[1] These downright and frank modes of action were not confined to King's Chapel. On the Records of Christ Church [Vestry] we read: —

"April 18, 1745. Whereas Robt Boning hath been Voted on Easter Monday . . . to be a Vestry Man for this Church, and was Duly Notifyd to Attend ye Church Wardens and Vestry to Tranceact ye business of the Church, and for Answare Returned To them That he had no business with them nor ye Church, Neithe Should he Ever meet them, — So It is Now *Voted*, He is not Worthy of the Station The Church thought proper to Chuse him In. And Therefore Unianimusly Voted him Out of ye Vestry, and that 9 be ye Number of ye Vestry this Year."

procure a lock to be put on ye door of ye pew, N. 6, and to deliver ye key to Messrs Frankland and Lightfoot.

Oct. 29, 1740. Whereas, at a Vestry held on ye 8 of September last it was *Voted*, That ye pew N°. 56, possesd by Mr Thos Green (who has left ye Chapel), be sold, and what money ye S^d Mr Green can make appear he paid to the Church for the purchase of ye Said pew be returned to him; and as it is Difficult to ascertain what has been paid by the original proprietor and his desendents for the purchase of ye same, Now it is —

Voted, That the Church Wardens shall pay to ye Said Mr Thos Green for himself and the other heirs of his late Mother, M^rs —— Green, who was entitled in her life time to one half part of ye said pew N. 56, The Sum of Twelve Pounds Ten Shillings, he and them relinquishing all the right and title or claim to ye same in favor of the King's Chapel.

£12. 10. 0.   BOSTON, Novemb^r 8, 1740.

Received of Mr James Gordon, Church Warden of King's Chapple in Boston, Twelve Pounds Ten Shillings, it being for one half of the Pew N°. 56 In said Church, according to the Vote of the Vestry of said Church, passed 29th of October last.   p THOS. GREENE.

Thus Mr. Greene came off victorious. In his departure from the church King's Chapel probably suffered the loss of the enduring memorial which still perpetuates his name in Trinity Church, where the Greene foundation, established by his heirs in 1763, originally a fund of £500, but now increased twenty-fold, furnishes a substantial addition to the resources of that parish.[1]

"Novr 7, 1740. The Gentlemen of ye Vestry, Considering the deficiency of the Contribution and the arreare due to ye Minister and officers of ye Chapel, thought proper to promote a voluntary Subscription for this Year, Viz., from Easter last past to Easter to come, to be Signed by the proprietors of ye Severall pews if willing, and to ascertain ye Sum each person is to pay, and to begin and incourge ye said Subscription. The Gentlemen of ye Vestry Severally promised to pay for this Year as p the preamble to Said Subscription paper.

It is not strange that Mr. Price wrote to the bishop, May 9, 1740,[2] —

..."The troubles of my Church daily increase, and my desire of quitting this Station increases with them. There is at present a warm con-

---

[1] The income of the Greene foundation in Trinity Church now sustains two Assistant ministers.   [2] Church Docs. Mass. p. 340.

test in my congregation relating to the Sale of the Pews belonging to the Members of the New Church, who still continue to vote, and thereby ferment quarrels in mine. The consequence of this despute (as indeed of most others in the Church) *is the non payment of my Salary*, — the dissatisfied party commonly withdrawing their Contribution, — for which I have no remedy but Patience. If your Lordship would please to express such a disapprobation of this irregularity as to allow me to hold both places in the Church *till the Minister's Salary is fix'd upon some sure Basis, and to acquaint the People with the reason of this Indulgence,* I believe I should be able by this means to establish the State of this Church and Salary for the Future, which will hardly be effected when they have no favor to ask, and another Minister to officiate ; and, indeed, in this case my very Enemies would assist in it. . . ."

But the church insisted on their point, and Mr. Price yielded.

Coppy of the Letter to his L^{d}Ship the Bishop of London, wrote according to ye direction of ye Vestry, Signed by the Minister, Church Wardens, and Vestry.

BOSTON, Decem^r. 8, 1740.

May it please your L^{d}Ship, — Having lately received advice from Mr Sandford of his delivery of our Letter to Your L^{d}Ship requesting Your L^{d}Ship to appoint a new Lecturer of King's Chapel in ye room of the Revd Mr Davenport, now Minister of Trinity Church, and that upon our request your L^{d}Ship was pleased to discover an inclination to appoint ye Rev^d Mr. Stephen Rowe, of S^o Carolina, if ye Revd Mr Comisary Price had not wrote to Your L^{d}Ship desireing that he might succeed Mr Davenport in that Lecture, — We here make our most dutifull acknowledm^{ts} to your L^{d}Ship for Your Goodness to us in so farr hearkning to our request ; and as Mr Comissary has upon further consideration declined being Lecturer of ye King's Chapel, of wch he informs Your L^{d}Ship in his inclosed letter, wee begg leave to renew our request to your L^{d}Ship for the appointment of a new Lecturer, and that it may be in favour of Mr Rowe, having still ye Same oppinion of him wch wee expres'd in our former letter to Your L^{d}Ship, and being perswaded that his removal to Boston will not only be much to ye Satisfaction of the Congregation of ye King's Chapel, but also have a tendency, by God's blessing, to promote ye wellfare and increase of ye Church in this place, which wee shall ever earnestly endeavour and seek after. Wee have desired Mr Comissary Price to express his Concurrence w^h us in this Letter to your L^{d}Ship by signing the Same, wch he has accordingly done, — and remain

Your L^{d}Ships most Dutifull and most Obed^t Sons and Servants,

ROGER PRICE, Com^y.

JA. GORDON, } Wardens,
W^M SHIRLEY, }

and all ye Vestry Men.

In grouping together these facts we have anticipated the order of time in our narrative. During these years, while Trinity Church was slowly consolidating into a parish independent of the mother church, the course of national and of parochial affairs is faintly reflected in our records. Great public events again cast their shadow or light upon their pages. The little wooden church witnessed an impressive spectacle, when it shared in the mourning of Great Britain. The death of Queen Caroline removed from the scene of English affairs not merely a great personage, but the most influential character and the strongest personality. The Queen's intelligence, force, and capacity for government were prized at their full worth, though it could hardly have been known how coarse and sordid the Court of George II. would be without the finer elements which her presence had called around her. But the King's Chapel contained enough persons who had been bred or had travelled in England to insure a sympathetic audience for the encomiums which Commissary Price lavished upon her character; and its mourning was, for this reason, less merely official and more heartfelt. The service of public official mourning was appointed by the legislature to be held at the Thursday Lecture in the First Meeting-house; but it seemed well to the Church of England to hold a special service. The Vestry took occasion in notifying Governor Belcher of this to atone for an unintentional slight to his sensitive dignity, which was not very graciously received. It does not appear that he attended the service.

March 15, 1737-38. That whereas by Publick Notice from the Government the Malancholy news of the Queen's Death is Confirmed,

Voted, That the Pulpit and Desk be put in Mourning at the Charge of the Church, and that the Church Wardens take care of the same.

Voted, That the Church Wardens Wait on M.̈ Comissary Price and desire him to Preach a Sermon Suitable to that Malancholy occasion.

Voted, That on Thursday, the 23.̣ ins.̇, be a Day for Solemnizing the same.

Voted, That the Church Wardens Acquaint his Excellency the Governour, and his Hon.̈ the Leuetenant-Governour, with The Substance of the above Votes.

Voted, That the Church Wardens, w.̈ M.̈ Charles Paxton, wait on his Excellency the Governour w.ͭʰ a Letter of w.ᶜʰ y.ᵉ Underneath is a Coppy.

BOSTON, March 15.ᵗʰ, 1737-38.

S.ͬ, — We of the Vestry of the King's Chapple being Informed that y.̣ Excellency has taken Umbrage at Coll.̈ Barwick and his Family Sitting in the King's Pew, In Justice to our Conduct in that perticular we beg leave to Represent to your Excell^{ie} that our assent to that Gentlem^n being So placed proceeded from the Assurance we had that Your Excellency first made that Compliment; and the part that we acted therein was in Concurrance with the Previous Leave by you Given, wch at all times is in ye Excellency's Power to Withdraw.

We are wth Great Respect, S^r, Y^r Excellency's most Obediant Humble Servants,

JN^O GIBBINS.	W^M SHERLY.	EDW^D TYNG.
CHA. PAXTON.	FRA^S BRINLY.	ROGER PRICE.
SILVESTER GARDINER.	JOHN MERRETT.	THOMAS CHILD.
THO^S GREENE.	GEO. STEUART.	W^M COFFIN.
GEO. CRADOCK.	W^M SPEAKMAN.	ROB^T AUCHMUTY.

March 16^h, 1737-38. Agreable to the Vote above we waited on his Excellency the Governour and acquainted him that the Pulpit of the King's Chapple will be coverd wth Black Cloth, and a Funerall Sermon Preached by the Revd Mr Commissary Price on the Death of our Late Graceous Queene on ye 23^d Instant.

Also Deliver'd him the Letter, the Coppy as above. To which his Excellency answer'd, he never Gave Leave for any Person to Set in the King's Pew.

At the Request of the Church Wardens and Vestry the Revd Commissary Price will preach a Funeral Sermon at The King's Chapple on ye 23rd Ins^t on the Death of her Late Majesty, ye Service to begin at Eleven a Clock, upon wch occasion the Vestry has given directions to cover the Pulpit and reading Desk with Black Cloth.

At The same time this Advertisement was Ordered to be put in the publick Prints.

28th March, 1738. *Voted*, That the Church Wardens be desired to wait on Mr Comissary Price and Return him Thanks for his Sermon Preached at the King's Chapple on ye 23 Ins^t, and Desire he will have it Printed as soon as Conveniently may be.[1]

[1] It was published with the title, "A SERMON Preach'd at the KING'S CHAPPEL In BOSTON, *New England*, March 23, 1737: Being the Day appointed by Order of His EXCELLENCY the GOVERNOUR and COUNCIL, for the Solemnization of the Obsequies of her late MAJESTY QUEEN CAROLINE. By Roger Price, M. A., Rector of the said Chappel, and Commissary of the Episcopal Churches in *New England*. Preach'd and Publish'd at the Request of the Gentlemen of the Vestry of the said Chappel." *Boston:* Printed and Sold by S. KNEELAND and T. GREEN, in Queen-Street over against the Prison. MDCCXXXVIII.

Rev. S. Mather's "*The Fall of the* MIGHTY *Lamented.* A *Funeral* DISCOURSE upon the DEATH of Her most Excellent Majesty WILHEMINA DOROTHEA CAROLINA, Queen-Consort to His MAJESTY of *Great Britain, France,* and *Ireland:* Preach'd on March 23, 1737-8, In the Audience of His Excellency the GOVERNOUR, the honourable the Lieutenant-Governour, and the honourable *His Majesty's Council*, At the Thursday-Lecture in *Boston, New England*," was also printed.

The notice "in the publick prints" of the proposed sermon is perhaps the first instance of the advertisement of religious services which has swelled to such large proportions in recent times.

Mr. Price was an impressive preacher; and on this occasion the dignity of his theme and his official position as Commissary inspired him to an eloquence more effective, doubtless, while the halo of royalty still obscured the impartial vision of his hearers, than now, when Queen Caroline is seen with disenchanted eyes.

Mr. Price's text was Psalm xi. 3,—"If the foundations be destroyed, what can the righteous do?" He showed—

1. That " our principal Confidence in all human Occurrences should be built upon the Favour and Protection of GOD. . . .
2. That there is another *Foundation*, upon which we ought also to relie in subordination to our absolute Dependance upon God, which is the Power and Protection of Princes, whom GOD hath cloathed with a Portion of his Authority, that they may be nursing Fathers and nursing Mothers to his Church. . . .

Kings are the nearest Resemblances and Representatives of the divine Majesty on Earth, and invested by him with their Power and Dignity to answer the wise Ends of his Providence, in promoting his Glory and the Happiness of his People.

The *first* Duty we owe to the King is to Pray for him."

On this he enlarged, and also on the duties of obedience, of putting trust and confidence in kings, and on that of mourning for them. He said:—

"It has been the constant Practice of all civilized States to pay a very great Regard to the Memory of Virtuous Princes, Heroes, and Patriots, which they have express'd in pompous Funerals and excessive Lamentations, Insomuch that this high Respect often carried them to the sinful Extreme of Idolatry; And tho' Christianity restrains from this Excess of Adoration, yet it forbids us not to mourn for the Loss of our Benefactors, or to indulge, within the Bounds of Decency and a future Hope, that tender Passion which is inseperable from our Humanity. . . .

" Have we not lost a Mother in Israel? A Queen, who was a nursing Mother to our Church ! A Queen, whose early Indications of Wisdom and Piety, in the Prime of her Youth, had made her the Admiration of the *Christian World!* . . . Nor was our Royal Master insensible of the Blessing he had obtain'd in the Partner of his Bed, in whom he found a Mind so richly stor'd with great and good Qualities that he made her also the Partner of his Power; And with what Wisdom and Fidelity she executed that Important Trust, the daily Praises and Encomiums of all Orders and Ranks of men, who happily experienc'd her wise and gracious Administration, loudly proclaim. But her greatest and most studious Concern was for the Church of GOD, which she had reverenc'd from her Youth; And with what Care and Judgment she acted in this great Work, let those learned and pious Prelates testify, who were promoted to their high Stations thro' her Favour and Interest. . . .

"Such was the publick Part which she acted in *Church* and *State*. Nor is her Behaviour in her *Court* and *Drawing Room* to be pass'd by in Silence; There she was in a most true Sense the Great Example and Ornament of her Sex, ever using the Authority of her High Station and *Royal Person*, which had a majestick Dignity happily temper'd with an attractive Sweetness, and could have added lustre to the most splendid *Attire*, in discountenancing the reigning extravagance of *Dress* and Affectation of *foreign Modes*, by the *Modesty* and Plainness of her own Garb; thereby endeavouring to introduce Frugality into private Families, and to recommend the Use of *British* Manufactures in her Court, to the great Comfort of the Industrious Artificer and the general Benefit of all Ranks of People. . . .

"As it had pleas'd GOD to make her the joyful Mother of many Children, so she gratefully receiv'd them as his Gifts, and made it her first care to instil such solid Principles of Vertue and Religion into their tender Minds as should hereafter make them active Instruments of his Glory and the Nation's Felicity. And what Blessings may we not hope from her Royal Offspring, into whom she has thus transplanted her own Princely Virtues? . . . Thus did she *run the race which was set before her*, rejoycing like the Sun in his Course, who, whilst by his Power and Influence he Guides and Directs the several Planets in their proper orbits and Governs the various seasons of the Year, neglects not to shine upon the Poor Man's Glebe, and warms and cherishes the lowly Cottager.

"As it would be an unpardonable Insensibility not to mourn for that precious Life which is taken away, so it would be no less ungrateful to our merciful GOD not to be thankful for that more precious life which is continued to us.

"It has pleased GOD to take from our Royal Master the beloved and constant Companion of his Life, the Joy of his Heart, and the Delight of his Eyes; for this *his Heart is faint, and Tears are upon his Checks; He setteth desolate*, and hath none who can afford him comfort, — none but the Almighty GOD of *Jacob*, who is his Help. Let us then jointly Endeavour to alleviate his Sorrows, by ardently praying the good GOD, who is a never failing Support to the Afflicted, to Comfort the Royal Mourner; That he would give him a double Portion of his Wisdom and Favour, for the Loss of a faithful Counsellor and the dear object of his Love. Above all, that He would *grant the* KING *a Long Life*; And when his precious Breath shall go forth, and his earthly Tabenacle shall be dissolved, that he would Crown him with *Salvation* in his better Part, and let him reign in that city which hath *Foundations, whose Builder and Maker is* GOD. And GOD grant that there may never be wanting Princes of his Family and of the *true Catholick* Faith, to sit upon his Throne and continue the Blessings of his Reign to after Ages."

Such echoes of an Old World loyalty come to us out of a buried past, and are the strongest proof of the changes which have passed over the face of things. But they doubtless deeply moved the loyal congregation which listened while the Commissary uttered them with fervid conviction.

Mr. Price was indeed an eloquent and persuasive preacher. The dust of more than a century is enough to obscure the reputation and to dull the sound of the most persuasive voice; but there is an accent of power still in these sentences from his earliest printed discourse: —

"Pleasure . . . is like a false light hung out to Marriners at Sea, which draws them from their true Course till they run upon Rocks or Sholes, and so become an easy Prey to their betrayers. Wretched stupidity of Man, that when his native Country is so inviting, and the way so plain to it, should be entic'd aside by every trifling Gugaw the Devil sets in his view to deceive him; altho' he knows it is only to trapan his Soul to ruin !

"What can be more profitable or more terrible than the sight of a Dying Man, when he lies breathing out his Soul on his Death Bed ! To see how the ancient Society of the Soul and Body is rent asunder, and to see how they struggle at the parting, being in some doubt what shall become of them hereafter : The Spirits shrink inward and retire to the Anguish'd Heart; while that in the mean time pants with affrighting Pangs, and can hardly discharge its Office, and keep the Lagging Blood in its circulating Motion. To see how the Mind strives to express itself when the organs of the Voice are too weak for utterance. To see the Eye settled to a fixed dimness, which a little before was swift as the shoots of Lightning, nimbler than the Thought, and bright as the Polished Diamond. To see all his Friends like conduits dropping Tears about him, while he neither knows his Wants, nor they his Cure. To see the countenance, thro' which perhaps there shin'd a lovely Majesty, now altered to a Frightful paleness and the terrors of a ghastly look. To think how that which could reason and perswade, and govern a Family, is now become a thing so full of Horror that children are afraid to look at it.

．　　．　　．　　．　　．　　．　　．

O, what a bubble ! what a puff ! what but a wink of Life is Man ! and with what a general Whirlpool Death swallows up the whole World !"[1]

[1] "A Funeral Sermon, Occasioned by the much Lamented Death of JOHN JEKYLL. *Esq., Collector of His Majesty's Customs for the Port of* Boston, *etc.*, Who Departed this Life *December* 30, 1732, *Aetat.* 58. By the REVEREND Mr. *Roger Price*, A.M., Commissary of the *Episcopal* Churches in *New England*, and Rector of the King's Chappel in Boston. Psalm xxxvii. 37. . . . Printed in the Year 1733." Text Eccles. vii. 2.

Among the Price family relics is a watch, on the face of which the letters of the name "Joseph Jekyll" take the place of the figures for the hours.

An interesting letter among his family papers testifies further to his power as a preacher:—

BOSTON, Feby. 11, 1735.

REV^d SIR,—Your sermon on Sunday last, whether or no levelled at me, has had very good effect on me, so much that without any Dissimulation I am bound in Duty by discharging my Conscience to return you my grateful and hearty thanks for them; for I shall be benefitted by them in several respects, but particularly in taking a more circumspect guard over my Conduct, and not only that, but in Discharging my Duty to my Creator; for you so well illustrated ye great Duty of our preparing ourselves for Death, that I really believe there was not a guilty Conscience at Church but was forced to tremble, whether with or against their inclinations. If I have gotten yours or ye Church's sensure I am sorry for it, and hope that what time God Almighty pleases to give me further in this Life will be spent in such a manner as to deserve neither; so give me leave to conclude myself, what I really am,

Your obliged and humble servant to command,

W^M REYNOLLDS.

Such evidence of a preacher's success in moving the consciences and hearts of his hearers does not often survive the changes of a century and a half; and it may well cause us to believe that Mr. Price by his power in the pulpit increased the prestige of King's Chapel in a community which has always set a high value on such a gift, and offset in the minds of his own congregation the difficulties raised by his independent theories and conduct. But a preacher of a very different order of genius was soon to knock at the door of his church and receive a frosty welcome.

For now Boston was to feel the breath of the new power which was beginning to affect the Church of England. The great event which shook New England to its centre, and left traces not yet effaced from the character of its people, was the preaching of a young minister of the Church of England. George Whitefield arrived in Boston on Sept. 18, 1740, being then twenty-five years old.[1] His fame had preceded him, and here he won his greatest triumphs. The echo of that silver trumpet has not died away, though more than a century has elapsed since it was stilled by death. An untiring energy, rare personal attractions, a voice that could melt the cool Frank-

---

[1] Whitefield visited America seven times,—(1) in 1738, coming to Georgia only; (2) August, 1739, to March, 1741; (3) August, 1744, to June, 1748; (4) September, 1751, visiting Georgia and South Carolina only; (5) March, 1754, to May, 1755; (6) June, 1763, to July, 1765; (7) September, 1769, to September, 1770, dying in Newburyport.

lin's heart, and an apostolic zeal were joined in him to harsh judgments of other men's religion and an indiscreet speech, which increased the hostility to his methods of excitement, wherein the sober reason found much to disapprove. The arrival of this famous evangelist in Boston had been anticipated with anxiety by his brethren of the Church of England. The Commissary wrote to the Bishop of London, May 9, 1740: —

"MY LORD, — Mr. Whitefield, who is the occasion of much debate and enquiry, is expected here the next fall. I shall be glad to receive your Lordship's directions for my behaviour towards him."

It is probable that the bishop's advice had been received and was followed in the course pursued by Mr. Price.

What is known as "the Great Awakening" was covered by Whitefield's second and third visits to America. It has been estimated that from thirty to forty thousand persons were permanently added to the membership of the New England churches alone. To these are to be joined a great number who after a time fell away, besides the vaster multitudes who were "melted and made to weep by his eloquence, but were not converted." The great religious movement of which the brain was John Wesley, and which his brother Charles sang into the hearts of men, has long been seen to be from God. Coming to the Church of England when it was at its lowest ebb of spiritual life, it is not strange that prelates like Blackburne and Cornwallis should have hated and despised it; but it must remain one of the saddest mistakes for the cause of religion which have ever been, that the Church in whose midst the new power descended, instead of welcoming, drove it out to bless other fields, while its own lay unfruitful.

There was much in Whitefield's theory of religious excitement which peculiarly offended the taste and contravened the sober methods of piety familiar to American members of the Church of England; but one of the chief grievances against him was his neglect of his own Church and his intimate relations with many of the Congregational ministers. These things were set forth with a vivid pen by the rector of Christ Church, in letters which depict with much force the feelings of Massachusetts churchmen. It is easy to see why they may well have shrunk from attempting to direct the whirlwind. Yet it can hardly be doubted that if they could have done so, it would have filled the sails of their church and borne it on to a position of power in New England which it never attained. Their caution, however, was shared by many of the best men in the New England Congregational Church.

Notwithstanding the popular enthusiasm, the heads of religion in Massachusetts were largely opposed to Whitefield's methods. The minister of the First Church in Boston, who may be regarded in some sort as the bishop of the Congregational Church, the Massachusetts Convention of Ministers, and the Professor of Divinity in Harvard College lifted up grave warning voices against them.[1]

The great preacher at first approached his own brethren at King's Chapel: —

"Friday, Sept. 19. . . . At eleven I went to public worship at the Church of England, and afterwards went home with the commissary. He treated me very courteously; and it being the day whereon the

---

[1] (1) Rev. Charles Chauncy, D.D. (born in Boston, 1705, ordained colleague to Foxcroft, 1727; died 1787), published in 1742 "Enthusiasm described and cautioned against," etc., and in 1743, "Seasonable Thoughts on the State of Religion in New England." In his answer to this, Whitefield admits that he was wrong when he said, "*Many*, nay *most*, of the New England preachers did not experimentally know Christ." Foxcroft differed from Chauncy in favoring Whitefield.

(2) "The TESTIMONY OF THE *Pastors* of the *Churches* IN THE PROVINCE of the MASSACHUSETTS BAY IN NEW ENGLAND, at their *Annual* Convention in BOSTON, May, 25, 1743, Against several ERRORS IN DOCTRINE AND *Disorders in Practice* which have of late obtained in *various Parts of the Land;* as drawn up by a *Committee* chosen by the said Pastors, read and accepted Paragraph by Paragraph, and voted to be *sign'd* by the *Moderator* in their Name, and *Printed.* BOSTON: Printed by ROGERS and FOWLE, for S. ELIOT in Cornhill. 1743." This "Testimony" said: —

"Though we deny not that the Human Mind, under the operation of the Divine SPIRIT, may be overborn with *Terrors* or *Joys;* yet the many Confusions that have appeared in some Places, from the Vanity of Mind and ungoverned Passions of People either in the Excess of *Sorrow* or *Joy*, with the *disorderly Tu-* *mults* and *indecent Behaviours* of Persons, we judge to be so far from an Indication of the *special Presence of* GOD with those preachers that have industriously excited and countenanced them, or in the Assemblies where they prevail, that they are a plain Evidence of the Weakness of human Nature, — as the History of the *Enthusiasms* that have appear'd in the World, in several Ages, manifests, . . . and earnestly advise all our Brethren in the Ministry carefully to endeavour to preserve their Churches pure in their Doctrine, Discipline, and Manners, and guard them against the Intrusions of *Itinerants* and *Exhorters*, and to uphold the Spirit of Love towards one another and all Men; which, together with their fervent Prayers, will be the most likely Means, under GOD, to promote the true Religion of the *Holy* JESUS, and hand it uncorrupt to succeeding Generations."

(3) "Some *distinguishing Characters* of the *Extraordinary* and *Ordinary* Ministers of the Church of Christ. Briefly considered IN TWO DISCOURSES delivered at the PUBLICK LECTURES in HARVARD-COLLEGE, *November* 12th and 19th 1754, After the Reverend Mr. *Whitefield's* preaching at *Cambridge.* By *Edward Wigglesworth,* D.D. and *Hollisian* Professor of Divinity. Made Publick at the general Desire of the Hearers. BOSTON: Printed and Sold by *Thomas Fleet*, at the *Heart* and *Crown* in Cornhill. 1754."

clergy of the Established Church met, I had an opportunity of conversing with five of them. In the afternoon I preached to about 4000 in Dr. Colman's meeting-house, and afterwards exhorted and prayed with many who came to my lodgings."[1]

But no hint was given of any invitation to him to preach in the Chapel where he, the most eloquent preacher of his generation, had been that day a listener to Mr. Price.

A full account of the interview is preserved from the pen of Dr. Cutler:[2] —

"By Thursday night following he came to this Town, welcomed by all our Teachers. The next morning the Secretary of the Province, a Dissenter, waited on him to conduct him to the Rev^d the Commissary's; but understanding He was not at home he found him at 11 o'clock, at Prayers in his Church, where were present 5 more Clergymen of us. After prayers he saluted us all, whom with him the Commissary invited to his House, where we had not been long before he entered on Invectives against the corruptions and errors of the Church, but was more temperate in the use of that Talent than he commonly is; and we lightly traversed over all these subjects: A *Call to* the *Ministry; Regeneration;* the *Indwelling* of the Spirit; *Justification; Perseverance;* and in every one he contradicted himself, the Church, and whatever your Lordship has deliver'd on these Heads. He made no motion for our Pulpits, nor did we offer them; and after a very civil Intercourse on all sides, Dinner being at hand, he took his leave of us, excusing himself from the Commissary's Invitation by one prior to it. Nor did he ever visit our Persons or our Churches more, tho' he was in Town 3 Sundays where we had two successive Sacraments, and he was twice an hearer in Dissenting Congregations.

"Between 3 and 4 o'clock he left us, he was in Dr Colman's Pulpit, in his Gown (which he constantly wore in Town), before a large Audience of Teachers and People, Praying *extempore*, and Preaching; commending the Faith and Purity of this Country, the Design and Lives of our Forefathers who settled it, — and this was a topic he never forgot upon all Public occasions. He also reproved the People for their slack attendance on the Weekly Dissenters' Lectures; assign'd it to the late Fashionable Preaching among us. He also reproached the Church universally for her corruptions in the Faith and Deviation from her Articles."

A still more animated account of the after effects of the great excitement was given by Dr. Cutler, Sept. 24, 1743:[3] —

"In many conventicles and places of rendevous there has been checquered work indeed; several preaching, and several exhorting or

[1] Whitefield's Diary.
[2] Church Docs. Mass. p. 346.
[3] Nicholls's Illustrations of Literature, iv, 304.

praying at the same time, the rest crying or laughing, yelping, sprawling, fainting, — and this revel maintained, in 'some places, many days and nights together without intermission; and then there were the blessed outpourings of the Spirit! The new Lights have some overdone themselves by ranting and blasphemy, and are quite demolished; others have extremely weakened their interests, and others are terrified from going the lengths they incline to. On the other hand, the old Lights (thus are they distinguished) have been, many of them, forced to trim, and some have lost their Congregations, for they will soon raise up a new Conventicle in any new town where they are opposed; and I do not know but we have fifty in one place or other, and some of them large and much frequented.

"When Mr Whitfield first arrived here the whole town was alarmed. He made his first visit to church on a Friday, and conversed first with many of our clergy together, and belied them — me especially — when he had done. Being not invited into our pulpits, the Dissenters were highly pleased and engrossed him; and immediately the bells rung, and all hands went to Lecture; and this show kept on all the while he was here. The town was ever alarmed; the streets filled with people, with coaches and chaises, — all for the benefit of that holy man. The Conventicles were crowded; but he chose rather our Common, where multitudes might see him in all his awful postures; besides that in one crowded conventicle, before he came in, six were killed with fright.[1] The fellow treated the most venerable with an air of superiority. But he forever lashed and anathematized the Church of England, and that was enough.

"After him came one *Tennent*, — a monster! impudent and noisy, — and told them all they were damn'd, damn'd, damn'd! This charmed them; and, in the most dreadful winter I ever saw, people wallowed in the snow, night and day, for the benefit of his beastly brayings, and many ended their days under these fatigues. Both of them carried more money out of these parts than the poor could be thankful for."

Whitefield had been followed by Rev. Gilbert Tennent, of New Jersey, a Presbyterian minister, whose preaching is described by more friendly hearers as "searching and rousing," and was

---

[1] This is a sad illustration of the bitterness into which dislike could betray a Christian minister. It is instructive to compare Whitefield's own account in his Diary: "Monday, September 22. . . . In the afternoon I went to preach at the Rev. Mr. Checkley's meeting-house; but God was pleased to humble us by a very awful providence. The meeting-house being filled, on a sudden all the people were in an uproar, and so unaccountably surprised, that some threw themselves out of the windows, others threw themselves out of the gallery, and others trampled upon one another, so that five were actually killed, and others dangerously wounded. I happened to come in the midst of the uproar, and saw two or three lying on the ground in a pitiable condition. I gave notice I would immediately preach upon the Common. The weather was wet, but many thousands followed me."

welcomed by the serious Congregationalists. But the unfavorable side of these religious excitements was manifest when James Davenport, of Long Island, a man of fervid but unbalanced mind, followed, provoking the ministers, by his violent assaults on their religious character, to shut their pulpits against him, and stirring a bitter spirit which convulsed the churches.[1] The intense New England interest in religion showed that it had only slumbered.

A contemporary letter described the sensation aroused by Whitefield's first visit: [2] —

"[BOSTON], Oct. 22, 1740.

"I perceive you are impatient to know what manner of entering in Mr. Whitefield had among us. *His own received him not;* but *we* (ministers, rulers, and people) generally received him as an angel of God, or as Elias, or John the Baptist risen from the dead. When he preached his farewell sermon on our Common there were, at a moderate computation, twenty-three thousand present. Such a power and presence of God with a preacher, and in religious assemblies, I never saw before, and am ready to fear I shall never see again. . . . Our Governor [Belcher] can call him nothing less than the Apostle Paul. He has shown him the highest respect; carried him in his coach from place to place, and could not help following him fifty miles out of town."

The Episcopal clergy in New England were absolutely in accord in this matter. Mr. Brockwell, who was soon to be assistant at King's Chapel, wrote to the Bishop of London, June 15, 1741: [3] —

". . . But now a more melancholy scene seems to open upon us; the Wesleys are expected in the fall. Men every way superior to those have already appeared, and therefore (if enemies) still capable of greater mischief. Conscious, my Lord, of my own weakness, not daring to rely on my own shallow judgment, I humbly crave your Lordship's direction. Believe me, in a young (I may say as yet unsettled) church much depends on my deportment in this critical juncture, which makes me thus pressingly intreat your Lordship's direction whether to receive them as brother clergymen into my church or Pulpit, or to reject them as those that are under the censure or displeasure of my Diocesan. . . ."

The same clergyman wrote to the Secretary: [4] —

[1] Rev. Andrew Croswell's Church was organized by the followers of Davenport, February, 1748.
[2] Letter published in postscript to "South Carolina Gazette," No. 361, quoted in Tyerman's "Whitefield," i. 421.
[3] Church Docs. Mass. p. 356.
[4] Ibid. p. 357.

"SALEM, New Engl^d, June 15th, 1741.

"The Wesleys and Whitfield are expected here in the fall. We universally dread the consequences of their coming, and I am sure as to myself I shall be glad of the Society's direction how to behave in such perilous times. The two former, if enemies, are powerful ones, — men of great capacities, and fortify'd by a large fund of learning, whereof Whitfield is destitute, and therefore the victory over him is neither difficult nor glorious, however he may boast in his lying and scandalous Journals. If the venerable Society please to favour us with their instructions how we are to treat these itinerant Preachers, the sooner the better, that we may be armed against the approach of (I fear) these enemies to our Church and Constitution."

The Commissary was equally firm in his opposition.

One of the best of the Boston ministers, Rev. William Cooper, declared, in 1743, just before his death, that "since the year 1740 more people had come to him in concern about their souls" than during the whole of his previous ministry. But this view of the subject does not appear to have impressed the Commissary or his brethren of the English Church. He wrote to the Society for Propagating the Gospel,[1] "that they have been in some Confusion in that Country by the means of Enthusiasts; but, God be praised! the Church hath stood steady in that Storm, which hath considerably shaken the Dissenters." And again, Jan. 29, 1742, "that their whole Attention at that time was taken up with the strange Effects produced by the Doctrines of Mr. Whitefield and his Followers, who prevailed chiefly in Country Towns, tho' they were not wanting in their Endeavours in that City; but the Church of England had escaped beyond expectation."

Dr. Cutler wrote to the Secretary, Nov. 18, 1745:[2] —

"I am exceedingly obliged to the Society for those Tracts against Enthusiasm.... There being none here very able to blow the coals

---

[1] Anniversary Sermons, 1740–41, 1741–42.

[2] Church Docs. Mass. p. 394. This watchful solicitude of the Church of England clergy against "enthusiasm" in their parishioners marked their preaching to the sober and moderate congregations who would seem to have been least likely to be injured if some spark of Whitefield's fire had kindled them. The Rev. Mr. Browne, the society's missionary at Portsmouth in New Hampshire, wrote, Sept. 28, 1741, "that the Town and District of Portsmouth contains between 600 and 700 Families, whereof between 50 and 60 are of the Church of England, and all the rest Independents, there being neither Quaker, Baptist, Papist, Heathen, or Infidel, that he knows of, among them; he reads prayers every morning at seven o'clock from May to September, and Preaches a weekly Lecture to strengthen his Flock, and guard them against the pernicious Doctrine of Enthusiasts, — besides his constant Duty on Sundays." — *Abstract of the Society's Proceedings.*

M.[r] Whitefield has kindled, the parts of the Country about this Town are quiet, a few Bickerings and Contentions excepted among those who encouraged the Disorders we have been under. But we have evidence enough that M.[r] Whitefield's Person and Principles remain yet in great estimation, which ever pretends Danger and demands Care."

Among Mr. Price's manuscripts is one in his own handwriting, apparently a sermon preached by him about this time, which states his opinion of Whitefield and his preaching, and deserves to be put on record as the most careful utterance of the English clergy here in relation to this question: —

"I come now, in the order of this Discourse, to take notice of his personal Character; and upon this Head I do readily assent to the just observation of two eminent Men upon this subject, in the Preface to Mr. Smith's Sermon, that he is the Wonder of the age; for what can be more surprising than that a Young Person just stept into the World, with little learning and less experience, with principles inconsistent and contradictory, in opposition to Scripture and reason, should so successfully prosecute a Chimerical projection founded without Judgment or a Moral probability of success, only by the force and prevalency of sound and Confidence, that a base prostitution of Religion and fulsom addresses to the foibles of every Sect should so engage the affections and approbation of the Multitude as to make them blind to the Breach of all the rules of order and decency, of all Divine and Humane Obligations. . It is a Melancholy Consideration that Christians should be educated in such gross ignorance and such strong prejudices as not to be able or willing to distinguish between the most glaring and evident truths of the Gospel and the delusive, trifling arguments of a party flatterer, and liable to be so easily imposed upon by crafty and designing men that lye in wait to deceive. It is further observed by these Preface Writers, that no Man more employs the Pens and fills up the Conversation of People than he does at this day. This I will not deny; but what is the Substance and Matter of their Writings and discourses? As to the Writings on his side, what are they but mean, nausious flatteries, and almost adorations of their beloved Idol, or false and scandalous abuses of their adversaries, or antiquated and perplex'd defences of errors which have been long since fully answer'd and confuted? As to the Writings occasion'd on the other side in Vindication of the Characters of pious and eminent Men in the Church, which have been basely attack'd and vilified by this Mighty Champion and his adherents, and in defence of the great truths of Christianity which have been perverted to wicked uses and wrested to the maintaining abominable Opinions, — these are thrown by, unregarded, unanswer'd, as the works of Carnal, unregenerate Men. Again, if we examine the Conversation his preaching has given life to among us, is it profitable and edifying; does it promote true Christian knowledge and increase Charity; do Men begin now to search deeper into the sublime truths of Christianity, and reform their Manners? So far from it that they are only the deeper and firmer rooted in their old errours and sinful habits. He that was dishonest is dishonest still; he that was before unfriendly and uncharitable is now unbridled and unbounded in lying and defamation. Have patience with me while I pay one Complement more to the Opinions of these learned Gentlemen, which with some alteration I readily joyn in.

"None more admired and applauded, by some contemned and reproached by others, the common lot of every remarkable Heretick and Sysmatick the world has ever had to show. Here again, let me ask by whom has this man been applauded and by whom condemned? Is it not the weak and ignorant Vulgar that make up the much greater of his admirers? or the Softer sex, and these we know are sooner worked upon by passion and Surprise than by reason and Judgment. Is it not the Heretick and Sysmatick whom he artfully sooths and confirms in their errours and follies? To the Quaker he becomes a Quaker; to the Anabaptist an Anabaptist; to the Presbeterian and Independent, a Presbeterian and Independent, — not that he may bring them into one fold under one Government, and unite them in one Communion with the bands of Love, which would be a stronger demonstration of the power and guidance of the Holy Spirit within him than Preaching with the eloquence of an Angel, and contribute more to revive the dying spirit of Christianity and restore the Church to her Primitive Glory and Power, than exorcising Rivers of Tears from the eyes or loads of money from the Pockets of the People, while they are encouraged to persevere in their unreasonable Separation from the Established Church of England, to contemn all lawful Ecclesiastical government and authority, and fondly taught to expect no other proof of their acceptance with God than a fit of Madness and Enthusiasm. These are his admirers and these his methods of persuasion; but ask the Opinion of the most sober and Judicious men in all places where he has Publickly appeared. Some, indeed, will speak with caution and reserve; others do absolutely condemn his proceedings and abhor his Character. And that for the following reasons: I shall now offer the two principal things that appear evidently Criminal in his Character and conduct, — immorality and insincerity. I am sensible I am now writing in a stile very different from what this part of the World has of late been accustomed to. The Press has long labour'd in publishing praises and Panegericks upon this strange Phenominon. Whatever, therefore, should venture out in contradiction to the general received Opinion now deeply rivited in the Hearts and Minds of the Multitude, and press'd home by their Guides and Teachers, must expect to meet with the severest Examination and Censure. This will keep me upon my guard, and check all unjust, ungrounded reflections. And, indeed, as the design of this discourse is not level'd against the Person, but his erroneous Doctrines, and to prevent, as far as I am able, the fatal Consequence of imbibing principles that are subversive of the very essence of Christianity, which are the more dangerous when enforced and recommended by an esteem of the person that delivers them. With this view I shall be under the less Temptation of exceeding the bounds of truth and Charity. I must own it seems a little harsh to suspect the Morality of a Christian, and especially of a Minister of the Christian Church, for without this the most specious pretences, the most Zealous protestations, are all but formal Cant and Hypocritical delusion; but when a Criminal and unjustifiable behaviour is represented as Zeal for the Glory of God and the most effectual means to promote the suffering cause of Christianity, it is time then to beat down the untemper'd Morter, to tear of the Mask and show it in its true light and Colours; to bring it to the touchstone, the Law, and the Testimony, and expose its blackness and deformity.

"I am ready to own that he is very industrious and diligent about the Work he is engaged in, and that he has encompassed sea and land to make proselytes; and our Saviour tells us the Pharisees would do the same, and if we may judge of the fruit in other parts by what has been observed here, I am inclined to think much to the same purpose, — to make them two fold more the children of Hell than before. For what dismal effects have we heard of and seen from this gentleman's labours! — discord and division in Societies and Families; maddness and Spiritual Pride, dispair, Idleness, lying, slander, and defamation. We are told, indeed, of strange feelings and Wonderful Operations of the Spirit, but I can find Nothing of this Nature since the age of Miracles promised in Scripture; and whatever some warm Visionary Men may work themselves up to by the strength of Imagination and a Splenetick Constitution, Yet to Men in their Sences the reflection upon a holy and useful Life, and a sincere and hearty endeavour to discharge our Christian Obligations to God and Man, steadily adhering to this resolution, with an Humble dependence upon the all-sufficient merits and satisfaction of our Saviour for the Pardon of our sins and the acceptance of our imperfect endeavours, will afford a more rational and solid Comfort than all the raptures of Enthusiasm or the violent effects of the most passionate and moving Harrangue. Not that we are sufficient of ourselves to think anything as of ourselves, but our sufficiency is of God; our Weakness is made strong by his Grace, and this Grace is promised to every Worthy Supplicant. This is a Faith which inspires us with Zeal and activity in our duty, the genuine fruits of which are peace and Joy in the Holy Ghost.

"But what fruit can be expected from the frigid, uncomfortable doctrine of the absolute and unconditional decrees of God concerning Election and reprobation? What but presumption on one side and dispair on the other? Farewell to all the motives to Repentance, Obedience, and a New Life, when Men are no better than mere Machines, actuated and compell'd by an irresistible impulse! Farewell all reverent and Worthy conceptions of the Divine Mercy and Justice, when much the greatest part of Mankind are forc'd into the World to fall the Innocent and Wretched Victims to Almighty Wrath and Vengeance! And, indeed, farewell Christianity! for it is much easier to believe there is no God, no Saviour, no future state, than to believe a doctrine so inconsistent with the Divine attributes, so contradictory to the Whole scope of the Gospel, and so repugnant to the general sence and apprehension of Mankind. What encouragement is there given to Licentiousness and Immorality by his inconsistent and false explanation of the doctrine of Faith and good Works in contradiction to one grand design of our Saviour's Mission, which was to purchase to himself a peculiar People, Zealous of good Works; but the importance and necessity of a holy Life, and the care and anxiety which all Christians should have to preserve a Conscience void of offence towards God and Man is greatly lessen'd and abated by his puzeling and unnatural distinctions, in favour of his beloved principle, —our Justification by faith only. And no wonder he is an enemy to good works, when most of his actions are of a very different nature; for how can he who hath solemnly vowed to observe the rules and Cannons of the Church of England at his Ordination, which I presume he had considered before he entered into that sacred engagement, reconcile his irrregular preaching in Conventicles, and disuse of the Public prayers of the Church, which are enjoined in those Cannons to that known command of our Saviour,—thou shalt not forsware thyself, but perform unto the Lord thy Vows? How can he reconcile his contempt of the Episcopal Authority to which he has likewise sworn Obedience to that injunction of Saint Paul,—'Obey them that have the Rule over you in the Lord and admonish you;' and how can he vindicate his insolent treatment of his Diocesan from the character S! Jude gives the false Teachers in his time,—'they despise Dominion and speak evil of Dignities'? How can his Joyning with every Sysmatical Sect upon the Continent be consistent with S! Paul's exhortations and Orders not to foment Divisions in the Church, to promote Unity and Peace, and Observe the rules he had established among them for the sake of order and decency,—these disturbers and dividers of the Church at Corinth?

". . . Having proceeded thus far in the sentiments of Mr. Whitfield's Advocates concerning his personal character, I hope it will be pardon'd me if I should presume to dissent from them in my opinion of the consequence of his irregular and illegal behaviour. I think it requires no Prophetical spirit to prognosticate the event. If we look back into the History of former times, we may read of many such strange appearances of deceitful or enthusiastic Men who aroused the World for a time and raised the expectations of the Populace with wonderful promises. Such was he that lead four Thousand Jews into the Wilderness, under the character of the Messias, who all perished in that way. Such a leader was he, also, that headed armies in Holland and endanger'd the Republick; and many such have started up in our own Nation, some of which have left a Memorial behind them to their Eternal Infamy, and some there are whose names are perished as though they had never been born. And as for . . . what can we expect but that from his Example and Doctrine our Sons and Daughters will be all fill'd with a plentiful portion of his Spirit, and Prophane the Christian Religion in every green Field and under every spreading Tree? And Jonathan also will be among the Prophets; till at length the Parent of this New light shall meet the fate of every irregular, excentrick Body, having spent himself in a Blaze shall go off like a Sky Rocket in a Bound, and all the little sparks that break from him vanish and expire in stink and vapour. I shall conclude this Preface with a short address to all that profess themselves Members of the Church of England. When the Jews Apostatised from their Religion and fell into the Idolatries of the Heathen Nations, God threatens them in this manner: 'I will provoke you to Jealousy by them that are No People, and by a foolish Nation I will anger you.' This has often been the unhappy case of our Church, and with shame we must ackknowledge the punishment to be just; for what corrections do we not deserve for the decay of our Christian Zeal, our deadness in the service of God, our unconcern and indifference for the honour of our Church, and our too frequent mixing with the assemblies of Separists? Let us heartily repent of these and all other sins in time, least a greater Judgment fall upon us. Let us be as active and industrious in defending the Christian Religion and our most excellent Established Church as our Enemies are in undermining and destroying it; and let us devoutly Implore the Divine Assistance in so good a Cause. We may then rest assured that the God of Peace and Order, who has already rescued us out of the paws of the Lyon and the Bear, from Popish and Fanatical fury, will also deliver us from the Rage of this Uncircumcised Philistine."

In all this, as the history of English Methodism abundantly shows, the commissary simply took the tone of the body of bishops and clergy of the Church of England at home. Bishop Gibson, indeed, with a wiser spirit, though publishing a pastoral letter "against enthusiasm," included "lukewarmness" in the same condemnation.[1] Mr. Whitefield was not, however, wholly without friends among members of the Church of England. In Virginia, Commissary Blair had received him kindly, as a servant of that church; and in New England all did not follow the lead of the minister of King's Chapel. On his second visit to Boston, in 1747, the "New England Gazette" announced: "Mr. Whitefield came, July 21, to the seat of his friend, Isaac Royal, Esq., at Charlestown," who was one of the prominent members of King's Chapel; and among the pall-bearers at Whitefield's funeral was the Rev. Edward Bass, then missionary in Newburyport, and afterward first bishop of the Protestant Epis-

[1] Republished at Philadelphia, 1740.

copal Church in Massachusetts. But the church was little affected, either for good or evil, by the great preacher, and went on the even tenor of its way; while all around it the New England parishes were convulsed by the strong spirit which wrought so mightily upon them. In Whitefield's later visits he went more and more outside the Episcopal body, whose relation to his work was that of expectant heirs of some benefit by the reaction in cooler spirits from his method of excitement to the sober moderation of the English Church.

Roger Price, after his marriage, lived in Boston in a large house belonging to Mrs. Price's uncle, Stephen Greenleaf, "the old sheriff of Suffolk under the stormy administration of Governor Bernard." It had a large garden, which extended from what is now Temple Place to West Street. Here two, if not three, of his children were born. Afterward the house and grounds became a place of public resort, known at that time as the Washington Gardens. The other residence of Roger Price in Boston was at the corner of Summer and Sea streets. This house, near Bull's Wharf, belonged to his wife.[1] But his favorite residence was in Hopkinton, in the beautiful tract of lands where he hoped to find a fortune for his family, and where the gayer and more free-living members of his church made a summer colony, to whom he preached and ministered in the little church, which it was his chief aim to persuade the Society for Propagating the Gospel to adopt and support. The centre of the gay life in this Arcadia was Charles Henry Frankland, a descendant of Oliver Cromwell, and heir presumptive to the family baronetcy, with the estates of Thirkleby and Mattersea, — a young man of fortune and education. The romantic story of her who later became Lady Frankland has been told in prose, and by one of our own poets in exquisite verse.[2] It is a story of sin and penitence, of wonderful escape and of strangely varied fortunes, such as no poet's fancy could ideally surpass. The beautiful girl, Agnes Surriage, whom the young collector found in poverty, scrubbing the floor of the Marblehead inn, was educated by him, and finally shared his home at Hopkinton. Through the years 1743-44, 1746-54, he was elected annually a member of the Vestry of King's Chapel; but the displeasure with which his mode of life was regarded in Boston,

[1] A portion of this estate is now occupied by the New York and New England Railroad Co. as a passenger station.

[2] By Rev. Elias Nason, A. M., in his "Boston in the Colonial Times," 1865, and by Dr. O. W. Holmes.

outside the circle of those who made ample allowance for courtly English fashions, notwithstanding the baronetcy which devolved upon him in 1747, caused him to remove to the country estate which he had purchased amid that charming landscape. Here Mr. Price found a social group not unlike what might have been seen at that time in many a country seat in the mother country, and which was very foreign in its habits and moral theories to the New England society around it. But all was soon changed. While visiting Lisbon in 1755, as Frankland was driving on All Saints' Day with a lady, the earthquake which destroyed sixty thousand lives overwhelmed them. His carriage was crushed, the horses killed, and his companion in her dying agony struck her teeth into his arm so as to bite out a piece of flesh. There he lay, buried among the ruins, when Agnes, who had rushed from the house to seek him, heard his voice "uttering vows in which her name was joined." She found men to lift off the weight, and he was saved. As soon as his wound would allow, he atoned for his wrong to her by making her his wife; and his relatives in England received with open arms the poor fisherman's daughter who had saved their son. He came back again to Boston an altered man. In his beautiful mansion at Hopkinton was a shut-up chamber, in which were kept the lime-covered garments and bent scabbard which he had worn on the day of his miraculous deliverance; and, on the anniversary, there he watched alone with fasting and prayer. But as yet all this, for the convivial company at Hopkinton, lay undreamed of in the future, and the later scenes in which the name of Lady Frankland will mingle again with our story, under the darkening sky of the Revolution, belong in a subsequent period.

Mr. Price's interest in the Episcopal colony and church at Hopkinton had so much to do with the growing dissatisfaction of the congregation at King's Chapel, and entered so largely into his own ministerial plans, that it is too intimately interwoven with our narrative to be passed by without further notice. The town of Hopkinton, in Worcester County, incorporated in 1715, owed its name to Edward Hopkins of London, an early governor of Connecticut, and one of the first settlers of Hartford, who returning later to England had bequeathed £500 to Harvard College. On receiving this money in 1713 the college had invested it in this extensive tract of land, giving the name "in honor of the donor."[1]

---

[1] See Quincy's "Harvard College," i. 205; Mass. Hist. Soc. Proc., 1871-73, p. 411. "Rev. Nathanael Howe's Century Sermon, at Hopkinton, Dec. 24, 1815,

Country Home of Rev. Roger Price,
(near the First Parish Church)
at Hopkinton.

Country Home of Rev. James Freeman, D. D.
at Newton.

About the year 1736 Roger Price there purchased a large tract of land on the banks of a "noble river." Here he built a church at his own expense, and obtained for it an endowment of a glebe of one hundred and seventy acres for the use of the Episcopal Church.[1] He also gave a church-yard containing an acre and a half, as a burial-place for the church people. His two children who died in this country are buried in this ground. When his surviving children returned to America in 1783, this church was found in such a dilapidated condition that it was taken down, and a new church built on the site, his children giving the timber and contributing funds.

Roger Price also purchased of Charles Morris an unfinished house and large tract of land with a fine grove, in the centre of the town of Hopkinton, finishing the house and occupying it during the summer months. In all the letters this house is mentioned as the "Mansion House." After Roger Price returned to England this mansion was leased by Sir Charles Henry Frankland, and occupied by him while his own manor-house was building. The Price mansion was leased to different parties until the return of the eldest son and daughter to America in 1783, when they repaired it, and made it their permanent place of abode.[2]

4th ed., with Memoir and notes by Elias Nason, A. M., Boston, 1851," gives an account of Edward Hopkins, and the foundation of the town.

[1] Howe's Century Sermon states that after Mr. Price went to England Rev. Mr. Troutbeck officiated for some time. "Since his removal there have been only a few solitary instances of that mode of worship for nearly sixty years. Some years since a new church was erected, and public worship is attended some part of the time." After the death of his children this church also fell into decay. The glebe was claimed by parties to whom it was leased. It was regained by the Episcopal Society, and the Rev. Alfred L. Baury during his life preached once a month in the church in order to hold it. A few years ago the old church was burned to the ground. The communion service, font, Bibles, and old chairs were saved, and are now in the possession of those who saved them, the Episcopal Society taking little interest in preserving the few relics left of this old Price Church. From Mr. Lawton's deed of gift, dated Aug. 28, 1739, it appears that Mr. Price was only the trustee of this glebe, and not, as stated by Sprague (Annals, v. 73), its donor: —

"Know all men by these presents, That I, Christopher Jacob Lawton, of Leicester, . . . for the good will I have for the Church established by Law, to wit, the Episcopal Church of England, give and grant the Farm within mentioned, in trust with the Revd Roger Price of Boston, for the use of an Episcopal Minister of the Church of England, which Minister to be appointed by the Society for the propagation of the Gospel in Foreign parts during the term they shall allow a mission there, and when the Mission is withdrawn the choice of a Minister to revert to the Trustee and his heirs forever; and in case of the failure of heirs in his family, the choice to be in the Bishop that shall preside over the Churches in this Province; and upon his omission for twelve months, to be in the Episcopal Church of that town, or in the Episcopal Ministers of the town of Boston," etc. — *Church Docs. Mass.* p. 375. See also p. 519, *post.*

[2] This mansion-house was purchased, in an unfinished condition, of " Charles Morris of Hopkinston, gent, for and in

The necessity and propriety of establishing such a mission at all, in a country town where there were already 'gospel privileges,' were stoutly denied by the native New-Englanders, and specially by the terrible pen of Jonathan Mayhew,[1] who quoted a letter from the Rev. Samuel Barrett to "the Honourable Society," in reference to a petition, in the handwriting of Commissary Price, from inhabitants of Hopkinton, asking the Society to aid their church. This petition, he said, stated that —

> "Were it not for ye kind assistance of ye Rev. Mr Commissary Price, who once a month visits and performs divine service among us, we sh'd be utterly deprived of all regular and public worship, and ourselves and families in danger of falling into ye deplorable ignorance of ye native Indians. . . . We are as great objects of ye Society's compassion as any of our brethren of ye episcopal Churche in New England."

It was said that some non-churchmen signed this, Mr. Price Consideration of the sum of two hundred pounds in province Bills, well and truly paid by Roger Price of Boston, Clerk, on the 15th day of August, 1746." Rev. Roger Price finished the house. He and his family resided in it after he resigned his rectorship of King's Chapel in Boston. He then built the first Episcopal church in Hopkinton. In 1753 Rev. Roger Price and family returned to England. Previous to leaving America Mr. Price leased his mansion-house to "Sir Henry Frankland, of Hopkinston, Baronett of Great Brittain. Also the Barn, with 15 acres of Land adjoining, with a garden and other Improvements thereon, . . . for the term of two years from the 25th of March Last past; and in consideration hereof that the sd. Sir Henry Frankland pays the yearly Rent or sum of 10 pounds old tenner or other Lawfull money, at or before the 21st day of March next ensuing, yearly, and every year during the term afors^d., and to keep down the Bushes where it is now cleared, etc."

Sir Henry Frankland occupied this house while building his manor-house at the lower part of the town of Hopkinton, — a house so famous in poetry and romance as identified with his own romantic life. After Sir Henry left the Roger Price mansion-house it had many tenants, — among them the Rev. John Troutbeck, who officiated at the Episcopal church as curate. In 1783 Major William and Elizabeth Price, the eldest son and daughter of Rev. Roger and Elizabeth (Bull) Price, returned to this country to regain their property in Boston and Hopkinton. They found the house in a dilapidated condition, and after repairing it resided there for many years. Major Price died Dec. 7, 1802. His sister, known as Madam Price, occupied the house until 1820, when she removed to Boston to live with her niece, Mary Ann, wife of Lawson Valentine. Madam Price died July 23, 1826, and was buried in the church-yard at Hopkinton. In 1821 the house was leased to Charles Valentine, who occupied it until 1825. Benjamin Herrick then took it, living in it until it was sold to Colonel Joseph Valentine. Soon after, the house was burned. Colonel Valentine built the present brick building, living in it for many years. It then passed into the hands of Hon. William Claflin, who made it a residence for some years. It was then occupied by Mr. Parker Coburn. From him it passed into the hands of the Catholic priest, who occupied it until his removal from the parish. The Hopkinton Bank purchased it, and at present occupy it for their banking-house. The heliotype of the old house is from a copy, by Mrs. Weston, of a small India-ink drawing, made in 1805, by Miss Sally Dupee, who was a great-niece of Lady Frankland.

[1] "Defence of the Observations," etc., 1763, pp. 126-130.

being their landlord. It was also complained that the petition "forbears to give the least hint that there hath been for this fourteen years a congregational church settled in Hopkinton, which holds fast the profession of the same faith that is contained in the doctrinal articles of the Church of England, and in which some of the members of Mr. Price's own church have been admitted to communion, in the ordinances of baptism and the Lord's Supper."

Mr. Price pressed anxiously and repeatedly for the support of a mission in this place. He wrote to the Lord Bishop of London, July 3, 1736:[1] —

"Some gentlemen of the Church of England have purchased a considerable number of Farms, almost to the half of a Town, about thirty Miles distant from Boston, with a view of settling a church there, and making it a Sanctuary for persecuted Churchmen who are drove from other places.

"There is a Church already built for this purpose. It would be of mighty advantage if the Society would please to take this place under their care and allow something towards the support of a Minister there. One of the best of the Farms, with a house and Barn and a good orchard upon it, is set apart for this use, which in time will alone be a sufficient maintenance."

Mr. Price proposed to the Bishop of London (Oct. 16, 1736) that an allowance be made for a minister at Hopkinton; he having already secured one farm of one hundred and sixty acres, with house and barn, and the promise of another, both worth upwards of £20 sterling per annum. He observes "that the *Schoolmasters' Salaries* would be much better applied to this use."[2]

". . . I cannot but repeat the request I have already made, for some small allowance to a Minister at Hopkinton, a considerable Town in the heart of the country, and surrounded by many other flourishing Towns, each of them desirous of an Episcopal Minister. I have conducted this affair alone, and taken great pains to form a Church there, and so successfully that I believe, upon the arrival of a Minister, no less than Sixty Families will come over to it. I have likewise obtained one good Farm alreddy, containing a hundred and sixty acres, with a house and Barn, towards the support of a Minister forever, and the promise of another upon the Societie's allowing a Missionary. . . ."

The plan of persuading the Society to establish a mission here was seconded by the clergy in their convention, in May, 1740.[3]

[1] Church Docs. Mass. p. 313.   [2] Ibid. p. 316.   [3] Ibid. Conn. i. 170.

"REVEREND SIR,— We, the Clergy of New England, convened at New London, beg leave to represent to the honourable Society the state of a considerable congregation of the Church of England settled at Hopkinston and the parts adjacent. This town has been for some years a place of resort to several creditable families of Conformists, whose inclination or employment has caused them to remove from Boston into the country; to whom many of the old inhabitants, both of the Church and dissenting persuasions, have united themselves in promoting the Episcopal Church, being induced thereto by a monthly lecture preached among them, and some encouragement they received of being recommended to the Society's favour. There is likewise a probability of a large increase by the addition of many others who have purchased farms in the same town, so as to possess near a third part of the township, in order to settle themselves or children thereon, provided they can enjoy a constant public worship of the Church of England, and procure some assistance toward the support of an Episcopal Minister to reside with them, which they express an earnest desire of, and a readiness to contribute to the utmost of their ability towards his comfortable subsistence."

After this support from his brethren, it must have been a sore trial to Mr. Price to see the Vestries of Christ Church and Trinity Church uniting with that of his own King's Chapel to protest against the plan.[1]

"We have heard that the clergy in their last convention were induced to give their voices in favor of a small town in this Province, known by the name of Hopkinton. This at first surprized us, not till we recollected that this meeting was held at New London, in Connecticutt, a hundred miles distant from it, that not a Clergyman there scarce ever heard or knew of it, the Gentleman alone excepted who was the chief in that convention, whose heart and treasure is buried in that obscure village, and whose pompous representation of it was the sole cause of their delusion.

"But it is amazing that the Commissary could forget the dying church at Scituate, or the frequent application of Bridgewater and Taunton for his Mediation with the Society on their behalf, and venture to commend an unknown solitude not to be mentioned with those other great towns.

"We should rejoice to see the Church lifting up her head everywhere around us; but it would be for a triumph to our Enemies should Hopkinton be preferred and Scituate neglected, — a town of such note and consequence that truth and justice compel us to say, that if the Society have any charity to bestow this way, it cannot better be disposed of than to their relief. . . ."

[1] From the United Vestries to the Secretary, Boston, Jan. 5, 1740. Church Docs. Mass. p. 334.

Still Mr. Price hoped to carry out his project, and the more his disquiet at King's Chapel increased, the more did his heart turn to the quiet country refuge as a haven of rest. When he finally left his church it was with the hope of this, but even the Governor, his friend, gave him so cool an indorsement that it must have hurt more than it helped him; and in this he was a disappointed man. Governor Shirley wrote to the Secretary, June 6, 1747:[1] —

". . . M^r. Commissary Price, who now goes home chiefly with a view of procuring a Mission for a Church wch he has been gathering for some years at Hopkinton, where he has considerable Interest in Lands, and is desirous of residing as the Minister of it, has apply'd to me to recommend his case to the Society. I need not mention, Sir, that it would give a particular pleasure to see the number of the Churches increase in the Province under my own Government, but I cant help saying at the same time that I think the state of the several Churches in Connecticutt requires the more immediate assistance of the Society, at least so far as to prevent a decay of 'em. When this is done, wch seems nearly to concern the general Interest of the Church in these parts, I would recommend the case of the particular congregation now collecting at Hopkinton to the favorable consideration of the Society, and heartily wish it may be provided for. . . ."

Thus failed Mr. Price's darling hope.

The church ledger supplies some financial facts belonging to this period, when his rectorship was drawing to a close: —

		£ s. d.
1737. July 10.	By Wm Sherly for ye Pew N° 96	25. 00. 00
1740–41. Aprile 1.	By Bad and Ragged bills Exchang'd	3. 15. 00
	By Sundry Land Bank bills Chang'd . . .	2. 10. 06
1737. July 4.	To mony Return'd wch was put in ye box by mistake	1. 08. 00
1737–38. April 3.	To p^d H. Laughton for blak Cloth for pulpit and Desk	29. 17. 06
1740. May 19.	To p^d Jno Indicot, Carpenter, in part for repairing ye Church p Agreem^t	80. 00. 00
August 12.	Do.	40. 00. 00
1740–41. March 25.	P^d John Indicott, Carpt^r, forbearance money and for Sundry Jobbs done	5. 00. 00

[1] Church Docs. Mass. p. 410.

		£. s. d.
1740–41. February 9.	No Contribution gathered this Sunday; only a Collection of Charity for y.ᵉ poor w.ᶜʰ amounted to £134. 10. 00, given into y.ᵉ hands of y.ᵉ Overseers for y.ᵉ town	
1741. Nov.ʳ 2.	To Cash pᵈ Tho.ˢ Baxter for a new chair for the Gov. Seat	16. 13. 11
1744. Sept.ʳ 15.	To Cash pᵈ M.ʳ Price in full Exch.ᵉ 470 p Cent settled by y.ᵉ superior Court, which is agree.ᵈ to the vote of the Church last Easter and comes out at £12. 01. 02 p Week, so that y.ᵉ above is what was deficient	
1744–45. April 15.	To Will.ᵐ Bowen for Shores for Gallerys and putting up, p bill	9. 05. 00
1746–47.	P.ᵈ one ⅓ p.ᵗ of the Charge of An Entertainment at y.ᵉ Royal Exch.ᵉ Tavern last Easter, in Conjunction w.ᵗʰ y.ᵉ Wardens of Christ and Trinity Churches, made for y.ᵉ Ministers at y.ᵉ Convention. Am.ᵗ to £22. 10. 00 .	7. 10. 00

A note each year in the ledger records the steady degradation of the currency, as the Province floundered deeper and deeper in that quagmire, and paid for the glories of the French war in paper of ever lessening value: —

1730–31.	Silver Money at or about 18/ p ounce N. Engl.ᵈ Curr.ʸ or Exch.ᵃ w.ᵗ London	260 p Cent.
1732.	Silver Money at or about 19/ p ounce N. Engl.ᵈ Curr.ʸ or Exch.ᵃ w.ᵗ London	280 p Cent.
1734.	Silver Money at or about 21/ p ounce N. Engl.ᵈ Curr.ʸ or Exch.ᵃ w.ᵗ London	320 p Cent.
1735.	Silver Money at or about 27/ p ounce N. Engl.ᵈ Curr.ʸ or Exch.ᵃ w.ᵗ London	440 p Cent.
1737.	Silver Money at or about 26/ p ounce N. Engl.ᵈ Curr.ʸ or Exch.ᵃ w.ᵗ London	430 p Cent.
1739.	Silver Money at or about 30/ p ounce N. Engl.ᵈ Curr.ʸ or Exch.ᵃ w.ᵗ London	500 p Cent.
1740.	Silver Money from 28 6 to 29/ p ounce N. Engl.ᵈ Curr.ʸ or Exch.ᵃ w.ᵗ London	480 p Cent.
1741.	Silver Money at or about 28/ p ounce N. Engl.ᵈ Curr.ʸ or Exch.ᵃ w.ᵗ London	460 p Cent.
1742.	Silver Money at or about 29/6 p ounce N. Engl.ᵈ Curr.ʸ or Exch.ᵃ w.ᵗ London	490 p Cent.

1743.	Silver Money at or about 29/4 to 30/ p ounce N. Engl^d Curr^y or Exch^a w^t London . . .	500 p Cent.
1744–45.	Silver Money at or about 32/ @ 33/ p ounce N. Engl^d Curr^y or Exch^a w^t London	545 p Cent.
1745.	Silver Money at or about 36/ p ounce N. Engl^d Curr^y or Exch^a w^t London	620 p Cent.
1747.	Silver Money at or about 38/ @ 40/ p ounce N. Engl^d Curr^y or Exch^a w^t London, about . .	700 p Cent.

A few entries may here be selected from the Register of Marriages during the Commissary's ministry: —

1732.	Dec. 11.	Silvester Gardiner and Ann Gibbins.
1738.	Mar. 27.	Isaac Royal and Elizabeth McIntosh. He of Mystick; she of Boston.
1738.	May 9.	Addington Davenport and Ann Faneuil.
1742.	Nov. 26.	William Primus and Damson, Negroes.
1743.	Sept. 8.	William Bollan and Frances Shirley.
1744.	May 6.	Luke Vardy and Jane Carson.
1746/7.	Mar. 2.	Barlow Trecothick and Grizel Apthorp.

[True copy from Mr. Price's Register.]

The number of vestrymen was curiously varied from year to year: —

April 11, 1737. *Voted,* That the number of Vestry Men be Twenty-one, and that Seven be a Quorum to doe Business; ye whole to be warned.

Easter Monday ye 3^d Aprill, 1738. *Voted,* That Mr Commissary Price be p^d Eleven pounds p week to this day.

Voted, That Mr Comissary Price's Sallary be computed at 400 p c^ts for the year ensueing.

Voted, That there be 24 Vestry Men chosen, and that 7 be a Quorum.

May 25, 1740. It was unanimously agreed that Capt. Edwd Tyng was chosen of ye Vestry on Easter Monday last, tho' not entered in ye Books as such, and the number Compleated without him; therefore the Vote relating to ye number of Vestrymen on Easter Monday last was reconsidered, and —

Voted, That ye number of Vestrymen for this year shall consist of Seventeen; and to compleat ye Number —

Voted, That Peter Fanneuil, Esqr, be one of ye Vestry for this year.

A subscription to rebuild the church was started at this time by a warden of the church, who was soon to win a distinguished place in the history of the country: —

Oct. 21, 1740. Mem^o, This Vestry requested the favour of Wm Shirley, Esqr, one of our Wardens, to draw up the preamble to a Subscription

· paper w{ch} is to be presented to such well-disposed persons as are willing to Contribute towards rebuilding y{e} King's Chapel, — w{ch} M{r} Shirley undertook, and is to be laid before y{e} Vestry at their next meeting.

The plan, however, which was to have much success a little later, came to nothing at this time. The Records also proceed:

December 5, 1740. *Agreed also*, That y{e} Voluntary Subscription for raising a Sum sufficient to defray the Charges of the current year be promoted, and the preamble thereof be written on large paper and presented to all the propriet{s} of pews and other members of the Chapel, for them to subscribe what Sum they thought proper. It was likewise agreed by a majority that y{e} Same should be presented to his Excellency the Governour.

March 30, 1741. *Voted*, That y{e} Church Wardens take an Acc{t} of y{e} Defficiencys of y{e} Severall Proprietors of pews, etc., in their Contributions for y{e} year last, and call in the money due to y{e} Chapel from them and the Subscribers this week, in Order to pay of the Debts of the Chapel this week before the last Year's Acc{ts} are closed by the Church Wardens, and to return the names and numbers of the pews of those that are delinquent and refractory to the Vestry or Congregation at their next meeting.

Voted, That wee now proceed to choose Twenty Vestry-men for this year, Seven of whom Shall be a quorum to act upon any occasion.

The Church Officers for this Year, Voted unanimously and Seperatly, —
Powers Merrit, Clerk, with the Same Sallery as last year, £50 p an.
Stephen De Blois, Organist, w{h} y{e} Same Sallery as last year, p £50.
W{m} Ruleau, Sexton, w{h} y{e} Same Salery as last year, viz., 12/ p week.
Stephen Ruleau, Assistant to y{e} Sexton, w{h} y{e} Same Salery as last y{r}, £5, and to keep Boys and Negroes in good order in time of Divine Service.

April 18{th}, 1742. *Voted*, That the Number of Vestrymen for the Ensuing year consist of fifteen and no more, and that [   ] of w{ch} be a Quorum; and here follows the Names of the Gentlemen chose to Serve as Vestrymen as they were severally voted, viz.: His Excellency [etc.].

Voted, That M{r} Ch. Paxton, and M{r} Gorden, and the Church-Wardens be a Committee to inquire into the State of the Church, to find out the deficient Proprietors for the two last years, to get their arrears and further subscriptions for the Currant year.

Easter Monday, April 4{th}, 1743. *Voted*, That the Church Wardens shall not give any Proprietor of a Pew Credit for any Sum or Sums of money put into the Box, unless his name be properly fixt to it, that it may be certain who the Donor is; neither shall any Proprietor be allow'd to have paid anything towards the support of his Pew, unless he Complys with the above prescribed method, or some other as Satisfactory to the Church Wardens.

The correspondence with the Bishop of London,[1] in connection with Mr. Davenport's departure from King's Chapel to assume the cure of Trinity Church, shows that, after a delay of a year, he had been succeeded by the person desired. Not much is known of the life or history of the new King's Lecturer thus appointed against the Commissary's wish, but in compliance with what the result shows to have been a mistaken partiality of the congregation.

Rev. Stephen Rowe, M.A., who had previously succeeded Rev. Francis Varnod as missionary of the Society for Propagating the Gospel, to St. George's Parish, Dorchester, S. C., " was licensed to that Parish by the Bishop of London, March 19, 1736. He was ordained deacon, June 15, 1730, by Dr. Synge, Archbishop of Tuam, and priest, June 5, 1732, by Dr. Hoadly, Archbishop of Dublin."[2] He remained in Dorchester, S. C., which at that time contained about three hundred and fifty persons, till his removal to Boston, where Mr. Rowe entered on his duties in 1741. In 1743 " the Venerable Society " established a grammar school in Boston, although it could hardly have seemed to be needful where the famous Latin school was directly under the eaves of the church, and Mr. Rowe was installed in charge of it. But a cloud upon his personal character soon caused him to be removed from his situation. Of all this the Records are silent, but a letter of Commissary Price to the Secretary, May 5, 1744, says:[3] —

"You remark that the Society, out of regard to the favor Governor Shirley show'd the Church and promises to do, and at his request, hath resolved to appoint M! Roe schoolmaster in Boston. . . . The Governor declared to me that he thought M! Roe's behaviour with regard to his marriage and courtship was excusable. I may add that it is very discouraging to the elder ministers in this province, who have labored many years with great pain in the service of the Church, and unwilling to be burdensome to the Society, to see a person with no uncommon qualifications but the art of inveigling, — forced out of his own country by guilt and shame, just landed among us, — thus distinguished with an uncommon share of the Society's bounty and favors."

The enemies of the Episcopal Church were not slow in taking notice of this unfortunate event: —

"The Society themselves say, *Abstr.* 1743, that they have 'tho't proper to establish a Catechetical Lecture, and for Gramar Learning, at

---

[1] See p. 497, *ante.*
[2] Dalcho's Episcopal Church in South Carolina, p. 348.
[3] Church Docs. Mass. p. 380.

Boston, with the Advice and under the Inspection of the Honourable *William Shirley*, Esq., the worthy Governor of the Province;' and the Advantage they propose in it is (among other Things) that it will 're-commend the Principles of the Church of *England* with great advantage and success.' Accordingly they appointed Mr. *Roe* their Catechist at *Boston*. What the success was, and with how 'great Advantage' it recommended the Church of *England* in *Boston*, is so generally known that I need say nothing of it."[1]

At this time, also, another attempt was made to increase the interest in the Episcopal Church, by the establishment of a monthly lecture in King's Chapel, under the supervision of the Society for Propagating the Gospel in Foreign Parts. Of this our Records bear no trace, but the correspondence of the secretary of that Society gives the whole brief history,[2] after the first chapter, which is gathered from the "Abstract" appended to their Anniversary Sermons:[3] —

"The Society, encouraged by the Success of the last Collection to promote their good Designs, hath thought proper to establish a Catechetical Lecture, and for Grammar Learning, at *Boston*, with the Advice and under the Inspection of the Honourable *William Shirley*, Esq., the worthy Governour of the Province, who thinks that such a School there, under the Blessing of Heaven, would prove an useful Seminary of Religion and good Literature throughout the Land, and recommend the Principles of the Church of England with great Advantage and Success. And Mr. *Shirley* much approves of the Society's Missionary at S! George's, Dorchester, in *South Carolina*, but promoted by the Lord Bishop of *London* to the King's Chapel in *Boston*, to be Schoolmaster; as to the Governour's certain knowledge, Mr. Roe performs Divine Service with much Propriety and advantage to the Liturgy, is a sensible, good Preacher, attends the Duty of visiting the Sick, is of good Abilities in Classic Learning, and in his opinion very fit for such an Undertaking."

The salary of Mr. Rowe was £60; but in 1744 he —

"Proved himself, by his bad Behaviour, unworthy of that Employment, and therefore hath been dismissed by the Society from it, which is at present carried on by the Reverend Mr. Commissary *Price*, till the Society shall appoint a new Catechist, or come to some other Resolution about that matter."

Governor Shirley wrote to the Secretary about Rev. Mr. Hooper, Nov. 26, 1746: —

---

[1] Hobart's Second Address, etc., p. 144.
[2] Printed in Church Docs. Mass. pp. 400, 404, 411, 414, 428.
[3] Quoted in Batchelder's Eastern Diocese, pp. 392-394.

"I promised to recommend him to the Society for the Catechetical Lecture lately design'd by 'em for Mr Rowe (without the School, which Mr Hooper would not undertake in conjunction with his cure), in case they should revive their design of supporting such a Lecture. . . . As to the usefulness of such a Lecture in this Town, provided the doctrines of the Church, or rather points of less consequence, which the Dissenters misunderstand or stumble at through prejudice, were to be explained on some week day once in a month, or oftener, after public catechism in the King's Chapel, with the same perspicuity, moderation, and Christian spirit as I find some of 'em have been in little Tracts sent over here by the Society, and in terms that had a tendency to heal differences and reconcile prejudiced minds, and not in the least to inflame 'em by railing accusations and stigmatizing men for errors imbibed by education, but with the utmost appearance of Charity and Brotherhood, I am persuaded it would have a good influence and effect for bringing people into Communion with the Church. Besides, the frequency of Lectures and Sermons on week days in the Meeting-House (whereas there is nothing of this sort in the Church) is what the Dissenters here extremely value themselves and their ministers upon, esteeming it a sure mark of the piety of what they call their Congregational Churches, and undervalue the Episcopal Clergy and Laity for their neglect of. . . ."

Again the Governor wrote, Dec. 1, 1746: —

" . . . And I should think a monthly meeting on every Friday before the Sacrament might be kept up in the King's Chappel in Boston by the Clergy, without any great Burthen to 'em. However, I daresay the allowance of a Guinea for every Sermon would maintain it. . . . "

And again, Jan. 6, 1747, after mentioning the lecture formerly kept up by Mr. Myles: —

"The neglect of it seems, I must own, to have the appearance of indifference and Coolness in both Ministers and people. . . . "

Mr. Hooper also wrote to the Secretary, Aug. 31, 1747: —

"I make no doubt, Sir, you'll do what you can in the Society towards establishing the Lecture in Boston proposed to you by our Governour. Everybody here is of opinion that it may be of great service to the Church. But we do not think it best to have it carried on by all the Ministers in the Province; That would be attended with many inconveniences. The four Ministers in Boston are sufficient for the support of it. We might have it once a month in the King's Chapel, because that Church is most in the centre of the Town; and as to the day of the week, and the time of ye day fittest for ye service, I hope you will leave that to us as we shall judge most convenient. I beg of you, Sir, to promote this affair. I am sure it will do more towards making converts to the Church and promoting religion than many missions you have established in America at very great expence. I could name several in New England not worthy ye supporting, and y^t reflect no honour upon the Society; and if Hopkinton should be added to them, that would be still a greater waste of money and discredit to the Society. . . ."

The experiment, however, was not successful. Dr. Cutler wrote to the Secretary, Dec. 26, 1748: —

"I have Had the opportunity to observe the condition of the Monthly Lecture at the Chapel, hitherto carried on by some of us at the motion of the Society for the Propagation of the Gospel; and I am able to say that from the beginning of it to the present time we have not had one congregation numerous enough to show any considerable respect to it, and we seem to lessen in number every term of the Lecture. Mr Hooper has never performed, and Mr Brockwell is so discouraged that he has given over, and there remains only Mr Caner, Dr Millar, and myself in the Service. For which reasons I would humbly beg the allowance of the Society also to lay down this Service, of whose usefulness I have so little prospect. . . ."

The hand of the new Governor in some of these letters shows that a churchman was once more at the helm of State.

By a strange retribution, Governor Belcher had fallen from office through being accused of plotting with the Episcopalians against the Congregational interest.[1] An anonymous letter was sent to Mr. Holden, the leading person among the English Dissenters, under a cover superscribed by Dr. Colman, who was ignorant of the contents, professing to be "the letter of many of the principal ministers of New England, who were afraid to publish their names lest Mr. Belcher should ruin them. The charge against him was a secret undermining of the Congregational interest in concert with Commissary Price and Dr. Cutler, while at the same time he pretended to Mr. Holden and other Dissenters in England to have it much at heart." Although this charge was entirely unfounded, it procured the desired result.[2]

Belcher had entered office the most popular man in the country; he left it with a host of enemies, whom he had raised through successive controversies in his opposition to the emis-

---

[1] Hutchinson, ii. 397.

[2] The Governor's demonstrative piety was shown by his letter to Dr. Watts on this occasion: "If the late change that has passed over me, from a glaring public station to an obscure private life, may lead me to a more close communion with God, *even to a life hid with Christ in God*, happy, forever happy and glorious, will be the exchange!" At that time his brother-in-law in London was intriguing to get him a governorship elsewhere, and in 1746 he was sent to New Jersey, where he died In 1757, being buried in Cambridge.

sion of new paper bills, in the boundary dispute between Massachusetts and New Hampshire, and in his hostility to the "Land-Bank" scheme. But the ecclesiastical question finally decided his removal.

To Mr. Price and his church the rumor of the Governor's approaching fall was grateful. He wrote to his sister: —

"There is a current report here that our present Governour, Mr Belcher, who is a rigid Dissenter and a bitter Enemy to the Church, is in some danger of being put out of his Government for Male administration; which is matter of great joy to the Majority of the people here, and in particular, you may judge, to every true member of the Church, under whose despite and Oppression we have long groan'd. It is likewise rumour'd that Mr. Shirley, an Old England Gentleman, not unknown to the Duke of Newcastle, is like to succeed him. This doubly adds to the publick satisfaction, which is as general as can well be imagin'd, from the good character the Gentleman has establish'd here, by his Generous and Courteous behaviour and experienc'd abilities; and so unexceptionable will this change be, that I believe Mr. Belcher's own Friends, which indeed are but few, would scarce murmur at it. I must own I heartily wish him success."

Mr. Shirley was indeed well known in the King's Chapel, of which he had been a member since his first coming to America.

The new governor was appointed in conformity with the recommendations of Lieut.-Governor Dunbar, of New Hampshire, who wrote some years before: [1] —

"It would not be for his Majesty's service to have any native of this country appointed Governor, even though he were of the Church of England."

And again to the Board of Trade: —

"New England might be made a very useful colony. It is very populous, and the people generally deem themselves independent, as is their religion. Were the Church of England encouraged, it would bring them to better principles than they now are of, being generally Republicans."

The Christ Church Vestry-book records: —

"Aug. 3, 1741. *Voted*, That ye 2 Church Wardins, With Mr Robt Jarvis, Mr Willm Price, Mr Robt Jenkins, and Mr Hugh McDaniel, Vestry men of Christ Church, Do attend The Reve^d Doc^r Timo^y Cutler To Joyn

[1] British Colonial Papers, and Chalmer's "Revolt," quoted in Palfrey, iv. 568, 575.

with y⁶ Rev⁴ M⁶ Commissary Price and y⁶ Rev⁴ M⁶ Adington Devinport, and their Comit⁶. Apointed for that Purpose, To Congratulate The Honerable Willm Shirley, Esqr, on y⁶ Arivale of his Commission as Governer of this provens, In the Behalf of Christ Church."

And so the first of the congratulatory processions, so many times to be repeated, took its way from King's Chapel to the Province House, down School Street, and up the paved courtyard, through the stately hall into the reception-room; the clergy in their robes, and their committees in rich garb of purple or crimson velvet and satin, are heralded as they come to Governor Shirley, proud in his new dignity, as viceroy of the English Crown. Their address to him survives, though his reply has perished: —

"We, Episcopal Ministers, with the Wardens and Vestry of the Several Churches in Boston, Beg leave to Congratulate your Excellency on your filling the Chair of this Government, and to express our most grateful sense of that goodness in His Sacred Majesty (whom God long preserve!) which has placed you there. That Wisdom and Learning, that Humanity and Integrity, which have so long pre-engag'd our Esteem of you, is one discovery how Royal favours are dispens'd, and a happy Omen of Universal Good. Your Excellency's strong affection and firm adherence to the Church of England leaves us no room to doubt of your Concern and care for the peace and Prosperity of it.

"As we have upon all occasions demonstrated our Loyalty and affection to our most Gracious Sovereign and his Illustrious Family, so we shall still endeavour to distinguish ourselves in this Character, and shall chearfully contribute to the utmost of our power, in our several Capacities, to render your Excellency's Administration easy to yourself and Happy to the Province."[1]

By the accession of the new governor the King's Chapel immediately gained a closer connection with the representative of the Crown than it had enjoyed for half a century. A traveller at this date wrote:[2] —

"King's Chapel . . . has a handsome organ, and a magnificent seat for the Governor, who goes to this place when of the Church of England."

Born in London, 1693, and emigrating to Boston about 1734, William Shirley was a prominent lawyer in this town. It had been his hope to obtain the lucrative place of collector of the

---

[1] This address has been preserved among Mr. Price's papers.
[2] Bennett's History of New England, 1740. Mass. Hist. Soc. Proc., 1861–62.

port on the death of the younger Jekyll, but that position had been given to Frankland; and Mrs. Shirley, a lady of rare charm, who was then in London, obtained for her husband the less desirable post of governor. The administration of Governor Shirley was marked by distinction to himself and lustre to New England in the reduction of Louisburg, and brought again to King's Chapel the brilliant array of officers in His Majesty's Service, who came, as a matter of course, to say their prayers in the church where the bishop's commissary and the king's lecturer read the petitions that George II. might have "victory over all his enemies," while the Governor and his little court mustered in the state pew. To him, more than to any other, the church was indebted for great services in the plans for building the new King's Chapel, which his generosity and public spirit carried through to complete success a few years after the time embraced in this chapter.

Although King's Chapel was independent of the Society for Propagating the Gospel, etc., Mr. Price, in his capacity as overseer of the other churches and missionaries, wrote occasionally to the Secretary; and the "Abstracts" appended to the Anniversary Sermons quote from his letters: —

"The Reverend Mr. Commissary Price, by a letter dated Boston, Aug. 9, 1741, acquaints the Society with the Satisfaction which the Episcopal Churches there have in their new Governour, and with their Hopes that thro' his Excellency's Probity and Justice they shall be eased from some Grievances they have laboured under, but yet that it is the Society which they must depend upon for their Life and Vigour; and that he receiveth continual Applications for Episcopal Ministers in several Country Places, but he hath not dared to give them Encouragement to Petition the Society in its present low Circumstances thro' the great Increase of Missions."[1]

"And the Society hath the Pleasure of being further informed by a second Letter from the Commissary, that the Assembly of the Province of *Massachusetts Bay*, of which *Boston* is the Capital, hath at length (under the Influence of their new Governour, William Shirley, Esq., a worthy Member of the Church of England) past a Law which frees the Members of the Church of *England* in that Province from paying to the Support of what the Independents there call the established Religion."

It was a great gain to Mr. Price to have the governor a parishioner and friend, who soon showed his kindness by an offer which was received by the Vestry in a manner that must

---

[1] See Batchelder's Eastern Diocese, pp. 392-394.

have reminded the Commissary of a similar episode in which he had himself sided with them against Mr. Harward: —

19 of July, 1742. After a Debate on the Commissary's Leaving his Church and Attending his Excellency the Govern. to the Eastward in his intended Interview with the Indians, on his Excellency's Invitation, The Question was put whether the Vestry then mett Consented to Mr Commissary Price's attending the Govern. to the Eastward, and passed in the negative.

Voted, That Mr Brinley, Mr Cradock, and Mr Apthorp, with the Church Wardens, wait on his Excellency, Govr Shirley, to acquaint him with the proceeding of ye Vestry so far as it related the Commissary's attending him to the Eastward.

Voted, That the Revd Mr Roe has the Consent of the Vestry to attend his Excellency as Chappling in his Easter voy.^e, provided his Excellency should please to ask him.

22nd of July, 1742. After debating on the Vote that pass'd ye 19th Inst, relating Mr Commissary Price's attending the Govr to the Eastward, The Question was put whether the Vestry would reconsider Said vote; it pass'd in the affirmative, nem Contra. Then another Question was put, Whether ye Vestry consented to ye Revd Mr Price's attending his Excellency, Govr Shirley, to the Eastward, notwithstanding the Vote it pass'd ye 19th Inst on y.^t Head, and it pass'd in the Affirmative.

Voted, That John Read, Esq., Geo. Cradock, Esq., with the Ch. Wardens, wait on the Gov. to acquaint his Excellency That ye Vestry had reconsidered their vote of the 19th Inst, relating the Commissary's attending him to the Eastward, and voted him their Consent to Accept of his Excellency's Invitation.

The Governor was, however, attended by Mr. Rowe, who wrote, Aug. 28, 1742:[1] —

". . . My Duty as Lecturer of the King's Chapel has led me to attend his Excellency, the Governor of this Province (who is, blessed be God! a Member of our Church), wth a Committee of ye Council and assembly, as Chaplain, in a progress thro' the North East parts of ye Province, to ye distance of 50 or 60 leagues by Sea and Land, in order to renew and establish a Treaty of peace and commerce wth ye Indian Tribes in those parts. . . ."

In the picturesque grouping of dusky savages and English officials round the council-fire, which prefigured so many similar meetings all the way across the continent, we are thus enabled to imagine the King's Chapel not only represented by the king's governor and other dignitaries, but by the king's

---

[1] Mr. Rowe to the Secretary. Church Docs. Mass. p. 364.

lecturer in cassock and bands, lending, in the wondering eyes of the Indians, a supernatural shadow and sanction to the scene.

Mr. Price found and left in Boston an eminent roll of names in the ministers of the other churches of the town, — "meeting-houses" as they were called, — while the stanch churchmen of his congregation, when they stood high enough on tiptoe to look over their own enclosure and see any person outside, called these ministers "Dissenting Teachers." To the earlier list of Mr. Myles's contemporaries [1] should now be added the younger Cooper, colleague since 1744, as his father's successor, with Dr. Colman at Brattle Square. He was to be known later, in days preceding the Revolution, as "Silver-tongued Sam," in the un-reverential phrase of the time. Rev. Andrew Eliot at the New North, Mather Byles at Hollis Street, and Chauncy at the First Church were now associated with the elder men. To these Congregational ministers is to be added one who became more directly concerned with Mr. Price, — the Rev. William Hooper. This gentleman, a Scotchman by birth and education, was the first minister of the West Church, which had been formed in 1737, and was an eloquent and popular preacher. He seems, however, to have been oppressed by the rigid Calvinism, not indeed of the West Church, — for that church always leaned to greater breadth than its sister societies, — but of the surrounding ministers who had sharply criticised him in a correspondence on doctrinal points, wherein he expresses himself with much sweetness and nobleness of spirit. After nine years' ministry at the West Church he suddenly resigned, being dismissed Nov. 19, 1746, and on the same day being chosen minister of Trinity Church, — Mr. Davenport, who had gone to England for his health in 1744, having died in London Sept. 8, 1746. It may well be imagined that Mr. Hooper's change without warning brought a storm about his ears. Not only did his Congregational associates ban him, but Mr. Commissary Price also unsuccessfully opposed his receiving ordination from the Bishop of London, for reasons in which, however conscientiously, the commissary did an injustice to an excellent man.

"Common report," Mr. Price wrote the bishop, "had not been at all favourable to him, either in respect to his principles or morals. . . . Taking such suspicious ministers into the Church might rather be a means of destroying Christianity, which is already in this town too much tinctured with base opinions." [2]

[1] See p. 363, *ante.*
[2] Mr. Price to the Bp. of London, Nov. 22, 1746, in Church Docs. Mass. p. 398.

Governor Shirley, however, did not indorse this view of Mr. Hooper, but wrote to the secretary, Nov. 26, 1746:[1] —

"This Gentleman . . . came from Scotland about twelve years ago to be Tutor to a Gentleman's Son here, where he soon distinguished himself by his natural abilities, acquired Learning, and an agreeable Conversation, but especially by his Talent for preaching, and was in great Vogue in this Town as a preacher, both among the Dissenting Ministers — the principal of which invited him into their pulpits — and the people, among whom a Number of persons, considerable for their Substance and character, form'd themselves into a Congregation, and built a new Meeting-house about nine years ago, in order to give him a Call; and he was accordingly made what they term their Ordain'd Minister, the Solemnity of doing which was performed by Dr. Colman, the principal Minister among the Presbytery here, and others of next note to him, in the new meeting-house; and as far as I am a Judge, I think from the Sermon I had the curiosity to hear him preach upon that occasion, without notes, that he has a prompt Elocution, a winning address, and good sense and learning in the pulpit. During his nine years' Ministry in this Meeting house he has maintained the Character of an Extraordinary preacher, and rather increas'd than diminish'd it; was united with the Ministers of the Association (as they are call'd) in preaching at the publick Lecture, and constantly preserved their good opinion and esteem, and had in a remarkable manner the affections and hearts of his people, and what is Esteem'd among the Dissenting Congregations here a liberal support from them. . . . His life has been unblameable and becoming a Minister of the Gospel. . . . Upon Trinity Church's becoming vacant, M' Hooper took occasion to signify to me what I thought I could discover before from his declared Sentiments in conversation with him some years since (when I had more leisure to converse than I have now), that he was disposed to come over to the Church of England; and I thereupon propos'd his succeeding M' Davenport in his late Cure, which offer was most readily embrac'd by the proprietors of Trinity Church. . . . There is a general expectation among the members of the several Episcopal Congregations in this Town that M' Hooper's coming over may be of considerable advantage, and add members to it. . . ."

His opposition to Mr. Hooper's new charge must have been one of the latest acts of Rev. Roger Price before leaving his charge here. Four days after his letter to the bishop Mr. Price resigned his place at King's Chapel, and was succeded by Rev. Henry Caner. In due time came back from England the report of his action in regard to Mr. Hooper. The Vestry of Trinity Church met May 21, 1747, and recorded: —

[1] Church Docs. Mass. p. 399.

"Several letters being read informing that Mr Hooper, who this Church hath presented to the Bishop of London for Holy Orders, has been opposed by Mr Com^y Price by representations directly contradicting the Testimonal the Church and many other persons have given, The Vestry taking into consideration this unjust behaviour look upon it highly injurious to this Church, who are intirely satisfied of the good Character of Mr Hooper, and that this opposition can be designed for no other end than the detriment (as far as laith in his power) of this church: It is therefore unanimously *Voted*, y^t, as a token of this Church just resentment of such unchristian Usage, said Mr Price be notified that the Vestry desire No more of his Service in this Church, as they have of late kindly Invited and employed Him to perform; and of this discharge the Wardens are desired to give Him Notice.

"*Voted*, That the Wardens apply to the Revd Mr Canner and Mr Brockwell, Ministers of ye King's Chappel, to desire them to Officiate in Trinity Church untill the s^d Church is Supplied, to pay them as p^d Mr Price and Mr Brockwell.

"The Wardens went to ye Revd Mr Price's House, he not being at Home, and Saturday Night left a letter there as followeth: —

"Rev^D S^R, — We are desired and ordered by the Vestry of Trinity Church to informe you that they have rec^d letters acquainting them that you have unjustly and in an unfair Manner opposed the Revd Mr Hooper, who this Church hath presented to ye Lord B^{ip} of Lond^n for Holy Orders, by representing him directly contradictory to their representations, which this Church look upon as highly injurious; they have therefore Unanimously Voted that they desire no further Service from you in said Church. We sign in behalf of an injured Church, Rev^d S^r,

"Y^r, etc.

"The Sunday following, Mr Canner and Mr Brockwell had promised to comply with the desire of the Vestry, but when the Congreg^n were Mett, Mr Brockwell not coming as expected was sent for. He returned Answer, Mr Price, as the Bishop's Com^y, had forbid His and Mr Canner officiating in Trinity Church, so the Congregation dismised and no Service that Day. The Sunday following, Mr Canner and Mr Brockwell entered upon the care of Trinity Church, and continued so till the Arrival of the Revd Mr Hooper, which was on ye 24th of August following."

Trinity Church also appealed to the mother church for assistance in this dilemma, with the satisfactory result which our records show: —

At a meeting of the Minister, Church Wardens, and Vestry of King's Chappel, on Thursday, June 4, 1747, . . . *A letter Directed To Mr James Gordon to be communicated to ye Minister, Wardens, and Vestry of King's Chappel, Boston*, of wch here follows a Copy : —

GENTLEMEN AND BRETHREN, — The proprietors of the Pews in Trinity Church haveing Chosen Mr Wm Hooper of this Town for their Minister, they presented him to their Diocesan, the Ld B.^{p} of London, for Holy Orders, giveing Testimonials that he had Lived in this Town a number of Years, and that he had been a Person of good life and conversation, of Repute and good Creditt here ; but to our great Surprise wee are informed that a Caveat hath been made to his Ordination, by representing him to his L.^{d}ship as a Person of whom Common Fame doth say he is neither of good Principals nor Morals. Wee therefore begg of you, Gentlem^n, as Brethren together with us and of the same Town, to signifie whether this Gentleman hath not been of a fair Character, or to give Such other representations of him as Y^o may think just, that such insinuations may not affect his reputation nor frustrate the designs of Our Church, wch are in haveing a Usefull Minister that may not only promote our Own good, but be instrumental in ye general benefit of the Church of Engl^d amongst us. Wee beg you candidly to consider this affair, and act with and for us as Brethren, wch will be thankfully acknowledged by the Church that wee have the honour to represent.

Wee are, Gentlem^n, Your Most humble Serv^{ts},

Jo.^{n} DOWSE, } Wardens of Trinity Church.
Wm PRICE,

Which letter being twice Read the Vestry Concurrd in An Answer by delivering to them the following letter to the Lord Bishop of London, to be Sign'd by the Wardens and Vestry, a copy whereof here follows : —

May it Pleas your Lordship, — Our Brethren of Trinity Church being under verry great Difficultys and Discouragements by reason of Mr Wm Hooper's Ordination being put off on acc.^{t}, as we hear, of some representations made of him to your L.^{d}Ship as a person whom Common Fame reports to be of bad morals ; and haveing desired us to acquaint y.^{r} L.^{d}Ship with Mr Hooper's Character, So far as we able, Since his first Settlement at New Boston to his departure last Fall, — Wee, the Church Wardens and Vestry of King's Chapel, Doe Solemnly Declare that wee know not of any Immoralitys he has been charged with Since he has been a Dissenting Teacher in this Town, but he has maintained a Verry fair Character here ; and from his constantly takeing his turn with the rest of the Teachers in this Town in the Weekly Lectures, and the great Love and Esteem his People had for him till he left them, must be of Opinion that he is a Gentleman of good Moralls.

Without the necessity of these further testimonials, however, Mr. Hooper obtained his reordination from the bishop, being "licensed to the Plantations" by him, June 10, 1747, and returning hither was minister of Trinity Church until his death in 1767. Whatever feeling may have rankled among his earlier parishioners on account of his sudden change of ecclesiastical relations, may be offset by the words of his latest successor at the West Church concerning his transition to Episcopacy: [1] —

"I . . . rank him in the class of intellectual and religious pioneers. Though he seemed to go back when he joined the Establishment, he really went forward, as the apparent retrogradation of a planet is an actual speeding, with undiminished velocity, on its way. . . . If he had faults, of which the register does not appear, — though some may think his desertion of his people implied them, — I am confident they were not those of hypocrisy or double-dealing in any form; and his summary leave-taking showed, perhaps, only a nature whose first necessity, like that of all great natures, was conformity between its action and its thought."

"It does not sound strange to us 'after this," adds his latest successor at Trinity Church, "that his son was one of the signers of the Declaration of Independence." [2]

Mr. Hooper seems to have retained a friendly fellowship, also, with his Congregational brethren; for in this sense, rather than as a covert rebuke to one who had crossed the line between one church and another, should be interpreted a letter to him from Mr. Barnard, of Salem, to whom he had applied for a just and honest character of Mr. Walter, a candidate for the place of his assistant minister: [3] —

"I hope he will never undergo such a miraculous change in his mental eyesight, of which there have been instances, as to view all without his future pale in the light of raw head and bloody bones. Most seriously I hope he 'll never get so buried in the fringes of religion as to lose sight of the substance of it, nor imagine he shall serve his master by smiting his 'Brethren engaged in the same Service."

The difficulties of the new parish now came to an end, and its history henceforward is probably even more independent of King's Chapel from the fact that this church was no longer governed by a commissary with official primacy before his brethren, but by the new minister, Mr. Caner, whose ministry began almost simultaneously with that of Mr. Hooper.

Until the Revolution, indeed, the two churches continued to be closely affiliated, and though in the eventful changes which then took place there were various doctrinal and ecclesiastical entanglements in the network of crossing threads in their relations, as will later appear in our narrative, the social and family

---

[1] Bartol's History of the West Church, p. 65.
[2] Brooks's Historical Sermon, etc., 1877, p. 33.
[3] Church Docs. Mass. p. 507.

ties between the two parishes were too strong to be broken, and have continued to the present day with undiminished force. In the gentler spirit which now prevails, Christians of every name find it less difficult than formerly to recognize that even where there are "differences of administration," there is "the same Lord."

The later history of Trinity Church falls, for the most part, beyond the scope of our narrative. With Mr. Hooper's final settlement, the parish entered on a long period of prosperity, not without varying fortunes, under a succession of able ministers, culminating in the large and brilliant position of usefulness and distinction which it now occupies in Boston, with a ministry whose influence extends far beyond its walls. The wooden church which was built almost as an appendage to King's Chapel, before the new parish took form, gave place in 1825 to the more stately tower of gray granite which perished in the great conflagration of 1872; and when Trinity Church in 1877 entered the noble building which is its latest home, no parish in the city can have rejoiced with more friendly sympathy in its religious and temporal prosperity than that of the ancient mother church.

The Records indicate that Mr. Price's final separation from the church in 1747 was strongly foreshadowed some years before.

At a meeting of the Congregation in the King's Chapple on Sunday, 5th Feb^y, 1743, on Mr Comiss^y Price's acquainting them that he was desirous of going to England to make a visit to his Relations and settle his own private affairs. It was

Voted, That Mr Read, Mr Cradock, and Mr Gordon, with the present Church Wardens, should be a Comittee to Consider how far and on what terms Mr Comiss^y Price's Request might be granted consistent with the well-being and Maintenance of the privileges of the said Chapple, and make their Report to the Congregation at their next meeting.

At a meeting of the Congregation in the King's Chapple on Sunday the 19th Feby Ins^t, ye before nam'd Committee presented the following proposals: —

In pursuance of the foregoing vote on Sunday ye 5th of this Ins^t, We the Committee for the said Church propose that upon the first assurance Mr Commissary can give us of a Clergyman provided in his stead and ready to embarke for this place, he may depart on his intended visit.

That we shall weekly pay his Vicar's dues according to his appointment out of his standing Salary, and ye rest of his Salary to his Order here.

That we are content that he continue in England upon his visit a twelve month from his first arrival there, and no longer without special occasion signified to and allow'd by the Church.

And, lastly, in Case he shall not incline to return to us again within the time herein limited, or such further time as may hereafter be allowed by the Congregation, that then the Church shall be declar'd and deem'd vacant, and may immediately proceed to the choice of a Minister.

These things we propose, and (on M! Commissary's agreeing thereto with the Congregation, or such person or persons as they shall see meet to appoint for that purpose) we think may be safely Comply'd with, leaving it to his own discretion when to go, wishing him a safe and prosperous Voyage.

The foregoing proposals being read to the Congregation they

Voted, That M! Commissary's Request should be granted on the terms therein mentioned, and that the Gentlemen of the Committee are desired in behalf of the Church to settle an Agreement with M! Commissary agreeable to their report.

March 26, 1744. *Voted*, That the present Church Wardens, with M! Read, E^m Hutchinson, and M! Gorden, be a Committee to assess the pews agreeable to the proposalls made by the late Church Wardens, wch the chief part of the proprietors subscribed to.

Voted, That M! Commissary Price's Salary be paid agreeable to the Exchange settled by this Government.

Easter Monday, April 15, 1745. *Voted*, That what is deficient of the Exchange in M! Price's Salary during M! Sam! Wentworth's Churchwardenship be settled by the present Church Wardens.

Mem^o, April 5, 1746. The Exch^e as it is Settled by the Governm! w^h Great Brittain is £500 p C!, at wch Exch^e the Rev^d M! Roger Price his yearly Salary, being £110 Sterling, Am^{ts} to old Ten! £660 p Ann,— £12. 13. 10. p Week, accounting 52 Weeks to ye year, wch Weekly allowance is to Continue till ye Governm! aters the Exch^a., and then it is to be Computed accordingly. But as there is 55 Sundays in ye following year, from Easter to Easter (ye last Inclusive), It is exactly £12 old Tin! p week to make up M! Price's Salery, unless ye Exch^e is alterd by the Governm! as aforesaid.

June 20, 1746. *Voted*, That the Pews (in the King's Chapel) of those persons that have not paid the full of their Contribution to the satisfaction of the Church-Wardens for the two years last past, According to the last Assesment, are forfeited according to the Rules and Votes of the Church, of wch the Church-Wardens may give them One more notice ; and if they doe not then pay their arrears of Contribution, Shall and may dispose of all, or any, of the Said pews as occasion offers.

At a meeting of the Congregation of the Church called King's Chapel, on Thursday, Nov. 27, 1746, Appointed for a General Thanksgiveing, after morning Servis in Said Chappel, The Rever! M! Roger Price, Rector of Said Chapel, Signified to the Congregation his Intention of goeing to

England, and quitting the Rectorship and Cure of Said Church, by reading his letter to the Congregation and then delivering the same to James Gordon the first Warden, of which here follows a true Copy: —

BOSTON, NEW ENGL^D, Novr 21, 1746.

To the Congregation of King's Chapel:

Haveing an intention of goeing to England in the Mermaid, Man-of-War, which will sail about four Months hence, I take this first opportunity to acquaint you with it, that you may procure a Minister in my Stead, to whom I am at any time ready to resign, for the Success of whose labours in your Servis I shall never cease to pray, And hope that all good Offices may Still Continue between my Congregation of King's Chappell and their Affectionate and Unworthy Minister, etc.

(Signed) ROGER PRICE.

Testis, JAMES GORDON, first Church Warden.

A suggestive proof of the stability of the ministerial relation at King's Chapel may be found in the fact that this is the only accepted letter of resignation on the Records, during nearly two centuries of church life.

The congregation now resolved to choose their minister to suit themselves, from among the persons "in holy orders" in New England, instead of asking the Bishop of London to send them one from abroad. It may be that their imperfect harmony with Mr. Price, whom the Bishop had picked out for them, had something to do with this state of mind; it may be that they apprehended that Mr. Price would make difficulty about his successor, as he had done about Mr. Hooper's going to Trinity church. We know not. The dust of more than a century rests on their reasons, and we cannot brush it away if we would.

The Rev. Henry Caner was then chosen "by a great majority," and was inducted April 11, 1747, Mr. Price assisting. All this is fully recorded. Dr. Caner's long and eventful ministry was cast in the times immediately preceding the Revolution, and is in many respects the most interesting period in our Annals, passing beyond the limits of mere parochial events and entering as an important force into the great history of the transformation of a British Province into an American State. But all this, and the later changes which make the story of the church, since the Revolution and during its second century, as marked theologically as was its earlier story politically, were as yet unimagined. When the Bishop's Commissary inducted his successor, it simply seemed that one minister was giving place to another in a system as stable as the imperial power of Eng-

TRINITY CHURCH.—A CLOSING EPOCH. 541

land, while in reality the church was entering on the prelude to a new epoch.

Although his ministry at King's Chapel was thus closed, by his own voluntary act, Commissary Price did not finally terminate his residence here until several years later, living for the most part on his estate in Hopkinton, occupied in its improvement and in the agreeable little society which was planted like an English exotic on that New England soil. There was, doubtless, disappointment on both sides in the long course of events which had loosened and at length severed the ties which bound the Bishop's Commissary and King's Chapel to each other; but it is not necessary to search for causes beneath the surface; records and letters tell the whole story in ample detail. A hundred years after Mr. Price preached and printed his sermon on the death of Mr. Jekyll, his successor wrote:[1] "Though he had not lived on the happiest terms with his people, his talents were good and his morals irreproachable. His great failing was that he could not accommodate himself to the country to which he had come, and was always wishing to live more like a dignitary of the Church at home than the habits of this country would bear."

In June, 1747, not long after his successor's induction at King's Chapel, Roger Price sailed in the "Mermaid," man-of-war, for England, taking his eldest son William with him to be educated in England, leaving his wife and four children in Boston in the Bull house. It appears from a letter written by the Rev. Thomas Valentine, of Epsom, England, to "Rev.ᵈ Roger Price, at Mrs. Westron's at the Golden Hartichoak, near the new Church in the Strand," that he must have returned to America in August, 1748. He remained in Hopkinton for several years, but finally went to England, arriving in London with his family Dec. 16, 1753. He now took his family to his living at Leigh, Essex, where he was "Incumbent of the Parish of Leigh in the Deanry of Braughing and Archdeaconry of St. Albans." But neither Mr. Price nor his family were pleased with their residence at Leigh, and he made several attempts to obtain a more agreeable place of abode, yet without success. The property in America was badly managed, and returned small interest for the amount invested. Two estates in Boston were lost through the carelessness of his agents, besides much of the land at Hopkinton. In 1757 a commission in the 25th regiment of Foot in the English army for his eldest son William

[1] Greenwood, p. 107.

was sent to Mr. Price by Mr. Stone, a relative and warm friend of the family, who became, in 1761, treasurer to the Queen's household. "I hope," wrote his father to the young lieutenant, while serving with the British forces in Germany, "you are not forgetful to return thanks to God for your many deliverances, which is the best means to obtain his protection:"

June 30, 1759, Roger Price applied for the living of Fobbing. A letter to him states "that it was promised three years before to a person of rank," but hopes he will bear his disappointment with the same constancy he has shown on former occasions.

Aug. 12, 1762, his brother-in-law, Rev. William Fletcher, enclosed to Roger Price a certificate of his birth, from the register at Whitefield, which was required, as he had applied for some benefaction which His Grace of Canterbury was to assist in procuring for him. The time was drawing near when death was to release him from all further trials and disappointments, in a life varied with much romance, great labor, and heavy responsibilities, through all of which he had showed himself a man of remarkable talent and earnestness. Letters from an intimate friend, Sir Peter Rivers, to Captain William Price, of the 25th regiment, then at Gibraltar, give the following account of the last days on earth of the Rev. Roger Price: —

WHITEHALL, Nov. 26th 1762.

I received a visitor this evening who brings a very melancholy account of your Father, insomuch that his life is in great danger from an inflammatory fever, which succeeded to a bad fit of the ague. He was under the necessity of attending his duty, one of these miserable foggy nights, in the church-yard, where he was so violently seized that he was obliged to be brought home by two men, and there is small hopes of his recovery."

Dec. 17, 1762, he wrote again: —

"He languished till the 8th when he died, which was on Wednesday, and the Monday following was to be buried. Should you find there is a necessity on this melancholy occasion to come to England, or that it is your choice so to do, my brother is told that General Conway has orders to permit it; but you must judge for yourself, and according to the present circumstances of things, which is most advisable or necessary, to come hither or stay with your Regiment: you are entirely at liberty to act either way as you shall judge best for your advantage or convenience.

"I cannot close this letter without expressing my real concern for your great loss, in which my Brother sincerely joins with me. Your

Father was an honest man and a truly good Christian, and I doubt not but he now reaps the full fruits of his labours, which in this world did by no means meet that compensation which was due to him."

The Rev. Roger Price died at Leigh, Essex, Dec. 8, 1762.[1] Some account of the subsequent history of his family may properly be given here. After his death, his family removed at once from the rectory at Leigh, to make room for the new incumbent, the Rev. Mr. Parker. The living at Durrington was given to the curate, the Rev. R. Head. The family took up their residence at Hammersmith, Middlesex. In 1763 Mary Ann Price, the second daughter, died with the small-pox. She was very beautiful and talented. Elizabeth, the eldest daughter, was also stricken with the same disease, which completely destroyed her beauty and almost cost her her life. Mrs. Price was exceedingly opposed to vaccination, and would not permit her children to be inoculated, but mourned bitterly her short-sightedness when too late.

May 8, 1764, we find Mrs. Price petitioning to the "Governors of the Charity for the Relief of Widows and children of clergymen": —

"That your Petitioner, aged forty-seven, now living in the Hamlet of Hammersmith, in the County of Middlesex, is the widow of the Rev. Roger Price, late Rector of Leigh, in the County of Essex, who died in the year 1762; that your Petitioner hath five children, — Elizabeth, aged 26 years, William, 25, Henry Yelverton, 23, Thomas, 14, Andrew, 9 years; that William has a commission in the Army, Henry Yelverton, in the East India companies' service, the other three are with your Petitioner unprovided for; that your Petitioner has no salary, annuity, estate, Pension, or Provision whatsoever (excepting a small estate in New England, from which she has received no advantage since the death of her Husband). Wherefore your Petitioner humbly prays to be admitted a Pensioner of this Corporation."

She was admitted, but we do not know the amount of benefit she received. Her friends were not pleased with this application for relief.

After this Mrs. Price resided principally among her friends,

---

[1] The following are his children, born in America and England: Elizabeth, born April 3, 1737; William, born April 14, 1739; Henry Yelverton, born Feb. 26, 1740; John, Mary (both died in infancy); Mary Ann, born 1745; John and James, twins, of whom James died an infant, John died when four years old (the Burial Register of King's Chapel records: "1747. Sept. 22, James, of Rev. Roger & Eliz^a Price, 8 months"); Thomas, born 1749; Andrew, born 1752, died in infancy at Boston; Andrew, born 1753, at Leigh, Essex, England.

of whom she possessed many warm and constant ones, judging from the letters still in existence.

Jan. 9, 1770, Thomas Price was drowned in the Serpentine River, Hyde Park, by breaking through the ice while skating. He was a very promising young man, and had nearly reached his twenty-first year. His death was a severe blow to the family and friends.

Mrs. Roger Price died at Beckley, Aug. 5, 1780, aged 63 years. Her second son, Henry Yelverton, died in London on the 14th of August, 1780, aged 39 years. Major William Price obtained leave of absence to visit America to look after the property and prove his father's will. He arrived in Boston Oct. 10, 1764, and left it Jan. 20, 1766, thoroughly disgusted with the condition of the American property. He obtained leave again for eight months, April 9, 1783; and, leaving England with his sister Elizabeth June 9, arrived here Aug. 4, 1783. The following year he sold his commission in the English army and retired on half pay. He repaired the mansion-house at Hopkinton, and he and his sister made it their permanent abode. Major William Price died at Hopkinton, Dec. 7, 1802. The "New England Palladium" mentions his death as follows: —

"Major William Price, eldest son of the late Commissary Price, in the 65th year of his age, 27 years of which he spent in His Britannic Majesty's service. He was present at the famous battle of Munden and the still more remarkable siege of Gibraltar during the American War, at the conclusion of which he retired to his native country. He was eminent for his military talents and social qualities. His hospitable table was open to every one, and the poor of Hopkinton will long regret his loss. His remains were interred on Friday with military honors, and a large concourse of the most respectable inhabitants of the neighbouring towns attended, to whom his hospitality and extensive charity had endeared him."

Major Price received much attention in England, and had many warm friends among the nobility and in the British army. The Duke of Kent, when in Boston, contemplated visiting him at Hopkinton, to enjoy a few days of hunting, but was prevented by unexpected commands to leave for England. An autograph letter from the duke expressing his regret was long preserved in the family. The female portion of the family were greatly relieved, the duties of entertaining the king's son being more than they cared to undertake. The duke, in speaking of Major Price, said he was one of the handsomest and most gentlemanly men he met while in America. Major Price was knighted for his bravery, but never assumed the title.[1]

Elizabeth Price, known in Hopkinton and Boston as Madam Price, continued to live in the old mansion-house after her brother's death, and had the charge of his daughters up to the year 1818, when she had become too old and feeble. She accordingly removed to Boston to live with a niece, and the mansion-house was rented once more. Finally the old house was burned to the ground, and many old documents and relics perished in the flames. Madam Price had a large circle of friends among the old families in Boston, who continued their interest in her up to the time of her death, although for many years her mind was entirely gone. She died in Boston, July 3, 1826, in her ninety-second year, and was buried in the Price tomb at Hopkinton, by the side of her brother, in the old churchyard, which was given by her father for a burial-ground.[2] Madam Price was a woman of strong character, sturdy in maintaining her opinions, fearless in righting what she considered wrong, and probably was more like her father than any of the other children, both mentally and physically. Although sought by many in marriage both in England and America, she preferred to live single. Her brother Andrew, the youngest son and last survivor of Roger Price's large family, was educated at Oxford, and after graduating obtained a fellowship at Magdalen College, which he retained for many years. He then took orders and obtained a living at Bromley, where he remained for some years, when the rectory at Britwell, Salome, near Tetsworth, Oxfordshire, became vacant, and he was urged to take it, which he did, and lived and died there. He never visited this country, and was the only child not born here. The property known as Bull's wharf, in which he had an interest, was almost wrested from the

---

[1] Major Price left two daughters: (1) Olivia, who married Benjamin Homer Hall, son of Judge Hall, of Vermont; Mrs. Hall died in Rochester, N. Y., March 1, 1852, leaving one child, Elizabeth Price Hall. (2) Mary Ann Price, married (1) Lawson Valentine, of Boston; they had four children,— Andrew Price, William Price, Edward Lawson, and Frances Erving Valentine; Mr. Valentine died in 1828. She married, Aug. 2, 1841, (2) Isaac Peabody Osgood, a lawyer of Boston, who died in Roxbury, Jan. 12, 1867. Mrs. Osgood died May, 1881, aged 89 years. To the end of her long life she retained her mind, and was bright, energetic, and active, attending perfectly to business affairs, while her memory was a wonderful treasury of the things of a former generation.

[2] The tomb at Hopkinton was built by Major Price. When it was finished, he said that in all probability he would be buried under arms, and therefore wished to know, while living, how it would seem to have a volley fired over him. Accordingly, shortly before his death, he shut himself up in the tomb, and had a company of militia fire the volley over it while he was inside.

family by an unjust lawsuit, which claimed, as it was owned by *aliens*, that the property was forfeited. A letter from Madam Price to her brother Andrew turned the scale of justice. Andrew Price died at Bromley, June 7, 1851. His mental faculties had failed him more than his bodily strength. He had nearly completed his ninety-seventh year. The rectory where he died had been in his wife's family over four hundred years. He was the last of his race in England, and the last of the name belonging to Roger Price's branch of the family.

A few of the prominent persons in the church during Commissary Price's ministry at King's Chapel have been noted in our narrative of this period; but there were many others, who for the most part outlived Mr. Price's stay at the church, and will claim recognition in the remarkable group of parishioners who gave character to it when Mr. Caner entered upon its cure. Indeed, a striking proof of the vitality of the church and of its special hold both on the respect of the community and on the affection of most of its members, is the fact that it had borne the exhaustion consequent on the internal dissensions which we have been obliged to relate, as well as the depletion of twice colonizing a daughter church out of its numbers, and yet retained a vigor which insured a prosperity greater than ever before, as will be related hereafter. While this is largely due to the able and faithful work of Caner in his long ministry, it must be recognized that he could have done little without the exceptional constituency which he found here. Such a body of parishioners, interested and loyal to the church of which they were proud, was a constant argument against the dislikes and suspicions of the descendants of the Puritans around it. While less austere, doubtless, and representing a more ample social type, with the freer habits of living congenial to greater wealth and leisure, they were neither irreligious nor profane. A fragment of the Old World in the New, and taking their tone from the echo of English society in the numerous body of king's officials who worshipped there, they constituted a unique feature of life in the Province of Massachusetts Bay, gathering, as it were, into a focus all the influences from the English church and crown. The potent effect of these influences in shaping thought and action in New England, from the granting of the second charter till the outbreak of the Revolution, has hardly been adequately grasped by our historians, who are inclined to slight our history as *Englishmen* in tracing the growth of our national spirit as *Americans*. To the Congregational churches around it, in its less rigid temper, King's Chapel may have stood for a real lack of the vital substance of religion; and in tracing a history so full of disputes and controversies, it may be that our readers have asked if this feeling had not a just foundation. It is to be remembered, however, that while the dissensions recorded themselves, the quiet course of religious life under sober preaching and the serious influence of the Book of Common Prayer, with its devout and uplifting form of worship, flowed on silent and unrecorded, but not the less deep and strong. Many hearts and lives were trained in piety and virtue, though in the midst of external bickerings. Moreover, it should not be forgotten that the age was a contentious one, not only in matters of religion, but in other ways. By its semi-political attitude, King's Chapel was naturally in a position of antagonism to much of the order of things around it; while its internal dissensions could be in a great degree paralleled in the history of neighboring societies if their records had been as fully kept. The convincing proof of the real character of the teaching and influence of the church is given by the character of the persons composing it. After almost a century and a half, we can clearly discern that many of them were held in marked respect and honor, as lawyers, merchants, and high officials, not merely receiving lip-service on account of their wealth or office, but trusted with an exceptional confidence. Such names, besides those already chronicled, as those of John Read, Robert Auchmuty, and John Overing, attorneys at law; Jonathan Pue, John Box, Job Lewis, and Peter Faneuil, in business; General Estes Hatch and Captain Edward Tyng; Thomas Letchmere, in His Majesty's Customs; Governor Shirley, and the group of younger men like Dr. Gardiner and Charles Paxton, who guided the fortunes of the church during the thirty years which preceded the Revolution, — all members of the Vestry, — should testify not only to the social character, but to the moral and religious tone of their church.

So far as can be gathered from the names which appear at this period through the records,[1] the parish now contained blended within it several elements. While the ruling class in it was that of official servants of the Crown, and a large proportion of the parishioners consisted of English emigrants in the

---

[1] Lists of all the persons who have been connected as parishioners with the church, so far as they can be gleaned, though imperfectly, from the Records, will be found at the close of Vol. II.

first or second generation, there was a sprinkling of persons of earlier New England descent, and a cosmopolitan quality was given to the congregation by other admixtures. The Scotch-Irish emigration of 1717 infused into the church strong Jacobite sympathies, which, as has been related, disturbed its peace and divided its counsels for years. This element was represented by Captain Robert Temple,[1] whose son Robert married Governor Shirley's daughter.

The church was the gainer also by the arrival of many French Protestants, and the names of Faneuil and Brimmer could have been ill spared from its roll of parishioners.[2]

Mr. Price also reckoned among his parishioners, and was evidently reluctant to part with, the whole group of persons who founded Trinity Church, some of whom indeed retained a connection with King's Chapel and later returned thither; but others separated permanently from it, like Thomas Greene,[3] whose "Foundation" has added greatly to the resources and power of usefulness of Trinity, and William Coffin, a warden of each church, father of Sir Thomas Aston Coffin, and brother of Admiral Sir Isaac Coffin, of the British navy.

A touch of human pathos is added to the shadowy group of parishioners whom we try to conjure up, as we look into the Governor's pew and see there his son, William Shirley, Jr., a warden in 1745, soon to be killed at Braddock's defeat in 1755, while acting as an aid to that unfortunate commander. There, too, is William Bollan, a lawyer, English born and bred, the husband of Governor Shirley's beautiful daughter Frances, whose monument is one of the greatest treasures of the church, in its stately Latin inscription perpetuating a sorrow for her early

---

[1] He was a descendant of Sir Thomas Temple, of Stowe, Bart. His second son, John, whose daughter married the late Lieut.-Governor Thomas Lindall Winthrop, received the baronetcy in 1786. "Memorial History," ii. 540.

[2] Martin Brimmer and other French Protestants were made Denizens of this Province, Feb. 25, 1730–31. See N. E. Hist. and Geneal. Reg., v. 374.

[3] Of Mr. Greene (1705–1764), as a former warden of King's Chapel (1734–1736), whose name is perpetuated by the permanent religious memorial which his heirs thus helped to constitute in the parish where he later belonged, a further notice may here be added to the reference to him on pp. 495–496, ante. He was descended from John Greene who came to America in 1635, was a surgeon in Providence and one of the original purchasers of the Narraganset tract, where he died in 1658. The four sons of this ancestor were: (1) John, an assistant governor of Rhode Island; (2) Peter, who married a daughter of Samuel Gorton, the heresiarch, "whom he aided in upholding the equal rights of such as agreed with their religious views;" (3) James, grandfather of General Nathaniel Greene, the Revolutionary hero; (4) Thomas, grandfather of the Thomas who was warden of King's Chapel, etc. "The Greene Foundation," etc. Boston: 1875.

death, which still draws tears to the reader's eyes, though the sorrow was assuaged more than a century ago.[1]

Among the worshippers also was Peter Pelham, the engraver, whose skill perpetuates the faces of many noted men of that generation, the step-father of young Copley, who perhaps caught with wondering eye, as he sat in Pelham's pew, the gleam of the brocades and velvets which he later threw on the canvas.[2]

There were some proselytes, like the wife of Lieut.-Governor Spencer Phips, 1733-41, of whom Dr. Cutler wrote to Gray, Nov. 8, 1734: —

"Our Lieut.-Governor's lady, a sober, virtuous woman, has, after mature consideration, come into the communion of our Church, — and so possesses those honours that her husband seems not fond of."

The church saw all the rich costumes and striking groupings of that picturesque age gathered, in that ancient day, within its walls. Chariots with liveried black footmen brought thither titled gentlemen and fine ladies; and the square pews were gay with modes of dress which must have brightened the sober New England life, — as the ruffled sleeves and powdered wigs, and swords; the judges whose robes were thought to give dignity and reverence to their high office as they sat upon the bench; the scarlet uniforms of British officers in army and navy, — all mingling with the beauty and fashion which still look down from old family portraits the special flavor of an age very different from our own. With such an assembly of worshippers the imagination peoples the church, as we "take such a glimpse of its venerable interior as the mist of dim ages will allow to us," — such as a successor of Mr. Price has described it.[3]

---

[1] See a sketch of William Bollan, husband of Frances Shirley, copied from Eliot's sketch of him. N. E. Hist. and Geneal. Reg. xx. 245.

[2] See Mass. Hist. Soc. Proc., 1866-67, pp. 197-204, for a notice of Peter Pelham, by W. H. Whitmore. To the prominent names in the parish during Mr. Price's ministry may be added the following: George Shores, Captain Brett, John Briggs, Henry Caswall, Captain John Cox, Alice Quick, Peter Stone, George Featherstone, Captain Doubt, Jonathan Pew, John Deacon, Thomas Bennet, Thomas Inches, Captain Trecothick, Peter Roe, John Brights, James Monk, Captain John Eastwick, Paul Mascarene, Esq., Henry Lloyd, John Oulton, Esq., James Smith, Powers Marriot, Thomas Hawding, Gilbert Warner, George Arthur, William Randell, Henry Franklyn, Charles Apthorp, Richard Hall, Ambrose Vincent, John Greaton, Thomas Pearson, Captain Wybert, Thomas Phillips (warden, 1727; probably son of Nicholas Phillips), Eliakim Hutchinson, Esq., Captain James Forbes, James Gordon, William Speakman, George Ruggles, Rowland Howghton, Captain Francis Wells, John Johnson, Andrew Hallyburton, Roger Hardcastle, Thomas Wroe.

[3] Greenwood, History, etc., p. 125. The reader may be aided in a mental

"Since the enlargement of the Chapel in 1710, and the erection subsequently of galleries, it contained one hundred and twenty-two pews, of which number eighty-two were on the ground-floor. But these pews must have been small, as the present church contains no more. The pulpit was on the north side of the church, at about the midst. A finely decorated pew for the governors, who sat successively in it, was opposite; and near it there was another pew reserved for officers of the British army and navy. In the west gallery of this first Episcopal church was the first organ which ever pealed to the praise of God in this country; while displayed along its walls and suspended from its pillars, after the manner of foreign churches, were escutcheons and coats of arms, — being those of the King, Sir Edmund Andros, Francis Nicholson, Captain Hamilton, and Governors Dudley, Shute, Burnet, Belcher, and Shirley. In the pulpit there was an hour-glass, according to the old fashion, mounted on a large and elaborate stand of brass. At the east end there was 'the Altar-piece, whereon was the Glory painted, the Ten Commandments, the Lord's Prayer, the Creed, and some texts of Scripture.' It was a strange sight among the bare churches of New England. Much that was in it has gone, never to return. We do not desire that it should return. But the mind may muse on these tokens of rejected royalty and forgotten heraldry, if without regret, yet with that tenderness which pays a due respect to things which were venerated aforetime, and which, with other shadows of earth, have passed away."

But, as will appear more clearly in the later course of our narrative, the real church itself, which was only tabernacled among these shadows of the past, contained enduring elements and vital characteristics which continued and shaped all its subsequent history. There must have been a solid weight of character in the men and women composing it, to give it the force to build its new and nobler church, and to enable even the fragment of the parish that remained through the Revolution to survive the tremendous losses by war and exile, and to carry into its second century a sincerity of conscience which could pass through a profound change of opinion without losing the spirit of religious faith, or breaking the bond of its traditionary form of worship. As we trace the story through later generations,

---

restoration of this picturesque interior of King's Chapel as it was in the reign of George II., by grouping together the escutcheons which adorned it, and which are delineated on pp. 61, 70, 84, 140, 140, 267, 297, 379, 397. Governor Shirley's arms, which were also hung in the church, will be found in Vol. II.

it will appear that the genuine qualities which marked the substance of the parish in the time when it stood for English loyalty to Church and King, and which gave it a fibre like heart of oak to grow sturdily on New England soil, ran through the succeeding generations and had not faded out when in our own day the young men of King's Chapel showed the same, yet nobler, loyalty to the American Constitution and the Republic. If history shall show that the sober religious temper and instinct, the tenacious habits and fixed traditions of the churchmen of the Georgian Age have mellowed into a more earnest spirit and a larger catholicity, without losing their essential quality of conviction and devout habit; that the church has added to its faith charity, without losing its faith; that though the superstructure is changed in much, it is still "built upon the chief corner-stone," — the secret of its continued life will be revealed.

FAC-SIMILE FROM THE COVER OF
THE OLD BIBLE.

www.ingramcontent.com/pod-product-compliance
Lightning Source LLC
Chambersburg PA
CBHW031936290426
44108CB00011B/571